BERLITZ POCKET DICTIONARIES FOR TRAVELLERS

GB USA CDN — Danish, Dutch, Finnish, French, German, Italian, Norwegian, Spanish, Spanish (Latin-American), Swedish

F B CH — Allemand, Anglais, Danois, Espagnol, Finlandais, Italien, Néerlandais, Norvégien, Suédois

D A CH — Dänisch, Englisch, Finnisch, Französisch, Italienisch, Niederländisch, Norwegisch, Spanisch, Schwedisch

NL B — Duits, Engels, Frans, Italiaans, Spaans

I CH — Danese, Finlandese, Francese, Inglese, Norvegese, Olandese, Spagnolo, Svedese, Tedesco

E MEX — Alemán, Danés, Finés, Francés, Holandés, Inglés, Italiano, Noruego, Sueco

DK — Engelsk, Fransk, Italiensk, Spansk, Tysk

SF — Englanti, Espanja, Italia, Ranska, Ruotsi, Saksa

N — Engelsk, Fransk, Italiensk, Spansk, Tysk

S — Engelska, Finska, Franska, Italienska, Spanska, Tyska

BERLITZ®

german-english
english-german
dictionary

---

wörterbuch
deutsch-englisch
englisch-deutsch

By the Staff of Editions Berlitz S.A., Lausanne, Switzerland

Copyright © 1974 by Editions Berlitz S.A.

Library of Congress Catalog Card Number: 74-1982

First Printing
Printed in France
Imprimerie Bussière
18200 – Sᵗ-Amand (480).

Editions Berlitz S.A.
8, avenue Bellefontaine
1003 Lausanne, Switzerland

CONTENTS

INHALTSVERZEICHNIS

PREFACE

In creating a new pocket dictionary series, Berlitz was particularly eager to make each book highly practical for travellers, tourists, students, businessmen. Our series contains just about everything you normally find in dictionaries, including grammar and irregular verbs. But as a bonus Berlitz has also provided:

* Imitated pronunciation next to each foreign-word entry in a script almost as easy to read as your own language.
* A major supplement to help you read a restaurant menu – a novel and very useful feature in a pocket dictionary. In French, German, Italian and Spanish dictionaries, Berlitz has also added maps of principal wine regions.
* Practical information on opening and closing hours, public holidays, telling time, trains, road signs, using the telephone, basic phrases. And on the cover for quick reference, there's a tipping chart.

The dictionary contains idioms and some colloquial expressions as well as simple words. As in a glossary of idiomatic expressions, these may often be listed under the first word of the expression, usually a preposition.

In selecting approximately 9,000 words or expressions in each language for this dictionary, the editors had a traveller's needs in mind. Thus, this book – which like our successful phrase-book series is designed to slip into your pocket or purse easily – should prove valuable in the jumbo-jet age we live in. By the same token, it also offers a student the basic vocabulary he is most likely to encounter and use.

Usually, it is quite difficult and costly to update a pocket dictionary, and revisions are hence infrequent. This is not the case with Berlitz. Because these dictionaries were created with the aid of a computer data bank, we are able to revise rapidly and regularly. Thus, if you run into a word on your trip which you feel belongs in a Berlitz dictionary, tell us. Just write the word on a postcard and mail it to our editors. We thank you in advance.

We are most grateful to Mr. Alan R. Beesley for the basic research on the word list and menu reader, and to Dr. T.J.A. Bennett who devised the phonetic transcription. We also wish to thank the staff of Keter Publishing House Ltd., Jerusalem, for their invaluable editorial and technical aid and Marie-Françoise Allard, Christine Baan, Ingeborg Fumagalli, Heidi Gieseler, Roger Haigh, Rosmarie Suss, Rainer Wörlen and Birgitta Zirbs for their assistance.

VORWORT

Mit diesem Band aus einer neuen Reihe von Berlitz-Taschenwörterbüchern legen wir eine praktische Verständigungshilfe für Urlaubs-, Studien- oder Geschäftsreise vor. Unsere Reihe enthält so ziemlich alles, was üblicherweise in Wörterbüchern zu finden ist, einschließlich einer Grundgrammatik und einer Liste unregelmäßiger Verben. Zusätzlich bietet sie Ihnen aber noch:

* Aussprachebezeichnung jedes fremdsprachigen Wortes in einer Lautschrift, die sich beinahe so fließend liest wie Deutsch;
* einen besonderen Anhang, der Ihnen beim Lesen der Speisekarte helfen soll – eine nützliche und in diesem Umfang ungewöhnliche Bereicherung eines Taschenwörterbuches. In einigen Ausgaben (Französisch, Italienisch, Spanisch) finden Sie zudem eine Karte mit den wichtigsten Weinbaugebieten;
* eine Menge Auskünfte über Geschäftszeiten, öffentliche Feiertage, Uhrzeit, Eisenbahn, Verkehrstafeln und Telephonbenutzung sowie einige brauchbare Sätze und Redewendungen. Auf den Innenseiten des Umschlags finden Sie eine Tabelle zum raschen Nachschlagen der Trinkgelder.

Das Wörterverzeichnis enthält nebst einfachen Wörtern auch Ausdrücke der Umgangssprache und idiomatische Redensarten. Sie sind unter dem ersten Wort der Redewendung, meist einer Präposition, aufgeführt.

Bei der Auswahl der ungefähr 9000 Wörter und Redewendungen ließen sich die Herausgeber vor allem vom Gedanken an die Wünsche und Bedürfnisse des Reisenden von heute leiten. Für ihn sollte sich deshalb dieses Buch – im gleichen praktischen Taschenformat wie unsere erfolgreichen Reisesprachführer – als besonders nützlich erweisen. Gleichzeitig bietet es jedem, der eine Sprache erlernen will, den unentbehrlichen Grundwortschatz.

Ein Taschenwörterbuch auf den neuesten Stand zu bringen, ist im allgemeinen eine recht schwierige und kostspielige Angelegenheit, weshalb Überarbeitungen ziemlich selten sind. Nicht so bei Berlitz: da unsere Wörterbücher mit Hilfe eines elektronischen Datenverarbeitungsgeräts geschaffen wurden, können sie ohne Schwierigkeiten rasch und regelmäßig überarbeitet werden. Sollten Sie auf Ihrer Reise einem Wort begegnen, das Ihrer Meinung nach in ein Berlitz-Wörterbuch gehört, zögern Sie also nicht, es uns mitzuteilen. Senden Sie das Wort einfach auf einer Postkarte an die Herausgeber. Wir danken Ihnen im voraus für Ihre Mithilfe.

Unser aufrichtiger Dank gebührt Herrn Alan R. Beesley für die grundlegende Arbeit am Wörterverzeichnis und am Führer durch die Speisekarte sowie Herrn Dr. T.J.A. Bennett für die Erstellung der Lautschrift. Ferner sind wir den Mitarbeitern von Keter Publishing House Ltd., Jerusalem, für ihre unschätzbare redaktionelle und technische Hilfe verbunden. Zum Gelingen des Werkes haben ebenfalls beigetragen: Marie-Françoise Allard, Christine Baan, Ingeborg Fumagalli, Heidi Gieseler, Roger Haigh, Rosmarie Suss, Rainer Wörlen und Birgitta Zirbs.

german-english
_____

deutsch-englisch

GUIDE TO PRONUNCIATION

Each entry in this dictionary is followed by a phonetic transcription in brackets which shows you how to pronounce the foreign word. This imitated pronunciation should be read as if it were your own language.

The symbols for sounds that do not exist in English should, however, be pronounced as described in the appropriate section of the following guide.

The divisions between syllables are marked by hyphens, and stressed syllables are printed in capital letters.

Of course, the sounds of any two languages are never exactly the same, but, if you follow carefully the indications of our Guide to Pronunciation, you should have no difficulty in reading the transcriptions in such a way as to make yourself understood. After that, listening to native speakers and constant practice will help you to improve your accent.

Letter	Approximate pronunciation	Symbol		Example	

Consonants

f, h, k, l, m, n, p, t, x	normally pronounced as in English				
b	1) at the end of a word, or between a vowel and a consonant, like p in up	p	**ab**	ahp	
	2) elsewhere as in English	b	**bis**	bis	
c	1) before e, i, ö, and ä, like ts in hits	ts	**Celsius**	TSEHL-zee-oos	
	2) elsewhere like c in cat	k	**Café**	kah-FAY	
ch	like ch in Scottish loch	kh	**ich**	ikh	
d	1) at the end of a word, or between a vowel and a consonant, like t in eat	t	**Rad**	rart	
	2) elsewhere, like d in do	d	**durstig**	DOORS-tikh	
g	always hard as in go, but, at the end of a word, more like ck in tack	g	**gehen**	GAY-ern	
		k	**weg**	vehk	
j	like y in yes	y	**ja**	yar	
qu	like k followed by v in vat	kv	**Quark**	kvahrk	
r	generally rolled in the back of the mouth	r	**warum**	vah-ROOM	
s	1) before or between vowels like z in zoo	z	**sie**	zee	
	2) before p and t, at the beginning of a syllable, like sh in shut	sh	**spät**	shpait	
	3) elsewhere, like s in sit	s	**es**	ehs	
ß	always like s in sit	s	**heiß**	highs	
sch	like sh in shut	sh	**schnell**	shnehl	
tsch	like ch in chip	ch	**deutsch**	doych	
tz	like ts in hits	ts	**Platz**	plahts	
v	like f in for	f	**vier**	feer	
w	like v in vice	v	**wie**	vee	
z	like ts in hits	ts	**zeigen**	TSIGH-gern	

Vowels

N.B. In German, vowels are generally long when followed by **h** or by one consonant and short when followed by two or more consonants.

a	1) short, like **u** in cut	ah	**hat**	haht
	2) long, like **a** in car	ar	**Abend**	AR-bernt
ä	1) short, like **e** in let	eh	**nächst**	nehkhst
	2) long, like **ai** in hair	ai	**spät**	shpait
e	1) short, like **e** in let	eh	**sprechen**	SHPREH-khern
	2) long, like **a** in late	ay	**gehen**	GAY-ern
	3) in unstressed syllables, it is generally	er	**bitte**	BI-ter
	pronounced like **er** in other		**geben**	GAY-bern
i	1) short, like **i** in hit	i	**bis**	bis
	2) long, like **ee** in meet	ee	**ihm**	eem
ie	like **ee** in bee	ee	**hier**	heer
o	1) short, like **o** in got	o	**voll**	fol
	2) long, like **o** in note	oa	**ohne**	OA-ner
ö	like **ur** in fur (long or short)	ur	**können**	KUR-nern
u	like **oo** in moon (long or short)	oo	**gut**	goot
ü	like French **u** in une; no English equivalent. Round your lips and try to say **ea** as in mean (long or short)	ew	**über**	EW-berr
y	like German **ü**	ew	**Symphonie**	zewm-foa-NEE

Diphthongs

ai, ay, ei, ey	like **igh** in high	igh	**mein**	mighn
au	like **ow** in now	ow	**auf**	owf
äu, eu	like **oy** in boy	oy	**neu**	noy

BASIC GERMAN GRAMMAR

Articles

Nouns in German are **masculine, feminine** or **neuter** and are classified by the article which precedes them.

Definite articles ("the") are: *der* (masc.), *die* (fem.), *das* (neuter) and *die* (plur. all genders).

Indefinite articles ("a", "an") are: *ein* (masc. and neuter), *eine* (fem.).

	der Mann	*die Männer*
	die Frau	*die Frauen*
	das Kind	*die Kinder*
	ein Zug, Züge	
	eine Reise, Reisen	
	ein Flugzeug, Flugzeuge	

Declension*

	der (masc.)	die (fem.)	das (neuter)
Nominative	*der*	*die*	*das*
Accusative	*den*	*die*	*das*
Genitive	*des*	*der*	*des*
Dative	*dem*	*der*	*dem*

	ein (masc.)	eine (fem.)	ein (neuter)
Nominative	*ein*	*eine*	*ein*
Accusative	*einen*	*eine*	*ein*
Genitive	*eines*	*einer*	*eines*
Dative	*einem*	*einer*	*einem*

Nouns

German nouns are written with a capital letter. According to their **function** in the sentence, they change their endings. Since articles and modifying adjectives undergo related changes, the tables below show the declension of all three parts of speech.

Der Lehrer hat uns eingeladen. The teacher has invited us. (*Der Lehrer* is the subject.) *Wir haben den Lehrer eingeladen.* We have invited the teacher. (*Den Lehrer* is the object.)

Masculine singular

Nom.	*der reiche Mann*	*ein reicher Mann*
Acc.	*den reichen Mann*	*einen reichen Mann*
Gen.	*des reichen Mannes*	*eines reichen Mannes*
Dat.	*dem reichen Mann*	*einem reichen Mann*

Masculine plural

Nom.	*die reichen Männer*	*reiche Männer*
Acc.	*die reichen Männer*	*reiche Männer*
Gen.	*der reichen Männer*	*reicher Männer*
Dat.	*den reichen Männern*	*reichen Männern*

* **Nominative** corresponds to the subject, **accusative** is generally the equivalent of the direct object, **dative** of the indirect object and **genitive** of the complement of the noun ("of the...").

Feminine singular

Nom.	*die schöne Frau*	*eine schöne Frau*
Acc.	*die schöne Frau*	*eine schöne Frau*
Gen.	*der schönen Frau*	*einer schönen Frau*
Dat.	*der schönen Frau*	*einer schönen Frau*

Feminine plural

Nom.	*die schönen Frauen*	*schöne Frauen*
Acc.	*die schönen Frauen*	*schöne Frauen*
Gen.	*der schönen Frauen*	*schöner Frauen*
Dat.	*den schönen Frauen*	*schönen Frauen*

Neuter singular

Nom.	*das kleine Kind*	*ein kleines Kind*
Acc.	*das kleine Kind*	*ein kleines Kind*
Gen.	*des kleinen Kindes*	*eines kleinen Kindes*
Dat.	*dem kleinen Kind*	*einem kleinen Kind*

Neuter plural

Nom.	*die kleinen Kinder*	*kleine Kinder*
Acc.	*die kleinen Kinder*	*kleine Kinder*
Gen.	*der kleinen Kinder*	*kleiner Kinder*
Dat.	*den kleinen Kindern*	*kleinen Kindern*

Nouns designating a boy or a man almost always have a **feminine** (woman or girl) formed by adding *-in* to the masculine.

der Arbeiter (the worker, male)
die Arbeiterin (the worker, female)
der Schweizer, die Schweizerin
der Koch, die Köchin
der Franzose, die Französin

All nouns are listed in the dictionary together with their corresponding plural forms.

Note:

Some nouns have two different plural forms, giving two different meanings, e.g.:

die Bank
die Banken the banks
die Bänke the benches

Prepositions

Always followed by the accusative: *durch, für, gegen, ohne, um.*

ohne ihn without him

Prepositions always followed by the dative: *aus, bei, mit, nach, seit, von, zu.*

nach der Mahlzeit after the meal

Prepositions followed either by the **dative** (when no movement is involved) or by the **accusative** (when movement is implied): *an, auf, hinter, in, neben, über, unter, vor, zwischen.*

Er ist im Garten. He's in the garden.
Er geht in den Garten. He goes to the garden.

Pronouns

Personal pronouns

	nom.	acc.	dat.
I	*ich*	*mich*	*mir*
you (fam. sing.)	*du*	*dich*	*dir*
he	*er*	*ihn*	*ihm*
she	*sie*	*sie*	*ihr*
it	*es*	*es*	*ihm*
we	*wir*	*uns*	*uns*
you (fam. plur.)	*ihr*	*euch*	*euch*
they	*sie*	*sie*	*ihnen*
you (polite, sing. and plur.)	*Sie*	*Sie*	*Ihnen*

Note: There are three forms for "you" in German. *Du* is used when talking to relatives, close friends, children, and between young people in the same cases; *ihr* is employed in the same cases, but when speaking to several people. *Sie* (written with a capital) is the polite form, both singular and plural, the verb taking the third person plural ending in both cases.

Interrogative pronouns

Nominative	*wer*	who
Accusative	*wen*	whom
Genitive	*wessen*	whose
Dative	*wem*	to whom

Wer ist da? Who's there?
Wen haben Sie getroffen? Whom did you meet?
Wessen Haus? Whose house?
Wem gehört dieses Auto? To whom does this car belong?

Interrogative adjectives

"What" or "which" followed by a noun:

masculine	*welcher Mann?*	what man? which man?
feminine	*welche Frau?*	what woman?
neuter	*welches Kind?*	what child?

Same declension as *der, die, das* (see above).

Exclamative adjectives

"What a" followed by a noun:

masculine	*welch ein Mann!*	what a man!
feminine	*welch eine Frau!*	what a woman!
neuter	*welch ein Kind!*	what a child!

Same declension as *ein, eine, ein* (see above), *welch* remaining unchanged.

Indefinite pronouns

"One", "they", "you", etc., are translated by *man* when used in an indefinite sense.

Man sagt, er sei verschwunden. People say he's disappeared.

Demonstrative adjectives

Singular	masculine	feminine	neuter
this	*dieser*	*diese*	*dieses*
that	*jener*	*jene*	*jenes*

Plural

these	*diese*
those	*jene*

"He who" or "the one who" is translated by: *derjenige, der ...,*
diejenige, die ... or *dasjenige, das ...*

Possessive adjectives

These agree in number and gender with the noun they modify.

	masculine or neuter singular	feminine or plural
my	*mein*	*meine*
your	*dein*	*deine*
his, its	*sein*	*seine*
her	*ihr*	*ihre*
our	*unser*	*unsere*
your	*euer*	*euere*
their	*ihr*	*ihre*
your (pol.)	*Ihr*	*Ihre*

Possessive adjectives are declined like *ein, eine*.

Note that *Ihr* meaning "your" in the polite form is capitalised.

As for the possessive pronoun (mine, yours, etc.), it is formed
by putting the article before the adjective (*der meine, die
meine,* or *das meine, der deine,* etc.).

Adjectives

Adjectives agree in gender and number with the noun they
modify. To decline them, refer to the "nouns" table.
Adjectives are invariable when they follow the noun.

Das Haus ist weiß. The house
is white.
but: *Das weiße Haus.*

Comparatives and **superlatives** are formed by adding *-er (-r)*
and *-est (-st)* respectively, very often together with an
umlaut ("").
They are regularly declined:

alt	älter	ältest
kurz	kürzer	kürzest

ein längeres Kleid a longer dress

Irregularities:

nah	näher	der nächste	am nächsten	
hoch	höher	der höchste	am höchsten	
gut	besser	der beste	am besten	Adverbial forms
viel	mehr	die meisten	am meisten	
gern	lieber		am liebsten	
(adv.)				

Adverbs

Many adjectives are used in their undeclined form as adverbs.	*schnell* quick, quickly
	gut good, well

There are a few **irregularities:**

glücklich	happy
glücklicherweise	happily, fortunately
anders	differently
besonders	especially
gleichfalls	as well, (the) same

Viel indicates quantity and *sehr* intensity:	*Er arbeitet viel.* He works a lot.
	Er ist sehr müde. He's very tired.
"Only" is translated by *nur* when expressing quantity and by *erst* when indicating a precise point in time.	*Sie kam um drei Uhr und blieb nur zehn Minuten.* She only came at three o'clock and only stayed ten minutes.

Verbs

Verbs fall into three main categories: weak, strong and mixed, according to their conjugations. In addition, there is a special conjugation for the "modal auxiliaries". All verbs are listed in the infinitive in the dictionary. Irregular verbs are preceded by an asterisk and listed separately.	weak: *begegnen*, pret. *begegnete*, past part. *begegnet* strong: *singen*, pret. *sang*, past part. *gesungen* mixed: *bringen*, *brachte*, *gebracht*
The **infinitive** always ends in *-en.*	*haben, gehen,* etc.
The **present participle** ends in *-end.* When used as an adjective, it agrees with the noun it modifies.	*liebend, sehend,* etc. *das singende Kind*
The **future** is formed by using the present of *werden* followed by the infinitive (which is placed at the end of the proposition), but the present is commonly used instead.	*Ich werde ihn nicht sehen.* I shan't see him.
The **conditional** is formed by using the past subjunctive of *werden* followed by the infinitive.	*Sie würden weggehen, wenn Sie es könnten.* You would leave if you could.
Other compound tenses are formed by using the auxiliary *haben* with the past participle which is placed at the end of the proposition.	*Sie haben ihm nicht geantwortet.* You didn't answer him.
Sein, bleiben and many intransitive verbs indicating motion or change of state employ *sein* ("to be") instead of *haben.*	*Ich bin geblieben.* I stayed or I have stayed. *Sie sind gegangen.* You went or you've gone.
The **imperative** in the second person singular (the *du* form) is the same as the present (but without the *-st* ending).	*hör!* listen! *komm!* come!
The second person plural (*ihr*) and the polite form *(Sie)* are both the same as in the present, but in the second person plural, the pronoun *ihr* is dropped and in the polite form *Sie* is placed after the verb.	*hört! hören Sie!* listen! *kommt! kommen Sie!* come!
The first person plural *(wir)* is the same as in the present (with inversion of the pronoun).	*gehen wir!* let's go!

Conjugations

Pres.	Pret.	Pres. perf.	Pres. subj.
haben ("to have")			
habe	*hatte*	*habe*	*habe*
hast	*hattest*	*hast*	*habest*
hat	*hatte*	*hat gehabt*	*habe*
haben	*hatten*	*haben*	*haben*
habt	*hattet*	*habt*	*habet*
haben	*hatten*	*haben*	*haben*
sein ("to be")			
bin	*war*	*bin*	*sei*
bist	*warst*	*bist*	*seiest*
ist	*war*	*ist gewesen*	*sei*
sind	*waren*	*sind*	*seien*
seid	*wart*	*seid*	*seiet*
sind	*waren*	*sind*	*seien*
werden ("to become")			
werde	*wurde*	*bin*	*werde*
wirst	*wurdest*	*bist*	*werdest*
wird	*wurde*	*ist geworden*	*werde*
werden	*wurden*	*sind*	*werden*
werdet	*wurdet*	*seid*	*werdet*
werden	*wurden*	*sind*	*werden*

Pres.	Pret.	Pres.	Pret.
fragen ("to ask")–weak		*kennen* ("to know")–mixed	
frage	*fragte*	*kenne*	*kannte*
fragst	*fragtest*	*kennst*	*kanntest*
fragt	*fragte*	*kennt*	*kannte*
fragen	*fragten*	*kennen*	*kannten*
fragt	*fragtet*	*kennt*	*kanntet*
fragen	*fragten*	*kennen*	*kannten*
tragen ("to carry")–strong		*können* ("to be able to")	
trage	*trug*	*kann*	*konnte*
trägst	*trugst*	*kannst*	*konntest*
trägt	*trug*	*kann*	*konnte*
tragen	*trugen*	*können*	*konnten*
tragt	*trugt*	*könnt*	*konntet*
tragen	*trugen*	*können*	*konnten*

Können is what is called a modal auxiliary. Like *müssen*, *sollen*, *dürfen* and *wollen*, it is used without *zu* before an infinitive.

When do I need to use the **subjunctive**? After a verb expressing doubt, fear, hope or a wish in a past tense.

Er hoffte, daß er einen Brief bekommen würde. He was hoping that he'd get a letter. *Ich fürchtete, daß er nie wiederkommen würde.* I was afraid that he'd never come again.

Also, in indirect speech after verbs like *antworten, behaupten, denken, erklären, erzählen, fragen, glauben, meinen, sagen* or *schreiben*.

Separable verbs: the prefix is stressed.

In the simple tenses, the particle is separated from the verb. But in the compound tenses, as well as in a dependent clause, the particle is combined with the verb.

*auf**machen*** (stress is on the prefix *auf*)
Er macht die Tür auf. He opens the door.
Er hat das Fenster zugemacht. He's closed the window.
Ich möchte, daß er die Tür aufmache. I'd like him to open the door.

Impersonal verbs are conjugated in the third person only. Some verbs are sometimes personal and sometimes impersonal: *geschehen, scheinen, genügen, gelten, sich handeln um, vorkommen, schlagen (Uhr)*.

es freut mich	I'm happy, glad
es wundert mich	I'm surprised
es gelingt mir	I succeed in…
es gefällt mir	I like it
es tut mir leid	I'm sorry
es fällt mir ein	It occurs to me
es fehlt mir	It's missing
es geht mir gut	I'm fine

Negatives are formed with *nicht*.

Er ist nicht hier. He isn't here.

Questions are formed by inverting the subject and the verb.

Sprechen Sie Englisch? Do you speak English?

A few words on German syntax

The infinitive and the participle are placed at the end of the proposition. The same applies to the verb in a subordinate clause.

The complement of time precedes that of place.

Ich habe sie letzten Sommer in Frankreich getroffen. I met her in France last summer.

If two object pronouns are present, the accusative precedes the dative.
It is the opposite for nouns where the dative precedes the accusative.

Ich habe es ihm gegeben. I gave it to him.
Ich habe meiner Mutter einen Brief geschrieben. I wrote a letter to my mother.

GERMAN IRREGULAR VERBS

Since the plural persons of the present tense are always regular in German, you will only find the singular below. Many verbs in German add prefixes to stem verbs. As these derivatives are conjugated like the stem verbs, they will not be given in this list. Just remember that conjugations of verbs beginning by *ab-, an-, auf-, aus-, be-, bei-, ein-, emp-, er-, ent-, ge-, in-, mit-, nach-, um-, ver-, vor-, zer-,* etc. will be found under the stem verb. (Thus, *einsteigen* follows the same pattern as *steigen; ankommen* will be found under *kommen*, etc.)

backen	*Pres:* backe, bäckst, bäckt	
	Pret: backte	*Past part:* gebacken
befehlen	*Pres:* befehle, befiehlst, befiehlt	
	Pret: befahl	*Past part:* befohlen
beginnen	*Pres:* beginne, beginnst, beginnt	
	Pret: begann	*Past part:* begonnen
beißen	*Pres:* beiße, beißt, beißt	
	Pret: biß	*Past part:* gebissen
betrügen	*Pres:* betrüge, betrügst, betrügt	
	Pret: betrog	*Past part:* betrogen
bewegen*	*Pres:* bewege, bewegst, bewegt	
	Pret: bewog	*Past part:* bewogen
biegen	*Pres:* biege, biegst, biegt	
	Pret: bog	*Past part:* gebogen
bieten	*see* **biegen**	
binden	*see* **finden**	
bitten	*Pres:* bitte, bittest, bittet	
	Pret: bat	*Past part:* gebeten
blasen	*Pres:* blase, bläst, bläst	
	Pret: blies	*Past part:* geblasen
bleiben	*Pres:* bleibe, bleibst, bleibt	
	Pret: blieb	*Past part:* geblieben
braten	*Pres:* brate, brätst, brät	
	Pret: briet	*Past part:* gebraten
brechen	*see* **helfen**	
brennen	*Pres:* brenne, brennst, brennt	
	Pret: brannte	*Past part:* gebrannt
bringen	*Pres:* bringe, bringst, bringt	
	Pret: brachte	*Past part:* gebracht
denken	*Pres:* denke, denkst, denkt	
	Pret: dachte	*Past part:* gedacht
dringen	*Pres:* dringe, dringst, dringt	
	Pret: drang	*Past part:* gedrungen
dürfen	*Pres:* darf, darfst, darf	
	Pret: durfte	*Past part:* gedurft
empfehlen	*see* **befehlen**	
erschrecken**	*Pres:* erschrecke, erschrickst, erschrickt	
	Pret: erschrak	*Past part:* erschrocken
essen	*Pres:* esse, ißt, ißt	
	Pret: aß	*Past part:* gegessen
fahren	*Pres:* fahre, fährst, fährt	
	Pret: fuhr	*Past part:* gefahren

* In a figurative meaning; verb is weak meaning "to move".
** Intransitive; verb is weak when transitive.

fallen	*Pres:* falle, fällst, fällt	
	Pret: fiel	*Past part:* gefallen
fangen	*Pres:* fange, fängst, fängt	
	Pret: fing	*Past part:* gefangen
finden	*Pres:* finde, findest, findet	
	Pret: fand	*Past part:* gefunden
fliegen	*see* **biegen**	
fliehen	*Pres:* fliehe, fliehst, flieht	
	Pret: floh	*Past part:* geflohen
fließen	*see* **gießen**	
fressen	*see* **essen**	
frieren	*Pres:* friere, frierst, friert	
	Pret: fror	*Past part:* gefroren
geben	*Pres:* gebe, gibst, gibt	
	Pret: gab	*Past part:* gegeben
gehen	*Pres:* gehe, gehst, geht	
	Pret: ging	*Past part:* gegangen
gelingen	*Pres:* es gelingt *(3rd pers. only)*	
	Pret: gelang	*Past part:* gelungen
gelten	*Pres:* gelte, giltst, gilt	
	Pret: galt	*Past part:* gegolten
genießen	*Pres:* genieße, genießt, genießt	
	Pret: genoß	*Past part:* genossen
geschehen	*Pres:* es geschieht *(3rd pers. only)*	
	Pret: geschah	*Past part:* geschehen
gewinnen	*see* **beginnen**	
gießen	*Pres:* gieße, gießt, gießt	
	Pret: goß	*Past part:* gegossen
gleichen	*Pres:* gleiche, gleichst, gleicht	
	Pret: glich	*Past part:* geglichen
graben	*Pres:* grabe, gräbst, gräbt	
	Pret: grub	*Past part:* gegraben
greifen	*Pres:* greife, greifst, greift	
	Pret: griff	*Past part:* gegriffen
haben	*see* conjugation	
halten	*Pres:* halte, hältst, hält	
	Pret: hielt	*Past part:* gehalten
hängen *	*Pres:* hänge, hängst, hängt	
	Pret: hing	*Past part:* gehangen
heben	*Pres:* hebe, hebst, hebt	
	Pret: hob	*Past part:* gehoben
heißen	*Pres:* heiße, heißt, heißt	
	Pret: hieß	*Past part:* geheißen
helfen	*Pres:* helfe, hilfst, hilft	
	Pret: half	*Past part:* geholfen
kennen	*see* **brennen**	
klingen	*Pres:* klinge, klingst, klingt	
	Pret: klang	*Past part:* geklungen
kommen	*Pres:* komme, kommst, kommt	
	Pret: kam	*Past part:* gekommen
können	*Pres:* kann, kannst, kann	
	Pret: konnte	*Past part:* gekonnt
laden	*Pres:* lade, lädst, lädt	
	Pret: lud	*Past part:* geladen

*Intransitive. Regular when used transitively.

lassen	*Pres:* lasse, läßt, läßt	
	Pret: ließ	*Past part:* gelassen
laufen	*Pres:* laufe, läufst, läuft	
	Pret: lief	*Past part:* gelaufen
leiden	*Pres:* leide, leidest, leidet	
	Pret: litt	*Past part:* gelitten
leihen	*Pres:* leihe, leihst, leiht	
	Pret: lieh	*Past part:* geliehen
lesen	*Pres:* lese, liest, liest	
	Pret: las	*Past part:* gelesen
liegen	*Pres:* liege, liegst, liegt	
	Pret: lag	*Past part:* gelegen
lügen	*Pres:* lüge, lügst, lügt	
	Pret: log	*Past part:* gelogen
messen	*Pres:* messe, mißt, mißt	
	Pret: maß	*Past part:* gemessen
mögen	*Pres:* mag, magst, mag	
	Pret: mochte	*Past part:* gemocht
müssen	*Pres:* muß, mußt, muß	
	Pret: mußte	*Past part:* gemußt
nehmen	*Pres:* nehme, nimmst, nimmt	
	Pret: nahm	*Past part:* genommen
nennen	*see* **brennen**	
pfeifen	*Pres:* pfeife, pfeifst, pfeift	
	Pret: pfiff	*Past part:* gepfiffen
raten	*Pres:* rate, rätst, rät	
	Pret: riet	*Past part:* geraten
reißen	*Pres:* reiße, reißt, reißt	
	Pret: riß	*Past part:* gerissen
reiten	*Pres:* reite, reit(e)st, reitet	
	Pret: ritt	*Past part:* geritten
rennen	*see* **brennen**	
riechen	*Pres:* rieche, riechst, riecht	
	Pret: roch	*Past part:* gerochen
ringen	*see* **finden**	
rufen	*Pres:* rufe, rufst, ruft	
	Pret: rief	*Past part:* gerufen
scheiden	*Pres:* scheide, scheidest, scheidet	
	Pret: schied	*Past part:* geschieden
scheinen	*see* **scheiden**	
schieben	*Pres:* schiebe, schiebst, schiebt	
	Pret: schob	*Past part:* geschoben
schießen	*Pres:* schieße, schießt, schießt	
	Pret: schoß	*Past part:* geschossen
schlafen	*Pres:* schlafe, schläfst, schläft	
	Pret: schlief	*Past part:* geschlafen
schließen	*see* **gießen**	
schmelzen	*Pres:* schmelze, schmilzt, schmilzt	
	Pret: schmolz	*Past part:* geschmolzen
schneiden	*see* **leiden**	
schreiben	*see* **scheiden**	
schreien	*Pres:* schreie, schreist, schreit	
	Pret: schrie	*Past part:* geschrie(e)n

schreiten	*see* **greifen**
schweigen	*Pres:* schweige, schweigst, schweigt
	Pret: schwieg *Past part:* geschwiegen
schwimmen	*Pres:* schwimme, schwimmst, schwimmt
	Pret: schwamm *Past part:* geschwommen
schwinden	*Pres:* schwinde, schwindest, schwindet
	Pret: schwand *Past part:* geschwunden
sehen	*Pres:* sehe, siehst, sieht
	Pret: sah *Past part:* gesehen
sein	*see conjugation*
senden	*Pres:* sende, sendest, sendet
	Pret: sandte *Past part:* gesandt
singen	*see* **finden**
sinken	*Pres:* sinke, sinkst, sinkt
	Pret: sank *Past part:* gesunken
sitzen	*Pres:* sitze, sitzt, sitzt
	Pret: saß *Past part:* gesessen
sprechen	*Pres:* spreche, sprichst, spricht
	Pret: sprach *Past part:* gesprochen
springen	*see* **finden**
stechen	*see* **helfen**
stehen	*Pres:* stehe, stehst, steht
	Pret: stand *Past part:* gestanden
stehlen	*Pres:* stehle, stiehlst, stiehlt
	Pret: stahl *Past part:* gestohlen
steigen	*Pres:* steige, steigst, steigt
	Pret: stieg *Past part:* gestiegen
sterben	*Pres:* sterbe, stirbst, stirbt
	Pret: starb *Past part:* gestorben
stoßen	*Pres:* stoße, stößt, stößt
	Pret: stieß *Past part:* gestoßen
streichen	*Pres:* streiche, streichst, streicht
	Pret: strich *Past part:* gestrichen
streiten	*see* **leiden**
tragen	*Pres:* trage, trägst, trägt
	Pret: trug *Past part:* getragen
treffen	*Pres:* treffe, triffst, trifft
	Pret: traf *Past part:* getroffen
treiben	*Pres:* treibe, treibst, treibt
	Pret: trieb *Past part:* getrieben
treten	*Pres:* trete, trittst, tritt
	Pret: trat *Past part:* getreten
trinken	*Pres:* trinke, trinkst, trinkt
	Pret: trank *Past part:* getrunken
tun	*Pres:* tue, tust, tut
	Pret: tat *Past part:* getan
verderben	*see* **sterben**
vergessen	*Pres:* vergesse, vergißt, vergißt
	Pret: vergaß *Past part:* vergessen
verlieren	*Pres:* verliere, verlierst, verliert
	Pret: verlor *Past part:* verloren
wachsen	*Pres:* wachse, wächst, wächst
	Pret: wuchs *Past part:* gewachsen
waschen	*Pres:* wasche, wäschst, wäscht
	Pret: wusch *Past part:* gewaschen

weisen	*Pres:* weise, wei(se)st, weist	
	Pret: **wies**	*Past part:* gewiesen
wenden	*see* **senden**	
werden	*Pres:* werde, wirst, wird	
	Pret: **wurde**	*Past part:* geworden
werfen	*see* **helfen**	
wiegen	*Pres:* wiege, wiegst, wiegt	
	Pret: **wog**	*Past part:* gewogen
wissen	*Pres:* weiß, weißt, weiß	
	Pret: **wußte**	*Past part:* gewußt
wollen	*Pres:* will, willst, will	
	Pret: **wollte**	*Past part:* gewollt
ziehen	*Pres:* ziehe, ziehst, zieht	
	Pret: **zog**	*Past part:* gezogen
zwingen	*see* **finden**	

KEY TO SYMBOLS AND ABBREVIATIONS

ERKLÄRUNG DER ABKÜRZUNGEN

adjective	**adj**	Adjektiv
adverb	**adv**	Adverb
article	**art**	Artikel
conjunction	**conj**	Konjunktion
feminine	**f**	Femininum
invariable	**inv**	unveränderlich
masculine	**m**	Maskulinum
noun	**n**	Substantiv
neuter	**nt**	Neutrum
past tense (preterite)	**p**	Präteritum (Imperfekt)
plural	**pl**	Plural
past participle	**pp**	Partizip Perfekt
present participle	**ppr**	Partizip Präsens
present tense	**pr**	Präsens
prefix	**pref**	Präfix
preposition	**prep**	Präposition
pronoun	**pron**	Pronomen
singular	**sing**	Singular
verb, compound verb	**v**	Verb
irregular verb	*	unregelmäßiges Verb
see (cross-reference)	→	siehe

Note: Adjective and adverb phrases are sometimes classified under adjectives and adverbs. Those forms (such as *Bundes-*), which cannot be used except in compound words (like *Bundesrepublik* and *Bundesbank*), are treated like prefixes.

german-english

Aal [arl] m (pl ~e) eel

ab [ahp] prep as from

abändern [AHP-ehn-derrn] v
alter

Abänderung [AHP-ehn-der-
roong] f (pl ~en) variation

abdrehen [AHP-dray-ern] v turn
off

Abend [AR-bernt] m (pl ~e)
evening

Abenddämmerung [AR-bernt-
deh-mer-roong] f dusk

Abendessen [AR-bernt-eh-sern]
nt supper

Abenteuer [AR-bern-toy-err] nt
(pl ~) adventure

aber [AR-berr] conj but

* **abfahren** [AHP-far-rern] v pull
out

Abfahrt [AHP-far-rt] f departure

Abfahrtszeit [AHP-farrts-tsight] f
(pl ~en) time of departure

Abfall [AHP-fahl] m (pl ~e)
refuse; rubbish; litter

* **abfallen** [AHP-fah-lern] v slope

abfertigen [AHP-fehr-ti-gern] v
dispatch

Abfluß [AHP-floos] m (pl ~e)
drain

Abführmittel [AHP-fewr-mi-terl]
nt (pl ~) laxative

* **abgeben** [AHP-gay-bern] v
check

abgelegen [AHP-ger-lay-gern] adj
far-off

abgemacht [AHP-ger-mahkht]
adj agreed

abgenutzt [AHP-ger-nootst] adj
worn-out

abgerundet [AHP-ger-roon-dert]
adj rounded

abgeschieden [AHP-ger-shee-
dern] adj isolated

Abgrund [AHP-groont] m (pl ~e)
precipice

Abhang [AHP-hahng] m (pl ~e)
slope

* **abhängen** [AHP-hehng-ern] v
depend

* **abheben** [AHP-hay-bern] v draw

Abkommen [AHP-ko-mern] nt (pl
~) agreement

* **abladen** [AHP-lar-dern] v unload

Ablagerung [AHP-lar-ger-roong] f
(pl ~en) deposit

Ablauf [AHP-lowf] m expiry

* **ablaufen** [AHP-low-fern] v
expire

Ablenkung [AHP-lehng-koong] f
diversion

abmelden (sich) [zikh-AHP-
mehl-dern] v check out

Abnahme [AHP-nar-mer] f (pl
~n) decrease

Abreise [AHP-righ-zer] f parting

abreisen [AHP-righ-zern] v
depart; set out

Absatz [AHP-zahts] m (pl ˜e)
paragraph

abschalten [AHP-shahl-tern] v
cut off

abscheulich [ahp-SHOY-likh] adj
hideous

Abschlagszahlung [AHP-shlarks-
tsar-loong] f (pl ~en)
instalment

Abschnitt [AHP-shnit] m (pl ~e)
section

abschrauben [AHP-shrow-bern] v
unscrew

Abschrift [AHP-shrift] f (pl ~en)
copy

* **absenden** [AHP-zehn-dern] v
send off

Absicht [AHP-zikht] f (pl ~en)
intention; purpose

absichtlich [ahp-ZIKHT-likh] adj
intentional; adv deliberately

absperren [AHP-shpeh-rern] v
lock

Abstieg [AHP-shteek] m (pl ~e)
descent

Abstinenzler [ahp-sti-NEHNTS-
lerr] m (pl ~; f ~in) teetotaller

abstoßend [AHP-shtoa-sernt] adj
repellent

abstrakt [ahp-STRAHKT] adj
abstract

absurd [ahp-ZOORT] adj absurd

Abtei [ahp-TIGH] f (pl ~en) abbey

Abteil [ahp-TIGHL] nt (pl ~e)
compartment

Abteilung [ahp-TIGH-loong] f (pl
~en) department

* **abtragen** [AHP-trar-gern] v wear
out

abwärts [AHP-vehrts] adv
downwards

* **abwaschen** [AHP-vah-shern] v
wash up

abwechselnd [AHP-veh-kserlnt]
adj alternate

abwesend [AHP-vay-zernt] adj
absent; away

Abwesenheit [AHP-vay-zern-
hight] f absence

abzeichnen [AHP-tsighkh-nern] v
initial

* **abziehen** [AHP-tsee-ern] v
deduct

Abzug [AHP-tsook] m (pl ˜e)
print

Achse [AH-kser] f (pl ~n) axle

acht [ahkht] adj eight

achte [AHKH-ter] adj eighth

achten [AHKH-tern] v respect

achten auf [AHKH-tern-owf] v
mind

achtzehn [AHKH-tsayn] adj
eighteen

achtzehnte [AHKH-tsayn-ter] adj
eighteenth

achtzig [AHKH-tsikh] adj eighty

addieren [ah-DEE-rern] v add

Addition [ah-di-TSYOAN] f (pl
~en) addition

Ader [AR-derr] f (pl ~n) vein

Adreßbuch [ah-DREHS-bookh] nt
(pl ˜er) directory

Adressat [ah-dreh-SART] m (pl
~en; f ~in) addressee

adressieren [ah-dreh-SEE-rern] v
address

Adverb [aht-VEHRP] nt adverb

Afrika [AHF-ri-kar] nt Africa

Afrikaner [ahf-ri-KAR-nerr] m (pl

~; *f* ~in) African

afrikanisch [ahf-ri-KAR-nish] *adj* African

Ägypten [ai-GEWP-tern] *nt* Egypt

Ägypter [ai-GEWP-terr] *m* (*pl* ~; *f* ~in) Egyptian

ägyptisch [ai-GEWP-tish] *adj* Egyptian

ähnlich [AIN-likh] *adj* similar; alike

Ähnlichkeit [AIN-likh-kight] *f* (*pl* ~en) similarity

Akademie [ah-kah-der-MEE] *f* (*pl* ~n) academy

Akkreditiv [ah-kray-di-TEEF] *nt* (*pl* ~e) letter of credit

Akt [ahkt] *m* (*pl* ~e) act

Akte [AHK-ter] *f* (*pl* ~n) record

Aktenmappe [AHK-tern-mah-per] *f* (*pl* ~n) briefcase

Aktentasche [AHK-tern-tah-sher] *f* (*pl* ~n) attaché-case

Aktie [AHK-tsyer] *f* (*pl* ~n) share

Aktien [AHK-tsyern] *fpl* stock

Aktiva [ahk-TEE-vah] *ntpl* assets *pl*

Akzent [ahk-TSEHNT] *m* (*pl* ~e) accent

Alarm [ah-LAHRM] *m* alarm

alarmieren [ah-lahr-MEE-rern] *v* alarm

albern [AHL-berrn] *adj* silly

Alkohol [AHL-koa-hoal] *m* alcohol

alkoholfreies Getränk [AHL-koa-hoal-frigh-ers-gay-TREHNGK] *nt* soft drink

alkoholisch [ahl-koa-HOA-lish] *adj* alcoholic

alle [AH-ler] *adj* all

Allee [ah-LAY] *f* (*pl* ~n) avenue

allein [ah-LIGHN] *adv* alone; by oneself

alles [AH-lers] *pron* everything

alles inbegriffen [AH-lers-IN-ber-gri-fern] all in

allgemein [ahl-ger-MIGHN] *adj* general

allmählich [ahl-MAI-likh] *adj* gradual

alltäglich [ahl-TAIK-likh] *adj* everyday

Alpinismus [ahl-pi-NIS-moos] *m* mountaineering

als [ahls] *conj* than

als Antwort [ahls-AHNT-vort] in reply

als ob [ahls-OP] as if

also [AHL-zoa] *conj* so

alt [ahlt] *adj* ancient; aged; old

Altar [ahl-TARR] *m* (*pl* ~e) altar

altbacken [AHLT-bah-kern] *adj* stale

alte Jungfer [AHL-ter-YOONG-ferr] *f* spinster

älter [EHL-terr] *adj* elder; older

Alter [AHL-terr] *nt* age

Alternative [ahl-terr-nah-TEE-ver] *f* (*pl* ~n) alternative

Altertum [AHL-terr-toom] *nt* antiquity

Altertümer [AHL-terr-tew-merr] *ntpl* antiquities *pl*

älteste [EHL-ters-ter] *adj* oldest; eldest

ältlich [EHLT-likh] *adj* elderly

altmodisch [AHLT-moa-dish] *adj* old-fashioned

Ameise [AR-migh-zer] *f* (*pl* ~n) ant

Amerika [ah-MAY-ri-kah] *nt* America

Amerikaner [ah-may-ri-KAR-nerr] *m* (*pl* ~; *f* ~in) American

amerikanisch [ah-may-ri-KAR-nish] *adj* American

Amethyst [ah-may-TIST] *m* (*pl*

~en) amethyst

Ammoniak [AH-moan-yahk] *nt*
ammonia

Amulett [ah-moo-LEHT] *nt* (*pl*
~e) charm; lucky charm

amüsant [ah-mew-ZAHNT] *adj*
amusing; entertaining

amüsieren [ah-mew-ZEE-rern] *v*
amuse

an Bord [ahn-BORT] aboard

Analyse [ah-nah-LEW-zer] *f* (*pl*
~n) analysis

analysieren [ah-nah-lew-ZEE-
rern] *v* analyse

Ananas [AH-nah-nahs] *f*
pineapple

* **anbieten** [AHN-bee-tern] *v* offer

Anblick [AHN-blik] *m* look

Andenken [AHN-dehng-kern] *nt*
(*pl* ~) souvenir

andere [AHN-der-rer] *adj* other

ändern [EHN-derrn] *v* change

anders [AHN-derrs] *adv*
otherwise

anderswo [AHN-derrs-voa] *adv*
elsewhere

Änderung [EHN-der-roong] *f* (*pl*
~en) change; alteration

andrehen [AHN-dray-ern] *v* turn
on

Anerkennung [AHN-ehr-keh-
noong] *f* (*pl* ~en) recognition

Anfang [AHN-fahng] *m* (*pl* ~̈e)
beginning; start

* **anfangen** [AHN-fahng-ern] *v*
start; commence

Anfänger [AHN-fehng-err] *m* (*pl*
~; *f* ~in) beginner; learner

Anfangsbuchstabe [AHN-fahngs-
bookh-shtar-ber] *m* (*pl* ~n)
initial

anfeuchten [AHN-foykh-tern] *v*
moisten

anfordern [AHN-for-derrn] *v*
demand

Anführungszeichen [AHN-few-
roongs-tsigh-khern] *ntpl*
quotation marks *pl*

Angebot [AHN-ger-boat] *nt* (*pl*
~e) offer

angeekelt [AHN-ger-ay-kerlt] *adj*
disgusted

Angelegenheit [AHN-ger-lay-
gern-hight] *f* (*pl* ~en) affair;
matter

Angelgerät [AHNG-erl-ger-rait] *nt*
(*pl* ~e) fishing tackle

Angelhaken [AHNG-erl-har-kern]
m (*pl* ~) fishing hook

Angeln [AHNG-erln] *nt* fishing

Angelrute [AHNG-erl-roo-ter] *f* (*pl*
~n) fishing rod

Angelschein [AHNG-erl-shighn]
m (*pl* ~e) fishing licence

Angelschnur [AHNG-erl-shnoor] *f*
(*pl* ~̈e) fishing line

angemessen [AHN-ger-meh-sern]
adj adequate; appropriate

angenehm [AHN-ger-naym] *adj*
agreeable; pleasing; pleasant;
enjoyable

angenommen daß [AHN-ger-no-
mern-dahs] *conj* supposing
that

Angestellte [AHN-ger-shtehl-ter]
m (*pl* ~n; *f* ~) employee

* **angreifen** [AHN-grigh-fern] *v*
attack

anhaken [AHN-har-kern] *v* tick

* **anhalten** [AHN-hahl-tern] *v* pull
up; halt

Anhänger [AHN-hehng-err] *m* (*pl*
~) pendant; trailer; tab

anhäufen [AHN-hoy-fern] *v* pile

ankleben [AHN-klay-bern] *v* stick

ankleiden (sich) [zikh-AHN-
kligh-dern] *v* dress

ankommend [AHN-ko-mernt] *adj*

incoming

ankündigen [AHN-kewn-di-gern] *v* announce

Ankündigung [AHN-kewn-di-goong] *f* (*pl* ~en) announcement

Ankunft [AHN-koonft] *f* arrival

Ankunftszeit [AHN-koonfts-tsight] *f* (*pl* ~en) time of arrival

Anlasser [AHN-lah-serr] *m* (*pl* ~) starter

Anleihe [AHN-ligh-er] *f* (*pl* ~n) loan

Anmeldebogen [AHN-mehl-der-boa-gern] *m* (*pl* ~) registration form

anmelden (sich) [zikh-AHN-mehl-dern] *v* check in

anmerken [AHN-mehr-kern] *v* note

Anmut [AHN-moot] *f* grace

anmutig [AHN-moo-tikh] *adj* graceful

annähen [AHN-nai-ern] *v* sew on

* **annehmen** [AHN-nay-mern] *v* suppose; adopt; accept

annullieren [ah-noo-LEE-rern] *v* cancel

Annullierung [ah-noo-LEE-roong] *f* cancellation

anonym [ah-noa-NEWM] *adj* anonymous

anpassen [AHN-pah-sern] *v* adjust

Anprobe [AHN-proa-ber] *f* (*pl* ~n) fitting

Anproberaum [AHN-proa-ber-rowm] *m* (*pl* ~e) fitting room

anprobieren [AHN-proa-bee-rern] *v* try on

Anruf [AHN-roof] *m* (*pl* ~e) call

* **anrufen** [AHN-roo-fern] *v* call; call up; ring up

Anschauung [AHN-show-oong] *f* (*pl* ~en) outlook

Anschluß [AHN-shloos] *m* (*pl* ~e) connection

* **anschreiben** [AHN-shrigh-bern] *v* score

Anschrift [AHN-shrift] *f* (*pl* ~en) address

* **ansehen** [AHN-zay-ern] *v* look at

Ansichtskarte [AHN-zikhts-kahr-ter] *f* (*pl* ~n) picture postcard

Anspannung [AHN-shpah-noong] *f* (*pl* ~en) strain

* **ansprechen** [AHN-shpreh-khern] *v* address

Anspruch [AHN-shprookh] *m* (*pl* ~e) claim

anständig [AHN-shtehn-dikh] *adj* decent

anstatt [ahn-SHTAHT] *prep* instead of

anstecken [AHN-shteh-kern] *v* infect

ansteckend [AHN-shteh-kernt] *adj* infectious; contagious

anstellen [AHN-shteh-lern] *v* employ

Anstoß [AHN-shtoas] *m* kick-off

anstößig [AHN-shtur-sikh] *adj* shocking; offensive

Anteil [AHN-tighl] *m* (*pl* ~e) share

Antenne [ahn-TEH-ner] *f* (*pl* ~n) aerial

Antibiotikum [ahn-ti-bi-OA-ti-koom] *nt* (*pl* ~a) antibiotic

antik [ahn-TEEK] *adj* antique

Antiquität [ahn-ti-kvi-TAIT] *f* (*pl* ~en) antique

antiseptisches Mittel [ahn-ti-ZEHP-ti-shers-MI-terl] *nt* antiseptic

* **antreiben** [AHN-trigh-bern] *v* propel

Antwort [AHNT-vort] *f* (*pl* ~en) reply; answer

antworten [AHNT-vor-tern] *v* reply

anvertrauen [AHN-fehr-trow-ern] *v* commit

Anwalt [AHN-vahlt] *m* (*pl* ~e; *f* ~in) attorney; solicitor

Anweisung [AHN-vigh-zoong] *f* (*pl* ~en) money order

Anweisungen [AHN-vigh-zoong-ern] *fpl* directions *pl*

anwesend [AHN-vay-zernt] *adj* present

Anwesenheit [AHN-vay-zern-hight] *f* presence

Anzahl [AHN-tsarl] *f* number

Anzeichen [AHN-tsigh-khern] *nt* (*pl* ~) indication

Anzeige [AHN-tsigh-ger] *f* (*pl* ~n) notice; advertisement

* **anziehen** [AHN-tsee-ern] *v* attract; put on

anziehend [AHN-tsee-ernt] *adj* attractive

Anzug [AHN-tsook] *m* (*pl* ~e) business suit; suit

anzünden [AHN-tsewn-dern] *v* light

Anzünder [AHN-tsewn-derr] *m* (*pl* ~) lighter

Aperitif [ah-peh-ri-TEEF] *m* aperitif

Apfel [AH-pferl] *m* (*pl* ~) apple

Apfelsine [ah-pferl-ZEE-ner] *f* (*pl* ~n) orange

Apotheke [ah-poa-TAY-ker] *f* (*pl* ~n) pharmacy; drugstore

Apotheker [ah-poa-TAY-kerr] *m* (*pl* ~; *f* ~in) druggist; chemist

Apparat [ah-pah-RART] *m* (*pl* ~e) gadget

Appell [ah-PEHL] *m* (*pl* ~e) appeal

Appetit [ah-per-TEET] *m* appetite

Appetithappen [AH-pay-TEET-hah-pern] *m* (*pl* ~) appetiser

Aprikose [ah-pri-KOA-zer] *f* (*pl* ~n) apricot

April [ah-PRIL] *m* April

Aquarell [ah-kvah-REHL] *nt* (*pl* ~e) water-colour

Äquator [eh-KVAR-tor] *m* equator

Araber [ah-RAR-berr] *m* (*pl* ~; *f* ~in) Arab

arabisch [ah-RAR-bish] *adj* Arab

Arbeit [AHR-bight] *f* (*pl* ~en) work; labour

arbeiten [AHR-bigh-tern] *v* work; operate

Arbeiter [AHR-bigh-terr] *m* (*pl* ~) workman; worker; labourer

Arbeitgeber [AHR-bight-gay-berr] *m* (*pl* ~) employer

Arbeitsbewilligung [AHR-bights-ber-VI-li-goong] *f* (*pl* ~en) labour permit; work permit

Arbeitskleidung [AHR-bights-kligh-doong] *f* overalls *pl*

arbeitslos [AHR-bights-loas] *adj* unemployed

Arbeitslosigkeit [AHR-bights-loa-zikh-kight] *f* unemployment

arbeitssparend [AHR-bights-shpar-rernt] *adj* labour-saving

Arbeitszimmer [AHR-bights-tsi-merr] *nt* (*pl* ~) study

Architekt [ahr-khi-TEHKT] *m* (*pl* ~en; *f* ~in) architect

Architektur [ahr-khi-tehk-TOOR] *f* architecture

ärgerlich [EHR-gerr-likh] *adj* annoying

Arkade [ahr-KAR-der] *f* (*pl* ~n) arcade

arm [ahrm] *adj* poor

Arm [ahrm] *m* (*pl* ~e) arm

Armaturenbrett [ahr-mah-TOOrern-breht] *nt* (*pl* ~er) dash-board

Armband [AHRM-bahnt] *nt* (*pl* ~er) bracelet

Armbanduhr [AHRM-bahnt-oor] *f* (*pl* ~en) wrist-watch

Armee [ahr-MAY] *f* (*pl* ~n) army

Ärmel [EHR-merl] *m* (*pl* ~) sleeve

Ärmelkanal [EHR-merl-kah-narl] *m* English Channel

Aroma [ah-ROA-mah] *nt* flavour

Art und Weise [ahrt-oont-VIGH-zer] way

Arterie [ahr-TAYR-yer] *f* (*pl* ~n) artery

Artikel [ahr-TI-kerl] *m* (*pl* ~) article

Artischocke [ahr-ti-SHO-ker] *f* (*pl* ~n) artichoke

Arznei [ahrts-NIGH] *f* (*pl* ~en) drug

Arzneimittel [ahrts-NIGH-mi-terl] *ntpl* pharmaceuticals *pl*

Arzt [ahrtst] *m* (*pl* ~e; *f* ~in) physician; doctor

As [ahs] *nt* (*pl* ~se) ace

Asche [AH-sher] *f* ashes *pl*

Aschenbecher [AH-shern-beh-kherr] *m* (*pl* ~) ashtray

Asiate [ahz-YAR-ter] *m* (*pl* ~n; *f* ~in) Asian

asiatisch [ahz-YAR-tish] *adj* Asian

Asien [AR-zyern] *nt* Asia

Aspirin [ahs-pi-REEN] *nt* aspirin

Assistent [ah-sis-TEHNT] *m* (*pl* ~en; *f* ~in) assistant

assortiert [ah-sor-TEERT] *adj* assorted

Ast [ahst] *m* (*pl* ~e) branch

Asthma [AHST-mah] *nt* asthma

Atem [AR-term] *m* breath

Athletik [aht-LAY-tik] *f* athletics *pl*

Atlantik [aht-LAHN-tik] *m* Atlantic

atmen [ART-mern] *v* breathe

Atmosphäre [aht-mos-FAI-rer] *f* atmosphere

Atmung [ART-moong] *f* breathing

Atombombe [ah-TOAM-bom-ber] *f* (*pl* ~n) atomic bomb

Aubergine [oa-behr-ZHEE-ner] *f* egg-plant

auch [owkh] *adv* too; also

auf [owf] *prep* upon

auf Bestellung gemacht [owf-ber-SHTEH-loong-ger-MAHKHT] made-to-order

auf halbem Wege [owf-HAHL-berm-VAY-ger] midway

auf jeden Fall [owf-YAY-dern-fahl] at any rate

auf Kredit [owf-kray-DEET] on credit

auf Urlaub [owf-OOR-lowp] on holiday

aufblähen [OWF-blai-ern] *v* inflate

aufblasbar [OWF-blars-barr] *adj* inflatable

aufdecken [OWF-deh-kern] *v* uncover

Aufenthaltsgenehmigung [ow-fehnt-hahlts-ger-nay-mi-goong] *f* (*pl* ~en) residence permit

auffallend [OWF-fah-lernt] *adj* striking

auffrischen [OWF-fri-shern] *v* touch up

Aufführung [OWF-few-roong] *f* (*pl* ~en) performance

Aufgabe [OWF-gar-ber] *f* (*pl* ~n) task

* **aufgeben** [OWF-gay-bern] *v* give up; post; quit; mail

aufgehalten [OWF-ger-hahl-tern]

adj detained

* **aufhalten (sich)** [zikh-OWF-hahl-tern] *v* stay

* **aufhängen** [OWF-hehng-ern] *v* hang

Aufhänger [OWF-hehng-err] *m* (*pl* ~) hanger

* **aufheben** [OWF-hay-bern] *v* pick up

aufheitern [OWF-high-terrn] *v* cheer

aufhören [OWF-hur-rern] *v* cease; stop

aufknöpfen [OWF-knur-pfern] *v* unbutton

aufknoten [OWF-knoa-tern] *v* untie

* **aufladen** [OWF-lar-dern] *v* recharge

auflauern [OWF-low-errn] *v* watch for

aufmachen [OWF-mah-khern] *v* undo; unfasten

Aufmerksamkeit [OWF-mehrk-zarm-kight] *f* attention

Aufmerksamkeit schenken [OWF-mehrk-zarm-kight-SHEHNG-kern] *v* pay attention to

* **aufnehmen** [OWF-nay-mern] *v* take in

aufpassen [OWF-pah-sern] *v* watch out

aufrecht [OWF-rehkht] *adj* upright

* **aufrechterhalten** [OWF-rehkht-ehr-hahl-tern] *v* maintain

aufregend [OWF-ray-gernt] *adj* exciting

Aufregung [OWF-ray-goong] *f* (*pl* ~en) excitement

aufreihen [OWF-righ-ern] *v* thread

aufrichtig [OWF-rikh-tikh] *adj* sincere

* **aufschieben** [OWF-shee-bern] *v* delay; postpone

* **aufschließen** [OWF-shlee-sern] *v* unlock

Aufseher [OWF-zay-err] *m* (*pl* ~; *f* ~in) supervisor; warden

Aufsichtsbeamte [OWF-zikhts-ber-ahm-ter] *m* (*pl* ~n; *f* ~in) inspector

* **aufstehen** [OWF-shtay-ern] *v* get up; rise

Aufstieg [OWF-shteek] *m* ascent; climb

aufwachen [OWF-vah-khern] *v* wake up

Aufwand [OWF-vahnt] *m* expenditure

aufwärts [OWF-vehrts] *adv* upwards

aufzeichnen [OWF-tsighkh-nern] *v* record

Aufzug [OWF-tsook] *m* (*pl* ~e) lift; elevator

Augapfel [OWK-ah-pferl] *m* (*pl* ~) eyeball

Auge [ow-ger] *nt* (*pl* ~n) eye

Augenarzt [ow-gern-ahrtst] *m* (*pl* ~e; *f* ~in) oculist

Augenblick [ow-gern-blik] *m* (*pl* ~e) instant; moment

augenblicklich [ow-gern-BLIK-likh] *adj* momentary

Augenbraue [ow-gern-brow-er] *f* (*pl* ~n) eyebrow

Augenbrauenstift [ow-gern-brow-ern-shtift] *m* (*pl* ~e) eye-pencil

Augenschminke [ow-gern-shming-ker] *f* eye-shadow

Augenwimper [ow-gern-vim-perr] *f* (*pl* ~n) eyelash

August [ow-GOOST] *m* August

Auktionator [owk-tsyoa-NAR-tor]

m (*pl* ~en) auctioneer

ausbessern [ows-beh-serrn] *v* mend

ausbilden [ows-bil-dern] *v* educate; train

Ausbildung [ows-bil-doong] *f* training

ausbreiten [ows-brigh-tern] *v* spread; expand

Ausdruck [ows-drook] *m* (*pl* ~e) expression; term

ausdrücken [ows-drew-kern] *v* express

Auseinandersetzung [ows-igh-NAHN-derr-zeh-tsoong] *f* (*pl* ~en) dispute; argument

Außenbezirke [ow-sern-ber-TSIR-ker] *mpl* outskirts *pl*

Außenbord . . . [ow-sern-bort] *pref* outboard

außer [ow-serr] *prep* except

außer Saison [ow-serr-seh-ZAWNG] off season

außer Sicht [ow-serr-ZIKHT] out of sight

außer wenn [ow-serr-VEHN] *conj* unless

außergewöhnlich [ow-serr-ger-vurn-likh] *adj* exceptional

auserlesen [ows-ehr-lay-zern] *adj* exquisite

äußerlich [OY-serr-likh] *adj* exterior

außerordentlich [ow-serr-OR-dernt-likh] *adj* extraordinary

äußerst [OY-serrst] *adj* extreme; utmost

ausfindig machen [ows-fin-dikh-mah-khern] locate

Ausflug [ows-flook] *m* (*pl* ~e) excursion

Ausfuhr [ows-foor] *f* exports *pl*

ausführen [ows-few-rern] *v* take out

ausfüllen [ows-few-lern] *v* fill out; fill in

Ausgabe [ows-gar-ber] *f* (*pl* ~n) expense; edition

Ausgang [ows-gahng] *m* (*pl* ~e) exit; way out

Ausgangspunkt [ows-gahngs-poongkt] *m* (*pl* ~e) starting point

* **ausgeben** [ows-gay-bern] *v* spend; issue

ausgedehnt [ows-ger-daynt] *adj* extensive

* **ausgehen** [ows-gay-ern] *v* go out

Ausgrabung [ows-grar-boong] *f* (*pl* ~en) excavation

Ausguß [ows-goos] *m* (*pl* ~e) sink

Auskunft [ows-koonft] *f* (*pl* ~e) information

Auskunftsbüro [ows-koonfts-bew-roa] *nt* (*pl* ~s) inquiry office; enquiry-office

* **ausladen** [ows-lar-dern] *v* discharge

Auslage [ows-lar-ger] *f* (*pl* ~n) display

ausländisch [ows-lehn-dish] *adj* alien

* **auslassen** [ows-lah-sern] *v* omit; leave out

auslegen [ows-lay-gern] *v* interpret

ausliefern [ows-lee-ferrn] *v* deliver

auslöschen [ows-lur-shern] *v* extinguish; put out

Ausnahme [ows-nar-mer] *f* (*pl* ~n) exception

* **ausnehmen** [ows-nay-mern] *v* exempt

auspacken [ows-pah-kern] *v* unwrap; unpack

Auspuff [ows-poof] *m* (*pl* ~e)
exhaust

Auspufftopf [ows-poof-topf] *m* (*pl*
~̈e) silencer

ausrechnen [ows-rehkh-nern] *v*
calculate

Ausreißer [ows-righ-serr] *m* (*pl*
~; *f* ~in) runaway

Ausruf [ows-roof] *m* (*pl* ~e)
exclamation

* **ausrufen** [ows-roo-fern] *v*
exclaim

ausruhen [ows-roo-ern] *v* pause

Ausrüstung [ows-rews-toong] *f*
(*pl* ~en) outfit; equipment;
gear; kit

ausrutschen [ows-roo-chern] *v*
slip

ausschalten [ows-shahl-tern] *v*
switch off

Ausschlag [ows-shlark] *m* (*pl*
~̈e) rash

* **ausschließen** [ows-shlee-sern]
v exclude

Ausschuß [ows-shoos] *m* (*pl* ~̈e)
reject; committee

Aussicht [ows-zikht] *f* (*pl* ~en)
sight; view

Aussprache [ows-shprar-kher] *f*
pronunciation

* **aussprechen** [ows-shpreh-
khern] *v* pronounce

ausstatten [ows-shtah-tern] *v*
equip

Ausstattung [ows-shtah-toong] *f*
(*pl* ~en) decor

* **aussteigen** [ows-shtigh-gern] *v*
get off

ausstellen [ows-shteh-lern] *v*
display; exhibit; show

Ausstellung [ows-shteh-loong] *f*
(*pl* ~en) exhibition

Ausstellungsraum [ows-shteh-
loongs-rowm] *m* (*pl* ~̈e)
showroom

Ausstoß [ows-shtoas] *m* output

austauschen [ows-tow-shern] *v*
exchange

Auster [ows-terr] *f* (*pl* ~n) oyster

Australien [ows-TRARL-yern] *nt*
Australia

Australier [ows-TRARL-yerr] *m*
(*pl* ~; *f* ~in) Australian

australisch [ow-STRAR-lish] *adj*
Australian

ausüben [ows-ew-bern] *v*
practise

ausverkauft [ows-fehr-kowft] *adj*
sold out

Auswahl [ows-varl] *f* (*pl* ~en)
selection; variety

Auswanderer [ows-vahn-der-
rerr] *m* (*pl* ~; *f* ~in) emigrant

auswandern [ows-vahn-derrn] *v*
emigrate

* **auswärts essen** [ows-vehrts-eh-
sern] *v* eat out

auswendig [ows-vehn-dikh] *adv*
by heart

* **ausziehen** [ows-tsee-ern] *v*
move out

Auto [ow-toa] *nt* (*pl* ~s)
automobile

Autobahnkreuz [ow-toa-barn-
kroyts] *nt* junction

Autofahren [ow-toa-far-rern] *nt*
motoring

Autofahrer [ow-toa-far-rerr] *m*
(*pl* ~; *f* ~in) motorist

Autokarte [ow-toa-kahr-ter] *f* (*pl*
~n) road map

Automat [ow-toa-MART] *m* (*pl*
~en) slot-machine

Automaten-Restaurant [ow-toa-
MAR-tern-rehs-toa-rahng] *nt*
automat

automatisch [ow-toa-MAR-tish]
adj automatic

Automobilklub [ow-toa-moa-BEEL-kloop] *m* (*pl* ~s) automobile club

autonom [ow-toa-NOAM] *adj* autonomous

Autor [OW-tor] *m* (*pl* ~en; *f* ~in) author

Autovermietung [ow-toa-fehr-mee-toong] *f* (*pl* ~en) car hire

Babysitter [BAY-bi-si-terr] *m* (*pl* ~) babysitter

Bach [bahkh] *m* (*pl* ~e) brook; stream

backen [BAH-kern] *v* bake

Backenbart [BAH-kern-barrt] *m* (*pl* ~e) whiskers *pl*

Backenknochen [BAH-kern-kno-khern] *m* (*pl* ~) cheek-bone

Bäcker [BEH-kerr] *m* (*pl* ~) baker

Bäckerei [beh-ker-RIGH] *f* (*pl* ~en) bakery

Backofen [BAHK-oa-fern] *m* (*pl* ~) oven

Backpflaume [BAHK-pflow-mer] *f* (*pl* ~n) prune

Bad [bart] *nt* (*pl* ~er) bath

Badeanzug [BAR-der-ahn-tsook] *m* (*pl* ~e) bathing suit; swim-suit

Badehose [BAR-der-hoa-zer] *f* (*pl* ~n) swimming trunks *pl*

Bademantel [BAR-der-mahn-terl] *m* (*pl* ~) bathrobe

Bademütze [BAR-der-mew-tser] *f* (*pl* ~n) bathing cap

baden [BAR-dern] *v* bathe

Badesalz [BAR-der-zahlts] *nt* (*pl* ~e) bath salts

Badetuch [BAR-der-tookh] *nt* (*pl* ~er) bath towel

Badewanne [BAR-der-vah-ner] *f* (*pl* ~n) tub

Badezimmer [BAR-der-tsi-merr] *nt* (*pl* ~) bathroom

Bahn [barn] *f* (*pl* ~en) track

Bahnhof [BARN-hoaf] *m* (*pl* ~e) depot; station

Bahnsteig [BARN-shtighk] *m* (*pl* ~e) platform

Bahnsteigkarte [BARN-shtighk-kahr-ter] *f* (*pl* ~n) platform ticket

Bahnübergang [BARN-ew-berr-gahng] *m* (*pl* ~e) level crossing

bald [bahlt] *adv* shortly; soon

Balkon [bahl-KAWNG] *m* (*pl* ~s) balcony; circle

Ball [bahl] *m* (*pl* ~e) ball

Ballett [bah-LEHT] *nt* ballet

Ballsaal [BAHL-zarl] *m* (*pl* ~e) ballroom

Banane [bah-NAR-ner] *f* (*pl* ~n) banana

Band [bahnt] *nt* (*pl* ~er) band; ribbon; tape; *m* volume

Bandit [bahn-DEET] *m* (*pl* ~en) bandit

Bandmaß [BAHNT-mars] *nt* tape measure

bange [BAHNG-er] *adj* afraid

Bank [bahngk] *f* (*pl* ~en) bank; bench

Bank-Einlage [BAHNGK-ighn-lar-ger] *f* (*pl* ~n) deposit

Bankettsaal [bahng-KEHT-zarl] *m* (*pl* ~e) banqueting-hall

Bankier [bahng-KYAY] *m* (*pl* ~s) banker

Bankkonto [BAHNGK-kon-toa] *nt* (*pl* ~en) bank account

Banknote [BAHNGK-noa-ter] *f* (*pl* ~n) bank-note; note

Bar [barr] *f* (*pl* ~s) bar; saloon

Bardame [BARR-dar-mer] *f* (*pl*

~n) barmaid

Bargeld [BARR-gehlt] *nt* cash

Barometer [bah-roa-MAY-terr] *nt* (*pl* ~) barometer

Barsch [bahrsh] *m* (*pl* ~e) bass; perch

Bart [bahrt] *m* (*pl* ~e) beard

Baseball [BAYS-bawl] *nt* baseball

Baskenmütze [BAHS-kern-mew-tser] *f* (*pl* ~n) beret

Batterie [bah-ter-REE] *f* (*pl* ~n) battery

Bau [bow] *m* (*pl* ~ten) construction

bauen [BOW-ern] *v* construct; build

Bauer [BOW-err] *m* (*pl* ~n; *f* ~in) peasant; farmer

Bauernhaus [BOW-errn-hows] *nt* (*pl* ~er) farmhouse

Bauernhof [BOW-errn-hoaf] *m* (*pl* ~e) farm

Bauholz [BOW-holts] *nt* (*pl* ~er) timber

Baum [bowm] *m* (*pl* ~e) tree

Baumwollsamt [BOWM-vol-zahmt] *m* velveteen

beabsichtigen [ber-AHP-zikh-ti-gern] *v* intend

beachten [ber-AHKH-tern] *v* observe

Beamte [ber-AHM-ter] *m* (*pl* ~n; *f* ~in) clerk

beanspruchen [ber-AHN-shproo-khern] *v* claim

beantworten [ber-AHNT-vor-tern] *v* answer

beaufsichtigen [ber-OWF-zikh-ti-gern] *v* supervise

bebauen [ber-BOW-ern] *v* cultivate

bebaut [ber-BOWT] *adj* cultivated

Becher [BEH-kherr] *m* (*pl* ~) tumbler; mug

Becken [BEH-kern] *nt* (*pl* ~) basin

bedauern [ber-DOW-errn] *v* regret

Bedauern [ber-DOW-errn] *nt* regret

bedecken [ber-DEH-kern] *v* cover

bedeutend [ber-DOY-ternd] *adj* substantial

Bedeutung [ber-DOY-toong] *f* (*pl* ~en) meaning

bedienen [ber-DEE-nern] *v* wait upon; serve

Bedienung [ber-DEE-noong] *f* service charge; service

bedingt [ber-DINGKT] *adj* conditional

Bedingung [ber-DING-oong] *f* (*pl* ~en) condition

Bedingungen [ber-DING-oong-ern] *fpl* conditions *pl*; terms *pl*

bedingungslos [ber-DING-oongs-loas] *adj* unconditional

bedrohen [ber-DROA-ern] *v* threaten

bedrohlich [ber-DROA-likh] *adj* threatening

Bedürfnis [ber-DEWRF-nis] *nt* (*pl* ~ se) need; want

beeindrucken [ber-IGHN-droo-kern] *v* impress

beeinflussen [ber-IGHN-floo-sern] *v* influence; affect

beenden [ber-EHN-dern] *v* finish; end

Beere [BAY-rer] *f* (*pl* ~n) berry

befähigen [ber-FAI-i-gern] *v* enable

Befähigung [ber-FAI-i-goong] *f* (*pl* ~en) qualification

befahrbar [ber-FARR-barr] *adj* navigable

befassen mit (sich) [zikh-ber-FAH-sern-mit] *v* deal with

* befehlen [ber-FAY-lern] *v* order; command

befestigen [ber-FEHS-ti-gern] *v* attach; pin; fasten

beflecken [ber-FLEH-kern] *v* stain

befleckt [ber-FLEHKT] *adj* stained

befragen [ber-FRAR-gern] *v* query

Befreiung [ber-FRIGH-oong] *f* (*pl* ~en) exemption

Befugnis [ber-FOOK-nis] *f* (*pl* ~se) authority

begabt [ber-GARPT] *adj* gifted

begegnen [ber-GAYG-nern] *v* encounter; come across

begeistert [ber-GIGHS-terrt] *adj* enthusiastic

begierig [ber-GEE-rikh] *adj* eager

* beginnen [ber-GI-nern] *v* begin

Beglaubigungsschreiben [ber-GLOW-bi-goongs-SHRIGH-bern] *nt* (*pl* ~) credentials *pl*

begleiten [ber-GLIGH-tern] *v* accompany

beglückwünschen [ber-GLEWK-vewn-shern] *v* congratulate; compliment

* begraben [ber-GRAR-bern] *v* bury

Begräbnis [ber-GRAIP-nis] *nt* (*pl* ~se) burial; funeral

behaglich [ber-HARK-likh] *adj* cosy

Behälter [ber-HEHL-terr] *m* (*pl* ~) container

behandeln [ber-HAHN-derln] *v* treat

Behandlung [ber-HAHN-dloong] *f* (*pl* ~en) treatment

beherbergen [ber-HEHR-behr-gern] *v* lodge

beherrschen [ber-HEHR-shern] *v* master

bei Nacht [bigh-NAHKHT] by night

bei Tage [bigh-TAR-ger] by day

bei weitem [bigh-VIGH-term] by far

beide [BIGH-der] *adj* both

Beifall [BIGH-fahl] *m* applause

beige [bayzh] *adj* beige

Beil [bighl] *nt* (*pl* ~e) axe

Beilage [BIGH-lar-ger] *f* (*pl* ~n) enclosure

beilegen [BIGH-lay-gern] *v* enclose

Bein [bighn] *nt* (*pl* ~e) leg

beinah [BIGH-nar] *adv* nearly

beinahe [BIGH-nar-er] *adv* almost

beiseite [bigh-ZIGH-ter] *adv* aside

* beißen [BIGH-sern] *v* bite

Beispiel [BIGH-shpeel] *nt* (*pl* ~e) instance; example

Beitrag [BIGH-trark] *m* (*pl* ~̈e) contribution

* beitragen [BIGH-trar-gern] *v* contribute

beiwohnen [BIGH-voa-nern] *v* attend

bejahend [ber-YAR-ernt] *adj* affirmative

Bekannte [ber-KAHN-ter] *m* (*pl* ~n; *f* ~) acquaintance

Bekanntmachung [ber-KAHNT-mah-khoong] *f* (*pl* ~en) public announcement

* bekommen [ber-KO-mern] *v* get

bekömmlich [ber-KURM-likh] *adj* wholesome

bekümmert [ber-KEW-merrt] *adj* sorry

belästigen [ber-LEHS-ti-gern] *v* annoy; bother

Belästigung [ber-LEHS-ti-goong] *f* bother

beleidigen [ber-LIGH-di-gern] *v* insult

Beleidigung [ber-LAHI-di-goong] *f* (*pl* ~en) insult

Beleuchtung [ber-LOYKH-toong] *f*
(*pl* ~en) lighting; illumination

Belgien [BEHL-gyern] *nt* Belgium

Belgier [BEHL-gyerr] *m* (*pl* ~; *f*
~in) Belgian

belgisch [BEHL-gish] *adj* Belgian

Belichtung [ber-LIKH-toong] *f*
exposure

Belichtungsmesser [ber-LIKH-
toongs-meh-serr] *m* (*pl* ~)
exposure metre

belohnen [ber-LOA-nern] *v*
reward

Belohnung [ber-LOA-noong] *f* (*pl*
~en) reward; award

bemerken [ber-MEHR-kern] *v*
notice; remark

bemerkenswert [ber-MEHR-
kerns-vayrt] *adj* remarkable

Bemerkung [ber-MEHR-koong] *f*
(*pl* ~en) remark

bemühen [ber-MEW-ern] *v*
trouble

Bemühung [ber-MEW-oong] *f* (*pl*
~en) effort

benachbart [ber-NAHKH-barrt]
adj neighbouring

benachrichtigen [ber-NARKH-
rikh-ti-gern] *v* notify

* **benehmen (sich)** [zikh-ber-
NAY-mern] *v* act; behave

Benennung [ber-NEH-noong] *f* (*pl*
~en) denomination

benötigen [ber-NUR-ti-gern] *v*
need

benutzen [ber-NOO-tsern] *v*
utilize

Benutzer [ber-NOO-tserr] *m* (*pl*
~; *f* ~in) user

Benzin [behn-TSEEN] *nt* fuel;
petrol; gasoline; gas

Benzinpumpe [behn-TSEEN-
poom-per] *f* (*pl* ~n) petrol
pump

Benzintank [behn-TSEEN-
tahngk] *m* petrol tank

beobachten [ber-OA-bahkh-tern]
v watch

Beobachtung [ber-OA-bahkh-
toong] *f* (*pl* ~en) observation

bequem [ber-KVAYM] *adj*
comfortable

berauscht [ber-ROWSHT] *adj*
intoxicated

Bereich [ber-RIGHKH] *m* (*pl* ~e)
range

bereisen [ber-RIGH-zern] *v* tour

bereit [ber-RIGHT] *adj* ready;
prepared

Berg [behrk] *m* (*pl* ~e)
mountain

bergab [behrk-AHP] *adv* downhill

bergan [behrk-AHN] *adv* uphill

Bergbau [BEHRK-bow] *m* mining

Bergkette [BEHRK-keh-ter] *f* (*pl*
~n) mountain range

Bergmann [BEHRK-mahn] *m* (*pl*
Bergleute) miner

Bergschlucht [BEHRK-shlookht] *f*
(*pl* ~en) glen

Bergwerk [BEHRK-vehrk] *nt* (*pl*
~e) mine

Bericht [ber-RIKHT] *m* (*pl* ~e)
report; account

berichten [ber-RIKH-tern] *v*
report

* **bersten** [BEHRS-tern] *v* burst

Beruf [ber-ROOF] *m* (*pl* ~e)
profession

beruflich [ber-ROOF-likh] *adj*
professional

beruhigen (sich) [zikh-ber-ROO-
i-gern] *v* calm down

Beruhigungsmittel [ber-ROO-i-
goongs-mi-terl] *nt* (*pl* ~)
sedative; tranquilliser

berühmt [ber-REWMT] *adj*
famous; noted

berühren [ber-REW-rern] v touch

besagen [ber-ZAR-gern] v imply

Besatzung [ber-ZAH-tsoong] f (pl
~en) crew

beschädigen [ber-SHAI-di-gern] v
damage

beschädigt [ber-SHAI-dikht] adj
damaged

beschaffen [ber-SHAH-fern] v
provide

beschäftigt [ber-SHEHF-tikht] adj
busy

Beschäftigung [ber-SHEHF-ti-
goong] f (pl ~en) business;
occupation; employment; job

beschämt [ber-SHAIMT] adj
ashamed

bescheiden [ber-SHIGH-dern] adj
humble; modest

beschleunigen [ber-SHLOY-ni-
gern] v accelerate

beschmutzt [ber-SHMOOTST] adj
soiled

beschränken [ber-SHREHNG-
kern] v limit

beschränkt [ber-SHREHNGKT] adj
limited

* **beschreiben** [ber-SHRIGH-bern]
v describe

Beschreibung [ber-SHRIGH-
boong] f (pl ~en) description

beschriften [ber-SHRIF-tern] v
label

beschuldigen [ber-SHOOL-di-
gern] v accuse; blame

Beschwerde [ber-SHVAYR-der] f
(pl ~n) complaint

beschweren (sich) [zikh-ber-
SHVAY-rern] v complain

beseitigen [ber-ZIGH-ti-gern] v
remove

Beseitigung [ber-ZIGH-ti-goong] f
(pl ~en) removal

besetzen [ber-ZEH-tsern] v

occupy

besetzt [ber-ZEHTST] adj
occupied; engaged

besichtigen [ber-ZIKH-ti-gern] v
view

besiegen [ber-ZEE-gern] v defeat;
beat

Besitz [ber-ZITS] m possession

* **besitzen** [ber-ZI-tsern] v
possess; own

Besitzer [ber-ZI-tserr] m (pl ~; f
~in) owner

besoldet [ber-ZOL-dert] adj
salaried

besonder [ber-ZON-derr] adj
particular

besonders [ber-ZON-derrs] adv
especially; most of all

besorgt [ber-ZORKT] adj
concerned; anxious

bespritzen [ber-SHPRI-tsern] v
splash

besser [BEH-serr] adj better

best [behst] adj best

beständig [ber-SHTEHN-dikh] adj
steady

bestätigen [ber-SHTAI-ti-gern] v
acknowledge; confirm

Bestätigung [ber-SHTAI-ti-goong]
f (pl ~en) confirmation

Besteck [ber-SHTEHK] nt cutlery

* **bestehen** [ber-SHTAY-ern] v
consist; insist

* **besteigen** [ber-SHTIGH-gern] v
mount

bestellen [ber-SHTEH-lern] v
order

Bestellung [ber-SHTEH-loong] f
(pl ~en) order

bestenfalls [BEHS-tern-fahls] adv
at best

besteuern [ber-SHTOY-errn] v tax

Besteuerung [ber-SHTOY-er-
roong] f taxation

bestimmt [ber-SHTIMT] *adj*
definite; certain

Bestimmungsort [ber-SHTI-moongs-ort] *m (pl ~e)*
destination

bestrebt [ber-SHTRAYPT] *adj*
anxious

bestürzt [ber-SHTEWRTST] *adj*
upset

Besuch [ber-ZOOKH] *m (pl ~e)*
visit; call

besuchen [ber-ZOO-khern] *v* call
on; visit

Besuchsstunden [ber-ZOOKHS-shtoon-dern] *fpl* visiting hours
pl

Betäubungsmittel [ber-TOY-boongs-mi-terl] *nt (pl ~)*
anaesthetic

Bete [BAY-ter] *f (pl ~n)* beetroot

beteiligt an [ber-TIGH-likht-ahn] *adj* connected with

beten [BAY-tern] *v* pray

betonen [ber-TOA-nern] *v*
emphasize; stress

Betonung [ber-TOA-noong] *f*
stress

betrachten [ber-TRAHKH-tern] *v*
regard; consider

Betrag [ber-TRARK] *m (pl ~̈e)*
amount

* **betragen** [ber-TRAR-gern] *v*
amount

Betragen [ber-TRAR-gern] *nt*
behaviour

* **betreffen** [ber-TREH-fern] *v*
concern; touch

betreffs [ber-TREHFS] *prep*
concerning

Betriebsanlage [ber-TREEPS-ahn-lar-ger] *f (pl ~n)* plant

Betrug [ber-TROOK] *m* fraud

* **betrügen** [ber-TREW-gern] *v*
cheat

betrunken [ber-TROONG-kern] *ãdj*
drunken

Bett [beht] *nt (pl ~en)* bed

betteln [BEH-terln] *v* beg

Bettler [BEHT-lerr] *m (pl ~; f
~in)* beggar

Bettzeug [BEHT-tsoyk] *nt* bedding

beunruhigen (sich) [zikh-ber-OON-roo-i-gern] *v* worry

beunruhigt [ber-OON-roo-ikht]
adj worried

Beutel [BOY-terl] *m (pl ~)* pouch

Bevölkerung [ber-FURL-ker-roong] *f (pl ~en)* population

bevor [ber-FOAR] *conj* before

bevorzugen [ber-FOAR-tsoo-gern]
v prefer

bewachen [ber-VAH-khern] *v*
guard

bewahren [ber-VAR-rern] *v*
preserve

Bewahrung [ber-VAR-roong] *f (pl
~en)* preservation

bewegen [ber-VAY-gern] *v* stir

beweglich [ber-VAYK-likh] *adj*
mobile; movable

Bewegung [ber-VAY-goong] *f (pl
~en)* motion; movement

Beweis [ber-VIGHS] *m (pl ~e)*
proof

* **beweisen** [ber-VIGH-zern] *v*
prove; show

bewillkommnen [ber-VIL-kom-nern] *v* welcome

bewirten [ber-VIR-tern] *v*
entertain

bewohnbar [ber-VOAN-barr] *adj*
habitable; inhabitable

bewohnen [ber-VOA-nern] *v*
inhabit

bewölkt [ber-VURLKT] *adj* cloudy

bewundern [ber-VOON-derrn] *v*
admire

Bewunderung [ber-VOON-der-roong] f admiration

bewußt [ber-VOOST] adj conscious

bewußtlos [ber-VOOST-loas] adj unconscious

bezahlen [ber-TSAR-lern] v pay

Bezahlung [ber-TSAR-loong] f (pl ~en) payment

bezaubernd [ber-TSOW-berrnt] adj enchanting; glamorous

Beziehungen [ber-TSEE-oong-ern] fpl relations pl; connections pl

Bezirk [ber-TSIRK] m (pl ~ e) district

Bezugschein [ber-TSOOKS-shighn] m (pl ~e) coupon

bezwecken [ber-TSVEH-kern] v aim

Bibel [BEE-berl] f (pl ~n) Bible

Bibliothek [bee-blioa-TAYK] f (pl ~en) library

* **biegen** [BEE-gern] v bend

Biegung [BEE-goong] f (pl ~en) bend; turn

Biene [BEE-ner] f (pl ~n) bee

Bilanz [bi-LAHNTS] f (pl ~en) balance sheet

Bild [bilt] nt (pl ~er) picture

Bildhauer [BILT-how-err] m (pl ~; f ~in) sculptor

Billard [BIL-yahrt] nt billiards

billig [BI-likh] adj cheap; inexpensive

billiger [BI-li-gerr] adj cheaper

billigst [BI-likst] adj cheapest

Billigung [BI-li-goong] f approval

Bimsstein [BIMS-shtighn] m (pl ~e) pumice stone

* **binden** [BIN-dern] v bind; tie

Bindestrich [BIN-der-shtrikh] m (pl ~e) hyphen

Binse [BIN-zer] f (pl ~n) rush

Biologie [bi-oa-loa-GEE] f biology

Birke [BIR-ker] f (pl ~n) birch

Birne [BIR-ner] f (pl ~n) bulb; pear

bis [bis] conj till; prep till; until

Biß [bis] m (pl ~e) bite

bis zu [bis-tsoo] prep to

Bißchen [BIS-khern] nt a little

Bischof [BI-shof] m (pl ~e) bishop

bisher [bis-HAYR] adv so far

Bissen [BI-sern] m (pl ~) bite

Bitte [BI-ter] f (pl ~n) request

* **bitten** [BI-tern] v request; ask

bitter [BI-terr] adj bitter

Blase [BLAR-zer] f (pl ~n) blister

* **blasen** [BLAR-zern] v blow

Blatt [blaht] nt (pl ~er) sheet; leaf

Blattgold [BLAHT-golt] nt gold leaf

blau [blow] adj blue

Blazer [BLAY-zerr] m (pl ~) blazer

Blei [bligh] nt lead

* **bleiben** [BLIGH-bern] v remain; stay

bleich [blighkh] adj pale

bleichen [BLIGH-khern] v bleach

Bleistift [BLIGH-shtift] m (pl ~e) pencil

Bleistiftspitzer [BLIGH-shtift-shpi-tserr] m (pl ~) pencil-sharpener

blind [blint] adj blind

Blinddarmentzündung [BLINT-dahrm-ehn-tsewn-doong] f appendicitis

Blitz [blits] m (pl ~e) lightning

Blitzlicht [BLITS-likht] nt (pl ~er) flash-bulb

blond [blont] adj fairhaired

Blondine [blon-DEE-ner] f (pl ~n) blonde

bloß [bloas] adj bare

Blue Jeans [bloo-JEENS] pl levis

Blume [BLOO-mer] *f* (*pl* ~n)
flower

Blumenblatt [BLOO-mern-blaht]
nt (*pl* ~er) petal

Blumenhändler [BLOO-mern-
hehn-dlerr] *m* (*pl* ~; *f* ~in)
florist

Blumenhandlung [BLOO-mern-
hahn-dloong] *f* (*pl* ~en)
flower-shop

Blumenkohl [BLOO-mern-koal] *m*
cauliflower

Bluse [BLOO-zer] *f* (*pl* ~n) blouse

Blut [bloot] *nt* blood

Blutarmut [BLOOT-ahr-moot] *f*
anaemia

Blutdruck [BLOOT-drook] *m*
blood-pressure

bluten [BLOO-tern] *v* bleed

Blutgefäß [BLOOT-ger-fais] *nt* (*pl*
~e) blood-vessel

Blutsturz [BLOOT-shtoorts] *m* (*pl*
~e) haemorrhage

Blutvergiftung [BLOOT-fehr-gif-
toong] *f* blood-poisoning

Boden [BOA-dern] *m* (*pl* ~)
bottom; ground

Bogen [BOA-gern] *m* (*pl* ~) arch

bogenförmig [BOA-gern-furr-
mikh] *adj* arched

Bohne [BOA-ner] *f* (*pl* ~n) bean

Bombe [BOM-ber] *f* (*pl* ~n) bomb

Bonbon [bawng-BAWNG] *nt* (*pl*
~s) candy

Boot [boat] *nt* (*pl* ~e) boat

Bootsführer [BOATS-few-rerr] *m*
(*pl* ~) boatman

borgen [BOR-gern] *v* borrow

Börse [BURR-zer] *f* (*pl* ~n) stock-
market; stock exchange

bösartig [BURS-ahr-tikh] *adj*
vicious

böse [BUR-zer] *adj* wicked

Botanik [boa-TAR-nik] *f* botany

botanischer Garten [boa-TAR-ni-
sherr-GAHR-tern] botanical
garden

Bote [BOA-ter] *m* (*pl* ~n; *f* ~in)
messenger

Botengang [BOA-tern-gahng] *m*
(*pl* ~e) errand

Botschaft [BOAT-shahft] *f* (*pl*
~en) embassy

Botschafter [BOAT-shahf-terr] *m*
(*pl* ~; *f* ~in) ambassador

Boutique [boo-TIK] *f* (*pl* ~n)
boutique

boxen [BOK-sern] *v* box

Boxkampf [BOKS-kahmpf] *m* (*pl*
~e) boxing match

Brandwunde [BRAHNT-voon-der]
f (*pl* ~n) burn

Brasilianer [brah-zil-YAR-nerr]
m (*pl* ~; *f* ~in) Brazilian

brasilianisch [brah-zil-YAR-nish]
adj Brazilian

Brasilien [brah-ZEEL-yern] *nt*
Brazil

Brassen [BRAH-sern] *m* (*pl* ~)
bream

* **braten** [BRAR-tern] *v* fry

Bratrost [BRART-rost] *m* grill

Brauch [browkh] *m* (*pl* ~e)
usage

brauchbar [BROWKH-barr] *adj*
usable

Brauerei [brower-RIGH] *f* (*pl*
~en) brewery

braun [brown] *adj* brown; tan

Braut [browt] *f* (*pl* ~e) bride

* **brechen** [BREH-khern] *v* break;
fracture

breit [bright] *adj* broad; wide

Breite [BRIGH-ter] *f* (*pl* ~n)
width; breadth

Breitling [BRIGHT-ling] *m* (*pl* ~e)
whitebait

Bremse [BREHM-zer] *f* (*pl* ~n)

brake

Bremslicht [BREHMS-likht] *nt* (*pl* ~er) brake lights *pl*

Brennpunkt [BREHN-poongkt] *m* (*pl* ~e) focus

Brennstoff [BREHN-shtof] *m* (*pl* ~e) fuel

Brett [breht] *nt* (*pl* ~er) board; plank

Bridge [brich] *nt* bridge

Brief [breef] *m* (*pl* ~e) letter

Briefkasten [BREEF-kahs-tern] *m* (*pl* ~) letterbox; mail-box; pillar-box

Briefmarke [BREEF-mahr-ker] *f* (*pl* ~n) postage stamp; stamp

Briefpapier [BREEF-pah-peer] *nt* (*pl* ~e) notepaper

Brieftasche [BREEF-tah-sher] *f* (*pl* ~n) pocket-book; wallet

Briefumschlag [BREEF-oom-shlark] *m* (*pl* ~e) envelope

Briefwechsel [BREEF-veh-kserl] *m* (*pl* ~) correspondence

Bries [brees] *nt* sweetbread

Brillantine [bril-yahn-TEE-ner] *f* brilliantine

Brille [BRI-ler] *f* (*pl* ~n) spectacles *pl*; glasses *pl*

Brillengestell [BRI-lern-ger-shtehl] *nt* (*pl* ~e) frames *pl*

*** bringen** [BRING-ern] *v* bring

Brise [BREE-zer] *f* (*pl* ~n) breeze

britisch [BRI-tish] *adj* British

Brokat [broa-KART] *m* brocade

Brombeere [BROM-bay-rer] *f* (*pl* ~n) blackberry

Bronchitis [bron-KHEE-tis] *f* bronchitis

Bronze [BRAWNG-ser] *f* bronze

Brosche [BRO-sher] *f* (*pl* ~n) brooch

Broschüre [bro-SHEW-rer] *f* (*pl* ~n) brochure

Brot [broat] *nt* (*pl* ~e) bread

Brotbeutel [BROAT-boy-terl] *m* (*pl* ~) haversack

Brötchen [BRURT-khern] *nt* (*pl* ~) bun; roll

Bruch [brookh] *m* hernia; fracture

Bruchstück [BROOKH-shtewk] *nt* (*pl* ~e) fraction

Brücke [BREW-ker] *f* (*pl* ~n) bridge

Bruder [BROO-derr] *m* (*pl* ~) brother

Brünette [brew-NEH-ter] *f* (*pl* ~n) brunette

Brunnen [BROO-nern] *m* (*pl* ~) well

Brunnenkresse [BROO-nern-kreh-ser] *f* watercress

Brust [broost] *f* (*pl* ~e) breast

Brustkasten [BROOST-kahs-tern] *m* chest

brutto [BROO-toa] *adj* gross

Bube [BOO-ber] *m* (*pl* ~n) knave; jack

Buch [bookh] *nt* (*pl* ~er) book

buchen [BOO-khern] *v* book

Bücherstand [BEW-kherr-shtahnt] *m* (*pl* ~e) bookstand

Buchhändler [BOOKH-hehn-dlerr] *m* (*pl* ~) bookseller

Buchhandlung [BOOKH-hahn-dloong] *f* (*pl* ~en) bookstore

Buchmacher [BOOKH-mah-kherr] *m* (*pl* ~) bookmaker

Büchse [BEW-kser] *f* (*pl* ~n) can; tin

Büchsen . . . [BEW-ksern] *pref* canned

Büchsenöffner [BEW-ksern-urf-nerr] *m* (*pl* ~) can opener

buchstabieren [bookh-shtah-BEE-rern] *v* spell

Bucht [bookht] *f* (*pl* ~en) creek;

bay; inlet

Budget [bew-JAY] *nt (pl ~s)*
budget

Büfett [bew-FAY] *nt (pl ~s)* buffet

Bügeleisen [BEW-gerl-igh-zern]
nt (pl ~) iron

bügelfrei [BEW-gerl-frigh] *adj*
wash and wear; drip-dry

bügeln [BEW-gerln] *v* iron; press

Bügeln [BEW-gerln] *nt* pressing

Bühne [BEW-ner] *f (pl ~n)* stage

Bühnenautor [BEW-nern-ow-tor]
m (pl ~en; f ~in) playwright

Bühnenbild [BEW-nern-bilt] *nt*
(pl ~er) scene

bummeln [BOO-merln] *v* stroll

Bummelzug [BOO-merl-tsook] *m*
local train

Bündel [BEWN-derl] *nt (pl ~)*
bunch of keys; bundle

Bundes . . . . [BOON-ders] *pref*
federal

bündig [BEWN-dikh] *adj* brief

buntes Glas [BOON-ters-GLARS]
stained glass

Burg [boork] *f (pl ~en)* castle

Bürge [BEWR-ger] *m (pl ~n)*
guarantor

Bürger [BEWR-gerr] *m (pl ~ ; f*
~in) citizen

Bürger . . . [BEWR-gerr] *pref*
civic

Bürgermeister [BEWR-gerr-
mighs-terr] *m (pl ~; f ~in)*
mayor

Bürgersteig [BEWR-gerr-shtighk]
m (pl ~e) pavement; sidewalk

Büro [bew-ROA] *nt (pl ~s)* office

Büroarbeit [bew-ROA-ahr-bight]
f (pl ~en) office work

Bürokratie [bew-roa-krah-TEE] *f*
bureaucracy

Bürostunden [bew-ROA-shtoon-
dern] *fpl* office hours *pl*

Bursche [BOOR-sher] *m (pl ~n)*
lad

Bürste [BEWRS-ter] *f (pl ~n)*
brush

bürsten [BEWRS-tern] *v* brush

Bus [boos] *m (pl ~se)* bus

Busch [boosh] *m (pl ~e)* bush

Büstenhalter [BEWS-tern-hahl-
terr] *m (pl ~)* bra; brassiere

Butter [BOO-terr] *f* butter

Camping [KEHM-ping] *nt*
camping

Campingplatz [KEHM-ping-
plahts] *m (pl ~e)* camping site

Chalet [shah-LAY] *nt (pl ~s)*
chalet

Chancen [SHAHNG-sern] *fpl* odds
pl

Charakter [kah-RAHK-terr] *m (pl*
~e) character

charakterisieren [kah-rahk-ter-
ri-ZEE-rern] *v* characterize

charakteristisch [kah-rahk-ter-
RIS-tish] *adj* characteristic

Charterflug [SHAHR-terr-flook] *m*
(pl ~e) charter flight

chartern [SHAHR-tern] *v* charter

Chauffeur [sho-FURR] *m (pl ~e)*
chauffeur; driver

Chaussee [shoa-SAY] *f (pl ~n)*
causeway

Chef [shehf] *m (pl ~s; f ~in)*
boss

Chemie [khay-MEE] *f* chemistry

chemisch reinigen [KHAY-mish-
RIGH-ni-gern] *v* dry-clean

chemische Reinigung [KHAY-mi-
sher-RIGH-ni-goong] *f* dry-
cleaner

China [KHEE-nah] *nt* China

Chinese [khi-NAY-zer] *m (pl ~n;*
f ~in) Chinese *inv*

chinesisch [khi-NAY-zish] *adj*
Chinese

Chinin [khi-NEEN] *nt* quinine

Chirurg [khi-ROORK] *m* (*pl* ~en; *f*
~in) surgeon

Choke [shoak] *m* (*pl* ~s) choke

Chor [koar] *m* (*pl* ~̈e) choir

Christ [krist] *m* (*pl* ~en; *f* ~in)
Christian

Christus [KRIS-toos] Christ

Chrom [kroam] *nt* chromium

chronisch [KROA-nish] *adj*
chronic

Cocktail [KOK-tayl] *m* (*pl* ~s)
cocktail

cold cream [koald-KREEM] *f* cold
cream

Corn-flakes [KORN-flayks] *pl*
cornflakes *pl*

Couch [kowch] *f* (*pl* ~en) couch

Cousin [koo-ZANG] *m* (*pl* ~s ; *f*
~e) cousin

Curry [KUR-ri] *m* curry

Dach [dahkh] *nt* (*pl* ~̈er) roof

damals [DAR-marls] *adv* then

Dame [DAR-mer] *f* (*pl* ~n) lady

Damenbinde [DAR-mern-bin-
der] *f* (*pl* ~n) sanitary napkin

Damentoilette [DAR-mern-toaah-
leh-ter] *f* (*pl* ~n) powder-
room; ladies' room

Damenunterwäsche [dar-mern-
OON-terr-veh-sher] *f* lingerie

Damespiel [DAR-mer-shpeel] *nt*
(*pl* ~e) draughts *pl*

Damm [dahm] *m* (*pl* ~̈e) dam;
embankment

Dampf [dahmpf] *m* (*pl* ~̈e)
steam

Dampfer [DAHM-pferr] *m* (*pl* ~)
steamer

Däne [DAI-ner] *m* (*pl* ~n; *f* ~in)
Dane

Dänemark [DAI-ner-mahrk] *nt*
Denmark

dänisch [DAI-nish] *adj* Danish

Dank [dahngk] *m* thanks *pl*

dankbar [DAHNGK-barr] *adj*
thankful; grateful

Dankbarkeit [DAHNGK-barr-
kight] *f* gratitude

danken [DAHNG-kern] *v* thank

dann [dahn] *adv* then

darlegen [DAR-lay-gern] *v* state

Darm [dahrm] *m* (*pl* ~̈e)
intestine

Darstellung [DARR-shteh-loong] *f*
(*pl* ~en) version

darum [DAR-room] *conj* therefore

daß [dahs] *conj* that

das [dahs] *pron* that

Dattel [DAH-terl] *f* (*pl* ~n) date

Datum [DAR-toom] *nt* date

Dauerbügelfalte [DOW-err-bew-
gerl-fahl-ter] *f* (*pl* ~n)
permanent press

dauerhaft [DOW-err-hahft] *adj*
lasting

Dauerkarte [DOW-err-kahr-ter] *f*
(*pl* ~n) season ticket

dauern [DOW-errn] *v* last

dauernd [DOW-errnt] *adj*
permanent

Dauerwelle [DOW-err-veh-ler] *f*
(*pl* ~n) perm

Daumen [DOW-mern] *m* (*pl* ~)
thumb

Daunendecke [DOW-nern-deh-
ker] *f* (*pl* ~n) eiderdown

Deck [dehk] *nt* (*pl* ~s) deck

Decke [DEH-ker] *f* (*pl* ~n) ceiling

Deckel [DEH-kerl] *m* (*pl* ~) lid

Deckkajüte [DEHK-kah-yew-ter]
f (*pl* ~n) deck-cabin

definieren [day-fi-NEE-rern] *v*
define

definiert [day-fi-NEERT] *adj* defined

Definition [day-fi-ni-tsyoan] *f* (*pl* ~en) definition

Defizit [DAY-fi-tsit] *nt* (*pl* ~e) deficit

dehnen [DAY-nern] *v* stretch

dein [dighn] *adj* your

deklarieren [day-klah-REE-rern] *v* declare

Demokratie [day-moa-krah-TEE] *f* (*pl* ~n) democracy

demokratisch [day-moa-KRAR-tish] *adj* democratic

Demonstration [day-mon-strah-TSYOAN] *f* (*pl* ~en) demonstration

* **denken** [DEHNG-kern] *v* think; mean

* **denken an** [DEHNG-kern-AHN] *v* think of

Denker [DEHNG-kerr] *m* (*pl* ~) thinker

Denkmal [DEHNGK-marl] *nt* (*pl* ~er) memorial; monument

denkwürdig [DEHNK-vewr-dikh] *adj* memorable

dennoch [DEH-nokh] *conj* yet ; *adv* still

Deodorant [day-oa-der-RAHNG] *nt* deodorant

Depesche [day-PEH-sher] *f* (*pl* ~n) despatch

deponieren [day-poa-NEE-rern] *v* bank

der [dayr] *art* (*f* **die**, *nt* **das**, *pl* **die**) the; *pron* that; which

der erste Mai [dayr-AYRS-ter-MIGH] May Day

der Länge nach [dayr-LEHNG-er-narkh] lengthways

Desinfektionsmittel [dehs-in-fehk-TSYOANS-mi-terl] *nt* (*pl* ~) disinfectant

desinfizieren [dehs-in-fi-TSEE-rern] *v* disinfect

destilliertes Wasser [dehs-ti-LEER-ters-VAH-serr] *nt* distilled water

deutsch [doych] *adj* German

Deutsche [DOY-cher] *m* (*pl* ~n; *f* ~) German

Deutschland [DOYCH-lahnt] *nt* Germany

Dezember [day-TSEHM-berr] *m* December

Dia [DEE-ah] *nt* (*pl* ~s) slide

Diabetiker [diah-BAY-ti-kerr] *m* (*pl* ~ ; *f* ~in) diabetic

Diagnose [diah-GNOA-zer] *f* (*pl* ~n) diagnosis

diagnostizieren [diah-gnos-ti-TSEE-rern] *v* diagnose

diagonal [diah-goa-NARL] *adj* diagonal

Diagramm [diah-GRAHM] *nt* (*pl* ~e) chart

Diamant [diah-MAHNT] *m* (*pl* ~en) diamond

Diät [di-AIT] *f* (*pl* ~en) diet

dich [dikh] *pron* yourself

dicht [dikht] *adj* dense; thick

dicht besiedelt [dikht-ber-ZEE-derlt] *adj* populous

Dichter [DIKH-terr] *m* (*pl* ~; *f* ~in) poet

Dichtung [DIKH-toong] *f* (*pl* ~en) poetry

dick [dik] *adj* thick; fat

Dicke [DI-ker] *f* (*pl* ~n) thickness

die [dee] *art* (→ **der**)

Dieb [deep] *m* (*pl* ~e) thief

Diebstahl [DEEP-shtarl] *m* (*pl* ~e) theft

Diener [DEE-nerr] *m* (*pl* ~; *f* ~in) servant; valet

Dienstag [DEENS-tark] *m*

Tuesday

Dienstmädchen [DEENST-mait-khern] *nt* (*pl* ~) maid

Dienstpflichtige [DEENST-pflikh-ti-ger] *m* (*pl* ~n) conscript

diese [DEE-zer] *pron* these

Diesel [DEE-zerl] *m* diesel

dieser [DEE-zerr] *pron* this; *adj* this

diesig [DEE-zikh] *adj* hazy

Diktaphon [dik-tah-FOAN] *nt* (*pl* ~e) dictaphone

Diktat [dik-TART] *nt* (*pl* ~e) dictation

diktieren [dik-TEE-rern] *v* dictate

Ding [ding] *nt* (*pl* ~e) thing

Diphtherie [dif-ter-REE] *f* diphtheria

Diplomat [di-ploa-MART] *m* (*pl* ~en ; *f* ~in) diplomat

dir [deer] *pron* you

direkt [di-REHKT] *adj* direct

Direktor [di-REHK-tor] *m* (*pl* ~en ; *f* ~in) director; manager; principal

Dirigent [di-ri-GEHNT] *m* (*pl* ~en) conductor

dirigieren [di-ri-GEE-rern] *v* conduct

Diskontsatz [dis-KONT-zahts] *m* (*pl* ~e) bank-rate

Diskussion [dis-koo-SYOAN] *f* (*pl* ~en) discussion

diskutieren [dis-koo-TEE-rern] *v* argue

docken [DO-kern] *v* dock

dolmetschen [DOL-meh-chern] *v* interpret

Dolmetscher [DOL-meh-cherr] *m* (*pl* ~ ; *f* ~in) interpreter

Donner [DO-nerr] *m* thunder

Donnerstag [DO-nerrs-tark] *m* Thursday

Doppelbett [DO-perl-beht] *nt* (*pl* ~en) twin beds *pl*; double bed

Doppelte [DO-perl-ter] *nt* double

doppelte Fahrbahn [DO-perl-ter-FARR-barn] *f* dual carriage-way

Doppelzimmer [DO-perl-tsi-merr] *nt* (*pl* ~) double room

Dorf [dorf] *nt* (*pl* ~er) village

Dorn [dorn] *m* (*pl* ~en) thorn

dort [dort] *adv* there

Dosenöffner [DOA-zern-urf-nerr] *m* (*pl* ~) tin-opener; opener

Dosis [DOA-zis] *f* (*pl* **Dosen**) dose

Draht [drart] *m* (*pl* ~e) wire

Drama [DRAR-mah] *nt* (*pl* **Dramen**) drama

Dramatiker [drah-MAR-ti-kerr] *m* (*pl* ~) dramatist

dramatisch [drah-MAR-tish] *adj* dramatic

draußen [DREROO-sern] *adv* outside; outdoors

drei [drigh] *adj* three

Dreieck [DRIGH-ehk] *nt* (*pl* ~e) triangle

dreieckig [DRIGH-eh-kikh] *adj* triangular

dreissig [DRIGH-sikh] *adj* thirty

dreissigste [DRIGH-sikhs-ter] *adj* thirtieth

dreiviertel [drigh-FIR-terl] *adj* three-quarter

dreizehn [DRIGH-tsayn] *adj* thirteen

dreizehnte [DRIGH-tsayn-ter] *adj* thirteenth

dringend [DRING-ernt] *adj* pressing; urgent

Dringlichkeit [DRING-likh-kight] *f* urgency

Drink [dringk] *m* (*pl* ~s) drink

drinnen [DRI-nern] *adv* inside

dritte [DRI-ter] *adj* third

Drohung [DROA-oong] *f* (*pl* ~en) thread

drüben [DREW-bern] *adv* over
there; across
Druck [drook] *m* pressure
drücken [DREW-kern] *v* press
drucken [DROO-kern] *v* print
Drüse [DREW-zer] *f (pl ~n)* gland
Dschungel [JOONG-erl] *m (pl ~)*
jungle
du [doo] *pron* you
du selbst [doo-ZEHLPST] *pron*
yourself
dumm [doom] *adj* stupid
dunkel [DOONG-kerl] *adj* dark
dünn [dewn] *adj* sheer; thin;
weak
Dunst [doonst] *m (pl ~̈e)* haze;
vapour
durch [doorkh] *prep* through
durchaus [doorkh-OWS] *adv* quite
durchbohren [doorkh-BOA-rern]
v pierce
Durcheinander [doorkh-igh-
NAHN-derr] *nt* muddle
* **durcheinanderbringen**
[doorkh-igh-NAHN-derr-bring-
ern] *v* muddle up
Durchfall [DOORKH-fahl] *m (pl
~̈e)* diarrhoea
durchführen [DOORKH-few-rern]
v carry out
durchgebraten [DOORKH-ger-
brar-tern] *adj* well-done
durchgehender Zug [DOORKH-
gay-ern-derr-TSOOK] *m*
through train
durchmachen [DOORKH-mah-
khern] *v* go through
durchnässen [doorkh-NEH-sern]
v soak
durchqueren [doorkh-KVAY-rern]
v pass through
Durchreise [DOORKH-righ-zer] *f*
passage
Durchschnitt [DOORKH-shnit] *m*

average; mean
durchschnittlich [DOORKH-shnit-
likh] *adj* average; on the
average
durchsichtig [DOORKH-zikh-tikh]
adj transparent
durchstochen [doorkh-SHTO-
khern] *adj* punctured
dürr [dewr] *adj* arid
Dürre [DEW-rer] *f (pl ~n)*
drought
Durst [doorst] *m* thirst
durstig [DOORS-tikh] *adj* thirsty
Dusche [DOO-sher] *f (pl ~n)*
shower
Düsenflugzeug [DEW-zern-flook-
tsoyk] *nt (pl ~e)* jet
Düsterkeit [DEWS-terr-kight] *f*
gloom
Dutzend [DOO-tsernt] *nt (pl ~e)*
dozen
Dynamo [dew-NAR-moa] *m (pl
~s)* dynamo

Ebbe [EH-ber] *f* low tide
eben [AY-bern] *adj* level
Ebene [AY-ber-ner] *f (pl ~n)*
plain
ebenfalls [AY-bern-fahls] *adv* as
well; likewise
Ebenholz [AY-bern-holts] *nt*
ebony
Echo [EH-khoa] *nt* echo
echt [ehkht] *adj* genuine;
authentic
Ecke [EH-ker] *f (pl ~n)* corner
Edelstein [AY-derl-shtighn] *m (pl
~e)* gem; stone
Ehe [AY-er] *f (pl ~n)* marriage
Ehepaar [AY-er-parr] *nt (pl ~e)*
married couple
eher [AY-err] *adv* sooner; rather
Ehering [AY-er-ring] *m (pl ~e)*

wedding ring

ehrbar [AYR-barr] *adj* respectable

Ehre [AY-rer] *f (pl ~n)* honour

ehrenwert [AY-rern-vayrt] *adj* honorable

ehrerbietig [AYR-ehr-bee-tikh] *adj* respectful

ehrgeizig [AYR-gigh-tsikh] *adj* ambitious

ehrlich [AYR-likh] honest; *adv* honestly

Ehrlichkeit [AYR-likh-kight] *f* honesty

Ei [igh] *nt (pl ~er)* egg

Eiche [IGH-kher] *f (pl ~n)* oak

Eierbecher [IGH-err-beh-kherr] *m (pl ~)* egg-cup

eifersüchtig [IGH-ferr-zewkh-tikh] *adj* jealous

eigen [IGH-gern] *adj* own

Eigenschaftswort [IGH-gern-shahfts-vort] *nt (pl ~er)* adjective

Eigentum [IGH-gern-toom] *nt* property

Eigentümer [IGH-gern-tew-merr] *m (pl ~; f ~in)* proprietor

eigentümlich [IGH-gern-tewm-likh] *adj* peculiar

eignen (sich) [zikh-IGH-gnern] *v* qualify

Eil . . . . [ighl] *pref* express

Eilbrief [IGHL-breef] *m (pl ~e)* express letter

Eile [IGH-ler] *f* hurry; haste

eilen [IGH-lern] *v* hasten; hurry; rush

eilig [IGH-likh] *adv* in a hurry

Eilpost [IGHL-post] special delivery

Eimer [IGH-merr] *m (pl ~)* pail; bucket

ein [ighn] *art (f eine nt ein)* a; *adj* one

ein anderer [ighn-AHN-der-rerr] another

einander [igh-NAHN-derr] *pron* each other

Einbahnstraße [IGHN-barn-shtrar-ser] *f (pl ~n)* one-way traffic

Einband [IGHN-bahnt] *m (pl ~e)* binding

* **eindringen** [IGHN-dring-ern] *v* invade

Eindruck [IGHN-drook] *m (pl ~e)* impression

eindrucksvoll [IGHN-drooks-fol] *adj* impressive

eine [IGH-ner] *art (→ ein)* a

* **eine Panne haben** [ahi-ner-PAH-ner-har-bern] *v* break down

einer von beiden [IGH-nerr-fon-BIGH-dern] either

einfach [IGHN-fahkh] *adj* simple; *adv* simply

einfache Fahrkarte [IGHN-fah-kher-FARR-kahr-ter] single ticket

* **einfahren** [IGHN-far-rern] *v* pull in

Einfluß [IGHN-floos] *m (pl ~e)* influence

einflußreich [IGHN-floos-righkh] *adj* influential

einfügen [IGHN-few-gern] *v* insert

einführen [IGHN-few-rern] *v* import; introduce

Einführung [IGHN-few-roong] *f (pl ~en)* introduction

Einfuhrzoll [IGHN-foor-tsol] *m (pl ~e)* import duty

Eingang [IGHN-gahng] *m (pl ~e)* way in; entrance

eingeführt [IGHN-ger-fewrt] *adj* imported

eingehend [IGHN-gay-ernt] *adj*
detailed

eingeschlossen [IGHN-ger-shlo-sern] *adj* included

eingeschriebene Brief [IGHN-ger-shree-ber-ner-BREEF] *m*
registered letter

Eingeweide [IGHN-ger-vigh-der] *ntpl* bowels *pl; nt* insides *pl*

Eingreifen [IGHN-grigh-fern] *nt*
interference

einheimisch [IGHN-high-mish]
adj native

Einheit [IGHN-hight] *f (pl ~en)*
unit

einhüllen (sich) [zikh-IGHN-hew-lern] *v* wrap up

einige [IGH-ni-ger] *adj* some;
couple of

einkassieren [IGHN-kah-see-rern] *v* cash

Einkauf [IGHN-kowf] *m (pl ~e)*
shopping

einkaufen [IGHN-kow-fern] *v*
shop

Einkaufstasche [IGHN-kowfs-tah-sher] *f (pl ~n)* shopping
bag

Einkaufszentrum [IGHN-kowfs-tsehn-troom] *nt (pl ~zentren)*
shopping centre

einkerkern [IGHN-kehr-kerrn] *v*
imprison

Einkerkerung [IGHN-kehr-ker-roong] *f* imprisonment

Einkommen [IGHN-ko-mern] *nt*
(pl ~) income; revenue

Einkommenssteuer [IGHN-ko-merns-shtoy-err] *f* income-tax

einkreisen [IGHN-krigh-zern] *v*
encircle

* **einladen** [IGHN-lar-dern] *v*
invite; ask

Einladung [IGHN-lar-doong] *f (pl*
~en) invitation

* **einlassen** [IGHN-lah-sern] *v*
admit

einmal [IGHN-marl] *adv* once;
some time

einmischen (sich) [zikh-IGHN-mi-shern] *v* interfere with

* **einnehmen** [IGHN-nay-mern] *v*
take

einpacken [IGHN-pah-kern] *v*
pack up

einrichten [IGHN-rikh-tern] *v*
furnish; institute

Einrichtung [IGHN-rikh-toong] *f*
(pl ~en) installation

Einrichtungen [IGHN-rikh-toong-ern] *fpl* facilities *pl*

einsam [IGHN-zarm] *adj* lonely

einschalten [IGHN-shahl-tern] *v*
switch on

einschiffen (sich) [zikh-IGHN-shi-fern] *v* embark

Einschiffung [IGHN-shi-foong] *f*
embarkation

* **einschließen** [IGHN-shlee-sern]
v shut; include; comprise

einschließlich [IGHN-shlees-likh]
adj inclusive

* **einschreiben** [IGHN-shrigh-bern] *v* register

* **einschreiben (sich)** [zikh-IGHN-shrigh-bern] *v* register

* **einschreiten** [IGHN-shrigh-tern]
v interfere

einsperren [IGHN-shpeh-rern] *v*
lock up

einspritzen [IGHN-shpri-tsern] *v*
inject

* **einsteigen** [IGHN-shtigh-gern] *v*
get on

einstellen [IGHN-shteh-lern] *v*
garage; tune in

Einstellung [IGHN-shteh-loong] *f*
(pl ~en) attitude

einstöpseln [IGHN-shturp-serln] *v*
plug in

einstufen [IGHN-shtoo-fern] *v*
grade

* **eintragen** [IGHN-trar-gern] *v* list

einträglich [IGHN-traik-likh] *adj*
profitable

Eintragung [IGHN-trar-goong] *f*
(*pl* ~en) registration; entry

* **eintreffen** [IGHN-treh-fern] *v*
arrive

* **eintreten** [IGHN-tray-tern] *v*
enter

Eintritt [IGHN-trit] *m* entry;
admission

Eintritt verboten [IGHN-trit-fehr-
BOA-tern] no entry

Einwand [IGHN-vahnt] *m* (*pl* ~̈e)
objection

Einwanderer [IGHN-vahn-der-
rerr] *m* (*pl* ~; *f* ~in)
immigrant

einwandern [IGHN-vahn-derrn] *v*
immigrate

* **einwenden** [IGHN-vehn-dern] *v*
object

einwickeln [IGHN-vi-kerln] *v*
wrap

einwilligen [IGHN-vi-li-gern] *v*
consent

Einwohner [IGHN-voa-nerr] *m* (*pl*
~) inhabitant

Einzahl [IGHN-tsarl] *f* singular

Einzelbett [IGHN-tserl-beht] *nt*
(*pl* ~en) single bed

Einzelheit [IGHN-tserl-hight] *f* (*pl*
~en) detail

Einzelheiten [IGHN-tserl-high-
tern] *fpl* particulars *pl*

Einzelzimmer [IGHN-tserl-tsi-
merr] *nt* (*pl* ~) single room

* **einziehen** [IGHN-tsee-ern] *v*
move in

einzig [IGHN-tsikh] *adj* single;
sole; only

einzigartig [IGHN-tsikh-ahr-tikh]
adj unique

Eis [ighs] *nt* ice; ice-cream

Eisbahn [IGHS-barn] *f* (*pl* ~en)
rink

Eisbeutel [IGHS-boy-terl] *m* (*pl*
~) icebag

Eisdiele [IGHS-dee-ler] *f* (*pl* ~n)
soda-fountain

Eisen [IGH-zern] *nt* iron

Eisenbahn [IGH-zern-barn] *f* (*pl*
~en) railway; railroad

Eisenbahnfähre [IGH-zern-barn-
fai-rer] *f* (*pl* ~n) train-ferry

Eisenhütte [IGH-zern-hew-ter] *f*
(*pl* ~n) ironworks

Eisenwaren [IGH-zern-var-rern]
fpl hardware

Eisenwarenhandlung [IGH-zern-
var-rern-hahn-dloong] *f* (*pl*
~en) hardware store

eisgekühltes Getränk [IGHS-ger-
kewl-ters-ger-TREHNGK] *nt* iced
drink

eisig [IGH-zikh] *adj* freezing

Eiswasser [IGHS-vah-serr] *nt* ice-
water

ekelhaft [AY-kerl-hahft] *adj*
disgusting

elastische Hose [ay-LAHS-ti-
sher-HOA-zer] *f* panty-girdle

elastischer Strumpf [ay-LAHS-ti-
sherr-SHTROOMPF] *m* (*pl* ~̈e)
support hose *pl*

elegant [ay-lay-GAHNT] *adj*
elegant

Eleganz [ay-lay-GAHNTS] *f*
elegance

Elektriker [ay-LEHK-tri-kerr] *m*
(*pl* ~) electrician

elektrisch [ay-LEHK-trish] *adj*
electric

Elektrizität [ay-lehk-tri-tsi-TAIT]

f electricity

Element [ay-lay-MEHNT] *nt* (*pl* ~e) element

elend [AY-lehnt] *adj* miserable

Elend [AY-lehnt] *nt* misery

Elendsviertel [AY-lehnts-fir-terl] *nt* slum

elf [ehlf] *adj* eleven

Elfenbein [EHL-fern-bighn] *nt* ivory

elfte [EHLF-ter] *adj* eleventh

Ellbogen [EHL-boa-gern] *m* (*pl* ~) elbow

Eltern [EHL-terrn] *pl* parents *pl*

Emaille [ay-MAHL-yer] *nt* enamel

Empfang [ehm-PFAHNG] *m* (*pl* ~e) reception

*** empfangen** [ehm-PFAHNG-ern] *v* receive

empfängnisverhütendes Mittel [ehm-PFEHNG-nis-fehr-hew-tern-ders-MI-terl] *nt* contraceptive

Empfangsdame [ehm-PFAHNGS-dar-mer] *f* (*pl* ~n) receptionist

*** empfehlen** [ehm-PFAY-lern] *v* recommend

Empfehlung [ehm-PFAY-loong] *f* (*pl* ~en) recommendation

Empfehlungen [ehm-PFAY-loong-ern] *fpl* respects *pl*

empfindlich [ehm-PFINT-likh] *adj* sensitive

Empfindung [ehm-PFIN-doong] *f* (*pl* ~en) sensation

empfohlen [ehm-PFOA-lern] *adj* recommended

Ende [EHN-der] *nt* (*pl* ~n) end; ending

Endivie [ehn-DEE-vyer] *f* (*pl* ~n) endive

endlich [EHNT-likh] *adv* at last

Endstation [EHNT-shtah-tsyoan] *f* (*pl* ~en) terminus

Energie [ay-nehr-GEE] *f* (*pl* ~n) energy

energisch [ay-NEHR-gish] *adj* energetic

eng [ehng] *adj* narrow

Engel [EHNG-erl] *m* (*pl* ~) angel

England [EHNG-lahnt] *nt* England

Engländer [EHNG-lehn-derr] *m* (*pl* ~; *f* ~in) Englishman

englisch [EHNG-lish] *adj* English

Enkel [EHNG-kerl] *m* (*pl* ~) grandson

Enkelin [EHNG-ker-lin] *f* (*pl* ~nen) granddaughter

entbehren [ehnt-BAY-rern] *v* spare

entdecken [ehnt-DEH-kern] *v* discover; detect

Entdeckung [ehnt-DEH-koong] *f* (*pl* ~en) discovery

Ente [EHN-ter] *f* (*pl* ~n) duck

entfalten [ehnt-FAHL-tern] *v* unfold

entfernt [ehnt-FEHRNT] *adj* distant; faraway; remote

entferntest [ehnt-FEHRN-terst] *adj* furthest

Entfernung [ehnt-FEHR-noong] *f* (*pl* ~en) distance

Entfernungsmesser [ehnt-FEHR-noongs-meh-serr] *m* (*pl* ~) range-finder

entgegengesetzt [ehnt-GAY-gern-ger-ZEHTST] *adj* opposite; contrary

*** enthalten** [ehnt-HAHL-tern] *v* contain

entkleiden (sich) [zikh-ehnt-KLIGH-dern] *v* undress

*** entkommen** [ehnt-KO-mern] *v* escape

entkorken [ehnt-KOR-kern] *v* uncork

entlang [ehnt-LAHNG] *prep* along

* **entlassen** [ehnt-LAH-sern] *v* fire; dismiss

entlegen [ehnt-LAY-gern] *adj* out of the way

Entlohnung [ehnt-LOA-noong] *f* (*pl* ~en) remuneration

entschädigen [ehnt-SHAI-di-gern] *v* remunerate

* **entscheiden** [ehnt-SHIGH-dern] *v* decide

Entscheidung [ehnt-SHIGH-doong] *f* (*pl* ~en) decision

entschieden [ehnt-SHEE-dern] *adj* decided

entschlossen [ehnt-SHLO-sern] *adj* determined

entschuldigen [ehnt-SHOOL-di-gern] *v* excuse

entschuldigen (sich) [zikh-ehnt-SHOOL-di-gern] *v* apologize

Entschuldigung [ehnt-SHOOL-di-goong] *f* (*pl* ~en) apology

entsetzlich [ehnt-ZEHTS-likh] *adj* horrible

entspannen (sich) [zikh-ehnt-SHPAH-nern] *v* relax

Entspannung [ehnt-SHPAH-noong] *f* (*pl* ~en) relaxation

enttäuschen [ehnt-TOY-shern] *v* disappoint

enttäuscht [ehnt-TOYSHT] *adj* disappointed

entweder....oder [EHNT-vay-derr-OA-derr] *conj* either... or

* **entwerfen** [ehnt-VEHR-fern] *v* design

entwerten [ehnt-VAYR-tern] *v* devalue

Entwertung [ehnt-VAYR-toong] *f* (*pl* ~en) devaluation

entwickeln [ehnt-VI-kerln] *v* develop

Entwicklung [ehnt-VIK-loong] *f* (*pl* ~en) development

entwischen [ehnt-VI-shern] *v* slip

Entwurf [ehnt-VOORF] *m* (*pl* ~e) design

entzückend [ehnt-TSEW-kernt] *adj* delightful

entzückt [ehnt-TSEWKT] *adj* delighted

entzündbar [ehnt-TSEWNT-barr] *adj* inflammable

Entzündung [ehnt-TSEWN-doong] *f* (*pl* ~en) inflammation

Enzyklopädie [ehn-tsew-kloa-pai-DEE] *f* (*pl* ~n) encyclopaedia

Epidemie [ay-pi-day-MEE] *f* (*pl* ~n) epidemic

Epilepsie [ay-pi-lehp-SEE] *f* epilepsy

er [ayr] *pron* he

er selbst [ayr-ZEHLPST] *pron* himself

* **erbrechen** [ehr-BREH-khern] *v* vomit

Erbrechen [ehr-BREH-khern] *nt* vomiting

Erbse [EHR-pser] *f* (*pl* ~n) pea

Erdball [AYRT-bahl] *m* globe

Erdbeben [AYRT-bay-bern] *nt* (*pl* ~) earthquake

Erdbeere [AYRT-bay-rer] *f* (*pl* ~n) strawberry

Erde [AYR-der] *f* soil; earth; Earth

Erdgeschoß [AYRT-ger-shos] *nt* ground-floor

Erdichtung [ehr-DIKH-toong] *f* (*pl* ~en) fiction

Erdkunde [AYRT-koon-der] *f* geography

Erdnuß [AYRT-noos] *f* (*pl* ~e) peanut

Erdteil [AYRT-tighl] *m* (*pl* ~e) continent

ereignen (sich) [zikh-ehr-IGHK-nern] *v* occur; happen

Ereignis [ehr-IGHK-nis] *nt* (*pl* ~se) happening; occurrence; event

erfahren [ehr-FAR-rern] *adj* experienced

Erfahrung [ehr-FAR-roong] *f* (*pl* ~en) experience

* **erfinden** [ehr-FIN-dern] *v* invent

Erfinder [ehr-FIN-derr] *m* (*pl* ~; *f* ~in) inventor

Erfindung [ehr-FIN-doong] *f* (*pl* ~en) invention

Erfolg [ehr-FOLK] *m* (*pl* ~e) success

erfolglos [ehr-FOLK-loas] *adj* unsuccessful

erfolgreich [ehr-FOLK-righkh] *adj* successful

erforderlich [ehr-FOR-derr-likh] *adj* requisite

erfordern [ehr-FOR-derrn] *v* require

Erfordernis [ehr-FOR-derr-nis] *nt* (*pl* ~se) requirement

erforschen [ehr-FOR-shern] *v* explore

erfreut [ehr-FROYT] *adj* pleased

erfrischen [ehr-FRI-shern] *v* refresh

Erfrischung [ehr-FRI-shoong] *f* refreshment

ergeben [ehr-GAY-bern] *adj* devoted

* **ergeben (sich)** [zikh-ehr-GAY-bern] *v* result

Ergebnis [ehr-GAYP-nis] *nt* (*pl* ~se) result

* **ergreifen** [ehr-GRIGH-fern] *v* grasp; seize

* **erhalten** [ehr-HAHL-tern] *v* obtain

* **erheben (sich)** [zikh-ehr-HAY-bern] *v* arise

Erhebung [ehr-HAY-boong] *f* (*pl* ~en) mound

Erholung [ehr-HOA-loong] *f* recreation; recovery

Erholungsheim [ehr-HOA-loongs-highm] *nt* (*pl* ~e) recreation centre; rest-house

Erholungsort [ehr-HOA-loongs-ort] *m* (*pl* ~e) resort

erinnern [ehr-IN-nerrn] *v* remind

erinnern (sich) [zikh-ehr-IN-nerrn] *v* remember

Erkältung [ehr-KEHL-toong] *f* (*pl* ~en) cold

* **erkennen** [ehr-KEH-nern] *v* recognise

erklären [ehr-KLAI-rern] *v* explain

Erklärung [ehr-KLAI-roong] *f* (*pl* ~en) explanation; declaration; statement

erkundigen (sich) [zikh-ehr-KOON-di-gern] *v* enquire; inquire

Erkundigung [ehr-KOON-di-goong] *f* (*pl* ~en) enquiry

erlauben [ehr-LOW-bern] *v* permit; allow

erlaubt [ehr-LOWPT] *adj* allowed

erleben [ehr-LAY-bern] *v* experience

erledigen [ehr-LAY-di-gern] *v* attend

erleichtern [ehr-LIGHKH-terrn] *v* relieve

erleichtert [ehr-LIGHKH-terrt] *adj* relieved

Erleichterung [ehr-LIGHKH-ter-roong] *f* (*pl* ~en) relief

* **erleiden** [ehr-LIGH-dern] *v* suffer

erlesen [ehr-LAY-zern] *adj* select

erleuchten [ehr-LOYKH-tern] *v* illuminate

ermüden [ehr-MEW-dern] *v* tire

ermüdend [ehr-MEW-dernt] *adj* tiring

ernähren [ehr-NAI-rern] *v* feed

erneuern [ehr-NOY-errn] *v* renew

ernst [ehrnst] *adj* severe; serious; grave

Ernte [EHRN-ter] *f (pl* ~n) crop; harvest

erörtern [ehr-URR-terrn] *v* discuss

erregen [ehr-RAY-gern] *v* excite

Erregung [ehr-RAY-goong] *f (pl* ~en) emotion

erreichen [ehr-RIGH-khern] *v* reach

errichten [ehr-RIKH-tern] *v* erect

Ersatz [ehr-ZAHTS] *m* substitute

Ersatzfüllung [ehr-ZAHTS-few-loong] *f (pl* ~en) refill

Ersatzteil [ehr-ZAHTS-tighl] *nt (pl* ~e) spare part

Ersatzteile [ehr-ZAHTS-tigh-ler] *ntpl* spares *pl*

erschallen [ehr-SHAH-lern] *v* sound

* **erscheinen** [ehr-SHIGH-nern] *v* appear

Erscheinung [ehr-SHIGH-noong] *f* appearance

erschöpft [ehr-SHURPFT] *adj* exhausted

* **erschrecken** [ehr-SHREH-kern] *v* frighten; terrify; scare

erschütternd [ehr-SHEW-terrnt] *adj* distressing

ersetzen [ehr-ZEH-tsern] *v* substitute; replace

Ersparnisse [ehr-SHPARR-ni-ser] *fpl* savings *pl*

erstaunen [ehr-SHTOW-nern] *v* amaze

erstaunlich [ehr-SHTOWN-likh] *adj* astonishing

erste [AYRS-ter] *adj* first; initial

erste Hilfe [AYRS-ter-HIL-fer] first aid

erstrangig [AYRST-rahng-ikh] *adj* first-rate

Ertrag [ehr-TRARK] *m (pl* ~e) produce

* **ertragen** [ehr-TRAR-gern] *v* bear

* **ertrinken** [ehr-TRING-kern] *v* drown

erwachsen [ehr-VAH-ksern] *adj* adult

Erwachsene [ehr-VAH-kser-ner] *m (pl* ~n) adult; grown-up

erwähnen [ehr-VAI-nern] *v* mention

Erwähnung [ehr-VAI-noong] *f (pl* ~en) mention

erwarten [ehr-VAHR-tern] *v* await; anticipate; expect

erweitern [ehr-VIGH-terrn] *v* widen

* **erwerben** [ehr-VEHR-bern] *v* acquire

Erzählung [ehr-TSAI-loong] *f (pl* ~en) tale

Erzbischof [EHRTS-bi-shof] *m (pl* ~e) archbishop

erzeugen [ehr-TSOY-gern] *v* generate

Erziehung [ehr-TSEE-oong] *f* education

es [ehs] *pron* it

es gibt [ehs-GIPT] there are; there is

eßbar [EHS-barr] *adj* edible

Esel [AY-zerl] *m (pl* ~) donkey; ass

Eßlöffel [EHS-lur-ferl] *m (pl* ~) tablespoon

Essay [EH-say] *m (pl* ~s) essay

esse [AYS-say] *pron* (→ **essi**) abbreviation

* **essen** [EH-sern] *v* eat; dine

Essig [EH-sikh] *m* vinegar

Etikett [ay-ti-KEHT] *nt* (*pl* ~**e**) label; tag

etwa [EHT-vah] *adv* about

etwas [EHT-vahs] *pron* something

etwas mehr [EHT-vahs-MAYR] some more

euch [oykh] *pron* you; yourselves

euer [OY-err] *adj* your

euere [OY-rer] *adj* your

Europa [oy-ROA-pah] *nt* Europe

Europäer [oy-roa-PAI-err] *m* (*pl* ~; *f* ~**in**) European

europäisch [oy-roa-PAI-ish] *adj* European

Examen [eh-KSAR-mern] *nt* (*pl* ~) examination

Exemplar [ehk-sehm-PLARR] *nt* (*pl* ~**e**) copy; specimen

existieren [eh-ksis-TEE-rern] *v* exist

exklusiv [ehks-kloo-ZEEF] *adj* exclusive

Expedition [ehks-pay-di-TSYOAN] *f* (*pl* ~**en**) expedition

Experiment [ehks-pay-ri-MEHNT] *nt* (*pl* ~**e**) experiment

experimentieren [ehks-pay-ri-mehn-TEE-rern] *v* experiment

explodieren [ehks-ploa-DEE-rern] *v* explode

exportieren [ehks-por-TEE-rern] *v* export

extravagant [EHKS-trah-vah-gahnt] *adj* extravagant

Eyeliner [IGH-ligh-nerr] *m* eyeliner

Fabrik [fah-BREEK] *f* (*pl* ~**en**) factory

Fabrikant [fah-bri-KAHNT] *m* (*pl* ~**en**) manufacturer

fabrizieren [fah-bri-TSEE-rern] *v* manufacture

fabriziert [fah-bri-TSEERT] *adj* manufactured

Fachmann [FAHKH-mahn] *m* (*pl* **Fachleute**) expert

Faden [FAR-dern] *m* (*pl* ~) thread

fähig [FAI-ikh] *adj* able; capable

Fähigkeit [FAI-ikh-kight] *f* (*pl* ~**en**) capacity; ability; faculty

Fahne [FAR-ner] *f* (*pl* ~**n**) flag

Fährboot [FAIR-boat] *nt* (*pl* ~**e**) ferry boat

* **fahren** [FAR-rern] *v* drive; ride; sail; motor

Fahren [FAR-rern] *nt* driving

Fahrgeld [FARR-gehlt] *nt* (*pl* ~**er**) fare; carfare

Fahrgestell [FARR-ger-shtehl] *nt* (*pl* ~**e**) chassis *inv*

Fahrkartenautomat [FARR-kahr-tern-ow-toa-mart] *m* (*pl* ~**en**) ticket machine *m*

Fahrkartenschalter [FARR-kahr-tern-shahl-terr] *m* (*pl* ~) ticket office

Fahrplan [FARR-plarn] *m* (*pl* ~**e**) timetable

Fahrrad [FAR-raht] *nt* (*pl* ~**er**) bicycle

Fahrt [farrt] *f* (*pl* ~**en**) ride; drive

Fahrzeug [FARR-tsoyk] *nt* (*pl* ~**e**) vehicle

fakturieren [fahk-too-REE-rern] *v* bill

Fakultät [fah-kool-TAIT] *f* (*pl* ~**en**) faculty

Fall [fahl] *m* (*pl* ~**e**) case

Falle [FAH-ler] *f* (*pl* ~**n**) trap

* **fallen** [FAH-lern] *v* fall

* **fallen lassen** [FAH-lern-lah-sern] *v* drop

fällig [FEH-likh] *adj* due

falsch [fahlsh] *adj* false;

mistaken; wrong

* falsch aussprechen [fahlsh-ows-shpreh-khern] *v* mispronounce

Falte [FAHL-ter] *f (pl ~n)* crease

falten [FAHL-tern] *v* fold

Familie [fah-MEEL-yer] *f (pl ~n)* family

Familienname [fah-MEEL-yern-nar-mer] *m (pl ~n)* surname

* fangen [FAHNG-ern] *v* catch

Farbe [FAHR-ber] *f (pl ~n)* colour; paint; suit; dye

Färbemittel [FEHR-ber-mi-terl] *nt (pl ~)* colourant

färben [FEHR-bern] *v* dye

farbenprächtig [FAHR-bern-prehkh-tikh] *adj* colourful

Farbfilm [FAHRP-film] *m (pl ~e)* colour-film

farbig [FAHR-bikh] *adj* coloured

Farbton [FAHRP-toan] *m (pl ~e)* shade

Faß [fahs] *nt (pl ~er)* cask; barrel

Fasan [fah-ZARN] *m (pl ~e)* pheasant

Fäßchen [FEHS-khern] *nt (pl ~)* keg

Faser [FAR-zerr] *f (pl ~n)* fibre

Fassade [fah-SAR-der] *f (pl ~n)* facade

fassen [FAH-sern] *v* grip

faul [fowl] *adj* lazy

Faust [fowst] *f (pl ~e)* fist

Fausthandschuhe [FOWST-hahnt-shoo-er] *mpl* mittens *pl*

Faustschlag [FOWST-shlark] *m (pl ~e)* punch

Favorit [fah-voa-REET] *m (pl ~en)* favourite

Fayence [fah-YAHNGS] *f* faience

Februar [FAY-broo-arr] *m* February

Feder [FAY-derr] *f (pl ~n)* feather; pen

fegen [FAY-gern] *v* sweep

fehlend [FAY-lernt] *adj* missing

Fehler [FAY-lerr] *m (pl ~)* mistake; fault

fehlerhaft [FAY-lerr-hahft] *adj* faulty

Fehltritt [FAYL-trit] *m (pl ~e)* slip

Feier [FIGH-err] *f (pl ~n)* celebration

feierlich [FIGH-err-likh] *adj* solemn

Feierlichkeit [FIGH-err-likh-kight] *f (pl ~en)* ceremony

feiern [FIGH-errn] *v* celebrate

Feiertag [FIGH-err-tark] *m (pl ~e)* holiday

Feige [FIGH-ger] *f (pl ~n)* fig

Feigling [FIGHK-ling] *m (pl ~e)* coward

Feile [FIGH-ler] *f (pl ~n)* file

fein [fighn] *adj* fine; delicate

Feind [fighnt] *m (pl ~e; f ~in)* enemy

Feinkost [FIGHN-kost] *f* delicatessen

Feld [fehlt] *nt (pl ~er)* field

Feldbett [FEHLT-beht] *nt (pl ~en)* cot; camp-bed

Feldflasche [FEHLT-flah-sher] *f (pl ~n)* water-canteen

Feldstecher [FEHLT-shteh-kherr] *m (pl ~)* field glasses *pl*

Felge [FEHL-ger] *f (pl ~n)* rim

Felsblock [FEHLS-blok] *m (pl ~e)* boulder

Felsen [FEHL-zern] *m (pl ~)* rock

felsig [FEHL-zikh] *adj* rocky

Fenster [FEHNS-terr] *nt (pl ~)* window

Fensterladen [FEHNS-terr-lar-dern] *m (pl ~)* shutter

Ferien [FAYR-yern] *pl* vacation

Ferienlager [FAYR-yern-lar-gerr] *nt* (*pl* ~) holiday camp

fern [fehrn] *adj* far

ferner [FEHR-nerr] *adj* farther; further

Ferngespräch [FEHRN-ger-shpraikh] *nt* (*pl* ~e) trunk-call

* **fernhalten (sich)** [zikh-FEHRN-hahl-tern] *v* keep off

Fernsehapparat [FEHRN-zay-ah-pah-rart] *m* (*pl* ~e) television set

Fernsehen [FEHRN-zay-ern] *nt* television

Fernsprechzelle [FEHRN-shprehkh-tseh-ler] *f* (*pl* ~n) telephone booth

fernst [fehrnst] *adj* farthest

Ferse [FEHR-zer] *f* (*pl* ~n) heel

Fertigkeit [FEHR-tikh-kight] *f* skill; art

fest [fehst] *adj* solid; firm; fixed; *adv* tight

Fest [fehst] *nt* (*pl* ~e) feast

feste Speisenfolge [fehs-ter-SHPIGH-zern-fol-ger] table d'hôte

fester Preis [FEHS-terr-PRIGHS] fixed price

festes Menü [FEHS-ters-may-NEW] set menu

* **festhalten (sich)** [zikh-FEHST-hahl-tern] *v* hold on

Festival [FEHS-ti-verl] *nt* (*pl* ~s) festival

Festkörper [FEHST-kurr-perr] *m* (*pl* ~) solid

Festland [FEHST-lahnt] *nt* mainland

festlich [FEHST-likh] *adj* festive

Festmahl [FEHST-marl] *nt* (*pl* ~er) banquet

festsetzen [FEHST-zeh-tsern] *v* stipulate

Festung [FEHS-toong] *f* (*pl* ~en) fortress

fett [feht] *adj* fat

Fett [feht] *nt* (*pl* ~e) fat

fettig [FEH-tikh] *adj* fatty; greasy

feucht [foykht] *adj* damp; humid; moist

Feuchtigkeit [FOYKH-tikh-kight] *f* moisture

Feuchtigkeitskrem [FOYKH-tikh-kights-kraym] *f* (*pl* ~s) moisturizing cream

feudal [foy-DARL] *adj* feudal

Feuer [FOY-err] *nt* (*pl* ~) fire

Feueralarm [FOY-err-ah-lahrm] *m* fire alarm

feuerfest [FOY-err-fehst] *adj* fireproof

Feuerlöscher [FOY-err-lur-sherr] *m* (*pl* ~) fire extinguisher; extinguisher

Feuerstein [FOY-err-shtighn] *m* (*pl* ~e) flint

Feuerzeug [FOY-err-tsoyk] *nt* (*pl* ~e) cigarette-lighter

Fieber [FEE-berr] *nt* fever

Fieberblase [FEE-berr-blar-zer] *f* (*pl* ~n) fever blister

fiebrig [FEE-brikh] *adj* feverish

Filet [fi-LAY] *nt* (*pl* ~s) tenderloin steak

Film [film] *m* (*pl* ~e) film; movie

filmen [FIL-mern] *v* film

Filmkamera [FILM-kah-mer-rah] *f* (*pl* ~s) movie camera

Filmleinwand [FILM-lighn-vahnt] *f* screen

Filter [FIL-terr] *m* (*pl* ~) filter

Filtermundstück [FIL-terr-moont-shtewk] *nt* (*pl* ~e) filter tip

Filz [filts] *m* (*pl* ~e) felt

finanziell [fi-nahn-TSYEHL] *adj* financial

*finden [FIN-dern] *v* find

Finger [FING-err] *m* (*pl* ~) finger

Fingergelenk [FING-err-ger-lehngk] *nt* (*pl* ~ e) knuckle

Fingerhut [FING-err-hoot] *m* (*pl* ~ e) thimble

Fingernagel [FING-err-nar-gerl] *m* (*pl* ~) nail

Finne [FI-ner] *m* (*pl* ~n; *f* **Finnin**) Finn

finnisch [FI-nish] *adj* Finnish

Finnland [FIN-lahnt] *nt* Finland

Firma [FIR-mah] *f* (*pl* **Firmen**) firm

Firnis [FIR-nis] *m* varnish

Fisch [fish] *m* (*pl* ~e) fish

fischen [FI-shern] *v* fish

Fischer [FI-sherr] *m* (*pl* ~) fisherman

Fischhandlung [FISH-hahn-dloong] *f* (*pl* ~en) fish shop

Fischnetz [FISH-nehts] *nt* (*pl* ~e) fishing net

Fjord [fyort] *m* (*pl* ~e) fjord

flach [flahkh] *adj* flat

Fläche [FLEH-kher] *f* (*pl* ~n) area

Flachzange [FLAHKH-tsahng-er] *f* (*pl* ~n) pliers *pl*

Flamme [FLAH-mer] *f* (*pl* ~n) flame

Flanell [flah-NEHL] *m* flannel

Flasche [FLAH-sher] *f* (*pl* ~n) bottle

Flaschenöffner [FLAH-shern-urf-nerr] *m* (*pl* ~) bottle opener

Fleck [flehk] *m* (*pl* ~e) stain; spot

fleckenlos [FLEH-kern-loas] *adj* spotless; stainless

Fleckenreinigungsmittel [fleh-kern-RIGH-ni-goongs-mi-terl] *nt* (*pl* ~) stain remover

Fleisch [flighsh] *nt* flesh; meat

Fleischer [FLIGH-sherr] *m* (*pl* ~)

butcher

fleißig [FLIGH-sikh] *adj* industrious

flicken [FLI-kern] *v* patch

Flicken [FLI-kern] *m* (*pl* ~) patch

Fliege [FLEE-ger] *f* (*pl* ~n) bow tie; fly

*fliegen [FLEE-gern] *v* fly

*fließen [FLEE-sern] *v* flow

fließend [FLEE-sernt] *adj* fluent

fließendes Wasser [FLEE-sern-ders-VAH-serr] *nt* running water

Flitterwochen [FLI-terr-vo-khern] *fpl* honeymoon

Flotte [FLO-ter] *f* (*pl* ~n) fleet

Fluch [flookh] *m* (*pl* ~ e) curse

fluchen [FLOO-khern] *v* curse; swear

*flüchtig ansehen [flewkh-tikh-AHN-zay-ern] *v* glance

flüchtig erblicken [FLEWKH-tikh-ehr-BLI-kern] *v* glimpse

flüchtiger Blick [FLEWKH-ti-gerr-BLIK] glance; glimpse

Flug [flook] *m* (*pl* ~ e) flight

Flügel [FLEW-gerl] *m* (*pl* ~) wing

Flughafen [FLOOK-har-fern] *m* (*pl* ~) airport

Fluglinie [FLOOK-leen-yer] *f* (*pl* ~n) airline

Flugplatz [FLOOK-plahts] *m* (*pl* ~ e) airfield

Flugzeug [FLOOK-tsoyk] *nt* (*pl* ~e) airplane; aircraft; aeroplane; plane

Flur [floor] *m* (*pl* ~e) corridor

Fluß [floos] *m* (*pl* ~ e) river

Flußkrebs [FLOOS-krayps] *m* (*pl* ~e) crayfish

Flußlauf [FLOOS-lowf] *m* course

flüssig [FLEW-sikh] *adj* liquid

Flüssigkeit [FLEW-sikh-kight] *f* (*pl* ~en) fluid

flüstern [FLEWS-terrn] *v* whisper

Flußufer [FLOOS-oo-ferr] *nt* (*pl* ~)
riverside; river-bank

Flut [floot] *f* high tide

Föderation [fur-der-rah-TSYOAN]
f federation

Föhn [furn] *m* (*pl* ~e) hair-dryer

folgen [FOL-gern] *v* follow

folgend [FOL-gernt] *adj* following;
subsequent

folglich [FOLK-likh] *adv*
consequently

foppen [FO-pern] *v* kid

Forelle [foa-REH-ler] *f* (*pl* ~n)
trout

Form [form] *f* (*pl* ~en) form;
shape

Formalität [for-mah-li-TAIT] *f* (*pl*
~en) formality

Formel [FOR-merl] *f* (*pl* ~n)
formula

formen [FOR-mern] *v* form

förmlich [FURRM-likh] *adj* formal

Formular [for-moo-LARR] *nt* (*pl*
~e) form

Forschung [FOR-shoong] *f* (*pl*
~en) research

** **fortfahren** [FORT-far-rern] *v*
proceed; go on; go ahead; keep
on

Fortschritt [FORT-shrit] *m* (*pl* ~e)
progress

fortschrittlich [FORT-shrit-likh]
adj progressive

fortsetzen [FORT-zeh-tsern] *v*
continue

Foyer [foaah-YAY] *nt* (*pl* ~s) hall;
foyer

Fracht [frahkht] *f* (*pl* ~en)
freight; cargo

Frage [FRAR-ger] *f* (*pl* ~n)
question; query

fragen [FRAR-gern] *v* ask

fragen (sich) [zikh-FRAR-gern] *v*
wonder

fragend [FRAR-gernt] *adj*
interrogative

Fragezeichen [FRAR-ger-tsigh-
khern] *nt* (*pl* ~) question
mark

frankieren [frahng-KEE-rern] *v*
stamp

Frankreich [FRAHNGK-righkh] *nt*
France

Franzose [frahn-TSOA-zer] *m* (*pl*
~n; *f* ~in) Frenchman

französisch [frahn-TSUR-zish]
adj French

Frau [frow] *f* (*pl* ~en) woman

Frauenarzt [FROW-ern-ahrtst] *m*
(*pl* ~e; *f* ~in) gynaecologist

Fräulein [FROY-lighn] *nt* miss

frei [frigh] *adj* vacant; free

freigestellt [FRIGH-ger-shtehlt]
adj optional

** **freihalten** [FRIGH-hahl-tern] *v*
hold

Freiheit [FRIGH-hight] *f* liberty;
freedom

Freikarte [FRIGH-kahr-ter] *f* (*pl*
~n) free ticket

Freitag [FRIGH-tark] *m* Friday

freiwillig [FRIGH-vi-likh] *adj*
voluntary

Freiwillige [FRIGH-vi-li-ger] *m* (*pl*
~n; *f* ~) volunteer

Freizeit [FRIGH-tsight] *f* spare
time

fremd [frehmt] *adj* strange;
foreign

Fremde [FREHM-der] *m* (*pl* ~n; *f*
~) stranger; foreigner

fremde Währung [frehm-der-
VAI-roong] foreign currency

Fremdenheim [FREHM-dern-
highm] *nt* (*pl* ~e) guest-house

Fremdenverkehr [FREHM-dern-
fehr-kayr] *m* tourism

Freude [FROY-der] *f* (*pl* ~n) joy;
pleasure

freudig [FROY-dikh] *adj* joyful

Freund [froynt] *m* (*pl* ~e; *f* ~in)
friend

freundlich [FROYNT-likh] *adj* kind

Freundschaft [FROYNT-shahft] *f*
(*pl* ~en) friendship

freundschaftlich [FROYNT-shahft-
likh] *adj* friendly

Frieden [FREE-dern] *m* peace

Friedensrichter [FREE-derns-
RIKH-terr] *m* (*pl* ~) magistrate

Friedhof [FREET-hoaf] *m* (*pl* ~e)
cemetery

friedlich [FREET-likh] *adj*
peaceful

frisch [frish] *adj* fresh

frisches Gemüse [FRI-shers-ger-
MEW-zer] greens *pl*

Friseur [fri-ZURR] *m* (*pl* ~e; *f*
Friseuse) barber; hairdresser

Frist [frist] *f* (*pl* ~en) term

Frisur [fri-ZOOR] *f* (*pl* ~en)
setting; hair set

froh [froa] *adj* glad

fröhlich [FRUR-likh] *adj* jolly;
merry

Fröhlichkeit [FRUR-likh-kight] *f*
gaiety

Frosch [frosh] *m* (*pl* ~e) frog

Frost [frost] *m* frost

Frostbeule [FROST-boy-ler] *f* (*pl*
~n) chilblain

Frösteln [FRURS-terln] *nt* chill

fröstelnd [FRURS-terlnt] *adj*
shivery

Frottierstoff [FRO-teer-shtof] *m*
(*pl* ~e) towelling

fruchtbar [FROOKHT-barr] *adj*
fertile

Fruchtsaft [FROOKHT-zahft] *m* (*pl*
~e) squash

früh [frew] *adj* early; *adv* early

früher [FREW-err] *adv* formerly;
adj former

Frühling [FREW-ling] *m* spring

Frühlingszeit [FREW-lings-tsight]
f springtime

Frühstück [FREW-shtewk] *nt*
breakfast

Fuchs [fooks] *m* (*pl* ~e) fox

fühlen [FEW-lern] *v* feel

führen [FEW-rern] *v* lead; guide

führend [FEW-rernt] *adj* leading

Führer [FEW-rerr] *m* (*pl* ~; *f* ~in)
leader; guide

Führerschein [FEW-rerr-shighn]
m (*pl* ~e) driving licence

Fülle [FEW-ler] *f* plenty

füllen [FEW-lern] *v* fill

Füller [FEW-lerr] *m* (*pl* ~)
fountain pen

Füllung [FEW-loong] *f* (*pl* ~en)
filling; stuffing

Fundbüro [FOONT-bew-roa] *nt* (*pl*
~s) lost property office

fünf [fewnf] *adj* five

fünfhundert [fewnf-HOON-derrt]
adj five hundred

fünfte [FEWNF-ter] *adj* fifth

fünfzehn [FEWNF-tsayn] *adj*
fifteen

fünfzehnte [FEWNF-tsayn-ter] *adj*
fifteenth

fünfzig [FEWNF-tsikh] *adj* fifty

funkelnd [FOONG-kerlnt] *adj*
sparkling

Funken [FOONG-kern] *m* (*pl* ~)
spark

Funktion [foongk-TSYOAN] *f* (*pl*
~en) function; operation

funktionieren [foongk-tsyoa-
NEE-rern] *v* work

funktionsunfähig [foongk-
tsyoans-OON-fai-ikh] *adj* out of
order

für [fewr] *prep* for

Furcht [foorkht] *f* fear

fürchten [FEWRKH-tern] *v* fear

Fürsorge [FEWR-zor-ger] *f* welfare

Furt [foort] *f* (*pl* ~en) ford

Furunkel [foo-ROONG-kerl] *m* (*pl* ~) boil

Fürwort [FEWR-vort] *nt* (*pl* ˜er) pronoun

Fuß [foos] *m* (*pl* ˜e) foot

Fußball [FOOS-bahl] *m* (*pl* ˜e) football; soccer

Fußballspiel [FOOS-bahl-shpeel] *nt* (*pl* ˜e) football match

Fußboden [FOOS-boa-dern] *m* (*pl* ˜) floor

Fußbremse [FOOS-brehm-zer] *f* (*pl* ~n) foot-brake

Fußgänger [FOOS-gehng-err] *m* (*pl* ~; *f* ~in) pedestrian

Fußgänger verboten [FOOS-gehng-err-fehr-BOA-tern] no pedestrians

Fußgängerübergang [FOOS-gehng-err-ew-berr-gahng] *m* (*pl* ˜e) pedestrian crossing

Fußknöchel [FOOS-knur-kherl] *m* (*pl* ~) ankle

Fußpfleger [FOOS-pflay-gerr] *m* (*pl* ~; *f* ~in) pedicure; chiropodist

Fußpuder [FOOS-poo-derr] *nt* foot powder

Fußweg [FOOS-vayk] *m* (*pl* ~e) footpath

Futterstoff [FOO-terr-shtof] *m* (*pl* ~e) lining

Gabel [GAR-berl] *f* (*pl* ~n) fork

gabeln (sich) [zikh-GAR-berln] *v* fork; branch off

Gabelung [GAR-ber-loong] *f* (*pl* ~en) fork

gähnen [GAI-nern] *v* yawn

Galerie [gah-ler-REE] *f* (*pl* ~n) gallery

Gang [gahng] *m* (*pl* ˜e) course; aisle

Gangschaltung [GAHNG-shahl-toong] *f* gear-lever

Gans [gahns] *f* (*pl* ˜e) goose

ganz [gahnts] *adv* entirely; *adj* entire; whole

ganz gewiß [gahnts-ger-VIS] without fail

Ganze [GAHN-tser] *nt* whole

gänzlich [GEHNTS-likh] *adv* wholly

gar nicht [GARR-nikht] not at all

Garage [gah-RAR-zher] *f* (*pl* ~n) garage

Garantie [gah-rahn-TEE] *f* (*pl* ~n) guarantee

garantieren [gah-rahn-TEE-rern] *v* guarantee

Garderobe [gahr-DROA-ber] *f* (*pl* ~n) wardrobe; cloak-room; check-room

Garn [gahrn] *nt* (*pl* ~e) yarn

Garnele [gahr-NAY-ler] *f* (*pl* ~n) shrimp

garstig [GAHRS-tikh] *adj* nasty

Garten [GAHR-tern] *m* (*pl* ˜) garden

Gärtner [GEHRT-nerr] *m* (*pl* ~; *f* ~in) gardener

Gas [gars] *nt* (*pl* ~e) gas

Gäßchen [GEHS-khern] *nt* (*pl* ~) alley

Gasherd [GARS-hayrt] *m* (*pl* ~e) gas cooker

Gasofen [GARS-oa-fern] *m* (*pl* ˜) gas stove

Gaspedal [GARS-pay-darl] *nt* (*pl* ~e) accelerator

Gast [gahst] *m* (*pl* ˜e) visitor; guest

Gästezimmer [GEHS-ter-tsi-merr] *nt* (*pl* ~) spare room

gastfreundlich [GAHST-froynt-likh] *adj* hospitable

Gastfreundschaft [GAHST-froynt-shahft] *f* hospitality

Gastgeber [GAHST-gay-berr] *m* (*pl* ~) host

Gastgeberin [GAHST-gay-ber-rin] *f* (*pl* ~nen) hostess

Gasthof [GAHST-hoaf] *m* (*pl* ~e) inn

gastrisch [GAHS-trish] *adj* gastric

Gaststätte [GAHST-shteh-ter] *f* (*pl* ~n) roadhouse

Gastwirt [GAHST-virt] *m* (*pl* ~e) innkeeper

Gastzimmer [GAHST-tsi-merr] *nt* (*pl* ~) guest-room

Gaswerk [GARS-vehrk] *nt* (*pl* ~e) gasworks

Gattin [GAH-tin] *f* (*pl* ~nen) wife

Gaze [GAR-zer] *f* gauze

Gebäude [ger-BOY-der] *nt* (*pl* ~) building

* **geben** [GAY-bern] *v* give; deal

Gebet [ger-BAYT] *nt* (*pl* ~e) prayer

Gebiet [ger-BEET] *nt* (*pl* ~e) region

gebirgig [ger-BIR-gikh] *adj* mountainous

Gebirgspaß [ger-BIRKS-pahs] *m* (*pl* ~e) pass

Gebiß [ger-BIS] *nt* (*pl* ~e) denture

geboren [ger-BOA-rern] *adj* born

gebraten [ger-BRAR-tern] *adj* fried

Gebrauch [ger-BROWKH] *m* use

gebrauchen [ger-BROW-khern] *v* use

gebraucht [ger-BROWKHT] *adj* used; second-hand

gebügelt [ger-BEW-gerlt] *adj* pressed

Gebühr [ger-BEWR] *f* (*pl* ~en) charge

Gebühren [ger-BEW-rern] *fpl* dues *pl*

Geburt [ger-BOORT] *f* (*pl* ~en) birth

Geburtsort [ger-BOORTS-ort] *m* (*pl* ~e) birthplace

Geburtsschein [ger-BOORTS-shighn] *m* (*pl* ~e) birth certificate

Geburtstag [ger-BOORTS-tark] *m* (*pl* ~e) birthday

Gedächtnis [ger-DEHKHT-nis] *nt* (*pl* ~se) memory

Gedanke [ger-DAHNG-ker] *m* (*pl* ~n) thought

Gedeckkosten [ger-DEHK-kos-tern] *pl* cover charge

Gedicht [ger-DIKHT] *nt* (*pl* ~e) poem

Geduld [ger-DOOLT] *f* patience

geduldig [ger-DOOL-dikh] *adj* patient

geeignet [ger-IGH-gnert] *adj* proper; suitable

Gefahr [ger-FARR] *f* (*pl* ~en) danger

gefährlich [ger-FAIR-likh] *adj* dangerous

* **gefallen** [ger-FAH-lern] *v* please

Gefallen finden an [ger-FAH-lern-fin-dern-ahn] fancy

gefällig [ger-FEH-likh] *adj* obliging

Gefälligkeit [ger-FEH-likh-kight] *f* (*pl* ~en) favour

Gefängnis [ger-FEHNG-nis] *nt* (*pl* ~se) gaol; prison; jail

Gefäß [ger-FAIS] *nt* (*pl* ~e) vessel

Geflügel [ger-FLEW-gerl] *nt* poultry; fowl

Geflüster [ger-FLEWS-terr] *nt*
whisper

* **gefrieren** [ger-FREE-rern] *v*
freeze

Gefrierpunkt [ger-FREER-
poongkt] *m* (*pl* ~e) freezing
point

Gefrierschutzmittel [ger-FREER-
shoots-mi-terl] *nt* (*pl* ~)
antifreeze

Gefrierwaren [ger-FREER-var-
rern] *fpl* frozen food

gefroren [ger-FROA-rern] *adj*
frozen

Gefühl [ger-FEWL] *nt* (*pl* ~e)
feeling

gefüllt [ger-FEWLT] *adj* stuffed

gegen [GAY-gern] *prep* against;
versus

Gegenstand [GAY-gern-shtahnt]
m (*pl* ~e) article; object

* **gegenstoßen** [GAY-gern-shtoa-
sern] *v* knock against

gegenüber [gay-gern-EW-berr]
prep opposite

* **gegenüberstehen** [gay-gern-
EW-berr-shtay-ern] *v* face

gegenwärtig [gay-gern-VEHR-
tikh] *adj* current; present

gegrillt [ger-GRILT] *adj* grilled

Gehalt [ger-HAHLT] *nt* (*pl* ~er)
salary

geheim [ger-HIGHM] *adj* secret

Geheimnis [ger-HIGHM-nis] *nt* (*pl*
~se) secret; mystery

geheimnisvoll [ger-HIGHM-nis-
fol] *adj* mysterious

* **gehen** [GAY-ern] *v* walk; go

Gehirn [ger-HIRN] *nt* (*pl* ~e)
brain

Gehirnerschütterung [ger-HIRN-
ehr-shew-ter-roong] *f*
concussion

Gehör [ger-HURR] *nt* hearing

gehorchen [ger-HOR-khern] *v*
obey

gehören [ger-HUR-rern] *v* belong

gehorsam [ger-HOAR-zarm] *adj*
obedient

Gehorsam [ger-HOAR-zarm] *m*
obedience

Geige [GIGH-ger] *f* (*pl* ~n) violin

Geist [gighst] *m* (*pl* ~er) ghost;
spirit

geistig [GIGHS-tikh] *adj* mental

Geistliche [GIGHST-li-kher] *m* (*pl*
~n) minister; clergyman

geistreich [GIGHST-righkh] *adj*
witty

gekocht [ger-KOKHT] *adj* cooked;
boiled

Gekreisch [ger-KRIGHSH] *nt*
shriek

gekrümmt [ger-KREWMT] *adj*
curved

Gelächter [ger-LEHKH-terr] *nt* (*pl*
~) laughter

gelähmt [ger-LAIMT] *adj*
paralysed

Gelände [ger-LEHN-der] *nt* site

Geländer [ger-LEHN-derr] *nt* (*pl*
~) rail

gelb [gehlp] *adj* yellow

Gelbsucht [GEHLP-zookht] *f*
jaundice

Geld [gehlt] *nt* money

Geldmittel [GEHLT-mi-terl] *ntpl*
means *pl*

Geldstrafe [GEHLT-shtrar-fer] *f*
(*pl* ~n) fine

Gelee [zhay-LAY] *nt* (*pl* ~s) jelly

gelegen [ger-LAY-gern] *adj*
situated

Gelegenheit [ger-LAY-gern-
hight] *f* (*pl* ~en) occasion;
opportunity

Gelegenheitskauf [ger-LAY-gern-
hights-kowf] *m* (*pl* ~e)

bargain

gelegentlich [ger-LAY-gernt-likh] *adv* occasionally

Gelehrte [ger-LAYR-ter] *m* (*pl* ~n) scholar

Geleit [ger-LIGHT] *nt* (*pl* ~e) escort

geleiten [ger-LIGH-tern] *v* escort

Gelenk [ger-LEHNGK] *nt* (*pl* ~e) joint

* **gelingen** [ger-LING-ern] *v* succeed

Gemälde [ger-MAIL-der] *nt* (*pl* ~) painting

gemalt [ger-MARLT] *adj* painted

gemäß [ger-MAIS] *prep* according to

gemein [ger-MIGHN] *adj* vulgar

Gemeinde [ger-MIGHN-der] *f* (*pl* ~n) congregation; community

gemeinsam [ger-MIGHN-zarm] *adj* common; *adv* jointly

gemischt [ger-MISHT] *adj* mixed

Gemüse [ger-MEW-zer] *nt* vegetable

Gemüsehändler [ger-MEW-zer-hehn-dlerr] *m* (*pl* ~; *f* ~in) greengrocer

genau [ger-NOW] *adj* exact; accurate; precise; *adv* exactly; just

genehmigen [ger-NAY-mi-gern] *v* approve

Genehmigung [ger-NAY-mi-goong] *f* (*pl* ~en) permit

General [gay-ner-RARL] *m* (*pl* ~e) general

Generation [gay-ner-rah-TSYOAN] *f* (*pl* ~en) generation

Generator [gay-ner-RAR-tor] *m* (*pl* ~en) generator

* **genießen** [ger-NEE-sern] *v* enjoy

genug [ger-NOOK] *adj* enough

genügen [ger-NEW-gern] *v* suffice

genügend [ger-NEW-gernt] *adj* sufficient

Genugtuung [ger-NOOK-too-oong] *f* satisfaction

geographisches Lexikon [gayoa-GRAR-fi-shers-LEH-ksi-kon] *nt* gazetteer

Geologie [gayoa-loa-GEE] *f* geology

Geometrie [gayoa-may-TREE] *f* geometry

Gepäck [ger-PEHK] *nt* baggage; luggage

Gepäckaufbewahrung [ger-PEHK-owf-ber-VAR-roong] *f* left luggage office

Gepäckaufgabe [ger-PEHK-owf-gar-ber] *f* baggage office

Gepäcknetz [ger-PEHK-nehts] *nt* (*pl* ~e) rack; luggage rack

Gepäckwagen [ger-PEHK-var-gern] *m* (*pl* ~) luggage van

Geplauder [ger-PLOW-derr] *nt* chat

gepökelt [ger-PUR-kerlt] *adj* pickled

gerade [GRAR-der] *adj* straight

geradeaus [ger-RAR-der-ows] *adv* straight on; straight ahead

geradewegs [ger-RAR-der-VAYKS] *adv* straight

Gerät [ger-RAIT] *nt* (*pl* ~e) appliance; utensil; implement

geräuchert [ger-ROY-kherrt] *adj* smoked

geräumig [ger-ROY-mikh] *adj* spacious; roomy

gerecht [ger-REHKHT] *adj* fair; just

Gerechtigkeit [ger-REHKH-tikh-kight] *f* justice

Gericht [ger-RIKHT] *nt* (*pl* ~e) court; dish

Gerichtshof [ger-RIKHTS-hoaf] *m*

(*pl* ~e) law courts *pl*

Gerichtsverfahren [ger-RIKHTS-fehr-far-rern] *nt* (*pl* ~) trial

geringer [ger-RING-err] *adj* minor

geringfügig [ger-RING-few-gikh] *adj* petty

* **gerinnen** [ger-RI-nern] *v* coagulate

* **gern mögen** [gehrn-MUR-gern] *v* like

* **gerne haben** [GEHR-ner-har-bern] *v* care for

Gerste [GEHRS-ter] *f* barley

Geruch [ger-ROOKH] *m* (*pl* ~e) odour; smell

Gerücht [ger-REWKHT] *nt* (*pl* ~e) rumour

Gesamtsumme [ger-ZAHMT-zoo-mer] *f* (*pl* ~n) total

Gesandtschaft [ger-ZAHNT-shahft] *f* (*pl* ~en) legation

Geschäft [ger-SHEHFT] *nt* (*pl* ~e) deal; shop

Geschäftigkeit [ger-SHEHF-tikh-kight] *f* bustle

geschäftlich [ger-SHEHFT-likh] on business

Geschäftsführer [ger-SHEHFTS-few-rerr] *m* (*pl* ~) executive

Geschäftsmann [ger-SHEHFTS-mahn] *m* (*pl* **Geschäftsleute**) tradesman; businessman

Geschäftsreise [ger-SHEHFTS-righ-zer] *f* (*pl* ~n) business trip

Geschäftsschluß [ger-SHEHFTS-shloos] *m* closing time

Geschäftszeit [ger-SHEHFTS-tsight] *f* (*pl* ~en) business hours *pl*

gescheit [ger-SHIGHT] *adj* smart

Geschenk [ger-SHEHNGK] *nt* (*pl* ~e) gift; present

Geschichte [ger-SHIKH-ter] *f* (*pl*

~n) story; history

geschichtlich [ger-SHIKHT-likh] *adj* historical

geschickt [ger-SHIKT] *adj* skillful; skilled

geschieden [ger-SHEE-dern] *adj* divorced

Geschlecht [ger-SHLEHKHT] *nt* (*pl* ~er) gender; sex

Geschlechtskrankheit [ger-SHLEHKHTS-krahngk-hight] *f* (*pl* ~en) venereal disease

geschlossen [ger-SHLO-sern] *adj* shut; closed

Geschmack [ger-SHMAHK] *m* taste

geschmacklos [ger-SHMAHK-loas] *adj* tasteless

geschmolzen [ger-SHMOL-tsern] *adj* melted

Geschöpf [ger-SHURPF] *nt* (*pl* ~e) creature

geschwind [ger-SHVINT] *adj* swift

Geschwindigkeit [ger-SHVIN-dikh-kight] *f* (*pl* ~en) speed; gear

Geschwindigkeitsbegrenzung [ger-SHVIN-dikh-kights-ber-GREHN-tsoong] *f* speed limit

Geschwindigkeitsmesser [ger-SHVIN-dikh-kights-meh-serr] *m* speedometer

Geschwulst [ger-SHVOOLST] *f* (*pl* ~e) swelling

Geschwür [ger-SHVEWR] *nt* (*pl* ~e) ulcer

Gesellschaft [ger-ZEHL-shahft] *f* (*pl* ~en) society; company

Gesellschaftsanzug [ger-ZEHL-shahfts-ahn-tsook] *m* (*pl* ~e) evening dress

Gesellschaftsraum [ger-ZEHL-shahfts-rowm] *m* (*pl* ~e) lounge

Gesellschaftsreise [ger-ZEHL-shahfts-righ-zer] *f (pl ~n)* conducted tour

Gesetz [ger-ZEHTS] *nt (pl ~e)* law

gesetzlich [ger-ZEHTS-likh] *adj* legal; lawful

gesetzt [ger-ZEHTST] *adj* sedate

Gesicht [ger-ZIKHT] *m (pl ~er)* face

Gesichtskrem [ger-ZIKHTS-kraym] *f* face cream

Gesichtsmassage [ger-ZIKHTS-mah-sar-zher] *f (pl ~n)* face massage

Gesichtspackung [ger-ZIKHTS-pah-koong] *f (pl ~en)* face pack

Gesichtszug [ger-ZIKHTS-tsook] *m (pl ~e)* feature

Gespräch [ger-SHPRAIKH] *nt (pl ~e)* talk; conversation

Gestalt [ger-SHTAHLT] *f (pl ~en)* figure

Geständnis [ger-SHTEHNT-nis] *nt (pl ~se)* confession

gestern [GEHS-terrn] *adv* yesterday

gestreift [ger-SHTRIGHFT] *adj* striped

Gestrüpp [ger-SHTREWP] *nt (pl ~e)* scrub

gesund [ger-ZOONT] *adj* healthy

Gesundheit [ger-ZOONT-hight] *f* health

Gesundheitsbescheinigung [ger-ZOONT-hights-ber-shigh-ni-goong] *f (pl ~en)* health certificate

Getränk [ger-TREHNGK] *nt (pl ~e)* beverage

Getreideflocken [ger-TRAHI-der-flo-kern] *fpl* cereal

getrennt [ger-TREHNT] *adv* apart; *adj* separate

Getriebe [ger-TREE-ber] *nt* gearbox

getrocknet [ger-TROK-nert] *adj* dried

Getue [ger-TOO-er] *nt* fuss

Gewächshaus [ger-VEHKS-hows] *nt (pl ~er)* greenhouse

gewahr [ger-VARR] *adj* aware

gewähren [ger-VAI-rern] *v* grant

gewalttätig [ger-VAHLT-tai-tikh] *adj* violent

Gewalttätigkeit [ger-VAHLT-tai-tikh-kight] *f (pl ~en)* violence

Gewebe [ger-VAY-ber] *nt (pl ~)* fabric

Gewehr [ger-VAYR] *nt (pl ~e)* rifle

Gewerkschaft [ger-VEHRK-shahft] *f (pl ~en)* trade-union

Gewicht [ger-VIKHT] *nt (pl ~e)* weight

Gewinn [ger-VIN] *m (pl ~e)* winnings *pl;* gain; profit

* **gewinnen** [ger-VI-nern] *v* gain; win

gewinnend [ger-VI-nernt] *adj* winning

Gewissen [ger-VI-sern] *nt* conscience

Gewitter [ger-VI-terr] *nt (pl ~)* thunderstorm

gewitterschwül [ger-VI-terr-shvewl] *adj* thundery

Gewohnheit [ger-VOAN-hight] *f (pl ~en)* custom; habit

gewöhnlich [ger-VURN-likh] *adj* usual; ordinary

gewohnt [ger-VOANT] *adj* accustomed; habitual

* **gewöhnt sein** [ger-VURNT-zighn] *v* used to (be)

Gewölbe [ger-VURL-ber] *nt (pl ~)* vault

Gewürz [ger-VEWRTS] *nt (pl ~e)*

seasoning; spice

gewürzt [ger-VEWRTST] *adj* spiced

Gezeit [ger-TSIGHT] *f (pl* ~**en)** tide

Gicht [gikht] *f* gout

Giebel [GEE-berl] *m (pl* ~) gable

Gier [geer] *f* greed

gierig [GEE-rikh] *adj* greedy

* **gießen** [GEE-sern] *v* pour

Gift [gift] *nt (pl* ~e) poison

giftig [GIF-tikh] *adj* poisonous

Gipfel [GI-pferl] *m (pl* ~) peak; top; summit

Gips [gips] *m* plaster

Gitarre [gi-TAH-rer] *f (pl* ~**n)** guitar

Gitter [GI-terr] *nt (pl* ~) railing; grating

glänzend [GLEHN-tsernt] *adj* glossy; brilliant

Glas [glars] *nt (pl* ~̈er) glass; jar

glasieren [glah-ZEE-rern] *v* glaze

glatt [glaht] *adj* smooth

Glattbutt [GLAHT-boot] *m (pl* ~e) brill

Glaube [GLOW-ber] *m* belief; faith

glauben [GLOW-bern] *v* believe

gleich [glighkh] *adv* alike; *adj* equal; like

gleich hier [glighkh-HEER] right here

* **gleichen** [GLIGH-khern] *v* resemble

Gleichgewicht [GLIGHKH-ger-vikht] *nt* balance

Gleichheit [GLIGHKH-hight] *f* equality

Gleichstrom [GLIGHKH-shtroam] *m* direct current

gleichwertig [GLIGHKH-vayr-tikh] *adj* equivalent

gleichzeitig [GLIGHKH-tsigh-tikh] *adj* simultaneous

Gleis [glighs] *nt (pl* ~e) track

* **gleiten** [GLIGH-tern] *v* slide; glide

Gleiten [GLIGH-tern] *nt* slide

Gletscher [GLEH-cherr] *m (pl* ~) glacier

Glied [gleet] *nt (pl* ~er) limb

Glocke [GLO-ker] *f (pl* ~**n)** bell

Glück [glewk] *nt* luck; happiness; fortune

glücklich [GLEWK-likh] *adj* fortunate; happy; lucky

Glücksspiel [GLEWKS-shpeel] *nt (pl* ~e) gambling

Glückwünsche [GLEWK-vewn-sher] *mpl* congratulations *pl*

Glühbirne [GLEW-bir-ner] *f (pl* ~**n)** light bulb

glühen [GLEW-ern] *v* glow

Glut [gloot] *f* glow

gnädige Frau [GNAIDI-ger-FROW] *f* madam

Gobelin [goa-ber-LANG] *m (pl* ~s) tapestry

Gold [golt] *nt* gold

golden [GOL-dern] *adj* golden

Goldgrube [GOLT-groo-ber] *f (pl* ~**n)** goldmine

Goldschmied [GOLT-shmeet] *m (pl* ~e) goldsmith

Golf [golf] *nt* golf; *m* gulf

Golfklub [GOLF-kloop] *m (pl* ~s) golf-club

Golfplatz [GOLF-plahts] *m (pl* ~̈e) golf-links; golf-course; links *pl*

Gondel [GON-derl] *f (pl* ~**n)** gondola

Gosse [GO-ser] *f (pl* ~**n)** gutter

Gott [got] *m* God

Gottesdienst [GO-ters-deenst] *m (pl* ~e) worship

Gouvernante [goo-vehr-NAHN-ter] *f (pl* ~**n)** governess

Gouverneur [goo-vehr-NURR] *m (pl* ~e) governor

Grab [grarp] *nt (pl ⁓er)* grave; tomb

** **graben** [GRAR-bern] *v* dig

Graben [GRAR-bern] *m (pl ⁓)* ditch

Grabstein [GRARP-shtighn] *m (pl ⁓e)* gravestone

Grad [grart] *m* degree

Grad Celsius [grart-TSEHL-zyoos] centigrade

graduieren [grah-doo-EE-rern] *v* graduate

Gram [grarm] *m* grief

Gramm [grahm] *nt* gram

Grammatik [grah-MAH-tik] *f* grammar

grammatikalisch [grah-mah-ti-KAR-lish] *adj* grammatical

Grammophon [grah-moa-FOAN] *nt (pl ⁓e)* gramophone

Granit [grah-NEET] *m* granite

Graphik [GRAR-fik] *f (pl ⁓en)* graph

graphisch [GRAR-fish] *adj* graphic

Gras [grars] *nt* grass

grasig [GRAR-zikh] *adj* grassy

Grat [grart] *m (pl ⁓e)* ridge

grau [grow] *adj* grey

gravieren [grah-VEE-rern] *v* engrave

grelles Licht [GREH -lers-LIKHT] glare

Grenze [GREHN-tser] *f (pl ⁓n)* frontier; border; boundary; limit

Grieche [GREE-kher] *m (pl ⁓n; f Griechin)* Greek

Griechenland [GREE-khern-lahnt] *nt* Greece

griechisch [GREE-khish] *adj* Greek

grillen [GRI-lern] *v* grill

Grillroom [GRIL-room] *m* grill-

room

grinsen [GRIN-zern] *v* grin

Grinsen [GRIN-zern] *nt* grin

Grippe [GRI-per] *f* flu; influenza

grob [grop] *adj* rude

groß [groas] *adj* big; large; great; tall

großartig [GROAS-ahr-tikh] *adj* terrific; grand

Großbritannien [groas-bri-TAHN-yern] *nt* Great Britain

Größe [GRUR-ser] *f (pl ⁓n)* size

Großeltern [GROAS-ehl-terrn] *pl* grandparents *pl*

größer [GRUR-serr] *adj* major; bigger

Großhandel [GROAS-hahn-derl] *m* wholesale

Großmutter [GROAS-moo-terr] *f (pl ⁓)* grandmother

größte [GRURS-ter] *adj* biggest

Großvater [GROAS-far-terr] *m (pl ⁓)* grandfather

** **großziehen** [GROAS-tsee-ern] *v* rear

großzügig [GROAS-tsew-gikh] *adj* generous

Grotte [GRO-ter] *f (pl ⁓n)* grotto

grün [grewn] *adj* green

Grund [groont] *m (pl ⁓e)* reason

gründen [GREWN-dern] *v* found

Grundlage [GROONT-lar-ger] *f (pl ⁓n)* base; basis

grundlegend [GROONT-lay-gernt] *adj* basic

gründlich [GREWNT-likh] *adj* thorough

Grundstück [GROONT-shtewk] *nt (pl ⁓e)* grounds *pl*

grüne Karte [grew-ner-KAHR-ter] green card

Gruppe [GROO-per] *f (pl ⁓n)* group; set; party

Grüße [GREW-ser] *mpl* regards *pl*;

greetings *pl*

grüßen [GREW-sern] *v* greet

Gummi [GOO-mi] *nt* rubber

Gummiband [GOO-mi-bahnt] *nt* (*pl* ̈er) elastic

Gummilinse [GOO-mi-lin-zer] *f* (*pl* ~n) zoom lens *pl*

günstig [GEWNS-tikh] *adj* favourable

gurgeln [GOOR-gerln] *v* gargle

Gurke [GOOR-ker] *f* (*pl* ~n) cucumber

Gürtel [GEWR-terl] *m* (*pl* ~) belt

Gußeisen [GOOS-igh-zern] *nt* cast-iron

gut [goot] *adv* all right; well; *adj* good; well

gutartig [GOOT-ahr-tikh] *adj* good-tempered

gute Manieren [GOO-ter-mah-NEE-rern] *fpl* amenities *pl*

Güter [GEW-terr] *ntpl* goods *pl*

Güterzug [GEW-terr-tsook] *m* (*pl* ̈e) goods-train

gutgebaut [goot-ger-BOWT] *adj* well-made

gutgelaunt [goot-ger-LOWNT] *adj* good-humoured

gutmütig [GOOT-mew-tikh] *adj* good-natured

Gutschein [GOOT-shighn] *m* (*pl* ~e) voucher

* **gutschreiben** [GOOT-shrigh-bern] *v* credit

Gymnasium [gewm-NAR-zyoom] *nt* (*pl* **Gymnasien**) grammar school

Haar [harr] *nt* (*pl* ~e) hair

Haarbürste [HARR-bewrs-ter] *f* (*pl* ~n) hairbrush

Haarfixativ [HARR-fik-sah-teef] *nt* setting lotion

Haarklemme [HARR-kleh-mer] *f* (*pl* ~n) hairgrip; bobby-pin

Haarkrem [HARR-kraym] *f* hair cream

Haarnadel [HARR-nar-derl] *f* (*pl* ~n) hairpin

Haarnetz [HARR-nehts] *nt* (*pl* ~e) hairnet

Haaröl [HARR-url] *nt* (*pl* ~e) hair-oil

Haarschnitt [HARR-shnit] *m* (*pl* ~e) haircut

Haarspülmittel [HARR-shpewl-mi-terl] *nt* (*pl* ~) rinse

Haarwickler [HARR-vik-lerr] *m* (*pl* ~) curlers *pl*

Haarwuchsmittel [HARR-vooks-mi-terl] *nt* hair tonic

Habe [HAR-ber] *f* possessions *pl* belongings *pl*

* **haben** [HAR-bern] *v* have

Hafen [HAR-fern] *m* (*pl* ̈) harbour; port

Hafenanlagen [HAR-fern-ahn-lar-gern] *fpl* docks *pl*

Hafer [HAR-ferr] *m* oats *pl*

Häftling [HEHFT-ling] *m* (*pl* ~e) prisoner

Hagel [HAR-gerl] *m* hail

Hahn [harn] *m* (*pl* ̈e) tap

Hain [highn] *m* (*pl* ~e) grove

Haken [HAR-kern] *m* (*pl* ~) hook

halb [hahlp] *adj* half; *adv* half

halber Fahrpreis [HAHL-berr-FARR-prighs] *m* half fare

halber Preis [HAHL-berr-prighs] half price

halbieren [hahl-BEE-rern] *v* halve

Halbinsel [HAHLP-in-zerl] *f* (*pl* ~n) peninsula

Halbkreis [HAHLP-krighs] *m* (*pl* ~e) semicircle

halbmondförmig [HAHLP-moantfurr-mikh] *adj* crescent

Hälfte [HEHLF-ter] *f (pl ~n)* half

Hals [hahls] *m (pl ~̈ e)* neck

Halsband [HAHLS-bahnt] *nt (pl ~̈ er)* beads *pl*

Halskette [HAHLS-keh-ter] *f (pl ~n)* necklace

Halsschmerzen [HAHLS-shmehr-tsern] *mpl* sore throat

* **halten** [HAHL-tern] *v* hold; keep

* **halten für** [HAHL-tern-fewr] *v* reckon

Haltestelle [HAHL-ter-shteh-ler] *f (pl ~n)* stop

Hammelfleisch [HAH-merl-flighsh] *nt* mutton

Hammer [HAH-merr] *m (pl ~̈)* hammer

Hämorrhoiden [hai-mo-roa-EE-dern] *fpl* haemorrhoids *pl*; piles *pl*

Hand [hahnt] *f (pl ~̈e)* hand

Handarbeit [HAHNT-ahr-bight] *f (pl ~ en)* needlework; handwork

Handbremse [HAHNT-brehm-zer] *f (pl ~n)* hand-brake

Handbuch [HAHNT-bookh] *nt (pl ~̈ er)* handbook

Handel [HAHN-derl] *m* trade; commerce

handeln [HAHN-derln] *v* bargain; trade

Handelsgesellschaft [HAHN-derls-ger-zehl-shahft] *f (pl ~en)* company

Handfläche [HAHNT-fleh-kher] *f (pl ~n)* palm

handgearbeitet [HAHNT-ger-ahr-bigh-tert] *adj* handmade

Handgelenk [HAHNT-ger-lehngk] *nt (pl ~e)* wrist

Handgepäck [HAHNT-ger-pehk] *nt* hand baggage

Handgriff [HAHNT-grif] *m (pl ~e)* handle

handhaben [HAHNT-har-bern] *v* handle

Handkoffer [HAHNT-ko-ferr] *m (pl ~)* suitcase

Handköfferchen [HAHNT-kur-ferr-khern] *nt (pl ~)* grip

Handkrem [HAHNT-kraym] *f* hand cream

Händler [HEHN-dlerr] *m (pl ~)* dealer; trader

handlich [HAHNT-likh] *adj* handy

Handlung [HAHNT-dloong] *f (pl ~en)* plot; action

Handschrift [HAHNT-shrift] *f (pl ~en)* handwriting

Handschuh [HAHNT-shoo] *m (pl ~e)* glove

Handtasche [HAHNT-tah-sher] *f (pl ~n)* handbag; bag

Handtuch [HAHNT-tookh] *nt (pl ~̈ er)* towel

Handvoll [HAHNT-fol] *f* handful

Handwerk [HAHNT-vehrk] *nt (pl ~e)* handicraft; trade

Hang [hahng] *m (pl ~̈e)* hillside

Hängematte [HEHNG-er-mah-ter] *f (pl ~n)* hammock

harmlos [HAHRM-loas] *adj* harmless

hart [hahrt] *adv* hard; *adj* hard

Haß [hahs] *m* hate

häßlich [HEHS-likh] *adj* ugly

hassen [HAH-sern] *v* hate

hastig [HAHS-tikh] *adj* hasty

Haufen [HOW-fern] *m (pl ~)* heap; bunch; pile

häufig [HOY-fikh] *adj* frequent

Häufigkeit [HOY-fikh-kight] *f* frequency

Haupt . . . [howpt] *pref* chief

Hauptbahnhof [HOWPT-barn-hoaf] *m (pl ~̈e)* central station

Hauptmahlzeit [HOWPT-marl-tsight] f (pl ~en) dinner

Hauptquartier [HOWPT-kvahr-teer] nt (pl ~e) headquarters

hauptsächlich [HOWPT-zehkh-likh] adv mostly; adj primary

Hauptstadt [HOWPT-shtaht] f (pl ~e) capital

Hauptstraße [HOWPT-shtrar-ser] f (pl ~n) main street; main road

Hauptstrecke [HOWPT-shtrehker] f (pl ~n) main line

Hauptverkehrsstraße [howpt-fehr-kayrs-shtrar-ser] f (pl ~n) thoroughfare

Hauptverkehrszeit [HOWPT-fehr-KAYRS-tsight] f (pl ~en) rush-hour

Hauptwort [HOWPT-vort] nt (pl ~e) noun

Haus [hows] nt (pl ~er) house

Hausangestellte [HOWS-ahn-ger-shtehl-ter] f (pl ~n) housemaid

Hausbesitzer [HOWS-ber-zi-tserr] m (pl ~) landlord

Häuserblock [HOY-zerr-blok] m (pl ~s) block

Häusermakler [HOY-zerr-mark-lerr] m (pl ~) house-agent

Hausfrau [HOWS-frow] f (pl ~en) housewife

Haushalt [HOWS-hahlt] m (pl ~e) household

Haushälterin [HOWS-hehl-ter-rin] f (pl ~nen) housekeeper

Haushaltsarbeiten [HOWS-hahlts-ahr-bigh-tern] fpl housework

Haushaltung [HOWS-hahl-toong] f housekeeping

Hauslehrer [HOWS-lay-rerr] m (pl ~; f ~in) tutor

Hausmeister [HOWS-mighs-terr] m (pl ~) concierge

Hausschlüssel [HOWS-shlew-serl] m (pl ~) latchkey

Haut [howt] f (pl ~e) skin

Hautkrem [HOWT-kraym] f skin cream

Hebel [HAY-berl] m (pl ~) lever

* **heben** [HAY-bern] v lift; raise

Hebräisch [hay-BRAI-ish] nt Hebrew

Hecht [hehkht] m (pl ~e) pike

Hecke [HEH-ker] f (pl ~n) hedge

heftig [HEHF-tikh] adj acute

Heftpflaster [HEHFT-pflahs-terr] nt (pl ~) adhesive tape; Band-Aid

Heide [HIGH-der] f (pl ~n) heath

Heidekraut [HIGH-der-krowt] nt heather

Heideland [HIGH-der-lahnt] nt moor

Heilbad [HIGHL-bart] nt (pl ~er) spa

Heilbutt [HIGHL-boot] m (pl ~e) halibut

heilen [HIGH-lern] v cure; heal

heilig [HIGH-likh] holy; adj sacred

Heilige [HIGH-li-ger] m (pl ~n; f ~) saint

Heilmittel [HIGHL-mi-terl] nt (pl ~) remedy

Heim [highm] nt (pl ~e) home

Heimatland [HIGH-mart-lahnt] nt (pl ~er) native country

* **heimgehen** [HIGHM-gay-ern] v go home

Heimweh [HIGHM-vay] nt homesickness

heiraten [HIGH-rar-tern] v marry

heiß [highs] adj hot

heiser [HIGH-zerr] adj hoarse

heiter [HIGH-terr] adj cheerful

Heizkissen [HIGHTS-ki-sern] nt

(*pl* ~) heating pad

Heizkörper [HIGHTS-kurr-perr] *m* (*pl* ~) radiator

Heizofen [HIGHTS-oa-fern] *m* (*pl* ~) heater

Heizöl [HAHITS-url] *nt* (*pl* ~e) oil fuel

Heizung [HIGH-tsoong] *f* (*pl* ~en) heating

Held [hehlt] *m* (*pl* ~en; *f* ~in) hero

helfen [HEHL-fern] *v* (*) help; assist; aid

Helfer [HEHL-ferr] *m* (*pl* ~; *f* ~in) helper

hell [hehl] *adj* light; bright

hellviolett [HEHL-vi-oa-LEHT] *adj* mauve

Hemd [hehmt] *nt* (*pl* ~en) shirt

Henne [HEH-ner] *f* (*pl* ~n) hen

herab [heh-RAHP] *adv* down

herabsetzen [heh-RAHP-zeh-tsern] *v* reduce

* **herabsteigen** [heh-RAHP-shtigh-gern] *v* descend

herannahend [heh-RAHN-nar-ernt] *adj* oncoming

* **herausnehmen** [heh-ROWS-nay-mern] *v* take out

herausputzen (sich) [zikh-heh-ROWS-poo-tsern] *v* dress up

heraussuchen [heh-ROWS-zoo-khern] *v* look up

Herberge [HEHR-behr-ger] *f* (*pl* ~n) hostel

Herbst [hehrpst] *m* autumn

Herd [hayrt] *m* (*pl* ~e) hearth

Herde [HAYR-der] *f* (*pl* ~n) herd; flock

hereinplatzen [heh-RIGHN-plah-tsern] *v* pop in

hergestellt aus [HAYR-ger-shtehlt-ows] *adj* made of

Hering [HAY-ring] *m* (*pl* ~e) herring

Herr [hehr] *m* (*pl* ~en) gentleman

Herrentoilette [HEH-rern-toaah-leh-ter] *f* (*pl* ~n) men's room

herrlich [HEHR-likh] *adj* splendid

Herrschaft [HEHR-shahft] *f* (*pl* ~en) reign

herrschaftliches Wohnhaus [HEHR-shahft-li-khers-VOAN-hows] mansion

Herrschaftshaus [HEHR-shahfts-hows] *nt* (*pl* ~er) manor house

herrschen [HEHR-shern] *v* rule

Herrscher [HEHR-sherr] *m* (*pl* ~; *f* ~in) ruler

herstellen [HAYR-shteh-lern] *v* produce

hervorragend [hehr-FOAR-rar-gernt] *adj* outstanding; excellent

Herz [hehrts] *nt* (*pl* ~en) heart; hearts *pl*

herzlich [HEHRTS-likh] *adj* hearty; cordial

Herzmuscheln [HEHRTS-moo-sherln] *fpl* cockles *pl*

Heu [hoy] *nt* hay

Heuschnupfen [HOY-shnoo-pfern] *m* hay-fever

heute [HOY-ter] *adv* today

heute abend [HOY-ter-AR-bernt] tonight

heutzutage [HOYT-tsoo-tar-ger] *adv* nowadays

Hexenschuß [HEH-ksern-shoos] *m* lumbago

hier [heer] *adv* here

Hi-Fi [HIGH-figh] hi-fi

Hilfe [HIL-fer] *f* help; aid

hilfreich [HILF-righkh] *adj* helpful

hilfsbereit [HILFS-ber-right] *adj* co-operative

Himbeere [HIM-bay-rer] *f (pl* ~n)
raspberry

Himmel [HI-merl] *m* heaven; sky

himmlisch [HIM-lish] *adj*
heavenly

Hin- und Rückfahrt [HIN-oont-
REWK-farrt] round trip

hin und wieder [HIN-oont-VEE-
derr] now and then

hinauf [hi-NOWF] *adv* up

* **hinaufsteigen** [hi-NOWF-shtigh-
gern] *v* ascend

hinaus [hi-NOWS] *adv* out

hindern [HIN-derrn] *v* hinder

Hindernis [HIN-derr-nis] *nt (pl*
~se) obstacle

hinein [hi-NIGHN] *adv* in

* **hineingehen** [hi-NIGHN-gay-
ern] *v* go in

hinken [HING-kern] *v* limp

hinsichtlich [HIN-zikht-likh]
prep with reference to;
regarding

hinten [HIN-tern] *adv* behind

hinter [HIN-terr] *prep* behind

hinterlegen [hin-terr-LAY-gern] *v*
deposit

Hinterrad [HIN-terr-rart] *nt (pl*
~er) rear wheel

Hinterseite [HIN-terr-zigh-ter] *f*
(pl ~n) rear

* **hinübergehen** [hi-NEW-berr-
gay-ern] *v* cross over

* **hinweisen** [HIN-vigh-zern] *v*
point

Hirt [hirt] *m (pl* ~en; *f* ~in)
shepherd

Historiker [his-TOA-ri-kerr] *m*
(pl ~; *f* ~in) historian

historisch [his-TOA-rish] *adj*
historic

Hitze [HI-tser] *f* heat

hoch [hoakh] *adj* high; tall

hoch und runter [HOAKH-oont-
ROON-terr] up and down

Hochland [HOAKH-lahnt] *nt*
upland

Hochsaison [HOAKH-sai-zàwng] *f*
(pl ~s) high season; peak
season

Hochsommer [HOAKH-zo-merr]
m midsummer

Hochspannungsmast [HOAKH-
shpah-noongs-mahst] *m (pl*
~en) pylon

Hochzeit [HOKH-tsight] *f (pl* ~en)
wedding

Hockey [HO-ki] *nt* hockey

Hof [hoaf] *m (pl* ~̈e) yard

hoffen [HO-fern] *v* hope

Hoffnung [HOF-noong] *f (pl* ~en)
hope

hoffnungsvoll [HOF-noongs-fol]
adj hopeful

höflich [HURF-likh] *adj* polite;
civil

Höhe [HUR-er] *f (pl* ~n) altitude;
height

höhere Lehranstalt [hur-er-rer-
LAYR-ahn-shtahlt] *f (pl* ~en)
college

hohl [hoal] *adj* hollow

Höhle [HUR-ler] *f (pl* ~n) cave

holen [HOA-lern] *v* fetch

Holland [HO-lahnt] *nt* Holland

Holländer [HO-lehn-derr] *m (pl*
~; *f* ~in) Dutchman

holländisch [HO-lehn-dish] *adj*
Dutch

Hölle [HUR-ler] *f* hell

holperig [HOL-per-rikh] *adj*
bumpy; rough

Holz [holts] *nt (pl* ~̈er) wood

hölzern [HURL-tserrn] *adj*
wooden

Holzhammer [HOLTS-hah-merr]
m (pl ~) mallet

Holzkohle [HOLTS-koa-ler] *f*

charcoal

Honig [HOA-nikh] *m* honey

Honorar [hoa-noa-RARR] *nt (pl ~e)* fee

Hopfen [HO-pfern] *m* hops *pl*

hören [HUR-rern] *v* hear

Horizont [hoa-ri-TSONT] *m* horizon

Hose [HOA-zer] *f (pl ~n)* slacks *pl;* trousers *pl;* pants *pl*

Hosenanzug [HOA-zern-ahn-tsook] *m (pl ~̈e)* pantsuit

Hosenträger [HOA-zern-trai-gerr] *mpl* suspenders *pl*

Hotel [hoa-TEHL] *nt (pl ~s)* hotel

Hotelpage [hoa-TEHL-par-zher] *m (pl ~n)* pageboy; bellboy

hübsch [hewpsh] *adj* nice; pretty; good-looking

Hubschrauber [HOOP-shrow-berr] *m (pl ~)* helicopter

Hüfte [HEWF-ter] *f (pl ~n)* hip

Hüfthalter [HEWFT-hahl-terr] *m (pl ~)* girdle; suspender belt

Hügel [HEW-gerl] *m (pl ~)* hill

hügelig [HEW-ger-likh] *adj* hilly

Hügelspitze [HEW-gerl-shpi-tser] *f (pl ~n)* hilltop

Huhn [hoon] *nt (pl ~̈er)* chicken

Hühnerauge [HEW-nerr-ow-ger] *nt (pl ~n)* corn

Hummer [HOO-merr] *m (pl ~)* lobster

Humor [hoo-MOAR] *m* humour

humorvoll [hoo-MOAR-fol] *adj* humorous

Hund [hoont] *m (pl ~e)* dog

Hundehütte [HOON-der-hew-ter] *f (pl ~n)* kennel

hundert [HOON-derrt] *adj* hundred

Hunger [HOONG-err] *m* hunger

hungrig [HOONG-rikh] *adj* hungry

Hupe [HOO-per] *f (pl ~n)* horn;

hooter

hupen [HOO-pern] *v* hoot

hüpfen [HEW-pfern] *v* hop

husten [HOOS-tern] *v* cough

Husten [HOOS-tern] *m* cough

Hustenbonbons [HOOS-tern-bawng-bawngs] *ntpl* cough-drops *pl*

Hustenpastillen [HOOS-tern-pahs-ti-lern] *fpl* cough-lozenges *pl*

Hustentropfen [HOOS-tern-tro-pfern] *pl* cough-mixture

Hut [hoot] *m (pl ~̈e)* hat

hüten (sich) [zikh-HEW-tern] *v* beware

Hütte [HEW-ter] *f (pl ~n)* cabin; hut

Hydrant [hew-DRAHNT] *m (pl ~en)* fire hydrant

hygienisch [hew-GYAY-nish] *adj* hygienic

Hymne [HEWM-ner] *f (pl ~n)* hymn

Hypothek [hew-poa-TAYK] *f (pl ~en)* mortgage

hysterisch [hews-TAY-rish] *adj* hysterical

ich [ikh] *pron* I

ich selbst [ikh-ZEHLPST] *pron* myself

ideal [i-day-ARL] *adj* ideal

Ideal [i-day-ARL] *nt (pl ~e)* ideal

Idee [i-DAY] *f (pl ~n)* idea

Identifizierung [i-dehnt-ti-fi-TSEE-roong] *f (pl ~en)* identification

identisch [i-DEHN-tish] *adj* identical

Identität [i-dehn-ti-TAIT] *f* identity

Idiom [i-DYOAM] *nt (pl ~s)* idiom

idiomatisch [i-dyoa-MAR-tish]
  adj idiomatic
Idiot [i-DYOAT] *m* (*pl* ~en; *f* ~in)
  idiot
ignorieren [ig-noa-REE-rern] *v*
  ignore
ihm [eem] *pron* him
ihn [een] *pron* him
ihnen [EE-nern] *pron* them
Ihnen [EE-nern] *pron* you
ihr [eer] *pron* you; her; *adj* her;
  their
Ihr [eer] *adj* your
ihr selbst [eer-ZEHLPST] *pron*
  yourselves
Illustration [i-loos-trah-TSYOAN] *f*
  (*pl* ~en) illustration
illustrieren [i-loos-TREE-rern] *v*
  illustrate
im allgemeinen [im-ahl-ger-
  MIGH-nern] in general
im Ausland [im-OWS-lahnt]
  abroad
im Freien [im-FRIGH-ern] *adv*
  open air
im Haus [im-HOWS] indoors;
  indoor
im kleinen verkaufen [im-KLIGH-
  nern-fehr-KOW-fern] *v* retail
im Namen von [im-NAR-mern-
  fon] *prep* on behalf of
im Ruhestand [im-ROO-er-
  shtahnt] retired
im Schlaf [im-SHLARF] asleep
imaginär [i-mah-gi-NAIR] *adj*
  imaginary
Imbiß [IM-bis] *m* (*pl* ~e) snack
Imitation [i-mi-tah-TSYOAN] *f* (*pl*
  ~en) imitation
Imitationsschmuck [i-mi-tah-
  TSYOANS-shmook] *m* costume
  jewellery
immer [I-merr] *adv* always
immer mehr [I-merr-MAYR] more

and more
immunisieren [i-moo-ni-ZEE-
  rern] *v* immunize
Immunität [i-moo-ni-TAIT] *f*
  immunity
imperialistisch [im-pehr-yah-
  LIS-tish] *adj* imperial
impfen [IM-pfern] *v* inoculate;
  vaccinate
Impfung [IM-pfoong] *f*
  vaccination; inoculation
Import [IM-port] *m* imports *pl*
Importeur [im-por-TURR] *m* (*pl*
  ~e) importer
imposant [im-poa-ZAHNT] *adj*
  imposing
Impuls [im-POOLS] *m* (*pl* ~e)
  impulse
impulsiv [im-pool-ZEEF] *adj*
  impulsive
in [in] *prep* in; into
in Abständen anordnen [in-AHP-
  shtehn-dern-AHN-ord-nern] *v*
  space
in Anbetracht [in-AHN-ber-
  trahkht] *prep* considering
*** in den Ruhestand treten** [in-
  dayn-ROO-er-shtahnt-TRAY-
  tern] *v* retire
in der Regel [in-dayr-RAY-gerl]
  as a rule
in Gang bringen [in-GAHNG-
  bring-ern] *v* launch
in Ordnung [in-ORD-noong] in
  order
in Scheiben geschnitten [in-
  SHIGH-bern-ger-SHNI-tern]
  sliced
*** in Unordnung bringen** [in-OON-
  ord-noong-BRING-ern] *v* mess
  up
in Verbindung stellen mit (sich)
  [zikh-in-fehr-BIN-doong-
  SHTEH-lern-mit] *v* contact

* **in Verlegenheit bringen** [in-fehr-LAY-gern-hight-BRING-ern] *v* embarrass

Inder [IN-derr] *m (pl ~; f ~in)* Indian

Index [IN-dehks] *m (pl ~e)* index

Indien [IN-dyern] *nt* India

indirekt [IN-di-rehkt] *adj* indirect

individuell [in-di-vi-doo-EHL] *adj* individual

Individuum [in-di-VEE-doo-oom] *nt (pl* **Individuen**) individual

indossieren [in-do-SEE-rern] *v* endorse

Industrie [in-doos-TREE] *f (pl ~n)* industry

industriell [in-doos-tri-EHL] *adj* industrial

Infanterie [in-fahn-ter-REE] *f* infantry

Infektion [in-fehk-TSYOAN] *f (pl ~en)* infection

Infinitiv [IN-fi-ni-teef] *m (pl ~e)* infinitive

Inflation [in-flah-TSYOAN] *f* inflation

infolge [in-FOL-ger] *prep* owing to

informieren [in-for-MEE-rern] *v* inform

infrarot [in-frah-ROAT] *adj* infra-red

Ingenieur [in-zhayn-YURR] *m (pl ~e)* engineer

Ingwer [ING-verr] *m* ginger

Inhaber [IN-har-berr] *m (pl ~; f ~in)* occupant; bearer

Inhalt [IN-hahlt] *m* contents *pl*

Injektion [in-yehk-TSYOAN] *f (pl ~en)* injection

inländisch [IN-lehn-dish] *adj* domestic

inmitten [in-MI-tern] *prep*

amidst

inner [I-nerr] *adj* inside

Innere [I-ner-rer] *nt* interior

innerhalb [I-nerr-hahlp] *prep* within

Inschrift [IN-shrift] *f (pl ~en)* inscription

Insekt [in-ZEHKT] *nt (pl ~en)* insect

Insektengift [in-ZEHK-tern-gift] *nt (pl ~e)* insecticide

Insektenschutzmittel [in-ZEHK-tern-shoots-mi-terl] *nt (pl ~)* insect repellent

Insektenstich [in-ZEHK-tern-shtikh] *m (pl ~e)* insect bite

Insel [IN-zerl] *f (pl ~n)* island

insgesamt [ins-ger-ZAHMT] *adv* altogether

Inspektion [in-spehk-TSYOAN] *f (pl ~en)* inspection

inspizieren [in-spi-TSEE-rern] *v* inspect

Installateur [in-stah-lah-TURR] *m (pl ~e)* plumber

installieren [in-stah-LEE-rern] *v* install

Instandhaltung [in-SHTAHNT-hahl-toong] *f* maintenance

Institut [in-sti-TOOT] *nt (pl ~e)* institute

Institution [in-sti-too-TSYOAN] *f (pl ~en)* institution

Instrument [in-stroo-MEHNT] *nt (pl ~e)* instrument

intellektuell [in-teh-lehk-too-EHL] *adj* intellectual

intelligent [in-teh-li-GEHNT] *adj* intelligent

Intelligenz [in-teh-li-GEHNTS] *f* intelligence

intensiv [in-tehn-ZEEF] *adj* intense

interessant [in-ter-reh-SAHNT]

adj interesting

Interesse [in-ter-REH-ser] *nt (pl ~n)* interest

interessieren [in-ter-reh-SEE-rern] *v* interest

interessiert [in-ter-reh-SEERT] *adj* interested

intern [in-TEHRN] *adj* internal

international [in-terr-nah-tsyoa-NARL] *adj* international

Intervall [in-terr-VAHL] *nt (pl ~e)* interval

Interview [in-terr-VYOO] *nt (pl ~s)* interview

intim [in-TEEM] *adj* intimate

invalide [in-vah-LEE-der] *adj* invalid

Invalide [in-vah-LEE-der] *m (pl ~n)* invalid

Inventar [in-vehn-TARR] *nt (pl ~e)* inventory

investieren [in-vehs-TEE-rern] *v* invest

Investition [in-vehs-ti-TSYOAN] *f (pl ~en)* investment

inwendig [IN-vehn-dikh] *adj* inner

inzwischen [in-TSVI-shern] *adv* in the meantime

Ire [EE-rer] *m (pl ~n; f ~in)* Irish

irgend etwas [IR-gernt-EHT-vahs] *pron* anything

irgend jemand [IR-gernt-YAY-mahnt] *pron* anybody

irgendein [IR-gernt-ighn] *adj* any

irgendwie [ir-gernt-VEE] *adv* anyhow

irgendwo [IR-gernt-voa] *adv* somewhere

irisch [EE-rish] *adj* Irish

Irland [IR-lahnt] *nt* Ireland

irren (sich) [zikh-I-rern] *v* err

irritieren [i-ri-TEE-rern] *v* irritate

Irrtum [IR-toom] *m (pl ~̈er)* error

Island [EES-lahnt] *nt* Iceland

Isolation [i-zoa-lah-TSYOAN] *f* insulation

Isolator [i-zoa-LAR-tor] *m (pl ~en)* insulator

isolieren [i-zoa-LEE-rern] *v* insulate

Isolierung [i-zoa-LEE-roong] *f* isolation

Israel [EES-rah-ehl] *nt* Israel

Israeli [ees-rah-AY-li] *m (pl ~s; f ~n)* Israeli

israelisch [is-rah-AY-lish] *adj* Israeli

Italien [i-TARL-yern] *nt* Italy

Italiener [i-tahl-YAY-nerr] *m (pl ~; f ~in)* Italian

italienisch [i-tahl-YAY-nish] *adj* Italian

ja [yar] yes

Jacht [yahkht] *f (pl ~en)* yacht

Jacke [YAH-ker] *f (pl ~n)* jacket

Jade [YAR-der] *f* jade

Jagd [yarkt] *f* hunt

jagen [YAR-gern] *v* hunt

Jäger [YAI-gerr] *m (pl ~)* hunter

Jahr [yarr] *nt (pl ~e)* year

Jahrestag [YAR-rers-tark] *m (pl ~e)* anniversary

Jahreszeit [YAR-rers-tsight] *f (pl ~en)* season

Jahrgang [YARR-gahng] *m (pl ~̈e)* vintage

Jahrhundert [yarr-HOON-derrt] *nt (pl ~e)* century

jährlich [YAIR-likh] *adv* per annum; *adj* yearly

Jalousie [zhah-loo-ZEE] *f (pl ~n)*

blind

Januar [YAH-noo-arr] *m* January

Japan [YAR-pahn] *nt* Japan

Japaner [yah-PAR-nerr] *m (pl ~;
f ~in)* Japanese

japanisch [yah-PAR-nish] *adj*
Japanese

Jazz [jehs] *m* jazz

Jeans [jeens] *pl* jeans *pl*

jede Nacht [yay-der-NAHKHT]
nightly

jeder [YAY-derr] *adj* every; each;
pron each one

jedermann [YAY-derr-mahn]
pron everyone; everybody;
anyone

jederzeit [yay-derr-TSIGHT] *adv*
at any time

jedoch [yay-DOKH] *conj* however

Jeep [jeep] *m (pl ~s)* jeep

jemand [YAY-mahnt] *pron*
somebody; someone

jene [YAY-ner] *pron* those; *adj*
those

jener [YAY-nerr] *pron* that; *adj*
that

jenseits [YEHN-zights] *prep*
across; beyond; *adv* beyond

Jersey [JURR-si] *nt* jersey

jetzt [yehtst] *adv* now

jeweilig [YAY-vigh-likh] *adj*
respective

Jockei [JO-ki] *m (pl ~s)* jockey

Jod [yoat] *nt* iodine

Johannisbeere [yoa-HAH-nis-
bay-rer] *f (pl ~n)* black-
currant

Joker [JOA-kerr] *m (pl ~)* joker

Jolle [YO-ler] *f (pl ~n)* dinghy

Journalismus [zhoor-nah-LIS-
moos] *m* journalism

Journalist [zhoor-nah-LIST] *m (pl
~en; f ~in)* journalist

Jucken [YOO-kern] *nt* itch

Jude [YOO-der] *m (pl ~n; f ~in)*
Jew

jüdisch [YEW-dish] *adj* Jewish

Jugend [YOO-gernt] *f* youth

Jugendherberge [YOO-gernt-
HEHR-behr-ger] *f (pl ~n)* youth
hostel

jugendlich [YOO-gernt-likh] *adj*
juvenile

Jugoslawe [yoo-goa-SLAR-ver] *m
(pl ~n; f Jugoslawin)*
Jugoslav; Yugoslav

Jugoslawien [yoo-goa-SLAR-
vyern] *nt* Yugoslavia;
Jugoslavia

jugoslawisch [yoo-goa-SLAR-
vish] *adj* Jugoslav

Juli [YOO-li] *m* July

Jumper [JAHM-perr] *m (pl ~)*
jumper

jung [yoong] *adj* young

Junge [YOONG-er] *m (pl ~n)* boy

junger Hecht [YOONG-err-
HEHKHT] *m* pickerel

Jungfrau [YOONGK-frow] *f (pl
~en)* virgin

Junggeselle [YOONG-ger-zeh-ler]
m (pl ~n) bachelor

jüngst [YEWNGST] *adj* recent

Juni [YOO-ni] *m* June

Juwel [yoo-VAYL] *nt (pl ~en)*
jewel

Juwelier [yoo-vay-LEER] *m (pl
~e)* jeweller

Kabarett [kah-bah-REHT] *nt (pl
~s)* revue; floor-show

Kabel [KAR-berl] *nt (pl ~)* flex

Kabeljau [KAR-berl-yow] *m (pl
~e)* cod

Kachel [KAH-kherl] *f (pl ~n)* tile

Kaffee [kah-FAY] *m* coffee; café

Kaffeehaus [kah-FAY-hows] *nt*

(*pl* ̃**er**) café
Kaffeemaschine [KAH-fay-mah-shee-ner] *f* (*pl* ～**n**) percolator
kahl [karl] *adj* bald
Kai [kigh] *m* (*pl* ～**s**) quay; wharf
Kakao [kah-KOW] *m* cocoa
Kalb [kahlp] *nt* (*pl* ̃**er**) calf
Kalbfleisch [KAHLP-flighsh] *nt* veal
Kalbleder [KAHLP-lay-derr] *nt* calfskin
Kalender [kah-LEHN-derr] *m* (*pl* ～) calendar
Kalkulation [kahl-koo-lah-TSYOAN] *f* (*pl* ～**en**) calculation
Kalorie [kah-loa-REE] *f* (*pl* ～**n**) calorie
kalt [kahlt] *adj* cold
Kälte [KEHL-ter] *f* cold
kaltes Büfett [kahl-ters-bew-FAY] *nt* cold buffet
Kamera [KAH-mer-rah] *f* (*pl* ～**s**) camera
Kamin [kah-MEEN] *m* (*pl* ～**e**) fireplace
Kamm [kahm] *m* (*pl* ̃**e**) comb
kämmen [KEH-mern] *v* comb
Kammgarnstoff [KAHM-gahrn-shtof] *m* (*pl* ～**e**) worsted
Kammuschel [KAHM-moo-sherl] *f* (*pl* ～**n**) scallop
Kampf [kahmpf] *m* (*pl* ̃**e**) fight
kämpfen [KEHM-pfern] *v* fight; struggle
Kanada [KAH-nah-dah] *nt* Canada
Kanadier [kah-NAR-dyerr] *m* (*pl* ～; *f* ～**in**) Canadian
kanadisch [kah-NAR-dish] *adj* Canadian
Kanal [kah-NARL] *m* (*pl* ̃**e**) canal; channel
Kaninchen [kah-NEEN-khern] *nt* (*pl* ～) rabbit

Kanone [kah-NOA-ner] *f* (*pl* ～**n**) gun
Kanu [KAR-noo] *nt* (*pl* ～**s**) canoe
Kap [kahp] *nt* (*pl* ～**s**) cape
Kapelle [kah-PEH-ler] *f* (*pl* ～**n**) chapel; band
kapern [KAR-perrn] *v* hijack
Kapital [kah-pi-TARL] *nt* capital
Kapitalgeber [kah-pi-TARL-gay-berr] *m* (*pl* ～) investor
Kapitän [kah-pi-TAIN] *m* (*pl* ～**e**) captain
Kapsel [KAHP-serl] *f* (*pl* ～**n**) capsule
Karaffe [kah-RAH-fer] *f* (*pl* ～**n**) carafe
Karamelle [kah-rah-MEH-ler] *nt* (*pl* ～**n**) caramel
Karat [kah-RART] *nt* carat
Karbolseife [kahr-BOAL-zahi-fer] *f* (*pl* ～**n**) carbolic soap
karmesinrot [kahr-mer-ZEEN-roat] *adj* crimson
Karneval [KAHR-ner-vahl] *m* carnival
Karo [KAR-roa] *nt* diamonds *pl*
Karotte [kah-RO-ter] *f* (*pl* ～**n**) carrot
Karpfen [KAHR-pfern] *m* (*pl* ～) carp
Karren [KAH-rern] *m* (*pl* ～) cart
Karriere [kahr-YAY-rer] *f* (*pl* ～**n**) career
Karte [KAHR-ter] *f* (*pl* ～**n**) ticket
Kartenspiel [KAHR-tern-shpeel] *nt* (*pl* ～**e**) deck; cards *pl*; pack of cards
Kartoffel [kahr-TO-ferl] *f* (*pl* ～**n**) potato
Karton [kahr-TAWNG] *m* (*pl* ～**s**) carton
Kaschmir [KAHSH-meer] *m* cashmere
Käse [KAI-zer] *m* cheese

Kaserne [kah-ZEHR-ner] *f* (*pl* ~n) barracks *pl*

Kasino [kah-ZEE-noa] *nt* (*pl* ~s) casino

Kasse [KAH-ser] *f* (*pl* ~n) box office; pay-desk

Kassierer [kah-SEE-rerr] *m* (*pl* ~; *f* ~in) cashier

Kastanie [kahs-TARN-yer] *f* (*pl* ~n) chestnut

Katakombe [kah-tah-KOM-ber] *f* (*pl* ~n) catacomb

Katalog [kah-tah-LOAK] *m* (*pl* ~e) catalogue

Katarrh [kah-TAHR] *m* catarrh

Katastrophe [kah-tahs-TROA-fer] *f* (*pl* ~n) disaster

Kategorie [kah-tay-goa-REE] *f* (*pl* ~n) category

Kathedrale [kah-tay-DRAR-ler] *f* (*pl* ~n) cathedral

katholisch [kah-TOA-lish] *adj* Catholic

Kattun [kah-TOON] *m* cotton

Katze [KAH-tser] *f* (*pl* ~n) cat

kauen [KOW-ern] *v* chew

Kauf [kowf] *m* (*pl* ~e) purchase

kaufen [KOW-fern] *v* purchase; buy

Käufer [KOY-ferr] *m* (*pl* ~; *f* ~in) buyer; purchaser

Kaufhaus [KOWF-hows] *nt* (*pl* ~er) department store

Kaufmann [KOWF-mahn] *m* (*pl* **Kaufleute**) merchant

Kaugummi [KOW-goo-mi] *nt* (*pl* ~s) gum; chewing gum

kaum [kowm] *adv* barely; scarcely; hardly

Kaution [kow-TSYOAN] *f* (*pl* ~en) bail

Kaviar [KAR-vi-ahr] *m* caviar

Kegelbahn [KAY-gerl-barn] *f* (*pl* ~en) bowling alley

Kegeln [KAY-gerln] *nt* bowling

Kehle [KAY-ler] *f* (*pl* ~n) throat

Keil [kighl] *m* (*pl* ~e) wedge

Keim [kighm] *m* (*pl* ~e) germ

kein [kighn] *adj* no

kein Eingang [kighn-IGHN-gahng] no admittance

keiner [KIGH-nerr] *pron* none

keiner von beiden [KIGH-nerr-fon-BIGH-dern] *pron* neither

keinesfalls [KIGH-ners-fahls] *adv* by no means

Keks [kayks] *m* (*pl* ~e) biscuit; cracker

Keller [KEH-lerr] *m* (*pl* ~) cellar

Kellermeister [KEH-lerr-mighs-terr] *m* (*pl* ~) wine-waiter

Kellner [KEHL-nerr] *m* (*pl* ~; *f* ~in) waiter

Kellnerin [KEHL-ner-rin] *f* (*pl* ~nen) waitress

*** kennen** [KEH-nern] *v* know

Kenntnis [KEHNT-nis] *f* (*pl* ~ se) knowledge

Keramik [kay-RAR-mik] *f* (*pl* ~en) ceramics *pl*

Kerosin [kay-roa-ZEEN] *nt* kerosene

Kerze [KEHR-tser] *f* (*pl* ~n) candle

Kessel [KEH-serl] *m* (*pl* ~) kettle

Kette [KEH-ter] *f* (*pl* ~n) chain

Khaki [KAR-ki] *nt* khaki

Kiefer [KEE-ferr] *m* (*pl* ~) jaw

Kies [kees] *m* gravel

Kieselstein [KEE-zerl-shtighn] *m* (*pl* ~e) pebble

Kilo [KEE-loa] *nt* (*pl* ~s) kilogram

Kilometer [kee-loa-MAY-terr] *m* (*pl* ~) kilometre

Kind [kint] *nt* (*pl* ~er) kid; youngster; child

Kindergarten [KIN-derr-gahr-tern] m (pl ∼) kindergarten

Kinderkrippe [KIN-derr-kri-per]
f (pl ∼n) nursery

Kinderwagen [KIN-derr-var-
gern] m (pl ∼) carriage; pram

Kinn [kin] nt chin

Kino [KEE-noa] nt (pl ∼s)
cinema; pictures pl

Kiosk [ki-OSK] m (pl ∼e) kiosk

Kirche [KIR-kher] f (pl ∼n)
church

Kirchhof [KIRKH-hoaf] m (pl ∼̈e)
churchyard; graveyard

Kirchspiel [KIRKH-shpeel] nt (pl
∼e) parish

Kirchturm [KIRKH-toorm] m (pl
∼̈e) steeple

Kirsche [KIR-sher] f (pl ∼n)
cherry

Kissen [KI-sern] nt (pl ∼)
cushion

Kissenbezug [KI-sern-ber-tsook]
m (pl ∼̈e) pillowcase

Klammer [KLAH-merr] f (pl ∼n)
clamp

klar [klarr] adj clear

klären [KLAI-rern] v clarify

Klasse [KLAH-ser] f (pl ∼n) class

Klassenzimmer [KLAH-sern-tsi-
merr] nt (pl ∼) classroom

klassisch [KLAH-sish] adj
classical

Klatsch [klahch] m gossip

klatschen [KLAH-chern] v gossip;
clap

Klaue [KLOW-er] f (pl ∼n) claw

Klausel [KLOW-zerl] f (pl ∼n)
stipulation

Klavier [klah-VEER] nt (pl ∼e)
piano

klebrig [KLAY-brikh] adj sticky

Klebstoff [KLAYP-shtof] m (pl ∼e)
gum

Klecks [klehks] m (pl ∼e) blot

Kleid [klight] nt (pl ∼er) gown;
dress; frock

Kleiderbügel [KLIGH-derr-bew-
gerl] m (pl ∼) coat-hanger

Kleiderbürste [KLIGH-derr-
bewrs-ter] f (pl ∼n) clothes-
brush

Kleiderhaken [KLIGH-derr-har-
kern] m (pl ∼) peg

Kleidung [KLAHI-doong] f clothes
pl

klein [klighn] adj small; little

kleine Summen [KLIGH-ner-ZOO-
mern] petty cash

kleiner Hügel [kligh-nerr-HEW-
gerl] hillock

Kleingeld [KLIGHN-gehlt] nt
small change

Kleinhandel [KLIGHN-hahn-derl]
m retail trade

Kleinhändler [KLIGHN-hehn-
dlerr] m (pl ∼; f ∼in) retailer

Kleinlieferwagen [KLIGHN-lee-
ferr-var-gern] m (pl ∼) pick-
up

kleinste [KLIGHNS-ter] adj least

Klima [KLEE-mah] nt climate

Klimaanlage [KLEE-mah-ahn-
lar-ger] f (pl ∼n) air
conditioner

klimatisiert [klee-mah-ti-ZÉERT]
adj air conditioned

Klinge [KLING-er] f (pl ∼n) blade

Klingeln [KLING-erln] nt ring

*__klingen__ [KLING-ern] v sound

Klinik [KLEE-nik] f (pl ∼en)
clinic

Klippe [KLI-per] f (pl ∼n) cliff

klopfen [KLO-pfern] v knock

Klopfen [KLO-pfern] nt knock;
tap

Kloster [KLOAS-terr] nt (pl ∼̈)
monastery; convent

Klotz [klots] m (pl ∼̈e) block; log

Klub [kloop] *m* (*pl* ~s) club

klug [klook] *adj* clever; bright

klumpig [KLOOM-pikh] *adj* lumpy

knapp [knahp] *adj* scarce; tight

Knappheit [KNAHP-hight] *f* shortage

* **kneifen** [KNIGH-fern] *v* pinch

Knie [knee] *nt* (*pl* ~ e) knee

knien [KNEE-ern] *v* kneel

Kniff [knif] *m* (*pl* ~e) trick

Knoblauch [KNOAB-lowkh] *m* garlic

Knochen [KNO-khern] *m* (*pl* ~) bone

Knopf [knopf] *m* (*pl* ~e) button

Knopf [knopf] *m* (*pl* ~ e) knob

Knopfloch [KNOPF-lokh] *nt* (*pl* ~er) buttonhole

Knospe [KNOS-per] *f* (*pl* ~n) bud

Knoten [KNOA-tern] *m* (*pl* ~) knot

Knüppel [KNEW-perl] *m* (*pl* ~) club

knusperig [KNOOS-prikh] *adj* crisp

Koch [kokh] *m* (*pl* ~e ; *f* ~in) cook

Kochbuch [KOKH-bookh] *nt* (*pl* ~er) cookery-book

kochen [KO-khern] *v* cook; boil

Kochen [KO-khern] *nt* cooking

Kocher [KO-kherr] *m* (*pl* ~) cooker

Kodein [koa-day-EEN] *nt* codeine

Köder [KUR-derr] *m* (*pl* ~) bait

Koffein [ko-fay-EEN] *nt* caffeine

Koffer [KO-ferr] *m* (*pl* ~) case; bag; trunk

Kofferraum [KO-ferr-rowm] *m* trunk; boot

Kohl [koal] *m* cabbage

Kohle [KOA-ler] *f* (*pl* ~n) coal

Kohlepapier [KOA-ler-pah-peer] *nt* (*pl* ~e) carbon paper

Koje [KOA-yer] *f* (*pl* ~n) berth

Kokosnuß [KOA-kos-noos] *f* (*pl* ~e) coconut

Koks [koaks] *m* coke

Kolben [KOL-bern] *m* (*pl* ~) piston

Kolbenstange [KOL-bern-shtahng-er] *f* (*pl* ~n) piston-rod

Kollege [ko-LAY-ger] *m* (*pl* ~n ; *f* ~in) colleague

Kolonie [koa-loa-NEE] *f* (*pl* ~n) colony

Koma [KOA-mah] *nt* coma

Kombination [kom-bi-nah-TSYOAN] *f* (*pl* ~en) combination

kombinieren [kerm-bi-NEE-rern] *v* combine

Komfort [kom-FAWR] *m* comfort

Komiker [KOA-mi-kerr] *m* (*pl* ~) comedian

komisch [KOA-mish] *adj* comic; funny

* **kommen** [KO-mern] *v* come

* **kommen lassen** [KO-mern-LAH-sern] *v* send for

Kommentar [ko-mehn-TARR] *m* (*pl* ~e) comment

kommentieren [ko-mehn-TEE-rern] *v* comment

kommerziell [ko-mehr-TSYEHL] *adj* commercial

Kommission [ko-mi-SYOAN] *f* (*pl* ~en) commission

Kommode [ko-MOA-der] *f* (*pl* ~n) bureau

Kommune [ko-MOO-ner] *f* (*pl* ~n) commune

Kommunismus [ko-moo-NIS-moos] *m* communism

Kommunist [ko-moo-NIST] *m* (*pl* ~en; *f* ~in) communist

Kompaß [KOM-pahs] *m* (*pl* ~e) compass

Komplex [kom-PLEHKS] *m* (*pl* ~e) complex

Kompliment [kom-pli-MEHNT] *nt* (*pl* ~e) compliment

Komponist [kom-poa-NIST] *m* (*pl* ~en; *f* ~in) composer

Komposition [kom-poa-zi-TSYOAN] *f* (*pl* ~en) composition

Kondensator [kon-dehn-ZAR-tor] *m* (*pl* ~en) condenser

Kondensmilch [kon-DEHNS-milkh] *f* condensed milk

Konditor [kon-DEE-tor] *m* (*pl* ~en) confectioner

Konditorei [kon-dee-toa-RIGH] *f* (*pl* ~en) pastry shop

Konfektions . . . [kon-fehk-TSYOANS] *pref* ready-made

Kongress [kon-GREHS] *m* (*pl* ~e) congress

König [KUR-nikh] *m* (*pl* ~e; *f* ~in) king

Königin [KUR-ni-gin] *f* (*pl* ~nen) queen

königlich [KUR-nik-likh] *adj* royal

Königreich [KUR-nikh-righkh] *nt* (*pl* ~e) kingdom

Konkurrent [kon-koo-REHNT] *m* (*pl* ~en ; *f* ~in) competitor

Konkurrenz [kon-koo-REHNTS] *f* competition

* **können** [KUR-nern] *v* can

konservativ [KON-zehr-vah-teef] *adj* conservative

Konserven [kon-ZEHR-vern] *fpl* tinned food

Konsul [KON-zool] *m* (*pl* ~n) consul

Konsulat [kon-zoo-LART] *nt* (*pl* ~e) consulate

Konsultation [kon-zool-tah-TSYOAN] *f* (*pl* ~en) consultation

konsultieren [kon-zool-TEE-rern] *v* consult

Konsument [kon-zoo-MEHNT] *m* (*pl* ~en; *f* ~in) consumer

Kontaktlinsen [kon-TAHKT-lin-zern] *fpl* contact lenses *pl*

kontinental [kon-ti-nehn-TARL] *adj* continental

Konto [KON-toa] *nt* (*pl* ~en) account

Kontrast [kon-TRAHST] *m* (*pl* ~e) contrast

Kontrollabschnitt [kon-TROL-ahp-shnit] *m* (*pl* ~e) counterfoil; stub

Kontrolle [kon-TRO-ler] *f* (*pl* ~n) control

kontrollieren [kon-troa-LEE-rern] *v* control

Kontrolluntersuchung [kon-TROL-oon-terr-zoo-khoong] *f* (*pl* ~en) check-up

Konzentration [kon-tsehn-trah-TSYOAN] *f* concentration

konzentrieren [kon-tsehn-TREE-rern] *v* concentrate

Konzern [kon-TSEHRN] *m* (*pl* ~e) concern

Konzert [kon-TSEHRT] *nt* (*pl* ~e) concert

Konzertsaal [kon-TSEHRT-zarl] *m* (*pl* ~e) concert hall

Konzession [kon-tseh-SYOAN] *f* (*pl* ~en) licence

konzessionieren [kon-tsehs-yoa-NEE-rern] *v* license

Kopf [kopf] *m* (*pl* ~e) head

Kopfkissen [KOPF-ki-sern] *nt* (*pl* ~) pillow

Kopfschmerzen [KOPF-shmehr-tsern] *mpl* headache

Koralle [koa-RAH-ler] *f* (*pl* ~n) coral

Korb [korp] *m* (*pl* ~e) basket

Kordsamt [KORT-zahmt] *m*

corduroy

Korinthe [koa-RIN-ter] f (pl ∼n)
currant

Korken [KOR-kern] m (pl ∼) cork

Korkenzieher [KOR-kern-tsee-
err] m (pl ∼) corkscrew

Korn [korn] nt grain

Kornfeld [KORN-fehlt] nt (pl ∼er)
cornfield

Körper [KURR-perr] m (pl ∼)
body

korpulent [kor-poo-LEHNT] adj
stout

korrespondieren [ko-rehs-pon-
DEE-rern] v correspond

Korsett [kor-ZEHT] nt (pl ∼s)
corset

kosmetische Behandlung [kos-
MAY-ti-sher-ber-HAHN-dloong] f
beauty treatment

kostbar [KOST-barr] adj precious

kosten [KOS-tern] v cost; taste

Kosten [KOS-tern] pl cost

kostenlos [KOS-tern-loas] adj
free of charge

Kostgänger [KOST-gehng-err] m
(pl ∼; f ∼in) boarder

köstlich [KURST-likh] adj
delicious

Kotelette [kot-LEH-ter] f (pl ∼n)
sideburns pl

Kotflügel [KOAT-flew-gerl] m (pl
∼) mud-guard; fender

Krabbe [KRAH-ber] f (pl ∼n) crab

Krach [krahkh] m (pl ∼̈e) row

Kraft [krahft] f (pl ∼̈e) power;
strength; force

Kraftwagen [KRAHFT-var-gern] m
(pl ∼) motorcar

Kraftwerk [KRAHFT-vehrk] nt (pl
∼e) power station

Kragen [KRAR-gern] m (pl ∼)
collar

Krampf [krahmpf] m (pl ∼̈e)

cramp

Krampfader [KRAHMPF-ar-derr] f
(pl ∼n) varicose vein

krank [krahnk] adj ill; sick

Krankenhaus [KRAHNG-kern-
hows] nt (pl ∼̈er) hospital

Krankenrevier [KRAHNG-kern-
ray-veer] nt (pl ∼e) infirmary

Krankenschwester [KRAHNG-
kern-shvehs-terr] f (pl ∼n)
nurse

Krankenwagen [KRAHNG-kern-
var-gern] m (pl ∼) ambulance

Krankheit [KRAHNGK-hight] f (pl
∼en) illness; sickness; disease

kratzen [KRAH-tsern] v scratch

Kraut [krowt] nt (pl ∼̈er) herb

Krawatte [krah-VAH-ter] f (pl ∼
n) necktie; tie

Krebs [krayps] m cancer

Kredit [kray-DEET] nt (pl ∼e)
credit

Kreditkarte [kray-DEET-kahr-
ter] f (pl ∼n) credit card;
charge plate

Kreditkonto [kray-DEET-kon-toa]
nt (pl ∼konten) charge
account

Kreis [krighs] m (pl ∼e) sphere

kreischen [KRIGH-shern] v shriek

Kreislauf [KRIGHS-lowf] m
circulation

Kreisverkehr [KRIGHS-fehr-kayr]
m roundabout

Krem [kraym] f (pl ∼s) cream

kremfarben [KRAYM-fahr-bern]
adj cream

Kreuz [kroyts] nt (pl ∼e) cross

Kreuzung [KROY-tsoong] f (pl
∼en) intersection

Kricket [KRI-kert] nt cricket

* **kriechen** [KREE-khern] v creep

Krieg [kreek] m (pl ∼e) war

Kriminalroman [kri-mi-NARLroa-marn] *m* (*pl* ~e) detective story

Kristall [kris-TAHL] *nt* crystal

Kritiker [KREE-ti-kerr] *m* (*pl* ~ ; *f* ~in) critic

kritisch [KREE-tish] *adj* critical

kritisieren [kri-ti-ZEE-rern] *v* criticize

Krone [KROA-ner] *f* (*pl* ~n) crown

Krug [krook] *m* (*pl* ~e) jug

Krümel [KREW-merl] *m* (*pl* ~) crumb

Kruste [KROOS-ter] *f* (*pl* ~n) crust

Kruzifix [KROO-tsi-FIKS] *nt* (*pl* ~e) crucifix

Küche [KEW-kher] *f* (*pl* ~ n) kitchen

Kuchen [KOO-khern] *m* (*pl* ~) cake

Küchenchef [KEW-khern-shehf] *m* (*pl* ~s; *f* ~in) chef

Kugel [KOO-gerl] *f* (*pl* ~n) sphere

Kugelschreiber [KOO-gerl-shrigh-berr] *m* (*pl* ~) Biro; ballpoint-pen

Kuh [koo] *f* (*pl* ~e) cow

kühl [kewl] *adj* cool; chilly

Kühlschrank [KEWL-shrahnk] *m* (*pl* ~e) refrigerator; fridge

kühn [kewn] *adj* bold

kultiviert [kool-ti-VEERT] *adj* cultured

Kultur [kool-TOOR] *f* (*pl* ~en) culture

Kummer [KOO-merr] *m* sorrow; trouble

kümmern (sich) [zikh-KEW-merrn] *v* look after

kümmern um (sich) [zikh-KEW-merrn-oom] *v* mind; take care of

Kunde [KOON-der] *m* (*pl* ~n; *f*

~in) customer; client; patron

Kunst [koonst] *f* (*pl* ~e) art

Kunstausstellung [KOONST-ows-shteh-loong] *f* (*pl* ~en) art exhibition

Kunstgalerie [KOONST-gah-ler-ree] *f* (*pl* ~n) art gallery

Künstler [KEWNST-lerr] *m* (*pl* ~; *f* ~in) artist

künstlerisch [KEWNST-ler-rish] *adj* artistic

künstlich [KEWNST-likh] *adj* artificial

künstliches Gebiß [KEWNST-li-khers-ger-BIS] *nt* false teeth *pl*

Kunstsammlung [KOONST-zahm-loong] *f* (*pl* ~en) art collection

Kunstseide [KOONST-zigh-der] *f* rayon

Kunststoff [KOONST-shtof] *m* (*pl* ~e) plastic

Kunstwerk [KOONST-vehrk] *nt* (*pl* ~e) work of art

Kupfer [KOO-pferr] *nt* copper

Kupferstich [KOO-pferr-shtikh] *m* (*pl* ~e) engraving

Kuppel [KOO-perl] *f* (*pl* ~n) dome

Kupplung [KOOP-loong] *f* (*pl* ~en) clutch

Kur [koor] *f* (*pl* ~en) cure

Kurator [koo-RAR-tor] *m* (*pl* ~en) curator

Kürbis [KEWR-bis] *m* (*pl* ~se) squash

Kurs [koors] *m* (*pl* ~e) rate of exchange

Kürschner [KEWRSH-nerr] *m* (*pl* ~) furrier

Kursivschrift [koor-ZEEF-shrift] *f* italics *pl*

Kurve [KOOR-ver] *f* (*pl* ~n) curve; turning

kurz [koorts] *adj* short

kurze Hose [KOOR-tser-HOA-zer]

shorts *pl*

Kurzschluß [KOORTS-shloos] *m* (*pl ~̈e*) short circuit

kurzsichtig [KOORTS-zikh-tikh] *adj* short-sighted

Kurzwarengeschäft [KOORTS-var-rern-ger-shehft] *nt* (*pl ~e*) haberdashery

Kurzwarenhändler [KOORTS-var-rern-hehn-dlerr] *m* (*pl ~*) haberdasher

Kuß [koos] *m* (*pl ~̈e*) kiss

küssen [KEW-sern] *v* kiss

Küste [KEWS-ter] *f* (*pl ~n*) shore; seaside; coast

Laboratorium [lah-boa-rah-TOAR-yoom] *nt* (*pl* **Laboratorien**) laboratory

lächeln [LEH-kherln] *v* smile

Lächeln [LEH-kherln] *nt* smile

lachen [LAH-khern] *v* laugh

Lachen [LAH-khern] *nt* laugh

lächerlich [LEH-kherr-likh] *adj* ridiculous

Lachs [lahks] *m* salmon

Lack [lahk] *m* (*pl ~e*) lacquer

*** laden** [LAR-dern] *v* load

Laden [LAR-dern] *m* (*pl ~̈*) store

Ladeninhaber [LAR-dern-in-har-berr] *m* (*pl ~; f ~in*) shopkeeper

Ladentisch [LAR-dern-tish] *m* (*pl ~e*) counter

Laderaum [LAR-der-rowm] *m* (*pl ~̈e*) hold

Lage [LAR-ger] *f* location; situation

Lager [LAR-gerr] *nt* (*pl ~*) camp

lagern [LAR-gerrn] *v* store

Lagerung [LAR-ger-roong] *f* storage

lahm [larm] *adj* lame

lähmen [LAI-mern] *v* paralyse

Laib [lighp] *m* (*pl ~e*) loaf

Laken [LAR-kern] *nt* (*pl ~*) sheet

Lakritze [lah-KRI-tser] *f* liquorice

Lamm [lahm] *nt* (*pl ~̈er*) lamb

Lampe [LAHM-per] *f* (*pl ~n*) lamp

Lampenschirm [LAHM-pern-shirm] *m* (*pl ~e*) lampshade

Land [lahnt] *nt* land; country

landen [LAHN-dern] *v* land; disembark

Landenge [LAHNT-ehng-er] *f* (*pl ~n*) isthmus

Landhaus [LAHNT-hows] *nt* (*pl ~̈er*) country house

Landkarte [LAHNT-kahr-ter] *f* (*pl ~n*) map

ländlich [LEHNT-likh] *adj* rustic; rural

Landschaft [LAHNT-shahft] *f* (*pl ~en*) scenery; countryside; landscape

Landsitz [LAHNT-zits] *m* (*pl ~e*) estate

Landsmann [LAHNTS-mahn] *m* (*pl* **Landsleute**) countryman

Landstraße [LAHNT-shtrar-ser] *f* (*pl ~n*) highway

Landung [LAHN-doong] *f* (*pl ~en*) landing

Landwirtschaft [LAHNT-virt-shahft] *f* agriculture

Landzunge [LAHNT-tsoong-er] *f* (*pl ~n*) headland

lang [lahng] *adj* long

Länge [LEHNG-er] *f* (*pl ~n*) length

Längengrad [LEHNG-ern-grart] *m* (*pl ~e*) longitude

länger [LEHNG-err] *adj* longer

länglich [LEHNG-likh] *adj* oblong

langsam [LAHNG-zarm] *adj* slow

Langspielplatte [LAHNG-shpeel-plah-ter] *f* (*pl ~n*) long-playing record

langweilen [LAHNG-vigh-lern] *v* bore

langweilig [LAHNG-vigh-likh] *adj* boring; dull

Lärm [lehrm] *m* noise

lärmend [LEHR-mernt] *adj* noisy

* **lassen** [LAH-sern] *v* let; leave

Last [lahst] *f* (*pl* ~**en**) load

lästig [LEHS-tikh] *adj* troublesome

Lastwagen [LAHST-var-gern] *m* (*pl* ~) truck; lorry

Lateinamerika [lah-TIGHN-ah-MAY-ri-kah] *nt* Latin America

Lateinamerikaner [lah-TIGHN-ah-may-ri-kar-nerr] *m* (*pl* ~) Latin American

lateinamerikanisch [lah-TIGHN-ah-may-ri-KAR-nish] *adj* Latin American

Laterne [lah-TEHR-ner] *f* (*pl* ~**n**) lantern

Laternenpfahl [lah-TEHR-nern-pfarl] *m* (*pl* ~**e**) lamp-post

* **laufen** [LOW-fern] *v* run

Laufplanke [LOWF-plahng-ker] *f* (*pl* ~**n**) gangway

Laune [LOW-ner] *f* (*pl* ~**n**) fancy; spirit

laut [lowt] *adv* aloud; *adj* loud

läuten [LOY-tern] *v* ring

Lautsprecher [LOWT-shpreh-kherr] *m* (*pl* ~) loud-speaker

lauwarm [low-VAHRM] *adj* lukewarm; tepid

Lawine [lah-VEE-ner] *f* (*pl* ~**n**) avalanche

leben [LAY-bern] *v* live

Leben [LAY-bern] *nt* living; life; lifetime

lebend [LAY-bernt] *adj* live; alive

Lebensmittel [LAY-berns-mi-terl] *pl* groceries *pl*

Lebensmittelgeschäft [LAY-berns-mi-terl-ger-shehft] *nt* (*pl* ~**e**) grocery

Lebensmittelhändler [LAY-berns-mi-terl-hehn-dlerr] *m* (*pl* ~) grocer

Lebensstandard [LAY-berns-shtahn-dahrt] *m* standard of living

Lebensversicherung [LAY-berns-fehr-zɪ-kher-roong] *f* (*pl* ~**en**) life insurance

Leber [LAY-berr] *f* liver

lebhaft [LAYP-hahft] *adj* lively; vivid; brisk

Leck [lehk] *nt* leak

lecken [LEH-kern] *v* leak

lecker [LEH-kerr] *adj* appetising

Leckerbissen [LEH-kerr-bi-sern] *m* (*pl* ~) delicacy

Leder [LAY-derr] *nt* (*pl* ~) leather

ledig [LAY-dikh] *adj* single

leer [layr] *adj* empty; blank

legen [LAY-gern] *v* lay

lehnen [LAY-nern] *v* lean

Lehnstuhl [LAYN-shtool] *m* (*pl* ~**e**) armchair; easy chair

Lehrbuch [LAYR-bookh] *nt* (*pl* ~**er**) textbook

Lehre [LAY-rer] *f* (*pl* ~**n**) teachings *pl*

lehren [LAY-rern] *v* teach

Lehrer [LAY-rerr] *m* (*pl* ~; *f* ~**in**) teacher; schoolteacher; instructor

leicht [lighkht] *adj* light; slight; easy

leicht verderblich [lighkht-fehr-DEHRP-likh] *adj* perishable

leichte Mahlzeit [LIGHKH-ter-MARL-tsight] *f* light meal

* **leiden** [LIGH-dern] *v* suffer

Leiden [LIGH-dern] *nt* (*pl* ~) suffering; ailment

leider [LIGH-derr] *adv*
unfortunately

* **leihen** [LIGH-ern] *v* lend

Leim [lighm] *m* (*pl* ~e) glue

Leine [LIGH-ner] *f* (*pl* ~n) lead

Leinen [LIGH-nern] *nt* linen

leisten [LIGHS-tern] *v* achieve

leisten (sich) [zikh-LIGHS-tern] *v*
afford

Leistung [LIGHS-toong] *f* (*pl* ~en)
achievement

leistungsfähig [LIGHS-toongs-fai-
ikh] *adj* efficient

Leiter [LIGH-terr] *f* (*pl* ~n) ladder

Lektion [lehk-TSYOAN] *f* (*pl* ~en)
lesson

Lektor [LEHK-tor] *m* (*pl* ~en)
lecturer

Lendenstück [LEHN-dern- ,
shtewk] *nt* (*pl* ~e) sirloin

lernen [LEHR-nern] *v* learn

Leselampe [LAY-zer-lahm-per] *f*
(*pl* ~n) reading-lamp

* **lesen** [LAY-zern] *v* read

Lesen [LAY-zern] *nt* reading

Lesesaal [LAY-zer-zarl] *m* (*pl* ~e)
reading-room

letzt [lehtst] *adj* latest; last;
terminal; final

leuchtend [LOYKH-ternt] *adj*
luminous

Leuchtturm [LOYKHT-toorm] *m*
(*pl* ~e) lighthouse

leugnen [LOY-gnern] *v* deny

Leute [LOY-ter] *pl* people

liberal [li-bay-RARL] *adj* liberal

Licht [likht] *nt* (*pl* ~er) light

Lichtbild [LIKHT-bilt] *nt* (*pl* ~er)
photograph

Lichtung [LIKH-toong] *f* (*pl* ~en)
clearing

lieb [leep] *adj* dear; sweet

Liebe [LEE-ber] *f* love

lieben [LEE-bern] *v* love

Liebesgeschichte [LEE-bers-ger-
SHIKH-ter] *f* (*pl* ~n) love-story

Liebling [LEEP-ling] *m* (*pl* ~e)
sweetheart; darling

Lieblingstier [LEEP-lings-teer] *nt*
(*pl* ~e) pet

Liebschaft [LEEP-shahft] *f* (*pl*
~en) affair

Lied [leet] *nt* (*pl* ~er) song

Lieferauto [LEE-ferr-ow-toa] *nt*
(*pl* ~s) van

liefern [LEE-fehrn] *v* supply

Lieferung [LEE-fer-roong] *f* (*pl*
~en) supply; delivery

* **liegen** [LEE-gern] *v* lie

Liegestuhl [LEE-ger-shtool] *m* (*pl*
~e) deck-chair

Lift [lift] *m* (*pl* ~s) ski-lift

Limone [li-MOA-ner] *f* (*pl* ~n)
lime

Lineal [li-nay-ARL] *nt* (*pl* ~e)
ruler

Linienschiff [LEEN-yern-shif] *nt*
(*pl* ~e) liner

linke [LING-ker] *adj* left-hand;
left

Linse [LIN-zer] *f* (*pl* ~n) lens

Lippe [LI-per] *f* (*pl* ~n) lip

Lippensalbe [LI-pern-zahl-ber] *f*
(*pl* ~n) lipsalve

Lippenstift [LI-pern-shtift] *m* (*pl*
~e) lipstick

Liste [LIS-ter] *f* (*pl* ~n) list

Liter [LEE-terr] *m* (*pl* ~n) litre

literarisch [li-ter-RAR-rish] *adj*
literary

Literatur [li-ter-rah-TOOR] *f*
literature

Lob [loap] *nt* praise

loben [LOA-bern] *v* praise

Loch [lokh] *nt* (*pl* ~er) hole

Locke [LO-ker] *f* (*pl* ~n) curl

locken [LO-kern] *v* curl

Lockenwickler [LO-kern-vik-lerr] *m* (*pl* ~) hair rollers *pl*

lockern [LO-kerrn] *v* loosen

lockig [LO-kikh] *adj* curly

Löffel [LUR-ferl] *m* (*pl* ~) spoon

Löffelvoll [LUR-ferl-fol] *m* spoonful

Logik [LOA-gik] *f* logic

Lohn [loan] *m* (*pl* ~e) wages *pl*

lohnen (sich) [zikh-LOA-nern] *v* worthwhile (be)

Lokomotive [loa-koa-moa-TEE-ver] *f* (*pl* ~n) locomotive

Lord [lort] *m* (*pl* ~) lord

Los [loas] *nt* (*pl* ~e) lot

lose [LOA-zer] *adj* loose

lösen [LUR-zern] *v* solve

löslich [LURS-likh] *adj* soluble

losmachen [LOAS-mah-khern] *v* detach

Lösung [LUR-zoong] *f* (*pl* ~en) solution

Lotterie [lo-ter-REE] *f* (*pl* ~n) lottery

loyal [loaah-YARL] *adj* loyal

Lücke [LEW-ker] *f* (*pl* ~n) gap

Luft [looft] *f* air

lüften [LEWF-tern] *v* air; ventilate

Luftkissenfahrzeug [LOOFT-ki-sern-farr-tsoyk] *nt* (*pl* ~e) hovercraft

Luftkrankheit [LOOFT-krahngk-hight] *f* air sickness

Luftpost [LOOFT-post] *f* air mail

Luftzug [LOOFT-tsook] *m* draught

Lüge [LEW-ger] *f* (*pl* ~n) lie

Lügen [LEW-gern] *nt* lying

Luke [LOO-ker] *f* (*pl* ~n) porthole

Lumpen [LOOM-PERN] *m* (*pl* ~) rag

Lunge [LOONG-er] *f* (*pl* ~n) lung

Lungenentzündung [LOONG-ern-ehn-tsewn-doong] *f* pneumonia

lustig [LOOS-tikh] *adj* gay

Lustspiel [LOOST-shpeel] *nt* (*pl* ~e) comedy

lutschen [LOO-chern] *v* suck

luxuriös [loo-ksoor-YURS] *adj* luxurious

Luxus [LOO-ksoos] *m* luxury

machen [MAH-khern] *v* make

Macht [mahkht] *f* (*pl* ~e) might; power

mächtig [MEHKH-tikh] *adj* powerful; mighty

Mädchen [MAIT-khern] *nt* (*pl* ~) girl

Mädchenname [MAIT-khern-nar-mer] *m* (*pl* ~n) maiden name

Magen [MAR-gern] *m* (*pl* ~) stomach

Magengeschwür [MAR-gern-ger-shvewr] *nt* (*pl* ~e) gastric ulcer

Magenschmerzen [MAR-gern-shmehr-tsern] *mpl* stomach ache

Magenverstimmung [MAR-gern-fehr-shti-moong] *f* indigestion

mager [MAR-gerr] *adj* lean; thin

Magnet [mahg-NAYT] *m* (*pl* ~en) magneto

magnetisch [mahg-NAY-tish] *adj* magnetic

mahlen [MAR-lern] *v* grind

Mahlzeit [MARL-tsight] *f* (*pl* ~en) meal

Mai [migh] *m* May

Mais [mighs] *m* maize

Maiskolben [MIGHS-kol-bern] *m* (*pl* ~) corn-on-the-cob

Make-up-Unterlage [mayk-AHP-oon-terr-lar-ger] *f* foundation cream

Makrele [mah-KRAY-ler] *f* (*pl* ~n) mackerel

Mal [marl] *nt* (*pl* ~**e**) time

Malaria [mah-LAR-riah] *f* malaria

Maler [MAR-lerr] *m* (*pl* ~; *f* ~**in**) painter

malerisch [MAR-ler-rish] *adj* picturesque; scenic

Malkasten [MARL-kahs-tern] *m* (*pl* ~̈) paintbox

man [mahn] *pron* one

manchmal [MAHNKH-marl] *adv* sometimes

Mandarine [mahn-dah-REE-ner] *f* (*pl* ~**n**) tangerine; mandarin

Mandel [MAHN-derl] *f* (*pl* ~**n**) almond

Mandelentzündung [MAHN-derl-ehn-tsewn-doong] *f* tonsillitis

Mandeln [MAHN-derln] *fpl* tonsils *pl*

Mangel [MAHNG-erl] *m* (*pl* ~̈) scarcity; lack

mangelhaft [MAHNG-erl-hahft] *adj* defective

mangeln [MAHNG-erln] *v* lack

Manieren [mah-NEE-rern] *fpl* manners *pl*

Maniküre [mah-ni-KEW-rer] *f* (*pl* ~**n**) manicure

maniküren [mah-ni-KEW-rern] *v* manicure

Mann [mahn] *m* (*pl* ~̈**er**) man; husband

Mannequin [MAH-ner-kang] *nt* (*pl* ~**s**) mannequin

männlich [MEHN-likh] *adj* masculine; male

Mannschaft [MAHN-shahft] *f* (*pl* ~**en**) team

Manschetten [mahn-SHEH-tern] *fpl* cuffs *pl*

Manschettenknöpfe [mahn-SHEH-tern-knur-pfer] *mpl* cuff-links *pl*; links *pl*

Mantel [MAHN-terl] *m* (*pl* ~̈) overcoat; coat

Manuskript [mah-noo-SKRIPT] *nt* (*pl* ~**e**) manuscript

Margarine [mahr-gah-REE-ner] *f* margarine

Marine [mah-REE-ner] *f* navy

maritim [mah-ri-TEEM] *adj* maritime

Marke [MAHR-ker] *f* (*pl* ~**n**) brand

Markenautomat [MAHR-kern-ow-toa-mart] *m* (*pl* ~**en**) stamp machine

Markstein [MAHRK-shtighn] *m* (*pl* ~**e**) landmark

Markt [mahrkt] *m* (*pl* ~̈**e**) market

Marktplatz [MAHRKT-plahts] *m* (*pl* ~̈**e**) market place

Marmelade [mahr-mer-LAR-der] *f* (*pl* ~**n**) marmalade

Marmor [MAHR-mor] *m* marble

Marsch [mahrsh] *m* (*pl* ~̈**e**) march

marschieren [mahr-SHEE-rern] *v* march

März [mehrts] *m* March

Maß [mars] *nt* (*pl* ~**e**) measure

Maschine [mah-SHEE-ner] *f* (*pl* ~**n**) machine

maschinengeschrieben [mah-SHEE-nern-ger-shree-bern] *adj* typewritten

Masern [MAR-zerrn] *pl* measles

mäßig [MAI-sikh] *adj* moderate

Massage [mah-SAR-zher] *f* (*pl* ~**n**) massage

Masse [MAH-ser] *f* (*pl* ~**n**) bulk

Massenproduktion [MAH-sern-proa-dook-tsyoan] *f* mass-production

Masseur [mah-SURR] *m* (*pl* ~**e**; *f* **Masseuse**) masseur

massieren [mah-SEE-rern] *v*
massage

massiv [mah-SEEF] *adj* massive

Maßstab [MARS-shtarp] *m* (*pl* ~e)
scale

Material [mah-tayr-YARL] *nt* (*pl*
~ien) material

Materie [mah-TAYR-yer] *f* (*pl* ~n)
matter

Mathematik [mah-tay-mah-
TEEK] *f* mathematics

Matratze [mah-TRAH-tser] *f* (*pl*
~n) mattress

Matrose [mah-TROA-zer] *m* (*pl*
~n) sailor; seaman

Matsch [mahch] *m* slush

matt [maht] *adj* dull

Matte [MAH-ter] *f* (*pl* ~n) mat

Mauer [MOW-err] *f* (*pl* ~n) wall

Maulbeere [MOWL-bay-rer] *f* (*pl*
~n) mulberry

Maus [mows] *f* (*pl* ~e) mouse

Mechaniker [may-KHAR-ni-kerr]
m (*pl* ~; *f* ~in) mechanic

mechanisch [may-KHAR-nish]
adj mechanical

Mechanismus [may-khah-NIS-
moos] *m* (*pl* **Mechanismen**)
mechanism; machinery

Medaille [may-DAHL-yer] *f* (*pl*
~n) medal

Medizin [may-di-TSEEN] *f*
medicine

medizinisch [may-di-TSEE-nish]
adj medical

Meer [mayr] *nt* (*pl* ~e) sea

Meeräsche [MAYR-eh-sher] *f* (*pl*
~n) mullet

Meeresblick [MAY-rers-blik] *m*
seascape

Meeresküste [MAY-rers-kews-
ter] *f* (*pl* ~n) seashore;
seacoast

Meerrettich [MAYR-reh-tikh] *m*
horse-radish

Meerwasser [MAYR-vah-serr] *nt*
sea-water

Mehl [mayl] *nt* flour

mehr [mayr] *adj* more

Mehrheit [MAYR-hight] *f* (*pl* ~en)
majority

Mehrzahl [MAYR-tsarl] *f* plural

Meile [MIGH-ler] *f* (*pl* ~n) mile

Meilenstand [MIGH-lern-shtahnt]
m mileage

Meilenstein [MIGH-lern-shtighn]
m (*pl* ~e) milestone

mein [mighn] *adj* my

mein Herr [mighn-HEHR] *m* sir

Meinung [MIGH-noong] *f* (*pl* ~en)
opinion

Meißel [MIGH-serl] *m* (*pl* ~)
chisel

meist [mighst] *adj* most

Meister [MIGHS-terr] *m* (*pl* ~; *f*
~in) master

Meisterstück [MIGHS-terr-
shtewk] *nt* (*pl* ~e)
masterpiece

Melodie [may-loa-DEE] *f* (*pl* ~n)
melody; tune

melodisch [may-LOA-dish] *adj*
tuneful

Melodrama [may-loa-DRAR-mah]
nt (*pl* **Melodramen**)
melodrama

Melone [may-LOA-ner] *f* (*pl* ~n)
melon

Memorandum [may-moa-RAHN-
doom] *nt* (*pl* **Memoranden**)
memo

memorieren [may-moa-REE-
rern] *v* memorize

Menge [MEHNG-er] *f* (*pl* ~n)
mass; lot; crowd; amount

Mensch [mehnsh] *m* (*pl* ~en)
human being

Menschheit [MEHNSH-hight] *f*

humanity; mankind

menschlich [MEHNSH-likh] *adj*
human

Meßgerät [MEHS-ger-rait] *nt* (*pl*
~e) gauge

Messe [MEH-ser] *f* (*pl* ~n) fair;
Mass

* **messen** [MEH-sern] *v* measure

Messer [MEH-serr] *nt* (*pl* ~) knife

Messing [MEH-sing] *nt* brass

Metall [may-TAHL] *nt* (*pl* ~e)
metal

metallisch [may-TAH-lish] *adj*
metal

Meter [MAY-terr] *nt* metre

Methode [may-TOA-der] *f* (*pl* ~n)
method

methodisch [may-TOA-dish] *adj*
methodical

metrisch [MAY-trish] *adj* metric

Mexikaner [meh-ksi-KAR-nerr]
m (*pl* ~; *f* ~in) Mexican

mexikanisch [meh-ksi-KAR-nish]
adj Mexican

Mexiko [MEH-ksi-koa] *nt* Mexico

mich [mikh] *pron* myself; me

Miete [MEE-ter] *f* (*pl* ~n) rental;
rent

mieten [MEE-tern] *v* rent; hire;
engage

Mieter [MEE-terr] *m* (*pl* ~; *f* ~in)
tenant; lodger

Mietvertrag [MEET-fehr-trark] *m*
(*pl* ~e) lease

Migräne [mi-GRAI-ner] *f*
migraine

Mikrophon [mi-kroa-FOAN] *nt* (*pl*
~e) microphone

Milch [milkh] *f* milk

Milchbar [MILKH-barr] *f* (*pl* ~s)
milk-bar

milchig [MIL-khikh] *adj* milky

Milchmann [MILKH-mahn] *m* (*pl*
~er) milkman

Milchpulver [MILKH-pool-verr] *nt*
powdered milk

Milchshake [MILKH-shayk] *m* (*pl*
~s) milk-shake

mild [milt] *adj* mild; mellow

mildern [MIL-derrn] *v* soften

militärisch [mi-li-TAI-rish] *adj*
military

Million [mil-YOAN] *f* (*pl* ~en)
million

Millionär [mil-yoa-NAIR] *m* (*pl*
~e; *f* ~in) millionaire

Minderheit [MIN-derr-hight] *f* (*pl*
~en) minority

minderjährig [MIN-derr-yai-rikh]
adj under-age

minderwertig [MIN-derr-vayr-
tikh] *adj* inferior

Mineral [mi-ner-RARL] *nt* (*pl* ~e)
mineral

Mineralwasser [mi-ner-RARL-
vah-serr] *nt* mineral water

Miniatur [mi-niah-TOOR] *f* (*pl*
~en) miniature

Minimum [MI-ni-moom] *nt*
minimum

Minister [mi-NIS-terr] *m* (*pl* ~; *f*
~in) minister

Ministerium [mi-nis-TAYR-yoom]
nt (*pl* **Ministerien**) ministry

Minute [mi-NOO-ter] *f* (*pl* ~n)
minute

Minze [MIN-tser] *f* (*pl* ~n) mint

mir [meer] *pron* me

mißbilligen [mis-BI-li-gern] *v*
disapprove

mischen [MI-shern] *v* shuffle;
mix

Mischung [MI-shoong] *f* (*pl* ~en)
mixture

Mißerfolg [MIS-ehr-folk] *m* (*pl*
~e) failure

* **mißfallen** [mis-FAH-lern] *v*
displease

Mißgeschick [MIS-ger-shik] *nt* (*pl* ~e) misfortune

Mißverständnis [MIS-fehr-shtehnt-nis] *nt* (*pl* ~se) misunderstanding

* **mißverstehen** [MIS-fehr-shtay-ern] *v* misunderstand

mit [mit] *prep* with

mit der Hand gemacht [mit-dayr-HAHNT-ger-MAHKHT] manual

mitfühlend [MIT-few-lernt] *adj* sympathetic

Mitgefühl [MIT-ger-fewl] *nt* sympathy

Mitglied [MIT-gleet] *nt* (*pl* ~er) member

Mitgliedschaft [MIT-gleet-shahft] *f* membership

Mitleid [MIT-light] *nt* pity

Mitschuldige [MIT-shool-di-ger] *m* (*pl* ~n; *f* ~) accessary

Mittag [MI-tark] *m* noon; midday

Mittagessen [MI-tark-eh-sern] *nt* (*pl* ~) luncheon; lunch

Mittagszeit [MI-tarks-tsight] *f* lunch time

mitteilen [MI-tigh-lern] *v* communicate

Mitteilung [MI-tigh-loong] *f* (*pl* ~en) communication; message

Mittel [MI-terl] *nt* (*pl* ~) means *pl*

mittelalterlich [MI-terl-ahl-terr-likh] *adj* mediaeval

Mittelmeer [MI-terl-mayr] *nt* Mediterranean

Mittelstand [MI-terl-shtahnt] *m* middle-class

Mitternacht [MI-terr-nahkht] *f* midnight

mittlere [MIT-ler-rer] *adj* medium; middle

mittlerweile [mit-lerr-VIGH-ler] *adv* meanwhile

Mittwoch [MIT-vokh] *m* Wednesday

Mixer [MI-kserr] *m* (*pl* ~) mixer

Möbel [MUR-berl] *ntpl* furniture

möblierte Wohnung [mur-BLEER-ter-VOA-noong] *f* (*pl* ~en) furnished flat

möbliertes Zimmer [mur-BLEER-ters-TSI-merr] *nt* (*pl* ~) furnished room

Mode [MOA-der] *f* fashion

Modell [moa-DEHL] *nt* (*pl* ~e) model

modern [moa-DEHRN] *adj* modern; fashionable

Modetorheit [MOA-der-toar-hight] *f* (*pl* ~en) fad

modifizieren [moa-di-fi-TSEE-rern] *v* modify

Modistin [moa-DIS-tin] *f* (*pl* ~nen) milliner

* **mögen** [MUR-gern] *v* may

möglich [MURK-likh] *adj* possible

Möglichkeit [MURK-likh-kight] *f* (*pl* ~en) possibility

Mohair [moa-HAIR] *m* mohair

Molkerei [mol-ker-RIGH] *f* (*pl* ~en) dairy

Monat [MOA-naht] *m* (*pl* ~e) month

monatlich [MOA-naht-likh] *adj* monthly

Mönch [murnkh] *m* (*pl* ~e) monk

Mond [moant] *m* (*pl* ~e) moon

Mondlicht [MOANT-likht] *nt* moonlight

Monopol [moa-noa-POAL] *nt* (*pl* ~e) monopoly

monoton [moa-noa-TOAN] *adj* monotonous

Montag [MOAN-tark] *m* Monday

Moorhuhn [MOAR-hoon] *nt* (*pl ~er*) grouse *inv*

Moral [moa-RARL] *f* morality

moralisch [moa-RAR-lish] *adj* moral

Mord [mort] *m* (*pl ~e*) murder

morden [MOR-dern] *v* murder

morgen [MOR-gern] *adv* tomorrow

Morgen [MOR-gern] *m* (*pl ~*) morning

Morgendämmerung [MOR-gern-deh-mer-roong] *f* dawn

Morgenrock [MOR-gern-rok] *m* (*pl ~e*) dressing gown

Morphium [MORF-yoom] *nt* morphia

Mosaik [moa-zah-EEK] *nt* (*pl ~en*) mosaic

Moschee [mo-SHAY] *f* (*pl ~n*) mosque

Moskito [mos-KEE-toa] *m* (*pl ~s*) mosquito

Moskitonetz [mos-KEE-toa-nehts] *nt* (*pl ~e*) mosquito net

Moskitostich [mos-KEE-toa-shtikh] *m* (*pl ~e*) mosquito bite

Motel [MOA-tehl] *nt* (*pl ~s*) motel

Motor [MOA-tor] *m* (*pl ~en*) motor; engine

Motorboot [MOA-tor-boat] *nt* (*pl ~e*) motorboat

Motorhaube [MOA-tor-how-ber] *f* (*pl ~n*) hood; bonnet

Motorrad [MOA-tor-rart] *nt* (*pl ~er*) motorcycle

Motorroller [moa-TOAR-ro-lerr] *m* (*pl ~*) scooter

Motte [MO-ter] *f* (*pl ~n*) moth

Möve [MUR-ver] *f* (*pl ~n*) seagull

müde [MEW-der] *adj* weary; tired

Mühe [MEW-er] *f* (*pl ~n*) pains *pl*

Mühle [MEW-ler] *f* (*pl ~n*) mill

Müll [mewl] *m* garbage

Müller [MEW-lerr] *m* (*pl ~*; *f ~in*) miller

Multiplikation [mool-ti-pli-kah-TSYOAN] *f* (*pl ~en*) multiplication

multiplizieren [mool-ti-pli-TSEE-rern] *v* multiply

Mumps [moomps] *m* mumps

Mund [moont] *m* (*pl ~er*) mouth

Mundart [MOONT-ahrt] *f* (*pl ~en*) dialect

mündlich [MEWNT-likh] *adj* verbal; oral

Mundwasser [MOONT-vah-serr] *nt* mouthwash

Münze [MEWN-tser] *f* (*pl ~n*) coin; token

Münzwäscherei [MEWNTS-veh-sher-righ] *f* (*pl ~en*) launderette

murren [MOO-rern] *v* grumble

Muschel [MOO-sherl] *f* (*pl ~n*) shell; mussel; sea-shell

Muße [MOO-ser] *f* leisure

Museum [moo-ZAY-oom] *nt* (*pl Museen*) museum

Musical [MYOO-zi-kerl] *nt* musical comedy

müßig [MEW-sikh] *adj* idle

Musik [moo-ZEEK] *f* music

musikalisch [moo-zi-KAR-lish] *adj* musical

Musiker [MOO-zi-kerr] *m* (*pl ~*; *f ~in*) musician

Musikgeschäft [moo-ZEEK-ger-shehft] *nt* (*pl ~e*) music shop

Musikinstrument [moo-ZEEK-in-stroo-mehnt] *nt* (*pl ~e*) musical instrument

Muskatnuß [moos-KART-noos] *f* (*pl ~e*) nutmeg

Muskel [MOOS-kerl] *m* (*pl ~n*) muscle

Musselin [moo-ser-LEEN] *m*
muslin

* **müssen** [MEW-sern] *v* must;
need; have to

Muster [MOOS-terr] *nt (pl ∼)*
sample; pattern

Mut [moot] *m* courage

mutig [MOO-tikh] *adj* courageous

Mutter [MOO-terr] *f (pl ∼)* mother

Muttersprache [MOO-terr-
shprar-kher] *f (pl ∼n)* mother
tongue; native language

Mütze [MEW-tser] *f (pl ∼n)* cap

Mythos [MEW-tos] *m (pl* **Mythen**)
myth

nach [narkh] *prep* after; to;
towards

nach draußen [narkh-DROW-
sern] outwards

nach innen [narkh-I-nern]
inwards

nach Maß [narkh-MARS] tailor-
made

nach und nach [NARKH-oont-
NARKH] little by little

nachahmen [NARKH-ar-mern] *v*
imitate

Nachbar [NAHKH-barr] *m (pl ∼n;
f ∼in)* neighbour

Nachbarschaft [NAHKH-barr-
shahft] *f (pl ∼ en)*
neighbourhood; vicinity

nachdem [narkh-DAYM] *conj*
after

* **nachdenken über** [NARKH-
dehng-kern-EW-berr] *v* think
about

nachdenklich [NARKH-dehngk-
likh] *adj* thoughtful

Nachfrage [NARKH-frar-ger] *f (pl
∼n)* inquiry

* **nachgeben** [NARKH-gay-bern] *v*
give in

nachher [narkh-HAYR] *adv*
afterwards

Nachmittag [NARKH-mi-tark] *m
(pl ∼e)* afternoon

Nachname [NARKH-nar-mer] *m
(pl ∼n)* family name

nachprüfen [NARKH-prew-fern] *v*
verify

Nachrichten [NARKH-rikh-tern]
fpl news

* **nachsenden** [NARKH-zehn-dern]
v forward

nächste [NAIKHS-ter] *adj* nearest

nächstfolgend [naikhst-FOL-
gernt] *adj* next

Nacht [nahkht] *f (pl ∼ e)* night

Nachteil [NARKH-tighl] *m (pl ∼e)*
disadvantage

Nachtflug [NAHKHT-flook] *m (pl
∼ e)* night-flight

Nachthemd [NAHKHT-hehmt] *nt
(pl ∼ en)* nightdress

Nachtisch [NARKH-tish] *m*
dessert; sweet

Nachtklub [NAHKHT-kloop] *m (pl
∼s)* cabaret

Nachtkrem [NAHKHT-kraym] *f (pl
∼s)* night-cream

Nachtlokal [NAHKHT-loa-karl] *nt
(pl ∼ e)* night-club

Nachttarif [NAHKHT-tah-reef] *m
(pl ∼ e)* night-rate

Nachtzug [NAHKHT-tsook] *m (pl
∼ e)* night train

nackt [nahkt] *adj* naked

Nadel [NAR-derl] *f (pl ∼ n)* needle

Nagel [NAR-gerl] *m (pl ∼)* nail

Nagelbürste [NAR-gerl-bewrs-
ter] *f (pl ∼ n)* nail-brush

Nagelfeile [NAR-gerl-figh-ler] *f
(pl ∼ n)* nail-file

Nagelschere [NAR-gerl-shay-rer]
f (pl ∼ n) nail-scissors *pl*

nahe [NAR-er] *adj* near; nearby; close

nähen [NAI-ern] *v* sew

näher [NAI-err] *adj* nearer

Näherei [nai-er-RIGH] *f (pl ~en)* sewing

nähern (sich) [zikh-NAI-errn] *v* approach

Nähmaschine [NAI-mah-shee-ner] *f (pl ~n)* sewing-machine

nahrhaft [NARR-hahft] *adj* nutritious

Nahrung [NAR-roong] *f* food

Nahrungsmittel [NAR-roongs-mi-terl] *ntpl* food-stuffs *pl*

Nahrungsmittelvergiftung [NAR-roongs-mi-terl-fehr-GIF-toong] *f* food poisoning

Naht [nart] *f (pl ~e)* seam

nahtlos [NART-loas] *adj* seamless

Name [NAR-mer] *m (pl ~ n)* name

Narbe [NAHR-ber] *f (pl ~n)* scar

naß [nahs] *adj* wet

Nase [NAR-zer] *f (pl ~n)* nose

Nasenloch [NAR-zern-lokh] *nt (pl ~er)* nostril

Nation [nah-TSYOAN] *f (pl ~ en)* nation

national [nah-tsyoa-NARL] *adj* national

Nationalhymne [nah-tsyoa-NARL-hewm-ner] *f (pl ~ n)* national anthem

Natur [nah-TOOR] *f* nature

natürlich [nah-TEWR-likh] *adj* natural

Naturschutzpark [nah-TOOR-shoots-pahrk] *m (pl ~s)* national park

Navigation [nah-vi-gah-TSYOAN] *f* navigation

Nebel [NAY-berl] *m (pl ~)* mist; fog

neben [NAY-bern] *prep* next to; beside

nebenan [nay-bern-AHN] *adv* next-door

Nebenanschluß [NAY-bern-ahn-shloos] *m (pl ~e)* extension

Nebenfluß [NAY-bern-floos] *m (pl ~e)* tributary

Nebengebäude [NAY-bern-ger-boy-der] *nt (pl ~)* annex

neblig [NAY-blikh] *adj* foggy; misty

Neffe [NEH-fer] *m (pl ~ n)* nephew

negativ [NAY-gah-teef] *adj* negative

Negativ [NAY-gah-teef] *nt (pl ~ e)* negative

Neger [NAY-gerr] *m (pl ~; f ~in)* negro

Negligé [nay-gli-ZHAY] *nt (pl ~ s)* negligee

* **nehmen** [NAY-mern] *v* take

Neid [night] *m* envy

neigen [NIGH-gern] *v* tend

neigen (sich) [zikh-NIGH-gern] *v* slant

Neigung [NIGH-goong] *f (pl ~en)* incline

nein [nighn] no

* **nennen** [NEH-nern] *v* name

Neon [NAY-on] *nt* neon

Nerv [nehrf] *m (pl ~ en)* nerve

nervös [nehr-VURS] *adj* nervous

Nest [nehst] *nt (pl ~ er)* nest

Netz [nehts] *nt (pl ~ e)* net; network; mesh

neu [noy] *adj* new

neugierig [NOY-gee-rikh] *adj* inquisitive; curious

Neuigkeiten [NOY-ikh-kigh-tern] *fpl* news

Neujahr [NOY-yarr] *nt* New Year

Neujahrstag [NOY-yarrs-tark] *m*

New Year's Day

neun [noyn] *adj* nine

neunte [NOYN-ter] *adj* ninth

neunzehn [NOYN-tsayn] *adj* nineteen

neunzehnte [NOYN-tsayn-ter] *adj* nineteenth

neunzig [NOYN-tsikh] *adj* ninety

Neuralgie [noy-rahl-GEE] *f (pl ~ n)* neuralgia

Neurose [noy-ROA-zer] *f (pl ~ n)* neurosis

neutral [noy-TRARL] *adj* neutral

nicht [nikht] *adv* not

nicht mehr [NIKHT-mayr] no more; no longer

* **nicht mögen** [nikht-MUR-gern] *v* dislike

nicht übereinstimmen [nikht-ew-berr-IGHN-shti-mern] *v* disagree

Nichte [NIKH-ter] *f (pl ~ n)* niece

nichtrostender Stahl [NIKHT-ros-tern-derr-SHTARL] stainless steel

nichts [nikhts] nothing

nichtsdestoweniger [nikhts-dehs-toa-VAY-ni-gerr] *adv* nevertheless

Nicken [NI-kern] *nt* nod

Niedergeschlagenheit [NEE-derr-ger-shlar-gern-hight] *f* depression

Niederlande [NEE-derr-lahn-der] *f* Netherlands *pl*

* **niederlassen (sich)** [zikh-NEE-derr-lah-sern] *v* settle down

niederlegen (sich) [zikh-NEE-derr-lay-gern] *v* lie down

* **niederschlagen** [NEE-derr-shlar-gern] *v* knock down

niederträchtig [NEE-derr-trehkh-tikh] *adj* mean

niedrig [NEE-drikh] *adj* low

niemals [NEE-mahls] *adv* never

niemand [NEE-mahnt] *pron* nobody; no one

Niere [NEE-rer] *f (pl ~ n)* kidney

niesen [NEE-zern] *v* sneeze

Niesen [NEE-zern] *nt* sneezing

nirgends [NIR-gerns] *adv* nowhere

noch [nokh] *adv* yet; still

noch ein [NOKH-ighn] another

noch einmal [NOKH-ighn-marl] once more

Nonne [NO-ner] *f (pl ~ n)* nun

Nord . . . [nort] *pref* northern

Norden [NOR-dern] *m* north

nördlich [NURRT-likh] *adj* northerly

Nordosten [nort-OS-tern] *m* north-east

nordwärts [NORT-vehrts] *adv* northwards

Nordwesten [nort-VEHS-tern] *m* north-west

normal [nor-MARL] *adj* normal

Norwegen [NOR-vay-gern] *nt* Norway

Norweger [NOR-vay-gerr] *m (pl ~; f ~in)* Norwegian

norwegisch [NOR-vay-gish] *adj* Norwegian

Notausgang [NOAT-ows-gahng] *m (pl ~e)* emergency exit

Notfall [NOAT-fahl] *m (pl ~e)* emergency

Notiz [noa-TEETS] *f (pl ~en)* note

Notizbuch [noa-TEETS-bookh] *nt (pl ~er)* notebook

Nottreppe [NOAT-treh-per] *f (pl ~n)* fire escape

notwendig [NOAT-vehn-dikh] *adj* necessary

Notwendigkeit [noat-VEHN-dikh-kight] *f (pl ~ en)* necessity

November [noa-VEHM-berr] *m*

November

nuklear [noo-klay-ARR] *adj* nuclear

Null [nool] *f* nil; zero

Nummer [NOO-merr] *f (pl ~n)* number; size

nur [noor] *adv* only

Nuß [noos] *f (pl ~e)* nut

Nutzen [NOO-tsern] *m* utility; benefit

nützlich [NEWTS-likh] *adj* useful

nutzlos [NOOTS-loas] *adj* useless

Nylon [NIGH-lon] *nt* nylon

ob [op] *conj* whether

ob . . . oder [op-OA-derr] *conj* whether . . . or

oben [OA-bern] *adv* above; overhead; upstairs

obenauf [OA-bern-OWF] *prep* on top of

* **obenauf schwimmen** [oa-bern-OWF-shvi-mern] *v* float

obere [OA-ber-rer] *adj* upper; superior

obere Koje [OA-ber-rer-KOA-yer] *f* upper berth

oberes Bett [OA-ber-rers-BEHT] *nt* upper bed

Oberfläche [OA-berr-fleh-kher] *f (pl ~n)* surface

Oberkellner [OA-berr-kehl-nerr] *m (pl ~)* head-waiter

Oberschenkel [OA-berr-shehn-kerl] *m (pl ~)* thigh

Oberseite [OA-berr-zigh-ter] *f (pl ~n)* upside

oberst [oa-berrst] *adj* top

obgleich [op-GLIGHKH] *conj* though

Obhut [OP-hoot] *f* custody

Oblate [oa-BLAR-ter] *f (pl ~n)* wafer

obligatorisch [o-bli-gah-TOA-rish] *adj* compulsory

Observatorium [op-zehr-vah-TOAR-yoom] *nt (pl Observatorien)* observatory

Obst [oapst] *nt* fruit

Obstgarten [OAPST-gahr-tern] *m (pl ~)* orchard

Obus [OA-boos] *m (pl ~se)* trolley-bus

obwohl [op-VOAL] *conj* although

Ochse [OK-ser] *m (pl ~n)* ox

oder [OA-derr] *conj* or

Ofen [OA-fern] *m (pl ~)* stove

offen [o-fern] *adj* open

offensichtlich [o-fern-ZIKHT-likh] *adj* apparent; evident; obvious

öffentlich [UR-fernt-likh] *adj* public

offiziell [o-fi-TSYEHL] *adj* official

offizielle Bekanntgabe [o-fi-TSYEH-ler-ber-KAHNT-gar-ber] *f* public notice

Offizier [o-fi-TSEER] *m (pl ~e)* officer

öffnen [URF-nern] *v* open

Öffnung [URF-noong] *f (pl ~en)* opening

oft [oft] *adv* often

ohne [OA-ner] *prep* without

ohne Chauffeur [OA-ner-sho-FURR] self-drive

ohne Zweifel [OA-ner-TSVIGH-ferl] without doubt

ohnehin [oa-ner-HIN] *adv* anyway

* **ohnmächtig werden** [OAN-mehhk-tikh-vayr-dern] *v* faint

Ohr [oar] *nt (pl ~en)* ear

Ohrenschmerzen [OA-rern-shmehr-tsern] *mpl* earache

Ohropax [oa-roa-PAHKS] *nt* earplug

Ohrringe [OAR-ring-er] *mpl*

earrings

Oktober [ok-TOA-berr] *m* October

Öldruck [URL-drook] *m* oil pressure

Ölgemälde [URL-ger-mail-der] *nt* (*pl* ~) oil-painting

ölig [UR-likh] *adj* oily

Olive [oa-LEE-ver] *f* (*pl* ~n) olive

Olivenöl [oa-LEE-vern-url] *nt* olive oil

Ölquelle [URL-kveh-ler] *f* (*pl* ~n) oil-well

Onkel [ONG-kerl] *m* (*pl* ~) uncle

Opal [oa-PARL] *m* (*pl* ~e) opal

Oper [OA-perr] *f* (*pl* ~n) opera

Operation [oa-per-rah-TSYOAN] *f* (*pl* ~en) operation; surgery

Operette [oa-per-REH-ter] *f* (*pl* ~n) operetta

Opernglas [OA-perrn-glars] *nt* (*pl* ~̈er) binoculars *pl*

Opernhaus [OA-perrn-hows] *nt* (*pl* ~̈er) opera house

Opfer [o-pferr] *nt* (*pl* ~) casualty; sacrifice

Optiker [OP-ti-kerr] *m* (*pl* ~; *f* ~in) optician

orange [oa-RAHNG-zher] *adj* orange

Orchester [or-KEHS-terr] *nt* (*pl* ~) orchestra

Orchestersitz [or-KEHS-terr-zits] *m* (*pl* ~e) orchestra seat

ordentlich [OR-dernt-likh] *adj* tidy

ordnen [ORD-nern] *v* arrange

Organisation [or-gah-ni-zah-TSYOAN] *f* organisation

organisch [or-GAR-nish] *adj* organic

organisieren [or-gah-ni-ZEE-rern] *v* organize

Orient [OA-ri-ehnt] *m* Orient

orientalisch [oa-ri-ehn-TAR-lish]
adj Oriental

orientieren (sich) [zikh-or-yehn-TEE-rern] *v* orientate

originell [oa-ri-gi-NEHL] *adj* original

Orlon [OR-lon] *nt* orlon

ornamental [or-nah-mehn-TARL] *adj* ornamental

Ort [ort] *m* (*pl* ~e) place

orthodox [or-toa-DOKS] *adj* orthodox

örtlich [URRT-likh] *adj* regional; local

Örtlichkeit [URRT-likh-kight] *f* (*pl* ~en) locality

Ortsansässige [ORTS-ahn-zeh-si-ger] *m* (*pl* ~n; *f* ~) resident

Ortsgespräch [ORTS-ger-shpraikh] *nt* (*pl* ~e) local call

Ortsnetz-Kennzahl [ORTS-nehts-KEHN-tsarl] *f* (*pl* ~en) area code

Osten [os-tern] *m* east

Ostern [OAS-terrn] *nt* Easter

Österreich [URS-ter-righkh] *nt* Austria

Österreicher [URS-ter-righ-kherr] *m* (*pl* ~; *f* ~in) Austrian

österreichisch [UR-ster-righ-khish] *adj* Austrian

östlich [URST-likh] *adj* eastern

Ouvertüre [oo-vehr-TEW-rer] *f* (*pl* ~n) overture

oval [oa-VARL] *adj* oval

Ozean [OA-tsay-arn] *m* (*pl* ~e) ocean

Paar [parr] *nt* (*pl* ~e) couple; pair

Päckchen [PEHK-khern] *nt* (*pl* ~) packet

packen [PAH-kern] *v* pack

Packkorb [PAHK-korp] *m* (*pl* ∼e)
hamper

Packpapier [PAHK-pah-peer] *nt*
wrapping paper

Paddel [PAH-derl] *nt* (*pl* ∼)
paddle

paddeln [PAH-derln] *v* paddle

Paket [pah-KAYT] *nt* (*pl* ∼e)
parcel; package

Pakistan [PAR-kis-tarn] *nt*
Pakistan

Pakistaner [par-kis-TAR-nerr] *m*
(*pl* ∼; *f* ∼in) Pakistani

Palast [pah-LAHST] *m* (*pl* ∼e)
palace

Palme [PAHL-mer] *f* (*pl* ∼n) palm

Pampelmuse [pahm-perl-MOO-
zer] *f* (*pl* ∼n) grapefruit

Panne [PAH-ner] *f* (*pl* ∼n)
breakdown

Pantoffel [pahn-TO-ferl] *m* (*pl*
∼n) slipper

Paperback [PAY-perr-behk] *nt*
paper-back

Papier [pah-PEER] *nt* (*pl* ∼e)
paper

Papiere [pah-PEE-rer] *ntpl*
papers *pl*

Papierkorb [pah-PEER-korp] *m*
(*pl* ∼e) wastepaper-basket

Papierserviette [pah-PEER-zehr-
VYEH-ter] *f* (*pl* ∼n) paper
napkin

Papiertaschentuch [pah-PEER-
tah-shern-tookh] *nt* (*pl* ∼ er)
kleenex

Pappe [PAH-per] *f* cardboard

Papst [parpst] *m* (*pl* ∼e) pope

Parade [pah-RAR-der] *f* (*pl* ∼n)
parade

parallel [pah-rah-LAYL] *adj*
parallel

Parfüm [pahr-FEWM] *nt* perfume;
scent

Park [pahrk] *m* (*pl* ∼s) park

parken [PAHR-kern] *v* park

Parken [PAHR-kern] *nt* parking

Parken verboten [PAHR-kern-
fehr-BOA-tern] no parking

Parkgebühr [PAHRK-ger-bewr] *f*
(*pl* ∼en) parking fee

Parkleuchte [PAHRK-loykh-ter] *f*
(*pl* ∼n) parking light

Parkplatz [PAHRK-plahts] *m* (*pl*
∼e) park; car park

Parkuhr [PAHRK-oor] *f* (*pl* ∼en)
parking meter

Parkzeit [PAHRK-tsight] *f* parking
time

Parkzone [PAHRK-tsoa-ner] *f* (*pl*
∼n) parking zone

Parlament [pahr-lah-MEHNT] *nt*
(*pl* ∼e) parliament

Partei [pahr-TIGH] *f* (*pl* ∼en) side

Partie [pahr-TEE] *f* (*pl* ∼n) batch

Partner [PAHRT-nerr] *m* (*pl* ∼; *f*
∼in) partner

Party [PAHR-ti] *f* (*pl* **Parties**)
party

Parzelle [pahr-TSEH-ler] *f* (*pl* ∼n)
plot

Paß [pahs] *m* (*pl* ∼e) passport

Paßkontrolle [PAHS-kon-tro-ler] *f*
(*pl* ∼n) passport control

Paßphoto [PAHS-foa-toa] *nt* (*pl*
∼s) passport photograph

Passagier [pah-sah-ZHEER] *m* (*pl*
∼e; *f* ∼in) passenger

Passant [pah-SAHNT] *m* (*pl* ∼en; *f*
∼in) passer-by

passen [PAH-sern] *v* fit; suit

passend [PAH-sernt] *adj*
convenient

passiv [PAH-seef] *adj* passive

Paste [PAHS-ter] *f* (*pl* ∼n) paste

Pastinake [pahs-ti-NAR-ker] *f* (*pl*
∼n) parsnip

Pastor [PAHS-tor] *m* (*pl* ∼en)

rector

Patient [pah-TSYEHNT] *m* (*pl* ~en; *f* ~in) patient

Patriot [pah-tri-OAT] *m* (*pl* ~en; *f* ~in) patriot

Patrone [pah-TROA-ner] *f* (*pl* ~n) cartridge

Pauschalsumme [pow-SHARL-zoo-mer] *f* (*pl* ~n) lump sum

Pause [POW-zer] *f* (*pl* ~n) intermission; pause

Pavillon [PAH-vil-yawng] *m* (*pl* ~s) pavilion

Pedal [pay-DARL] *nt* (*pl* ~en) pedal

peinlich [PIGHN-likh] *adj* awkward

Peitsche [PIGH-cher] *f* (*pl* ~n) whip

Pelz [pehlts] *m* (*pl* ~e) fur

Pelzmantel [PEHLTS-mahn-terl] *m* (*pl* ~̈) fur coat

Penicillin [pay-ni-tsi-LEEN] *nt* penicillin

Pension [pahng-SYOAN] *f* (*pl* ~en) pension; boarding house

per Bahn [pehr-BARN] by train

per Bus [pehr-BOOS] by bus

per Flugzeug [pehr-FLOOK-tsoyk] by air

per Nachnahme [pehr-NARKH-nar-mer] cash on delivery

per Schiff [pehr-SHIF] by sea

periodisch [payr-YOA-dish] *adv* periodically

Perle [PEHR-ler] *f* (*pl* ~n) pearl

perlend [PEHR-lernt] *adj* sparkling

Perlmutt [pehrl-MOOT] *nt* mother-of-pearl

Person [pehr-ZOAN] *f* (*pl* ~en) person

Personal [pehr-zoa-NARL] *nt* personnel; staff

Personalausweis [pehr-zoa-NARL-ows-vighs] *m* (*pl* ~e) identity card

Personenzug [pehr-ZOA-nern-tsook] *m* (*pl* ~̈e) passenger train

persönlich [pehr-ZURN-likh] *adj* personal

Persönlichkeit [pehr-ZURN-likh-kight] *f* (*pl* ~en) personality

Perücke [peh-REW-ker] *f* (*pl* ~n) wig

Petersilie [pay-terr-ZEEL-yer] *f* parsley

Petroleum [pay-TROA-lay-oom] *nt* paraffin; petroleum; oil

Pfad [pfart] *m* (*pl* ~e) path; trail

Pfandleiher [PFAHNT-ligh-err] *m* (*pl* ~) pawnbroker

Pfanne [PFAH-ner] *f* (*pl* ~n) pan; saucepan

Pfarre [PFAH-rer] *f* (*pl* ~n) rectory

Pfarrhaus [PFAHR-hows] *nt* (*pl* ~̈er) parsonage; vicarage

Pfeffer [PFEH-ferr] *m* pepper

Pfefferminze [pfeh-ferr-MIN-tser] *f* peppermint

Pfeife [PFIGH-fer] *f* (*pl* ~n) pipe; whistle

* **pfeifen** [PFIGH-fern] *v* whistle

Pfeifenreiniger [PFIGH-fern-righ-ni-gerr] *m* (*pl* ~) pipe cleaner

Pfeil [pfighl] *m* (*pl* ~e) arrow

Pferd [pfayrt] *nt* (*pl* ~e) horse

Pferderennen [PFAYR-der-reh-nern] *nt* (*pl* ~) horse-race

Pferdeschlitten [PFAYR-der-shli-tern] *m* (*pl* ~) sleigh

Pferdestärke [PFAYR-der-shtehr-ker] *f* (*pl* ~n) horse-power

Pfingsten [PFINGS-tern] *nt* Whitsuntide

Pfirsich [PFIR-zikh] *m* (*pl* ~e)

peach

Pflanze [PFLAHN-tser] f (pl ~n)
plant

pflanzen [PFLAHN-tsern] v plant

Pflaume [PFLOW-mer] f (pl ~n)
plum

Pflug [pflook] m (pl ~̈e) plough

Pfosten [PFOS-tern] m (pl ~) post;
pole

Pfund [pfoont] nt (pl ~e) pound

phantastisch [fahn-TAHS-tish]
adj fantastic

Philosoph [fi-loa-ZOAF] m (pl
~en; f ~in) philosopher

Philosophie [fi-loa-zoa-FEE] f
philosophy

phonetisch [foa-NAY-tish] adj
phonetic

Photogeschäft [FOA-toa-ger-
shehft] nt (pl ~e) camera store

Photograph [foa-toa-GRARF] m (pl
~en; f ~in) photographer

Photographie [foa-toa-grah-FEE]
f (pl ~n) photo; photography

photographieren [foa-toa-grah-
FEE-rern] v photograph

Photokopie [foa-toa-koa-PEE] f
(pl ~n) photostat

Photoladen [FOA-toa-lar-dern] m
(pl ~̈) photo store

physich [FEW-zish] adj physical

Physik [few-ZEEK] f physics

Physiker [FEW-zi-kerr] m (pl ~; f
~in) physicist

Pianist [piah-NIST] m (pl ~en; f
~in) pianist

Pickel [PI-kerl] m (pl ~) pimple

Pickles [PI-kerls] pl pickles pl

Picknick [PIK-nik] nt picnic

picknicken [PIK-ni-kern] v picnic

Pier [peer] f (pl ~s) pier; m jetty

Pik [peek] spades pl

pikant [pi-KAHNT] adj spicy

Pilger [PIL-gerr] m (pl ~; f ~in)

pilgrim

Pilgerfahrt [PIL-gerr-farrt] f (pl
~en) pilgrimage

Pille [PI-ler] f (pl ~n) pill

Pilot [pi-LOAT] m (pl ~en) pilot

Pilz [pilts] m (pl ~e) mushroom

Pinsel [PIN-zerl] m (pl ~)
paintbrush

Pinzette [pin-TSEH-ter] f (pl ~n)
tweezers pl

Pistole [pis-TOA-ler] f (pl ~n)
pistol

Plan [plarn] m (pl ~̈e) plan;
schedule

Plane [PLAR-ner] f (pl ~n)
tarpaulin

planen [PLAR-nern] v plan

Planet [plah-NAYT] m (pl ~en)
planet

Planetarium [plah-nay-TAR-
rioom] nt planetarium

Plantage [plahn-TAR-zher] f (pl
~n) plantation

Platin [PLAR-teen] nt platinum

Plattenspieler [PLAH-tern-shpee-
lerr] m (pl ~) record player

Platz [plahts] m (pl ~̈e) seat;
spot; square

Platzanweiser [PLAHTS-ahn-vigh-
zerr] m (pl ~) usher

Platzanweiserin [PLAHTS-ahn-
vigh-zer-rin] f (pl **~nen**)
usherette

Plombe [PLOM-ber] f (pl ~n)
filling

Plötze [PLUR-tser] f (pl ~n) roach

plötzlich [PLURTS-likh] adj
sudden

Plunder [PLOON-derr] m junk

plus [ploos] prep plus

pneumatisch [pnoy-MAR-tish]
adj pneumatic

pochen [PO-khern] v tap

Pocken [PO-kern] fpl smallpox

Police [poa-LEE-ser] *f* (*pl* ~**n**) policy

polieren [poa-LEE-rern] *v* polish

Politik [poa-li-TEEK] *f* politics *pl*; policy

Politiker [poa-LEE-ti-kerr] *m* (*pl* ~; *f* ~**in**) politician

politisch [poa-LEE-tish] *adj* political

Polizei [poa-li-TSIGH] *f* police *inv*

Polizeistation [poa-li-TSIGH-shtah-tsyoan] *f* (*pl* ~**en**) police-station

Polizist [poa-li-TSIST] *m* (*pl* ~**en**; *f* ~**in**) policeman

Polster [POL-sterr] *nt* (*pl* ~) pad

Polyp [poa-LEWP] *m* (*pl* ~**en**) octopus

Pony [PO-ni] *nt* (*pl* ~**s**) pony

Popelin [poa-per-LEEN] *nt* poplin

Popmusik [POP-moo-zeek] *f* pop music

populär [poa-poo-LAIR] *adj* popular

Portemonnaie [PORT-mo-nai] *nt* (*pl* ~**s**) purse

Portier [port-YAY] *m* (*pl* ~**s**) doorman; door-keeper

Portion [por-TSYOAN] *f* (*pl* ~**en**) portion; helping

Porto [POR-toa] *nt* postage

Porträt [por-TRAI] *nt* (*pl* ~**s**) portrait

Portugal [POR-too-gahl] *nt* Portugal

Portugiese [por-too-GEE-zer] *m* (*pl* ~**n**; *f* ~**in**) Portuguese

portugiesisch [por-too-GEE-zish] *adj* Portuguese

Porzellan [por-tser-LARN] *nt* porcelain; china

Position [poa-zi-TSYOAN] *f* (*pl* ~**en**) position

positiv [POA-zi-teef] *adj* positive

Positiv [POA-zi-teef] *nt* (*pl* ~**e**) positive

Post [post] *f* post; mail

Postamt [POST-ahmt] *nt* (*pl* ~**er**) post-office

Postanweisung [POST-ahn-vigh-zoong] *f* (*pl* ~**en**) postal order

Postbote [POST-boa-ter] *m* (*pl* ~**n**) postman

Postdienst [POST-deenst] *m* postal service

Posten [POS-tern] *m* (*pl* ~) post; item

Postkarte [POST-kahr-ter] *f* (*pl* ~**n**) postcard; card

postlagernd [POST-lar-gerrnt] poste restante

Postleitzahl [POST-light-tsarl] *f* (*pl* ~**en**) zip code

Pracht [prahkht] *f* glory

prächtig [PREHKH-tikh] *adj* glorious; gorgeous; superb; magnificent

Präfix [PRAI-fiks] *nt* (*pl* ~**e**) prefix

praktisch [PRAHK-tish] *adj* practical

praktischer Arzt [PRAHK-ti-sherr-AHRTST] general practitioner

Prämie [PRAIM-yer] *f* (*pl* ~**n**) premium

Präposition [prai-poa-zi-TSYOAN] *f* (*pl* ~**en**) preposition

Präsident [prai-zi-DEHNT] *m* (*pl* ~**en**) president

Praxis [PRAH-ksis] *f* practice

Preis [prighs] *m* (*pl* ~**e**) prize; price

Preis ansetzen [prighs-AHN-zeh-tsern] *v* price

Preisgericht [PRIGHS-ger-rikht] *nt* (*pl* ~**e**) jury

Preisliste [PRIGHS-lis-ter] *f* (*pl*

~n) price list

Preisnachlaß [PRIGHS-narkh-lahs] *m* reduction

Premierminister [prerm-YAY-mi-nis-terr] *m* (*pl* ~) premier

Presse [PREH-ser] *f* press

Priester [PREES-terr] *m* (*pl* ~) priest

Prinz [prints] *m* (*pl* ~en) prince

Prinzessin [prin-TSEH-sin] *f* (*pl* ~nen) princess

Prinzip [prin-TSEEP] *nt* (*pl* ~ien) principle

privat [pri-VART] *adj* private

Privateigentum [pri-VART-igh-gern-toom] *nt* (*pl* ~er) private property

Privathaus [pri-VART-hows] *nt* (*pl* ~er) private house

Privatleben [pri-VART-lay-bern] *nt* privacy

pro Person [proa-pehr-ZOAN] per person

pro Tag [proa-TARK] per day

Problem [proa-BLAYM] *nt* (*pl* ~e) problem

Produkt [proa-DOOKT] *nt* (*pl* ~e) product

Produktion [proa-dook-TSYOAN] *f* production

Produzent [proa-doo-TSEHNT] *m* (*pl* ~en) producer

Professor [proa-FEH·sor] *m* (*pl* ~en; *f* ~in) professor

Programm [proa-GRAHM] *nt* (*pl* ~e) programme

Projekt [proa-YEHKT] *nt* (*pl* ~e) project

Promenade [proa-mer-NAR-der] *f* (*pl* ~n) promenade; esplanade

Propaganda [proa-pah-GAHN-dah] *f* propaganda

Propeller [proa-PEH-lerr] *m* (*pl* ~) propeller

Prospekt [proa-SPEHKT] *m* (*pl* ~e) prospectus

Protest [proa-TEHST] *m* (*pl* ~e) protest

protestantisch [proa-tehs-TAHN-tish] *adj* Protestant

protestieren [proa-tehs-TEE-rern] *v* protest

Provinz [proa-VINTS] *f* (*pl* ~en) province

provinziell [proa-vin-TSYEHL] *adj* provincial

Prozent [proa-TSEHNT] *nt* percent

Prozentsatz [proa-TSEHNT-zahts] *m* percentage

prüfen [PREW-fern] *v* examine; test

Psychiater [psew-KHAR-terr] *m* (*pl* ~) psychiatrist

Psychoanalytiker [psew-khoa-ah-nah-LEW-ti-kerr] *m* (*pl* ~) psychoanalyst; analyst

Psychologe [psew-khoa-LOA-ger] *m* (*pl* ~n; *f* ~in) psychologist

Psychologie [psew-khoa-loa-GEE] *f* psychology

psychologisch [psew-khoa-LOA-gish] *adj* psychological

Public Relations [PAHB-lik-ri-LEH-sherns] public relations *pl*

Publikum [POO-bli-koom] *nt* public; audience

Puder [POO-derr] *nt* powder; face powder

Puderdose [POO-derr-doa-zer] *f* (*pl* ~n) compact

Puderquaste [POO-derr-kvahs-ter] *f* (*pl* ~n) powder-puff

Pullmanwagen [POOL-mahn-var-gern] *m* (*pl* ~) Pullman car

Pullover [poo-LOA-verr] *m* (*pl* ~) pullover

Puls [pools] *m* pulse

Pumpe [POOM-per] *f* (*pl* ~n)

pump

pumpen [POOM-pern] *v* pump

Pumpernickel [POOM-perr-ni-kerl] *m* pumpernickel

Punkt [poongkt] *m* (*pl* ~e) point; full stop

pünktlich [PEWNKT-likh] *adj* punctual

Puppe [POO-per] *f* (*pl* ~n) doll

purpur [POOR-poor] *adj* purple

Pyjama [pew-ZHAR-mah] *m* (*pl* ~) pyjamas *pl*

Quadrat [kvah-DRART] *nt* (*pl* ~e) square

quadratisch [kvah-DRAR-tish] *adj* square

Qualität [kvah-li-TAIT] *f* (*pl* ~en) quality

Quantität [kvahn-ti-TAIT] *f* (*pl* ~en) quantity

Quarantäne [kah-rahn-TAI-ner] *f* quarantine

Quelle [KVEH-ler] *f* (*pl* ~n) spring

quetschen [KVEH-chern] *v* bruise

Quetschung [KVEH-choong] *f* (*pl* ~en) bruise

Quittung [KVI-toong] *f* (*pl* ~en) receipt

Quiz [kvis] *nt* quiz

Quote [KVOA-ter] *f* (*pl* ~n) quota

Rabatt [rah-BAHT] *m* (*pl* ~e) rebate; discount

Rad [rart] *nt* (*pl* ~er) wheel

Radfahrer [RART-far-rerr] *m* (*pl* ~ ; *f* ~in) cyclist

Radiergummi [rah-DEER-goo-mi] *m* (*pl* ~s) eraser; rubber

Radio [RAR-dyoa] *nt* (*pl* ~s) radio; wireless

Rahmen [RAR-mern] *m* (*pl* ~) frame

Rakete [rah-KAY-ter] *f* (*pl* ~n) rocket

Rampe [RAHM-per] *f* (*pl* ~n) ramp

Rand [rahnt] *m* (*pl* ~er) rim; edge; margin; verge

Randstein [RAHNT-shtighn] *m* (*pl* ~e) curb

Rang [rahng] *m* (*pl* ~e) grade; rank

ranzig [RAHN-tsikh] *adj* rancid

Rarität [rah-ri-TAIT] *f* (*pl* ~en) curio

rasen [RAR-zern] *v* speed

Rasen [RAR-zern] *m* (*pl* ~) lawn

rasend [RAR-zernt] *adj* delirious

Rasierapparat [rah-ZEER-ah-pah-rart] *m* (*pl* ~e) shaver; electric razor; razor; safety razor

rasieren (sich) [zikh-rah-ZEE-rern] *v* shave

Rasierklinge [rah-ZEER-kling-er] *f* (*pl* ~n) razor-blade

Rasierkrem [rah-ZEER-kraym] *f* shaving-cream

Rasierpinsel [rah-ZEER-pin-zerl] *m* (*pl* ~) shaving-brush

Rasierseife [rah-ZEER-zigh-fer] *f* shaving-soap

Rasierwasser [rah-ZEER-vah-serr] *nt* aftershave lotion

raspeln [RAHS-perln] *v* grate

Rasse [RAH-ser] *f* (*pl* ~n) breed; race

Rassen . . . [RAH-sern] *pref* racial

Rast [rahst] *f* rest

Rat [rart] *m* (*pl* ~e) board; advice; council

* **raten** [RAR-tern] *v* advise; guess

Rathaus [RART-hows] *nt* (*pl* ~er) town hall

Rätsel [RAI-tserl] *nt* (*pl* ~) puzzle

Ratte [RAH-ter] *f* (*pl* ~n) rat

Raub [rowp] *m* robbery

rauben [ROW-bern] *v* rob

Räuber [ROY-berr] *m* (*pl* ~; *f* ~in) robber

Rauch [rowkh] *m* smoke

rauchen [ROW-khern] *v* smoke

Rauchen verboten [ROW-khern-fehr-BOA-tern] no smoking

Raucher [ROW-kherr] *m* (*pl* ~; *f* ~in) smoker

Raucherabteil [ROW-kherr-ahp-tighl] *nt* (*pl* ~e) smoking compartment

rauchlos [ROWKH-loas] *adj* smokeless

Rauchzimmer [ROWKH-tsi-merr] *nt* (*pl* ~) smoke-room

Raum [rowm] *m* (*pl* ~̈e) space

räumen [ROY-mern] *v* vacate

Rauschgift [ROWSH-gift] *nt* (*pl* ~e) narcotic

Rechenschaft ablegen über [REH-khern-shahft-AHP-lay-gern-EW-berr] *v* account for

Rechnen [REHKH-nern] *nt* arithmetic

Rechnung [REHKH-noong] *f* (*pl* ~en) bill; check; invoice

* **Rechnung begleichen** [REHKH-noong-ber-GLIGH-khern] *v* settle up

recht [rehkht] *adj* right; right-hand

Recht [rehkht] *nt* (*pl* ~e) rights *pl*

Rechteck [REHKHT-ehk] *nt* (*pl* ~e) rectangle

rechteckig [REHKHT-eh-kikh] *adj* rectangular

Rechtsanwalt [REHKHTS-ahn-vahlt] *m* (*pl* ~̈e; *f* ~in) barrister; lawyer

Rechtschreibung [REHKHT-shrigh-boong] *f* spelling

rechtsgültig [REHKHTS-gewl-tikh] *adj* valid

rechtzeitig [REHKHT-tsigh-tikh] *adv* in time; on time

Rede [RAY-der] *f* (*pl* ~n) speech

Redewendung [RAY-der-vehn-doong] *f* (*pl* ~en) phrase

Referenz [ray-fay-REHNTS] *f* (*pl* ~en) reference

Reflektor [ray-FLEHK-tor] *m* (*pl* ~en) reflector

Regal [ray-GARL] *nt* (*pl* ~e) shelf

Regatta [ray-GAH-tah] *f* (*pl* **Regatten**) regatta

regelmäßig [RAY-gerl-mai-sikh] *adj* regular

regeln [RAY-gerln] *v* regulate; settle

Regen [RAY-gern] *m* rain

Regenbogen [RAY-gern-boa-gern] *m* (*pl* ~) rainbow

Regenguß [RAY-gern-goos] *m* (*pl* ~̈e) downpour

Regenmantel [RAY-gern-mahn-terl] *m* (*pl* ~̈) raincoat; mackintosh

Regenschauer [RAY-gern-show-err] *m* (*pl* ~) rainfall

Regenschirm [RAY-gern-shirm] *m* (*pl* ~e) umbrella

Regenwasser [RAY-gern-vah-serr] *nt* rain-water

Regierung [ray-GEE-roong] *f* (*pl* ~en) government

regnen [RAY-gnern] *v* rain

regnerisch [RAYG-ner-rish] *adj* rainy

rehbraun [RAY-brown] *adj* fawn

* **reiben** [RIGH-bern] *v* rub

reich [righkh] *adj* rich; wealthy

Reich [righkh] *nt* (*pl* ~e) empire

Reichtum [RIGHKH-toom] *m* (*pl*

~er) wealth

Reichtümer [RIGHKH-tew-merr] *mpl* riches *pl*

reif [righf] *adj* ripe; mature

Reife [RIGH-fer] *f* maturity

Reifen [RIGH-fern] *m* (*pl* ~) tyre

Reifendruck [RIGH-fern-drook] *m* tyre pressure

Reifenpanne [RIGH-fern-pah-ner] *f* (*pl* ~n) flat; puncture; blow-out

Reihe [RIGH-er] *f* (*pl* ~n) rank; row; file; line

Reim [righm] *m* (*pl* ~e) rhyme

rein [righn] *adj* pure

reinigen [RIGH-ni-gern] *v* clean

Reinigung [RIGH-ni-goong] *f* cleaning

Reinigungsmittel [RIGH-ni-goongs-mi-terl] *nt* (*pl* ~) cleaning fluid; detergent

Reis [righs] *m* rice

Reise [RIGH-zer] *f* (*pl* ~n) passage; travel; trip; journey; voyage

Reisebüro [RIGH-zer-bew-roa] *nt* (*pl* ~s) travel agent; travel agency ; tourist office

Reisebus [RIGH-zer-boos] *m* (*pl* ~se) coach

Reiseführer [RIGH-zer-few-rerr] *m* (*pl* ~) guidebook

reisen [RIGH-zern] *v* travel

Reisen [RIGH-zern] *nt* travelling

Reisende [RIGH-zern-der] *m* (*pl* ~n; *f* ~) traveller

Reiseplan [RIGH-zer-plarn] *m* (*pl* ~e) itinerary

Reisescheck [RIGH-zer-shehk] *m* (*pl* ~s) traveller's cheque

Reisespesen [RIGH-zer-shpay-zern] *pl* travelling expenses *pl*

Reiseversicherung [RIGH-zer-fehr-zi-kher-roong] *f* travel

insurance

Reißnagel [RIGHS-nar-gerl] *m* (*pl* ~) thumbtack

Reißverschluß [RIGHS-fehr-shloos] *m* (*pl* ~e) zip; zipper

Reißzwecke [RIGHS-tsveh-ker] *f* (*pl* ~n) drawing pin

Reiten [RIGH-tern] *nt* riding

Reiter [RIGH-terr] *m* (*pl* ~; *f* ~in) rider

Reiz [rights] *m* (*pl* ~e) attraction

reizbar [RIGHTS-barr] *adj* irritable

Reizmittel [RIGHTS-mi-terl] *nt* (*pl* ~) stimulant

Reklame [ray-KLAR-mer] *f* (*pl* ~n) publicity

Rekrut [ray-KROOT] *m* (*pl* ~en; *f* ~in) recruit

relativ [ray-lah-TEEF] *adj* relative

Relief [rayl-YEHF] *nt* (*pl* ~s) relief

Religion [ray-li-GYOAN] *f* (*pl* ~en) religion

religiös [ray-li-GYURS] *adj* religious

Reliquie [ray-LEE-kvier] *f* (*pl* ~n) relic

Rennbahn [REHN-barn] *f* (*pl* ~en) race-track; racecourse; course

Rennen [REH-nern] *nt* (*pl* ~) race

Rennpferd [REHN-pfayrt] *nt* (*pl* ~e) racehorse

Rente [REHN-ter] *f* (*pl* ~n) pension

Reparatur [ray-pah-rah-TOOR] *f* (*pl* ~en) repairs *pl*

Reparaturwerkstatt [ray-pah-rah-TOOR-vehrk-shtaht] *f* (*pl* ~en) repair shop

reparieren [ray-pah-REE-rern] *v* repair

repräsentativ [ray-preh-zehn-tah-TEEF] *adj* representative

Reproduktion [ray-proa-dook-TSYOAN] *f* (*pl* ~en)
reproduction

reproduzieren [ray-proa-doo-TSEE-rern] *v* reproduce

Reptil [rehp-TEEL] *nt* (*pl* ~e)
reptile

Republik [ray-poo-BLEEK] *f* (*pl* ~en) republic

republikanisch [ray-poo-bli-KAR-nish] *adj* republican

Reserverad [ray-ZEHR-ver-rart] *nt* (*pl* ~er) spare wheel

Reserveschlauch [ray-ZEHR-ver-shlowkh] *m* (*pl* ~e) spare tyre

reservieren [ray-zehr-VEE-rern] *v* reserve

reserviert [ray-zehr-VEERT] *adj* reserved

reservierter Platz [ray-zehr-VEER-terr-PLAHTS] *m* reserved seat

Reservierung [ray-zehr-VEE-roong] *f* (*pl* ~en) reservation; booking

Reservoir [ray-zehr-voa-ARR] *nt* (*pl* ~s) reservoir

Rest [rehst] *m* (*pl* ~e) rest; remainder

Restaurant [rehs-toa-RAHNG] *nt* (*pl* ~s) restaurant

retten [REH-tern] *v* rescue; save

Retter [REH-terr] *m* (*pl* ~; *f* ~in) saviour

Rettich [REH-tikh] *m* (*pl* ~e) radish

Rettung [REH-toong] *f* (*pl* ~en) rescue

Revolution [ray-voa-loo-TSYOAN] *f* (*pl* ~en) revolution

Revolver [ray-VOL-verr] *m* (*pl* ~) gun

Rezept [ray-TSEHPT] *nt* (*pl* ~e) recipe; prescription

Rezeption [ray-tsehp-TSYOAN] *f* reception office

Rhabarber [rah-BAHR-berr] *m* rhubarb

Rheumatismus [roy-mah-TIS-moos] *m* rheumatism

Rhythmus [REWT-moos] *m* (*pl* **Rhythmen**) rhythm

richten [RIKH-tern] *v* fix

Richter [RIKH-terr] *m* (*pl* ~) judge

richtig [RIKH-tikh] *adj* right; correct

Richtung [RIKH-toong] *f* (*pl* ~en) direction

* **riechen** [REE-khern] *v* smell

Riemen [REE-mern] *m* (*pl* ~) strap

riesig [REE-zikh] *adj* huge

Riff [rif] *nt* (*pl* ~e) reef

Rille [RI-ler] *f* (*pl* ~n) groove

Rindfleisch [RINT-flighsh] *nt* beef

Ring [ring] *m* (*pl* ~e) ring

Rippe [RI-per] *f* (*pl* ~n) rib

Riß [ris] *m* (*pl* ~e) crack; tear

Risiko [REE-zi-koa] *nt* (*pl* **Risiken**) risk

riskant [ris-KAHNT] *adj* risky

Rizinusöl [REE-tsi-noos-url] *nt* castor-oil

Rock [rok] *m* (*pl* ~e) skirt

Rock-and-Roll [ROK-ehnt-ROL] *m* rock-and-roll

Rockaufschlag [ROK-owf-shlark] *m* (*pl* ~e) lapel

Rogen [ROA-gern] *m* roe

roh [roa] *adj* raw

Rohmaterial [ROA-mah-tayr-yarl] (*pl* ~ien) raw material

Rohr [roar] *nt* (*pl* ~e) pipe; tube

Rolle [RO-ler] *f* (*pl* ~n) roll

rollen [RO-lern] *v* roll

Rollschuhfahren [ROL-shoo-FAR-rern] *nt* roller-skating

Rolltreppe [ROAL-treh-per] *f* (*pl* ~n) escalator

Roman [roa-MARN] *m* (*pl* ~e) novel

Romanschriftsteller [roa-MARN-shrift-shteh-lerr] *m* (*pl* ~ ; *f* ~in) novelist

romantisch [roa-MAHN-tish] *adj* romantic

Romanze [roa-MAHN-tser] *f* (*pl* ~n) romance

Röntgenbild [RURNT-gern-bilt] *nt* (*pl* ~er) X-ray

rosa [ROA-zah] *adj* pink

rosarot [ROA-zah-roat] *adj* rose

Rose [ROA-zer] *f* (*pl* ~n) rose

Rosenkohl [ROA-zern-koal] *m* Brussels-sprouts; sprouts *pl*

Rosenkranz [ROA-zern-krahnts] *m* (*pl* ~e) rosary

Rosine [roa-ZEE-ner] *f* (*pl* ~n) raisin

Rost [rost] *m* rust

rostig [ROS-tikh] *adj* rusty

rot [roat] *adj* red

Rote Kreuz [roa-ter-KROYTS] *nt* Red Cross

Rotwild [ROAT-vilt] *nt* deer *inv*

Rouge [roozh] *nt* rouge

Roulett [roo-LEHT] *nt* roulette

Route [ROO-ter] *f* (*pl* ~n) route

Routine [roo-TEE-ner] *f* routine

Rubin [roo-BEEN] *m* (*pl* ~e) ruby

Rücken [REW-kern] *m* (*pl* ~) back

Rückenschmerzen [REW-kern-shmehr-tsern] *mpl* backache

Rückfahrkarte [REWK-farr-kahr-ter] *f* (*pl* ~n) return ticket

Rückfahrt [REWK-farrt] *f* (*pl* ~en) return journey

Rückflug [REWK-flook] *m* (*pl* ~e) return flight

Rückgrat [REWK-rart] *nt* (*pl* ~e) spine

Rückkehr [REWK-kayr] *f* return

Rücklicht [REWK-likht] *nt* (*pl* ~er) tail-light

Rucksack [ROOK-zahk] *m* (*pl* ~e) rucksack; knapsack

Rückschlag [REWK-shlark] *m* (*pl* ~e) reverse

rücksichtsvoll [REWK-zikhts-fol] *adj* considerate

Rücktritt [REWK-trit] *m* (*pl* ~e) resignation

rückvergüten [REWK-fehr-gew-tern] *v* refund

Rückvergütung [REWK-fehr-gew-toong] *f* (*pl* ~en) refund

* **rückwärts fahren** [REWK-vehrts-FAR-rern] *v* reverse

Rückwärtsgang [REWK-vehrts-gahng] *m* reverse

Rückzahlung [REWK-tsar-loong] *f* (*pl* ~en) repayment

Ruder [ROO-derr] *nt* (*pl* ~) oar

Ruderboot [ROO-derr-boat] *nt* (*pl* ~e) rowing-boat

rudern [ROO-derrn] *v* row

Ruf [roof] *m* (*pl* ~e) call

* **rufen** [ROO-fern] *v* call; shout

ruhen [ROO-ern] *v* rest

ruhig [ROO-ikh] *adj* restful; tranquil

Ruhm [room] *m* fame

Ruhr [roor] *f* dysentery

rühren [REW-rern] *v* stir

rührig [REW-rikh] *adj* active

Ruinen [roo-EE-nern] *fpl* ruins *pl*

ruinieren [roo-i-NEE-rern] *v* ruin

rund [roont] *adj* round

rundherum [roont-heh-ROOM] *adv* around

Rundreise [ROONT-righ-zer] *f* (*pl* ~n) tour

Saal [zarl] *m* (*pl* ̃e) hall

Saccharin [zah-khah-REEN] *nt* saccharin

sächlich [ZEHKH-likh] *adj* neuter

Sack [zahk] *m* (*pl* ̃e) sack; bag

Sackgasse [ZAHK-gah-ser] *f* (*pl* ~n) cul-de-sac

säen [ZAI-ern] *v* sow

Safe [sayf] *m* (*pl* ~s) safe

Saft [zahft] *m* (*pl* ̃e) juice

saftig [ZAHF-tikh] *adj* juicy

Säge [ZAI-ger] *f* (*pl* ~n) saw

sagen [ZAR-gern] *v* say; tell

Sahne [ZAR-ner] *f* cream

sahnig [ZAR-nikh] *adj* creamy

Salami [zah-LAR-mi] *f* salami

Salat [zah-LART] *m* lettuce

Salatöl [zah-LART-url] *nt* (*pl* ~e) salad oil

Salbe [ZAHL-ber] *f* (*pl* ~n) salve; ointment

Salon [zah-LAWNG] *m* (*pl* ~s) salon

Salz [zahlts] *nt* salt

Salzfäßchen [ZAHLTS-fehs-khern] *nt* (*pl* ~) saltcellar

salzig [ZAHL-tsikh] *adj* salty

Samen [ZAR-mern] *m* (*pl* ~) seed

sammeln [ZAH-merln] *v* collect

Sammelplatz [ZAH-merl-plahts] *m* (*pl* ̃e) meeting-place

Sammler [ZAHM-lerr] *m* (*pl* ~ ; *f* ~in) collector

Sammlung [ZAHM-loong] *f* (*pl* ~en) collection

Samt [zahmt] *m* velvet

Sand [zahnt] *m* sand

Sandale [zahn-DAR-ler] *f* (*pl* ~n) sandal

sandig [ZAHN-dikh] *adj* sandy

Sandwich [SEHND-vich] *nt* (*pl* ~es) sandwich

sanft [zahnft] *adj* gentle

Sänger [ZEHNG-err] *m* (*pl* ~ ; *f* ~in) singer; vocalist

sanitär [zah-ni-TAIR] *adj* sanitary

Saphir [zah-FEER] *m* sapphire

Sardelle [zahr-DEH-ler] *f* (*pl* ~n) anchovy

Sardine [zahr-DEE-ner] *f* (*pl* ~n) sardine; pilchard

Sattel [ZAH-terl] *m* (*pl* ̃) saddle

Satz [zahts] *m* (*pl* ̃e) sentence

sauber [ZOW-berr] *adj* clean

sauer [ZOW-err] *adj* sour

Sauerstoff [ZOW-err-shtof] *m* oxygen

Säugetier [ZOY-ger-teer] *nt* (*pl* ~e) mammal

Säugling [ZOYK-ling] *m* (*pl* ~e) infant; baby

Säule [ZOY-ler] *f* (*pl* ~n) column; pillar

Saum [zowm] *m* (*pl* ̃e) hem

Sauna [ZOW-nah] *f* sauna

schaben [SHAR-bern] *v* scrape

Schach [shahkh] *nt* chess

Schachtel [SHAHKH-terl] *f* (*pl* ~n) box

schade [SHAR-der] *pity*

Schädel [SHAI-derl] *m* (*pl* ~) skull

schaden [SHAR-dern] *v* harm

Schaden [SHAR-dern] *m* (*pl* ̃) harm; damage

schädlich [SHAIT-likh] *adj* harmful; hurtful

Schaf [sharf] *nt* (*pl* ~e) sheep *inv*

*** schaffen** [SHAH-fern] *v* create

Schaffner [SHAHF-nerr] *m* (*pl* ~ ; *f* ~in) conductor; ticket collector

Schal [sharl] *m* (*pl* ~s) shawl; scarf

Schale [SHAR-ler] *f* (*pl* ~n) peel;

bowl

schälen [SHAI-lern] *v* peel

Schalentier [SHAR-lern-teer] *nt* (*pl* ∼e) shell-fish

Schall [shahl] *m* sound

schalldicht [SHAHL-dikht] *adj* soundproof

Schallplatte [SHAHL-plah-ter] *f* (*pl* ∼n) disc; record

Schallplattenladen [SHAHL-plah-tern-lar-dern] *m* (*pl* ∼̈) record shop

Schalotte [shah-LO-ter] *f* (*pl* ∼n) scallion

Schaltbrett [SHAHLT-breht] *nt* (*pl* ∼er) switchboard

Schalter [SHAHL-terr] *m* (*pl* ∼) switch

Schaltjahr [SHAHLT-yarr] *nt* (*pl* ∼e) leap-year

Schande [SHAHN-der] *f* shame

Schankkellner [SHAHNK-kehl-nerr] *m* (*pl* ∼) bartender; barman

scharf [shahrf] *adj* sharp; keen

schärfen [SHEHR-fern] *v* sharpen

scharlachrot [SHAHR-lahkh-roat] *adj* scarlet

Scharnier [shahr-NEER] *nt* (*pl* ∼e) hinge

Schatten [SHAH-tern] *m* (*pl* ∼) shade; shadow

schattig [SHAH-tikh] *adj* shady

Schatz [shahts] *m* (*pl* ∼̈e) treasure

Schatzamt [SHAHTS-ahmt] *nt* (*pl* ∼̈er) treasury

schätzen [SHEH-tsern] *v* estimate; value; appreciate

Schätzung [SHEH-tsoong] *f* appreciation

schauen [SHOW-ern] *v* look

Schauer [SHOW-err] *m* (*pl* ∼) shower

Schaufenster [SHOW-fehns-terr] *nt* (*pl* ∼) shop-window

schaukeln [SHOW-kerln] *v* swing; rock

Schauspiel [SHOW-shpeel] *nt* (*pl* ∼e) play; spectacle

Schauspieler [SHOW-shpee-lerr] *m* (*pl* ∼) actor

Schauspielerin [SHOW-shpee-ler-rin] *f* (*pl* ∼nen) actress

Scheck [shehk] *m* (*pl* ∼s) cheque; check

Scheckbuch [SHEHK-bookh] *nt* (*pl* ∼̈er) cheque-book; check-book

Scheidung [SHIGH-doong] *f* (*pl* ∼en) divorce

∗ **scheinen** [SHIGH-nern] *v* appear; seem

Scheinwerfer [SHIGHN-vehr-ferr] *m* (*pl* ∼) headlamp; headlight

Scheitel [SHIGH-terl] *m* (*pl* ∼) parting

Schellfisch [SHEHL-fish] *m* (*pl* ∼e) haddock

schelmisch [SHEHL-mish] *adj* mischievous

Schema [SHAY-mah] *nt* (*pl* ∼ta) diagram; scheme

Schenke [SHEHN-ker] *f* (*pl* ∼n) tavern

Schenkung [SHEHNG-koong] *f* (*pl* ∼en) donation

Schere [SHAY-rer] *f* (*pl* ∼n) scissors *pl*

scheuern [SHOY-errn] *v* scrub

Scheune [SHOY-ner] *f* (*pl* ∼n) barn

Schicksal [SHIK-zarl] *nt* (*pl* ∼e) fate

Schiedsrichter [SHEETS-rikh-terr] *m* (*pl* ∼) umpire

Schiene [SHEE-ner] *f* (*pl* ∼n) splint

* **schießen** [SHEE-sern] *v* shoot

Schiff [shif] *nt* (*pl* ~e) ship; vessel

Schiffahrt [SHIF-farrt] *f* (*pl* ~en) sailing

Schiffahrtslinie [SHIF-farrts-leen-yer] *f* (*pl* ~n) shipping line

Schilfrohr [SHILF-roar] *nt* (*pl* ~e) reed

schimpfen [SHIM-pfern] *v* scold

Schinken [SHING-kern] *m* ham

Schlacht [shlahkht] *f* (*pl* ~en) battle

Schlaf [shlarf] *m* sleep

* **schlafen** [SHLAR-fern] *v* sleep

schlaff [shlahf] *adj* limp

Schlaflosigkeit [SHLARF-loa-zikh-kight] *f* insomnia

Schlafmittel [SHLARF-mi-terl] *nt* (*pl* ~) sleeping-pill

schläfrig [SHLAIF-rikh] *adj* sleepy

Schlafsaal [SHLARF-zarl] *m* (*pl* ~e) dormitory

Schlafsack [SHLARF-zahk] *m* (*pl* ~e) sleeping-bag

Schlafwagen [SHLARF-var-gern] *m* (*pl* ~) sleeping-car

Schlafwagenbett [SHLARF-var-gern-beht] *nt* (*pl* ~en) sleeping-berth

Schlafzimmer [SHLARF-tsi-merr] *nt* (*pl* ~) bedroom

Schlag [shlark] *m* (*pl* ~e) blow

Schlaganfall [SHLARK-ahn-fahl] *m* (*pl* ~e) stroke

* **schlagen** [SHLAR-gern] *v* strike; beat; hit; whip

Schlager [SHLAR-gerr] *m* (*pl* ~) hit

Schlagzeile [SHLARK-tsigh-ler] *f* (*pl* ~n) headline

Schlamm [shlahm] *m* mud

schlammig [SHLAH-mikh] *adj* muddy

Schlange [SHLAHNG-er] *f* queue

* **Schlange stehen** [SHLAHNG-er-SHTAY-ern] *v* queue

schlank [shlahngk] *adj* slim; slender

Schlauch [shlowkh] *m* (*pl* ~e) inner tube

schlecht [shlehkht] *adj* evil; bad

schlechter [SHLEHKH-terr] *adj* worse; *adv* worse

schlechtest [SHLEHKH-terst] *adj* worst; *adv* worst

Schleier [SHLIGH-err] *m* (*pl* ~) veil

schleppen [SHLEH-pern] *v* tow; tug

Schlepper [SHLEH-perr] *m* (*pl* ~) tug

schleudern [SHLOY-derrn] *v* skid

schlicht [SHLIKHT] *adj* plain

* **schließen** [SHLEE-sern] *v* close; shut

schließlich [SHLEES-likh] *adv* eventually

Schlitten [SHLI-tern] *m* (*pl* ~) sledge

Schlittschuh [SHLIT-shoo] *m* (*pl* ~e) skate

Schlittschuh laufen [SHLIT-shoo-LOW-fern] skate

Schlittschuhbahn [SHLIT-shoo-barn] *f* (*pl* ~en) skating-rink

Schlittschuhlaufen [SHLIT-shoo-low-fern] *nt* skating

Schlitz [shlits] *m* (*pl* ~e) slot

Schloß [shlos] *nt* (*pl* ~er) lock

Schluckauf [SHLOOK-owf] *m* hiccup

Schlückchen [SHLEWK-khern] *nt* (*pl* ~) tot

schlucken [SHLOO-kern] *v* swallow

Schlüpfer [SHLEW-pferr] *m* (*pl* ~)

panties *pl*

schlüpfrig [SHLEWPF-rikh] *adj* slippery

Schluß [shloos] *m* (*pl* ~e) end; finish; conclusion

Schlußlicht [SHLOOS-likht] *nt* (*pl* ~er) rear-light

Schlüssel [SHLEW-serl] *m* (*pl* ~) key

Schlüsselbein [SHLEW-serl-bighn] *nt* (*pl* ~e) collar-bone

Schlüsselloch [SHLEW-serl-lokh] *nt* (*pl* ~er) keyhole

Schlußverkauf [SHLOOS-fehr-kowf] *m* (*pl* ~e) sales *pl*

schmackhaft [SHMAHK-hahft] *adj* savoury; tasty

Schmalz [shmahlts] *nt* lard

* **schmelzen** [SHMEHL-tsern] *v* melt

Schmerz [shmehrts] *m* (*pl* ~en) ache

schmerzen [SHMEHR-tsern] *v* ache

schmerzhaft [SHMEHRTS-hahft] *adj* painful

schmerzlos [SHMEHRTS-loas] *adj* painless

Schmetterling [SHMEH-terr-ling] *m* (*pl* ~e) butterfly

Schmied [shmeet] *m* (*pl* ~e) blacksmith; smith

schmieren [SHMEE-rern] *v* grease; lubricate

Schmierfett [SHMEER-feht] *nt* (*pl* ~e) grease

Schmieröl [SHMEER-url] *nt* (*pl* ~e) lubrication oil

Schmiersystem [SHMEER-zews-taym] *nt* (*pl* ~e) lubrication system

Schmierung [SHMEE-roong] *f* lubrication

Schminke [SHMING-ker] *f* (*pl* ~n)

make-up

Schmuck [shmook] *m* jewellery

schmuggeln [SHMOO-gerln] *v* smuggle

Schmutz [shmoots] *m* dirt

schmutzig [SHMOO-tsikh] *adj* dirty; filthy

Schnalle [SHNAH-ler] *f* (*pl* ~n) buckle

Schnappschuß [SHNAHP-shoos] *m* (*pl* ~e) snapshot

Schnecke [SHNEH-ker] *f* (*pl* ~n) snail

Schnee [shnay] *m* snow

schneebedeckt [SHNAY-ber-dehkt] *adj* snowy

Schneesturm [SHNAY-shtoorm] *m* (*pl* ~e) snowstorm; blizzard

* **schneiden** [SHNIGH-dern] *v* cut

Schneider [SHNIGH-derr] (*pl* ~; *f* ~in) tailor

Schneiderin [SHNIGH-der-rin] *f* (*pl* ~nen) dressmaker

schneien [SHNIGH-ern] *v* snow

schnell [shnehl] *adj* fast; quick; rapid; *adv* quick

Schnellzug [SHNEHL-tsook] *m* (*pl* ~e) express train

Schnitt [shnit] *m* (*pl* ~e) cut

Schnitte [SHNI-ter] *f* (*pl* ~n) slice; rasher

Schnittlauch [SHNIT-lowkh] *m* chives *pl*

schnitzen [SHNI-tsern] *v* carve

Schnitzerei [shni-tser-RIGH] *f* (*pl* ~en) carving

Schnorchel [SHNOR-kherl] *m* (*pl* ~) snorkel

Schnur [shnoor] *f* (*pl* ~e) string; twine

Schnürbänder [SHNEWR-behn-derr] *ntpl* laces *pl*

Schnurrbart [SHNOOR-barrt] *m* (*pl* ~e) moustache

Schnürsenkel [SHNEWR-zehng-kerl] *mpl* shoe-lace

Schock [shoak] *m* shock

schokieren [sho-KEE-rern] *v* shock

Schokolade [shoa-koa-LAR-der] *f* chocolate

Scholle [SHO-ler] *f(pl* ~n) plaice

schön [shurn] *adj* beautiful; lovely

schon [shoan] *adv* already

Schönheitsmittel [SHURN-hights-mi-terl] *nt(pl* ~) cosmetics *pl*

Schönheitssalon [SHURN-hights-zah-lawng] *m(pl* ~s) beauty salon; beauty parlour

Schornstein [SHORN-shtighn] *m(pl* ~e) chimney

Schotte [SHO-ter] *m(pl* ~n; *f* ~in) Scot

schottisch [SHO-tish] *adj* Scottish; Scotch

Schottland [SHOT-lahnt] *nt* Scotland

schräg [shraik] *adj* sloping; slanting

Schramme [SHRAH-mer] *f(pl* ~n) scratch

Schrank [shrahngk] *m(pl* ~̈e) cupboard

Schranke [SHRAHNG-ker] *f(pl* ~n) barrier

Schraube [SHROW-ber] *f(pl* ~n) screw

schrauben [SHROW-bern] *v* screw

Schraubenmutter [SHROW-bern-moo-terr] *f(pl* ~n) nut

Schraubenschlüssel [SHROW-bern-shlew-serl] *m(pl* ~) wrench

Schraubenzieher [SHROW-bern-tsee-err] *m(pl* ~) screwdriver

Schreck [shrehk] *m* fright

schrecklich [SHREHK-likh] *adj* frightful; terrible; awful

Schrei [shrigh] *m(pl* ~e) scream; cry; shout

Schreibblock [SHRIGHP-blok] *m(pl* ~s) writing pad

* **schreiben** [SHRIGH-bern] *v* write

Schreiber [SHRIGH-berr] *m(pl* ~; *f* ~in) writer

Schreibmaschine [SHRIGHP-mah-shee-ner] *f(pl* ~n) typewriter

Schreibmaschinenpapier [SHRIGHP-mah-shee-nern-pah-peer] *nt* typing paper

Schreibpapier [SHRIGHP-pah-peer] *nt(pl* ~e) writing paper

Schreibtisch [SHRIGHP-tish] *m(pl* ~e) desk

Schreibwarenhandlung [SHRIGHP-var-rern-hahn-dloong] *f(pl* ~en) stationer; stationery

* **schreien** [SHRIGH-ern] *v* cry; scream

Schrein [shrighn] *m(pl* ~e) shrine

Schrift [shrift] *f(pl* ~en) writing

schriftlich [SHRIFT-likh] *adv* in writing

schroff [shrof] *adj* harsh

schrumpfen [SHROOM-pfern] *v* shrink

Schublade [SHOOP-lar-der] *f(pl* ~n) drawer

schüchtern [SHEWKH-terrn] *adj* shy; timid

Schuh [shoo] *m(pl* ~e) shoe

Schuhgeschäft [SHOO-ger-shehft] *nt(pl* ~e) shoe-shop

Schuhkrem [SHOO-kraym] *f* shoe polish; polish

Schuhmacher [SHOO-mah-kherr] *m(pl* ~) shoemaker

Schuhputzen [SHOO-poo-tsern] *nt* shoe-shine

Schuhwerk [SHOO-vehrk] *nt* footwear

Schuld [shoolt] *f (pl ~en)* debt; blame

schulden [SHOOL-dern] *v* owe

schuldig [SHOOL-dikh] *adj* guilty

Schuldirektor [SHOOL-di-rehk-tor] *m (pl ~en)* schoolmaster; headmaster

Schule [SHOO-ler] *f (pl ~n)* school

Schüler [SHEW-lerr] *m (pl ~)* schoolboy; pupil

Schülerin [SHEW-ler-rin] *f (pl ~nen)* schoolgirl

Schulter [SHOOL-terr] *f (pl ~n)* shoulder

Schuppen [SHOO-pern] *m (pl ~)* shed; *fpl* dandruff

Schürze [SHEWR-tser] *f (pl ~n)* apron

Schuß [shoos] *m (pl ~e)* shot

schütteln [SHEW-terln] *v* shake

Schutz [shoots] *m* shelter; protection

Schutzbrille [SHOOTS-bri-ler] *f (pl ~n)* goggles *pl*

schützen [SHEW-tsern] *v* shelter; protect

Schutzschirm [SHOOTS-shirm] *m (pl ~e)* screen

schwach [shvahkh] *adj* feeble; faint; weak

Schwäche [SHVEH-kher] *f (pl ~n)* weakness

Schwager [SHVAR-gerr] *m (pl ~)* brother-in-law

Schwägerin [SHVAI-ger-rin] *f (pl ~nen)* sister-in-law

Schwamm [shvahm] *m (pl ~e)* sponge

schwanger [SHVAHNG-err] *adj* pregnant

Schwanz [shvahnts] *m (pl ~e)* tail

schwarz [shvahrts] *adj* black

Schwarzmarkt [SHVAHRTS-mahrkt] *m (pl ~e)* black market

Schwede [SHVAY-der] *m (pl ~n; f ~in)* Swede

Schweden [SHVAY-dern] *nt* Sweden

schwedisch [SHVAY-dish] *adj* Swedish

Schwein [shvighn] *nt (pl ~e)* pig

Schweinefleisch [SHVIGH-ner-flighsh] *nt* pork

Schweinsleder [SHVIGHNS-lay-derr] *nt* pigskin

Schweiß [shvighs] *m* perspiration; sweat

Schweiz [shvights] *f* Switzerland

Schweizer [SHVIGH-tserr] *m (pl ~; f ~in)* Swiss

schweizerisch [SHVIGH-tser-rish] *adj* Swiss

* **schwellen** [SHVEH-lern] *v* swell

schwer [shvayr] *adj* heavy

schwerfällig [SHVAYR-feh-likh] *adj* slow

Schwert [shvayrt] *nt (pl ~er)* sword

Schwester [SHVEHS-terr] *f (pl ~n)* sister

Schwiegereltern [SHVEE-gerr-ehl-terrn] *pl* parents-in-law *pl*

Schwiegermutter [SHVEE-gerr-moo-terr] *f (pl ~)* mother-in-law

Schwiegersohn [SHVEE-gerr-zoan] *m (pl ~e)* son-in-law

Schwiegervater [SHVEE-gerr-far-terr] *m (pl ~)* father-in-law

schwierig [SHVEE-rikh] *adj* difficult

Schwierigkeit [SHVEE-rikh-kight] *f (pl ~en)* difficulty; inconvenience

Schwimmbad [SHVIM-bart] *nt* (*pl* ̈er) swimming pool

* **schwimmen** [SHVI-mern] *v* swim

Schwimmer [SHVI-merr] *m* (*pl* ~; *f* ~in) swimmer

Schwimmsport [SHVIM-shport] *m* swimming

Schwindelanfall [SHVIN-derl-ahn-fahl] *m* (*pl* ̈e) vertigo

Schwindelgefühl [SHVIN-derl-ger-fewl] *nt* giddiness

schwindlig [SHVIN-dlikh] *adj* giddy; dizzy

Schwitzbad [SHVITS-bart] *nt* (*pl* ̈er) Turkish bath

schwitzen [SHVI-tsern] *v* sweat ; perspire

sechs [zehks] *adj* six

sechste [ZEHKS-ter] *adj* sixth

sechzehn [ZEHKH-tsayn] *adj* sixteen

sechzehnte [ZEHKH-tsayn-ter] *adj* sixteenth

sechzig [ZEHKH-tsikh] *adj* sixty

See [zay] *m* (*pl* ~n) lake

Seebad [ZAY-bart] *nt* (*pl* ̈er) seaside resort

Seehafen [ZAY-har-fern] *m* (*pl* ̈) seaport

Seeigel [ZAY-ee-gerl] *m* (*pl* ~) sea-urchin

Seekiste [ZAY-kis-ter] *f* (*pl* ~n) packing case

Seekrankheit [ZAY-krahngk-hight] *f* seasickness

Seele [ZAY-ler] *f* (*pl* ~n) soul

Seereise [ZAY-righ-zer] *f* (*pl* ~n) cruise

Seeufer [ZAY-oo-ferr] *nt* (*pl* ~) lakeside

Seevogel [ZAY-foa-gerl] *m* (*pl* ̈) sea-bird

Seezunge [ZAY-tsoong-er] *f* (*pl* ~n) sole

Segel [ZAY-gerl] *nt* (*pl* ~) sail

Segelboot [ZAY-gerl-boat] *nt* (*pl* ~e) sailing boat

Segelflugzeug [ZAY-gerl-flook-tsoyk] *nt* (*pl* ~e) glider

Segelklub [ZAY-gerl-kloop] *m* (*pl* ~s) yacht club

Segelsport [ZAY-gerl-shport] *m* yachting

Segen [ZAY-gern] *m* (*pl* ~) blessing

segnen [ZAY-gnern] *v* bless

* **sehen** [ZAY-ern] *v* see

Sehenswürdigkeiten [ZAY-erns-vewr-dikh-kigh-tern] *fpl* sights *pl*

sehnen nach (sich) [zikh-ZAY-nern-narkh] *v* long for

sehr [zayr] *adv* very

seicht [zighkht] *adj* shallow

Seide [ZIGH-der] *f* (*pl* ~n) silk

seiden [ZIGH-dern] *adj* silken

Seidenpapier [ZIGH-dern-pah-peer] *nt* tissue paper

Seidensatin [ZIGH-dern-zah-tang] *m* satin

Seife [ZIGH-fer] *f* (*pl* ~n) soap

Seifenpulver [ZIGH-fern-pool-verr] *nt* soap powder

Seil [zighl] *nt* (*pl* ~e) rope

* **sein** [zighn] *v* be; *adj* his

seit [zight] *prep* since

seitdem [zight-DAYM] *conj* since

Seite [ZIGH-ter] *f* (*pl* ~n) side; page

Seitenlicht [ZIGH-tern-likht] *nt* (*pl* ~er) sidelight

seither [zight-HAYR] *adv* since

seitwärts [ZIGHT-vehrts] *adv* sideways

Sekretärin [zay-kray-TAI-rin] *f* (*pl* ~nen) secretary

Sekunde [zay-KOON-der] *f* (*pl*

~n) second

selbe [ZEHL-ber] *adj* same

selbst [zehlpst] *pron* oneself

selbständig [ZEHLP-shtehn-dikh] *adj* self-employed

Selbstbedienung [ZEHLPST-ber-dee-noong] *f* self-service

Selbstbedienungsrestaurant [ZEHLPST-ber-dee-noongs-rehs-toa-rahng] *nt (pl ~s)* self-service restaurant; cafeteria

selbstgemacht [ZEHLPST-ger-mahkht] *adj* home-made

Selbstklebeband [ZEHLPST-klay-ber-bahnt] *nt (pl ~er)* scotch tape

Selbstlaut [ZEHLPST-lowt] *m (pl ~e)* vowel

selbstlos [ZEHLPST-loas] *adj* unselfish

Selbstmord [ZEHLPST-mort] *m (pl ~e)* suicide

selbstsüchtig [ZEHLPST-zewkh-tikh] *adj* selfish

selbstverständlich [zehlpst-fehr-SHTEHNT-likh] *adv* of course

Selbstverwaltung [ZEHLPST-fehr-vahl-toong] *f (pl ~en)* self-government

Sellerie [ZEH-ler-ree] *m* celery

selten [ZEHL-tern] *adv* seldom; *adj* rare; infrequent

Selterswasser [ZEHL-terrs-vah-serr] *nt* seltzer

seltsam [ZEHLT-zarm] *adj* quaint; curious

Senat [zay-NART] *m* senate

Senator [zay-NAR-tor] *m (pl ~en)* senator

* **senden** [ZEHN-dern] *v* send; transmit

Sendung [ZEHN-doong] *f (pl ~en)* transmission; broadcast; consignment

Senf [zehnf] *m* mustard

senkrecht [ZEHNGK-rehkht] *adj* vertical; perpendicular

Sensation [zehn-zah-TSYOAN] *f (pl ~en)* sensation

sensationell [zehn-zah-tsyoa-NEHL] *adj* sensational

sentimental [zehn-ti-mehn-TARL] *adj* sentimental

September [zehp-TEHM-berr] *m* September

septisch [ZEHP-tish] *adj* septic

Serie [ZAYR-yer] *f (pl ~n)* series

Serum [ZAY-room] *nt (pl Seren)* serum

Serviette [zehr-VYEH-ter] *f (pl ~n)* serviette; napkin

setzen (sich) [zikh-ZEH-tsern] *v* sit down

Shampoo [SHAHM-poo] *nt* shampoo

sich [zikh] *pron* themselves; himself; herself

sicher [ZI-kherr] *adj* sure; secure; safe

Sicherheit [ZI-kherr-hight] *f (pl ~en)* safety

Sicherheitsgurt [ZI-kherr-hights-goort] *m (pl ~e)* safety belt; seat belt

Sicherheitsnadel [ZI-kherr-hights-nar-derl] *f (pl ~n)* safety pin

sicherlich [ZI-kherr-likh] *adv* surely

Sicherstellung [ZI-kherr-shteh-loong] *f (pl ~en)* indemnity

Sicherung [ZI-kher-roong] *f (pl ~en)* fuse

sichtbar [ZIKHT-barr] *adj* visible

Sichtweite [ZIKHT-vigh-ter] *f (pl ~n)* visibility

sie [zee] *pron* her; them; she; they

Sie [zee] *pron* you

sie selbst [zee-ZEHLPST] *pron* herself; themselves

Sie selbst [zee-ZEHLPST] *pron* yourself; yourselves

sieben [ZEE-bern] *adj* seven

siebente [ZEE-bern-ter] *adj* seventh

siebzehn [ZEEP-tsayn] *adj* seventeen

siebzehnte [ZEEP-tsayn-ter] *adj* seventeenth

siebzig [ZEEP-tsikh] *adj* seventy

siedendes Wasser [ZEE-dern-ders-VAH-serr] *nt* boiling water

Sieg [zeek] *m* (*pl* ~e) victory

Siegel [ZEE-gerl] *nt* (*pl* ~) seal

Sieger [ZEE-gerr] *m* (*pl* ~; *f* ~in) winner

Signal [zig-NARL] *nt* (*pl* ~e) signal

Silbe [ZIL-ber] *f* (*pl* ~n) syllable

Silber [ZIL-berr] *nt* silverware; silver

silberig [ZIL-brikh] *adj* silvery

Silberschmied [ZIL-berr-shmeet] *m* (*pl* ~e) silversmith

* **singen** [ZING-ern] *v* sing

* **sinken** [ZING-kern] *v* sink

Sinn [zin] *m* (*pl* ~e) sense

sinnlos [ZIN-loas] *adj* meaningless

Siphon [ZI-fon] *m* siphon; syphon

Sirup [ZEE-roop] *m* syrup

Sitten [ZI-tern] *fpl* morals *pl*

Sitz [zits] *m* (*pl* ~e) seat

* **sitzen** [ZI-tsern] *v* sit

sitzend [ZI-tsernt] *adj* seated

Skelett [skay-LEHT] *nt* (*pl* ~e) skeleton

Ski [shee] *m* (*pl* ~er) ski

Ski laufen [SHEE-low-fern] ski

Skihose [SHEE-hoa-zer] *f* (*pl* ~n) ski-pants *pl*

Skilauf [SHEE-lowf] *m* skiing

Skiläufer [SHEE-loy-ferr] *m* (*pl* ~; *f* ~in) skier

Skischuhe [SHEE-shoo-er] *mpl* ski boots *pl*

Skisprung [SHEE-shproong] *m* (*pl* ~e) ski-jump

Skistöcke [SHEE-shtur-ker] *mpl* ski-poles *pl*

Skizze [SKI-tser] *f* (*pl* ~n) sketch

Skizzenbuch [SKI-tsern-bookh] *nt* (*pl* ~er) sketchbook

skizzieren [ski-TSEE-rern] *v* sketch

Sklave [SKLAR-ver] *m* (*pl* ~n; *f* ~in) slave

Skulptur [skoolp-TOOR] *f* (*pl* ~en) sculpture

Slang [slehng] *nt* slang

Smaragd [smah-RAHKT] *m* (*pl* ~e) emerald

Smog [smog] *m* smog

dinner jacket

Snackbar [SNEHK-barr] *f* (*pl* ~s) snack-bar

so [zoa] *adv* so; thus

so daß [zoa-DAHS] *conj* so that

sobald als [zoa-BAHLT-ahls] as soon as

Socke [ZO-ker] *f* (*pl* ~n) sock

Sodawasser [ZOA-dah-vah-serr] *nt* soda-water

Sodbrennen [ZOAT-breh-nern] *nt* heartburn

Sofa [ZOA-fah] *nt* (*pl* ~s) sofa

sofort [soa-FORT] *adv* straight away; immediately; instantly; at once

sogar [zoa-GARR] *adv* even

sogenannte [ZOA-ger-nahn-ter] *adj* so-called

sogleich [zoa-GLIGHKH] *adv* right away; presently

Sohle [ZOA-ler] *f* (*pl* ~n) sole

Sohn [zoan] *m* (*pl* ~̈e) son

solch [zolkh] *adv* such; *adj* such

Soldat [zol-DART] *m* (*pl* ~en) soldier

Solistenkonzert [zoa-LIS-tern-kon-tsehrt] *nt* (*pl* ~e) recital

Soll [zol] *nt* debit

* **sollen** [zo-lern] *v* shall; ought

Sommer [zo-merr] *m* summer

Sommerhaus [zo-merr-hows] *nt* (*pl* ~̈er) cottage

Sommerzeit [zo-merr-tsight] *f* summertime

Sonderausgaben [ZON-derr-ows-gar-bern] *fpl* extras *pl*

sonderbar [ZON-derr-barr] *adj* funny; odd; queer

Sonnabend [ZON-ar-bernt] *m* Saturday

Sonne [zo-ner] *f* (*pl* ~n) sun

sonnen (sich) [zikh-zo-nern] *v* sunbathe

Sonnenaufgang [zo-nern-OWF-gahng] *m* (*pl* ~̈e) sunrise

Sonnenbrand [zo-nern-brahnt] *m* sunburn

Sonnenbräune [zo-nern-broy-ner] *f* suntan

Sonnenbrille [zo-nern-bri-ler] *f* (*pl* ~n) sunglasses *pl*

Sonnenlicht [zo-nern-likht] *nt* sunlight

Sonnenöl [zo-nern-url] *nt* suntan oil

Sonnenschein [zo-nern-shighn] *m* sunshine

Sonnenschirm [zo-nern-shirm] *m* (*pl* ~e) sunshade

Sonnenstich [zo-nern-shtikh] *m* sunstroke

Sonnenuntergang [zo-nern-OON-terr-gahng] *m* (*pl* ~̈e) sunset

sonnig [zo-nikh] *adj* sunny

Sonntag [ZON-tark] *m* Sunday

sonst [zonst] *adv* else; *conj* otherwise

Sorge [ZOR-ger] *f* (*pl* ~n) concern; care; worry

sorgen für [ZOR-gern-fewr] *v* see to

sorgen (sich) [zikh-ZOR-gern] *v* care

sorgfältig [ZORK-fehl-tikh] *adj* neat

Sorte [ZOR-ter] *f* (*pl* ~n) kind; sort

sortieren [zor-TEE-rern] *v* sort

Sortiment [zor-ti-MEHNT] *nt* (*pl* ~e) assortment

sozial [zoa-TSYARL] *adj* social

sozialistisch [zoa-tsyah-LIS-tish] *adj* socialist

spalten [SHPAHL-tern] *v* split

Spanien [SHPARN-yern] *nt* Spain

Spanier [SHPARN-yerr] *m* (*pl* ~; *f* ~in) Spanish

spanisch [SHPAR-nish] *adj* Spanish

Spannung [SHPAH-noong] *f* (*pl* ~en) voltage; stress; tension

sparen [SHPAR-rern] *v* economize; save

Spargel [SHPAHR-gerl] *m* asparagus

Sparkasse [SHPARR-kah-ser] *f* (*pl* ~n) savings bank

sparsam [SHPARR-zarm] *adj* economical

Spaß [shpars] *m* fun

spät [shpait] *adj* late

Spaten [SHPAR-tern] *m* (*pl* ~) spade

später [SHPAI-terr] *adj* later

spätestens [SHPAI-ters-terns] *adv* at the latest

Spaziergang [shpah-TSEER-gahng] *m* (*pl* ~e) walk

Spaziergänger [shpah-TSEER-gehng-err] *m* (*pl* ~; *f* ~in) walker

Spazierstock [shpah-TSEER-shtok] *m* (*pl* ~e) walking-stick

Speck [shpehk] *m* bacon

Speiche [SHPIGH-kher] *f* (*pl* ~n) spoke

Speisekammer [SHPIGH-zer-kah-merr] *f* (*pl* ~n) larder

Speisekarte [SHPIGH-zer-kahr-ter] *f* (*pl* ~n) menu

Speisewagen [SHPIGH-zer-var-gern] *m* (*pl* ~) dining car

Speisezimmer [SHPIGH-zer-tsi-merr] *nt* (*pl* ~) dining room

sperren [SHPEH-rern] *v* block

Sperrsitz [SHPEHR-zits] *m* (*pl* ~e) stall

spezialisieren (sich) [zikh-shpay-tsyah-li-ZEE-rern] *v* specialise

Spezialist [shpay-TSYAH-list] *m* (*pl* ~en) specialist

Spezialität [shpay-tsyah-li-TAIT] *f* (*pl* ~en) speciality

speziell [shpay-TSYEHL] *adj* special; *adv* in particular

Spiegel [SHPEE-gerl] *m* (*pl* ~) looking-glass; mirror

Spiegelung [SHPEE-ger-loong] *f* reflection

Spiel [shpeel] *nt* (*pl* ~e) match; game

spielen [SHPEE-lern] *v* play

spielen um Geld [SHPEE-lern-oom-gehlt] *v* gamble

Spieler [SHPEE-lerr] *m* (*pl* ~; *f* ~in) player

Spielkarte [SHPEEL-kahr-ter] *f* (*pl* ~n) card

Spielkarten [SHPEEL-kahr-tern] *fpl* playing-cards *pl*

Spielmarke [SHPEEL-mahr-ker] *f* (*pl* ~n) chip

Spielplatz [SHPEEL-plahts] *m* (*pl* ~e) playground; recreation ground

Spielwarenladen [SHPEEL-var-rern-lar-dern] *m* (*pl* ~) toyshop

Spielzeug [SHPEEL-tsoyk] *nt* toy

Spinat [shpi-NART] *m* spinach

* **spinnen** [SHPI-nern] *v* spin

Spirituosenladen [shpi-ri-too-OA-zern-lar-dern] *m* (*pl* ~) off-licence

Spirituskocher [SHPEE-ri-toos-KO-kherr] *m* (*pl* ~) spirit stove

spitz [shpits] *adj* pointed

Spitze [SHPI-tser] *f* (*pl* ~n) point; peak; tip; lace

Splitter [SHPLI-terr] *m* (*pl* ~) splinter

Sport [shport] *m* sport

Sportjacke [SHPORT-yah-ker] *f* (*pl* ~n) sports jacket

Sportkleidung [SHPORT-kligh-doong] *f* sportswear

Sportler [SHPORT-lerr] *m* (*pl* ~; *f* ~in) sportsman

Sportwagen [SHPORT-var-gern] *m* (*pl* ~) sports car

Sprache [SHPRAR-kher] *f* (*pl* ~n) speech; language

Sprachführer [SHPRARKH-few-rerr] *m* (*pl* ~) phrase book

* **sprechen** [SHPREH-khern] *v* speak; talk

Sprechzimmer [SHPREHKH-tsi-merr] *nt* (*pl* ~) surgery

Sprengstoff [SHPREHNG-shtof] *m* (*pl* ~e) explosive

Sprichwort [SHPRIKH-vort] *nt* (*pl* ~e) proverb

Springbrunnen [SHPRING-broo-nern] *m* (*pl* ~) fountain

* **springen** [SHPRING-ern] *v* jump; leap

Spritze [SHPRI-tser] *f* (*pl* ~n) syringe

Sprung [shproong] *m* (*pl* ~̈e) jump

Sprungfeder [SHPROONG-fay-derr] *f* (*pl* ~n) spring

spucken [SHPOO-kern] *v* spit

spüren [SHPEW-rern] *v* sense

Staat [shtart] *m* (*pl* ~en) state

Staatsangehörige [SHTARTS-ahn-ger-hur-ri-ger] *m* (*pl* ~n) subject

Staatsangehörigkeit [SHTARTS-ahn-ger-hur-rikh-kight] *f* citizenship; nationality

Staatsbeamte [SHTARTS-ber-ahm-ter] *m* (*pl* ~n; *f* ~in) civil servant

Staatsdienst [SHTARTS-deenst] *m* civil service

Staatsmann [SHTARTS-mahn] *m* (*pl* ~̈er) statesman

stabil [shtah-BEEL] *adj* stable

Stachelbeere [SHTAH-kherl-bay-rer] *f* (*pl* ~n) gooseberry

Stadion [SHTAR-dyon] *nt* stadium

Stadium [SHTAR-dyoom] *nt* (*pl* **Stadien**) stage

Stadt [shtaht] *f* (*pl* ~̈e) town; city; borough

Städter [SHTEH-terr] *mpl* townspeople *pl*

städtisch [SHTEH-tish] *adj* urban; municipal

Stadtverwaltung [SHTAHT-fehr-vahl-toong] *f* (*pl* ~en) municipality

Stadtviertel [SHTAHT-fir-terl] *nt* (*pl* ~) quarter

Stadtzentrum [SHTAHT-tsehn-troom] *nt* town centre

Stahl [shtarl] *m* steel

Stahlkammer [SHTARL-kah-merr] *f* (*pl* ~n) vault

Stamm [shtahm] *m* (*pl* ~̈e) tribe; trunk

Standard... [SHTAHN-dahrt] *pref* standard

Standbild [SHTAHNT-bilt] *nt* (*pl* ~er) statue

Stange [SHTAHNG-er] *f* (*pl* ~n) rod; bar

Stanniol [shtahn-YOAL] *nt* tinfoil

stark [shtahrk] *adj* strong

Stärke [SHTEHR-ker] *f* starch

stärken [SHTEHR-kern] *v* starch

Stärkungsmittel [SHTEHR-koongs-mi-terl] *nt* (*pl* ~) tonic

starr [shtahr] *adj* numb

starren [SHTAH-rern] *v* stare; gaze

Start [shtahrt] *m* take-off

Startbahn [SHTAHRT-barn] *f* (*pl* ~en) runway

starten [SHTAHR-tern] *v* take off

Stationsvorsteher [shtah-TSYOANS-foar-shtay-err] *m* (*pl* ~) station master

* **stattfinden** [SHTAHT-fin-dern] *v* take place

stattlich [SHTAHT-likh] *adj* handsome

Staub [shtowp] *m* dust

staubig [SHTOW-bikh] *adj* dusty

Staubsauger [SHTOWP-zow-gerr] *m* (*pl* ~) vacuum cleaner

Steak [stayk] *nt* (*pl* ~s) steak

* **stechen** [SHTEH-khern] *v* sting

Steckdose [SHTEHK-doa-zer] *f* (*pl* ~n) socket

Steckenpferd [SHTEH-kern-pfayrt] *nt* (*pl* ~e) hobby

Stecker [SHTEH-kerr] *m* (*pl* ~) plug

Stecknadel [SHTEHK-nar-derl] *f*

(*pl* ~n) pin
* **stehen** [SHTAY-ern] *v* stand
* **stehlen** [SHTAY-lern] *v* steal
steif [shtighf] *adj* stiff
* **steigen** [SHTIGH-gern] *v* climb
Steigung [SHTIGH-goong] *f* (*pl* ~en) gradient
steil [shtighl] *adj* steep
Stein [shtighn] *m* (*pl* ~e) stone
Steinbruch [SHTIGHN-brookh] *m* (*pl* ~̈e) quarry
Steinbutt [SHTIGHN-boot] *m* (*pl* ~s) turbot
Steingarnele [SHTIGHN-gahr-nay-ler] *f* (*pl* ~n) prawn
Steingut [SHTIGHN-goot] *nt* earthenware
steinig [SHTIGH-nikh] *adj* stony
Stelle [SHTEH-ler] *f* (*pl* ~n) station
stellen [SHTEH-lern] *v* place; put; set
Stellung [SHTEH-loong] *f* (*pl* ~en) position
Stellvertreter [SHTEHL-fehr-tray-terr] *m* (*pl* ~; *f* ~in) deputy
Stenograph [shtay-noa-GRARF] *m* (*pl* ~en; *f* ~in) stenographer
Stenographie [shtay-noa-grah-FEE] *f* shorthand
Stenotypistin [shtay-noa-tew-PIS-tin] *f* (*pl* ~nen) typist
Steppdecke [SHTEHP-deh-ker] *f* (*pl* ~n) quilt
* **sterben** [SHTEHR-bern] *v* die
sterilisieren [shtay-ri-li-ZEE-rern] *v* sterilize
sterilisiert [shtay-ri-li-ZEERT] *adj* sterilized
Stern [shtehrn] *m* (*pl* ~e) star
Steuer [SHTOY-err] *f* (*pl* ~n) tax
steuerfrei [SHTOY-err-frigh] *adj* tax-free
steuern [SHTOY-errn] *v* navigate

Steuerrad [SHTOY-err-rart] *nt* (*pl* ~̈er) steering-wheel
Steuerruder [SHTOY-err-roo-derr] *nt* (*pl* ~) rudder
Steuerung [SHTOY-er-roong] *f* controls *pl*; steering
Steward [STYOO-ahrt] *m* (*pl* ~s) steward
Stewardess [STYOO-ahr-dehs] *f* (*pl* ~en) stewardess
Stich [shtikh] *m* (*pl* ~e) sting; stitch; bite; print
Stickerei [shti-ker-RIGH] *f* (*pl* ~en) embroidery
stickig [SHTI-kikh] *adj* stuffy
Stiefel [SHTEE-ferl] *m* (*pl* ~) boot
Stier [shteer] *m* (*pl* ~e) bull
Stierkampf [SHTEER-kahmpf] *m* (*pl* ~̈e) bullfight
Stierkampfarena [SHTEER-kahmpf-ah-RAY-nah] *f* (*pl* ~arenen) bull-ring
Stiftung [SHTIF-toong] *f* (*pl* ~en) foundation
Stil [shteel] *m* (*pl* ~e) style
still [shtil] *adj* still; silent; calm; quiet
* **still sein** [SHTIL-zighn] *v* keep quiet
Stille [SHTI-ler] *f* silence
Stille Ozean [SHTI-ler-OA-tsay-arn] *m* Pacific Ocean
stillstehend [SHTIL-shtay-ernt] *adj* stationary
Stimme [SHTI-mer] *f* (*pl* ~n) voice; vote
stimmen [SHTI-mern] *v* vote
Stimmung [SHTI-moong] *f* (*pl* ~en) mood; atmosphere
Stipendium [shti-PEHN-dyoom] *nt* (*pl* Stipendien) scholarship; grant
Stirn [shtirn] *f* (*pl* ~en) forehead
Stock [shtok] *m* (*pl* ~̈e) stick

Stockwerk [SHTOK-vehrk] *nt (pl ~e)* storey; floor

Stoff [shtof] *m (pl ~e)* cloth

stolz [shtoalts] *adj* proud

Stolz [shtolts] *m* pride

stopfen [SHTO-pfern] *v* darn

Stopfgarn [SHTOPF-gahrn] *nt* darning wool

Stöpsel [STURP-serl] *m (pl ~)* stopper

stören [SHTUR-rern] *v* upset; disturb

Störung [SHTUR-roong] *f (pl ~en)* disturbance

Stoß [shtoas] *m (pl ~e)* bump

Stoßdämpfer [SHTOAS-dehm-pferr] *m (pl ~)* shock absorber

* **stoßen** [SHTOA-sern] *v* bump; push

Stoßstange [SHTOAS-shtahng-er] *f (pl ~n)* bumper; fender

Strafe [SHTRAR-fer] *f (pl ~n)* punishment; penalty

strafen [SHTRAR-fern] *v* punish

straffen [SHTRAH-fern] *v* tighten

Strahl [shtrarl] *m (pl ~en)* ray

strahlen [SHTRAR-lern] *v* shine

Strahlturbine [SHTRARL-toor-bee-ner] *f (pl ~n)* turbo-jet

Strand [shtrahnt] *m (pl ~e)* beach

Straße [SHTRAR-ser] *f (pl ~n)* road; street

Straßenarbeiten [SHTRAR-sern-ahr-bigh-tern] road up

Straßenbahn [SHTRAR-sern-barn] *f (pl ~en)* streetcar

Straßenbahnwagen [SHTRAR-sern-barn-var-gern] *m (pl ~)* tram

Straßenkreuzung [SHTRAR-sern-kroy-tsoong] *f (pl ~en)* cross-roads

Straßenseite [SHTRAR-sern-zigh-ter] *f (pl ~n)* roadside

Strauch [shtrowkh] *m (pl ~er)* shrub

Strauß [shtrows] *m (pl ~e)* bunch

Strecke [SHTREH-ker] *f (pl ~n)* stretch

Streichholz [SHTRIGHKH-holts] *nt (pl ~er)* match

Streichholzschachtel [SHTRIGHKH-holts-SHAHKH-terl] *f (pl ~n)* match-box

Streife [SHTRIGH-fer] *f (pl ~n)* patrol

Streifen [SHTRIGH-fern] *m (pl ~)* stripe; strip

Streik [shtrighk] *m (pl ~s)* strike

streiken [SHTRIGH-kern] *v* strike

* **streiten** [SHTRIGH-tern] *v* quarrel

streng [shtrehng] *adj* strict

Strichpunkt [SHTRIKH-poonkt] *m (pl ~e)* semicolon

stricken [SHTRI-kern] *v* knit

Strickzeug [SHTRIK-tsoyk] *nt (pl ~e)* knitting

Stroh [shtroal] *nt* straw

Strohdach [SHTROA-dahkh] *nt (pl ~er)* thatch

Strom [shtroam] *m (pl ~e)* current

stromabwärts [shtroam-AHP-vehrts] *adv* downstream

stromaufwärts [shtroam-OWF-vehrts] *adv* upstream

Stromschnelle [SHTROAM-shneh-ler] *f (pl ~n)* rapids *pl*

Strömung [SHTRUR-moong] *f (pl ~en)* current

Struktur [shtrook-TOOR] *f (pl ~en)* texture; structure

Strumpf [shtroompf] *m (pl ~e)* stocking

Strumpfhose [SHTROOMPF-hoa-zer] *f (pl ~n)* panty-hose

Strumpfwaren [SHTROOMPF-var-rern] *fpl* hosiery

Stück [shtewk] *nt (pl ~e)* lump; piece

Stückchen [SHTEWK-khern] *nt (pl ~)* scrap; bit

Student [shtoo-DEHNT] *m (pl ~en; f ~in)* student

studieren [shtoo-DEE-rern] *v* study

Studium [SHTOO-dyoom] *nt (pl ~ien)* study

Stufe [SHTOO-fer] *f (pl ~n)* step

Stuhl [shtool] *m (pl ~e)* chair

stumm [shtoom] *adj* dumb

stumpf [shtoompf] *adj* blunt

Stunde [SHTOON-der] *f (pl ~n)* hour

stündlich [SHTEWNT-likh] *adj* hourly

Sturm [shtoorm] *m (pl ~e)* gale; storm

stürmisch [SHTEWR-mish] *adj* stormy; gusty

Sturmlaterne [SHTOORM-lah-tehr-ner] *f (pl ~n)* hurricane lamp

Sturz [shtoorts] *m (pl ~e)* fall

stürzen [SHTEWR-tsern] *v* crash

stützen [SHTEW-tsern] *v* support; hold up

stutzen [SHTOO-tsern] *v* trim

Subjekt [zoop-yehkt] *nt (pl ~e)* subject

Substanz [zoops-TAHNTS] *f (pl ~en)* substance

subtrahieren [zoop-trah-HEE-rern] *v* subtract

Suche [zoo-kher] *f* search

suchen [zoo-khern] *v* seek; search; hunt for; look for

Sucher [zoo-kherr] *m (pl ~)* view-finder

Südafrika [zewt-AHF-ri-kah] *nt* South Africa

Süden [ZEW-dern] *m* south

südlich [ZEWT-likh] *adj* southern

Südosten [zewt-OS-tern] *m* south-east

südwärts [ZEWT-vehrts] *adv* southwards

Südwesten [zewt-VEHS-tern] *m* south-west

Summe [ZOO-mer] *f (pl ~n)* sum

Sumpf [zhoompf] *m (pl ~e)* marsh

sumpfig [ZOOM-pfikh] *adj* marshy

Supermarkt [ZOO-perr-mahrkt] *m (pl ~e)* supermarket

Suppenlöffel [ZOO-pern-lur-ferl] *m (pl ~)* soupspoon

Suppenteller [ZOO-pern-teh-lerr] *m (pl ~)* soup-plate

süß [zews] *adj* sweet

süßen [ZEW-sern] *v* sweeten

Süßigkeiten [ZEW-sikh-kigh-tern] *fpl* sweets *pl*

Süßwarengeschäft [ZEWS-var-rern-ger-shehft] *nt (pl ~e)* sweetshop

Süßwasser [SEWS-vah-serr] *nt* fresh water

Sweater [SVEH-terr] *m (pl ~)* sweater

Symphonie [zewm-foa-NEE] *f (pl ~n)* symphony

Symptom [zewmp-TOAM] *nt (pl ~e)* symptom

Synagoge [zew-nah-GOA-ger] *f (pl ~n)* synagogue

Synonym [zew-noa-NEWM] *nt (pl ~e)* synonym

synthetisch [zewn-TAY-tish] *adj* synthetic

System [zews-TAYM] *nt (pl ~e)* system

systematisch [zews-tay-MAR-tish] *adj* systematic

Tabak [TAH-bahk] *m* tobacco; pipe tobacco

Tabakhändler [TAH-bahk-HEHN-dlerr] *m* (*pl* ~) tobacconist

Tabaksbeutel [TAH-bahks-boy-terl] *m* (*pl* ~) tobacco pouch

Tabelle [tah-BEH-ler] *f* (*pl* ~n) table

Tablett [tah-BLEHT] *nt* (*pl* ~s) tray

Tablette [tah-BLEH-ter] *f* (*pl* ~n) tablet

Tag [tark] *m* (*pl* ~e) day

Tagebuch [TAR-ger-bookh] *nt* (*pl* ~er) diary

Tagesanbruch [TAR-gers-ahn-brookh] *m* daybreak

Tagesausflug [TAR-gers-ows-flook] *m* (*pl* ~e) day trip

Tageslicht [TAR-gers-likht] *nt* daylight

täglich [TAIK-likh] *adj* daily

Taille [TAHL-yer] *f* (*pl* ~n) waist

Tal [tarl] *nt* (*pl* ~er) valley

Talent [tah-LEHNT] *nt* (*pl* ~e) talent

Talkpuder [TAHLK-poo-derr] *nt* talcum powder

Tampon [tahm-PAWNG] *m* (*pl* ~s) tampon

Tank [tahngk] *m* (*pl* ~e) tank

Tankschiff [TAHNGK-shif] *nt* (*pl* ~e) tanker

Tankstelle [TAHNGK-shteh-ler] *f* (*pl* ~n) filling station; gas station; petrol station; service station

Tante [TAHN-ter] *f* (*pl* ~n) aunt

Tanz [tahnts] *m* (*pl* ~e) dance

tanzen [TAHN-tsern] *v* dance

Tänzer [TEHN-tserr] *m* (*pl* ~ ; *f* ~in) dancer

tapfer [TAH-pferr] *adj* brave

Tarif [tah-REEF] *m* (*pl* ~e) tariff

Tasche [TAH-sher] *f* (*pl* ~n) pocket

Taschenkamm [TAH-shern-kahm] *m* (*pl* ~e) pocket-comb

Taschenlampe [TAH-shern-lahm-per] *f* (*pl* ~n) torch; flash-light

Taschenmesser [TAH-shern-meh-serr] *nt* (*pl* ~) pocket-knife; penknife

Taschentuch [TAH-shern-tookh] *nt* (*pl* ~er) handkerchief

Taschenuhr [TAH-shern-oor] *f* (*pl* ~en) pocket-watch

Tasse [TAH-ser] *f* (*pl* ~n) cup

Tastsinn [TAHST-zin] *m* touch

Tat [tart] *f* (*pl* ~en) deed; act

Tätigkeit [TAI-tikh-kight] *f* (*pl* ~en) activity

Tatsache [TART-zah-kher] *f* (*pl* ~n) fact

tatsächlich [tart-ZEHKH-likh] *adj* factual; actual; *adv* as a matter of fact; in fact

Tau [tow] *m* dew

taub [towp] *adj* deaf

Taube [TOW-ber] *f* (*pl* ~n) pigeon

tauchen [TOW-khern] *v* dive

Tauchsieder [TOWKH-zee-derr] *m* (*pl* ~) immersion heater

tausend [TOW-zernt] *adj* thousand

Tauwetter [TOW-veh-terr] *nt* thaw

Taxameter [tahk-sah-MAY-terr] *m* (*pl* ~) taximeter

Taxi [TAHK-si] *nt* (*pl* ~s) taxi; cab

Taxichauffeur [TAHK-si-sho-FURR] *m* (*pl* ~e) taxi-driver

Taxifahrer [TAHK-si-far-rerr] *m*

(*pl* ～) cabdriver

Taxistand [TAHK-si-shtahnt] *m* (*pl* ̃e) taxi-stand; taxi-rank

Technik [TAYKH-nik] *f* (*pl* ～en) technique

Techniker [TEHKH-ni-kerr] *m* (*pl* ～; *f* ～in) technician

technisch [TEHKH-nish] *adj* technical

Tee [tay] *m* tea

Teekanne [TAY-kah-ner] *f* (*pl* ～n) teapot

Teelöffel [TAY-lur-ferl] *m* (*pl* ～) teaspoon

Teelöffelvoll [TAY-lur-ferl-fol] *m* teaspoonful

Teenager [TEEN-ay-jerr] *m* (*pl* ～) teenager

Teeservice [TAY-zehr-vees] *nt* tea-set

Teestube [TAY-shtoo-ber] *f* (*pl* ～n) tea-shop

Teetasse [TAY-tah-ser] *f* (*pl* ～n) teacup

Teich [tighkh] *m* (*pl* ～e) pond

Teig [tighk] *m* (*pl* ～e) dough

Teil [tighl] *m* (*pl* ～e) part

teilen [TIGH-lern] *v* share; divide

Teilhaber [TIGHL-har-berr] *m* (*pl* ～; *f* ～in) associate

* **teilnehmen** [TIGHL-nay-mern] *v* participate

Teilung [TIGH-loong] *f* (*pl* ～en) division

teilweise [TIGHL-vigh-zer] *adv* partly

Teilzahlungskauf [TIGHL-tsar-loongs-kowf] *m* (*pl* ̃e) hire-purchase

Teint [tang] *m* complexion

Telefonhörer [tay-lay-FOAN-hur-rerr] *m* (*pl* ～) receiver

Telegramm [tay-lay-GRAHM] *nt* (*pl* ～e) cable; telegram

telegraphieren [tay-lay-grah-FEE-rern] *v* telegraph; cable

Teleobjektiv [TAY-lay-op-yehk-teef] *nt* (*pl* ～e) telephoto lens *pl*

Telephon [tay-lay-FOAN] *nt* (*pl* ～e) telephone; phone

Telephonanruf [tay-lay-FOAN-ahn-roof] *m* (*pl* ～e) telephone call

Telephonanruf mit Voranmeldung [tay-lay-FOAN-ahn-roof-mit-FOAR-ahn-mehl-doong] personal call

Telephonbuch [tay-lay-FOAN-bookh] *nt* (*pl* ̃er) telephone book; telephone directory

telephonieren [tay-lay-foa-NEE-rern] *v* phone

Telephonistin [tay-lay-foa-NIS-tin] *f* (*pl* ～nen) operator; telephonist; telephone operator

Telephonzentrale [tay-lay-FOAN-tsehn-trar-ler] *f* (*pl* ～n) exchange

Telex [TAY-lehks] *nt* telex

Teller [TEH-lerr] *m* (*pl* ～) dish; plate

Tempel [TEHM-perl] *m* (*pl* ～) temple

Temperatur [tehm-per-rah-TOOR] *f* (*pl* ～en) temperature

Tempo [TEHM-poa] *nt* pace

Tennis [TEH-nis] *nt* tennis

Tennisplatz [TEH-nis-plahts] *m* (*pl* ̃e) tennis court; court

Tennisschläger [TEH-nis-shlai-gerr] *m* (*pl* ～) racquet

Teppich [TEH-pikh] *m* (*pl* ～e) carpet

Terpentin [tehr-pern-TEEN] *nt* turpentine

Terrasse [teh-RAH-ser] *f* (*pl* ～n)

terrace
Terylene [TEH-ri-layn] *nt*
Terylene
Test [tehst] *m (pl ~s)* test
Testament [tehs-tah-MEHNT] *nt*
(*pl ~e*) will
teuer [TOY-err] *adj* dear;
expensive
Teufel [TOY-ferl] *m (pl ~)* devil
Text [tehkst] *m (pl ~e)* text
Textilien [tehks-TEEL-yern] *pl*
textile
Theater [tay-AR-terr] *nt* theatre
Thema [TAY-mah] *nt (pl* **Themen**)
topic
Theorie [tayoa-REE] *f (pl ~n)*
theory
Therapie [tay-rah-PEE] *f (pl ~n)*
therapy
Thermometer [tehr-moa-MAY-
terr] *nt (pl ~)* thermometer
Thermosflasche [TEHR-mos-flah-
sher] *f (pl ~n)* thermos;
vacuum flask
Thunfisch [TOON-fish] *m (pl ~e)*
tuna
Thymian [TEWM-yarn] *m* thyme
tief [teef] *adj* deep
Tiefe [TEE-fer] *f (pl ~n)* depth
Tiefland [TEEF-lahnt] *nt* lowland
Tier [teer] *nt (pl ~e)* animal
Tierarzt [TEER-ahrtst] *m (pl ~e; f*
~in) veterinary surgeon
Tinte [TIN-ter] *f (pl ~n)* ink
tippen [TI-pern] *v* type
Tisch [tish] *m (pl ~e)* table
Tischler [TISH-lerr] *m (pl ~)*
carpenter
Tischtennis [TISH-teh-nis] *nt*
table tennis
Tischtuch [TISH-tookh] *nt (pl*
~er) tablecloth
Titel [TEE-terl] *m (pl ~)* title;
degree

Toast [toast] *m (pl ~e)* toast
Tochter [TOKH-terr] *f (pl ~)*
daughter
tödlich [TURT-likh] *adj* fatal
Toffee [TO-fi] *nt (pl ~s)* toffee
Toilette [toaah-LEH-ter] *f (pl ~n)*
toilet; lavatory
Toilettenartikel [toaah-LEH-
tern-ahr-ti-kerl] *mpl* toiletry
Toilettennecessaire [toaah-LEH-
tern-nay-seh-sair] *nt* toilet-
case
Toilettenpapier [toaah-LEH-tern-
pah-peer] *nt* toilet-paper
Toilettenwasser [toaah-LEH-
tern-vah-serr] *nt* toilet water
Tomate [toa-MAR-ter] *f (pl ~n)*
tomato
Ton [toan] *m (pl ~e)* tone; clay
Tonbandgerät [TOAN-bahnt-ger-
rait] *nt (pl ~e)* recorder; tape
recorder
Tonne [TO-ner] *f (pl ~n)* ton
Topf [topf] *m (pl ~e)* pot
Töpferware [TUR-pferr-var-rer] *f*
(pl ~n) crockery
Töpferwaren [TUR-pferr-var-
rern] *fpl* pottery
Tor [toar] *nt (pl ~e)* gate; goal
töricht [TUR-rikht] *adj* foolish
Torstand [TOAR-shtahnt] *m* score
Torwart [TOAR-vahrt] *m (pl ~e)*
goalkeeper
tot [toat] *adj* dead
total [toa-TARL] *adj* total
Totalisator [toa-tah-li-zAR-tor] *m*
(pl ~en) totalizator
tote Saison [TOA-ter-seh-zAWNG] *f*
low season
töten [TUR-tern] *v* kill
Toupet [too-PAY] *nt (pl ~s)* hair
piece
Tourist [too-RIST] *m (pl ~en; f*
~in) tourist

Touristenklasse [too-RIS-tern-klah-ser] *f* tourist class

toxisch [TOK-sish] *adj* toxic

Tracht [trahkht] *f* (*pl* ~**en**) national dress

Tradition [trah-di-TSYOAN] *f* (*pl* ~**en**) tradition

traditionell [trah-di-tsyoa-NEHL] *adj* traditional

tragbar [TRARK-barr] *adj* portable

* **tragen** [TRAR-gern] *v* carry; bear; wear

Träger [TRAI-gerr] *m* (*pl* ~) porter

tragisch [TRAR-gish] *adj* tragic

Tragödie [trah-GUR-dyer] *f* (*pl* ~**n**) tragedy

Traktor [TRAHK-tor] *m* (*pl* ~**en**) tractor

trampen [TREHM-pern] *v* hitchhike

Tramper [TREHM-perr] *m* (*pl* ~; *f* ~**in**) hitchhiker

Träne [TRAI-ner] *f* (*pl* ~**n**) tear

Transaktion [trahns-ahk-TSYOAN] *f* (*pl* ~**en**) transaction

transatlantisch [trahns-aht-LAHN-tish] *adj* transatlantic

Transformator [trahns-for-MAR-tor] *m* (*pl* ~**en**) transformer

Transistor [trahn-ZIS-tor] *m* (*pl* ~**en**) transistor

Transport [trahns-PORT] *m* transportation

transportieren [trahns-por-TEE-rern] *v* transport

Tratte [TRAH-ter] *f* (*pl* ~**n**) draft

träumen [TROY-mern] *v* dream

traurig [TROW-rikh] *adj* sad

Treff [trehf] club

* **treffen** [TREH-fern] *v* meet

Treffen [TREH-fern] *nt* (*pl* ~) meeting

Treibrad [TRIGHP-rart] *nt* (*pl* ~**er**) driving-wheel

trennen [TREH-nern] *v* disconnect; separate

Treppe [TREH-per] *f* (*pl* ~**n**) staircase; stairs *pl*

* **treten** [TRAY-tern] *v* step; kick

treu [troy] *adj* faithful

Tribüne [tri-BEW-ner] *f* (*pl* ~**n**) stand

Trichter [TRIKH-terr] *m* (*pl* ~) funnel

Trichtermündung [TRIKH-terr-mewn-doong] *f* (*pl* ~**en**) estuary

Trikot [tri-KOA] *nt* (*pl* ~**s**) tights *pl*

trinkbar [TRINGK-barr] *adj* potable

Trinkbrunnen [TRINGK-broo-nern] *m* (*pl* ~) drinking fountain

* **trinken** [TRING-kern] *v* drink

Trinkgeld [TRINGK-gehlt] *nt* (*pl* ~**er**) gratuity; tip

Trinkschokolade [TRINGK-shoa-koa-lar-der] *f* chocolate

Trinkspruch [TRINGK-shprookh] *m* (*pl* ~**e**) toast

Trinkwasser [TRINGK-vah-serr] *nt* drinking water

Triumph [tri-OOMF] *m* triumph

triumphierend [tri-oom-FEE-rernt] *adj* triumphant

trocken [TRO-kern] *adj* dry

trocknen [TROK-nern] *v* dry

Trockner [TROK-nerr] *m* (*pl* ~) dryer

Tropen [TROA-pern] *pl* tropics *pl*

Tropfen [TRO-pfern] *mpl* drops *pl; m* drop

tropisch [TROA-pish] *adj* tropical

trotz [trots] *prep* in spite of; despite

trübe [TREW-ber] *adj* dim

Truhe [TROO-er] f (pl ~n) chest

Trumpf [troompf] m (pl ~̈e) trump

Truppen [TROO-pern] fpl troops pl

Truthahn [TROOT-harn] m (pl ~̈e) turkey

Tuberkulose [too-behr-koo-LOA-zer] f tuberculosis

Tuchhändler [TOOKH-hehn-dlerr] m (pl ~) draper

Tuchwaren [TOOKH-var-rern] fpl drapery

Tugend [TOO-gernt] f (pl ~en) virtue

Tülle [TEW-ler] f (pl ~n) nozzle

Tumor [TOO-mawr] m (pl ~e) tumour

* **tun** [toon] v do

Tunika [TOO-ni-kah] f (pl **Tuniken**) tunic

Tunnel [TOO-nerl] m (pl ~) tunnel

Tür [tewr] f (pl ~en) door

Turbine [toor-BEE-ner] f (pl ~n) turbine

Türke [TEWR-ker] m (pl ~n; f ~in) Turk

Türkei [tewr-KIGH] f Turkey

türkisch [TEWR-kish] adj Turkish

Türklingel [TEWR-kling-erl] f (pl ~n) door-bell

Turm [toorm] m (pl ~̈e) tower

Turmspitze [TOORM-shpi-tser] f (pl ~n) spire

Turnen [TOOR-nern] nt gymnastics pl

Turner [TOOR-nerr] m (pl ~; f ~in) gymnast

Turnhalle [TOORN-hah-ler] f (pl ~n) gymnasium

Turnhose [TOORN-hoa-zer] f (pl ~n) trunks pl

Turnschuhe [TOORN-shoo-er] mpl sneakers pl; gym shoes pl

Tüte [TEW-ter] f (pl ~n) paper-bag

Tweed [tweet] m tweed

Typ [tewp] m (pl ~en) type

typisch [TEW-pish] adj typical

U-Bahn [OO-barn] f (pl ~en) Underground

Übelkeit [EW-berl-kight] f (pl ~en) nausea

* **übelnehmen** [EW-berl-nay-mern] v resent

übelriechend [EW-berl-ree-khernt] adj smelly

über [EW-berr] adv over; prep over; above; about; via

über Bord [ew-berr-BORT] overboard

über Nacht [ew-berr-NAHKHT] overnight

über See [ew-berr-ZAY] overseas

überall [EW-berr-ahl] adv anywhere; throughout; everywhere

überanstrengen [ew-berr-AHN-shtrehng-ern] v overwork

überarbeiten [ew-berr-AHR-bigh-tern] v revise

Überarbeitung [ew-berr-AHR-bigh-toong] f (pl ~en) revision

überdies [ew-berr-DEES] adv besides; furthermore; moreover

Übereinkunft [ew-berr-IGHN-koonft] f (pl ~̈e) settlement

übereinstimmen [ew-berr-IGHN-shti-mern] v agree

* **überessen (sich)** [zikh-ew-berr-EH-sern] v overeat

überfällig [EW-berr-feh-likh] adj overdue

überführen [ew-berr-FEW-rern] v

convict

überfüllt [ew-berr-FEWLT] *adj* crowded

Übergang [EW-berr-gahng] *m (pl* ~e) crossing

Übergewicht [EW-berr-ger-vikht] *nt* overweight; excess baggage

Übergröße [EW-berr-grur-ser] *f (pl* ~n) outsize

überhaupt [ew-berr-HOWPT] *adv* at all

überhöhte Geschwindigkeit [ew-berr-HUR-ter-ger-SHVIN-dikh-kight] *f* speeding

überholen [ew-berr-HOA-lern] *v* overhaul; overtake

Überholen verboten [ew-berr-HOA-lern-fehr-BOA-tern] no overtaking

überleben [ew-berr-LAY-bern] *v* survive

Überleben [ew-berr-LAY-bern] *nt* survival

überlegen [ew-berr-LAY-gern] *v* think over

übermüdet [ew-berr-MEW-dert] *adj* overtired

* **übernehmen** [ew-berr-NAY-mern] *v* take charge of

überprüfen [ew-berr-PREW-fern] *v* check in; review

überragend [ew-berr-RAR-gernt] *adj* superlative

überraschen [ew-berr-RAH-shern] *v* surprise

überraschend [ew-berr-RAH-shernt] *adj* surprising

überrascht [ew-berr-RAHSHT] *adj* surprised

Überraschung [ew-berr-RAH-shoong] *f (pl* ~en) surprise

überreden [ew-berr-RAY-dern] *v* persuade

Überrest [EW-berr-rehst] *m (pl*

~e) remnant

Überrock [EW-berr-rok] *m (pl* ~e) topcoat

* **überschreiten** [ew-berr-SHRIGH-tern] *v* exceed

Überschrift [EW-berr-shrift] *f (pl* ~en) heading

Überschuß [EW-berr-shoos] *m (pl* ~e) surplus

überschüssig [ew-berr-shew-sikh] *adj* spare

Überschwemmung [ew-berr-SHVEH-moong] *f (pl* ~en) flood

* **übersehen** [ew-berr-ZAY-ern] *v* overlook

übersetzen [ew-berr-ZEH-tsern] *v* translate

Übersetzer [ew-berr-ZEH-tserr] *m (pl* ~; *f* ~in) translator

Übersetzung [ew-berr-ZEH-tsoong] *f (pl* ~en) translation

Überstunden [ew-berr-shtoon-dern] *fpl* overtime

* **übertragen** [ew-berr-TRAR-gern] *v* transfer

* **übertreiben** [ew-berr-TRIGH-bern] *v* exaggerate

Übertreter [EW-berr-tray-terr] *m (pl* ~; *f* ~in) trespasser

* **überweisen** [ew-berr-VIGH-zern] *v* remit

Überweisung [ew-berr-VIGH-zoong] *f (pl* ~en) remittance

überzeugen [ew-berr-TSOY-gern] *v* convince

Überzeugung [ew-berr-TSOY-goong] *f (pl* ~en) conviction

üblich [EWP-likh] *adj* customary

übrig [EW-brikh] *adj* remaining

übrigens [EW-bri-gerns] *adv* by the way

Übung [EW-boong] *f (pl* ~en) exercise

Ufer [OO-ferr] *nt (pl* ~) bank

Uferschnecke [OO-ferr-shneh-ker] *f* (*pl* ~n) winkle

Uhr [oor] *f* (*pl* ~en) watch; clock

Uhrband [OOR-bahnt] *nt* (*pl* ~̃er) watch-strap

Uhrmacher [OOR-mah-kherr] *m* (*pl* ~) watchmaker

Ulme [OOL-mer] *f* elm

ultraviolett [OOL-trah-vioa-LEHT] *adj* ultra-violet

umadressieren [OOM-ah-dreh-see-rern] *v* readdress

umarmen [oom-AHR-mern] *v* embrace; hug

umdrehen (sich) [zikh-OOM-dray-ern] *v* turn round

umfangreich [OOM-fahng-righkh] *adj* bulky

* **umgeben** [oom-GAY-bern] *v* surround

Umgebung [oom-GAY-boong] *f* (*pl* ~en) surroundings *pl*; setting

* **umgehen** [oom-GAY-ern] *v* bypass

umgekehrt [OOM-ger-kayrt] upside down

Umhang [OOM-hahng] *m* (*pl* ~̃e) cape; cloak

um...herum [oom-heh-ROOM] *prep* around

umherwandern [oom-HAYR-vahn-derrn] *v* wander

umherziehend [oom-HAYR-tsee-ernt] *adj* itinerant

umkehren [OOM-kay-rern] *v* turn back

Umkreis [OOM-krighs] *m* radius

umkreisen [oom-KRIGH-zern] *v* circle

Umleitung [OOM-ligh-toong] *f* (*pl* ~en) bypass

umliegend [OOM-lee-gernt] *adj* surrounding

Umsatz [OOM-zahts] *m* (*pl* ~̃e)

turnover

Umsatzsteuer [OOM-zahts-shtoy-err] *f* turnover tax

Umschlag [OOM-shlark] *m* (*pl* ~̃e) cover

Umstände [OOM-shtehn-der] *mpl* circumstances *pl*

umstritten [oom-SHTRI-tern] *adj* controversial

Umweg [OOM-vayk] *m* (*pl* ~e) detour

* **umziehen** [OOM-tsee-ern] *v* move

Umzug [OOM-tsook] *m* (*pl* ~̃e) move

unabhängig [OON-ahp-hehng-ikh] *adj* independent

Unabhängigkeit [OON-ahp-hehng-ikh-kight] *f* independence

unabsichtlich [OON-ahp-zikht-likh] *adj* unintentional

unähnlich [OON-ain-likh] *adj* unlike

unangenehm [OON-ahn-ger-naym] *adj* unpleasant; disagreeable

unannehmbar [oon-ahn-NAYM-barr] *adj* unacceptable

unartig [OON-ahr-tikh] *adj* naughty

unaufrichtig [OON-owf-rikh-tikh] *adj* insincere

unbedeutend [OON-ber-doy-ternt] *adj* insignificant

unbefriedigend [OON-ber-free-di-gernt] *adj* unsatisfactory

unbefugt [OON-ber-fookt] *adj* unauthorized

unbefugt eindringen [OON-ber-fookt-IGHN-dring-ern] trespass

unbekannt [OON-ber-kahnt] *adj* unknown

unbeliebt [OON-ber-leept] *adj*

unpopular

unbeschränkt [OON-ber-shrehngkt] *adj* unlimited

unbesetzt [OON-ber-zehtst] *adj* unoccupied

unbesonnen [OON-ber-zo-nern] *adv* headlong

unbestimmt [OON-ber-shtimt] *adj* indefinite

unbewohnbar [OON-ber-voan-barr] *adj* uninhabitable

unbewohnt [OON-ber-voant] *adj* uninhabited

unbewußt [OON-ber-voost] *adj* unaware

unbezahlt [OON-ber-tsarlt] *adj* unpaid

und [oont] *conj* and

und so weiter [oont-zoa-VIGH-terr] and so on

undankbar [OON-dahngk-barr] *adj* ungrateful

undeutlich [OON-doyt-likh] *adj* indistinct

uneben [OON-ay-bern] *adj* uneven

unehrlich [OON-ayr-likh] *adj* dishonest; crooked

unempfindlich [OON-ehm-pfint-likh] *adj* insensible

unentdeckt [OON-ehnt-dehkt] *adj* undiscovered

unentgeltlich [OON-ehnt-gehlt-likh] *adj* gratis

unerfahren [OON-ehr-far-rern] *adj* inexperienced

unerkärlich [oon-ehr-KLAIR-likh] *adj* unaccountable

unermeßlich [oon-ehr-MEHS-likh] *adj* immense

unerschwinglich [oon-ehr-SHVING-likh] *adj* prohibitive

unerträglich [oon-ehr-traik-likh] *adj* unbearable

unerwartet [OON-ehr-vahr-tert] *adj* unexpected

unerwünscht [OON-ehr-vewnsht] *adj* undesirable

unfähig [OON-fai-ikh] *adj* unable; incapable; incompetent

Unfall [OON-fahl] *m* (*pl* ~e) accident

Unfallstation [OON-fahl-shtah-tsyoan] *f* (*pl* ~en) first-aid post

unformell [OON-for-MEHL] *adj* informal

unfreundlich [OON-froynt-likh] *adj* unfriendly; unkind

Unfug [OON-fook] *m* nuisance; mischief

ungangbar [OON-gahng-barr] *adj* impassable

Ungar [OON-gahr] *m* (*pl* ~n; *f* ~in) Hungarian

ungarisch [OONG-gar-rish] *adj* Hungarian

Ungarn [OON-gahrn] *nt* Hungary

ungebildet [OON-ger-bil-dert] *adj* uneducated

ungebraucht [OON-ger-browkht] *adj* unused

ungeduldig [OON-ger-dool-dikh] *adj* impatient

ungeeignet [OON-ger-igh-gnert] *adj* unsuitable

ungefähr [OON-ger-fair] *adv* approximately

ungehalten [OON-ger-hahl-tern] *adj* displeased

ungeheuer [OON-ger-hoy-err] *adj* enormous; tremendous

ungekocht [OON-ger-kokht] *adj* uncooked

ungelegen [OON-ger-lay-gern] *adj* inconvenient

ungelernt [OON-ger-lehrnt] *adj* unskilled

ungemütlich [OON-ger-mewt-likh] *adj* uncomfortable

ungenau [OON-ger-now] *adj* inaccurate; inexact

ungenießbar [OON-ger-nees-barr] *adj* inedible

ungenügend [OON-ger-new-gernt] *adj* insufficient

ungerade [OON-ger-rar-der] *adj* odd

ungerecht [OON-ger-rehkht] *adj* unfair; unjust

Ungerechtigkeit [OON-ger-rehkh-tikh-kight] *f (pl ~en)* injustice

ungeschickt [OON-ger-shikt] *adj* awkward; clumsy

ungeschützt [OON-ger-shewtst] *adj* unprotected

ungesehen [OON-ger-zay-ern] *adj* unseen

ungesetzlich [OON-ger-zehts-likh] *adj* unlawful; illegal

ungesund [OON-ger-zoont] *adj* insanitary; unsound; unhealthy

ungewöhnlich [OON-ger-vurn-likh] *adj* unusual; uncommon

ungewohnt [OON-ger-voant] *adj* unaccustomed

unglaublich [oon-GLOWP-likh] *adj* incredible

ungleich [OON-glighkh] *adj* unequal

unglücklich [OON-glewk-likh] *adj* unfortunate; unlucky; unhappy

ungünstig [OON-gewns-tikh] *adj* unfavourable

unheilbar [OON-highl-barr] *adj* incurable

unhöflich [OON-hurf-likh] *adj* impolite

Uniform [oo-ni-FORM] *f (pl ~en)*

uniform

universal [oo-ni-vehr-ZARL] *adj* universal

Universität [oo-ni-vehr-zi-TAIT] *f (pl ~en)* university

Unkraut [OON-krowt] *nt (pl ~er)* weed

unkultiviert [OON-kool-ti-veert] *adj* uncultivated

unlängst [oon-LEHNGST] *adv* lately

unleserlich [OON-lay-zerr-likh] *adj* illegible

unmittelbar [OON-mi-terl-barr] *adj* immediate

unmöbliert [OON-mur-bleert] *adj* unfurnished

unmöglich [OON-murk-likh] *adj* impossible

unnatürlich [OON-nah-tewr-likh] *adj* unnatural

unnötig [OON-nur-tikh] *adj* unnecessary

unordentlich [OON-or-dernt-likh] *adj* untidy

Unordnung [OON-ord-noong] *f* mess

unpassend [OON-pah-sernt] *adj* improper

unproduktiv [OON-proa-dook-teef] *adj* unproductive

unqualifiziert [OON-kvah-li-fi-tseert] *adj* unqualified

unrecht [OON-rehkht] *adj* wrong

Unrecht [OON-rehkht] *nt* wrong

*unrecht tun [OON-rehkht-toon] *v* wrong

unregelmäßig [OON-ray-gerl-mai-sikh] *adj* irregular

unrein [OON-righn] *adj* unclean

unrichtig [OON-rikh-tikh] *adj* incorrect

Unruhe [OON-roo-er] *f (pl ~n)* unrest

unruhig [OON-roo-ikh] *adj* uneasy; restless

uns [oons] *pron* us; ourselves

unschuldig [OON-shool-dikh] *adj* innocent

unser [OON-zerr] *adj* our

unsere [OON-zray] *adj* (→ **unser**)

unsicher [OON-zi-kherr] *adj* unsafe; uncertain

unsichtbar [OON-zikht-barr] *adj* invisible

Unsinn [OON-zin] *m* nonsense

unsinnig [OON-zi-nikh] *adj* senseless

unstet [OON-shtayt] *adj* unsteady

unten [OON-tern] *adv* underneath; downstairs; beneath; below

unter [OON-terr] *prep* among; under

* **unterbrechen** [oon-terr-BREH-khern] *v* interrupt

Unterbrechung [oon-terr-BREH-khoong] *f* (*pl* ~en) interruption

* **unterbringen** [OON-terr-bring-ern] *v* accommodate

unterbrochen [oon-terr-BRO-khern] *adj* discontinued

untere [OON-te-rer] *adj* lower

untere Koje [OON-te-rer-KOA-yer] *f* lower berth

untergeordnet [OON-terr-ger-ord-nert] *adj* secondary

Untergeschoß [OON-terr-ger-shos] *nt* basement

Untergrundbahn [OON-terr-groont-barn] *f* (*pl* ~en) subway

unterhalb [oon-terr-hahlp] *prep* below

Unterhalt [OON-terr-hahlt] *m* upkeep

* **unterhalten (sich)** [zikh-oon-

terr-HAHL-tern] *v* amuse

Unterhaltung [oon-terr-HAHL-toong] *f* entertainment

Unterhemd [OON-terr-hehmt] *nt* (*pl* ~en) undershirt

Unterhose [OON-terr-hoa-zer] *f* (*pl* ~n) underpants *pl*; shorts *pl*; briefs *pl*

unterirdisch [OON-terr-ir-dish] *adj* underground

Unterkunft [OON-terr-koonft] *f* (*pl* ~e) accommodations *pl*; lodgings *pl*

* **unternehmen** [oon-terr-NAY-mern] *v* undertake

Unternehmen [oon-terr-NAY-mern] *nt* (*pl* ~) enterprise

Unternehmung [oon-terr-NAY-moong] *f* (*pl* ~en) undertaking

unternehmungslustig [oon-terr-NAY-moongs-loos-tikh] *adj* enterprising

Unterrock [OON-terr-rok] *m* (*pl* ~e) slip

unterschätzen [oon-terr-SHEH-tsern] *v* underestimate

* **unterscheiden** [oon-terr-SHIGH-dern] *v* distinguish

* **unterscheiden (sich)** [zikh-oon-terr-SHIGH-dern] *v* differ

Unterschied [OON-terr-sheet] *m* (*pl* ~e) difference

* **unterschreiben** [oon-terr-SHRIGH-bern] *v* sign

Unterschrift [OON-terr-shrift] *f* (*pl* ~en) signature

* **unterstreichen** [oon-terr-SHTRIGH-khern] *v* underline

Unterströmung [OON-terr-shtrur-moong] *f* undertow

Unterstützung [oon-terr-SHTEW-tsoong] *f* (*pl* ~en) support

untersuchen [oon-terr-ZOO-khern] *v* investigate

Untersuchung [oon-terr-ZOO-khoong] f (pl ~en) medical examination

Untertasse [OON-terr-tah-ser] f (pl ~n) saucer

Untertitel [OON-terr-ti-terl] m (pl ~) sub-title

Unterwäsche [OON-terr-veh-sher] fpl underwear

Unterwasser . . . [oon-terr-VAH-serr] pref underwater

*__**unterweisen**__ [oon-terr-VIGH-zern] v instruct

Unterweisung [oon-terr-VIGH-zoong] f (pl ~en) instruction

*__**unterwerfen**__ [oon-terr-WEHR-fern] v subject

Unterzeichnete [oon-terr-TSIGHKH-ner-ter] m (pl ~n; f ~) undersigned

untreu [OON-troy] adj unfaithful

unüberlegt [OON-ew-berr-laykt] adj unwise

ununterbrochen [OON-oon-terr-BRO-khern] adj continuous

unverbindlich [OON-fehr-bint-likh] without obligation

unverdient [OON-fehr-deent] adj unearned

unverdünnt [OON-fehr-dewnt] adj neat

unverheiratet [OON-fehr-high-rar-tert] adj unmarried

unverkauft [OON-fehr-kowft] adj unsold

unverletzt [OON-fehr-lehtst] adj unhurt

unvermeidlich [OON-fehr-MIGHT-likh] adj unavoidable

unvernünftig [OON-fehr-newnf-tikh] adj unreasonable

unverschämt [OON-fehr-shaimt] adj insolent; impudent; impertinent

Unverschämtheit [OON-fehr-shaimt-hight] f impertinence

unversehrt [OON-fehr-zayrt] adj intact; unbroken

unverzüglich [oon-fehr-TSEWK-likh] adj prompt

unvollkommen [OON-fol-ko-mern] adj imperfect

unvollständig [OON-fol-shtehn-dikh] adj incomplete

unvorbereitet [OON-foar-ber-right-tert] adj unprepared

unwahr [OON-varr] adj untrue

unwahrscheinlich [OON-varr-shighn-likh] adj unlikely; improbable

unwichtig [OON-vikh-tikh] adj unimportant

unwillig [OON-vi-likh] adj unwilling

unwillkommen [OON-vil-ko-mern] adj unwelcome

unwirtlich [OON-virt-likh] adj inhospitable

unwissend [OON-vi-sernt] adj ignorant

unwohl [OON-voal] adj unwell

unzerbrechlich [OON-tsehr-brehkh-likh] adj unbreakable

unzufrieden [OON-tsoo-free-dern] adj discontented; dissatisfied

unzugänglich [OON-tsoo-gehng-likh] adj inaccessible

unzulänglich [OON-tsoo-lehng-likh] adj inadequate

unzuverlässig [OON-tsoo-fehr-leh-sikh] adj untrustworthy; unreliable

Urin [oo-REEN] m urine

Urkunde [OOR-koon-der] f (pl ~n) document

Urlaub [OOR-lowp] m holidays pl

Ursache [OOR-zah-kher] f (pl ~n)

cause

Ursprung [OOR-shproong] *m* (*pl* ~̈e) origin

Urteil [OOR-tighl] *nt* (*pl* ~e) sentence; judgment

urteilen [OOR-tigh-lern] *v* judge

Urteilsspruch [OOR-tighls-shprookh] *m* (*pl* ~̈e) verdict

Vakanz [vah-KAHNTS] *f* (*pl* ~en) vacancy

Vakuum [VAR-koo-oom] *nt* vacuum

Vanille [vah-NIL-yer] *f* vanilla

Varietétheater [vah-riay-TAY-tay-ar-terr] *nt* (*pl* ~) variety theatre; music hall

Varietévorstellung [vah-riay-TAY-foar-shteh-loong] *f* (*pl* ~en) variety show

Vase [VAR-zer] *f* (*pl* ~n) vase

Vaseline [vah-zer-LEE-ner] *f* vaseline

Vater [FAR-terr] *m* (*pl* ~̈) dad

Vaterland [FAR-terr-lahnt] *nt* (*pl* ~̈er) mother country

Vati [FAR-ti] *m* daddy

Vegetarier [vay-gay-TARR-yerr] *m* (*pl* ~) vegetarian

Vegetation [vay-gay-tah-TSYOAN] *f* vegetation

Veilchen [FIGHL-khern] *nt* (*pl* ~) violet

Ventil [vehn-TEEL] *nt* (*pl* ~e) valve

Ventilation [vehn-ti-lah-TSYOAN] *f* ventilation

Ventilator [vehn-ti-LAR-tor] *m* (*pl* ~en) ventilator; fan

Ventilatorriemen [vehn-ti-LAR-tor-ree-mern] *m* (*pl* ~) fan-belt

Venusmuschel [VAY-noos-moo-sherl] *f* (*pl* ~n) clams *pl*

Verabredung [fehr-AHP-ray-doong] *f* (*pl* ~en) appointment; engagement; date

verabscheuen [fehr-AHP-shoy-ern] *v* hate

verachten [fehr-AHKH-tern] *v* despise; scorn

Verachtung [fehr-AHKH-toong] *f* scorn

veraltet [fehr-AHL-tert] *adj* out of date

Veranda [vay-RAHN-dah] *f* (*pl* **Veranden**) veranda

veränderlich [fehr-EHN-derr-likh] *adj* variable

verängstigt [fehr-EHNGS-tikht] *adj* frightened

veranschlagen [fehr-AHN-shlar-gern] *v* evaluate

verantwortlich [fehr-AHNT-vort-likh] *adj* responsible; liable

Verantwortlichkeit [fehr-AHNT-vort-likh-kight] *f* liability

Verband [fehr-BAHNT] *m* (*pl* ~̈e) bandage

Verbandskasten [fehr-BAHNTS-kahs-tern] *m* (*pl* ~̈) first-aid kit

verbessern [fehr-BEH-serrn] *v* correct; improve

verbessert [fehr-BEH-serrt] *adj* improved

Verbesserung [fehr-BEH-ser-roong] *f* (*pl* ~en) improvement

* **verbieten** [fehr-BEE-tern] *v* prohibit; forbid

* **verbinden** [fehr-BIN-dern] *v* connect; link; join

Verbindungsglied [fehr-BIN-doongs-gleet] *nt* (*pl* ~er) link

verblassen [fehr-BLAH-sern] *v* fade

verblüffen [fehr-BLEW-fern] v
astonish

Verbot [fehr-BOAT] nt (pl ~e)
prohibition

verboten [fehr-BOA-tern] adj
prohibited

verbrauchen [fehr-BROW-khern]
v use up

Verbrauchssteuer [fehr-
BROWKHS-shtoy-err] f purchase
tax

Verbrechen [fehr-BREH-khern]
nt (pl ~) crime

Verbrecher [fehr-BREH-kherr] m
(pl ~) criminal

* **verbrennen** [fehr-BREH-nern] v
burn

* **verbringen** [fehr-BRING-ern] v
spend

Verdacht [fehr-DAHKHT] m
suspicion

verdächtig [fehr-DEHKH-tikh] adj
suspicious

verdampfen [fehr-DAHM-pfern] v
evaporate

verdauen [fehr-DOW-ern] v digest

verdaulich [fehr-DOW-likh] adj
digestible

Verdauung [fehr-DOW-oong] f
digestion

verdecken [fehr-DEH-kern] v
cover

* **verderben** [fehr-DEHR-bern] v
spoil

verdicken [fehr-DI-kern] v
thicken

verdienen [fehr-DEE-nern] v
deserve; earn; merit

Verdienst [fehr-DEENST] nt (pl
~e) merit; m earnings pl

verdrießlich [fehr-DREES-likh]
adj gloomy

verdünnen [fehr-DEW-nern] v
dilute

verdünnt [fehr-DEWNT] adj
diluted

verehren [fehr-AY-rern] v
worship

Verein [fehr-IGHN] m (pl ~e)
society

vereinigen [fehr-IGH-ni-gern] v
unite; associate

Vereinigte Staaten [fehr-IGH-
nik-ter-SHTAR-tern] mpl
United States; States, the pl

Vereinigung [fehr-IGH-ni-goong]
f (pl ~en) union; association

Verfahren [fehr-FAR-rern] nt (pl
~) procedure

verfärbt [fehr-FEHRPT] adj
discoloured

verfolgen [fehr-FOL-gern] v chase

verfügbar [fehr-FEWK-barr] adj
available

vergällter Spiritus [fehr-GEHL-
terr-SHPI-ri-toos] m
methylated spirits

vergangen [fehr-GAHNG-ern] adj
past

Vergangenheit [fehr-GAHNG-ern-
hight] f past

Vergaser [fehr-GAR-zerr] m (pl
~) carburettor

vergegenwärtigen (sich) [zikh-
fehr-gay-gern-VEHR-ti-gern] v
realise

Vergehen [fehr-GAY-ern] nt (pl
~) offence

* **vergehen (sich)** [zikh-fehr-GAY-
ern] v offend

* **vergessen** [fehr-GEH-sern] v
forget

vergeuden [fehr-GOY-dern] v
waste

Vergleich [fehr-GLAHIKH] m (pl
~e) comparison

* **vergleichen** [fehr-GLIGH-khern]
v compare

vergoldet [fehr-GOL-dert] *adj* gilt

vergrößern [fehr-GRUR-serrn] *v* enlarge; increase

Vergrößerung [fehr-GRUR-ser-roong] *f* (*pl* ~en) enlargement

verhaften [fehr-HAHF-tern] *v* arrest

Verhaftung [fehr-HAHF-toong] *f* (*pl* ~en) arrest

Verhältnis [fehr-HEHLT-nis] *nt* (*pl* ~se) proportion

verhandeln [fehr-HAHN-derln] *v* negotiate

Verhandlung [fehr-HAHN-dloong] *f* (*pl* ~ en) negotiation

verheiratet [fehr-HIGH-rar-tert] *adj* married

verhindern [fehr-HIN-derrn] *v* prevent

verhören [fehr-HUR-rern] *v* interrogate

Verkauf [fehr-KOWF] *m* (*pl* ~̈e) sale

verkaufen [fehr-KOW-fern] *v* sell

Verkäufer [fehr-KOY-ferr] *m* (*pl* ~) salesman; shop assistant

Verkäuferin [fehr-KOY-fer-rin] *f* (*pl* ~nen) salesgirl

verkäuflich [fehr-KOYF-likh] *adj* saleable

Verkehr [fehr-KAYR] *m* traffic

Verkehrsampel [fehr-KAYRS-ahm-perl] *f* (*pl* ~n) traffic light

Verkehrsstauung [fehr-KAYRS-shtow-oong] *f* (*pl* ~en) traffic jam

Verkehrsstockung [fehr-KAYRS-shto-koong] *f* (*pl* ~en) jam

verkürzen [fehr-KEWR-tsern] *v* shorten

verlangen [fehr-LAHNG-ern] *v* charge

verlängern [fehr-LEHNG-errn] *v* renew; extend; lengthen

Verlängerungsschnur [fehr-LEHNGER-roongs-shnoor] *f* (*pl* ~̈e) extension cord

verlangsamen [fehr-LAHNG-zar-mern] *v* slow down

* **verlassen** [fehr-LAH-sern] *v* leave

* **verlassen auf (sich)** [zikh-fehr-LAH-sern-owf] *v* rely

verlegen [fehr-LAY-gern] *v* mislay; *adj* embarrassed

Verleger [fehr-LAY-gerr] *m* (*pl* ~) publisher

verletzen [fehr-LEH-tsern] *v* injure; hurt

verletzt [fehr-LEHTST] *adj* injured

Verletzung [fehr-LEH-tsoong] *f* (*pl* ~en) injury

verliebt [fehr-LEEPT] *adj* in love

* **verlieren** [fehr-LEE-rern] *v* lose

verlobt [fehr-LOAPT] *adj* engaged

Verlobte [fehr-LOAP-ter] *m* (*pl* ~n) fiancé; *f* fiancée

Verlobungsring [fehr-LOA-boongs-ring] *m* (*pl* ~e) engagement ring

Verlust [fehr-LOOST] *m* (*pl* ~̈e) loss

Verlust- und Fundanzeigen [fehr-LOOST-oont-FOONT-ahn-tsigh-gern] *fpl* lost and found

* **vermeiden** [fehr-MIGH-dern] *v* avoid

Vermerkhäkchen [fehr-MEHRK-haik-khern] *nt* (*pl* ~) tick

vermieten [fehr-MEE-tern] *v* let

vermindern [fehr-MIN-derrn] *v* lessen; decrease

vermischt [fehr-MISHT] *adj* miscellaneous

Vermißte [fehr-MIS-ter] *m* (*pl* ~n) missing person

vermutlich [fehr-MOOT-likh] *adv*

presumably

Vermutung [fehr-MOO-toong] *f*
(*pl* ~en) guess

vernachlässigen [fehr-NARKH-leh-si-gern] *v* neglect

Vernachlässigung [fehr-NARKH-leh-si-goong] *f* (*pl* ~ en)
neglect

vernichten [fehr-NIKH-tern] *v*
wreck; destroy

vernünftig [fehr-NEWNF-tikh] *adj*
reasonable

veröffentlichen [fehr-UR-fernt-li-khern] *v* publish

Veröffentlichung [fehr-UR-fernt-li-khoong] *f* (*pl* ~en)
publication

Verpackung [fehr-PAH-koong] *f*
(*pl* ~en) packing

verpassen [fehr-PAH-sern] *v* miss

verpfänden [fehr-PFEHN-dern] *v*
pawn

verpflichtend [fehr-PFLIKH-ternt]
adj obligatory

verrenkt [fehr-REHNGKT] *adj*
dislocated

verrichten [fehr-RIKH-tern] *v*
perform

verrückt [fehr-REWKT] *adj* crazy;
mad

Vers [fehrs] *m* (*pl* ~e) verse

versagen [fehr-ZAR-gern] *v* fail

versammeln (sich) [zikh-fehr-ZAH-merln] *v* gather

Versammlung [fehr-ZAHM-loong]
f (*pl* ~en) rally

* **verschieben** [fehr-SHEE-bern] *v*
put off

verschieden [fehr-SHEE-dern] *adj*
distinct; different; varied

verschiedene [fehr-SHEE-der-ner] *adj* various; several

* **verschlafen** [fehr-SHLAR-fern] *v*
oversleep

Verschluß [fehr-SHLOOS] *m* (*pl* ~e) fastener

* **verschreiben** [fehr-SHRIGH-bern] *v* prescribe

verschütten [fehr-SHEW-tern] *v*
spill

verschwenderisch [fehr-SHVEHN-der-rish] *adj* wasteful

Verschwendung [fehr-SHVEHN-doong] *f* waste

* **verschwinden** [fehr-SHVIN-dern] *v* vanish; disappear

Versehen [fehr-ZAY-ern] *nt* (*pl* ~) oversight

* **versenden** [fehr-ZEHN-dern] *v*
ship

versichern [fehr-ZI-kherrn] *v*
assure; insure

Versicherung [fehr-ZI-kher-roong] *f* (*pl* ~en) insurance

Versicherungspolice [fehr-ZI-kher-roongs-poa-LEE-ser] *f* (*pl* ~n) insurance policy

* **versprechen** [fehr-SHPREH-khern] *v* promise

Versprechen [fehr-SHPREH-khern] *nt* (*pl* ~) promise

Verstand [fehr-SHTAHNT] *m*
sense; intellect; mind

verständig [fehr-SHTEHN-dikh]
adj sensible

Verständigung [fehr-SHTEHN-di-goong] *f* understanding

verstauchen [fehr-SHTOW-khern]
v sprain

Verstauchung [fehr-SHTOW-khoong] *f* (*pl* ~en) sprain

verstecken [fehr-SHTEH-kern] *v*
hide

* **verstehen** [fehr-SHTAY-ern] *v*
understand

Versteigerung [fehr-SHTIGH-ger-roong] *f* (*pl* ~en) auction

verstopft [fehr-SHTOPFT] *adj*

constipated

Verstopfung [fehr-SHTO-pfoong] *f* constipation

verstreuen [fehr-SHTROY-ern] *v* scatter

versuchen [fehr-ZOO-khern] *v* attempt; try; tempt

verteidigen [fehr-TIGH-di-gern] *v* defend

Verteidigung [fehr-TIGH-di-goong] *f* (*pl* ~en) defence

Verteiler [fehr-TIGH-lerr] *m* (*pl* ~) distributor

Vertrag [fehr-TRARK] *m* (*pl* ~e) contract

vertrauen [fehr-TROW-ern] *v* trust

Vertrauen [fehr-TROW-ern] *nt* trust

vertraulich [fehr-TROW-likh] *adj* confidential

vertraut [fehr-TROWT] *adj* familiar

* **vertreten** [fehr-TRAY-tern] *v* represent

Vertreter [fehr-TRAY-terr] *m* (*pl* ~; *f* ~in) agent

Vertretung [fehr-TRAY-toong] *f* (*pl* ~en) agency; representation

verursachen [fehr-OOR-zah-khern] *v* cause

verurteilen [fehr-OOR-tigh-lern] *v* sentence

verwalten [fehr-VAHL-tern] *v* manage

Verwaltung [fehr-VAHL-toong] *f* (*pl* ~en) management

verwandeln [fehr-VAHN-derln] *v* transform

verwandt [fehr-VAHNT] *adj* related

Verwandte [fehr-VAHN-ter] *m* (*pl* ~n; *f* ~) relative

verwechseln [fehr-VEHK-serln] *v* mistake

verweigern [fehr-VIGH-gerrn] *v* refuse

Verweigerung [fehr-VIGH-ger-roong] *f* (*pl* ~en) refusal

* **verweisen auf** [fehr-VIGH-zern-owf] *v* refer to

* **verwenden** [fehr-VEHN-dern] *v* apply; employ

verwickeln [fehr-VI-kerln] *v* involve

verwickelt [fehr-VI-kerlt] *adj* complex

verwirrt [fehr-VIRT] *adj* confused

Verwirrung [fehr-VI-roong] *f* (*pl* ~en) confusion

verwunden [fehr-VOON-dern] *v* wound

Verwunderung [fehr-VOON-der-roong] *f* wonder

* **verzeihen** [fehr-TSIGH-ern] *v* forgive

Verzeihung [fehr-TSIGH-oong] *f* pardon

verzichten auf [fehr-TSIKH-tern-owf] *v* do without

Verzierung [fehr-TSEE-roong] *f* (*pl* ~en) ornament

Verzögerung [fehr-TSUR-ger-roong] *f* (*pl* ~en) delay

verzweifelt [fehr-TSVIGH-ferlt] *adj* desperate

Vestibül [vehs-ti-BEWL] *nt* (*pl* ~e) lobby

Viadukt [viah-DOOKT] *m* (*pl* ~e) viaduct

vibrieren [vi-BREE-rern] *v* vibrate

Vibrieren [vi-BREE-rern] *nt* vibration

Vieh [fee] *nt* cattle

viel [feel] *adv* much

viele [FEE-ler] *adj* many

vielleicht [fee-LIGHKHT] *adv* maybe; perhaps

vier [feer] adj four

vierte [FEER-ter] adj fourth

Viertel [FIR-terl] nt (pl ~)
quarter

vierteljährlich [FIR-terl-yair-likh] adj quarterly

vierzehn [FIR-tsayn] adj fourteen

vierzehn Tage [FIR-tsayn-TAR-ger] mpl fortnight

vierzehnte [FIR-tsayn-ter] adj
fourteenth

vierzig [FIR-tsikh] adj forty

Vikar [vi-KARR] m (pl ~e) vicar

Villa [VI-lah] f (pl **Villen**) villa

Visitenkarte [vi-ZI-tern-kahr-ter] f (pl ~n) card; visiting
card

Visum [VEE-zoom] nt (pl **Visa**)
visa

Vitamin [vi-tah-MEEN] nt (pl ~e)
vitamin

Vizepräsident [FEE-tser-prai-zi-dehnt] m (pl ~en; f ~in) vice-
president

Vogel [FOA-gerl] m (pl ~) bird

Volk [folk] nt (pl ~er) folk;
people

Volkslied [FOLKS-leet] nt (pl ~er)
folk-song

Volkssagen [FOLKS-zar-gern] fpl
folklore

Volkstanz [FOLKS-tahnts] m (pl
~e) folk-dance

Volkswirt [FOLKS-virt] m (pl ~e)
economist

voll [fol] adj full

vollbesetzt [FOL-ber-ZEHTST] adj
full up

vollfüllen [FOL-few-lern] v fill up

völlig [FUR-likh] adv absolutely

vollkommen [fol-KO-mern] adj
perfect

Vollkornbrot [FOL-korn-broat] nt
(pl ~e) wholemeal bread

Vollpension [FOL-pahng-syoan] f
bed and board; board and
lodging; full board

vollständig [FOL-shtehn-dikh]
adj complete

Volt [volt] nt volt

von [fon] prep of; from

* **von Bedeutung sein** [fon-ber-DOY-toong-zighn] v matter

vor [foar] prep in front of; ahead
of; before

vor langer Zeit [foar-LAHNG-err-tsight] long ago

* **vorangehen** [foa-RAHN-gay-ern]
v precede

Voranschlag [FOAR-ahn-shlark]
m (pl ~e) estimate

vorausbezahlt [foa-ROWS-ber-tsarlt] adj prepaid

vorausgesetzt daß [foa-ROWS-ger-zehtst-dahs] conj provided

voraussagen [foa-ROWS-zar-gern]
v forecast

voraussetzen [foa-ROWS-zeh-tsern] v assume

vorbei [foar-BIGH] adj over

* **vorbeifahren** [foar-BIGH-far-rern] v pass

* **vorbeigehen** [foar-BIGH-gay-ern] v pass by

vorbereiten [FOAR-ber-righ-tern]
v prepare; arrange

Vorbereitung [FOAR-ber-righ-toong] f (pl ~en) preparation

Vorbereitungen [FOAR-ber-righ-toong-ern] fpl arrangements
pl

vorbeugend [FOAR-boy-gernt] adj
preventive

Vorbildung [FOAR-bil-doong] f
background

* **vorbringen** [FOAR-bring-ern] v
bring up

Vordergrund [FOR-derr-groont]
m foreground

Vorderseite [FOR-derr-zigh-ter] *f* (*pl* ~n) front

Vorfahr [FOAR-farr] *m* (*pl* ~en) ancestor

Vorfahrtsrecht [FOAR-farrts-rehkht] *nt* right-of-way

Vorgang [FOAR-gahng] *m* (*pl* ~e) process

* **vorgeben** [FOAR-gay-bern] *v* pretend

Vorhang [FOAR-hahng] *m* (*pl* ~e) drapes *pl;* curtain

Vorhängeschloß [FOAR-hehng-er-shlos] *nt* (*pl* ~er) padlock

vorher [FOAR-hayr] *adv* before; in advance

vorhergehend [foar-HAYR-gay-ernt] *adj* preceding; previous

Vorhersage [foar-HAYR-zar-ger] *f* (*pl* ~n) forecast

Vorkriegs... [FOAR-kreeks] *pref* pre-war

vorläufig [FOAR-loy-fikh] *adj* preliminary

Vorleger [FOAR-lay-gerr] *m* (*pl* ~) rug

Vorname [FOAR-nar-mer] *m* (*pl* ~n) Christian name; first name

Vorrang [FOAR-rahng] *m* (*pl* ~e) priority

Vorrat [FOA-rart] *m* (*pl* ~e) provisions *pl;* store; stock; supplies *pl*

* **vorrätig haben** [FOA-rai-tikh-HAR-bern] *v* stock

* **vorschießen** [FOAR-shee-sern] *v* advance

Vorschlag [FOAR-shlark] *m* (*pl* ~e) proposal; suggestion

* **vorschlagen** [FOAR-shlar-gern] *v* suggest; propose

Vorschrift [FOAR-shrift] *f* (*pl* ~en) regulation

Vorschuß [FOAR-shoos] *m* (*pl* ~e) advance

* **vorsehen (sich)** [zikh-FOAR-zay-ern] *v* look out

Vorsicht [FOAR-zikht] *f* caution

vorsichtig [FOAR-zikh-tikh] *adj* careful

Vorsichtsmaßregel [FOAR-zikhts-mars-ray-gerl] *f* (*pl* ~n) precaution

Vorsitzende [FOAR-zi-tsern-der] *m* (*pl* ~n ; *f* ~) chairman

Vorspeise [FOAR-shpahi-zer] *f* (*pl* ~n) hors-d'œuvre

* **vorsprechen** [FOAR-shpreh-khern] *v* drop in

Vorstadt [FOAR-shtaht] *f* (*pl* ~e) suburb

vorstädtisch [FOAR-shteh-tish] *adj* suburban

vorstellen [FOAR-shteh-lern] *v* introduce; present

vorstellen (sich) [zikh-FOAR-shteh-lern] *v* imagine

Vorstellung [FOAR-shteh-loong] *f* (*pl* ~en) introduction; show

Vorstellungskraft [FOAR-shteh-loongs-krahft] *f* imagination

Vorteil [FOAR-tighl] *m* (*pl* ~e) advantage

vorteilhaft [FOAR-tighl-hahft] *adj* advantageous

Vortrag [FOAR-trark] *m* (*pl* ~e) lecture

Vorwand [FOAR-vahnt] *m* (*pl* ~e) pretence

vorwärts [FOR-vehrts] *adv* ahead; onwards; forward

* **vorwärtskommen** [FOR-vehrts-ko-mern] *v* get on

Vorzug [FOAR-tsook] *m* (*pl* ~e) preference

vorzuziehend [FOAR-tsoo-tsee-ernt] *adj* preferable

Vulkan [vool-KARN] *m (pl ~e)*
volcano

Waage [VAR-ger] *f (pl ~n)*
weighing machine; scales *pl*
waagrecht [VARK-rehkht] *adj*
horizontal
wach [vahkh] *adj* awake
Wache [VAH-kher] *f (pl ~n)*
guard
Wachs [vahks] *nt* wax
*** wachsen** [VAH-ksern] *v* grow
Wachsfigurenkabinett [VAHKS-fi-
goo-rern-kah-bi-neht] *nt*
waxworks *pl*
Wachtel [VAHKH-terl] *f (pl ~n)*
quail
Waffe [VAH-fer] *f (pl ~n)* weapon
Waffel [VAH-ferl] *f (pl ~n)* waffle
Waffen [VAH-fern] *fpl* arms *pl*
wagen [VAR-gern] *v* dare
Wagen [VAR-gern] *m (pl ~)*
coach; car
Wagenheber [VAR-gern-HAY-berr]
m (pl ~) jack
Waggon [vah-GAWNG] *m (pl ~s)*
wagon
Wahl [varl] *f* choice; pick;
election
wählen [VAI-lern] *v* elect; pick;
choose; dial
Wählscheibe [VAIL-shigh-ber] *f*
(pl ~n) dial
wahnsinnig [VARN-zi-nikh] *adj*
insane
wahr [varr] *adj* true
während [VAI-rernt] *prep* during;
conj while
wahrhaft [VARR-hahft] *adj*
truthful
Wahrheit [VARR-hight] *f (pl ~en)*
truth
wahrnehmbar [VARR-naym-barr]

adj noticeable
wahrscheinlich [varr-SHIGHN-
likh] *adv* likely; *adj* probable
Währung [VAI-roong] *f (pl ~en)*
currency
Wald [vahlt] *m (pl ~̈er)* forest;
wood
Waldung [VAHL-doong] *f (pl ~en)*
woodland
Walnuß [VAHL-noos] *f (pl ~̈e)*
walnut
Walzer [VAHL-tserr] *m (pl ~)*
waltz
wandern [VAHN-derrn] *v* hike;
tramp
Wandschrank [VAHNT-shrahngk]
m (pl ~̈e) closet
Wange [VAHNG-er] *f (pl ~n)*
cheek
wann [vahn] *adv* when
wann immer [vahn-I-merr]
whenever
Wanze [VAHN-tser] *f (pl ~n)* bug
Ware [VAR-rer] *f (pl ~n)* wares *pl*;
merchandise
Warenhaus [VAR-rern-hows] *nt*
(pl ~̈er) warehouse
warm [vahrm] *adj* warm
Wärme [VEHR-mer] *f* warmth
wärmen [VEHR-mern] *v* warm;
heat
Wärmflasche [VEHRM-flah-sher] *f*
(pl ~n) hot-water bottle
warnen [VAHR-nern] *v* warn;
caution
Warnung [VAHR-noong] *f (pl
~en)* warning
Warteliste [VAHR-ter-lis-ter] *f (pl
~n)* waiting-list
warten [VAHR-tern] *v* wait
Warten [VAHR-tern] *nt* waiting
Wärter [VEHR-terr] *m (pl ~; f
~in)* attendant
Wartezimmer [VAHR-ter-tsi-

merr] *nt (pl ~)* waiting-room

warum [vah-ROOM] why

was [vahs] *pron* what

was . . . betrifft [vahs-ber-TRIFFT] as regards

was auch immer [vahs-owkh-I-merr] whatever

was noch [vahs-nokh] what else

waschbar [VAHSH-barr] *adj* washable

Waschbecken [VAHSH-beh-kern] *nt (pl ~)* wash-basin

Wäsche [VEH-sher] *f* washing; linen; laundry

* **waschen** [VAHSH- shern] *v* wash

Wäscherei [veh-sher-RIGH] *f (pl ~ en)* laundry

Waschmaschine [VAHSH-mah-shee-ner] *f (pl ~n)* washing-machine

Waschpulver [VAHSH-pool-verr] *nt (pl ~)* washing-powder

Waschraum [VAHSH-rowm] *m (pl ~e)* wash-room

Waschtisch [VAHSH-tish] *m (pl ~e)* wash-stand

Wasser [VAH-serr] *nt* water; lotion

wasserdicht [VAH-serr-dikht] *adj* waterproof; rainproof

Wasserfall [VAH-serr-fahl] *m (pl ~e)* waterfall

Wasserhahn [VAH-serr-harn] *m (pl ~e)* faucet

Wassermelone [VAH-serr-may-loa-ner] *f (pl ~n)* watermelon

Wasserskier [VAH-serr-SHEE-err] *mpl* water skis *pl*

Wasserstoff [VAH-serr-shtof] *m* hydrogen

Wasserstoffsuperoxyd [vah-serr-shtof-zoo-perr-ok-sewt] *nt* peroxide

Wasserstraße [VAH-serr-shtrar-ser] *f (pl ~n)* waterway

waten [VAR-tern] *v* wade

Watt [vaht] *nt* watt

Watte [VAH-ter] *f* cotton-wool

weben [VAY-bern] *v* weave

Weber [VAY-berr] *m (pl ~; f ~in)* weaver

Wechselgeld [VEHK-serl-gehlt] *nt* change

Wechselkurs [VEH-kserl-koors] *m (pl ~e)* exchange rate

wechseln [VEHK-serln] *v* switch; vary; change

Wechselstrom [VEHK-serl-shtroam] *m* alternating current

Wechselstube [VEH-kserl-shtoo-ber] *f (pl ~n)* exchange office; money exchange

wecken [VEH-kern] *v* wake; awake

Wecker [VEH-kerr] *m (pl ~)* alarm clock

weder . . . noch . . . [VAY-derr-nokh] neither . . . nor

Weg [vayk] *m (pl ~e)* way; lane; drive

Wegegeld [VAY-ger-gehlt] *nt* toll

wegen [VAY-gern] *prep* because of; on account of

* **weggehen** [VEHK-gay-ern] *v* go away

* **wegnehmen** [VEHK-nay-mern] *v* take away

Wegrand [VAYK-rahnt] *m (pl ~er)* wayside

Wegweiser [VAYK-vigh-zerr] *m (pl ~)* milepost; signpost

wegwerfbar [VEHK-vehrf-barr] *adj* disposable

weiblich [VIGHP-likh] *adj* female; feminine

weich [vighkh] *adj* soft

Weichmacher [VIGHKH-mah-kherr] *m (pl ~)* softener

weiden [VIGH-dern] *v* graze

Weihnachten [VIGH-nahkh-tern] *nt* Xmas; Christmas

weil [vighl] *conj* because

Weile [VIGH-ler] *f* while

Weiler [VIGH-lerr] *m (pl ~)* hamlet

Wein [vighn] *m (pl ~e)* wine

Weinberg [VIGHN-behrk] *m (pl ~e)* vineyard

weinen [VIGH-nern] *v* weep; cry

Weinflasche [VIGHN-flah-sher] *f (pl ~n)* wine bottle

Weinglas [VIGHN-glars] *nt (pl ~̃er)* wineglass

Weinhändler [VIGHN-hehn-dlerr] *m (pl ~)* wine-merchant

Weinkarte [VIGHN-kahr-ter] *f (pl ~n)* wine-list

Weinkeller [VIGHN-keh-lerr] *m (pl ~)* wine-cellar

Weinrebe [VIGHN-ray-ber] *f (pl ~n)* vine

Weintrauben [VIGHN-trow-bern] *fpl* grapes *pl*

weiß [vighs] *adj* white

weise [VIGH-zer] *adj* wise

Weiße [VIGH-ser] *f* whiteness

Weise [VIGH-zer] *f (pl ~n)* manner

* **weisen** [VIGH-zern] *v* direct

Weißfisch [VIGHS-fish] *m (pl ~e)* whiting

Weisheit [VIGHS-hight] *f (pl ~en)* wisdom

weit [vight] *adj* vast

weitermachen [VIGH-terr-mah-khern] *v* carry on

weitverbreitet [vight-fehr-BRIGH-tert] *adj* widespread

Weizen [VIGH-tsern] *m* wheat

welcher [VEHL-kherr] *pron* which; who

welcher auch immer [VEHL-kherr-owkh-I-merr] whichever

Welle [VEH-ler] *f (pl ~n)* wave

Wellenlänge [VEH-lern-lehng-er] *f (pl ~n)* wavelength

Wellenreiterbrett [VEH-lern-righ-terr-breht] *nt (pl ~er)* surfboard

wellig [VEH-likh] *adj* undulating; wavy

Welt [vehlt] *f (pl ~en)* world

Weltall [VEHLT-ahl] *nt* universe

weltberühmt [VEHLT-ber-rewmt] *adj* world famous

Weltkrieg [VEHLT-kreek] *m (pl ~e)* world war

weltumfassend [VEHLT-oom-fah-sernt] *adj* global

weltweit [VEHLT-vight] *adj* world-wide

wem [vaym] *pron* whom

wenden [VEHN-dern] *v* turn

Wendepunkt [VEHN-der-poongkt] *m (pl ~e)* turning point

wenige [VAY-ni-ger] *adj* few

weniger [VAY-ni-gerr] *prep* minus; *adv* less

Wenigste [VAY-niks-ter] *nt* least

wenigstens [VAY-nikh-sterns] *adv* at least

wenn [vehn] *conj* when; if

wer [vayr] *pron* who

wer auch immer [VAYR-owkh-I-merr] whoever

Werbesendung [VEHR-ber-zehn-doong] *f (pl ~en)* commercial

* **werden** [VAYR-dern] *v* become

* **werfen** [VEHR-fern] *v* cast; throw; toss

Werkmeister [VEHRK-mighs-terr] *m (pl ~)* foreman

Werkstatt [VEHRK-shtaht] *f (pl ~̃en)* workshop

Werktag [VEHRK-tark] *m* (*pl* ~e) working day

Werkzeug [VEHRK-tsoyk] *nt* (*pl* ~e) tool

Werkzeugtasche [VEHRK-tsoyk-tah-sher] *f* (*pl* ~n) tool-kit

Wert [vayrt] *m* (*pl* ~e) value; worth

* **wert sein** [VAYRT-zighn] *v* worth (be)

wertlos [VAYRT-loas] *adj* worthless

Wertsachen [VAYRT-zah-khern] *fpl* valuables *pl*

wertvoll [VAYRT-fol] *adj* valuable

Wesen [VAY-zern] *nt* essence; being

Wesensart [VAY-zerns-arrt] *f* nature

wesentlich [VAY-zernt-likh] *adj* vital; essential

Wespe [VEHS-per] *f* (*pl* ~n) wasp

Weste [VEHS-ter] *f* (*pl* ~n) waistcoat; vest

Westen [VEHS-tern] *m* west

Westindien [vehst-IN-dyern] *nt* West Indies *pl*

westlich [VEHST-likh] *adj* western

westwärts [VEHST-vehrts] *adv* westwards

Wettbewerb [VEHT-ber-vehrp] *m* (*pl* ~e) contest

Wettbüro [VEHT-bew-roa] *nt* (*pl* ~s) betting office

Wette [VEH-ter] *f* (*pl* ~n) bet

Wetter [VEH-terr] *nt* weather

Wetterbericht [VEH-terr-ber-rikht] *m* (*pl* ~e) weather report

wichtig [VIKH-tikh] *adj* important

Wichtigkeit [VIKH-tikh-kight] *f* importance

wichtigste [VIKH-tiks-ter] *adj* main; principal

widersetzen (sich) [zikh-vee-derr-ZEH-tsern] *v* oppose

widerspiegeln [VEE-derr-shpee-gerln] *v* reflect

* **widersprechen** [vee-derr-SHPREH-khern] *v* contradict

widmen [VIT-mern] *v* devote

wie [vee] *conj* as; *adv* how; *prep* like

wie zum Beispiel [vee-tsoom-BIGH-shpeel] *v* such as

wieder [VEE-derr] *adv* again

* **wieder beginnen** [vee-derr-ber-GI-nern] *v* recommence

wieder eröffnen [vee-derr-ehr-URF-nern] *v* reopen

wiedererlangen [VEE-derr-ehr-lahng-ern] *v* recover

wiedererstatten [VEE-derr-ehr-shtah-tern] *v* reimburse

wiederholen [vee-derr-HOA-lern] *v* repeat

Wiederholung [vee-derr-HOA-loong] *f* (*pl* ~en) repetition

Wiege [VEE-ger] *f* (*pl* ~n) cradle

* **wiegen** [VEE-gern] *v* weigh

Wiese [VEE-zer] *f* (*pl* ~n) meadow

wild [vilt] *adj* wild; savage; fierce

Wild [vilt] *nt* game

Wildbret [VILT-breht] *nt* venison

Wildleder [VILT-lay-derr] *nt* suede

Wille [VI-ler] *m* will

willig [VI-likh] *adj* willing

willkommen [vil-KO-mern] *adj* welcome

Willkommen [vil-KO-mern] *nt* welcome

Wimperntusche [VIM-perrn-TOO-sher] *f* (*pl* ~n) mascara

Wind [vint] *m* (*pl* ~e) wind

Windel [VIN-derl] *f* (*pl* ~ n) nappy; diaper

* **winden** [VIN-dern] *v* twist; wind

* **winden (sich)** [zikh-VIN-dern] *v* wind

windend (sich) [zikh-VIN-dernt] *adj* winding

windig [VIN-dikh] *adj* windy

Windmühle [VINT-mew-ler] *f (pl ~n)* windmill

Windpocken [VINT-po-kern] *fpl* chicken-pox

Windschutzscheibe [VINT-shoots-shigh-ber] *f (pl ~n)* windscreen; windshield

Windstoß [VINT-shtoas] *m (pl ~e)* gust

winken [VING-kern] *v* wave

Winker [VING-kerr] *m (pl ~)* indicator; trafficator

Winter [VIN-terr] *m* winter

winterlich [VIN-terr-likh] *adj* wintry

Wintersport [VIN-terr-shport] *m* winter sports *pl*

winzig [VIN-tsikh] *adj* minute; tiny

wir [veer] *pron* we

wir selbst [veer-ZEHLPST] *pron* ourselves

wirbeln [VIR-berln] *v* spin

Wirbelsturm [VIR-berl-shtoorm] *m (pl ~e)* hurricane

wirklich [VIRK-likh] *adv* indeed; really; *adj* real

Wirkung [VIR-koong] *f (pl ~en)* effect

wirkungslos [VIR-koongs-loas] *adj* inefficient

wirkungsvoll [VIR-koongs-foll] *adj* effective

Wirtin [VIR-tin] *f (pl ~nen)* landlady

Wirtschaft [VIRT-shahft] *f* economy

wirtschaftlich [VIRT-shahft-likh] *adj* economic

Wirtshaus [VIRTS-hows] *nt (pl ~er)* pub; public house

wischen [VI-shern] *v* wipe

* **wissen** [VI-sern] *v* know

Wissenschaft [VI-sern-shahft] *f (pl ~en)* science

Wissenschaftler [VI-sern-shahft-lerr] *m (pl ~; f ~in)* scientist

wissenschaftlich [VI-sern-shahft-likh] *adj* scientific

Witwe [VIT-ver] *f (pl ~n)* widow

Witwer [VIT-verr] *m (pl ~)* widower

Witz [vits] *m (pl ~e)* joke

wo [voa] *conj* where; where

wo immer [voa-I-merr] wherever

Woche [VO-kher] *f (pl ~n)* week

Wochenende [VO-khern-ehn-der] *nt (pl ~n)* weekend

Wochenschau [VO-khern-show] *f* news-reel

Wochentag [VO-khern-tark] *m (pl ~e)* weekday

wöchentlich [VUR-khernt-likh] *adj* weekly

woher [voa-HAYR] wherefrom

wohlbekannt [VOAL-ber-kahnt] *adj* well-known

wohlhabend [VOAL-har-bernt] *adj* prosperous

Wohlstand [VOAL-shtahnt] *m* prosperity

Wohlwollen [VOAL-vo-lern] *nt* good-will

Wohnblock [VOAN-blok] *m (pl ~e)* block of flats; apartment house

wohnen [VOA-nern] *v* reside

Wohnsitz [VOAN-zits] *m (pl ~e)* residence; domicile

Wohnung [VOA-noong] *f (pl ~en)* flat; apartment

Wohnzimmer [VOAN-tsi-merr] *nt*

(*pl* ~) sitting-room; living-room

Wolf [volf] *m* (*pl* ~e) wolf

Wolke [VOL-ker] *f* (*pl* ~n) cloud

Wolkenbruch [VOL-kern-brookh] *m* (*pl* ~e) cloudburst

Wolkenkratzer [VOL-kern-krah-tserr] *m* (*pl* ~) sky-scraper

Wolldecke [VOL-deh-ker] *f* (*pl* ~n) blanket

Wolle [VO-ler] *f* wool

wollen [VO-lern] *adj* woollen; *v* will; want

Wolljacke [VOL-yah-ker] *f* (*pl* ~n) cardigan

Wollpullover [VOL-poo-loa-verr] *m* (*pl* ~) jersey

Wonne [VO-ner] *f* (*pl* ~n) delight

Wort [vort] *nt* (*pl* ~er) word

Wörterbuch [VURR-terr-bookh] *nt* (*pl* ~er) dictionary

Wortschatz [VORT-shahts] *m* vocabulary

wozu [voa-TSOO] what for

Wrack [vrahk] *nt* (*pl* ~s) wreck

Wuchs [vooks] *m* growth

wund [voont] *adj* sore

Wunde [VOON-der] *f* (*pl* ~n) wound

wunde Stelle [VOON-der-SHTEH-ler] sore

Wunder [VOON-derr] *nt* (*pl* ~) miracle; marvel

wunderbar [VOON-derr-barr] *adj* marvellous; miraculous; wonderful

wundern (sich) [zikh-VOON-derrn] *v* marvel

Wunsch [voonsh] *m* (*pl* ~e) wish

wünschen [VEWN-shern] *v* wish; want; desire

wünschenswert [VEWN-sherns-vayrt] *adj* desirable

Würfel [VEWR-ferl] *m* (*pl* ~) dice; cube

Wurm [voorm] *m* (*pl* ~er) worm

Wurst [voorst] *f* (*pl* ~e) sausage

Würstchen [VEWRST-khern] *nt* (*pl* ~) sausages *pl*

Wurzel [VOOR-tserl] *f* (*pl* ~n) root

würzen [VEWR-tsern] *v* flavour

Wüste [VEWS-ter] *f* (*pl* ~n) desert

Wut [voot] *f* temper

wütend [VEW-ternt] *adj* furious

zäh [tsai] *adj* tough

zählen [TSAI-lern] *v* count

Zähler [TSAI-lerr] *m* (*pl* ~) meter

zahlreich [TSARL-righkh] *adj* numerous

Zahlungsbedingungen [TSAR-loongs-ber-ding-oong-ern] *fpl* terms of payment *pl*

Zahlungsempfänger [TSAR-loongs-ehm-PFEHNG-err] *m* (*pl* ~; *f* ~in) payee

zahm [tsarm] *adj* tame

Zahn [tsarn] *m* (*pl* ~e) tooth

Zahnarzt [TSARN-ahrtst] *m* (*pl* ~e ; *f* ~in) dentist

Zahnbürste [TSARN-bewrs-ter] *f* (*pl* ~n) toothbrush

Zahnfleisch [TSARN-flighsh] *nt* gum

Zahnpasta [TSARN-pahs-tah] *f* toothpaste

Zahnpulver [TSARN-pool-verr] *nt* tooth-powder

Zahnstocher [TSARN-shto-kherr] *m* (*pl* ~) toothpick

Zahnweh [TSARN-vay] *nt* toothache

Zange [TSAHNG-er] *f* (*pl* ~n) tongs *pl*

Zank [tsahngk] *m* quarrel

Zäpfchen [TSEHPF-khern] *nt* (*pl* ~) suppository

zart [tsahrt] *adj* tender

zärtlich [TSAIRT-likh] *adj* affectionate

Zauberei [tsow-ber-RIGH] *f* (*pl* ~en) magic

Zaun [tsown] *m* (*pl* ~̈e) fence

Zebrastreifen [TSAY-brah-shtrigh-fern] *m* (*pl* ~) crosswalk

Zehe [TSAY-er] *f* (*pl* ~n) toe

zehn [tsayn] *adj* ten

zehnte [TSAYN-ter] *adj* tenth

Zeichen [TSIGH-khern] *nt* (*pl* ~) sign; mark

zeichnen [TSIGHKH-nern] *v* mark; draw

Zeichnung [TSIGHKH-noong] *f* (*pl* ~en) drawing

zeigen [TSIGH-gern] *v* show; indicate

Zeile [TSIGH-ler] *f* (*pl* ~n) line

Zeit [tsight] *f* (*pl* ~en) time

Zeitabschnitt [TSIGHT-ahp-shnit] *m* (*pl* ~e) period

zeitgenössisch [TSIGHT-ger-nur-sish] *adj* contemporary

Zeitschrift [TSIGHT-shrift] *f* (*pl* ~en) periodical; review; magazine; journal

Zeitung [TSIGH-toong] *f* (*pl* ~ en) newspaper; paper

Zeitungshändler [TSIGH-toongs-hehn-dlerr] *m* (*pl* ~) newsagent

Zeitungsstand [TSIGH-toongs-shtahnt] *m* (*pl* ~̈ e) newsstand

zeitweilig [TSIGHT-vigh-likh] *adj* temporary

Zeitwort [TSIGHT-vort] *nt* (*pl* ~̈er) verb

Zelle [TSEH-ler] *f* (*pl* ~n) booth; cell

Zelt [tsehlt] *nt* (*pl* ~e) tent

zelten [TSEHL-tern] *v* camp

Zement [tsay-MEHNT] *m* cement

Zensor [TSEHN-zor] *m* (*pl* ~en) censor

Zensur [tsehn-ZOOR] *f* (*pl* ~en) censorship

Zentimeter [TSEHN-ti-may-terr] *m* (*pl* ~) centimetre

zentral [tsehn-TRARL] *adj* central

Zentralheizung [tsehn-TRARL-high-tsoong] *f* (*pl* ~en) central heating

zentralisieren [tsehn-trah-li-ZEE-rern] *v* centralize

Zentrum [TSEHN-troom] *nt* centre

zerbrechlich [tsehr-BREHKH-likh] *adj* fragile

zerhacken [tsehr-HAH-kern] *v* mince

zerknittern [tsehr-KNI-terrn] *v* crease

zerlegen [tsehr-LAY-gern] *v* carve

zerquetschen [tsehr-KVEH-chern] *v* crush

* **zerreißen** [tsehr-RIGH-sern] *v* tear

Zerstäuber [tsehr-SHTOY-berr] *m* (*pl* ~) atomizer

Zerstörung [tsehr-SHTUR-roong] *f* (*pl* ~en) destruction

Zeuge [TSOY-ger] *m* (*pl* ~n; *f* ~in) witness

Zeugnis [TSOYK-nis] *nt* (*pl* ~se) certificate

Ziege [TSEE-ger] *f* (*pl* ~n) goat

Ziegel [TSEE-gerl] *m* (*pl* ~) brick

Ziegenleder [TSEE-gern-lay-derr] *nt* kid

* **ziehen** [TSEE-ern] *v* pull; draw; extract

Ziehen [TSEE-ern] *nt* extraction

Ziehung [TSEE-oong] *f* (*pl* ~en) draw

Ziel [tseel] *nt* (*pl* ~e) goal; aim

ziemlich [TSEEM-likh] *adv* fairly; somewhat

Zigarette [tsi-gah-REH-ter] *f (pl ~n)* cigarette

Zigarettenetui [tsi-gah-REH-tern-ay-TVEE] *nt (pl ~s)* cigarette-case

Zigarettenspitze [tsi-gah-REH-tern-shpi-tser] *f (pl ~n)* cigarette-holder

Zigarre [tsi-GAH-rer] *f (pl ~n)* cigar

Zigarrenladen [tsi-GAH-rern-lar-dern] *m (pl ~)* cigar-store

Zigeuner [tsi-GOY-nerr] *m (pl ~; f ~in)* gypsy

Zimmer [TSI-merr] *nt (pl ~)* room

Zimmer mit Frühstück [TSI-merr-mit-FREW-shtewk] bed and breakfast

Zimmer mit Vollpension [TSI-merr-mit-FOL-pahng-syoan] room and board

Zimmerbedienung [TSI-merr-ber-DEE-noong] *f* room service

Zimmerflucht [TSI-merr-flookht] *f* suite

Zimmermädchen [TSI-merr-meht-khern] *nt (pl ~)* chambermaid

Zink [tsingk] *nt* zinc

Zinn [tsin] *nt* pewter

Zins [tsins] *m (pl ~en)* interest

Zirkus [TSIR-koos] *m* circus

Zitat [tsi-TART] *nt (pl ~e)* quotation

zitieren [tsi-TEE-rern] *v* quote

Zitrone [tsi-TROA-ner] *f (pl ~n)* lemon

zittern [TSI-terrn] *v* shiver; tremble

zivil [tsi-VEEL] *adj* civil

Zivilisation [tsi-vi-li-zah-TSYOAN] *f (pl ~en)* civilization

Zivilist [tsi-vi-LIST] *m (pl ~en)* civilian

zögern [TSUR-gerrn] *v* hesitate

Zoll [tsol] *m (pl ~̈e)* Customs duty; duty

Zollamt [TSOL-ahmt] *nt (pl ~̈er)* Customs house

Zollbehörde [TSOL-ber-hurr-der] *f (pl ~n)* Customs *pl*

zollfrei [TSOL-frigh] *adj* duty-free

Zollkontrolle [TSOL-kon-tro-ler] *f (pl ~n)* Customs examination

Zöllner [TSURL-nerr] *m (pl ~)* Customs officer

zollpflichtig [TSOL-pflikh-tikh] *adj* dutiable

Zone [TSOA-ner] *f (pl ~n)* zone

Zoo [tsoa] *m (pl ~s)* zoo

Zoologie [tsoa-oa-loa-GEE] *f* zoology

Zoologischer Garten [tsoa-oa-LOA-gi-sherr-GAHR-tern] zoological gardens *pl*

Zorn [tsorn] *m* anger

zornig [TSOR-nikh] *adj* angry

zu [tsoo] *adv* too; *prep* towards

zu Fuß [tsoo-FOOS] on foot; walking

zu verkaufen [tsoo-fehr-KOW-fern] for sale

zu vermieten [tsoo-fehr-MEE-tern] for hire

Zubehör [TSOO-ber-hurr] *nt* accessories *pl*

Zucker [TSOO-kerr] *m* sugar

Zuckerkrankheit [TSOO-kerr-krahngk-hight] *f* diabetes

zuerst [tsoo-AYRST] *adv* at first

Zufall [TSOO-fahl] *m (pl ~̈e)* chance

zufällig [TSOO-feh-likh] *adv* by chance; *adj* accidental; incidental zufällig **begegnen** [TSOO-feh-likh-ber-GAYG-nern] *v* run into

zufrieden [TSOO-FREE-dern] *adj* satisfied; contented; content

zufriedenstellen [TSOO-FREE-dern-shteh-lern] *v* satisfy

Zug [tsook] *m* (*pl* ~e) train

Zugang [TSOO-gahng] *m* approach

zügeln [TSEW-gerln] *v* curb

zuhause [tsoo-HOW-zer] *adv* at home

zuhören [TSOO-hur-rern] *v* listen

Zuhörer [TSOO-hur-rerr] *m* (*pl* ~; *f* ~in) listener

Zukunft [TSOO-koonft] *f* future

zum Beispiel [tsoom-BIGH-shpeel] for instance; for example

Zunahme [TSOO-nar-mer] *f* (*pl* ~n) increase

Zündkerze [TSEWNT-kehr-tser] *f* (*pl* ~n) sparking-plug

Zündung [TSEWN-doong] *f* (*pl* ~en) ignition

Zunge [TSOONG-er] *f* (*pl* ~n) tongue

zur Ansicht [tsoor-AHN-zikht] on approval

zurück [tsoo-REWK] *adv* backwards; back

* zurückbringen [tsoo-REWK-bring-ern] *v* bring back

* zurückgehen [tsoo-REWK-gay-ern] *v* go back; get back

zurückkehren [tsoo-REWK-kay-rern] *v* return

* zurücksenden [tsoo-REWK-zehn-dern] *v* send back

* zurücktreten [tsoo-REWK-tray-tern] *v* resign

* zurückweisen [tsoo-REWK-vigh-zern] *v* reject

zurückzahlen [tsoo-REWK-tsar-lern] *v* repay

* zurückziehen [tsoo-REWK-tsee-ern] *v* withdraw

zusammen [tsoo-ZAH-mern] *adv* together

Zusammenarbeit [tsoo-ZAH-mern-ahr-bight] *f* co-operation

* zusammenbrechen [tsoo-ZAH-mern-breh-khern] *v* collapse

Zusammenfassung [tsoo-ZAH-mern-fah-soong] *f* (*pl* ~en) summary

Zusammenkunft [tsoo-ZAH-mern-koonft] *f* (*pl* ~e) assembly

Zusammenstoß [tsoo-ZAH-mern-shtoas] *m* (*pl* ~e) collision; crash

* zusammenstoßen [tsoo-ZAH-mern-shtoa-sern] *v* collide

zusätzlich [tsoo-zehts-likh] *adj* additional; extra

Zuschauer [tsoo-show-err] *m* (*pl* ~; *f* ~in) spectator

Zuschlag [tsoo-shlark] *m* (*pl* ~e) surcharge

Zustand [tsoo-shtahnt] *m* (*pl* ~e) state

zustande bringen [tsoo-SHTAHN-der-bring-ern] *v* accomplish

zustimmen [tsoo-shti-mern] *v* agree

Zustimmung [tsoo-shti-moong] *f* (*pl* ~en) consent

Zutaten [tsoo-tar-tern] *fpl* ingredient

Zutritt [tsoo-trit] *m* admittance; access

zuverlässig [tsoo-fehr-leh-sikh] *adj* reliable; trustworthy

zuversichtlich [tsoo-fehr-zikht-likh] *adj* confident

zuviel [tsoo-FEEL] *adv* too much

zuviel fordern [tsoo-FIAYL-FOR-derrn] *v* overcharge

zwanglos [TSVAHNG-loas] *adj* casual

zwanzig [TSVAHN-tsikh] *adj* twenty

zwanzigste [TSVAHN-tsiks-ter] *adj* twentieth

zwei [tsvigh] *adj* two

zweifelhaft [TSVIGH-ferl-hahft] *adj* doubtful

zweifeln [TSVIGH-ferln] *v* doubt

Zweig [TSVIGHK] *m* (*pl* ~e) twig

Zweiggeschäft [TSVIGHK-ger-shehft] *nt* (*pl* ~e) chain-store

zweimal [TSVIGH-marl] *adv* twice

zweite [TSVIGH-ter] *adj* second

zweiteilig [TSVIGH-tigh-likh] *adj* two-piece

zweitklassig [TSVIGHT-klah-sikh] *adj* second-class

Zwiebel [TSVEE-berl] *f* (*pl* ~n) onion

Zwielicht [TSVEE-likht] *nt* twilight

Zwilling [TSVI-ling] *m* (*pl* ~e) twins *pl*

* **zwingen** [TSVING-ern] *v* force; compel

zwischen [TSVI-shern] *prep* between

Zwischenfall [TSVI-shern-fahl] *m* (*pl* ~e) incident

Zwischenraum [TSVI-shern-rowm] *m* (*pl* ~e) space

Zwischenspiel [TSVI-shern-shpeel] *nt* (*pl* ~e) interlude

Zwischenstock [TSVI-shern-shtok] *m* (*pl* ~e) mezzanine

Zwischenzeit [TSVI-shern-tsahit] *f* (*pl* ~en) interim

zwölf [tsvurlf] *adj* twelve

zwölfte [TSVURLF-ter] *adj* twelfth

Zyklus [TSEW-kloos] *m* (*pl* Zyklen) cycle

Zylinder [tsew-LIN-derr] *m* (*pl* ~) cylinder

Menu Reader

FOOD

Aal eel
  geräucherter ~ smoked eel
  ~**suppe** eel soup
Abendbrot, Abendessen evening dinner, supper
Allgäuer Bergkäse hard cow's milk cheese from Bavaria resembling *Emmentaler* (swiss cheese)
Allgäuer Rahmkäse a Bavarian cheese like French *brie,* it is creamy but milder
Altenburger a mild, soft goat's milk cheese (Thuringia)
Ananas (mit Sahne) pineapple (and cream)
Anis aniseed
Anken butter
Apfel apple
  ~**kuchen** apple cake
  ~**mus** apple sauce
  ~**saft** apple juice
  ~**schnitzchen** apple fritters
  ~**strudel** paper-thin layers of pastry filled with apple slices, nuts, raisins and jam
  ~**torte** apple tart
Apfelsine orange
Appenzeller (Käse) a mild, firm cheese (Swiss)
Appetithäppchen appetizers, e.g., canapes
Aprikose apricot

Artischocke (globe) artichoke
  ~**nboden** artichoke hearts (US artichoke bottoms)
Aubergine aubergine (US eggplant)
Auflauf 1) soufflé 2) a meat, fish, fowl, fruit or vegetable dish which is oven-browned
Aufschnitt cold cuts
Austern oysters
Backerbsensuppe broth served with small, round croutons
Backforelle baked trout
Backhuhn fried chicken
Backobst dried fruit
Backpflaumen prunes
Backsteinkäse strong cheese from Bavaria resembling *Limburger*
Backwerk pastries, baked goods
Banane banana
Barsch bass, sea perch
Bauernbrot rye or whole wheat bread
Bauernfrühstück "farmer's breakfast"; usually consists of eggs, bacon, potatoes
Bauernomelett diced bacon and onion omelet
Bauernschmaus sauerkraut garnished with bacon, smoked pork, sausages, dumplings, potatoes (Austria)
Bauernsuppe "farmer's soup"; a

thick soup of sliced frankfurters and cabbage

Baumnüsse walnuts

Bedienung service, service charge
~ **(e)inbegriffen** service included

Beefsteak beef steak
deutsches ~ a chopped beef patty sometimes topped with a fried egg

Beere berry

Beilage 1) side dish 2) sometimes a garnish

belegtes Brot open-face sandwich

Berliner Pfannkuchen jam-filled doughnut (US bismarck, jelly doughnut)

Berner Platte a mound of sauerkraut (or sometimes boiled potatoes) liberally garnished with pork chops, boiled bacon and beef, sausages, tongue, and/or ham (Swiss)

Beuschel pig's lung in a slightly sour sauce (Austria)

Bienenstich honey-almond cake

Bierrettich black-skinned or white radish, generally cut and salted as an accompaniment to beer

Biersuppe a sweet, spicy soup from beer

Birchermus, Birchermüsli a cold porridge with fruit and milk, often with nuts added

Birne pear

Bischofsbrot fruit-nut cake

Bismarckhering soused herring, seasoned with onions

Blätterteig puff pastry

blau "blue"; 1) of fish, usually trout, cooked very fresh 2) of meat, rare

Blaubeeren blueberries

Blaukraut red cabbage

Blumenkohl cauliflower

Blutwurst black (blood) pudding (sausage)

Bockwurst a larger variety of frankfurter

Bohnen beans
grüne ~ french beans (US green beans)
~**suppe** french bean soup with diced bacon
weiße ~ butter beans, dried white beans

Bouillon bouillon, broth, consommé
~ **mit Ei** with raw egg

Brachse, Brasse sea bream

Bratapfel baked apple

Braten roast, joint
~**sauce** gravy, sauce

Bratfisch fried fish

Brathähnchen, Brathendl, Brathuhn roast chicken

Bratkartoffeln roast potatoes

Bratwurst pork or veal frying sausage

Braunschweiger Kuchen "Brunswick cake"; rich fruit-almond cake

Brei porridge, mash, paste, purée

Brezel pretzel

Bries (gebacken) (fried) calf gland (Austria)
~ **chen,** ~ **el** veal sweetbreads

Brombeeren blackberries

Bröselbohnen french beans with toasted breadcrumbs (Austria)

Brot bread
Bauern~ rye or whole wheat bread
Grau~ grey bread
Schwarz~ black bread, pumpernickel
~**suppe** soup of stale bread

Weiß ~ white bread
Brötchen roll
Brühe broth, consommé
Brunnenkresse watercress
Brust breast
  ~ **stück** brisket
Bückling bloater, smoked herring
Bulette meat or fish ball
Bündnerfleisch cured, dried beef served in paper-thin slices (Grissons)
Butt flounder, turbot
Butter butter
  ~ **mit Brot** bread and butter
  ~ **milch** buttermilk
Champignon button mushroom
Chateaubriand thick steak of prime beef (US tenderloin)
Chicorée endive
Cornichons gherkins (pickles)
Creme cream, custard
  ~ **schnitten** napoleon
Dampfbraten stew (usually of beef)
Dampfnudeln steamed sweet dumplings
Datteln dates
deutsches Beefsteak a chopped beef patty sometimes topped with a fried egg
Dill dill
  ~ **sauce** dill sauce
Donaukarpfen Danube River carp
Dörrobst dried fruit
Dorsch a variety of codfish
Dotterkäse cheese made from skimmed milk and egg yolk
durchgebraten well-done, well-cooked
  nicht ~ underdone (US rare)
Edamer (Käse) German variety of *edam* cheese; firm and round, red rind and yellow interior
Egli perch

Ei egg
  ~ **dotter,** ~ **gelb** egg yolk
  hartgekochtes ~ hard-boiled egg
  ~ **schnee** beaten egg whites
  weichgekochtes ~ soft-boiled egg
  ~ **weiß** egg white
Eier eggs
  ~ **auflauf** omelet
  ~ **creme** custard
  gefüllte ~ stuffed eggs
  ~ **kuchen** a type of wheatflour pancake, sometimes filled
  Rühr ~ scrambled eggs
  russische ~ hard-boiled eggs served with diced, cooked vegetables in mayonnaise
  ~ **mit Speck** eggs and bacon
  ~ **speise** egg dish
  Spiegel ~ fried eggs, sunny side up
  verlorene ~ poached eggs
Eierschwämme, Eierschwammerl chanterelle mushrooms
einbegriffen included
  Bedienung ~ service included
eingemacht preserved (of fruit, vegetables, etc.)
Eintopf stew (usually of meat and vegetables)
Eis ice, ice-cream
  Erdbeer ~ strawberry ice-cream
  Mokka ~ coffee-flavoured ice-cream
  Vanille ~ vanilla ice-cream
Eisbein mit Sauerkraut pickled pig's knuckles with sauerkraut
Eisbombe ice-cream dessert
Eischnee beaten egg whites
Eiweiß egg white
Emmentaler (Käse) a semi-hard, robust cheese with holes, swiss cheese

Ente duck, duckling
  gebratene ~ roast duck
  ~nbrust breast of duck
  ~nleber duck liver
Erbsen peas
  ~suppe pea soup
Erdapfel potato
Erdbeeren strawberries
Erdnüsse peanuts
errötende Jungfrau "blushing virgin"; raspberries with cream
Essig vinegar
  ~gurke gherkin, pickle
  ~kren horseradish in vinegar, spices and sugar
  ~pilze pickled mushrooms
Eßkastanien chestnuts
Extraaufschlag extra charge, supplementary charge
Fadennudeln thin noodles, vermicelli
Fasan pheasant
faschierte Laibchen meat balls
Faschiertes minced meat, chopped meat
Feigen figs
Felchen lake salmon, salmon trout
Fenchel fennel
fertig ready, done
(zu) festem Preis meal at a set price
fett fat, greasy
Fett fat, lard
Filet fillet
Fisch fish
  ~croutons fishballs
  ~schüssel casserole of fish and diced bacon
  ~suppe fish soup
Fladen biscuits (US cookies), tart
Flädle, Flädli thin strips of pancake added to soup
flambiert flambé, a dish set aflame with alcohol
Flammeri a pudding usually made of semolina
Fleisch meat
  ~brühe consommé, broth
  ~eintopf meat stew
  ~gerichte meat dishes
  ~käse a type of meat loaf
  ~klöße meat balls
  ~pastete meat purée, pâté
  ~speise meat dish
  ~vögel slices of meat rolled around a filling and braised
Flunder flounder, sole
Forelle trout
  ~ blau very fresh trout poached in a vinegar broth
Frankfurter (Würstchen) frankfurter (sausages)
Frikadelle meat ball
frisch fresh, cool
Froschschenkel froglegs
Frucht fruit
  ~ nach Jahreszeit fruit in season
  ~salat fruit cocktail
Frühlingssuppe vegetable soup
Frühstück breakfast
  ~skäse a strong cheese with a smooth texture
Füllung stuffing, filling, forcemeat
Fürst-Pückler-Eisbombe lightly-frozen ice-cream dessert
Gabelfrühstück brunch
Gans goose
  gebratene ~ roast goose
Gänse geese
  ~brust breast of goose
  ~klein goose giblets
  ~leber goose liver
  ~leberpastete goose liver paste, goose pâté
Garnelen shrimp
Gebäck pastry

gebacken baked
gebraten roasted, fried
gedämpft steamed
Gedeck meal at a fixed price
gedünstet stewed, boiled
Geflügel fowl
  ~**frikassee** fricassee of chicken
  ~**klein** giblets
  ~**leber** chicken liver
  ~**salat** chicken salad
Gefrorenes ice-cream
gefüllt stuffed
  ~**e Eier** stuffed eggs
  ~**e Kalbsbrust** breast of veal stuffed and fried
  ~**e Kartoffeln** stuffed potatoes
  ~**e Paprika(schoten)** green peppers stuffed with minced meat and sometimes rice
  ~**e Tomaten** tomatoes filled with minced meat or rice
gegrillt grilled, broiled
gehackt minced, chopped, hashed, diced
Gehacktes minced meat (US chopped meat)
gekocht cooked, boiled
Gelee aspic, jelly
gemischt mixed
  ~**er Salat** mixed salad
Gemüse vegetables
  ~**salat** vegetable salad
gepökelt pickled, salted, cured
geräuchert smoked
  ~**er Aal** smoked eel
  ~**er Lachs** smoked salmon
geröstet roasted
Gerste barley
gesalzen salted
geschmort stewed, braised
  ~**e Rinderbrust** beef braised with vegetables
Geschnetzeltes meat cut into thin strips

Geselchtes smoked or salted meat (usually pork) (Bavaria, Austria)
gesotten stewed, simmered in its own juice
gesottenes Rindfleisch boiled beef and vegetables (often served with horseradish sauce)
gespickt larded
  ~**es Rinderfilet** larded beef tenderloin
gesülzt jellied, in aspic
Gewürz spice
  ~**kuchen** spiced cakes or biscuits (US ginger cookies)
  ~**nelken** cloves
gewürzt spiced
Gipfel crescent-shaped roll
Gitzi kid goat
Glace ice-cream
Gnagi cured pig's knuckle, shank
Granatapfel pomegranate
Grapefruit grapefruit
gratiniert oven-browned, gratinéed
Graupensuppe barley soup
Greyerzer (Käse) a cheese, rich in flavour, smooth in texture (Swiss)
Griebenwurst a sausage with chunks of rendered fat
Grieß semolina
  ~**klößchen** semolina dumplings
(vom) Grill, grilliert grilled
groß big
Gröstl hashed-browned potatoes (Austrian)
grün green
  ~**e Bohnen** green beans, string beans
  ~**e Oliven** green olives
Grünkohl kale
Gschwellti potato boiled in its jacket

Gugelhopf, Gugelhupf a moulded cake with a hole in the centre, usually has raisins and almonds

Güggeli spring chicken

Gulasch goulash

Gurke cucumber
~ **nsalat** cucumber salad

gut durchgebraten well-done, well-cooked

Hachse knuckle, shank

Hackbraten meat loaf, baked minced meat

Hackfleisch minced or chopped meat

Hafer oats
~ **brei**, ~ **grütze** oatmeal porridge
~ **flocken** oatmeal (flakes)
~ **suppe** oatmeal soup

Hähnchen spring chicken

halb half
~ **durchgebraten** medium-done (US medium-rare)

Hamme ham

Hammel(fleisch) mutton
~ **frikassee** mutton stew
~ **keule** leg of mutton
~ **kotelett** mutton chop
~ **schulter** shoulder of mutton

Handkäse piquant cheese with a pungent taste and smell; made from sour milk

Hase hare
~ **nbraten** roast hare
~ **npfeffer** jugged hare, fried and braised in its marinade liquid and sour cream

Haselnüsse hazelnuts

Haselnußtorte hazelnut tart

von Haus, hausgemacht home-made, home cooked

Hausmannskost good, simple meal

Haxe shank, knuckle

Hecht pike

Hefekranz ring-shaped coffee cake

Heidelbeeren bilberries (US blueberries)

Heilbutt halibut

heiß hot

Hering herring
~ **Hausfrauenart** "herring in the housewife's style"; herring fillet with onions in sour cream
Matjes~ salted sprats
Räucher~ smoked herring
~ **skartoffeln** a casserole of layers of herring and potatoes

Herz heart

Himbeeren raspberries

Himmel und Erde "heaven and earth"; a mixture of mashed potatoes, apple sauce, onions. diced bacon and meat

Hirn brains

Hirsch venison (deer)
~ **braten** roast venison
~ **keule** leg of venison

hohe Rippe prime ribs of beef

Holsteiner Schnitzel breaded veal cutlet served with vegetables and topped with a fried egg

Honig honey

Hörnchen crescent-shaped roll

Huhn hen

Hühnchen chicken

Hühnerbrühe chicken broth

Hühnerleber chicken liver

Hülsenfrüchte pulse, i.e., beans, peas, lentils, etc.

Hummer lobster

Hutzelbrot bread filled with raisins (or other dried fruit)

(gespickter) Igel "hedgehog"; a chocolate cake with almonds protruding from the top

Imbiß snack
inbegriffen included
   Bedienung ~ service included
Indianer(krapfen) chocolate meringue with whipped cream filling
Ingwer ginger
italienischer Salat diced vegetables in mayonnaise
(nach) Jägerart "in the hunter's style"; sautéed with mushrooms and sometimes onions
Joghurt yoghurt
Johannisbeeren red currants
   schwarze ~ black currants
jung young, spring
   ~e Erbsen spring peas
Jungfernbraten roast pork with bacon
Kabeljau cod
Kaffeekuchen coffee cake
Kaiserschmarren shredded pancake with raisins served with syrup
Kalb(fleisch) veal
   ~ sbraten roast veal
   ~ sbrust breast of veal
   ~ shachse, **~ shaxe** calf's knuckle, shank
   ~ shirn calf's brains
   ~ skopf calf's head
   ~ skotelett veal cutlet
   ~ sleber calf's liver
   ~ slende veal tenderloin, veal fillet
   ~ smilch veal sweetbreads
   ~ snierenbraten roast veal tenderloin, sometimes with kidney stuffing
   ~ srippchen veal cutlet, veal chop
   ~ sschnitzel veal scallop, veal cutlet
Kaldaunen tripe

kalt cold
   ~e Speisen cold cuts, cold dishes
   ~er Braten cold roast
Kaltschale chilled fruit soup
Kammuscheln scallops
kandierte Früchte candied fruit
Kaninchen rabbit
Kapaun capon
Kapern capers
Karamelcreme caramel custard
Karfiol cauliflower
Karotten carrots
Karpfen carp
Kartoffel potato
   ~ brei mashed potatoes
   ~ klöße, **~ knödel** potato dumplings
   gedämpfte ~n steamed potatoes
   gekochte ~n boiled potatoes
   geröstete ~ roast potatoes
   Pell ~n potatoes boiled in their jackets
   ~ puffer potato fritters
   ~ püree mashed potatoes
   ~ salat potato salad
   ~ stock mashed potatoes
   ~ suppe potato soup
   Petersil~n boiled potatoes garnished with minced parsley
Käse cheese
   ~ kuchen cheesecake
   ~ platte cheeseboard
   ~ stangen cheese straws, cheese sticks
Kasseler Rippchen or **Rippenspeer** smoked pork chops, often served with sauerkraut
Kastanien chestnuts
Katenrauchschinken country-style smoked ham
Katzenjammer cold slices of beef in mayonnaise with cucumbers

or gherkins

Kaviar caviar

Kekse biscuits (US cookies)

Kerbel chervil

Kesselfleisch fresh pork, boiled, garnished with vegetables

Keule leg, haunch

Kieler Sprotten smoked sprats

Kipfel crescent-shaped roll

Kirschen cherries

Kirschtorte cherry tart usually flavoured with *kirsch* (cherry brandy)

klein small

~**es Gebäck** sweet rolls, pastries

Klops fried meat ball

Kloß dumpling

Klößchen small dumpling

Knackwurst a lightly-flavoured garlic sausage, generally boiled

Knoblauch garlic

Knochen bone

Knödel dumpling

Kohl cabbage

~**roulade** cabbage leaves stuffed with minced meat

Konfitüre jam, jelly

Königinpastetchen puff-pastry shell filled with diced meat and mushrooms

Königinsuppe chicken soup with almonds and sour cream

Königsberger Klöpse cooked meat balls in white caper sauce

Köpfli a pudding usually made of semolina

Kopfsalat green salad, lettuce salad

Korinthen currants. raisins

Kotelett chop

Krabben prawns

Kraftbrühe broth, consommé

~ **mit Ei** with raw egg added

Krainer spiced pork sausage (Austria)

Kranzkuchen ring-shaped cake

Krapfen jelly doughnut (US bismarck) (Austria)

Kraut cabbage

~**wickel** cabbage leaves with minced meat stuffing

Krebs crayfish, crawfish

Kren horseradish

~**fleisch** cooked pork, usually the head

Kresse watercress

Kroketten croquettes

Kuchen cake

Kümmel caraway seed

~**brot** caraway bread

~**käse** cheese with caraway seeds

Kürbis pumpkin, gourd

Kutteln tripe

Labskaus thick stew of minced and marinated meat with mashed potatoes

Lachs salmon

~**forelle** salmon trout

geräucherter ~ smoked salmon

Lamm(fleisch) lamb

~**braten** roast lamb

~**keule** leg of lamb

~**kotelett** lamb chop

Languste spiny lobster

Lattich lettuce

Lauch(gemüse) leeks

Leber liver

~**käs** type of meat loaf

~**knödel,** ~**nockerln** liver dumplings

~**spätzle** small, short, thick liver noodles

~ **(Wiener) Art** grilled liver and onions

~**wurst** liver sausage

Lebkuchen gingerbread

Leckerli ginger biscuits (US ginger cookies) (Switzerland)

legiert thickened, usually with egg yolk (refers to sauces or soups)

Lende loin
~ **nbraten** roast sirloin
~ **nstück** choice fillet

Limburger yellowish, semi-hard cheese, smells and tastes strong

Linsen lentils
~ **suppe (mit Bauernwurst)** lentil soup (with spiced sausage)

Linzertorte almond cake or tart with a raspberry topping

Lunge lights (lungs of an animal)

Mahlzeit meal

Mainauer semi-hard, full-cream cheese; round with a red rind and yellow interior

Mainzer Rippchen pork chops

Mais maize, corn

Majoran marjoram

Makkaroni macaroni

Makrele mackerel

Makrone macaroon

Mandarine tangerine, mandarin

Mandel almond
~ **torte** almond cake

Marillen apricots
~ **knödel** apricot dumpling or fritter

mariniert marinated, pickled

Mark (bone) marrow
~ **knödel** marrow dumpling

Marmelade jam

Marmorgugelhupf a moulded cake with a marbled appearance; cake is moulded with a hole in the centre

Maronen roasted chestnuts

Marzipan marzipan, almond paste

Mastente fattened duckling

Masthähnchen fattened chicken

Matjeshering salted sprats

Matrosenbrot a sandwich with chopped hard-boiled eggs, anchovies and seasoning

Maultaschen small dough envelopes filled with meat, vegetables and seasoning

Mayonnaise mayonnaise

Meerrettich horseradish

Mehl flour
~ **nockerln** dumpling
~ **speise** pudding or pastry
~ **suppe** brown flour soup

Melone melon

Menü meal at a fixed price

Meringe meringue

Mettwurst highly-spiced sausage

Miesmuscheln mussels

Milke veal sweetbreads

Mirabelle small yellow plum

Mittagessen noon dinner, lunch

Mohn poppy seeds
~ **brötchen** poppy-seed rolls
~ **kuchen** poppy-seed cake

Mohrenkopf "Moor's head"; chocolate meringue with whipped cream filling

Mohrrüben carrots

Mondseer Austrian semi-hard fermented cheese

Morcheln morels

Morgenessen breakfast

Morgenrötesuppe thick soup of meat, tapioca, tomatoes, and chicken stock

Mostrich mustard

Mus mousse, stewed fruit

Muscheln shellfish, usually refers to mussels

Muskat(nuß) nutmeg

Nachspeise, Nachtisch dessert, sweet

natur plain

Nelken cloves

Nidel cream
Nieren kidneys
  ~**stück** loin
Nockerln dumplings
Nudel noodle
  ~**suppe** noodle soup
Nürnberger Bratwurst pork sausage flavoured with marjoram
Nuß nut
  ~**kipferl** nut-filled crescent-shaped rolls
  ~**strudel** layers of paper-thin pastry with nuts and honey
  ~**torte** nut cake
Obst fruit
  ~**kuchen** fruit cake
  ~**salat** fruit cocktail
  ~**sauce** sweet-sour sauce
  ~**torte** fruit tart
Ochs(enfleisch) beef
  ~**enauge** fried egg
  ~**enbraten** roast beef
  ~**enmaulsalat** cooked ox muzzle in vinegar dressing
  ~**enschwanzsuppe** oxtail soup with herbs and red wine
  ~**enzunge** ox tongue
Öl oil
  ~**sardinen** sardines in oil
Oliven olives
  ~**öl** olive oil
Omelett(e) omelet
Orange orange
  ~**nmarmelade** marmalade
Palatschinken pancakes usually filled with jam, cheese, sausages or nuts and sometimes served with a hot chocolate and nut topping (Austria)
Pampelmuse grapefruit
paniert breaded
  ~**e Eier** eggs fried in breadcrumbs
Paprika 1) paprika 2) sweet pepper
  gefüllte ~**(schoten)** sweet peppers filled with chopped meat and/or rice
  ~**gulasch** highly-seasoned goulash
Paradeis(er) tomato
Pastetchen filled puff-pastry shell
Pastete a purée or loaf of meat, fish, fowl or vegetables
Patisserie pastries
Pellkartoffeln potatoes boiled in their jackets
Petersilie parsley
Petersilkartoffeln parslied potatoes
Pfannkuchen pancake
Pfeffer pepper
  ~**kuchen** variety of gingerbread
Pfeffernüsse gingernuts
Pfifferlinge chanterelle mushrooms
Pfirsich peach
  ~ **Melba** peaches poached in syrup and topped with ice-cream and raspberry jam
Pflaumen plums
Pfluten a variety of dumpling
Pichelsteiner (Fleisch) a meat and vegetable stew
pikant piquant
Pilze mushrooms
Platte platter
Plattfisch plaice
Plätzchen biscuit (US cookie)
Plätzli scallop, cutlet
pochiert poached
Pökelfleisch marinated meat
Pomeranzensauce sauce of Seville oranges, wine and brandy, usually as an accompaniment to duck
Pommes frites chips (US french fries)

Poulet chicken
Pralinen pralines, chocolates with a sweet filling
Preiselbeeren cranberries
Preßkopf jellied head of pork
Printen honey-flavoured biscuits (US honey-flavoured cookies)
Pudding custard, pudding
Pumpernickel black rye bread, pumpernickel
Püree mash, purée
Puter turkey
~ **braten** roast turkey
Quargl a soft, small, round fermented cheese with a pungent taste and odor
Quark a mild cottage cheese
~ **speise** a mild cottage cheese mixed with sugar and served as dessert
Quitte quince
Radieschen radishes
Ragout stew
Rahm cream
~ **gulasch** goulash with cream sauce
~ **käse** cream cheese
~ **schnitzel** veal scallop in cream sauce
~ **torte** cream tart
Randen beetroot
Rast(aurations)brot large openface sandwich
Räucheraal smoked eel
Räucherhering smoked herring
Räucherlachs smoked salmon
Räucherspeck smoked bacon
Rebhuhn partridge
Rechnung bill (US check)
Regensburger (Wurst) a highly-spiced smoked pork sausage
Reh roe, venison
~ **braten** roast venison
~ **keule** haunch of venison

~ **rücken** saddle of venison
~ **schlegel** leg of venison
Reibekuchen potato fritters
Reibkäse grated cheese
Reineclaude greengage
Reis rice
~ **auflauf** rice pudding often served with fruit sauce
~ **fleisch** veal or pork braised with rice, tomatoes and other vegetables
Rettich large radish
Rhabarber rhubarb
Rheinsalm Rhine River salmon
Ribisel red currants
schwarze ~ black currants
Rind(fleisch) beef
~ **erbraten** roast beef
~ **erleber** beef liver
~ **ermark** beef marrow
~ **errouladen** beef olives; slices of beef rolled and stuffed with a variety of fillings
~ **schnitzel** beef steak
Ringlotte greengage
Rippe rib
Rippchen, Rippenspeer, Rippenstück, Rippli chop (usually smoked pork)
Rochen skate, ray
Rogen roe (generally cod's roe)
Roggenbrot rye bread
roh raw
~ **er Schinken** cured ham
Rohkost uncooked raw vegetables
Rollmops soused herring fillet rolled around chopped onions or gherkins
Rosenkohl brussels sprouts
Rosinen raisins
Rosmarin rosemary
Rostbraten pot roast
Rösti hashed-brown potatoes (Switzerland)

Röstkartoffeln fried potatoes
rot red
  ~**e Bete** beetroot (US beets)
  ~**e Grütze** tapioca and fruit juice served with cream
  ~**e Rübe** beetroot (US beets)
Rotkohl, Rotkraut red cabbage
Rotzunge lemon sole
Rouladen usually thin slices of beef, filled, rolled, and braised in brown gravy
Rüben turnips
Rüebli carrots
Rührreier scrambled eggs
Rumpsteak rump steak
russische Eier "Russian eggs"; hard-boiled eggs stuffed with peas and carrots in mayonnaise
Sachertorte rich chocolate layer cake with jam and coffee-flavoured cream filling
Safran saffron
Saft juice, gravy
Sahne cream
  ~**käse** cream cheese
  ~**kuchen** cream cake, cream tart
Saitenwurst a variety of frankfurter or wiener
Salat salad
  Bohnen~ bean salad
  Frucht~ fruit cocktail
  gemischter ~ mixed salad
  grüner ~ green salad
  Gurken~ cucumber salad
  Kartoffel~ potato salad
  Kraut~ cole slaw
  Obst ~fruit cocktail
  Randen ~ beet salad
  russischer ~ diced vegetables mixed with mayonnaise
  ~**sauce** salad dressing
Salbei sage
Salm salmon

Salz salt
  ~**fleisch** salted meat
  ~**gurke** pickled cucumber
  ~**kartoffeln** boiled potatoes
Salzburger Nockerln sweetened and beaten eggs baked in the oven (Salzburg)
Sardellen, Sardelles anchovies
  ~**ringe** rolled anchovies
Sardinen sardines, pilchards
Saubohnen broad beans (US fava beans)
Sauce sauce
  braune ~ brown sauce
  grüne ~ green sauce
  Käse~ cheese sauce
  Kräuter~ mixed-herb dressing
  Rahm~ cream sauce
  spanische ~ a brown sauce with herbs, spices and wine
  weiße ~ white sauce
sauer sour
Sauerampfer sorrel
Sauerbraten marinated pot roast with herbs
Sauerkraut sauerkraut
Schalotten shallots
Schaltiere shellfish
Schaschlik chunks of mutton, grilled, then braised in a spicy sauce of tomatoes, onions and bacon
Schaumrollen puff pastry rolls filled with whipped cream or custard
Scheibe slice
Schellfisch haddock
Schildkrötensuppe turtle soup
Schinken ham
  ~**brot** ham sandwich (usually open-faced)
  ~**omelett** ham omelet
Schlachtplatte platter of pork, liver sausage, sauerkraut

Schlagobers, Schlagrahm, Schlagsahne whipped cream

Schlegel leg, haunch of venison, veal, etc.

Schleie tench

Schmelzkäse soft cheese

Schmierkäse a soft and pungent cheese, usually for spreading on bread

Schmorbraten pot roast braised with mushrooms

Schnecke(nudel) cinnamon roll

Schnecken snails

Schnepfe snipe, woodcock

Schnittbohnen runner beans (US green beans)

Schnitte slice, cut

Schnittlauch chives

Schnitzel cutlet

  Holstein-~ breaded veal cutlet topped with fried egg and usually garnished with pieces of toast, anchovies, mussels, smoked salmon and vegetables

  Wiener ~ breaded veal cutlet

Schokolade chocolate

  ~neis chocolate ice-cream

Scholle plaice

Schulter shoulder

Schwämme, Schwammerl mushrooms

Schwanz tail

  Ochsen~ oxtail

schwarz black

  ~e Johannisbeeren black currants

Schwarzbrot black bread, rye bread

Schwarzwälder Kirschtorte "Black Forest cherry cake"; a chocolate layer cake filled with cream and cherries

Schwarzwurzeln black salsify

Schwein(efleisch) pork

~ebraten roast pork

~ekotelett pork chop

~erippchen small pork chop

~shachse, ~shaxe pig's knuckle, shank

~skeule leg of pork

~sstelze leg of pork

Seezunge sole

Selchfleisch smoked pork

Sellerie celery

Semmel roll

  ~brösel breadcrumbs

  ~knödel dumpling made of *Semmeln* crumbs

Senf mustard

Siedfleisch boiled beef

Sirup syrup

Soße sauce, gravy; see *Sauce*

Spaghetti spaghetti

Spanferkel suck(l)ing pig

Spargel asparagus

  ~suppe asparagus soup

Spätzle, Spätzli thick noodles

Speck bacon

  ~pfannkuchen pancake with bacon

Speise food

  ~eis ice-cream

  ~karte menu

Spekulatius almond biscuit (US almond cookie)

Spezialität speciality

  ~ des Hauses chef's speciality

  ~ des Tages the day's speciality

Spiegelei(er) fried egg(s), sunny-side up

Spieß spit

Spinat spinach

Sprossenkohl brussels sprouts

Sprotten sprats

Stachelbeeren gooseberries

Steckrübe turnip

Steinbuscher Käse semi-hard, creamy cheese; strong and

slightly bitter
Steinbutt turbot
Steingarnelen prawns
Steinpilze boletus mushrooms
Stelze leg (particularly of pork)
Stierenauge(n) fried egg(s)
Stock mashed potatoes
~**fisch** hake, dried codfish
Stollen loaf cake with raisins, al-
monds, nuts, candied lemon
peel
Stoßsuppe caraway soup
Stotzen leg
Strammer Max highly-spiced
minced pork served with eggs
and onions
Streichkäse any of a variety of
soft cheese spreads with dif-
ferent flavours
Streuselkuchen a type of coffee
cake with a crumbly topping
made of butter, sugar, flour,
cinnamon
Strudel paper-thin layers of pas-
try filled with apple slices, nuts,
raisins and jam
Stück piece, slice
Sülze 1) jellied, in aspic 2) brawn
(US head cheese)
Suppe soup
Aal~ eel soup
Erbsen~ pea soup
Fisch~ fish soup
Kartoffel~ potato soup
Mehl~ flour soup
Morgenröte~ broth with meat,
tapioca, tomatoes
Nieren~ kidney soup
Ochsenschwanz~ oxtail soup
Paradeis~ tomato soup
Rahm~ creamed soup
Schildkröten~ turtle soup
Tomaten~ tomato soup
süß sweet

~**-sauer** sweet-sour (of sauces)
Süßigkeiten sweets, confectionary
Süßspeise dessert, pudding
Tagesplatte day's special
Tagessuppe day's soup
Tascherln pastry turnovers with
meat, cheese, jam, etc., filling
Tatar raw, spiced minced beef
~**enbrot** open-face sandwich
with spiced minced beef
Taube pigeon
Teegebäck tea cakes (US cookies)
Teig dough
~**waren** noodles, spaghetti, etc.
Teller plate
~**gericht** a serving of a main
course only
~**service** serving of main
courses only
Thunfisch tunny (US tuna)
Thymian thyme
Tilsiter (Käse) semi-hard, strong
but bland cheese
Tomate tomato
~**nsuppe** tomato soup
Topfen mild cottage cheese
~**strudel** flaky pastry dough
filled with creamed cottage
cheese with vanilla flavouring,
rolled and baked
~**torte** tart with a mild cottage-
cheese filling
Topfkuchen moulded cake with
raisins
Törtchen small tart or cake
Torte layer cake, usually rich
Buttercreme~ layer cake with
butter-cream filling
Mokka~ coffee-flavoured cake
Sacher~ a rich chocolate layer
cake with jam and coffee-flavoured cream filling
Schwarzwälder Kirsch~ "Black
Forest cherry cake"; a layer

cake filled with cream and cherries

Trauben grapes

Trüffeln truffles

Truthahn turkey cock

Tunke sauce

Türkenkorn corn, maize

Vanille vanilla

~ **eis** vanilla ice-cream

~ **pudding** vanilla custard

~ **sauce** vanilla custard

verlorene Eier poached eggs

Voressen meat stew

Vorspeisen appetizers, first courses

Wacholderbeeren juniper berries

Wachtel quail

Waffel waffle

Walnüsse walnuts

warm warm

Wasserkresse watercress

Wassermelone watermelon

Weinbeißer ginger biscuits (US ginger snaps)

Weinbergschnecken Burgundy snails

Weinkarte wine list

Weinkraut white cabbage, often braised with apples and simmered in wine

weiß white

~ **e Bohnen** butter beans, haricot beans

Weißbrot white bread

Weißfisch whiting

Weißkäse cottage cheese

Weißkohl, Weißkraut white cabbage

Weißwurst white sausage (Bavaria)

Weizen wheat

Welschkohl, Welschkraut savoy cabbage

Welschkorn corn

Westfälischer Schinken a well-known raw smoked ham (Westphalia)

Wiener (Würstchen), Wienerli wiener, frankfurter

Wiener Schnitzel breaded veal cutlet

Wild game

Wildbraten roast game, usually venison

Wildente wild duck

Wildschwein(braten) (roast) wild boar

Wilstermarschkäse semi-hard cheese, not unlike *Tilsiter*

Windbeutel "wind bag"; cream puff

Wirsing(kohl) savoy cabbage

Wurst sausage

Würstchen small sausage

Würze condiment

würzig spiced

Zander pike

Ziege goat

Zieger a mild cottage cheese

Zimt cinnamon

~ **plätzchen** cinnamon cakes (US cinnamon cookies)

Zitrone lemon

Zucker sugar

Zunge tongue

Zutaten ingredients

Zwetsch(g)en plums

~ **knödel** plum dumplings

Zwieback rusks (US zwieback)

Zwiebel onion

~ **fleisch** beef sautéed with onions

~ **rostbraten** steak and onions

~ **suppe** onion soup with red wine and seasoning

Zwischenrippenstück rib steak

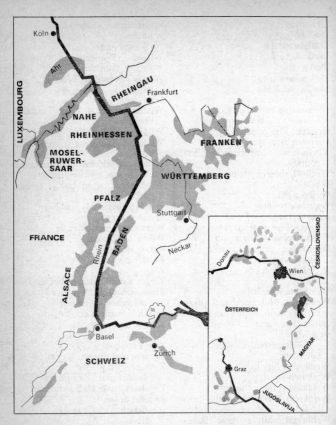

Wine-Producing Regions

Principal wine-producing regions are indicated in grey on the map. For fuller information on the wine of these regions, please refer to individual entries in the beverage section.

Abfüllung bottled, from wine bought directly from the grower

Abzug wine bottled on the estate or at the vineyard where the grapes were grown, e.g., *Schloßabzug, Kellerabzug*

Ahr the region, named for its tributary of the Rhine, has the continent's northern most vineyards; the red wine—pale, delicious with a fine aroma—is the best in Germany which produces little red wine; Ahr wine is rarely exported and has to be drunk young; try them around the towns of Ahrweiler, Neuenahr and Walporzheim

Apfelmost apple cider

Apfelsaft apple juice

Apfelwein apple cider with a high alcoholic content

Aprikosenlikör apricot liqueur

Auslese wine produced from choice grapes

Austria see *Österreich*

Baden this wine-producing region is located in the southwestern part of Germany with Switzerland to the south and Alsace, France, to the west; vineyards are especially found on the outskirts of the Black Forest facing the Rhine River valley; some examples of the wine are *Kaiserstuhl* produced on a volcanic islet to the west of Freiburg, *Markgräfler, Mauerwein* and *Seewein* from the Lake of Constance

Beerenauslese wine produced from very mature grapes resulting in a sweet dessert wine

Bier beer
  dunkles ~ dark beer
  helles ~ light beer
  (some examples of local beer are Austria's *Schwechater*, Switzerland's *Feldschlößchen*, West Germany's *Becks, Dortmunder Union, Löwenbräu, Spatenbräu*)

Bock(bier) a beer with a higher malt content

Bocksbeutel, Boxbeutel a squat flagon shaped like a wineskin and used for certain wine like *Mauerwein, Steinwein*

Branntwein brandy

Brauner coffee with milk
  kleiner ~ small cup of coffee with milk

Danziger Goldwasser an aniseed-flavoured liqueur flecked with tiny golden leaves

Doppelkorn grain liquor

Dornkaat a grain-distilled brandy, slightly flavoured with juniper berries

Eierlikör egg brandy, eggnog

Enzian a liquor distilled from gentian root

Exportbier a beer with a higher hops content than lager beer

Flasche bottle
   ~**nbier** bottled beer

Franken Franconia; the best vineyards of this Main River wine-producing region are located in the vicinity of Iphofen, Escherndorf, Randersacker, Rödelsee and Würzburg; the vineyards either belong to the state, a half-dozen noble families or benevolent foundations; Franconian wine is dry, strong and full-bodied; Würzburg produces one of the area's best wines under the name *Steinwein;* Franconia's wine is traditionally bottled in a *Bocksbeutel,* a squat flagon

Fruchtsaft fruit juice

Gewächs "growth"; used on a wine label with the name of the proprietor

gezuckert sugar added, sweetened

Glas glass

Himbeergeist raspberry brandy

Johannisbeersaft currant juice

Kabinett a term indicating that a wine is bottled exclusively

Kaffee coffee
   Eis~ iced coffee
   ~ **Haag** caffeine-free coffee
   Milch~ half coffee and half hot milk
   ~ **mit Sahne (und Zucker)** coffee with cream (and sugar)
   ~ **mit Schlag(obers)** coffee with whipped cream
   schwarzer ~ black coffee

Kakao cocoa

Kupuziner coffee with whipped cream and powdered chocolate

Kirsch(wasser) cherry brandy

Klosterlikör an herb liqueur

Kognak cognac; see also *Weinbrand*

Korn(branntwein) a grain-distilled liquor

Kümmel(branntwein) caraway-flavoured liquor

Likör liqueur, cordial

Limonade 1) soft drink 2) lemon drink

Malzbier malt beer, with a low alcoholic content

Märzenbier a special brew containing more malt than usual

Maß(krug) a large beer mug holding 1 litre (about 1 quart)

Milch milk
   ~**mix** milk shake

Mineralwasser mineral water

Mosel(-Saar-Ruwer) the official name of the Moselle region; the best Moselle wine is produced in only a part of the region, the mid-Moselle valley which runs from Trittenheim to Traben-Trarbach; the best vineyards are those of Bernkastel, Brauneberg, Graach, Piesport, Wehlen and Zeltingen

Most cider, new wine

Nahe a wine-producing region, named for its tributary of the Rhine River, in the vicinity of Bad Kreuznach; its white wine is full-bodied, usually excellent, and may be compared to the best wine of Rhenish Hesse; the most celebrated vineyard is Schloß Böckelheim, owned by the state; other excellent wine is produced in the vicinity of Bad Kreuznach, Bretzenheim, Münster, Niederhäuser, Norheim, Roxheim, Winzerheim

Naturwein unblended, unsweetened wine

Orangeade orangeade, orange drink

Österreich Austria exports very little of its wine; the red—mainly from Burgenland—is not especially notable and is usually drunk only locally; probably the best-known Austrian wine is *Gumpoldskirchener*, produced to the south of Vienna, a good white wine which generations of Viennese have enjoyed; along the banks of the Danube River to the west of Vienna, good white wine is produced in the Wachau area (e.g., *Dürnsteiner, Loibner, Kremser*); in the immediate vicinity of the Austrian capital, table wine is produced (e.g., *Nußberger, Wiener, Grinzinger*) of which the best is sometimes bottled and exported

Perlwein white, semi-sparkling wine

Pfalz Palatinate; in good years this region is often first among West Germany's wine-producing regions in terms of production, predominantly white wine; in medieval times, the Palatinate gained a reputation of being "the wine cellar of the Holy Roman Empire"; today's Palatinate is bounded on the north by Rhenish Hesse to the east by the Rhine River, to the south and west by Alsace and Lorraine, France; some examples: *Durkheimer, Forster, Deidesheimer, Ruppertsberger* for white, *Durkheimer* also for red

Pilsener a beer with a particularly strong aroma of hops

Pflümli(wasser) Swiss plum brandy

Portwein port

Rhein Rhine wine is produced in five regions on the Rhine River valley; the vineyards in Rheingau on the right bank between Wiesbaden and Rüdesheim are noted for offering the country's best white wine including the well-known *Johannisberger*; Rhenisch Hesse on the left bank south of Rheingau is renowned for its *Liebfraumilch*; the Palatinate is also located on the left bank near the Alsatian border; another region is located to the north of Rheingau between Rüdesheim and Coblence (middle Rhine) while Baden to the south faces Alsace and the Black Forest; on the banks of Rhine tributaries vineyards are also found including the vineyards of Nahe, those of Franconia in the Main River valley and the Ahr River valley which produces virtually only red wine

Rheingau the region, located at the foot of the Taunus Mountains facing the Rhine River, is noted for the high quality of its white wine; its wine of lesser quality usually has sugar added in order to obtain a minimum degree of alcohol; such wine may only be identified with the name of the village (such as *Johannisberger, Rüdesheimer*) while other wine of renowned quality can use the name of the vineyard from which it was produced (like *Steinberg, Schloß Vollrads, Markobrunn, Schloß Johannisberg;* Rheingau's best wines are dessert wines which can be compared to a fine *Sauternes;* a good red wine is produced in *Aßmannshausen*

Rheinhessen Rhenish Hesse, of which Mainz is the capital, is bounded on the east and north by the Rhine River, on the south by the Palatinate and to the west by the Nahe Valley; no less than 155 villages are dedicated to wine production but only ten of them produce wine of an exceptional quality: Alsheim, Bingen, Bodenheim, Dienheim, Guntersblum, Laubenheim, Nackenheim, Nierstein, Oppenheim and Worms; wine of lesser quality is sold in carafes or under the generic name of *Liebfraumilch* or *Domtal;* wine produced from the best vineyards is generally excellent, of a distinctive class and quality; as in Rheingau, wine which carries the term *Beerenauslese* are fine dessert wines which may be compared to *Sauternes*

Rum rum

Schillerwein rosé wine

Schloß castle, denotes a wine estate

Schnaps liquor

Schokolade chocolate

Schweiz Switzerland; while the nation's most notable wine is produced in French- and Italian-speaking cantons, predominantly red table wine is produced in the German-speaking region with the exception of vineyards on the shores of the Lake of Biel; some of the best light red wine is found in the cantons of Grisons, St. Gallen, Schaffhausen and Zurich

Sekt sparkling champagne-like wine (e.g., *Deinhard, Henkell*)

Sirup syrup

Sodawasser soda water

Spätlese wine produced from grapes picked late in the season, often resulting in robust wine

Spezialbier a more stronglybrewed beer than *Vollbier*

spritzig sparkling

Sprudel(wasser) mineral water

Starkbier a strong beer with a high malt content

Steinhäger juniper-berry brandy

Süßwein dessert wine

Tee tea

    Lindenblüten~ lime-blossom tea

    ~ mit Milch tea with milk

    Pfefferminz~ peppermint tea

    ~ mit Zitrone tea with lemon

Traube grape

trocken dry

Trockenbeerenauslese wine produced from specially-selected over-ripe grapes, usually results in a rich, full-bodied dessert wine

ungezuckert unsweetened

verbessert in reference to wine, improved or sweetened

Viertel ¼ litre (about ½ pint) of wine

Vollbier the typical German beer which 95% of the breweries produce with an alcoholic content of 3-4%

Wachstum "growth"; used on a wine label with the name of the proprietor

Wasser water

Wein wine

    Rosé~ rosé wine

    Rot~ red wine

    Schaum~ sparkling wine

    Süß~ dessert wine

    Weiß~ white wine

Weinbrand brandy (some names: *Asbach Uralt, Dujardin, Scharlachberg*)

(Berliner) Weißbier a light beer brewed from wheat

Wermut vermouth

Whisky whisky

Wodka vodka

Württemberg wine from this region, rarely exported, must be drunk very young; the term *Schillerwein* is employed in the region to denote rosé wine; best wine is produced at Cannstatt, Feuerbach, Untertürckheim; *Stettener Brotwasser* is a noted wine

Zitronensaft lemon squash (US lemon soda

Zwetschgenwasser plum brandy

GERMAN ABBREVIATIONS

ACS	Automobil-Club der Schweiz	Automobile Club of Switzerland
ADAC	Allgemeiner Deutscher Automobil-Club	German General Automobile Club
AG	Aktiengesellschaft	Ltd.
Anm.	Anmerkung	note
AvD	Automobilklub von Deutschland	Automobile Association of Germany
Bez.	Bezirk	district
BRD	Bundesrepublik Deutschland	Federal Republic of Germany
b.w.	bitte wenden	please turn over
bzw.	beziehungsweise	respectively
Co.	«Companie», (Handels)gesellschaft	company
DB	Deutsche Bundesbahn	German Federal Railways
DBP	Deutsche Bundespost	German Federal Post Office
DDR	Deutsche Demokratische Republik	German Democratic Republic
d.h.	das heißt	i.e.
DM	Deutsche Mark	(West) German mark
d.M.	des Monats	inst., of the month
Dr.	Doktor	Dr.
EWG	Europäische Wirtschaftsgemeinschaft	European Economic Community (Common Market)
ff.	folgende	following
Fr.	Franken	francs (Switzerland)
Frl.	Fräulein	Miss
G.	Gasse	small street, alley
g	Groschen	$1/100$ of a schilling
GmbH	Gesellschaft mit beschränkter Haftung	private firm with limited liability
Hbf.	Hauptbahnhof	main train station
Hr.	Herr	Mr.
Ing.	Ingenieur	engineer
i.R.	im Ruhestand	retired
i.V.	in Vertretung	by proxy

jr.	Junior	junior
KG	Kommanditgesellschaft	small, private company
LKW	Lastkraftwagen	lorry, truck
max.	maximal	maximum
min.	minimal	minimum
MWST	Mehrwertsteuer	value added tax
NATO	Nordatlantikpakt	NATO (North Atlantic Treaty Organization)
NB	notabene	please note
n.Chr.	nach Christus	A.D.
Nr.	Nummer	number
ÖAMTC	Österreichischer Automobil-, Motorrad- und Touring-Club	Austrian Automobile, Motorcycle and Touring Club
ÖBB	Österreichische Bundesbahnen	Austrian Railways
Pf	Pfennig	$1/100$ of a mark
PKW	Personenkraftwagen	automobile
Prof.	Professor	professor
PS	Pferdestärke	horsepower
P.S.	Postskriptum	postscript
PTT	Post, Telephon, Telegraph	Post, Telephone, Telegraph
Rp.	Rappen	$1/100$ of a franc
S	Schilling	Austrian schilling
SBB	Schweizerische Bundesbahnen	Swiss Federal Railways
St.	Sankt	saint
Str.	Straße	street
TCS	Touring-Club der Schweiz	Swiss Touring Club
TEE	Trans-Europ-Express	see *Trains*
u.a.	unter anderem	including
UNO	Vereinte Nationen	United Nations
usw.	und so weiter	etc.
v.Chr.	vor Christus	B.C.
vgl.	vergleiche	see
Wwe.	Witwe	widow
z.B.	zum Beispiel	for instance, e.g.

TIME AND MONEY

Time. Except for time-tables, the twelve-hour system is generally used in Germany, Austria and Switzerland.

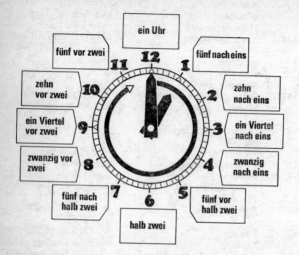

If you want to indicate a.m. or p.m. add *morgens, nachmittags* or *abends*. Thus:

acht Uhr morgens	eight a.m.
zwei Uhr nachmittags	two p.m.
acht Uhr abends	eight p.m.

Dates. In German, large amounts and years are expressed in a slightly different way.
Thus:

tausendzweihundert Stück	1,200 pieces
Neunzehnhundertdreiundsiebzig	1973

Currency. In Germany, the basic unit is the mark (*Deutsche Mark* ; abb. : DM) which is divided into 100 pfennings (German: *Pfennig*: abb.: Pf.).

Coins: 1, 2, 5, 10 and 50 Pf. ; 1, 2 and 5 DM
Bank-notes: 5, 10, 20, 50, 100, 500 and 1000 DM

In Austria, the basic unit is the *schilling* (abb.: S), divided into 100 *groschen* (abb.: g).

Coins: 1, 2, 5, 10, 20 and 50 g; 1, 5 and 10 S.
Bank-notes: 10, 20, 50, 100, 500 and 1000 S.

In Switzerland, the basic unit is the franc (German: Franken; abb.: Fr.), divided into 100 centimes (German: Rappen; abb.: Rp.).

Coins: 5, 10, 20 and 50 Rp.; 1, 2 and 5 Fr.
Bank-notes: 10, 20, 50, 100, 500 and 1000 Fr.

As rates of exchange fluctuate frequently, consult a bank for currency information.

BUSINESS HOURS

Banks:

Germany	Switzerland	Austria
9 a.m. to noon	8 a.m. to noon	8 a.m. to 1 p.m.
3 to 5 p.m.	2 to 4 p.m.	2 to 3.30 p.m.
		(Friday to 5.30 p.m.)

In Germany, as well as Switzerland and Austria, you will find several small currency-exchange offices *(Geldwechsel)* in most tourist centres, especially during the summer season. They are often open outside regular banking hours and even sometimes on Saturdays, Sundays and holidays.

Post offices:

Germany	Switzerland	Austria
8 a.m. to noon	7.30 a.m. to noon	8 a.m. to noon
2 to 5 p.m.	1.45 to 6.30 p.m.	2 to 5 p.m.
(Saturdays to noon)	(Saturdays to 11 a.m.)	(Saturdays to 10 a.m.)

Closed on Sundays and holidays.

In principal cities, some post offices are open outside of the normal hours.

Stores:

Germany	**Switzerland**	**Austria**
8 a.m. to 12.30 (1) p.m.	8 a.m. to noon (12.30 p.m.)	8 a.m. to noon
2 to 6 p.m.	1.30 to 6.30 (7) p.m.	2.30 (3) to 6 (6.30) p.m.
(Saturday from 8 a.m. to 1 p.m. except the first Saturday of the month when stores remain open until 5.30 p.m.)	(Saturdays until 5 p.m.)	(Saturdays closing at noon)

In Switzerland department stores generally remain open at noon but close Monday morning. Most shops close from half a day to a day weekly.

Offices:

Germany	**Switzerland**	**Austria**
8 a.m. to 12.30 p.m.	8 a.m. to noon	8 a.m. to noon
2 to 5.30 p.m.	2 to 5 p.m.	2 to 6 p.m.

Offices are usually closed on Saturday.

HOI IDAYS

While there may be additional regional holidays, only those are cited below that are *national* holidays in Germany (D), Austria (A) or Switzerland (CH).

January 1	**Neujahr**	New Year's Day	D A CH
January 2			CH*
January 6	**Heilige 3 Könige**	Epiphany	A
May 1	**Tag der Arbeit**	Labour Day	D A
August 15	**Mariä Himmelfahrt**	Assumption Day	A
October 26	**Nationalfeiertag**	National Day	A
November 1	**Allerheiligen**	All Saints' Day	A
December 8	**Unbefleckte Empfängnis**	Immaculate Conception	A
December 25	**1. Weihnachtstag**	1st Christmas Day	D A CH
December 26	**2. Weihnachtstag**	2nd Christmas Day	D A CH*
Movable dates:	**Karfreitag**	Good Friday	D CH*
	Ostermontag	Easter Monday	D A CH
	Christi Himmelfahrt	Ascension	D A CH
	Pfingstmontag	Whit Monday	D A CH
	Fronleichnam	Corpus Christi	A

* Most cantons.

TRAINS

If not otherwise indicated, these terms also apply to Switzerland and Austria:

TEE	Trans-Europ-Express; luxury continental service; first class with a supplementary fare required
Expreß (Austria, Germany)	Long-distance train, usually coming from or going abroad, stopping at principal stations
Fernschnellzug (Germany)	Equivalent of the express train
Schnellzug	Long-distance train making a few more stops than an express train
D-Zug (Germany)	Equivalent of the *Schnellzug*
Städteschnellzug (Switzerland)	Long-distance train connecting principal cities and stopping only there
Eilzug	Medium-distance train, not stopping at small stations
Personenzug	Local train stopping at all stations
Schienenbus (Germany)	Small diesel used on short runs
Triebwagen (Austria, Switzerland)	Equivalent of the *Schienenbus*
Triebwagenschnellzug (Austria)	Fast diesel used on long-distance runs
Autoreisezug	Motorail (piggy-back car train)
Schlafwagen	Sleeping-car with individual compartments (single, double, tourist) and toilette or lavatory facilities
Liegewagen	Sleeping-car with simple accommodation
Speisewagen	Dining car
Gepäckwagen	Baggage car with only registered luggage permitted

ROAD SIGNS

Written road signs are rarely found on the continent. These are the most important:

Blaue Zone	Blue zone (parking); special parking disc required
Durchgangsverkehr	Through traffic
Einbahnstraße	One way
Einordnen	Use appropriate lane
Ende des Parkverbots	End of no parking zone
Frostschäden	Ice damage
Gefährliche Kurve	Dangerous bend (curve)
Gefährliches Gefälle	Steep descent
Gefährliche Steigung	Steep hill
Halt, Polizei!	Stop, police
Hupen verboten	No honking
Kein Durchgang für Fußgänger	No pedestrians
Kurzparkzone	Limited parking zone
Lawinengefahr	Avalanche zone
LKW	Alternative route for heavy vehicles
Nur für Anlieger	Access to residents only
Parken erlaubt/verboten	Parking allowed/prohibited
Rechts/Links fahren	Keep right/left
Schlechte Fahrbahn (Wegstrecke)	Bad road surface
Steinschlag	Falling stones
Überholen verboten	No overtaking/passing
Umleitung	Diversion (detour)
Vorsicht Schule/Fußgänger/ Straßenarbeiten	Children/pedestrians/road works (men working)

TELEPHONING

In Germany and Switzerland the telephone network is virtually fully automatic and instructions are posted in every call box. But if you have to ask for a number at your hotel, you might say, for instance:

> *Bitte geben Sie mir null eins/zwounddreißig/achtzehn/vierzig.*
> "I want to call (01) 32 18 40."

In Austria there are still some out-of-the-way places where you may have to phone via an operator. In this case, you merely lift the receiver and wait for the operator. Otherwise, the instructions are the same as in Germany and Switzerland.

N.B. Usually in telephoning *zwei* becomes *zwo*.

Spelling code

A	Anton	**I**	Ida	**Q**	Quelle	**Y**	Ypsilon
B	Berta	**J**	Julius	**R**	Richard	**Z**	Zeppelin
C	Caesar	**K**	Konrad	**S**	Siegfried	**Ä**	A Umlaut
D	Dora	**L**	Ludwig	**T**	Theodor	**Ö**	O Umlaut
E	Emil	**M**	Martin	**U**	Ulrich	**Ü**	U Umlaut
F	Friedrich	**N**	Nordpol	**V**	Viktor		
G	Gustav	**O**	Otto	**W**	Wilhelm		
H	Heinrich	**P**	Paula	**X**	Xanten		

SOME BASIC PHRASES

EINIGE ALLGEMEINE AUSDRÜCKE

Please.	Bitte.
Thank you very much.	Vielen Dank.
That's all right.	Gern geschehen.
Good morning.	Guten Morgen.
Good afternoon.	Guten Tag.
Good evening.	Guten Abend.
Good night.	Gute Nacht.
Good-bye.	Auf Wiedersehen.
See you later.	Auf bald.
Where is...?	Wo ist...?
Where are...?	Wo sind...?
What do you call this?	Wie heißt dies?
What does that mean?	Was bedeutet das?
Do you speak English?	Sprechen Sie Englisch?
Do you speak German?	Sprechen Sie Deutsch?
Do you speak French?	Sprechen Sie Französisch?
Do you speak Spanish?	Sprechen Sie Spanisch?
Do you speak Italian?	Sprechen Sie Italienisch?
Could you speak more slowly, please?	Könnten Sie bitte langsamer sprechen?
I don't understand.	Ich verstehe nicht.
Can I have...?	Kann ich... haben?
Can you show me...?	Können Sie mir... zeigen?
Can you tell me...?	Können Sie mir sagen...?
Can you help me, please?	Können Sie mir bitte helfen?
I'd like...	Ich hätte gern...
We'd like...	Wir hätten gern...
Please give me...	Geben Sie mir bitte...
Please bring me...	Bringen Sie mir bitte...
I'm hungry.	Ich habe Hunger.
I'm thirsty.	Ich habe Durst.

I'm lost.	Ich habe mich verirrt.
Hurry up!	Beeilen Sie sich!
There is/There are...	Es gibt...
There isn't/There aren't...	Es gibt keinen/Es gibt keine/Es gibt kein...

Arrival

Ankunft

Your passport, please.	Ihren Paß, bitte.
Have you anything to declare?	Haben Sie etwas zu verzollen?
No, nothing at all.	Nein, gar nichts.
Can you help me with my luggage, please?	Können Sie mir mit meinem Gepäck helfen, bitte?
Where's the bus to the centre of town, please?	Wo ist der Bus zum Stadtzentrum, bitte?
This way, please.	Hier durch, bitte.
Where can I get a taxi?	Wo finde ich ein Taxi?
What's the fare to...?	Was kostet es bis...?
Take me to this address, please.	Fahren Sie mich bitte zu dieser Adresse.
I'm in a hurry.	Ich habe es eilig.

Hotel

Hotel

My name is...	Mein Name ist...
Have you a reservation?	Haben Sie vorbestellt?
I'd like a room with a bath.	Ich hätte gern ein Zimmer mit Bad.
What's the price per night?	Wieviel kostet es pro Nacht?
May I see the room?	Kann ich das Zimmer sehen?
What's my room number, please?	Welche Zimmernummer habe ich, bitte?
There's no hot water.	Es kommt kein warmes Wasser.
May I see the manager, please?	Kann ich bitte den Direktor sprechen?
Did anyone telephone me?	Hat mich jemand angerufen?

Is there any mail for me?	Ist Post für mich da?
May I have my bill, please?	Kann ich bitte meine Rechnung haben?

Eating out

Gaststätten

Do you have a fixed-price menu?	Haben Sie ein Menü?
May I see the menu?	Kann ich die Speisekarte sehen?
May we have an ashtray, please?	Können wir bitte einen Aschenbecher haben?
Where's the gentlemen's toilet (men's room)?	Wo ist die Herrentoilette?
Where's the ladies' toilet (ladies' room)?	Wo ist die Damentoilette?
I'd like some assorted appetizers.	Ich hätte gern gemischte Vorspeisen.
Have you any chicken soup?	Haben Sie Hühnersuppe?
I'd like some fish.	Ich hätte gern Fisch.
I'd like it steamed.	Ich hätte es gern gedämpft.
I'd like a beef steak.	Ich hätte gern ein Beefsteak.
What vegetables have you got?	Was für Gemüse haben Sie?
Nothing more, thanks.	Nein danke, nichts mehr.
What would you like to drink?	Was möchten Sie gern trinken?
I'll have a beer, please.	Ich nehme ein Bier, bitte.
I'd like a bottle of wine.	Ich möchte eine Flasche Wein.
Is service included?	Ist Bedienung inbegriffen?
Thank you, that was a very good meal.	Danke, das Essen war sehr gut.

Travelling

Reisen

Where's the railway station, please?	Wo ist der Bahnhof, bitte?
Where's the ticket office, please?	Wo ist der Fahrkartenschalter, bitte?
I'd like a ticket to...	Ich möchte eine Fahrkarte nach...
First or second class?	Erste oder zweite Klasse?

First class, please.	Erste Klasse, bitte.
Single or return (one way or roundtrip)?	Einfach oder hin und zurück?
Do I have to change trains?	Muß ich umsteigen?
What platform does the train leave from?	Auf welchem Bahnsteig fährt der Zug ab?
Where's the nearest underground (subway) station?	Wo ist die nächste U-Bahn-station?
Where's the bus station, please?	Wo ist der Busbahnhof, bitte?
When's the first bus to…?	Wann fährt der erste Bus nach…?
Please let me off at the next stop.	Bitte lassen Sie mich an der nächsten Haltestelle aussteigen.

Relaxing / Unterhaltung

What's on at the cinema (movies)?	Was gibt es im Kino zu sehen?
What time does the film begin?	Wann beginnt der Film?
Are there any tickets for tonight?	Gibt es noch Karten für heute abend?
Where can we go dancing?	Wohin können wir tanzen gehen?

Introductions — Dating / Vorstellung — Verabredung

How are you?	Wie geht es Ihnen?
Very well, thank you. And you?	Sehr gut, danke. Und Ihnen?
May I introduce Miss Philips?	Darf ich Fräulein Philips vorstellen?
My name is…	Ich heiße…
I'm very pleased to meet you.	Sehr erfreut.
How long have you been here?	Wie lange sind Sie schon hier?
It was nice meeting you.	Es war mir ein Vergnügen.
Would you like a cigarette?	Möchten Sie eine Zigarette?
May I get you a drink?	Darf ich Ihnen etwas zu trinken bestellen?
Do you have a light, please?	Haben Sie Feuer, bitte?

Are you free this evening? | Sind Sie heute abend frei?

Where shall we meet? | Wo treffen wir uns?

Shops, stores and services

Läden, Geschäfte usw.

Where's the nearest bank, please? | Wo ist die nächste Bank, bitte?

Where can I cash some traveller's cheques? | Wo kann ich Reiseschecks einlösen?

Can you give me some small change, please? | Können Sie mir bitte Kleingeld geben?

Where's the nearest chemist (pharmacy)? | Wo ist die nächste Apotheke?

How do I get there? | Wie komme ich dorthin?

Is it within walking distance? | Kann man zu Fuß gehen?

Can you help me, please? | Können Sie mir helfen, bitte?

How much is this? And that? | Wieviel kostet dies? Und das?

It's not quite what I want. | Es ist nicht ganz das, was ich möchte.

I like it. | Es gefällt mir.

Can you recommend something for sunburn? | Können Sie mir etwas gegen Sonnenbrand empfehlen?

I'd like a haircut, please. | Ich möchte mir das Haar schneiden lassen, bitte.

I'd like a manicure, please. | Ich möchte eine Maniküre.

Street directions

Wo? Wohin?

Can you show me on the map where I am? | Können Sie mir auf der Karte zeigen, wo ich bin?

You are on the wrong road. | Sie sind auf der falschen Straße.

Go straight ahead. | Fahren Sie geradeaus.

It's on the left/on the right. | Es ist linker Hand/rechter Hand.

Emergency

Im Notfall

Call a doctor quickly. | Rufen Sie schnell einen Arzt.

Call an ambulance. | Rufen Sie einen Krankenwagen.

Please call the police. | Rufen Sie bitte die Polizei.

englisch-deutsch

english-german

ANLEITUNG ZUR AUSSPRACHE

Hinter jedem Stichwort in diesem Wörterbuch finden Sie in eckigen Klammern die Aussprachebezeichnung. Die von uns gewählte vereinfachte Umschrift ist wie Deutsch zu lesen; besondere Ausspracheregeln werden unten erläutert.

Silbentrennung ist durch Bindestriche angegeben, wobei die betonten Silben in Großbuchstaben gedruckt sind.

Natürlich stimmen die Laute zweier verschiedener Sprachen nie ganz genau überein; aber wenn Sie die folgenden Anleitungen sorgfältig beachten, sollten Sie mit dem Lesen unserer Aussprachebezeichnung keine Mühe haben und sich in der fremden Sprache ohne weiteres verständlich machen können.

Buchstabe	Annähernde Aussprache	Lautschrift	Beispiel	
Konsonanten				
f, h, k, l, m, n, o, t, x	werden wie im Deutschen ausgesprochen			
b	immer wie in Ra**b**e, nie wie in a**b**	b	**b**uy	bai
c	1) vor e, **i, y** wie **ß** in Nu**ß**;	ss	re**c**eipt	ri-SSIET
	2) sonstwo wie **k** in **k**ein	k	**c**an	kæn
ch	wie **tsch** in rutschen	tsch	mu**ch**	matsch
d	immer wie in ba**d**en, nie wie in Ba**d**	d	**d**o	duh
g	1) gewöhnlich vor e, **i, y** wie **d** mit folgendem schwachem **sch**-Laut (wie **ge** in Gara**ge**);	dʒ	**g**in	dʒin
	2) sonstwo wie **g** in **g**ut	g	**g**ood	gud
j	wie **d** mit folgendem schwachem **sch**-Laut	dʒ	**j**am	dʒæm
r	ähnlich wie **ge** in Gara**ge**, aber mit offenerem Mund, und der Ausatmungsstrom ist weniger geräuschvoll	r	**r**eserve	ri-SÖHW
s	1) zwischen Vokalen und am Wortende wie **s** in Ro**s**e;	s	plea**s**e	plies
	2) sonstwo wie **ß** in Nu**ß**	ss	**s**ee	ssie
sh	wie **sch** in **sch**ön	sch	**sh**ut	schat
th	1) manchmal (besonders am Wortende) wie **s** in bi**s**, aber mit Lispeln;	θ	ber**th**	böhθ
	2) manchmal (besonders vor Vokal) wie **s** in Ro**s**e, aber mit Lispeln	ð	**th**is	ðiss
v	wie **w** in **W**ein	w	**v**ery	WÄ-ri
w	wie ein schwacher **u**-Laut	u	**w**e	uie
y	als Konsonant wie deutsches **j**	j	**y**ou	juh
z	wie **s** in Ro**s**e	s	**z**oo	suh

Vokale

a	1) vor Konsonanten außer **r** ähnlich wie **a** in hat, aber mit offenerem Mund;	æ	**that**	ðæt
	2) mit folgendem **r** wie **ah** in fahren;	ah	**car**	kah
	3) vor einem Konsonanten mit folgendem Vokal (besonders **e, i, y**) wie **ee** in See mit folgendem **j**-Laut	eej	**late**	leejt
e	1) vor Konsonanten wie **e** in beste;	ä	**red**	räd
	2) vor einem Konsonanten mit folgendem Vokal oft wie **ie** in dieser	ie	**these**	ðies
i	1) vor einem Konsonanten wie **i** in bitte;	i	**this**	ðiss
	2) vor einem Konsonanten mit folgendem Vokal gewöhnlich wie **ei** in kein	ai	**line**	lain
o	1) vor Konsonanten wie **o** in Post;	o	**hot**	hot
	2) vor einem Konsonanten mit folgendem Vokal wie **oh** in ohne;	oo	**hotel**	hoo-TÄL
	3) vor **r** wie **oh**, aber mit etwas offenerem Mund zwischen **ah** und **oh**	oh	**pork**	pohk
u	1) vor einem Konsonanten manchmal wie **u** in lustig;	u	**put**	put
	2) vor zwei Konsonanten und manchmal vor einem wie **a** in hat;	a	**must**	mast
	3) vor einem Konsonanten mit folgendem Vokal wie **ju** in jubeln	juh	**during**	DJUH-ring
y	1) in einsilbigen Wörtern wie **ei** in mein;	ai	**my**	mai
	2) sonstwo wie **ie** in tief	i	**very**	WÄ-ri

Laute, die mit 2 oder mehr Buchstaben geschrieben werden

ai, ay	wie **ä** in spät mit folgendem **j**-Laut	eej	**may**	meej
aw	wie **oh** in ohne, aber mit offenerem Mund	oh	**raw**	roh
ea, ee, (c)ei, ie	gewöhnlich wie **ie** in tief	ie	**leave**	liew
ew	wie **ju** in jubeln	juh	**new**	njuh
igh	wie **ei** in mein	ai	**high**	hai
ir, er, ur	wie **öh** in Löhne, aber mit gedehnten Lippen wie für **eh**	öh	**thirsty**	θÖH-ssti
oi, oy	wie **eu** in neu	eu	**boy**	beu
ou, ow	wie **au** in Haus	au	**now**	nau

NB: Unbetonte Vokale werden oft wie ein flüchtiges **e** in bitte ausgesprochen (in unserer Lautschrift **ö**).

197

ENGLISCHE GRUNDGRAMMATIK

Artikel

Der bestimmte Artikel hat nur eine Form: *the*.

the room	the rooms
the father	the fathers
the mother	the mothers

Der unbestimmte Artikel hat zwei Formen: man verwendet *a* vor einem Konsonanten (Mitlaut) und *an* vor einem Vokal (Selbstlaut) oder stimmlosen *h*.
Aber:

a coat, a week, an umbrella
an hour (stimmloses «*h*»)
a house (das «*h*» wird ausgesprochen)

Im Plural (Mehrzahl) wird der unbestimmte Artikel weggelassen.

people Leute
small houses kleine Häuser

Some deutet eine Menge oder eine unbestimmte Zahl an. Man verwendet es vor Substantiven im Singular (Einzahl) – nicht in der Aufzählung – sowie im Plural. Es entspricht den deutschen Ausdrücken «etwas» oder «einige».

I'd like some coffee, please. Ich möchte gerne etwas Kaffee, bitte.
Bring me some cigarettes, please. Bringen Sie mir bitte einige Zigaretten.

Any wird in Verneinungs- und Fragesätzen verwendet.

There isn't any soap. Es gibt keine Seife.
Have you got any stamps? Haben Sie Briefmarken?

Merke: In Großbritannien zieht man die Formulierung *have you any* vor, in den U.S.A. den Ausdruck *do you have. Have you got* ist in beiden Gebieten gebräuchlich.

Substantive

Der Plural der meisten Substantive (Hauptwörter) wird durch Anhängen von *-s* oder *-es* an den Singular gebildet. Wenn ein Substantiv auf *-y* endet, ist zu beachten, daß sich die Endung in *-ies* umwandelt, wenn dem *-y* ein Konsonant vorausgeht und einfach in *-ys*, wenn der vorausgehende Buchstabe ein Vokal ist.

cup	cups
car	cars
dress	dresses
lady	ladies
key	keys

Salmon, deer, sheep, trout, swine, grouse sind unveränderlich.

Substantive, die auf *-fe*, und einige, die auf *-f* enden, *(calf, loaf, self, sheaf, shelf, thief, wolf)*, bilden ihren Plural mit *-ves*.

knife	knives
wolf	wolves

Hier einige ganz unregelmäßige Pluralformen:

man	men
woman	women
child	children
foot	feet
tooth	teeth
mouse	mice

Ergänzung von Substantiven

1. Der Besitzer ist eine Person. Wenn das Substantiv oder der Name nicht auf *-s* enden, wird *'s* angefügt (sächsischer Genitiv).

the boy's room das Zimmer des Jungen
Anne's dress Annes Kleid
the children's clothes die Kleider der Kinder

Wenn das Substantiv auf -*s* endet, fügt man **einfach ein Apostroph** hinzu.

2. Wenn es sich bei dem zu ergänzenden Substantiv um eine Sache handelt, verwendet man die Präposition *of*.

the boys' room das Zimmer der Jungen
the key of the door der Schlüssel der Tür
the end of the journey das Ende der Reise

Demonstrativform

This (in Plural *these*) bezeichnet die räumliche oder zeitliche Nähe.
That (Plural *those*) bezeichnet die Entfernung. Beide können Adjektive oder Pronomen sein. In letzterem Fall hängt man im Englischen *one* an: *this one, that one*.

Is this seat taken? Ist dieser Platz besetzt?
That's my seat. Das ist mein Platz.
Those aren't my suitcases. Das sind nicht meine Koffer.

Adjektive

Das Adjektiv (Eigenschaftswort), das unveränderlich bleibt, wird vor das Substantiv gestellt.

A large brown suitcase. Ein großer brauner Koffer.

Steigerung:

Es gibt zwei Arten, um den **Komparativ** (1. Steigerungsstufe) und den **Superlativ** (2. Steigerungsstufe) der Adjektive zu bilden:

1. Einsilbige Adjektive und der größte Teil der zweisilbigen haben die Endung -*(e)r* und *(e)st*.

small   smaller   smallest
busy   busier   busiest
large   larger   largest

2. Die Adjektive, die aus mehr als zwei Silben bestehen, und gewisse Adjektive mit nur zwei Silben (z.B. solche, die auf -*ful* oder -*less* enden) bilden ihren Komparativ und Superlativ mit Hilfe von *more* und *most*.

expensive   more expensive
most expensive
useful   more useful
most useful

Folgende unregelmäßige Bildungen sind zu beachten:

good   better   best
bad   worse   worst
little   less   least
much }
many } *more   most*

Pronomen

Singular	Personalpronomen (persönliches Fürwort)		Possessivpronomen (besitzanzeigendes Fürwort)	
	Subjekt	Ergänzung	1	2
1. Person	*I*	*me*	*my*	*mine*
2. Person	*you*	*you*	*your*	*yours*
3. Person (m.)	*he*	*him*	*his*	*his*
3. Person (f.)	*she*	*her*	*her*	*hers*
3. Person (n.)	*it*	*it*	*its*	
Plural				
1. Person	*we*	*us*	*our*	*ours*
2. Person	*you*	*you*	*your*	*yours*
3. Person	*they*	*them*	*their*	*theirs*

Merke:

1. Das Englische kennt kein «du» (außer in Bezug auf Gott). Es gibt nur eine einzige Form, *you*, die «du» oder «Sie» bedeuten kann.

   Give it to me. Gib es mir/ Geben Sie es mir.

2. Die Ergänzung gebraucht man **auch** als Dativobjekt und nach Präpositionen (Verhältniswörtern).

   He came with us. Er kam mit uns.

3. Die erste Form des Possessivpronomens stellt das Adjektiv dar, die zweite Pronomen (man braucht sie also alleine).

   Where's my key? Wo ist mein Schlüssel?
   That's not mine. Das gehört nicht mir.

Adverb

Adverbien (Umstandswörter) werden gebildet, indem man -*ly* an das Adjektiv anhängt, ausgenommen, wenn diese Endung schon vorhanden ist. Adjektive, die auf -*y* enden (ausgenommen solche auf -*ly*), nehmen als Adverbien die Endung -*ily* an.

quick	*quickly*
easy	*easily*

Zu beachten:

good	*well*
fast	*fast*

Verben

Die englischen Verben (Zeitwörter) behalten die **Infinitivform** (Nennform) in allen Personen des Präsens (Gegenwart), außer in der 3. Person Singular, wo -*s* angehängt wird.

he walks er geht
he proposes er schlägt vor

Das Imperfekt (Vergangenheit) und das **Partizip Perfekt** (Mittelwort der vollendeten Vergangenheit) der regelmäßigen Verben werden durch Anhängen von -*d* oder -*ed* gebildet.

I walked ich ging (spaziere)
I have walked ich bin gegangen
I proposed ich schlug vor
I have proposed ich habe vorgeschlagen

Das **Partizip Präsens** bildet man, indem man -*ing* an den Infinitiv anhängt.

walking

Wenn das Verb mit einem Konsonanten endet, dem ein kurzer betonter Vokal vorausgeht, wird der Endkonsonant im Partizip (Präsens und Perfekt) und im Imperfekt verdoppelt.

stopped angehalten
stopping anhaltend

Verben mit der Endung -*y*, der ein Konsonant vorausgeht, enden in der 3. Person Singular im Präsens mit -*ies* und in der Vergangenheit mit -*ied*.

he satisfies er stellt zufrieden
he satisfied er stellte zufrieden
satisfied zufriedengestellt

Das englische **Futur** (Zukunft) wird mit zwei Hilfsverben (*shall* und *will*) und dem Infinitiv gebildet. Normalerweise benutzt man *shall* für die 1. Person und *will* für alle anderen.

I shall see ich werde sehen
we shall go wir werden gehen
you will give du wirst geben
they will arrive sie werden ankommen

Wird *will* in der 1. Person angewendet, zeigt es Bestimmtheit oder Willen an.

I will go ich will gehen.

Wenn *shall* in der zweiten und dritten Person angewendet wird, zeigt es einen Auftrag oder Zwang an.
Der Ausdruck *I am going to* drückt eine unmittelbar bevorstehende Zukunft aus.

you shall leave du sollst gehen (weil ich es will)
He's going to leave. Er ist im Begriff wegzugehen.

Die 2. Person des **Imperativs** (Befehlsform) lautet gleich wie der Infinitiv.
Die 2. und 3. Person werden mit *let* (lassen) gebildet, dem ein Personalpronomen und der Infinitiv des konjugierten Verbs folgen.

Go! Geh!
Let us go! Gehen wir!
Let him speak! Laß ihn sprechen!

Der Konditional (Bedingungsform) wird mit zwei Hilfsverben gebildet, mit *should* in der 1. Person und mit *would* in allen anderen.

I should say ich würde sagen
he would answer er würde antworten

Die Modalverben (Art und Weise betreffende Verben) haben meistens zwei Formen:
Can–could, may–might, will–would, shall–should.
Ought und *must* haben nur eine Form.
In den Zeiten, die ihnen fehlen, werden sie durch andere Verben ersetzt: *can* durch *to be able to; may* durch *to be allowed, to be permitted to; must* durch *to have to, to be obliged to.*

He was able to move. Er konnte sich bewegen.
I had to go. Ich mußte gehen.

Die **Verneinung** und die **Frage** wird mit dem Hilfsverb *to do* geformt. **Präsens:**

We do not (oder *don't*) *like this hotel.* Wir mögen dieses Hotel nicht.
Does he like this hotel? Gefällt ihm dieses Hotel?

Imperfekt (Vergangenheit):

We didn't like this hotel. Uns gefiel dieses Hotel nicht.
Did he like this hotel? Gefiel ihm dieses Hotel?

In den anderen Zeiten werden Frage und Verneinung mit ihren entsprechenden Hilfsverben *(have, shall, will, should, usw.)* gebildet.
Die Frageform des Hilfsverbs *to be* erhält man durch einfache Umstellung des Verbs und des Subjekts, die Verneinung durch Hinzufügung von *not*.

Are you happy? Sind Sie glücklich?
I'm not happy. Ich bin nicht glücklich.

Hilfsverben

to be (sein)

Präsens	abgekürzte Form
I am	*I'm*
you are	*you're*
he is	*he's*
she is	*she's*
it is	*it's*
we are	*we're*
they are	*they're*

Verneinung	abgekürzte Form
I am not	*I'm not*
you are not	*you're not* oder *you aren't*
he is not	*he's not* oder *he isn't*
she is not	*she's not* oder *she isn't*
we are not	*we're not* oder *we aren't*
they are not	*they're not* oder *they aren't*

Die deutsche Form «es gibt» hat im Englischen zwei Bedeutungen, je nachdem, ob das Verb von einem Substantiv im Singular *(there is)* oder Plural *(there are)* gefolgt wird.
Verneinung: *There isn't.* *There aren't.*
Frage: *Is there?* *Are there?*

To have (haben)

Präsens   abgekürzte Form

I have	*I've*	
you have	*you've*	
he has	*he's*	Verneinung: *I have not*
she has	*she's*	(*I haven't*)
it has	*it's*	Frage: *Have you?*
we have	*we've*	*Has he?*
they have	*they've*	

To do (tun, machen)

I do	
you do	
he does	Verneinung: *I do not*
she does	(*I don't*) *He does not*
we do	(*he doesn't*)
they do	Frage: *Do you? Does he?*

Merke: In der Umgangssprache verwendet man fast immer die abgekürzte Form.

Perfekt

Um diese Zeit zu bilden, benutzt man das Partizip Perfekt in Verbindung mit den konjugierten Formen des Hilfsverbs *to have*.

She's seen him. Sie hat ihn gesehen.
We've gone. Wir sind gegangen.

Die progressive Form

Diese Form entspricht dem Deutschen «ich bin gerade dabei zu...» und wird mit dem Hilfsverb *to be* gebildet, das vom Partizip Präsens eines Verbes gefolgt wird.

Infinitiv	Part. Präs.	Progressiv-Form
to read	*reading*	*I'm reading* usw.
to write	*writing*	*I'm writing* usw.

Der Ausdruck *would (used to)*, gefolgt von einem Infinitiv, entspricht dem Imperfekt einer Gewohnheit.

I would drink (I'd drink) coffee now and then. Hin und wieder trank ich Kaffee.
I used to take the train every day. Ich nahm jeden Tag den Zug.

ENGLISCHE UNREGELMÄSSIGE VERBEN

Hier sind nur die unregelmäßigen Formen angegeben.

Infinitiv	*Imperfekt*	*Partizip Perfekt*
arise	arose	arisen
awake	awoke	awoke (awaked *oder* awoken)
be	was	been
bear	bore	borne (born = geboren)
beat	beat	beaten
become	became	become
begin	began	begun
bend	bent	bent
beseech	besought	besought
bid	bade	bid (bidden)
bind	bound	bound
bite	bit	bit (bitten)
bleed	bled	bled
blow	blew	blown
break	broke	broken
breed	bred	bred
bring	brought	brought
build	built	built
burn	burnt	burnt
burst	burst	burst
buy	bought	bought
cast	cast	cast
catch	caught	caught
choose	chose	chosen
cling	clung	clung
come	came	come
cost	cost	cost
creep	crept	crept
cut	cut	cut
deal	dealt	dealt
dig	dug	dug
do (he does)	did	done
draw	drew	drawn
dream	dreamt	dreamt
drink	drank	drunk
drive	drove	driven
dwell	dwelt	dwelt
to eat	ate	eaten
fall	fell	fallen
feed	fed	fed
feel	felt	felt
fight	fought	fought
find	found	found
flee	fled	fled
fling	flung	flung
fly	flew	flown
forbid	forbade	forbidden
forget	forgot	forgotten
forgive	forgave	forgiven
freeze	froze	frozen

Infinitiv	Imperfekt	Partizip Perfekt
get	got	got
give	gave	given
go	went	gone
grow	grew	grown
hang	hung	hung
have	had	had
hear	heard	heard
hide	hid	hid (hidden)
hit	hit	hit
hold	held	held
hurt	hurt	hurt
keep	kept	kept
kneel	knelt	knelt
knit	knit	knit
know	knew	known
lay	laid	laid
lead	led	led
lean	leant	leant
leap	leapt	leapt
learn	learnt	learnt
leave	left	left
lie	lay	lain
light	lit	lit
lose	lost	lost
make	made	made
mean	meant	meant
meet	met	met
mistake	mistook	mistaken
mow	mowed	mown
pay	paid	paid
prove	proved	proved (proven)
put	put	put
read	read	read
rend	rent	rent
ride	rode	ridden
ring	rang	rung
rise	rose	risen
run	ran	run
saw	sawed	sawn
say	said	said
see	saw	seen
seek	sought	sought
sell	sold	sold
send	sent	sent
set	set	set
sew	sewed	sewn
shake	shook	shaken
shape	shaped	shaped
shave	shaved	shaved (shaven)
shine	shone	shone
shoot	shot	shot
show	showed	shown
shred	shred	shred
shrink	shrank	shrunk

Infinitiv	*Imperfekt*	*Partizip Perfekt*
shut	shut	shut
sing	sang	sung
sink	sank	sunk
sit	sat	sat
sleep	slept	slept
slide	slid	slid
sling	slung	slung
smell	smelt	smelt
sow	sowed	sown
speak	spoke	spoken
speed	sped	sped
spell	spelt	spelt
spend	spent	spent
spill	spilt	spilt
spin	spun	spun
spit	spit	spit
split	split	split
spoil	spoilt	spoilt
spread	spread	spread
spring	sprang	sprung
stand	stood	stood
steal	stole	stolen
stick	stuck	stuck
sting	stung	stung
strew	strewed	strewn
strike	struck	struck
string	strung	strung
swear	swore	sworn
sweat	sweat	sweat
sweep	swept	swept
swell	swelled	swollen
swim	swam	swum
take	took	taken
teach	taught	taught
tear	tore	torn
tell	told	told
think	thought	thought
throw	threw	thrown
understand	understood	understood
upset	upset	upset
wear	wore	worn
weave	wove	woven
win	won	won
wind	wound	wound
withdraw	withdrew	withdrawn
write	wrote	written

ERKLÄRUNG DER ABKÜRZUNGEN		KEY TO SYMBOLS AND ABBREVIATIONS
Adjektiv	**adj**	adjective
Adverb	**adv**	adverb
Artikel	**art**	article
Konjunktion	**conj**	conjunction
Femininum	**f**	feminine
unveränderlich	**inv**	invariable
Maskulinum	**m**	masculine
Substantiv	**n**	noun
Neutrum	**nt**	neuter
Präteritum (Imperfekt)	**p**	past tense (preterite)
Plural	**pl**	plural
Partizip Perfekt	**pp**	past participle
Partizip Präsens	**ppr**	present participle
Präsens	**pr**	present tense
Präfix	**pref**	prefix
Präposition	**prep**	preposition
Pronomen	**pron**	pronoun
Singular	**sing**	singular
Verb	**v**	verb, compound verb
unregelmäßiges Verb	*****	irregular verb
siehe	$\rightarrow$	see (cross-reference)

N.B. Bei aus mehreren Wörtern bestehenden Wendungen wird oft die sinngemäße Wortart angegeben.

englisch-deutsch

a [eej] *art* **(an)** ein; eine
a little [ö LIT-öl] *n* Bißchen *nt*
abbey [ÆB-i] *n* Abtei *f*
abbreviation [ö-brie-wi-EEJ-schön] *n* esse
ability [ö-BIL-i-ti] *n* Fähigkeit *f*
able [EEJ-böl] *adj* fähig
aboard [ö-BOHD] *adv* an Bord
about [ö-BAUT] *prep* über; *adv* etwa
above [ö-BAW] *prep* über; *adv* oben
abroad [ö-BROHD] *adv* im Ausland
absence [ÆB-ssönss] *n* Abwesenheit *f*
absent [ÆB-ssönt] *adj* abwesend
absolutely [ÆB-ssöl-uht-li] *adv* völlig
abstract [ÆB-sstrækt] *adj* abstrakt
absurd [öb-SSOHD] *adj* absurd
academy [ö-KÆD-ö-mi] *n* Akademie *f*
accelerate [æk-SSÄL-ör-eejt] *v* beschleunigen
accelerator [æk-SSÄL-ör-eej-tö] *n* Gaspedal *nt*
accent [ÆK-ssönt] *n* Akzent *m*

accept [ök-SSÄPT] *v* annehmen
access [ÆK-ssäss] *n* Zutritt *m*
accessary [æk-SSÄSS-ör-i] *n* Mitschuldige *m*
accessories [æk-SSÄSS-ör-is] *pl* Zubehör *nt*
accident [ÆK-ssi-dönt] *n* Unfall *m*
accidental [æk-ssi-DÄNT-öl] *adj* zufällig
accommodate [ö-KOM-ö-deejt] *v* unterbringen
accommodations [ö-kom-ö-DEEJ-schöns] *pl* Unterkunft *f*
accompany [ö-KAM-pö-ni] *v* begleiten
accomplish [ö-KOM-plisch] *v* zustande bringen
according to [ö-KOH-ding tuh] *prep* gemäß
account [ö-KAUNT] *n* Bericht *m;* Konto *nt*
account for [ö-KAUNT foh] *v* Rechenschaft ablegen über
accurate [ÆK-ju-rit] *adj* genau
accuse [ö-KJUHS] *v* beschuldigen
accustomed [ö-KASS-tömd] *adj* gewohnt
ace [eejss] *n* As *nt*

ache [eejk] *n* Schmerz *m*; *v* schmerzen

achieve [ö-TSCHIEW] *v* leisten

achievement [ö-TSCHIEW-mönt] *n* Leistung *f*

acknowledge [ök-NOL-idʒ] *v* bestätigen

acquaintance [ö-KUEEJN-tönss] *n* Bekannte *m*

acquire [ö-KUAIÖ] *v* erwerben

across [ö-KROSS] *adv* drüben; *prep* jenseits

act [äkt] *v* benehmen (sich); *n* Akt *m*; Tat *f*

action [ÄK-schön] *n* Handlung *f*

active [ÄK-tiw] *adj* rührig

activity [äk-TIW-i-ti] *n* Tätigkeit *f*

actor [ÄK-tö] *n* Schauspieler *m*

actress [ÄK-triss] *n* Schauspielerin *f*

actual [ÄK-tju-öl] *adj* tatsächlich

acute [ö-KJUHT] *adj* heftig

add [äd] *v* addieren

addition [ö-DISCH-ön] *n* Addition *f*

additional [ö-DISCH-ön-öl] *adj* zusätzlich

address [ö-DRÄSS] *n* Anschrift *f*; *v* adressieren; ansprechen

addressee [ä-drä-SSIE] *n* Adressat *m*

adequate [ÄD-i-kuit] *adj* angemessen

adhesive tape [öd-HIESS-iw teejp] *n* Heftpflaster *nt*

adjective [ÄDʒ-ik-tiw] *n* Eigenschaftswort *nt*

adjust [ö-DʒASST] *v* anpassen

admiration [äd-mö-REEJ-schön] *n* Bewunderung *f*

admire [öd-MAIÖ] *v* bewundern

admission [öd-MISCH-ön] *n* Eintritt *m*

* **admit** [öd-MIT] *v* einlassen

admittance [öd-MIT-önss] *n* Zutritt *m*

adopt [ö-DOPT] *v* annehmen

adult [ÄD-alt] *adj* erwachsen; *n* Erwachsene *m*

advance [öd-WAHNSS] *n* Vorschuß *m*; *v* vorschießen

advantage [öd-WAHNT-idʒ] *n* Vorteil *m*

advantageous [äd-wön-TEEJ-dʒöss] *adj* vorteilhaft

adventure [öd-WÄN-tschö] *n* Abenteuer *nt*

adverb [ÄD-wöhb] *n* Adverb *nt*

advertisement [öd-WÖHT-iss-mönt] *n* Anzeige *f*

advice [öd-WAISS] *n* Rat *m*

advise [öd-WAIS] *v* raten

aerial [ÄÖR-i-öl] *n* Antenne *f*

aeroplane [ÄÖR-ö-pleejn] *n* Flugzeug *nt*

affair [ö-FÄÖ] *n* Liebschaft *f*; Angelegenheit *f*

affect [ö-FÄKT] *v* beeinflussen

affectionate [ö-FÄK-schön-it] *adj* zärtlich

affirmative [ö-FÖHM-ö-tiw] *adj* bejahend

afford [ö-FOHD] *v* leisten (sich)

afraid [ö-FREEJD] *adj* bange

Africa [ÄF-ri-kö] *n* Afrika *nt*

African [ÄF-ri-kön] *n* Afrikaner *m*; *adj* afrikanisch

after [AHF-tö] *prep* nach; *conj* nachdem

afternoon [AHF-tö-nuhn] *n* Nachmittag *m*

aftershave lotion [AHF-tö-scheejw LOO-schön] *n* Rasierwasser *nt*

afterwards [AHF-tö-uöds] *adv* nachher

again [ö-GÄN] *adv* wieder

against [ö-GÄNSST] *prep* gegen

age [eejdʒ] n Alter nt
aged [EEJdʒ-id] adj alt
agency [EEJ-dʒön-ssi] n
  Vertretung f
agent [EEJ-dʒönt] n Vertreter m
agree [ö-GRIE] v
  übereinstimmen; zustimmen
agreeable [ö-GRIE-ö-böl] adj
  angenehm
agreed [ö-GRIED] adj abgemacht
agreement [ö-GRIE-mönt] n
  Abkommen nt
agriculture [ÆG-ri-kal-tschö] n
  Landwirtschaft f
ahead [ö-HÄD] adv vorwärts
ahead of [ö-HÄD OW] vor
aid [eejd] n Hilfe f; v helfen
ailment [EEJL-mönt] n Leiden nt
aim [eejm] v bezwecken; n Ziel
  nt
air [äö] v lüften; n Luft f
air conditioned [äö kön-DISCH-
  önd] adj klimatisiert
air conditioner [äö kön-DISCH-
  ön-ö] n Klimaanlage f
air mail [äö meejl] n Luftpost f
air sickness [äö SSIK-niss] n
  Luftkrankheit f
aircraft [ÄÖ-krahft] n Flugzeug
  nt
airfield [ÄÖ-field] n Flugplatz m
airline [ÄÖ-lain] n Fluglinie f
airplane [ÄÖ-pleejn] n Flugzeug
  nt
airport [ÄÖ-poht] n Flughafen m
aisle [ail] n Gang m
alarm [ö-LAHM] v alarmieren; n
  Alarm m
alarm clock [ö-LAHM klok] n
  Wecker m
alcohol [ÆL-kö-hol] n Alkohol m
alcoholic [æl-kö-HOL-ik] adj
  alkoholisch
alien [EEJL-jön] adj ausländisch

alike [ö-LAIK] adj ähnlich; adv
  gleich
alive [ö-LAIW] adj lebend
all [ohl] adj alle
all in [ohl in] alles inbegriffen
all right [ohl rait] gut
alley [ÆL-i] n Gäßchen nt
allow [ö-LAU] v erlauben
allowed [ö-LAUD] adj erlaubt
almond [AH-mönd] n Mandel f
almost [OHL-moosst] adv beinahe
alone [ö-LOON] adv allein
along [ö-LONG] prep entlang
aloud [ö-LAUD] adv laut
already [ohl-RAD-i] adv schon
also [OHL-ssoo] adv auch
altar [OHL-tö] n Altar m
alter [OHL-tö] v abändern
alteration [ohl-tö-REEJ-schön] n
  Änderung f
alternate [ohl-TÖH-nit] adj
  abwechselnd
alternating current [OHL-tö-
  neejt-ing KAR-önt] n
  Wechselstrom m
alternative [ohl-TÖH-nö-tiw] n
  Alternative f
although [ohl-ðoo] conj obwohl
altitude [ÆL-ti-tjuhd] n Höhe f
altogether [ohl-tö-GÄð-ö] adv
  insgesamt
always [OHL-uös] adv immer
am [æm] v (pr be)
amaze [ö-MEEJS] v erstaunen
ambassador [æm-BÆSS-ö-dö] n
  Botschafter m
ambitious [æm-BISCH-öss] adj
  ehrgeizig
ambulance [ÆM-bju-lönss] n
  Krankenwagen m
amenities [ö-MIEN-i-tis] pl gute
  Manieren fpl
America [ö-MÄR-i-kö] n Amerika
  nt

American [ö-MÄR-i-kön] *n*
Amerikaner *m; adj*
amerikanisch

amethyst [ÆM-i-Ɵisst] *n*
Amethyst *m*

amidst [ö-MIDSST] *prep* inmitten

ammonia [ö-MOON-jö] *n*
Ammoniak *nt*

among [ö-MANG] *prep* unter

amount [ö-MAUNT] *v* betragen; *n*
Menge *f;* Betrag *m*

amuse [ö-MJUHS] *v* amüsieren;
unterhalten (sich)

amusing [ö-MJUHS-ing] *adj*
amüsant

an [æn] *art* (→ **a**)

anaemia [ö-NIEM-jö] *n* Blutarmut
f

anaesthetic [æn-iss-Ɵät-ik] *n*
Betäubungsmittel *nt*

analyse [ÆN-ö-lais] *v* analysieren

analysis [ö-NÆL-ö-ssiss] *n* (*pl* -
ses) Analyse *f*

analyst [ÆN-ö-lisst] *n*
Psychoanalytiker *m*

ancestor [ÆN-ssiss-tö] *n* Vorfahr
m

anchovy [ÆN-tschöw-i] *n*
Sardelle *f*

ancient [EEJN-schönt] *adj* alt

and [ænd] *conj* und

and so on [önd ssoo on] und so
weiter

angel [EEJN-dȝöl] *n* Engel *m*

anger [ÆNG-gö] *n* Zorn *m*

angry [ÆNG-gri] *adj* zornig

animal [ÆN-i-möl] *n* Tier *nt*

ankle [ÆNG-köl] *n* Fußknöchel *m*

annex [ÆN-äkss] *n*
Nebengebäude *nt*

anniversary [æn-i-wöHSS-ö-ri] *n*
Jahrestag *m*

announce [ö-NAUNSS] *v*
ankündigen

announcement [ö-NAUNSS-mönt]
n Ankündigung *f*

annoy [ö-NEU] *v* belästigen

annoying [ö-NEU-ing] *adj*
ärgerlich

anonymous [ö-NON-i-möss] *adj*
anonym

another [ö-NAð-ö] *adj* ein
anderer; noch ein

answer [AHN-ssö] *n* Antwort *f; v*
beantworten

ant [ænt] *n* Ameise *f*

antibiotic [ÆN-ti-bai-OT-ik] *n*
Antibiotikum *nt*

anticipate [æn-TISS-i-peejt] *v*
erwarten

antifreeze [ÆN-ti-FRIES] *n*
Gefrierschutzmittel *nt*

antique [æn-TIEK] *n* Antiquität *f;
adj* antik

antiquities [æn-TIK-ui-tis] *pl*
Altertümer *ntpl*

antiquity [æn-TIK-ui-ti] *n*
Altertum *nt*

antiseptic [æn-ti-SSÄP-tik] *n*
antiseptisches Mittel *nt*

anxious [ÆNGK-schöss] *adj*
besorgt; bestrebt

any [AN-i] *adj* irgendein

anybody [AN-i-bod-il] *pron* irgend
jemand

anyhow [AN-i-hau] *adv* irgendwie

anyone [AN-i-uan] *pron*
jedermann

anything [AN-i-Ɵing] *pron* irgend
etwas

anyway [AN-i-ueej] *adv* ohnehin

anywhere [AN-i-uäö] *adv* überall

apart [ö-PAHT] *adv* getrennt

apartment [ö-PAHT-mönt] *n*
Wohnung *f*

apartment house [ö-PAHT-mönt
hauss] *n* Wohnblock *m*

aperitif [ö-PÄR-i-tiw] *n* Aperitif *m*

apologize [ö-POL-ö-dʒais] *v* entschuldigen (sich)

apology [ö-POL-ö-dʒi] *n* Entschuldigung *f*

apparent [ö-PÆR-önt] *adj* offensichtlich

appeal [ö-PIEL] *n* Appell *m*

appear [ö-PIÖ] *v* erscheinen; scheinen

appearance [ö-PIÖR-önss] *n* Erscheinung *f*

appendicitis [ö-pän-di-SSAI-tiss] *n* Blinddarmentzündung *f*

appetiser [ÆP-i-tais-ö] *n* Appetithappen *m*

appetising [ÆP-i-tais-ing] *adj* lecker

appetite [ÆP-i-tait] *n* Appetit *m*

applause [ö-PLOHS] *n* Beifall *m*

apple [ÆP-öl] *n* Apfel *m*

appliance [ö-PLAI-önss] *n* Gerät *nt*

apply [ö-PLAI] *v* verwenden

appointment [ö-PEUNT-mönt] *n* Verabredung *f*

appreciate [ö-PRIE-schi-eejt] *v* schätzen

appreciation [ö-pri-schi-EEJ-schön] *n* Schätzung *f*

approach [ö-PROOTSCH] *n* Zugang *m*; *v* nähern (sich)

appropriate [ö-PROO-pri-it] *adj* angemessen

approval [ö-PRUHW-öl] *n* Billigung *f*

approve [ö-PRUHW] *v* genehmigen

approximately [ö-PROKSS-im-öt-li] *adv* ungefähr

apricot [EEJ-pri-kot] *n* Aprikose *f*

April [EEJ-pröl] *n* April *m*

apron [EEJ-prön] *n* Schürze *f*

Arab [ÆR-öb] *n* Araber *m*; *adj* arabisch

arcade [ah-KEEJD] *n* Arkade *f*

arch [ahtsch] *n* Bogen *m*

archbishop [AHTSCH-bisch-öp] *n* Erzbischof *m*

arched [ahtscht] *adj* bogenförmig

architect [AHK-i-täkt] *n* Architekt *m*

architecture [AHK-i-täk-tschö] *n* Architektur *f*

are [ah] *v* (*pr* **be**)

area [ÄÖ-ri-ö] *n* Fläche *f*

area code [ÄÖ-ri-ö kood] *n* Ortsnetz-Kennzahl *f*

argue [AH-gjuh] *v* diskutieren

argument [AH-gju-mönt] *n* Auseinandersetzung *f*

arid [ÆR-id] *adj* dürr

*** arise** [ö-RAIS] *v* erheben (sich)

arisen [ö-RIS-ön] *v* (*pp* **arise**)

arithmetic [ö-RIΘ-mö-tik] *n* Rechnen *nt*

arm [ahm] *n* Arm *m*

armchair [AHM-tschäö] *n* Lehnstuhl *m*

arms [ahms] *pl* Waffen *fpl*

army [AHM-i] *n* Armee *f*

arose [ö-ROOS] *v* (*p* **arise**)

around [ö-RAUND] *adv* rundherum; *prep* um...herum

arrange [ö-REEJndʒ] *v* vorbereiten; ordnen

arrangements [ö-REEJndʒ-möntss] *pl* Vorbereitungen *fpl*

arrest [ö-RÄSST] *n* Verhaftung *f*; *v* verhaften

arrival [ö-RAIW-öl] *n* Ankunft *f*

arrive [ö-RAIW] *v* eintreffen

arrow [ÆR-oo] *n* Pfeil *m*

art [aht] *n* Fertigkeit *f*; Kunst *f*

art collection [aht kö-LÄK-schön] *n* Kunstsammlung *f*

art exhibition [aht äkss-i-BISCH-ön] *n* Kunstausstellung *f*

art gallery [aht GÆL-ö-ri] *n*

Kunstgalerie *f*

artery [AH-tö-ri] *n* Arterie *f*

artichoke [AH-ti-tschook] *n* Artischocke *f*

article [AH-ti-köl] *n* Gegenstand *m;* Artikel *m*

artificial [ah-ti-FISCH-öl] *adj* künstlich

artist [AH-tisst] *n* Künstler *m*

artistic [ah-TISS-tik] *adj* künstlerisch

as [æs] *conj* wie

as a matter of fact [æs ö MÆT-ö öw fækt] tatsächlich

as a rule [æs ö ruhl] in der Regel

as from [æs from] ab

as if [æs if] als ob

as regards [æs ri-GAHDS] wasâ.â.â.âbetrifft

as soon as [æs ssuhn æs] sobald als

as well [æs uäl] ebenfalls

ascend [ö-SSÄND] *v* hinaufsteigen

ascent [ö-SSÄNT] *n* Aufstieg *m*

ashamed [ö-SCHEEJMD] *adj* beschämt

ashes [ÆSCH-is] *pl* Asche *f*

ashtray [ÆSCH-treej] *n* Aschenbecher *m*

Asia [EEJSCH-ö] *n* Asien *nt*

Asian [EEJSCH-ön] *n* Asiate *m; adj* asiatisch

aside [ö-SSAID] *adv* beiseite

ask [ahssk] *v* einladen; bitten; fragen

asleep [ö-SSLIEP] *adj* im Schlaf

asparagus [öss-PÆR-ö-göss] *n* Spargel *m*

aspirin [ÆSS-pö-rin] *n* Aspirin *nt*

ass [æss] *n* Esel *m*

assembly [ö-SSÄM-bli] *n* Zusammenkunft *f*

assets [ÆSS-ätss] *pl* Aktiva *ntpl*

assist [ö-SSISST] *v* helfen

assistant [ö-SSISS-tönt] *n* Assistent *m*

associate [ö-SSOO-schi-eejt] *v* vereinigen; *n* Teilhaber *m*

association [ö-SSOO-ssi-EEJ-schön] *n* Vereinigung *f*

assorted [ö-SSOHT-id] *adj* assortiert

assortment [ö-SSOHT-mönt] *n* Sortiment *nt*

assume [ö-SSJUHM] *v* voraussetzen

assure [ö-SCHUHÖ] *v* versichern

asthma [ÆSS-mö] *n* Asthma *nt*

astonish [öss-TON-isch] *v* verblüffen

astonishing [öss-TON-isch-ing] *adj* erstaunlich

at all [æt ohl] überhaupt

at any rate [æt ÄN-i reejt] auf jeden Fall

at any time [æt ÄN-i taim] jederzeit

at best [æt bässt] bestenfalls

at first [æt föhsst] zuerst

at home [æt hoom] zuhause

at last [æt lahsst] endlich

at least [æt liesst] wenigstens

at once [æt uanss] sofort

at the latest [æt ðö LEEJT-isst] spätestens

ate [ät] *v* (*p* eat)

athletics [æΘ-LÄT-ikss] *pl* Athletik *f*

Atlantic [æt-LÆN-tik] *n* Atlantik *m*

atmosphere [ÆT-möss-fiö] *n* Atmosphäre *f;* Stimmung *f*

atomic bomb [ö-TOM-ik bom] *n* Atombombe *f*

atomizer [ÆT-öm-ais-ö] *n* Zerstäuber *m*

attach [ö-TÆTSCH] *v* befestigen

attaché-case [ö-TÆSCH-i-keejss

n Aktentasche *f*
attack [ö-TÆK] *v* angreifen
attempt [ö-TÄMPT] *v* versuchen
attend [ö-TÄND] *v* erledigen;
beiwohnen
attendant [ö-TÄND-önt] *n* Wärter
m
attention [ö-TÄN-schön] *n*
Aufmerksamkeit *f*
attitude [ÆT-i-tjuhd] *n*
Einstellung *f*
attorney [ö-TÖH-ni] *n* Anwalt *m*
attract [ö-TRÆKT] *v* anziehen
attraction [ö-TRÆK-schön] *n* Reiz
m
attractive [ö-TRÆK-tiw] *adj*
anziehend
auction [OHK-schön] *n*
Versteigerung *f*
auctioneer [ohk-schö-NIÖ] *n*
Auktionator *m*
audience [OHD-i-önss] *n*
Publikum *nt*
August [OH-gösst] *n* August *m*
aunt [ahnt] *n* Tante *f*
Australia [oss-TREEJL-jö] *n*
Australien *nt*
Australian [oss-TREEJL-jön] *n*
Australier *m; adj* australisch
Austria [oss-tri-ö] *n* Österreich
nt
Austrian [oss-tri-ön] *n*
Österreicher *m; adj*
österreichisch
authentic [oo-ΘÄNT-ik] *adj* echt
author [OHΘ-ö] *n* Autor *m*
authority [oh-ΘOR-it-i] *n*
Befugnis *f*
automat [OH-tö-mæt] *n*
Automaten-Restaurant *nt*
automatic [oh-tö-MÆT-ik] *adj*
automatisch
automobile [OH-tö-mö-biel] *n*
Auto *nt*

automobile club [OH-tö-mö-biel
klab] *n* Automobilklub *m*
autonomous [oh-TON-öm-öss] *adj*
autonom
autumn [OH-töm] *n* Herbst *m*
available [ö-WEEJL-ö-böl] *adj*
verfügbar
avalanche [ÆW-ö-lahnsch] *n*
Lawine *f*
avenue [ÆW-i-njuh] *n* Allee *f*
average [ÆW-ör-idʒ] *n*
Durchschnitt *m; adj*
durchschnittlich
avoid [ö-WEUD] *v* vermeiden
await [ö-UEEJT] *v* erwarten
awake [ö-UEEJK] *adj* wach; *v*
wecken
award [ö-UOHD] *n* Belohnung *f*
aware [ö-UÄÖ] *adj* gewahr
away [ö-UEEJ] *adv* abwesend
awful [OH-ful] *adj* schrecklich
awkward [OHK-uöd] *adj* peinlich;
ungeschickt
awoke [ö-UOOK] *v* (*p* awake)
axe [ækss] *n* Beil *nt*
axle [ÆKSS-öl] *n* Achse *f*

baby [BEEJ-bi] *n* Säugling *m*
babysitter [BEEJ-bi-ssIT-ö] *n*
Babysitter *m*
bachelor [BÆTSCH-öl-ö] *n*
Junggeselle *m*
back [bæk] *n* Rücken *m; adv*
zurück
backache [BÆK-eejk] *n*
Rückenschmerzen *mpl*
background [BÆK-graund] *n*
Vorbildung *f*
backwards [BÆK-uöds] *adv*
zurück
bacon [BEEJ-kön] *n* Speck *m*
bad [bæd] *adj* schlecht
bag [bæg] *n* Sack *m; Handtasche*

f; Koffer m
baggage [BÆG-idʒ] n Gepäck nt
baggage office [BÆG-idʒ OF-iss] n
Gepäckaufgabe f
bail [beejl] n Kaution f
bait [beejt] n Köder m
bake [beejk] v backen
baker [BEEJK-ö] n Bäcker m
bakery [BEEJK-ör-i] n Bäckerei f
balance [BÆL-önss] n
Gleichgewicht nt
balance sheet [BÆL-önss schiet]
n Bilanz f
balcony [BÆL-kö-ni] n Balkon m
bald [bohld] adj kahl
ball [bohl] n Ball m
ballet [BÆL-eej] n Ballett nt
ballpoint-pen [BOHL-peunt-PÄN]
n Kugelschreiber m
ballroom [BOHL-ruhm] n Ballsaal
m
banana [bö-NAH-nö] n Banane f
band [bænd] n Kapelle f; Band
nt
bandage [BÆND-idʒ] n Verband
m
Band-Aid [BÆND-eejd] n
Heftpflaster nt
bandit [BÆN-dit] n Bandit m
bank [bængk] v deponieren; n
Ufer nt; Bank f
bank account [bængk ö-KAUNT] n
Bankkonto nt
banker [BÆNGK-ö] n Bankier m
bank-note [BÆNGK-noot] n
Banknote f
bank-rate [BÆNGK-reejt] n
Diskontsatz m
banquet [BÆNGK-uit] n Festmahl
nt
banqueting-hall [BÆNGK-uit-ing-
hohl] n Bankettsaal m
bar [bah] n Stange f; Bar f
barber [BAHB-ö] n Friseur m

bare [bäö] adj bloß
barely [BÄÖ-li] adv kaum
bargain [BAH-gin] n
Gelegenheitskauf m; v
handeln
barley [BAH-li] n Gerste f
barmaid [BAH-meejd] n Bardame
f
barman [BAH-mön] n (pl -men)
Schankkellner m
barn [bahn] n Scheune f
barometer [bö-ROM-i-tö] n
Barometer nt
barracks [BÆR-ökss] pl Kaserne f
barrel [BÆR-öl] n Faß nt
barrier [BÆR-i-ö] n Schranke f
barrister [BÆR-iss-tö] n
Rechtsanwalt m
bartender [BAH-tönd-ö] n
Schankkellner m
base [beejss] n Grundlage f
baseball [BEEJSS-bohl] n Baseball
nt
basement [BEEJSS-mönt] n
Untergeschoß nt
basic [BEEJSS-ik] adj
grundlegend
basin [BEEJ-ssön] n Becken nt
basis [BEEJ-ssiss] n (pl -ses)
Grundlage f
basket [BAHSS-kit] n Korb m
bass [bæss] n Barsch m
batch [bætsch] n Partie f
bath [bahΘ] n Bad nt
bath salts [bahΘ ssohltss] n
Badesalz nt
bath towel [bahΘ TAU-öl] n
Badetuch nt
bathe [beejð] v baden
bathing cap [BEEJð-ing kæp] n
Bademütze f
bathing suit [BEEJð-ing ssuht] n
Badeanzug m
bathrobe [BAHΘ-roob] n

Bademantel *m*
bathroom [BAHΘ-ruhm] *n*
Badezimmer *nt*
battery [BÆT-ör-i] *n* Batterie *f*
battle [BÆT-öl] *n* Schlacht *f*
bay [beej] *n* Bucht *f*
* **be** [bie] *v* sein
beach [bietsch] *n* Strand *m*
beads [bieds] *pl* Halsband *nt*
bean [bien] *n* Bohne *f*
* **bear** [bäö] *v* ertragen; tragen
beard [biöd] *n* Bart *m*
bearer [BÄÖR-ö] *n* Inhaber *m*
* **beat** [biet] *v* besiegen; schlagen
beaten [BIET-ön] *v* (*pp* beat)
beautiful [BJUH-tö-full] *adj* schön
beauty parlour [BJUH-ti PAH-lö] *n*
Schönheitssalon *m*
beauty salon [BJUH-ti SSÆL-
ongng] *n* Schönheitssalon *m*
beauty treatment [BJUH-ti TRIET-
mönt] *n* kosmetische
Behandlung *f*
became [bi-KEEJM] *v* (*p* become)
because [bi-KOS] *conj* weil
because of [bi-KOS ow] wegen
* **become** [bi-KAM] *v* werden
bed [bäd] *n* Bett *nt*
bed and board [bäd önd bohd]
Vollpension *f*
bed and breakfast [bäd önd
BRÄK-fösst] Zimmer mit
Frühstück
bedding [BÄD-ing] *n* Bettzeug *nt*
bedroom [BÄD-ruhm] *n*
Schlafzimmer *nt*
bee [bie] *n* Biene *f*
beef [bief] *n* Rindfleisch *nt*
been [bien] *v* (*pp* be)
beetroot [BIET-ruht] *n* Bete *f*
before [bi-FOH] *adv* vorher; *prep*
vor; *conj* bevor
beg [bäg] *v* betteln
began [bi-GÆN] *v* (*p* begin)

beggar [BÄG-ö] *n* Bettler *m*
* **begin** [bi-GIN] *v* beginnen
beginner [bi-GIN-ö] *n* Anfänger
m
beginning [bi-GIN-ing] *n* Anfang
m
begun [bi-GAN] *v* (*pp* begin)
behave [bi-HEEJW] *v* benehmen
(sich)
behaviour [bi-HEEJW-jö] *n*
Betragen *nt*
behind [bi-HAIND] *prep* hinter;
adv hinten
beige [beejʒ] *adj* beige
being [BI-ing] *n* Wesen *nt*
Belgian [BÄL-dʒön] *n* Belgier *m*;
adj belgisch
Belgium [BÄL-dʒam] *n* Belgien *nt*
belief [bi-LIEF] *n* Glaube *m*
believe [bi-LIEW] *v* glauben
bell [bäl] *n* Glocke *f*
bellboy [BÄL-beu] *n* Hotelpage *m*
belong [bi-LONG] *v* gehören
belongings [bi-LONG-ings] *pl*
Habe *f*
below [bi-LOO] *adv* unten; *prep*
unterhalb
belt [bält] *n* Gürtel *m*
bench [bäntsch] *n* Bank *f*
* **bend** [bänd] *v* biegen; *n*
Biegung *f*
beneath [bi-NIEΘ] *adv* unten
benefit [BÄN-i-fit] *n* Nutzen *m*
bent [bänt] *v* (*p*, *pp* bend)
beret [BÄR-eej] *n* Baskenmütze *f*
berry [BÄR-i] *n* Beere *f*
berth [böhΘ] *n* Koje *f*
beside [bi-SSAID] *prep* neben
besides [bi-SSAIDS] *adv* überdies
best [bässt] *adj* best
bet [bät] *n* Wette *f*
better [BÄT-ö] *adj* besser
betting office [BÄT-ing OF-iss] *n*
Wettbüro *nt*

between [bi-TUIEN] *prep*
zwischen

beverage [BÄW-ör-idȝ] *n* Getränk
nt

beware [bi-UÄÖ] *v* hüten (sich)

beyond [bi-JOND] *prep* jenseits;
adv jenseits

Bible [BAI-böl] *n* Bibel *f*

bicycle [BAI-ssi-köl] *n* Fahrrad *nt*

big [big] *adj* groß

bigger [BIG-ö] *adj* größer

biggest [BIG-isst] *adj* größte

bill [bil] *v* fakturieren; *n*
Rechnung *f*

billiards [BIL-jöds] *n* Billard *nt*

*** bind** [baind] *v* binden

binding [BAIND-ing] *n* Einband *m*

binoculars [bi-NOK-ju-lös] *pl*
Opernglas *nt*

biology [bai-OL-ö-dȝi] *n* Biologie
f

birch [böhtsch] *n* Birke *f*

bird [böhd] *n* Vogel *m*

Biro [BAI-roo] *n* Kugelschreiber
m

birth [böhϴ] *n* Geburt *f*

birth certificate [böhϴ ssö-TIF-i-
kit] *n* Geburtsschein *m*

birthday [BÖHϴ-deej] *n*
Geburtstag *m*

birthplace [BÖHϴ-pleejss] *n*
Geburtsort *m*

biscuit [BISS-kit] *n* Keks *m*

bishop [BISCH-öp] *n* Bischof *m*

bit [bit] *v* (*p* **bite**); *n* Stückchen *nt*

*** bite** [bait] *v* beißen; *n* Bissen *m*;
Stich *m*; Biß *m*

bitten [BIT-ön] *v* (*pp* **bite**)

bitter [BIT-ö] *adj* bitter

black [blæk] *adj* schwarz

black market [blæk MAH-kit] *n*
Schwarzmarkt *m*

blackberry [BLÆK-bö-ri] *n*
Brombeere *f*

black-currant [BLÆK-KAR-önt] *n*
Johannisbeere *f*

blacksmith [BLÆK-ssmiϴ] *n*
Schmied *m*

blade [bleejd] *n* Klinge *f*

blame [bleejm] *n* Schuld *f*; *v*
beschuldigen

blank [blængk] *adj* leer

blanket [BLÆNGK-it] *n* Wolldecke
f

blazer [BLEEJS-ö] *n* Blazer *m*

bleach [blietsch] *v* bleichen

bled [blæd] *v* (*p, pp* **bleed**)

*** bleed** [blied] *v* bluten

bless [bläss] *v* segnen

blessing [BLÄSS-ing] *n* Segen *m*

blew [bluh] *v* (*p* **blow**)

blind [blaind] *adj* blind; *n*
Jalousie *f*

blister [BLISS-tö] *n* Blase *f*

blizzard [BLIS-öd] *n* Schneesturm
m

block [blok] *v* sperren; *n* Klotz
m; Häuserblock *m*

block of flats [blok öw flætss]
Wohnblock *m*

blonde [blond] *n* Blondine *f*

blood [blad] *n* Blut *nt*

blood-poisoning [BLAD-peus-ön-
ing] *n* Blutvergiftung *f*

blood-pressure [BLAD-präsch-ö]
n Blutdruck *m*

blood-vessel [BLAD-wäss-öl] *n*
Blutgefäß *nt*

blot [blot] *n* Klecks *m*

blouse [blaus] *n* Bluse *f*

*** blow** [bloo] *v* blasen; *n* Schlag *m*

blown [bloon] *v* (*pp* **blow**)

blow-out [BLOO-aut] *n*
Reifenpanne *f*

blue [bluh] *adj* blau

blunt [blant] *adj* stumpf

board [bohd] *n* Brett *nt*; Rat *m*

board and lodging [bohd önd

LOD3-ing] Vollpension *f*

boarder [BOHD-ö] *n* Kostgänger *m*

boarding house [BOHD-ing hauss] *n* Pension *f*

boat [boot] *n* Boot *nt*

boatman [BOOT-mön] *n* (*pl* -men) Bootsführer *m*

bobby-pin [BOB-i-pin] *n* Haarklemme *f*

body [BOD-i] *n* Körper *m*

boil [beul] *v* kochen; *n* Furunkel *m*

boiled [beuld] *adj* gekocht

boiling water [BEUL-ing UOH-tö] siedendes Wasser *nt*

bold [boold] *adj* kühn

bomb [bom] *n* Bombe *f*

bone [boon] *n* Knochen *m*

bonnet [BON-it] *n* Motorhaube *f*

book [buk] *n* Buch *nt; v* buchen

booking [BUK-ing] *n* Reservierung *f*

bookmaker [BUK-meejk-öl *n* Buchmacher *m*

bookseller [BUK-ssäl-ö] *n* Buchhändler *m*

bookstand [BUK-sstænd] *n* Bücherstand *m*

bookstore [BUK-sstoh] *n* Buchhandlung *f*

boot [buht] *n* Kofferraum *m;* Stiefel *m*

booth [buhð] *n* Zelle *f*

border [BOHD-ö] *n* Grenze *f*

bore [boh] *v* langweilen

boring [BOHR-ing] *adj* langweilig

born [bohn] *adj* geboren

borne [bohn] *v* (*pp* bear)

borough [BAR-ö] *n* Stadt *f*

borrow [BOR-oo] *v* borgen

boss [boss] *n* Chef *m*

botanical garden [boo-TÆN-ik-öl GAH-dön] *n* botanischer Garten

botany [BOT-ön-i] *n* Botanik *f*

both [booΘ] *adj* beide

bother [BOð-ö] *n* Belästigung *f; v* belästigen

bottle [BOOT-öl] *n* Flasche *f*

bottle opener [BOT-öl oo-pön-ö] *n* Flaschenöffner *m*

bottom [BOT-öm] *n* Boden *m*

bought [boht] *v* (*p, pp* buy)

boulder [BOOL-dö] *n* Felsblock *m*

bound [baund] *v* (*p, pp* bind)

boundary [BAUND-ör-i] *n* Grenze *f*

boutique [bu-TIEK] *n* Boutique *f*

bow tie [boo tai] *n* Fliege *f*

bowels [BAU-öls] *pl* Eingeweide *ntpl*

bowl [bool] *n* Schale *f*

bowling [BOOL-ing] *n* Kegeln *nt*

bowling alley [BOOL-ing ÆL-i] *n* Kegelbahn *f*

box [bokss] *n* Schachtel *f; v* boxen

box office [bokss OF-iss] *n* Kasse *f*

boxing match [BOKSS-ing mætsch] *n* Boxkampf *m*

boy [beu] *n* Junge *m*

bra [brah] *n* Büstenhalter *m*

bracelet [BREEJSS-lit] *n* Armband *nt*

brain [breejn] *n* Gehirn *nt*

brake [breejk] *n* Bremse *f*

brake lights [breejk laitss] *pl* Bremslicht *nt*

branch [brahntsch] *n* Ast *m*

branch off [brahntsch of] *v* gabeln (sich)

brand [brænd] *n* Marke *f*

brass [brahss] *n* Messing *nt*

brassiere [bræss-i-ö] *n* Büstenhalter *m*

brave [breejw] *adj* tapfer

Brazil [brö-SIL] *n* Brasilien *nt*

Brazilian [brö-SIL-jön] *adj*

brasilianisch; n Brasilianer m
bread [bräd] n Brot nt
breadth [bädΘ] n Breite f
* **break** [breejk] v brechen
break down [breejk daun] v eine
Panne haben
breakdown [BREEJK-daun] n
Panne f
breakfast [BRÄK-fösst] n
Frühstück nt
bream [briem] n Brassen m
breast [brässt] n Brust f
breath [bräΘ] n Atem m
breathe [brieð] v atmen
breathing [BRIEð-ing] n Atmung f
breed [bried] n Rasse f
breeze [bries] n Brise f
brewery [BRUH-ör-i] n Brauerei f
brick [brik] n Ziegel m
bride [braid] n Braut f
bridge [bridʒ] n Brücke f; Bridge
nt
brief [brief] adj bündig
briefcase [BRIEF-keejss] n
Aktenmappe f
briefs [briefss] pl Unterhose f
bright [brait] adj klug; hell
brill [bril] n Glattbutt m
brilliant [BRIL-jönt] adj glänzend
brilliantine [BRIL-jön-tien] n
Brillantine f
* **bring** [bring] v bringen
* **bring back** [bring bäk] v
zurückbringen
* **bring up** [bring ap] v
vorbringen
brisk [brissk] adj lebhaft
British [BRIT-isch] adj britisch
broad [brohd] adj breit
broadcast [BROHD-kahsst] n
Sendung f
brocade [broo-KEEJD] n Brokat m
brochure [broo-SCHUHÖ] n
Broschüre f

broke [brook] v (p break)
broken [BROOK-ön] v (pp break)
bronchitis [bron-KAIT-iss] n
Bronchitis f
bronze [brons] n Bronze f
brooch [brootsch] n Brosche f
brook [bruk] n Bach m
brother [BRAð-öl] n Bruder m
brother-in-law [BRAð-ör-in-loh]
n Schwager m
brought [broht] v (p, pp bring)
brown [braun] adj braun
bruise [bruhs] n Quetschung f; v
quetschen
brunette [bruh-NÄT] n Brünette f
brush [brasch] v bürsten; n
Bürste f
Brussels-sprouts [BRASS-öl-
ssPRAUTSS] n Rosenkohl m
bucket [BAK-it] n Eimer m
buckle [BAK-öl] n Schnalle f
bud [bad] n Knospe f
budget [BADʒ-it] n Budget nt
buffet [BU-feej] n Büfett nt
bug [bag] n Wanze f
* **build** [bild] v bauen
building [BILD-ing] n Gebäude nt
built [bilt] v (p, pp build)
bulb [balb] n Birne f
bulk [balk] n Masse f
bulky [BALK-i] adj umfangreich
bull [bul] n Stier m
bullfight [BUL-fait] n Stierkampf
m
bull-ring [BUL-ring] n
Stierkampfarena f
bump [bamp] v stoßen; n Stoß m
bumper [BAMP-ö] n Stoßstange f
bumpy [BAMP-i] adj holperig
bun [ban] n Brötchen nt
bunch [bantsch] n Strauß m;
Haufen m
bunch of keys [bantsch öw kies]
n Bündel nt

bundle [BAN-döl] *n* Bündel *nt*
bureau [bjuhö-ROO] *n* Kommode *f*
bureaucracy [bjuhö-ROK-rö-ssi] *n* Bürokratie *f*
burial [BÄR-i-öl] *n* Begräbnis *nt*
*burn [böhn] *v* verbrennen; *n* Brandwunde *f*
burnt [böhnt] *v* (*p, pp* **burn**)
*burst [böhsst] *v* bersten
bury [BÄR-i] *v* begraben
bus [bass] *n* Bus *m*
bush [busch] *n* Busch *m*
business [BIS-niss] *n* Beschäftigung *f*
business hours [BIS-niss auös] *pl* Geschäftszeit *f*
business suit [BIS-niss ssuht] *n* Anzug *m*
business trip [BIS-niss trip] *n* Geschäftsreise *f*
businessman [BIS-niss-mön] *n* (*pl* **-men**) Geschäftsmann *m*
bustle [BASS-öl] *n* Geschäftigkeit *f*
busy [BIS-i] *adj* beschäftigt
but [bat] *conj* aber
butcher [BUTSCH-ö] *n* Fleischer *m*
butter [BAT-ö] *n* Butter *f*
butterfly [BAT-ö-flai] *n* Schmetterling *m*
button [BAT-ön] *n* Knopf *m*
buttonhole [BAT-ön-hool] *n* Knopfloch *nt*
*buy [bai] *v* kaufen
buyer [BAI-ö] *n* Käufer *m*
by air [bai äö] per Flugzeug
by bus [bai bass] per Bus
by chance [bai tschahnss] zufällig
by day [bai deej] bei Tage
by far [bai fah] bei weitem
by heart [bai haht] auswendig
by night [bai nait] bei Nacht

by no means [bai noo miens] keinesfalls
by oneself [bai uan-SSÄLF] allein
by sea [bai ssie] per Schiff
by the way [bai öö ueej] übrigens
by train [bai treejn] per Bahn
bypass [BAI-pahss] *n* Umleitung *f*; *v* umgehen

cab [kæb] *n* Taxi *nt*
cabaret [KÆB-ö-reej] *n* Nachtklub *m*
cabbage [KÆB-idʒ] *n* Kohl *m*
cabdriver [KÆB-draiw-ö] *n* Taxifahrer *m*
cabin [KÆB-in] *n* Hütte *f*
cable [KEEJ-böl] *v* telegraphieren; *n* Telegramm *nt*
café [kæ-FEEJ] *n* Kaffee *m*; Kaffeehaus *nt*
cafeteria [kæf-i-TIÖR-i-ö] *n* Selbstbedienungsrestaurant *nt*
caffeine [KÆF-ien] *n* Koffein *nt*
cake [keejk] *n* Kuchen *m*
calculate [KÆL-kju-leejt] *v* ausrechnen
calculation [kæl-kju-LEEJ-schön] *n* Kalkulation *f*
calendar [KÆL-in-dö] *n* Kalender *m*
calf [kahf] *n* Kalb *nt*
calfskin [KAHF-sskin] *n* Kalbleder *nt*
call [kohl] *v* rufen; anrufen; *n* Ruf *m*; Anruf *m*; Besuch *m*
call on [kohl on] *v* besuchen
call up [kahl ap] *v* anrufen
calm [kahm] *adj* still
calm down [kahm daun] *v* beruhigen (sich)
calorie [KÆL-ör-i] *n* Kalorie *f*

came [keejm] v (p come)

camera [KÆM-ör-ö] n Kamera f

camera store [KÆM-ör-ö sstoh] n
Photogeschäft nt

camp [kæmp] n Lager nt; v
zelten

camp-bed [KÆMP-bäd] n Feldbett
nt

camping [KÆMP-ing] n Camping
nt

camping site [KÆMP-ing ssait] n
Campingplatz m

* can [kæn] v können; n Büchse f

can opener [kæn OO-pön-ö] n
Büchsenöffner m

Canada [KÆN-ö-dö] n Kanada nt

Canadian [kö-NEEJ-di-ön] n
Kanadier m; adj kanadisch

canal [kö-NÆL] n Kanal m

cancel [KÆN-ssöl] v annullieren

cancellation [kæn-ssä-LEEJ-
schön] n Annullierung f

cancer [KÆN-ssö] n Krebs m

candle [KÆN-döl] n Kerze f

candy [KÆN-di] n Bonbon nt

canned [kænd] adj
Büchsen . . .

cannot [KÆN-ot] v (can not)

canoe [kö-NUH] n Kanu nt

cap [kæp] n Mütze f

capable [KEEJP-ö-böl] adj fähig

capacity [kö-PÆSS-i-ti] n
Fähigkeit f

cape [keejp] n Umhang m; Kap
nt

capital [KÆP-it-öl] n Kapital nt;
Hauptstadt f

capsule [KÆP-ssjuhl] n Kapsel f

captain [KÆP-tin] n Kapitän m

car [kahr] n Wagen m

car hire [kah haiö] n
Autovermietung f

car park [kah pahk] n Parkplatz
m

carafe [kö-RAHF] n Karaffe f

caramel [KÆR-ö-mäl] n
Karamelle f

carat [KÆR-öt] n Karat nt

carbolic soap [kah-BOL-ik ssoop]
n Karbolseife f

carbon paper [KAH-bön PEEJ-pö]
n Kohlepapier nt

carburettor [KAH-bju-rät-ö] n
Vergaser m

card [kahd] n Postkarte f;
Spielkarte f; Visitenkarte f

cardboard [KAHD-bohd] n Pappe
f

cardigan [KAH-di-gön] n
Wolljacke f

cards [kahds] pl Kartenspiel nt

care [kaö] v sorgen (sich); n
Sorge f

care for [kaö foh] v gerne haben

career [kö-RIÖ] n Karriere f

careful [KAÖ-ful] adj vorsichtig

carfare [KAH-fäö] n Fahrgeld nt

cargo [KAH-goo] n Fracht f

carnival [KAH-ni-wöl] n Karneval
m

carp [kahp] n Karpfen m

carpenter [KAH-pin-tö] n Tischler
m

carpet [KAH-pit] n Teppich m

carriage [KÆR-idʒ] n
Kinderwagen m

carrot [KÆR-öt] n Karotte f

carry [KÆR-i] v tragen

carry on [KÆR-i on] v
weitermachen

carry out [KÆR-i aut] v
durchführen

cart [kaht] n Karren m

carton [KAH-tön] n Karton m

cartridge [KAH-tridʒ] n Patrone f

carve [kahw] v schnitzen;
zerlegen

carving [KAHW-ing] n Schnitzerei

f

case [keejss] *n* Fall *m*; Koffer *m*

cash [kæsch] *n* Bargeld *nt*; *v* einkassieren

cash on delivery [kæsch on di-LIW-ör-i] per Nachnahme

cashier [kæ-SCHIÖ] *n* Kassierer *m*

cashmere [KÆSCH-miö] *n* Kaschmir *m*

casino [kö-SSIE-noo] *n* Kasino *nt*

cask [kahssk] *n* Faß *nt*

* **cast** [kahsst] *v* werfen

cast-iron [KAHSST-AI-ön] *n* Gußeisen *nt*

castle [KAHSS-öl] *n* Burg *f*

castor-oil [KAHSS-tör-EUL] *n* Rizinusöl *nt*

casual [KÆ3-ju-öl] *adj* zwanglos

casualty [KÆ3-ju-öl-ti] *n* Opfer *nt*

cat [kæt] *n* Katze *f*

catacomb [KÆT-ö-koom] *n* Katakombe *f*

catalogue [KÆT-ö-log] *n* Katalog *m*

catarrh [kö-TAH] *n* Katarrh *m*

* **catch** [kætsch] *v* fangen

category [KÆT-i-gör-i] *n* Kategorie *f*

cathedral [kö-ΘIE-dröl] *n* Kathedrale *f*

Catholic [KÆΘ-ö-lik] *adj* katholisch

cattle [KÆT-öl] *n* Vieh *nt*

caught [koht] *v* (*p, pp* catch)

cauliflower [KOL-i-flau-ö] *n* Blumenkohl *m*

cause [kohs] *n* Ursache *f*; *v* verursachen

causeway [KOHS-ueej] *n* Chaussee *f*

caution [KOH-schön] *v* warnen; *n* Vorsicht *f*

cave [keejw] *n* Höhle *f*

caviar [KÆW-i-ah] *n* Kaviar *m*

cease [ssiess] *v* aufhören

ceiling [SSIEL-ing] *n* Decke *f*

celebrate [SSÄL-i-breejt] *v* feiern

celebration [ssäl-i-BREEJ-schön] *n* Feier *f*

celery [SSÄL-ör-i] *n* Sellerie *m*

cell [ssäl] *n* Zelle *f*

cellar [SSÄL-ö] *n* Keller *m*

cement [ssi-MÄNT] *n* Zement *m*

cemetery [SSÄM-i-tri] *n* Friedhof *m*

censor [SSÄN-ssö] *n* Zensor *m*

censorship [SSÄN-ssö-schip] *n* Zensur *f*

centigrade [SSÄN-ti-greejd] *adj* Grad Celsius

centimetre [SSÄN-ti-mie-tö] *n* Zentimeter *m*

central [SSÄN-tröl] *adj* zentral

central heating [SSÄN-tröl HIET-ing] *n* Zentralheizung *f*

central station [SSÄN-tröl SSTEEJ-schön] *n* Hauptbahnhof *m*

centralize [SSÄN-tröl-ais] *v* zentralisieren

centre [SSÄN-tö] *n* Zentrum *nt*

century [SSÄN-tschu-ri] *n* Jahrhundert *nt*

ceramics [ssi-RÆM-ikss] *pl* Keramik *f*

cereal [SSIÖR-i-öl] *n* Getreidéflocken *fpl*

ceremony [SSÄR-i-mö-ni] *n* Feierlichkeit *f*

certain [SSÖH-tön] *adj* bestimmt

certificate [ssö-TIF-i-kit] *n* Zeugnis *nt*

chain [tscheejn] *n* Kette *f*

chain-store [TSCHEEJN-sstoh] *n* Zweiggeschäft *nt*

chair [tschäö] *n* Stuhl *m*

chairman [TSCHÄÖ-mön] *n* (*pl* - men) Vorsitzende *m*

chalet [SCHÆL-eej] *n* Chalet *nt*

chambermaid [TSCHEEJM-bö-meejd] *n* Zimmermädchen *nt*

chance [tschahnss] *n* Zufall *m*

change [tscheejndʒ] *n* Wechselgeld *nt;* Änderung *f; v* wechseln; ändern

channel [TSCHÆN-öl] *n* Kanal *m*

chapel [TSCHÆP-öl] *n* Kapelle *f*

character [KÆR-ik-tö] *n* Charakter *m*

characteristic [kær-ik-tö-RISS-tik] *adj* charakteristisch

characterize [KÆR-ik-tö-rais] *v* charakterisieren

charcoal [TSCHAH-kool] *n* Holzkohle *f*

charge [tschahdʒ] *v* verlangen; *n* Gebühr *f*

charge account [tschahdʒ ö-KAUNT] *n* Kreditkonto *nt*

charge plate [tschahdʒ pleejt] *n* Kreditkarte *f*

charm [tschahm] *n* Amulett *nt*

chart [tschaht] *n* Diagramm *nt*

charter [TSCHAHT-ö] *v* chartern

charter flight [TSCHAHT-ö flait] *n* Charterflug *m*

chase [tscheejss] *v* verfolgen

chassis [SCHÆSS-i] *inv* Fahrgestell *nt*

chat [tschæt] *n* Geplauder *nt*

chauffeur [SCHOO-fö] *n* Chauffeur *m*

cheap [tschiep] *adj* billig

cheaper [TSCHIEP-ö] *adj* billiger

cheapest [TSCHIEP-isst] *adj* billigst

cheat [tschiet] *v* betrügen

check [tschäk] *v* abgeben; *n* Rechnung *f;* Scheck *m*

check in [tschäk in] *v* anmelden (sich); überprüfen

check out [tschäk aut] *v* abmelden (sich)

check-book [TSCHÄK-buk] *n* Scheckbuch *nt*

check-room [TSCHÄK-ruhm] *n* Garderobe *f*

check-up [TSCHÄK-ap] *n* Kontrolluntersuchung *f*

cheek [tschiek] *n* Wange *f*

cheek-bone [TSCHIEK-boon] *n* Backenknochen *m*

cheer [tschiö] *v* aufheitern

cheerful [TSCHIÖ-ful] *adj* heiter

cheese [tschies] *n* Käse *m*

chef [schäf] *n* Küchenchef *m*

chemist [KÄM-isst] *n* Apotheker *m*

chemistry [KÄM-iss-tri] *n* Chemie *f*

cheque [tschäk] *n* Scheck *m*

cheque-book [TSCHÄK-buk] *n* Scheckbuch *nt*

cherry [TSCHÄR-i] *n* Kirsche *f*

chess [tschäss] *n* Schach *m*

chest [tschässt] *n* Brustkasten *m;* Truhe *f*

chestnut [TSCHÄSS-nat] *n* Kastanie *f*

chew [tschuh] *v* kauen

chewing gum [TSCHUH-ing gam] *n* Kaugummi *nt*

chicken [TSCHIK-in] *n* Huhn *nt*

chicken-pox [TSCHIK-in-pokss] *n* Windpocken *fpl*

chief [tschief] *adj* Haupt . . .

chilblain [TSCHIL-bleejn] *n* Frostbeule *f*

child [tschaild] *n* (*pl* -ren) Kind *nt*

chill [tschil] *n* Frösteln *nt*

chilly [TSCHIL-i] *adj* kühl

chimney [TSCHIM-ni] *n* Schornstein *m*

chin [tschin] *n* Kinn *nt*

china [TSCHAI-nö] *n* Porzellan *nt*

China [TSCHAI-nö] n China nt

Chinese [tschai-NIES] inv Chinese m; adj chinesisch

chip [tschip] n Spielmarke f

chiropodist [ki-ROP-ö-disst] n Fußpfleger m

chisel [TSCHIS-öl] n Meißel m

chives [tschaiws] pl Schnittlauch m

chocolate [TSCHOK-ö-lit] n Schokolade f; Trinkschokolade f

choice [tscheuss] n Wahl f

choir [kuaiö] n Chor m

choke [tschook] n Choke m

* choose [tschuhs] v wählen

chose [tschoos] v (p choose)

chosen [TSCHOOS-ön] v (pp choose)

Christ [kraisst] Christus

Christian [KRISST-jön] n Christ m

Christian name [KRISST-jön neejm] n Vorname m

Christmas [KRISS-möss] n Weihnachten nt

chromium [KROO-mi-öm] n Chrom nt

chronic [KRON-ik] adj chronisch

church [tschöhtsch] n Kirche f

churchyard [TSCHÖHTSCH-jahd] n Kirchhof m

cigar [ssi-GAH] n Zigarre f

cigarette [ssig-ö-RÄT] n Zigarette f

cigarette-case [ssig-ö-RÄT-keejss] n Zigarettenetui nt

cigarette-holder [ssig-ö-RÄT-hoold-ö] n Zigarettenspitze f

cigarette-lighter [ssig-ö-RÄT-lait-öl] n Feuerzeug nt

cigar-store [ssi-GAH-sstoh] n Zigarrenladen m

cinema [SSIN-i-mö] n Kino nt

circle [SSÖH-köl] v umkreisen; n Balkon m

circulation [ssöh-kju-LEEJ-schön] n Kreislauf m

circumstances [SSÖH-köm-sstönss-is] pl Umstände mpl

circus [SSÖH-köss] n Zirkus m

citizen [SSIT-i-sön] n Bürger m

citizenship [SSIT-i-sön-schip] n Staatsangehörigkeit f

city [SSIT-i] n Stadt f

civic [SSIW-ik] adj Bürger . . .

civil [SSIW-il] adj höflich; zivil

civil servant [SSIW-il SSÖH-wönt] n Staatsbeamte m

civil service [SSIW-il SSÖH-wiss] n Staatsdienst m

civilian [ssi-WIL-jön] n Zivilist m

civilization [ssiw-il-ai-SEEJ-schön] n Zivilisation f

claim [kleejm] n Anspruch m; v beanspruchen

clamp [klämp] n Klammer f

clams [kläms] pl Venusmuschel f

clap [kläp] v klatschen

clarify [KLÄR-i-fai] v klären

class [klahss] n Klasse f

classical [KLÄSS-ik-öl] adj klassisch

classroom [KLAHSS-ruhm] n Klassenzimmer nt

claw [kloh] n Klaue f

clay [kleej] n Ton m

clean [klien] adj sauber; v reinigen

cleaning [KLIEN-ing] n Reinigung f

cleaning fluid [KLIEN-ing FLUH-id] n Reinigungsmittel nt

clear [kliö] adj klar

clearing [KLIÖR-ing] n Lichtung f

clergyman [KLÖH-dʒi-mön] n (pl -men) Geistliche m

clerk [klahk] n Beamte m

clever [KLÄW-ö] *adj* klug
client [KLAI-önt] *n* Kunde *m*
cliff [klif] *n* Klippe *f*
climate [KLAI-mit] *n* Klima *nt*
climb [klaim] *n* Aufstieg *m; v* steigen
clinic [KLIN-ik] *n* Klinik *f*
cloak [klook] *n* Umhang *m*
cloak-room [KLOOK-ruhm] *n* Garderobe *f*
clock [klok] *n* Uhr *f*
close [kloos] *v* schließen; *adj* nahe
closed [kloosd] *adj* geschlossen
closet [KLOS-it] *n* Wandschrank *m*
closing time [KLOOS-ing taim] *n* Geschäftsschluß *m*
cloth [kloΘ] *n* Stoff *m*
clothes [klooðs] *pl* Kleidung *f*
clothes-brush [KLOOS-brasch] *n* Kleiderbürste *f*
cloud [klaud] *n* Wolke *f*
cloudburst [KLAUD-böhsst] *n* Wolkenbruch *m*
cloudy [KLAUD-i] *adj* bewölkt
club [klab] *n* Knüppel *m;* Klub *m;* Treff
clumsy [KLAM-si] *adj* ungeschickt
clutch [klatsch] *n* Kupplung *f*
coach [kootsch] *n* Reisebus *m;* Wagen *m*
coagulate [koo-ÆG-ju-leejt] *v* gerinnen
coal [kool] *n* Kohle *f*
coast [koosst] *n* Küste *f*
coat [koot] *n* Mantel *m*
coat-hanger [KOOT-hæng-ö] *n* Kleiderbügel *m*
cockles [KOK-öls] *pl* Herzmuscheln *fpl*
cocktail [KOK-teejl] *n* Cocktail *m*
cocoa [KOO-koo] *n* Kakao *m*
coconut [KOO-kö-nat] *n* Kokosnuß *f*

cod [kod] *n* Kabeljau *m*
codeine [KOO-dien] *n* Kodein *nt*
coffee [KOF-i] *n* Kaffee *m*
coin [keun] *n* Münze *f*
coke [kook] *n* Koks *m*
cold [koold] *n* Kälte *f;* Erkältung *f; adj* kalt
cold buffet [koold BU-feej] *n* kaltes Büfett *nt*
cold cream [koold kriem] *n* cold cream *f*
collapse [kö-LÆPSS] *v* zusammenbrechen
collar [KOL-ö] *n* Kragen *m*
collar-bone [KOL-ö-boon] *n* Schlüsselbein *nt*
colleague [KOL-ieg] *n* Kollege *m*
collect [kö-LÄKT] *v* sammeln
collection [kö-LÄK-schön] *n* Sammlung *f*
collector [kö-LÄKT-ö] *n* Sammler *m*
college [KOL-idʒ] *n* höhere Lehranstalt *f*
collide [kö-LAID] *v* zusammenstoßen
collision [kö-LIʒ-ön] *n* Zusammenstoß *m*
colony [KOL-ön-i] *n* Kolonie *f*
colour [KAL-ö] *n* Farbe *f*
colourant [KAL-ö-önt] *n* Färbemittel *nt*
coloured [KAL-öd] *adj* farbig
colour-film [KAL-ö-film] *n* Farbfilm *m*
colourful [KAL-ö-ful] *adj* farbenprächtig
column [KOL-öm] *n* Säule *f*
coma [KOO-mö] *n* Koma *nt*
comb [koom] *n* Kamm *m; v* kämmen
combination [kom-bi-NEEJ-schön] *n* Kombination *f*

combine [kom-BAIN] v
kombinieren

* **come** [kam] v kommen

* **come across** [kam ö-KROSS] v
begegnen

comedian [kö-MIE-di-ön] n
Komiker m

comedy [KOM-i-di] n Lustspiel nt

comfort [KAM-föt] n Komfort m

comfortable [KAM-föt-ö-böl] adj
bequem

comic [KOM-ik] adj komisch

command [kö-MAHND] v befehlen

commence [kö-MÄNSS] v
anfangen

comment [KOM-önt] n
Kommentar m; v
kommentieren

commerce [KOM-öhss] n Handel
m

commercial [kö-MÖH-schöl] n
Werbesendung f; adj
kommerziell

commission [kö-MISCH-ön] n
Kommission f

commit [kö-MIT] v anvertrauen

committee [kö-MIT-i] n Ausschuß
m

common [KOM-ön] adj
gemeinsam

commune [KOM-juhn] n
Kommune f

communicate [kö-MJUH-ni-keejt]
v mitteilen

communication [kö-mjuh-ni-
KEEJ-schön] n Mitteilung f

communism [KOM-ju-nism] n
Kommunismus m

communist [KOM-ju-nisst] n
Kommunist m

community [kö-MJUHN-it-i] n
Gemeinde f

compact [KOM-pækt] n
Puderdose f

company [KAM-pö-ni] n
Gesellschaft f;
Handelsgesellschaft f

compare [köm-PÄÖ] v
vergleichen

comparison [köm-PÆR-i-ssön] n
Vergleich m

compartment [köm-PAHT-mönt]
n Abteil nt

compass [KAM-pöss] n Kompaß
m

compel [köm-PÄL] v zwingen

competition [kom-pi-TISCH-ön] n
Konkurrenz f

competitor [kom-PÄT-it-ö] n
Konkurrent m

complain [köm-PLEEJN] v
beschweren (sich)

complaint [köm-PLEEJNT] n
Beschwerde f

complete [köm-PLIET] adj
vollständig

complex [KOM-pläkss] n
Komplex m; adj verwickelt

complexion [köm-PLAK-schön] n
Teint m

compliment [kom-pli-MÄNT] v
beglückwünschen; n
Kompliment nt

composer [köm-POOS-ö] n
Komponist m

composition [kom-pö-SISCH-ön]
n Komposition f

comprise [köm-PRAIS] v
einschließen

compulsory [köm-PAL-ssö-ri] adj
obligatorisch

concentrate [KON-ssän-treejt] v
konzentrieren

concentration [kon-ssän-TREEJ-
schön] n Konzentration f

concern [kön-SSÖHN] v betreffen;
n Konzern m; Sorge f

concerned [kön-SSÖHND] adj

besorgt

concerning [kön-SSOHN-ing] *prep*
betreffs

concert [KON-ssöt] *n* Konzert *nt*

concert hall [KON-ssöt hohl] *n*
Konzertsaal *m*

concierge [kong-ssi-ÄÖ3] *n*
Hausmeister *m*

conclusion [kön-KLUH-3ön] *n*
Schluß *m*

concussion [kön-KASCH-ön] *n*
Gehirnerschütterung *f*

condensed milk [kön-DÄNSST
milk] *n* Kondensmilch *f*

condenser [kön-DÄNSS-ö] *n*
Kondensator *m*

condition [kön-DISCH-ön] *n*
Bedingung *f*

conditional [kön-DISCH-ön-öl] *adj*
bedingt

conditions [kön-DISCH-öns] *pl*
Bedingungen *fpl*

conduct [kön-DAKT] *v* dirigieren

conducted tour [kön-DAKT-id
tuhö] *n* Gesellschaftsreise *f*

conductor [kön-DAKT-ö] *n*
Schaffner *m*; Dirigent *m*

confectioner [kön-FÄK-schön-ö]
n Konditor *m*

confession [kön-FÄSCH-ön] *n*
Geständnis *nt*

confident [KON-fi-dönt] *adj*
zuversichtlich

confidential [kon-fi-DÄN-schöl]
adj vertraulich

confirm [kön-FÖHM] *v* bestätigen

confirmation [kon-fö-MEEJ-
schön] *n* Bestätigung *f*

confused [kön-FJUHSD] *adj*
verwirrt

confusion [kön-FJUH-3ön] *n*
Verwirrung *f*

congratulate [kön-GRÆT-ju-leejt]
v beglückwünschen

congratulations [kön-græt-ju-
LEEJ-schöns] *pl* Glückwünsche
mpl

congregation [kong-gri-GEEJ-
schön] *n* Gemeinde *f*

congress [KONG-gräss] *n*
Kongress *m*

connect [kö-NÄKT] *v* verbinden

connected with [kö-NÄKT-id uiö]
beteiligt an

connection [kö-NÄK-schön] *n*
Anschluß *m*

connections [kö-NÄK-schöns] *pl*
Beziehungen *fpl*

conscience [KON-schönss] *n*
Gewissen *nt*

conscious [KON-schöss] *adj*
bewußt

conscript [KON-sskript] *n*
Dienstpflichtige *m*

consent [kön-SSÄNT] *n*
Zustimmung *f*; *v* einwilligen

consequently [KON-ssi-kuönt-li]
adv folglich

conservative [kön-SSÖH-wö-tiw]
adj konservativ

consider [kön-SSID-ö] *v*
betrachten

considerate [kön-SSID-ör-it] *adj*
rücksichtsvoll

considering [kön-SSID-ör-ing]
prep in Anbetracht

consignment [kön-SSAIN-mönt] *n*
Sendung *f*

consist [kön-SSISST] *v* bestehen

constipated [kon-ssti-PEEJT-id]
adj verstopft

constipation [kon-ssti-PEEJ-
schön] *n* Verstopfung *f*

construct [kön-SSTRAKT] *v* bauen

construction [kön-SSTRAK-schön]
n Bau *m*

consul [KON-ssöl] *n* Konsul *m*

consulate [KON-ssjul-it] *n*

Konsulat *nt*

consult [kön-SSALT] *v* konsultieren

consultation [kon-ssöl-TEEJ-schön] *n* Konsultation *f*

consumer [kön-SSJUHM-ö] *n* Konsument *m*

contact [KON-tækt] *v* in Verbindung stellen mit (sich)

contact lenses [KON-tækt LÄNS-is] *pl* Kontaktlinsen *fpl*

contagious [kön-TEEJ-dʒöss] *adj* ansteckend

contain [kön-TEEJN] *v* enthalten

container [kön-TEEJN-ö] *n* Behälter *m*

contemporary [kön-TÄM-pör-ör-i] *adj* zeitgenössisch

content [kön-TÄNT] *adj* zufrieden

contented [kön-TÄNT-id] *adj* zufrieden

contents [KON-täntss] *pl* Inhalt *m*

contest [KON-tässt] *n* Wettbewerb *m*

continent [KON-tin-önt] *n* Erdteil *m*

continental [kon-ti-NÄN-töl] *adj* kontinental

continue [kön-TIN-juh] *v* fortsetzen

continuous [kön-TIN-ju-öss] *adj* ununterbrochen

contraceptive [kon-trö-SSÄP-tiw] *n* empfängnisverhütendes Mittel *nt*

contract [KON-trækt] *n* Vertrag *m*

contradict [kon-trö-DIKT] *v* widersprechen

contrary [KON-trör-i] *adj* entgegengesetzt

contrast [KON-trässt] *n* Kontrast *m*

contribute [kön-TRIB-juht] *v* beitragen

contribution [kon-tri-BJUH-schön] *n* Beitrag *m*

control [kön-TROOL] *n* Kontrolle *f*; *v* kontrollieren

controls [kön-TROOLS] *pl* Steuerung *f*

controversial [kon-trö-WÖH-schöl] *adj* umstritten

convenient [kön-WIEN-jönt] *adj* passend

convent [KON-wönt] *n* Kloster *nt*

conversation [kon-wö-SSEEJ-schön] *n* Gespräch *nt*

convict [kön-WIKT] *v* überführen

conviction [kön-WIK-schön] *n* Überzeugung *f*

convince [kön-WINSS] *v* überzeugen

cook [kuk] *v* kochen; *n* Koch *m*

cooked [kukd] *adj* gekocht

cooker [KUK-ö] *n* Kocher *m*

cookery-book [KUK-ör-i-buk] *n* Kochbuch *nt*

cooking [KUK-ing] *n* Kochen *nt*

cool [kuhl] *adj* kühl

co-operation [koo-op-ö-REEJ-schön] *n* Zusammenarbeit *f*

co-operative [koo-OP-ör-ö-tiw] *adj* hilfsbereit

copper [KOP-ö] *n* Kupfer *nt*

copy [KOP-i] *n* Abschrift *f*; Exemplar *nt*

coral [KOR-öl] *n* Koralle *f*

cordial [KOH-di-öl] *adj* herzlich

corduroy [KOH-dö-reu] *n* Kordsamt *m*

cork [kohk] *n* Korken *m*

corkscrew [KOHK-sskruh] *n* Korkenzieher *m*

corn [kohn] *n* Hühnerauge *nt*

corner [KOH-nö] *n* Ecke *f*

cornfield [KOHN-field] *n* Kornfeld *nt*

cornflakes [KOHN-fleejkss] *pl*

Corn-flakes *pl*

corn-on-the-cob [kohn-on-ðö-KOB] Maiskolben *m*

correct [kö-RÄKT] *adj* richtig; *v* verbessern

correspond [kor-i-SSPOND] *v* korrespondieren

correspondence [kor-i-SSPOND-önss] *n* Briefwechsel *m*

corridor [KOR-i-doh] *n* Flur *m*

corset [KOH-ssit] *n* Korsett *nt*

cosmetics [kos-MÄT-ikss] *pl* Schönheitsmittel *nt*

* **cost** [kosst] *v* kosten; *n* Kosten *pl*

costume jewellery [KOSS-tjuhm DʒUH-öl-ri] *n* Imitationsschmuck *m*

cosy [KOO-si] *adj* behaglich

cot [kot] *n* Feldbett *nt*

cottage [KOT-idʒ] *n* Sommerhaus *nt*

cotton [KOT-ön] *n* Kattun *m*

cotton-wool [KOT-ön-UUL] *n* Watte *f*

couch [kautsch] *n* Couch *f*

cough [kof] *v* husten; *n* Husten *m*

cough-drops [KOF-dropss] *pl* Hustenbonbons *ntpl*

cough-lozenges [KOF-LOS-indʒ-is] *pl* Hustenpastillen *fpl*

cough-mixture [KOF-mikss-tschö] *n* Hustentropfen *pl*

could [kud] *v* (*p* can)

council [KAUN-ssöl] *n* Rat *m*

count [kaunt] *v* zählen

counter [KAUNT-ö] *n* Ladentisch *m*

counterfoil [KAUN-tö-feull] *n* Kontrollabschnitt *m*

country [KAN-tri] *n* Land *nt*

country house [KAN-tri hauss] *n* Landhaus *nt*

countryman [KAN-tri-mön] *n* (*pl* - men) Landsmann *m*

countryside [KAN-tri-ssaid] *n* Landschaft *f*

couple [KAP-öl] *n* Paar *nt*

couple of [KAP-öl ow] einige

coupon [KUH-pon] *n* Bezugschein *m*

courage [KAR-idʒ] *n* Mut *m*

courageous [kö--REEJ-dʒöss] *adj* mutig

course [kohss] *n* Flußlauf *m*; Rennbahn *f*; Gang *m*

court [koht] *n* Tennisplatz *m*; Gericht *nt*

cousin [KAS-ön] *n* Cousin *m*

cover [KAW-ö] *n* Umschlag *m*; *v* bedecken; verdecken

cover charge [KAW-ö tschahdʒ] *n* Gedeckkosten *pl*

cow [kau] *n* Kuh *f*

coward [KAU-öd] *n* Feigling *m*

crab [kräb] *n* Krabbe *f*

crack [kräk] *n* Riß *m*

cracker [KRÄK-ö] *n* Keks *m*

cradle [KREEJ-döl] *n* Wiege *f*

cramp [krämp] *n* Krampf *m*

crash [kräsch] *v* stürzen; *n* Zusammenstoß *m*

crayfish [KREEJ-fisch] *n* Flußkrebs *m*

crazy [KREEJ-si] *adj* verrückt

cream [kriem] *n* Sahne *f*; Krem *f*; *adj* kremfarben

creamy [KRIEM-i] *adj* sahnig

crease [kriess] *v* zerknittern; *n* Falte *f*

create [kri-EEJT] *v* schaffen

creature [KRIE-tschö] *n* Geschöpf *nt*

credentials [kri-DÄN-schöls] *pl* Beglaubigungsschreiben *nt*

credit [KRÄD-it] *n* Kredit *nt*; *v* gutschreiben

credit card [KRÄD-it kahd] *n*

Kreditkarte f

creek [kriek] n Bucht f

* **creep** [kriep] v kriechen

crept [kräpt] v (p, pp **creep**)

crescent [KRÄSS-önt] adj halbmondförmig

crew [kruh] n Besatzung f

cricket [KRIK-it] n Kricket nt

cried [kraid] v (p, pp **cry**)

crime [kraim] n Verbrechen nt

criminal [KRIM-in-öl] n Verbrecher m

crimson [KRIM-sön] adj karmesinrot

crisp [krissp] adj knusperig

critic [KRIT-ik] n Kritiker m

critical [KRIT-ik-öl] adj kritisch

criticize [KRIT-i-ssais] v kritisieren

crockery [KROK-ör-i] n Töpferware f

crooked [KRUK-id] adj unehrlich

crop [krop] n Ernte f

cross [kross] n Kreuz nt

cross over [kross OOW-ö] v hinübergehen

crossing [KROSS-ing] n Übergang m

cross-roads [KROSS-roods] n Straßenkreuzung f

cross-walk [KROSS-uohk] n Zebrastreifen m

crowd [kraud] n Menge f

crowded [KRAUD-id] adj überfüllt

crown [kraun] n Krone f

crucifix [KRUH-ssi-fikss] n Kruzifix nt

cruise [kruhs] n Seereise f

crumb [kram] n Krümel m

crush [krasch] v zerquetschen

crust [krasst] n Kruste f

cry [krai] v schreien; weinen; Schrei m

crystal [KRISS-töl] n Kristall nt

cube [kjuhb] n Würfel m

cucumber [KJUH-köm-bö] n Gurke f

cuff-links [KAF-lingkss] pl Manschettenknöpfe mpl

cuffs [kafss] pl Manschetten fpl

cul-de-sac [KUL-dö-SSÆK] n Sackgasse f

cultivate [KAL-ti-weejt] v bebauen

cultivated [KAL-ti-weejt-id] adj bebaut

culture [KAL-tschö] n Kultur f

cultured [KAL-tschöd] adj kultiviert

cup [kap] n Tasse f

cupboard [KAB-öd] n Schrank m

curator [kjuhö-REEJT-ö] n Kurator m

curb [köhb] v zügeln; n Randstein m

cure [kjuhö] n Kur f; v heilen

curio [KJUHÖR-i-oo] n Rarität f

curious [KJUHÖ-ri-öss] adj neugierig; seltsam

curl [köhl] n Locke f; v locken

curlers [KÖHL-is] pl Haarwickler m

curly [KÖHL-i] adj lockig

currant [KAR-önt] n Korinthe f

currency [KAR-ön-ssi] n Währung f

current [KAR-önt] n Strömung f; Strom m; adj gegenwärtig

curry [KAR-i] n Curry m

curse [köhss] n Fluch m; v fluchen

curtain [KÖH-tön] n Vorhang m

curve [köhw] n Kurve f

curved [köhwd] adj gekrümmt

cushion [KUSCH-ön] n Kissen nt

custody [KASS-tö-di] n Obhut f

custom [KASS-töm] n Gewohnheit f

customary [KASS-töm-ör-i] *adj*
 üblich

customer [KASS-töm-ö] *n* Kunde
 m

Customs [KASS-töms] *pl*
 Zollbehörde *f*

Customs duty [KASS-töms DJUH-
 ti] *n* Zoll *m*

Customs examination [KASS-
 töms ig-sæm-i-NEEJ-schön] *n*
 Zollkontrolle *f*

Customs house [KASS-töms
 hauss] *n* Zollamt *nt*

Customs officer [KASS-töms OF-
 iss-ö] *n* Zöllner *m*

* **cut** [kat] *v* schneiden; *n* Schnitt
 m

* **cut off** [kat of] *v* abschalten

cutlery [KAT-lör-i] *n* Besteck *nt*

cycle [SSAI-köl] *n* Zyklus *m*

cyclist [SSAI-klisst] *n* Radfahrer
 m

cylinder [SSIL-in-dö] *n* Zylinder
 m

dad [dæd] *n* Vater *m*

daddy [DÆD-i] *n* Vati *m*

daily [DEEJ-li] *adj* täglich

dairy [DÄO-ri] *n* Molkerei *f*

dam [dæm] *n* Damm *m*

damage [DÆM-idȝ] *n* Schaden *m*;
 v beschädigen

damaged [DÆM-idȝd] *adj*
 beschädigt

damp [dæmp] *adj* feucht

dance [dahnss] *n* Tanz *m*; *v*
 tanzen

dancer [DAHNSS-ö] *n* Tänzer *m*

dandruff [DÆN-dröf] *n* Schuppen
 fpl

Dane [deejn] *n* Däne *m*

danger [DEEJN-dȝö] *n* Gefahr *f*

dangerous [DEEJN-dȝör-öss] *adj*
 gefährlich

Danish [DEEJN-isch] *adj* dänisch

dare [däö] *v* wagen

daren't [däönt] *v* (**dare not**)

dark [dahk] *adj* dunkel

darling [DAH-ling] *n* Liebling *m*

darn [dahn] *v* stopfen

darning wool [DAHN-ing uul] *n*
 Stopfgarn *nt*

dash-board [DÆSCH-bohd] *n*
 Armaturenbrett *nt*

date [deejt] *n* Verabredung *f*;
 Datum *nt*; Dattel *f*

daughter [DOH-tö] *n* Tochter *f*

dawn [dohn] *n*
 Morgendämmerung *f*

day [deej] *n* Tag *m*

day trip [deej trip] *n*
 Tagesausflug *m*

daybreak [DEEJ-breejk] *n*
 Tagesanbruch *m*

daylight [DEEJ-lait] *n* Tageslicht
 nt

dead [däd] *adj* tot

deaf [däf] *adj* taub

* **deal** [diel] *v* geben; *n* Geschäft
 nt

* **deal with** [diel uiȝ] *v* befassen
 mit (sich)

dealer [DIEL-ö] *n* Händler *m*

dealt [dält] *v* (*p, pp* **deal**)

dear [diö] *adj* lieb; teuer

debit [DÄB-it] *n* Soll *nt*

debt [dät] *n* Schuld *f*

December [di-SSÄM-bö] *n*
 Dezember *m*

decent [DIE-ssönt] *adj* anständig

decide [di-SSAID] *v* entscheiden

decided [di-SSAID-id] *adj*
 entschieden

decision [di-ssiȝ-ön] *n*
 Entscheidung *f*

deck [däk] *n* Kartenspiel *nt*;
 Deck *nt*

deck-cabin [DÄK-kæb-in] *n*
Deckkajüte *f*

deck-chair [DÄK-tschäö] *n*
Liegestuhl *m*

declaration [däk-lö-REEJ-schön]
n Erklärung *f*

declare [di-KLÄÖ] *v* deklarieren

decor [DEEJ-koh] *n* Ausstattung *f*

decrease [die-KRIESS] *v*
vermindern; *n* Abnahme *f*

deduct [di-DAKT] *v* abziehen

deed [died] *n* Tat *f*

deep [diep] *adj* tief

deer [diö] *inv* Rotwild *nt*

defeat [di-FIET] *v* besiegen

defective [di-FÄKT-iw] *adj*
mangelhaft

defence [di-FÄNSS] *n*
Verteidigung *f*

defend [di-FÄND] *v* verteidigen

deficit [DÄF-i-ssit] *n* Defizit *nt*

define [di-FAIN] *v* definieren

defined [di-FAIND] *adj* definiert

definite [DÄF-i-nit] *adj* bestimmt

definition [däf-i-NISCH-ön] *n*
Definition *f*

degree [di-GRIE] *n* Titel *m*; Grad
m

delay [di-LEEJ] *v* aufschieben; *n*
Verzögerung *f*

deliberately [di-LIB-ör-öt-li] *adv*
absichtlich

delicacy [DÄL-i-kö-ssi] *n*
Leckerbissen *m*

delicate [DÄL-i-kit] *adj* fein

delicatessen [däl-i-kö-TÄSS-ön] *n*
Feinkost *f*

delicious [di-LISCH-öss] *adj*
köstlich

delight [di-LAIT] *n* Wonne *f*

delighted [di-LAIT-id] *adj*
entzückt

delightful [di-LAIT-ful] *adj*
entzückend

delirious [di-LIR-i-öss] *adj*
rasend

deliver [di-LIW-ö] *v* ausliefern

delivery [di-LIW-ör-i] *n* Lieferung
f

demand [di-MAHND] *v* anfordern

democracy [di-MOK-rö-ssi] *n*
Demokratie *f*

democratic [däm-oo-KR -ik]
adj demokratisch

demonstration [däm-ön-sSTREEJ-
schön] *n* Demonstration *f*

Denmark [DÄN-mahk] *n*
Dänemark *nt*

denomination [di-nom-i-NEEJ-
schön] *n* Benennung *f*

dense [dänss] *adj* dicht

dentist [DÄN-tisst] *n* Zahnarzt *m*

denture [DÄN-tschö] *n* Gebiß *nt*

deny [di-NAI] *v* leugnen

deodorant [die-oo-dör-önt] *n*
Deodorant *nt*

depart [di-PAHT] *v* abreisen

department [di-PAHT-mönt] *n*
Abteilung *f*

department store [di-PAHT-mönt
sstoh] *n* Kaufhaus *nt*

departure [di-PAH-tschö] *n*
Abfahrt *f*

depend [di-PÄND] *v* abhängen

deposit [di-POS-it] *n* Ablagerung
f; Bank-Einlage *f*; *v*
hinterlegen

depot [DÄP-oo] *n* Bahnhof *m*

depression [di-PRÄSCH-ön] *n*
Niedergeschlagenheit *f*

depth [däpΘ] *n* Tiefe *f*

deputy [DÄP-ju-ti] *n*
Stellvertreter *m*

descend [di-sSÄND] *v*
herabsteigen

descent [di-sSÄNT] *n* Abstieg *m*

describe [di-sSKRAIB] *v*
beschreiben

description [diss-KRIP-schön] *n* Beschreibung *f*

desert [DÄS-öt] *n* Wüste *f*

deserve [di-SÖHW] *v* verdienen

design [di-SAIN] *v* entwerfen; *n* Entwurf *m*

desirable [di-SAIÖR-ö-böl] *adj* wünschenswert

desire [di-SAIÖ] *v* wünschen

desk [dässk] *n* Schreibtisch *m*

despatch [diss-PÆTSCH] *n* Depesche *f*

desperate [DÄSS-pör-it] *adj* verzweifelt

despise [diss-PAIS] *v* verachten

despite [diss-PAIT] *prep* trotz

dessert [di-SÖHT] *n* Nachtisch *m*

destination [däss-ti-NEEJ-schön] *n* Bestimmungsort *m*

destroy [diss-TREU] *v* vernichten

destruction [diss-TRAK-schön] *n* Zerstörung *f*

detach [di-TÆSCH] *v* losmachen

detail [DIE-teejl] *n* Einzelheit *f*

detailed [DIE-teejld] *adj* eingehend

detained [di-TEEJnd] *adj* aufgehalten

detect [di-TÄKT] *v* entdecken

detective story [di-TÄKT-iw sstoh-ri] *n* Kriminalroman *m*

detergent [di-TÖH-dʒönt] *n* Reinigungsmittel *nt*

determined [di-TÖH-mind] *adj* entschlossen

detour [di-TUHÖ] *n* Umweg *m*

devaluation [die-wæl-ju-EEJ-schön] *n* Entwertung *f*

devalue [die-WÆL-juh] *v* entwerten

develop [di-WÄL-öp] *v* entwickeln

development [di-WÄL-öp-mönt] *n* Entwicklung *f*

devil [DÄW-öl] *n* Teufel *m*

devote [di-WOOT] *v* widmen

devoted [di-WOOT-id] *adj* ergeben

dew [djuh] *n* Tau *m*

diabetes [dai-ö-BIE-ties] *n* Zuckerkrankheit *f*

diabetic [dai-ö-BÄT-ik] *n* Diabetiker *m*

diagnose [DAI-ög-noos] *v* diagnostizieren

diagnosis [dai-ög-NOO-ssiss] (*pl* -ses) Diagnose *f*

diagonal [dai-ÆG-ö-nöl] *adj* diagonal

diagram [DAI-ö-græm] *n* Schema *nt*

dial [DAI-öl] *n* Wählscheibe *f*; *v* wählen

dialect [DAI-ö-läkt] *n* Mundart *f*

diamond [DAI-ö-mönd] *n* Diamant *m*

diamonds [DAI-ö-mönds] *pl* Karo *nt*

diaper [DAI-ö-pö] *n* Windel *f*

diarrhoea [dai-ö-RI-ö] *n* Durchfall *m*

diary [DAI-ö-ri] *n* Tagebuch *nt*

dice [daiss] *n* Würfel *m*

dictaphone [DIK-tö-foon] *n* Diktaphon *m*

dictate [dik-TEEJT] *v* diktieren

dictation [dik-TEEJ-schön] *n* Diktat *nt*

dictionary [DIK-schön-ö-ri] *n* Wörterbuch *nt*

did [did] *v* (*p* **do**)

die [dai] *v* sterben

died [daid] *v* (*p* **die**)

diesel [DIES-öl] *n* Diesel *m*

diet [DAI-öt] *n* Diät *f*

differ [DIF-ö] *v* unterscheiden (sich)

difference [DIF-ör-önss] *n* Unterschied *m*

different [DIF-ör-önt] *adj*

verschieden

difficult [DIF-i-költ] *adj* schwierig

difficulty [DIF-i-köl-ti] *n*
Schwierigkeit *f*

* **dig** [dig] *v* graben

digest [di-DƷÄSST] *v* verdauen

digestible [di-DƷÄSST-ö-böl] *adj*
verdaulich

digestion [di-DƷÄSS-tschön] *n*
Verdauung *f*

dilute [dai-LJUHT] *v* verdünnen

diluted [dai-LJUHT-id] *adj*
verdünnt

dim [dim] *adj* trübe

dine [dain] *v* essen

dinghy [DING-gi] *n* Jolle *f*

dining car [DAIN-ing kah] *n*
Speisewagen *m*

dining room [DAIN-ing ruhm] *n*
Speisezimmer *nt*

dinner [DIN-ö] *n* Hauptmahlzeit *f*

dinner jacket [DIN-ö DƷÆK-it] *n*
Smoking *m*

diphtheria [dif-Θ IÖR-i-ö] *n*
Diphtherie *f*

diplomat [DIP-lö-mæt] *n*
Diplomat *m*

direct [di-RÄKT] *v* weisen; *adj*
direkt

direct current [di-RÄKT KAR-önt]
n Gleichstrom *m*

direction [di-RÄK-schön] *n*
Richtung *f*

directions [di-RÄK-schöns] *pl*
Anweisungen *fpl*

director [di-RÄK-tö] *n* Direktor *m*

directory [di-RÄK-tö-ri] *n*
Adreßbuch *nt*

dirt [döht] *n* Schmutz *m*

dirty [DÖHT-i] *adj* schmutzig

disadvantage [diss-öd-WAHN-tidƷ] *n* Nachteil *m*

disagree [diss-ö-GRIE] *v* nicht
übereinstimmen

disagreeable [diss-ö-GRIE-ö-böl]
adj unangenehm

disappear [diss-ö-PIÖ] *v*
verschwinden

disappoint [diss-ö-PEUNT] *v*
enttäuschen

disappointed [diss-ö-PEUNT-id]
adj enttäuscht

disapprove [diss-ö-PRUHW] *v*
mißbilligen

disaster [dis-AHSS-tö] *n*
Katastrophe *f*

disc [dissk] *n* Schallplatte *f*

discharge [diss-TSCHAHDƷ] *v*
ausladen

discoloured [diss-KAL-öd] *adj*
verfärbt

disconnect [diss-kö-NÄKT] *v*
trennen

discontented [diss-kön-TÄNT-id]
adj unzufrieden

discontinued [diss-kön-TIN-juhd]
adj unterbrochen

discount [DISS-kaunt] *n* Rabatt *m*

discover [diss-KAW-ö] *v*
entdecken

discovery [diss-KAW-ö-ri] *n*
Entdeckung *f*

discuss [diss-KASS] *v* erörtern

discussion [diss-KASCH-ön] *n*
Diskussion *f*

disease [di-SIES] *n* Krankheit *f*

disembark [diss-im-BAHK] *v*
landen

disgusted [diss-GASST-id] *adj*
angeekelt

disgusting [diss-GASST-ing] *adj*
ekelhaft

dish [dif] *n* Teller *m*; Gericht *nt*

dishonest [diss-ON-isst] *adj*
unehrlich

disinfect [diss-in-FÄKT] *v*
desinfizieren

disinfectant [diss-in-FÄKT-önt] *n*

Desinfektionsmittel *nt*
dislike [diss-LAIK] *v* nicht mögen
dislocated [diss-loo-KEEJT-id] *adj*
verrenkt
dismiss [diss-MISS] *v* entlassen
dispatch [diss-PÆTSCH] *v*
abfertigen
display [diss-PLEEJ] *v* ausstellen;
n Auslage *f*
displease [diss-PLIES] *v* mißfallen
displeased [diss-PLIESD] *adj*
ungehalten
disposable [diss-POOS-ö-böl] *adj*
wegwerfbar
dispute [diss-PJUHT] *n*
Auseinandersetzung *f*
dissatisfied [diss-SSÆT-iss-faid]
adj unzufrieden
distance [DISS-tönss] *n*
Entfernung *f*
distant [DISS-tönt] *adj* entfernt
distilled water [diss-TILD UOH-tö]
n destilliertes Wasser *nt*
distinct [diss-TINGKT] *adj*
verschieden
distinguish [diss-TING-guisch] *v*
unterscheiden
distressing [diss-TRÄSS-ing] *adj*
erschütternd
distributor [diss-TRIB-ju-tö] *n*
Verteiler *m*
district [DISS-trikt] *n* Bezirk *m*
disturb [diss-TÖHB] *v* stören
disturbance [diss-TÖHB-önss] *n*
Störung *f*
ditch [ditsch] *n* Graben *m*
dive [daiw] *v* tauchen
diversion [dai-WÖH-schön] *n*
Ablenkung *f*
divide [di-WAID] *v* teilen
division [di-WIʒ-ön] *n* Teilung *f*
divorce [di-WOHSS] *n* Scheidung *f*
divorced [di-WOHSST] *adj*
geschieden

dizzy [DIS-i] *adj* schwindlig
* **do** [duh] *v* tun
* **do without** [duh ui-ðAUT] *v*
verzichten auf
dock [dok] *v* docken
docks [dokss] *pl* Hafenanlagen
fpl
doctor [DOK-tö] *n* Arzt *m*
document [DOK-ju-mönt] *n*
Urkunde *f*
dog [dog] *n* Hund *m*
doll [dol] *n* Puppe *f*
dome [doom] *n* Kuppel *f*
domestic [dö-MÄSS-tik] *adj*
inländisch
domicile [DOM-i-ssail] *n*
Wohnsitz *m*
donation [doo-NEEJ-schön] *n*
Schenkung *f*
done [dan] *v* (*pp* **do**)
donkey [DONG-ki] *n* Esel *m*
don't [doont] *v* (**do not**)
door [doh] *n* Tür *f*
door-bell [DOH-böl] *n* Türklingel
f
door-keeper [DOH-kiep-ö] *n*
Portier *m*
doorman [DOH-mön] *n* (*pl* -**men**)
Portier *m*
dormitory [DOHM-i-tri] *n*
Schlafsaal *m*
dose [dooss] *n* Dosis *f*
double [DAB-öl] *n* Doppelte *nt*
double bed [DAB-öl bäd] *n*
Doppelbett *nt*
double room [DAB-öl ruhm] *n*
Doppelzimmer *nt*
doubt [daut] *v* zweifeln
doubtful [DAUT-ful] *adj*
zweifelhaft
dough [doo] *n* Teig *m*
down [daun] *adv* herab
downhill [daun-HIL] *adv* bergab
downpour [DAUN-poh] *n*

Regenguß *m*

downstairs [daun-SSTÄOS] *adv*
unten

downstream [daun-SSTRIEM] *adv*
stromabwärts

downwards [DAUN-uöds] *adv*
abwärts

dozen [DAS-ön] *n* Dutzend *nt*

draft [drahft] *n* Tratte *f*

drain [dreejn] *n* Abfluß *m*

drama [DRAHM-ö] *n* Drama *nt*

dramatic [drö-MÆT-ik] *adj*
dramatisch

dramatist [DRÆM-ö-tisst] *n*
Dramatiker *m*

drank [drængk] *v* (*p* **drink**)

draper [DREEJP-ö] *n* Tuchhändler
m

drapery [DREEJP-ör-i] *n*
Tuchwaren *fpl*

drapes [dreejpss] *pl* Vorhang *m*

draught [drahft] *n* Luftzug *m*

draughts [drahftss] *pl* Damespiel
nt

* **draw** [droh] *v* zeichnen; ziehen;
abheben; *n* Ziehung *f*

drawer [DROH-ö] *n* Schublade *f*

drawing [DROH-ing] *n* Zeichnung
f

drawing pin [DROH-ing pin] *n*
Reißzwecke *f*

drawn [drohn] *v* (*pp* **draw**)

* **dream** [driem] *v* träumen

dress [dräss] *v* ankleiden (sich);
n Kleid *nt*

dress up [dräss ap] *v*
herausputzen (sich)

dressing gown [DRÄSS-ing gaun]
n Morgenrock *m*

dressmaker [DRÄSS-meejk-ö] *n*
Schneiderin *f*

drew [druh] *v* (*p* **draw**)

dried [draid] *adj* getrocknet

drink [dringk] *n* Drink *m*; *v*

trinken

drinking fountain [DRINGK-ing
FAUN-tin] *n* Trinkbrunnen *m*

drinking water [DRINGK-ing UOH-
tö] *n* Trinkwasser *nt*

drip-dry [DRIP-drai] *adj* bügelfrei

drive [draiw] *n* Fahrt *f*; Weg *m*; *v*
fahren

driven [DRIW-ön] *v* (*pp* **drive**)

driver [DRAIW-ö] *n* Chauffeur *m*

driving [DRAIW-ing] *n* Fahren *nt*

driving licence [DRAIW-ing LAI-
ssönss] *n* Führerschein *m*

driving-wheel [DRAIW-ing-uiell] *n*
Treibrad *nt*

drop [drop] *n* Tropfen *m*; *v* fallen
lassen

drop in [drop in] *v* vorsprechen

drops [dropss] *pl* Tropfen *mpl*

drought [draut] *n* Dürre *f*

drove [droow] *v* (*p* **drive**)

drown [draun] *v* ertrinken

drug [drag] *n* Arznei *f*

druggist [DRAG-isst] *n* Apotheker
m

drugstore [DRAG-sstoh] *n*
Apotheke *f*

drunk [drangk] *v* (*pp* **drink**)

drunken [DRANGK-ön] *adj*
betrunken

dry [drai] *v* trocknen; *adj* trocken

dry-clean [DRAI-klien] *v*
chemisch reinigen

dry-cleaner [drai-KLIEN-ö] *n*
chemische Reinigung *f*

dryer [DRAI-ö] *n* Trockner *m*

dual carriage-way [DJUH-öl KÆR-
idʒ-ueej] *n* doppelte Fahrbahn
f

duck [dak] *n* Ente *f*

due [djuh] *adj* fällig

dues [djuhs] *pl* Gebühren *fpl*

dug [dag] *v* (*p, pp* **dig**)

dull [dal] *adj* langweilig; matt

dumb [dam] *adj* stumm

during [DJUHÖR-ing] *prep* während

dusk [dassk] *n* Abenddämmerung *f*

dust [dasst] *n* Staub *m*

dusty [DASST-i] *adj* staubig

Dutch [datsch] *adj* holländisch

Dutchman [DATSCH-mön] *n* (*pl - men*) Holländer *m*

dutiable [DJUH-ti-ö-böl] *adj* zollpflichtig

duty [DJUH-ti] *n* Zoll *m*

duty-free [DJUH-ti-frie] *adj* zollfrei

dye [dai] *n* Farbe *f; v* färben

dynamo [DAIN-ö-moo] *n* Dynamo *m*

dysentery [DISS-ön-tri] *n* Ruhr *f*

each [ietsch] *adj* jeder

each one [ietsch uan] *pron* jeder

each other [ietsch Að-ö] einander

eager [IEG-ö] *adj* begierig

ear [iö] *n* Ohr *nt*

earache [IÖR-eejk] *n* Ohrenschmerzen *mpl*

early [ÖH-li] *adj* früh; *adv* früh

earn [öhn] *v* verdienen

earnings [ÖHN-ings] *pl* Verdienst *m*

earplug [IÖ-plag] *n* Ohropax *nt*

earrings [IÖR-ings] *n* Ohrringe *mpl*

earth [öhϴ] *n* Erde *f*

Earth [öhϴ] *n* Erde *f*

earthenware [ÖHϴ-ön-uäö] *n* Steingut *nt*

earthquake [ÖHϴ-kueejk] *n* Erdbeben *nt*

east [iesst] *n* Osten *m*

Easter [IESST-ö] *n* Ostern *nt*

eastern [IESST-ön] *adj* östlich

easy [IES-i] *adj* leicht

easy chair [IES-i tschäö] *n* Lehnstuhl *m*

* eat [iet] *v* essen

eat out [iet aut] auswärts essen

eaten [IET-ön] (*pp* **eat**)

ebony [AB-ön-i] *n* Ebenholz *nt*

echo [ÄK-oo] *n* Echo *nt*

economic [ie-kö-NOM-ik] *adj* wirtschaftlich

economical [ie-kö-NOM-ik-öl] *adj* sparsam

economist [i-KON-ö-misst] *n* Volkswirt *m*

economize [i-KON-ö-mais] *v* sparen

economy [i-KON-ö-mi] *n* Wirtschaft *f*

edge [ädʒ] *n* Rand *m*

edible [AD-i-böl] *adj* eßbar

edition [i-DISCH-ön] *n* Ausgabe *f*

educate [AD-ju-keejt] *v* ausbilden

education [äd-ju-KEEJ-schön] *n* Erziehung *f*

eel [iel] *n* Aal *m*

effect [i-FÄKT] *n* Wirkung *f*

effective [i-FÄK-tiw] *adj* wirkungsvoll

efficient [i-FISCH-önt] *adj* leistungsfähig

effort [ÄF-öt] *n* Bemühung *f*

egg [äg] *n* Ei *nt*

egg-cup [ÄG-kap] *n* Eierbecher *m*

egg-plant [ÄG-plahnt] *n* Aubergine *f*

Egypt [IE-dʒipt] *n* Ägypten *nt*

Egyptian [i-DʒIP-schön] *n* Ägypter *m; adj* ägyptisch

eiderdown [AI-dö-daun] *n* Daunendecke *f*

eight [eejt] *adj* acht

eighteen [EEJ-tien] *adj* achtzehn

eighteenth [EEJ-tienϴ] *adj* achtzehnte

eighth [eejtΘ] *adj* achte
eighty [EEJ-ti] *adj* achtzig
either [AI-ðö] *pron* einer von
beiden
either... or [AI-ðö oh] *conj*
entweder....oder
elastic [i-LÆSS-tik] *n*
Gummiband *nt*
elbow [ÄL-boo] *n* Ellbogen *m*
elder [ALD-ö] *adj* älter
elderly [ALD-ö-li] *adj* ältlich
eldest [ALD-isst] *adj* älteste
elect [i-LÄKT] *v* wählen
election [i-LÄK-schön] *n* Wahl *f*
electric [i-LÄK-trik] *adj*
elektrisch
electric razor [i-LÄK-trik REEJS-ö]
n Rasierapparat *m*
electrician [äl-ik-TRISCH-ön] *n*
Elektriker *m*
electricity [äl-ik-TRISS-i-ti] *n*
Elektrizität *f*
elegance [ÄL-i-gönss] *n* Eleganz *f*
elegant [ÄL-i-gönt] *adj* elegant
element [AL-i-mönt] *n* Element
nt
elevator [ÄL-i-weejt-ö] *n* Aufzug
m
eleven [i-LÄW-ön] *adj* elf
eleventh [i-LÄW-önΘ] *adj* elfte
elm [älm] *n* Ulme *f*
else [älss] *adv* sonst
elsewhere [älss-UÄO] *adv*
anderswo
embankment [im-BÆNGK-mönt]
n Damm *m*
embark [im-BAHK] *v* einschiffen
(sich)
embarkation [äm-bah-KEEJ-
schön] *n* Einschiffung *f*
embarrass [im-BÆR-öss] *v* in
Verlegenheit bringen
embarrassed [im-BÆR-össt] *adj*
verlegen

embassy [AM-bö-ssi] *n* Botschaft
f
embrace [im-BREEJSS] *v*
umarmen
embroidery [im-BREUD-ör-i] *n*
Stickerei *f*
emerald [AM-ör-öld] *n* Smaragd
m
emergency [i-MÖH-dʒön-ssi] *n*
Notfall *m*
emergency exit [i-MÖH-dʒön-ssi
AKSS-it] *n* Notausgang *m*
emigrant [AM-i-grönt] *n*
Auswanderer *m*
emigrate [AM-i-greejt] *v*
auswandern
emotion [i-MOO-schön] *n*
Erregung *f*
emphasize [ÄM-fö-ssais] *v*
betonen
empire [AM-paiö] *n* Reich *nt*
employ [im-PLEU] *v* anstellen;
verwenden
employee [äm-pleu-IE] *n*
Angestellte *m*
employer [im-PLEU-ö] *n*
Arbeitgeber *m*
employment [im-PLEU-mönt] *n*
Beschäftigung *f*
empty [ÄMP-ti] *adj* leer
enable [i-NEEJ-böl] *v* befähigen
enamel [i-NÆM-öl] *n* Emaille *nt*
enchanting [in-TSCHAHNT-ing]
adj bezaubernd
encircle [in-SSÖH-köl] *v*
einkreisen
enclose [in-KLOOS] *v* beilegen
enclosure [in-KLOOʒ-ö] *n* Beilage
f
encounter [in-KAUNT-ö] *v*
begegnen
encyclopaedia [än-ssai-kloo-PIE-
di-ö] *n* Enzyklopädie *f*
end [änd] *v* beenden; *n* Schluß *m*;

Ende *nt*
ending [ÁND-ing] *n* Ende *nt*
endive [ÁN-diw] *n* Endivie *f*
endorse [in-DOHSS] *v* indossieren
enemy [ÁN-i-mi] *n* Feind *m*
energetic [än-ö-DʒÄT-ik] *adj*
energisch
energy [ÁN-ö-dʒi] *n* Energie *f*
engage [in-GEEJDʒ] *v* mieten
engaged [in-GEEJDʒD] *adj* besetzt;
verlobt
engagement [in-GEEJDʒ-mönt] *n*
Verabredung *f*
engagement ring [in-GEEJDʒ-
mönt ring] *n* Verlobungsring
m
engine [ÁN-dʒin] *n* Motor *m*
engineer [än-dʒi-NIÖ] *n*
Ingenieur *m*
England [ING-glönd] *n* England
nt
English [ING-glisch] *n* englisch
English Channel [ING-glisch
TSCHÆN-öl] *n* Ärmelkanal *m*
Englishman [ING-glisch-mön] *n*
(*pl* -men) Engländer *m*
engrave [in-GREEJW] *v* gravieren
engraving [in-GREEJW-ing] *n*
Kupferstich *m*
enjoy [in-DʒEU] *v* genießen
enjoyable [in-DʒEU-ö-böl] *adj*
angenehm
enlarge [in-LAHDʒ] *v* vergrößern
enlargement [in-LAHDʒ-mönt] *n*
Vergrößerung *f*
enormous [i-NOH-möss] *adj*
ungeheuer
enough [i-NAF] *adj* genug
enquire [in-KUAIÖ] *v* erkundigen
(sich)
enquiry [in-KUAIÖR-i] *n*
Erkundigung *f*
enquiry-office [in-KUAIÖR-i-of-
iss] *n* Auskunftsbüro *nt*

enter [ÁN-tö] *v* eintreten
enterprise [ÁN-tö-prais] *n*
Unternehmen *nt*
enterprising [ÁN-tö-prais-ing]
adj unternehmungslustig
entertain [än-tö-TEEJN] *v*
bewirten
entertaining [än-tö-TEEJN-ing]
adj amüsant
entertainment [än-tö-TEEJN-
mönt] *n* Unterhaltung *f*
enthusiastic [in-Θjuh-si-ÆSS-tik]
adj begeistert
entire [in-TAIÖ] *adj* ganz
entirely [in-TAIÖ-li] *adv* ganz
entrance [ÁN-trönss] *n* Eingang
m
entry [ÁN-tri] *n* Eintragung *f;*
Eintritt *m*
envelope [ÁN-wil-oop] *n*
Briefumschlag *m*
envy [ÁN-wi] *n* Neid *m*
epidemic [äp-i-DÄM-ik] *n*
Epidemie *f*
epilepsy [ÁP-i-läp-ssi] *n*
Epilepsie *f*
equal [IEK-uöl] *adj* gleich
equality [i-KUOL-i-ti] *n* Gleichheit
f
equator [i-KUEEJ-tö] *n* Äquator *m*
equip [i-KUIP] *v* ausstatten
equipment [i-KUIP-mönt] *n*
Ausrüstung *f*
equivalent [i-KUIW-ö-lönt] *adj*
gleichwertig
eraser [i-REEJS-ö] *n*
Radiergummi *m*
erect [i-RÄKT] *v* errichten
err [öh] *v* irren (sich)
errand [ÁR-önd] *n* Botengang *m*
error [ÁR-öl] *n* Irrtum *m*
escalator [ÁSS-kö-leejt-ö] *n*
Rolltreppe *f*
escape [iss-KEEJP] *v* entkommen

escort [iss-KOHT] v geleiten; n Geleit nt

especially [iss-PÄSCH-öl-i] adv besonders

esplanade [äss-plö-NAHD] n Promenade f

essay [ASS-eej] n Essay m

essence [ÄSS-önss] n Wesen nt

essential [i-SSÄN-schöl] adj wesentlich

estate [iss-TEEJT] n Landsitz m

estimate [ASS-ti-meejt] v schätzen; n Voranschlag m

estuary [ÄSS-tju-ör-i] n Trichtermündung f

Europe [JUHÖR-öp] n Europa nt

European [juhör-ö-PIE-ön] adj Europäer m; europäisch

evaluate [i-WÄL-ju-eejt] v veranschlagen

evaporate [i-WÄP-ör-eejt] v verdampfen

even [IEW-ön] adv sogar

evening [IEW-ning] n Abend m

evening dress [IEW-ning dräss] n Gesellschaftsanzug m

event [i-WÄNT] n Ereignis nt

eventually [i-WÄN-tju-öl-i] adv schließlich

every [AW-ri] adj jeder

everybody [AW-ri-bod-i] pron jedermann

everyday [AW-ri-deej] adj alltäglich

everyone [AW-ri-uan] pron jedermann

everything [AW-ri-Θing] pron alles

everywhere [AW-ri-uäö] adv überall

evident [AW-i-dönt] adj offensichtlich

evil [IE-wil] adj schlecht

exact [ig-SÄKT] adj genau

exactly [ig-SÄKT-li] adv genau

exaggerate [ig-SÄDЗ-ör-eejt] v übertreiben

examination [ig-säm-i-NEEJ-schön] n Examen nt

examine [ig-SÄM-in] v prüfen

example [ig-SAHM-pöl] n Beispiel nt

excavation [äkss-kö-WEEJ-schön] n Ausgrabung f

exceed [ik-SSIED] v überschreiten

excellent [AKSS-öl-önt] adj hervorragend

except [ik-SSÄPT] prep außer

exception [ik-SSÄP-schön] n Ausnahme f

exceptional [ik-SSÄP-schön-öl] adj außergewöhnlich

excess baggage [ik-SSÄSS BÄG-idЗ] n Übergewicht nt

exchange [ikss-TSCHEEJNDЗ] n Telephonzentrale f; v austauschen

exchange office [ĺkss-TSCHEEJNDЗ OF-iss] n Wechselstube f

exchange rate [ikss-TSCHEEJNDЗ reejt] n Wechselkurs m

excite [ik-SSAIT] v erregen

excitement [ik-SSAIT-mönt] n Aufregung f

exciting [ik-SSAIT-ing] adj aufregend

exclaim [ikss-KLEEJM] v ausrufen

exclamation [äkss-klö-MEEJ-schön] n Ausruf m

exclude [ikss-KLUHD] v ausschließen

exclusive [ikss-KLUHSS-iw] adj exklusiv

excursion [ikss-KÖH-schön] n Ausflug m

excuse [ikss-KJUHS] v entschuldigen

executive [ig-SÄK-ju-tiw] n

Geschäftsführer *m*

exempt [ig-SÄMPT] *v* ausnehmen

exemption [ig-SÄMP-schön] *n* Befreiung *f*

exercise [ÄKSS-ö-ssais] *n* Übung *f*

exhaust [ig-SOHSST] *n* Auspuff *m*

exhausted [ig-SOHSST-id] *adj* erschöpft

exhibit [ig-SIB-it] *v* ausstellen

exhibition [äkss-i-BISCH-ön] *n* Ausstellung *f*

exist [ig-SISST] *v* existieren

exit [AKSS-it] *n* Ausgang *m*

expand [ikss-PÄND] *v* ausbreiten

expect [ikss-PÄKT] *v* erwarten

expedition [äkss-pi-DISCH-ön] *n* Expedition *f*

expenditure [ikss-PÄND-i-tschö] *n* Aufwand *m*

expense [ikss-PÄNSS] *n* Ausgabe *f*

expensive [ikss-PÄNSS-iw] *adj* teuer

experience [ikss-PIÖR-i-önss] *n* Erfahrung *f*; *v* erleben

experienced [ikss-PIÖR-i-önsst] *adj* erfahren

experiment [ikss-PÄR-i-mänt] *v* experimentieren; *n* Experiment *nt*

expert [AKSS-pöht] *n* Fachmann *m*

expire [ikss-PAIÖ] *v* ablaufen

expiry [ikss-PAIÖR-i] *n* Ablauf *m*

explain [ikss-PLEEJN] *v* erklären

explanation [äkss-plö-NEEJ-schön] *n* Erklärung *f*

explode [ikss-PLOOD] *v* explodieren

explore [ikss-PLOH] *v* erforschen

explosive [ikss-PLOOSS-iw] *n* Sprengstoff *m*

export [äkss-POHT] *v* exportieren

exports [AKSS-pohtss] *pl* Ausfuhr *f*

exposure [ikss-POO-зö] *n* Belichtung *f*

exposure metre [ikss-POO-зö MIE-tö] *n* Belichtungsmesser *m*

express [ikss-PRÄSS] *adj* Eil . . . . *v* ausdrücken

express letter [ikss-PRÄSS LÄT-ö] *n* Eilbrief *m*

express train [ikss-PRÄSS treejn] *n* Schnellzug *m*

expression [ikss-PRÄSCH-ön] *n* Ausdruck *m*

exquisite [ÄKSS-kuis-it] *adj* auserlesen

extend [ikss-TÄND] *v* verlängern

extension [ikss-TÄN-schön] *n* Nebenanschluß *m*

extension cord [ikss-TÄN-schön kohd] *n* Verlängerungsschnur *f*

extensive [ikss-TÄNSS-iw] *adj* ausgedehnt

exterior [äkss-TIÖR-i-ö] *adj* äußerlich

extinguish [ikss-TING-guisch] *v* auslöschen

extinguisher [ikss-TING-guisch-ö] *n* Feuerlöscher *m*

extra [ÄKSS-trö] *adj* zusätzlich

extract [ikss-TRÄKT] *v* ziehen

extraction [ikss-TRÄK-schön] *n* Ziehen *nt*

extraordinary [ikss-TROHD-nör-i] *adj* außerordentlich

extras [ÄKSS-trös] *pl* Sonderausgaben *fpl*

extravagant [ikss-TRÄW-i-gönt] *adj* extravagant

extreme [ikss-TRIEM] *adj* äußerst

eye [ai] *n* Auge *nt*

eyeball [AI-bohl] *n* Augapfel *m*

eyebrow [AI-brau] *n* Augenbraue *f*

eyelash [AI-läsch] *n*

Augenwimper f
eye-liner [AI-lain-ö] n Eyeliner
m
eye-pencil [AI-pän-ssöl] n
Augenbrauenstift·m
eye-shadow [AI-schæd-oo] n
Augenschminke f

fabric [FÆB-rik] n Gewebe nt
facade [fö-SSAHD] n Fassade f
face [feejss] v gegenüberstehen;
n Gesicht m
face cream [feejss kriem] n
Gesichtskrem f
face massage [feejss mö-SSAH3]
n Gesichtsmassage f
face pack [feejss pæk] n
Gesichtspackung f
face powder [feejss PAU-dö] n
Puder nt
facilities [fö-SSIL-i-tis] pl
• Einrichtungen fpl
fact [fækt] n Tatsache f
factory [FÆK-tör-i] n Fabrik f
factual [FÆK-tju-öl] adj
tatsächlich
faculty [FÆK-öl-ti] n Fähigkeit f;
Fakultät f
fad [fæd] n Modetorheit f
fade [feejd] v verblassen
faience [feej-JANGSS] n Fayence f
fail [feejl] v versagen
failure [FEEJL-jö] n Mißerfolg m
faint [feejnt] adj schwach; v
ohnmächtig werden
fair [fää] adj gerecht; n Messe f
fairhaired [FÄÖ-häöd] adj blond
fairly [FÄÖ-li] adv ziemlich
faith [feejΘ] n Glaube m
faithful [FEEJΘ-ful] adj treu
fall [fohl] n Sturz m; v fallen
fallen [FOHL-ön] v (pp fall)
false [fohlss] adj falsch

false teeth [fohlss tieΘ] pl
künstliches Gebiß nt
fame [feejm] n Ruhm m
familiar [fö-MIL-jö] adj vertraut
family [FÆM-il-i] n Familie f
family name [FÆM-il-i neejm] n
Nachname m
famous [FEEJM-öss] adj berühmt
fan [fæn] ɔ Ventilator m
fan-belt [FÆN-bält] n
Ventilatorriemen m
fancy [FÆN-ssi] n Laune f; v
Gefallen finden an
fantastic [fæn-TÆSS-tik] adj
phantastisch
far [fah] adj fern
faraway [FAHR-ö-ueej] adj
entfernt
fare [fää] n Fahrgeld nt
farm [fahm] n Bauernhof m
farmer [FAHM-ö] n Bauer m
farmhouse [FAHM-hauss] n
Bauernhaus nt
far-off [FAHR-of] adj abgelegen
farther [FAH-ðö] adj ferner
farthest [FAH-ðisst] adj fernst
fashion [FÆSCH-ön] n Mode f
fashionable [FÆSCH-ön-ö-böl] adj
modern
fast [fahsst] adj schnell
fasten [FAHSS-ön] v befestigen
fastener [FAHSS-ön-ö] n
Verschluß m
fat [fæt] n Fett nt; adj fett; dick
fatal [FEEJT-öl] adj tödlich
fate [feejt] n Schicksal nt
father [FAH-ðö] n Vater m
father-in-law [FAH-ðör-in-loh] n
Schwiegervater m
fatty [FÆT-i] adj fettig
faucet [FOH-ssit] n Wasserhahn
m
fault [fohlt] n Fehler m
faulty [FOHLT-i] adj fehlerhaft

favour [FEEJW-ö] *n* Gefälligkeit *f*
favourable [FEEJW-ör-ö-böll] *adj*
  günstig
favourite [FEEJW-ör-it] *n* Favorit
  m
fawn [fohn] *adj* rehbraun
fear [fiö] *v* fürchten; *n* Furcht *f*
feast [fiesst] *n* Fest *nt*
feather [FÀð-ö] *n* Feder *f*
feature [FIE-tschö] *n* Gesichtszug
  m
February [FÀB-ru-ör-i] *n* Februar
  m
fed [fäd] *v* (*p, pp* **feed**)
federal [FÀD-ör-öl] *adj* Bundes
federation [fäd-ö-REEJ-schön]
  n Föderation *f*
fee [fie] *n* Honorar *nt*
feeble [FIE-böl] *adj* schwach
* **feed** [fiesst] *v* ernähren
* **feel** [fiel] *v* fühlen
feeling [FIEL-ing] *n* Gefühl *nt*
fell [fäl] *v* (*p* **fall**)
felt [fält] *n* Filz *m*
female [FIE-meejl] *adj* weiblich
feminine [FÀM-in-in] *adj*
  weiblich
fence [fänss] *n* Zaun *m*
fender [FÀN-dö] *n* Stoßstange *f*;
  Kotflügel *m*
ferry boat [FÀR-i boot] *n*
  Fährboot *nt*
fertile [FÖH-tail] *adj* fruchtbar
festival [FÀSS-töw-öl] *n* Festival
  nt
festive [FÀSS-tiw] *adj* festlich
fetch [fätsch] *v* holen
feudal [FJUHD-öl] *adj* feudal
fever [FIE-wö] *n* Fieber *nt*
fever blister [FIE-wö BLISS-tö] *n*
  Fieberblase *f*
feverish [FIE-wör-isch] *adj*
  fiebrig
few [fjuh] *adj* wenige

fiancé [fi-ANGN-sseej] *n* Verlobte
  m
fiancée [fi-ANGN-sseej] *n*
  Verlobte *f*
fibre [FAI-bö] *n* Faser *f*
fiction [FIK-schön] *n* Erdichtung
  f
field [field] *n* Feld *nt*
field glasses [field GLAHSS-is] *pl*
  Feldstecher *m*
fierce [fiöss] *adj* wild
fifteen [FIF-tien] *adj* fünfzehn
fifteenth [FIF-tienΘ] *adj*
  fünfzehnte
fifth [fifΘ] *adj* fünfte
fifty [FIF-ti] *adj* fünfzig
fig [fig] *n* Feige *f*
fight [fait] *n* Kampf *m*; *v*
  kämpfen
figure [FIG-ö] *n* Gestalt *f*
file [fail] *n* Feile *f*; Reihe *f*
fill [fil] *v* füllen
fill in [fil in] *v* ausfüllen
fill out [fil aut] *v* ausfüllen
fill up [fil ap] *v* vollfüllen
filling [FIL-ing] *n* Füllung *f*;
  Plombe *f*
filling station [FIL-ing SSTEEJ-
  schön] *n* Tankstelle *f*
film [film] *n* Film *m*; *v* filmen
filter [FIL-tö] *n* Filter *m*
filter tip [FIL-tö tip] *n*
  Filtermundstück *nt*
filthy [FILΘ-i] *adj* schmutzig
final [FAI-nöl] *adj* letzt
financial [fai-NÆN-schöll] *adj*
  finanziell
* **find** [faind] *v* finden
fine [fain] *adj* fein; *n* Geldstrafe *f*
finger [FING-gö] *n* Finger *m*
finish [FIN-isch] *v* beenden; *n*
  Schluß *m*
Finland [FIN-lönd] *n* Finnland *nt*
Finn [fin] *n* Finne *m*

Finnish [FIN-isch] *adj* finnisch

fire [schaiö] *v* entlassen; *n* Feuer *nt*

fire alarm [faiör ö-LAHM] *n* Feueralarm *m*

fire escape [faiö iss-KEEJP] *n* Nottreppe *f*

fire extinguisher [faiö ikss-TING-guisch-ö] *n* Feuerlöscher *m*

fire hydrant [faiö HAI-drönt] *n* Hydrant *m*

fireplace [FAIÖ-pleejss] *n* Kamin *m*

fireproof [FAIÖ-pruhf] *adj* feuerfest

firm [föhm] *adj* fest; *n* Firma *f*

first [föhsst] *adj* erste

first aid [föhsst eejd] *n* erste Hilfe

first-aid kit [FÖHSST-eejd kit] *n* Verbandskasten *m*

first-aid post [FÖHSST-eejd poosst] *n* Unfallstation *f*

first-rate [FÖHSST-reejt] *adj* erstrangig

fish [fisch] *v* fischen; *n* Fisch *m*

fish shop [fisch schop] *n* Fischhandlung *f*

fisherman [FISCH-ö-mön] *n* (*pl - men*) Fischer *m*

fishing [FISCH-ing] *n* Angeln *nt*

fishing hook [FISCH-ing huk] *n* Angelhaken *m*

fishing licence [FISCH-ing LAI-ssönss] *n* Angelschein *m*

fishing line [FISCH-ing lain] *n* Angelschnur *f*

fishing net [FISCH-ing nät] *n* Fischnetz *nt*

fishing rod [FISCH-ing rod] *n* Angelrute *f*

fishing tackle [FISCH-ing TÆK-öl]

n Angelgerät *nt*

fist [fisst] *n* Faust *f*

fit [fit] *v* passen

fitting [FIT-ing] *n* Anprobe *f*

fitting room [FIT-ing ruhm] *n* Anproberaum *m*

five [faiw] *adj* fünf

five hundred [faiw HAN-dröd] *adj* fünfhundert

fix [fikss] *v* richten

fixed [fiksst] *adj* fest

fixed price [fiksst praiss] *n* fester Preis

fjord [fjoord] *n* Fjord *m*

flag [flæg] *n* Fahne *f*

flame [fleejm] *n* Flamme *f*

flannel [FLÆN-öl] *n* Flanell *m*

flash-bulb [FLÆSCH-balb] *n* Blitzlicht *nt*

flash-light [FLÆSCH-lait] *n* Taschenlampe *f*

flat [flæt] *adj* flach; *n* Reifenpanne *f*; Wohnung *f*

flavour [FLEEJ-wö] *v* würzen; *n* Aroma *nt*

fleet [fliet] *n* Flotte *f*

flesh [fläsch] *n* Fleisch *nt*

flew [fluh] *v* (*p* fly)

flex [fläkss] *n* Kabel *nt*

flight [flait] *n* Flug *m*

flint [flint] *n* Feuerstein *m*

float [floot] *v* obenauf schwimmen

flock [flok] *n* Herde *f*

flood [flad] *n* Überschwemmung *f*

floor [floh] *n* Fußboden *m*; Stockwerk *nt*

floor-show [FLOH-sshoo] *n* Kabarett *nt*

florist [FLOR-isst] *n* Blumenhändler *m*

flour [flauö] *n* Mehl *nt*

flow [floo] *v* fließen

flower [FLAU-ö] *n* Blume *f*
flower-shop [FLAU-ö-schop] *n*
  Blumenhandlung *f*
flown [floon] *v* (*pp* fly)
flu [fluh] *n* Grippe *f*
fluent [FLUH-önt] *adj* fließend
fluid [FLUH-id] *n* Flüssigkeit *f*
fly [flai] *n* Fliege *f; v* fliegen
focus [FOO-köss] *n* Brennpunkt
  m
fog [fog] *n* Nebel *m*
foggy [FOG-i] *adj* neblig
fold [foold] *v* falten
folk [fook] *n* Volk *nt*
folk-dance [FOOK-dahnss] *n*
  Volkstanz *m*
folklore [FOOK-loh] *n* Volkssagen
  fpl
folk-song [FOOK-ssong] *n*
  Volkslied *nt*
follow [FOL-oo] *v* folgen
following [FOL-oo-ing] *adj*
  folgend
food [fuhd] *n* Nahrung *f*
food poisoning [fuhd PEUS-ön-
  ing] *n*
  Nahrungsmittelvergiftung *f*
food-stuffs [FUHD-sstafss] *pl*
  Nahrungsmittel *ntpl*
foolish [FUHL-isch] *adj* töricht
foot [fut] *n* (*pl* feet) Fuß *m*
foot powder [fut PAU-dö] *n*
  Fußpuder *nt*
football [FUT-bohl] *n* Fußball *m*
football match [FUT-bohl
  mætsch] *n* Fußballspiel *nt*
foot-brake [FUT-breejk] *n*
  Fußbremse *f*
footpath [FUT-pahӨ] *n* Fußweg *m*
footwear [FUT-uäö] *n* Schuhwerk
  nt
for [foh] *prep* für
for example [för ig-SAHM-pöl]
  zum Beispiel

for hire [fö haiö] zu vermieten
for instance [för IN-sstönss] zum
  Beispiel
for sale [fö sseejl] zu verkaufen
forbade [fö-BEEJD] *v* (*p* forbid)
* **forbid** [fö-BID] *v* verbieten
forbidden [fö-BID-ön] *v* (*pp*
  forbid)
force [fohss] *n* Kraft *f; v* zwingen
ford [fohd] *n* Furt *f*
* **forecast** [foh-KAHSST] *v*
  voraussagen; *n* Vorhersage *f*
foreground [FOH-graund] *n*
  Vordergrund *m*
forehead [FOR-id] *n* Stirn *f*
foreign [FOR-in] *adj* fremd
foreign currency [FOR-in KAR-ön-
  ssi] *n* fremde Währung
foreigner [FOR-in-ö] *n* Fremde *m*
foreman [FOH-mön] *n* (*pl* -men)
  Werkmeister *m*
forest [FOR-isst] *n* Wald *m*
forgave [fö-GEEJW] *v* (*p* forgive)
* **forget** [fö-GÄT] *v* vergessen
* **forgive** [fö-GIW] *v* verzeihen
forgiven [fö-GIW-ön] *v* (*pp*
  forgive)
forgot [fö-GOT] *v* (*p* forget)
forgotten [fö-GOT-ön] *v* (*pp*
  forget)
fork [fohk] *v* gabeln (sich); *n*
  Gabel *f; Gabelung *f*
form [fohm] *v* formen; *n* Form *f;*
  Formular *nt*
formal [FOHM-öl] *adj* förmlich
formality [foh-MÆL-i-ti] *n*
  Formalität *f*
former [FOHM-ö] *adj* früher
formerly [FOHM-ö-li] *adv* früher
formula [FOHM-ju-lö] *n* Formel *f*
fortnight [FOHT-nait] *n* vierzehn
  Tage *mpl*
fortress [FOH-triss] *n* Festung *f*
fortunate [FOH-tschö-nit] *adj*

glücklich

fortune [FOH-tschön] n Glück nt

forty [FOH-ti] adj vierzig

forward [FOH-uöd] adv vorwärts; v nachsenden

fought [foht] v (p, pp fight)

found [faund] v (p, pp find)

found [faund] v gründen

foundation [faun-DEEJ-schön] n Stiftung f

foundation cream [faun-DEEJ-schön kriem] n Make-up-Unterlage f

fountain [FAUN-tin] n Springbrunnen m

fountain pen [FAUN-tin pän] n Füller m

four [foh] adj vier

fourteen [FOH-tien] adj vierzehn

fourteenth [FOH-tienΘ] adj vierzehnte

fourth [fohΘ] adj vierte

fowl [faul] n Geflügel nt

fox [fokss] n Fuchs m

foyer [FEU-jöl] n Foyer nt

fraction [FRÆK-schön] n Bruchstück nt

fracture [FRÆK-tschö] n Bruch m; v brechen

fragile [FRÆ-dʒail] adj zerbrechlich

frame [freejm] n Rahmen m

frames [freejms] pl Brillengestell nt

France [frahnss] n Frankreich nt

fraud [frohd] n Betrug m

free [frie] adj frei

free of charge [frie öw tschahdʒ] kostenlos

free ticket [frie TIK-it] n Freikarte f

freedom [FRIE-döm] n Freiheit f

* **freeze** [fries] v gefrieren

freezing [FRIES-ing] adj eisig

freezing point [FRIES-ing peunt] n Gefrierpunkt m

freight [freejt] n Fracht f

French [fräntsch] adj französisch

Frenchman [FRÄNTSCH-mön] n (pl -men) Franzose m

frequency [FRIE-kuön-ssi] n Häufigkeit f

frequent [FRIE-kuönt] adj häufig

fresh [fräsch] adj frisch

fresh water [fräsch UOH-tö] n Süßwasser nt

Friday [FRAI-di] n Freitag m

fridge [fridʒ] n Kühlschrank m

fried [fraid] adj gebraten

friend [fränd] n Freund m

friendly [FRÄND-li] adj freundschaftlich

friendship [FRÄND-schip] n Freundschaft f

fright [frait] n Schreck m

frighten [FRAIT-ön] v erschrecken

frightened [FRAIT-önd] adj verängstigt

frightful [FRAIT-ful] adj schrecklich

frock [frok] n Kleid nt

frog [frog] n Frosch m

from [from] prep von

front [frant] n Vorderseite f

frontier [FRAN-tiö] n Grenze f

frost [frosst] n Frost m

frozen [FROOS-ön] adj gefroren

frozen food [FROOS-ön fuhd] n Gefrierwaren fpl

fruit [fruht] n Obst nt

fry [frai] v braten

fuel [FJU-öl] n Brennstoff m; Benzin nt

full [ful] adj voll

full board [ful bohd] n Vollpension f

full stop [ful sstop] *n* Punkt *m*

full up [ful ap] vollbesetzt

fun [fan] *n* Spaß *m*

function [FANGK-schön] *n* Funktion *f*

funeral [FJUHN-ör-öl] *n* Begräbnis *nt*

funnel [FAN-öl] *n* Trichter *m*

funny [FAN-i] *adj* sonderbar; komisch

fur [föh] *n* Pelz *m*

fur coat [föh koot] *n* Pelzmantel *m*

furious [FJUHÖR-i-öss] *adj* wütend

furnish [FÖH-nisch] *v* einrichten

furnished flat [FÖH-nischt flæt] *n* möblierte Wohnung *f*

furnished room [FÖH-nischt ruhm] *n* möbliertes Zimmer *nt*

furniture [FÖH-ni-tschö] *n* Möbel *ntpl*

furrier [FAR-i-ö] *n* Kürschner *m*

further [FÖH-ðöl] *adj* ferner

furthermore [FÖH-ðö-moh] *adv* überdies

furthest [FÖH-ðisst] *adj* entferntest

fuse [fjuhs] *n* Sicherung *f*

fuss [fass] *n* Getue *nt*

future [FJUH-tschö] *n* Zukunft *f*

gable [GEEJ-böl] *n* Giebel *m*

gadget [GÆDʒ-it] *n* Apparat *m*

gaiety [GEEJ-ö-ti] *n* Fröhlichkeit *f*

gain [geejn] *n* Gewinn *m; v* gewinnen

gale [geejl] *n* Sturm *m*

gallery [GÆL-ö-ri] *n* Galerie *f*

gamble [GÆM-böl] *v* spielen um Geld

gambling [GÆM-bling] *n* Glücksspiel *nt*

game [geejm] *n* Wild *nt;* Spiel *nt*

gangway [GÆNG-ueej] *n* Laufplanke *f*

gaol [dʒeejl] *n* Gefängnis *nt*

gap [gæp] *n* Lücke *f*

garage [GÆR-ahʒ] *n* Garage *f; v* einstellen

garbage [GAH-bidʒ] *n* Müll *m*

garden [GAH-dön] *n* Garten *m*

gardener [GAH-dön-ö] *n* Gärtner *m*

gargle [GAH-göl] *v* gurgeln

garlic [GAH-lik] *n* Knoblauch *m*

gas [gæss] *n* Benzin *nt;* Gas *nt*

gas cooker [gæss KUK-ö] *n* Gasherd *m*

gas station [gæss SSTEEJ-schön] *n* Tankstelle *f*

gas stove [gæss sstoow] *n* Gasofen *m*

gasoline [GÆSS-ö-lien] *n* Benzin *nt*

gastric [GÆSS-trik] *adj* gastrisch

gastric ulcer [GÆSS-trik UL-ssö] *n* Magengeschwür *nt*

gasworks [GÆSS-uöhkss] *n* Gaswerk *nt*

gate [geejt] *n* Tor *nt*

gather [GÆð-ö] *v* versammeln (sich)

gauge [geejdʒ] *n* Meßgerät *nt*

gauze [gohs] *n* Gaze *f*

gave [geejw] *v (p* **give)**

gay [geej] *adj* lustig

gaze [geejs] *v* starren

gazetteer [gæs-i-TIÖ] *n* geographisches Lexikon *nt*

gear [giö] *n* Ausrüstung *f;* Geschwindigkeit *f*

gear-box [GIÖ-bokss] *n* Getriebe *nt*

gear-lever [GIÖ-liew-ö] *n* Gangschaltung *f*

gem [dʒäm] *n* Edelstein *m*

gender [DʒäN-dö] *n* Geschlecht *nt*

general [DƷAN-ör-öl] n General m; adj allgemein

general practitioner [DƷAN-ör-öl præk-TISCH-ön-ö] n praktischer Arzt

generate [DƷAN-ör-eejt] v erzeugen

generation [dƷän-ö-REEJ-schön] n Generation f

generator [DƷAN-ör-eejt-ö] n Generator m

generous [DƷAN-ör-öss] adj großzügig

gentle [DƷAN-töl] adj sanft

gentleman [DƷAN-töl-mön] n (pl - men) Herr m

genuine [DƷAN-ju-in] adj echt

geography [dƷi-OG-rö-fi] n Erdkunde f

geology [dƷi-OL-ö-dƷi] n Geologie f

geometry [dƷi-OM-i-tri] n Geometrie f

germ [dƷöhm] n Keim m

German [DƷÖH-mön] n Deutsche m; adj deutsch

Germany [DƷÖH-mön-i] n Deutschland nt

* **get** [gät] v bekommen

* **get back** [gät bæk] v zurückgehen

* **get off** [gät of] v aussteigen

* **get on** [gät on] v vorwärtskommen; einsteigen

* **get up** [gät ap] v aufstehen

ghost [goosst] n Geist m

giddiness [GID-i-niss] n Schwindelgefühl nt

giddy [GID-i] adj schwindlig

gift [gift] n Geschenk nt

gifted [GIFT-id] adj begabt

gilt [gilt] adj vergoldet

ginger [DƷIN-dƷö] n Ingwer m

girdle [GÖH-döl] n Hüfthalter m

girl [göhl] n Mädchen nt

* **give** [giw] v geben

* **give in** [giw in] v nachgeben

* **give up** [giw ap] v aufgeben

given [GIW-ön] v (pp give)

glacier [GLÆSS-i-ö] n Gletscher m

glad [glæd] adj froh

glamorous [GLÆM-ör-öss] adj bezaubernd

glance [glahnss] n flüchtiger Blick; v flüchtig ansehen

gland [glænd] n Drüse f

glare [gläö] n grelles Licht

glass [glahss] n Glas nt

glasses [GLAHSS-is] pl Brille f

glaze [gleejs] v glasieren

glen [glän] n Bergschlucht f

glide [glaid] v gleiten

glider [GLAID-ö] n Segelflugzeug nt

glimpse [glimpss] n flüchtiger Blick; v flüchtig erblicken

global [GLOOB-öl] adj weltumfassend

globe [gloob] n Erdball m

gloom [gluhm] n Düsterkeit f

gloomy [GLUHM-i] adj verdrießlich

glorious [GLOH-ri-öss] adj prächtig

glory [GLOH-ri] n Pracht f

glossy [GLOSS-i] adj glänzend

glove [glaw] n Handschuh m

glow [gloo] n Glut f; v glühen

glue [gluh] n Leim m

* **go** [goo] v gehen

* **go ahead** [goo ö-HÄD] v fortfahren

* **go away** [goo ö-UEEJ] v weggehen

* **go back** [goo bæk] v zurückgehen

* **go home** [goo hoom] v heimgehen

* **go in** [goo in] *v* hineingehen
* **go on** [goo on] *v* fortfahren
* **go out** [goo aut] *v* ausgehen
* **go through** [goo Θruh] *v* durchmachen

goal [gool] *n* Tor *nt*; Ziel *nt*

goalkeeper [GOOL-kiep-ö] *n* Torwart *m*

goat [goot] *n* Ziege *f*

God [god] *n* Gott *m*

goggles [GOG-öls] *pl* Schutzbrille *f*

gold [goold] *n* Gold *nt*

gold leaf [goold lief] *n* Blattgold *nt*

golden [GOOL-dön] *adj* golden

goldmine [GOOLD-main] *n* Goldgrube *f*

goldsmith [GOOLD-ssmiΘ] *n* Goldschmied *m*

golf [golf] *n* Golf *nt*

golf-club [GOLF-klab] *n* Golfklub *m*

golf-course [GOLF-kohss] *n* Golfplatz *m*

golf-links [GOLF-lingkss] *n* Golfplatz *m*

gondola [GON-dö-lö] *n* Gondel *f*

gone [gon] *v* (*pp* go)

good [gud] *adj* gut

good-humoured [gud-HJUH-möd] *adj* gutgelaunt

good-looking [GUD-luk-ing] *adj* hübsch

good-natured [gud-NEEJ-tschöd] *adj* gutmütig

goods [guds] *pl* Güter *ntpl*

goods-train [GUDS-treejn] *n* Güterzug *m*

good-tempered [gud-TÄM-pöd] *adj* gutartig

good-will [gud-UIL] *n* Wohlwollen *nt*

goose [guhss] *n* (*pl* geese) Gans *f*

gooseberry [GUS-bö-ri] *n* Stachelbeere *f*

gorgeous [GOH-dʒöss] *adj* prächtig

gossip [GOSS-ip] *n* Klatsch *m*; *v* klatschen

got [got] *v* (*p,pp* get)

gout [gaut] *n* Gicht *f*

govern [GAW-ön] *v* regieren

governess [GAW-ö-nöss] *n* Gouvernante *f*

government [GAW-ö-mönt] *n* Regierung *f*

governor [GAW-ön-ö] *n* Gouverneur *m*

gown [gaun] *n* Kleid *nt*

grace [greejss] *n* Anmut *f*

graceful [GREEJSS-ful] *adj* anmutig

grade [greejd] *v* einstufen; *n* Rang *m*

gradient [GREEJD-i-önt] *n* Steigung *f*

gradual [GRÄD-ju-öl] *adj* allmählich

graduate [GRÄD-ju-eejt] *v* graduieren

grain [greejn] *n* Korn *nt*

gram [gräm] *n* Gramm *nt*

grammar [GRÄM-ö] *n* Grammatik *f*

grammar school [GRÄM-ö sskuhl] *n* Gymnasium *nt*

grammatical [grö-MÄT-ik-öl] *adj* grammatikalisch

gramophone [GRÄM-ö-foon] *n* Grammophon *nt*

grand [gränd] *adj* großartig

granddaughter [GRÄN-doh-tö] *n* Enkelin *f*

grandfather [GRÄN-fah-ðö] *n* Großvater *m*

grandmother [GRÄN-mað-ö] *n* Großmutter *f*

grandparents [GRÆN-päör-öntss] *pl* Großeltern *pl*

grandson [GRÆN-ssan] *n* Enkel *m*

granite [GRÆN-it] *n* Granit *m*

grant [grahnt] *v* gewähren; *n* Stipendium *nt*

grapefruit [GREEJP-fruht] *n* Pampelmuse *f*

grapes [greejpss] *pl* Weintrauben *fpl*

graph [grÆf] *n* Graphik *f*

graphic [GRÆF-ik] *adj* graphisch

grasp [grahssp] *v* ergreifen

grass [grahss] *n* Gras *nt*

grassy [GRAHSS-i] *adj* grasig

grate [greejt] *v* raspeln

grateful [GREEJT-ful] *adj* dankbar

grating [GREEJT-ing] *n* Gitter *nt*

gratis [GRÆ-tiss] *adv* unentgeltlich

gratitude [GRÆT-i-tjuhd] *n* Dankbarkeit *f*

gratuity [grö-TJUH-i-ti] *n* Trinkgeld *nt*

grave [greejw] *adj* ernst; *n* Grab *nt*

gravel [GRÆW-öl] *n* Kies *m*

gravestone [GREEJW-sstoon] *n* Grabstein *m*

graveyard [GREEJW-jahd] *n* Kirchhof *m*

graze [greejs] *v* weiden

grease [griess] *n* Schmierfett *nt*; *v* schmieren

greasy [GRIESS-i] *adj* fettig

great [greejt] *adj* groß

Great Britain [greejt BRIT-ön] *n* Großbritannien *nt*

Greece [griess] *n* Griechenland *nt*

greed [gried] *n* Gier *f*

greedy [GRIED-i] *adj* gierig

Greek [griek] *n* Grieche *m*; *adj* griechisch

green [grien] *adj* grün

green card [grien kahd] *n* grüne Karte

greengrocer [GRIEN-grooss-ö] *n* Gemüsehändler *m*

greenhouse [GRIEN-hauss] *n* Gewächshaus *nt*

greens [griens] *pl* frisches Gemüse

greet [griet] *v* grüßen

greetings [GRIET-ings] *pl* Grüße *mpl*

grew [gruh] *v* (*p* grow)

grey [greej] *adj* grau

grief [grief] *n* Gram *m*

grill [gril] *v* grillen; *n* Bratrost *m*

grilled [grild] *adj* gegrillt

grill-room [GRIL-ruhm] *n* Grillroom *m*

grin [grin] *v* grinsen; *n* Grinsen *nt*

* **grind** [graind] *v* mahlen

grip [grip] *n* Handköfferchen *nt*; *v* fassen

grocer [GROOSS-ö] *n* Lebensmittelhändler *m*

groceries [GROOSS-ör-is] *pl* Lebensmittel *pl*

grocery [GROOSS-ör-i] *n* Lebensmittelgeschäft *nt*

groove [gruhw] *n* Rille *f*

gross [grooss] *adj* brutto

grotto [GROT-oo] *n* Grotte *f*

ground [graund] *n* Boden *m*

ground-floor [GRAUND-floh] *n* Erdgeschoß *nt*

grounds [graunds] *pl* Grundstück *nt*

group [gruhp] *n* Gruppe *f*

grouse [grauss] *inv* Moorhuhn *nt*

grove [groow] *n* Hain *m*

* **grow** [groo] *v* wachsen

grown [groon] *v* (*pp* grow)

grown-up [GROON-ap] *n*

Erwachsene *m*

growth [grooⲐ] *n* Wuchs *m*

grumble [GRAM-böl] *v* murren

* **guarantee** [gær-ön-TIE] *v* garantieren; *n* Garantie *f*

guarantor [gær-ön-TOH] *n* Bürge *m*

guard [gahd] *v* bewachen; *n* Wache *f*

guess [gäss] *v* raten; *n* Vermutung *f*

guest [gässt] *n* Gast *m*

guest-house [GÄSST-hauss] *n* Fremdenheim *nt*

guest-room [GÄSST-ruhm] *n* Gastzimmer *nt*

guide [gaid] *n* Führer *m; v* führen

guidebook [GAID-buk] *n* Reiseführer *m*

guilty [GIL-ti] *adj* schuldig

guitar [gi-TAH] *n* Gitarre *f*

gulf [galf] *n* Golf *m*

gum [gam] *n* Klebstoff *m*; Kaugummi *nt*; Zahnfleisch *nt*

gun [gan] *n* Kanone *f*; Revolver *m*

gust [gasst] *n* Windstoß *m*

gusty [GASS-ti] *adj* stürmisch

gutter [GAT-ö] *n* Gosse *f*

gym shoes [dʒim schuhs] *pl* Turnschuhe *mpl*

gymnasium [dʒim-NEEJ-si-öm] *n* Turnhalle *f*

gymnast [DʒIM-næsst] *n* Turner *m*

gymnastics [dʒim-NÆSS-tikss] *pl* Turnen *nt*

gynaecologist [gain-i-KOL-ö-dʒisst] *n* Frauenarzt *m*

gypsy [DʒIP-ssi] *n* Zigeuner *m*

haberdasher [HÆB-ö-dæsch-ö] *n* Kurzwarenhändler *m*

haberdashery [HÆB-ö-dæsch-ör-i] *n* Kurzwarengeschäft *nt*

habit [HÆB-it] *n* Gewohnheit *f*

habitable [HÆB-it-ö-böl] *adj* bewohnbar

habitual [hö-BIT-ju-öl] *adj* gewohnt

had [hæd] *v* (*p,pp* have)

haddock [HÆD-ök] *n* Schellfisch *m*

hadn't [HÆD-önt] *v* (**had not**)

haemorrhage [HÄM-ör-idʒ] *n* Blutsturz *m*

haemorrhoids [HÄM-ör-euds] *pl* Hämorrhoiden *fpl*

hail [heejl] *n* Hagel *m*

hair [häö] *n* Haar *nt*

hair cream [häö kriem] *n* Haarkrem *f*

hair piece [häö piess] *n* Toupet *nt*

hair rollers [häö ROOL-äs] *pl* Lockenwickler *m*

hair set [häö ssät] *n* Frisur *f*

hair tonic [häö TON-ik] *n* Haarwuchsmittel *nt*

hairbrush [HÄÖ-brasch] *n* Haarbürste *f*

haircut [HÄÖ-kat] *n* Haarschnitt *m*

hairdresser [HÄÖ-dräss-ö] *n* Friseur *m*

hair-dryer [HÄÖ-drai-ö] *n* Föhn *m*

hairgrip [HÄÖ-grip] *n* Haarklemme *f*

hairnet [HÄÖ-nät] *n* Haarnetz *nt*

hair-oil [HÄÖR-eul] *n* Haaröl *nt*

hairpin [HÄÖ-pin] *n* Haarnadel *f*

half [hahf] *adv* halb; *n* Hälfte *f*; *adj* halb

half fare [hahf fäö] *n* halber Fahrpreis *m*

half price [hahf praiss] n halber Preis

halibut [HÆL-i-böt] n Heilbutt m

hall [hohl] n Foyer nt; Saal m

halt [hohlt] v anhalten

halve [hahw] v halbieren

ham [hæm] n Schinken m

hamlet [HÆM-lit] n Weiler m

hammer [HÆM-ö] n Hammer m

hammock [HÆM-ök] n Hängematte f

hamper [HÆM-pö] n Packkorb m

hand [hænd] n Hand f

hand baggage [hænd BÆG-id3] n Handgepäck nt

hand cream [hænd kriem] n Handkrem f

handbag [HÆND-bæg] n Handtasche f

handbook [HÆND-buk] n Handbuch nt

hand-brake [HÆND-breejk] n Handbremse f

handful [HÆND-ful] n Handvoll m

handicraft [HÆN-di-krahft] n Handwerk nt

handkerchief [HÆNG-kö-tschif] n Taschentuch nt

handle [HÆN-döl] v handhaben; n Handgriff m

handmade [HÆND-meejd] adj handgearbeitet

handsome [HÆN-ssöm] adj stattlich

handwork [HÆND-uöhk] n Handarbeit f

handwriting [HÆND-urait-ing] n Handschrift f

handy [HÆN-di] adj handlich

* **hang** [hæng] v aufhängen

hanger [HÆNG-ö] n Aufhänger m

happen [HÆP-ön] v ereignen (sich)

happening [HÆP-ön-ing] n Ereignis nt

happiness [HÆP-i-niss] n Glück nt

happy [HÆP-i] adj glücklich

harbour [HAH-bö] n Hafen m

hard [hahd] adv hart; adj hart

hardly [HAHD-li] adv kaum

hardware [HAHD-uäö] n Eisenwaren fpl

hardware store [HAHD-uäö sstoh] n Eisenwarenhandlung f

harm [hahm] v schaden; n Schaden m

harmful [HAHM-ful] adj schädlich

harmless [HAHM-liss] adj harmlos

harsh [hahsch] adj schroff

harvest [HAH-wisst] n Ernte f

has [hæs] v (pr **have**)

hasn't [HÆS-önt] v (**has not**)

haste [heejsst] n Eile f

hasten [HEEJSS-ön] v eilen

hasty [HEEJSS-ti] adj hastig

hat [hæt] n Hut m

hate [heejt] v hassen; verabscheuen; n Haß m

* **have** [hæw] v haben

* **have to** [hæw tu] v müssen

haven't [HÆW-önt] v (**have not**)

haversack [HÆW-ö-ssæk] n Brotbeutel m

hay [heej] n Heu nt

hay-fever [HEEJ-fiew-ö] n Heuschnupfen m

haze [heejs] n Dunst m

hazy [HEEJS-i] adj diesig

he [hie] pron er

head [häd] n Kopf m

headache [HÄD-eejk] n Kopfschmerzen mpl

heading [HÄD-ing] n Überschrift f

headlamp [HÄD-læmp] n Scheinwerfer m

headland [HÄD-lönd] *n*
Landzunge *f*

headlight [HÄD-lait] *n*
Scheinwerfer *m*

headline [HÄD-lain] *n* Schlagzeile
f

headlong [HÄD-long] *adv*
unbesonnen

headmaster [HÄD-mahss-tö] *n*
Schuldirektor *m*

headquarters [HÄD-kuoh-tös] *n*
Hauptquartier *nt*

head-waiter [häd-UEEJT-ö] *n*
Oberkellner *m*

heal [hiel] *v* heilen

health [hälⴲ] *n* Gesundheit *f*

health certificate [hälⴲ ssö-TIF-
i-kit] *n*
Gesundheitsbescheinigung *f*

healthy [HÄLⴲ-i] *adj* gesund

heap [hiep] *n* Haufen *m*

* **hear** [hiö] *v* hören

heard [höhd] *v (p, pp* hear)

hearing [HIÖR-ing] *n* Gehör *nt*

heart [haht] *n* Herz *nt*

heartburn [HAHT-böhn] *n*
Sodbrennen *nt*

hearth [hahⴲ] *n* Herd *m*

hearts [hahtss] *pl* Herz

hearty [HAHT-i] *adj* herzlich

heat [hiet] *v* wärmen; *n* Hitze *f*

heater [HIET-ö] *n* Heizofen *m*

heath [hieⴲ] *n* Heide *f*

heather [HÄⴁ-ö] *n* Heidekraut *nt*

heating [HIET-ing] *n* Heizung *f*

heating pad [HIET-ing pæd] *n*
Heizkissen *nt*

heaven [HÄW-ön] *n* Himmel *m*

heavenly [HÄW-ön-li] *adj*
himmlisch

heavy [HÄW-i] *adj* schwer

Hebrew [HIE-bruh] *n* Hebräisch
nt

hedge [hädʒ] *n* Hecke *f*

heel [hiel] *n* Ferse *f*

height [hait] *n* Höhe *f*

held [häld] *v (p,pp* **hold)**

helicopter [HÄL-i-kop-tö] *n*
Hubschrauber *m*

he'll [hiel] *v* (**he will**)

hell [häl] *n* Hölle *f*

help [hälp] *v* helfen; *n* Hilfe *f*

helper [HÄLP-ö] *n* Helfer *m*

helpful [HÄLP-ful] *adj* hilfreich

helping [HÄLP-ing] *n* Portion *f*

hem [häm] *n* Saum *m*

hen [hän] *n* Henne *f*

her [höh] *pron* ihr; sie; *adj* ihr

herb [höhb] *n* Kraut *nt*

herd [höhd] *n* Herde *f*

here [hiö] *adv* hier

hernia [HÖH-ni-ö] *n* Bruch *m*

hero [HIÖR-oo] *n* Held *m*

herring [HÄR-ing] *n* Hering *m*

herself [höh-SSÄLF] *pron* sie
selbst; sich

he's [hies] *v* (**he is, he has**)

hesitate [HÄS-i-teejt] *v* zögern

hiccup [HIK-ap] *n* Schluckauf *m*

* **hide** [haid] *v* verstecken

hideous [HID-i-öss] *adj*
abscheulich

hi-fi [HAI-FAI] *n* Hi-Fi

high [hai] *adj* hoch

high season [hai SSIES-ön] *n*
Hochsaison *f*

high tide [hai taid] *n* Flut *f*

highway [HAI-ueej] *n* Landstraße
f

hijack [HAI-dʒæk] *v* kapern

hike [haik] *v* wandern

hill [hil] *n* Hügel *m*

hillock [HIL-ök] *n* kleiner Hügel

hillside [HIL-ssaid] *n* Hang *m*

hilltop [HIL-top] *n* Hügelspitze *f*

hilly [HIL-i] *adj* hügelig

him [him] *pron* ihm; ihn

himself [him-SSÄLF] *pron* sich; er selbst

hinder [HIN-dö] *v* hindern

hinge [hindʒ] *n* Scharnier *nt*

hip [hip] *n* Hüfte *f*

hire [haiö] *v* mieten

hire-purchase [haiö-PÖH-tschöss] *n* Teilzahlungskauf *m*

his [his] *adj* sein

historian [hiss-TOO-ri-ön] *n* Historiker *m*

historic [hiss-TOR-ik] *adj* historisch

historical [hiss-TOR-ik-öl] *adj* geschichtlich

history [HISS-tör-i] *n* Geschichte *f*

* **hit** [hit] *v* schlagen; *n* Schlager *m*

hitchhike [HITSCH-haik] *v* trampen

hitchhiker [HITSCH-haik-ö] *n* Tramper *m*

hoarse [hohss] *adj* heiser

hobby [HOB-i] *n* Steckenpferd *nt*

hockey [HOK-i] *n* Hockey *nt*

* **hold** [hoold] *v* freihalten; halten; *n* Laderaum *m*

* **hold on** [hoold on] *v* festhalten (sich)

* **hold up** [hoold ap] *v* stützen

hole [hool] *n* Loch *nt*

holiday [HOL-ö-deej] *n* Feiertag *m*

holiday camp [HOL-ö-deej kæmp] *n* Ferienlager *nt*

holidays [HOL-ö-deejs] *pl* Urlaub *m*

Holland [HOL-önd] *n* Holland *nt*

hollow [HOL-oo] *adj* hohl

holy [HOO-li] *adj* heilig

home [hoom] *n* Heim *nt*

home-made [HOOM-meejd] *adj* selbstgemacht

homesickness [HOOM-ssik-niss] *n* Heimweh *nt*

honest [ON-isst] *adj* ehrlich

honestly [ON-isst-li] *adv* ehrlich

honesty [ON-iss-ti] *n* Ehrlichkeit *f*

honey [HAN-i] *n* Honig *m*

honeymoon [HAN-i-muhn] *n* Flitterwochen *fpl*

honorable [ON-ör-ö-böl] *adj* ehrenwert

honour [ON-ö] *n* Ehre *f*

hood [hud] *n* Motorhaube *f*

hook [huk] *n* Haken *m*

hoot [huht] *v* hupen

hooter [HUHT-ö] *n* Hupe *f*

hop [hop] *v* hüpfen

hope [hoop] *v* hoffen; *n* Hoffnung *f*

hopeful [HOOP-ful] *adj* hoffnungsvoll

hops [hopss] *pl* Hopfen *m*

horizon [hö-RAI-sön] *n* Horizont *m*

horizontal [hor-i-SON-töl] *adj* waagrecht

horn [hohn] *n* Hupe *f*

horrible [HOR-ö-böl] *adj* entsetzlich

hors-d'œuvre [] *n* Vorspeise *f*

horse [hohss] *n* Pferd *nt*

horse-power [HOHSS-pau-ö] *n* Pferdestärke *f*

horse-race [HOHSS-reejss] *n* Pferderennen *nt*

horse-radish [HOHSS-ræd-isch] *n* Meerrettich *m*

hosiery [HOO-ʒör-i] *n* Strumpfwaren *fpl*

hospitable [HOSS-pit-ö-böl] *adj* gastfreundlich

hospital [HOSS-pit-öl] *n* Krankenhaus *nt*

hospitality [hoss-pi-TÆL-i-ti] *n* Gastfreundschaft *f*

host [hoosst] *n* Gastgeber *m*

hostel [HOSS-töl] *n* Herberge *f*

hostess [HOOSS-tiss] *n* Gastgeberin *f*

hot [hot] *adj* heiß

hotel [hoo-TÁL] *n* Hotel *nt*

hot-water bottle [hot-UOH-tö BOT-öl] *n* Wärmflasche *f*

hour [auö] *n* Stunde *f*

hourly [AUÖ-li] *adj* stündlich

house [hauss] *n* Haus *nt*

house-agent [HAUSS-eej-dʒönt] *n* Häusermakler *m*

household [HAUSS-hoold] *n* Haushalt *m*

housekeeper [HAUSS-kiep-ö] *n* Haushälterin *f*

housekeeping [HAUSS-kiep-ing] *n* Haushaltung *f*

housemaid [HAUSS-meejd] *n* Hausangestellte *f*

housewife [HAUSS-uaif] *n* Hausfrau *f*

housework [HAUSS-uöhk] *n* Haushaltsarbeiten *fpl*

hovercraft [HOW-ö-krahft] *n* Luftkissenfahrzeug *nt*

how [hau] *adv* wie

however [hau-AW-ö] *conj* jedoch

hug [hag] *v* umarmen

huge [hjuhdʒ] *adj* riesig

human [HJUH-mön] *adj* menschlich

human being [HJUH-mön BIE-ing] *n* Mensch *m*

humanity [hju-MÆN-it-i] *n* Menschheit *f*

humble [HAM-böl] *adj* bescheiden

humid [HJUH-mid] *adj* feucht

humorous [HJUH-mör-öss] *adj* humorvoll

humour [HJUH-mö] *n* Humor *m*

hundred [HAN-dröd] *n* hundert

hung [hang] *v* (*p, pp* hang)

Hungarian [hang-GAÖR-i-ön] *n* Ungar *m*; *adj* ungarisch

Hungary [HANG-gör-i] *n* Ungarn *nt*

hunger [HANG-gö] *n* Hunger *m*

hungry [HANG-gri] *adj* hungrig

hunt [hant] *v* jagen; *n* Jagd *f*

hunt for [hant foh] *v* suchen

hunter [HAN-tö] *n* Jäger *m*

hurricane [HAR-i-kön] *n* Wirbelsturm *m*

hurricane lamp [HAR-i-kön læmp] *n* Sturmlaterne *f*

hurry [HAR-i] *n* Eile *f*; *v* eilen

* hurt [höht] *v* verletzen

hurtful [HÖHT-ful] *adj* schädlich

husband [HAS-bönd] *n* Mann *m*

hut [hat] *n* Hütte *f*

hydrogen [HAI-dri-dʒön] *n* Wasserstoff *m*

hygienic [hai-DʒIEN-ik] *adj* hygienisch

hymn [him] *n* Hymne *f*

hyphen [HAI-fön] *n* Bindestrich *m*

hysterical [hiss-TÄR-ik-öl] *adj* hysterisch

I [ai] *pron* ich

ice [aiss] *n* Eis *nt*

icebag [AISS-bæg] *n* Eisbeutel *m*

ice-cream [AISS-kriem] *n* Eis *nt*

iced drink [aisst dringk] *n* eisgekühltes Getränk *nt*

Iceland [AISS-lönd] *n* Island *nt*

ice-water [AISS-uoh-tö] *n* Eiswasser *nt*

I'd [aid] *v* (**I should, I would, I had**)

I'd rather [aid RAH-ðö] *v* (**I would rather**)

idea [ai-DI-ö] *n* Idee *f*

ideal [ai-DI-öl] *adj* ideal; *n* Ideal

nt
identical [ai-DÄN-tik-öl] *adj*
identisch
identification [ai-dän-ti-fi-KEEJ-schön] *n* Identifizierung *f*
identity [ai-DÄN-ti-ti] *n* Identität *f*
identity card [ai-DÄN-ti-ti kahd] *n* Personalausweis *m*
idiom [ID-i-öm] *n* Idiom *nt*
idiomatic [id-i-ö-MÆT-ik] *adj* idiomatisch
idiot [ID-i-öt] *n* Idiot *m*
idle [AI-döl] *adj* müßig
if [if] *conj* wenn
ignition [ig-NISCH-ön] *n* Zündung *f*
ignorant [IG-nör-önt] *adj* unwissend
ignore [ig-NOH] *v* ignorieren
ill [ill] *adj* krank
I'll [ail] *v* (I shall, I will)
illegal [i-LIEG-öl] *adj* ungesetzlich
illegible [i-LÄDʒ-ö-böl] *adj* unleserlich
illness [IL-niss] *n* Krankheit *f*
illuminate [i-LUH-min-eejt] *v* erleuchten
illumination [i-luh-mi-NEEJ-schön] *n* Beleuchtung *f*
illustrate [IL-öss-treejt] *v* illustrieren
illustration [il-öss-TREEJ-schön] *n* Illustration *f*
I'm [aim] *v* (I am)
imaginary [i-MÆDʒ-in-ör-i] *adj* imaginär
imagination [i-mædʒ-i-NEEJ-schön] *n* Vorstellungskraft *f*
imagine [i-MÆDS-in] *v* vorstellen (sich)
imitate [IM-i-teejt] *v* nachahmen
imitation [im-i-TEEJ-schön] *n* Imitation *f*

immediate [i-MIE-djöt] *adj* unmittelbar
immediately [i-MIE-djöt-li] *adj* sofort
immense [i-MÄNSS] *adj* unermeßlich
immersion heater [i-MÖH-schön HIET-ö] *n* Tauchsieder *m*
immigrant [IM-i-grönt] *n* Einwanderer *m*
immigrate [IM-i-greejt] *v* einwandern
immunity [i-MJUHN-it-i] *n* Immunität *f*
immunize [IM-juh-nais] *v* immunisieren
impassable [im-PAHSS-ö-böl] *adj* ungangbar
impatient [im-PEEJ-schönt] *adj* ungeduldig
imperfect [im-PÖH-fikt] *adj* unvollkommen
imperial [im-PIÖR-i-öl] *adj* imperialistisch
impertinence [im-PÖH-tin-önss] *n* Unverschämtheit *f*
impertinent [im-PÖH-tin-önt] *adj* unverschämt
implement [IM-pli-mönt] *n* Gerät *nt*
imply [im-PLAI] *v* besagen
impolite [im-pö-LAIT] *adj* unhöflich
import [im-POHT] *v* einführen
import duty [IM-poht DJUH-ti] *n* Einfuhrzoll *m*
importance [im-POHT-önss] *n* Wichtigkeit *f*
important [im-POHT-önt] *adj* wichtig
imported [im-POHT-id] *adj* eingeführt
importer [im-POHT-ö] *n* Importeur *m*

imports [IM-pohtss] *pl* Import *m*

imposing [im-POOS-ing] *adj*
imposant

impossible [im-POSS-i-böl] *adj*
unmöglich

impress [im-PRÄSS] *v*
beeindrucken

impression [im-PRÄSCH-ön] *n*
Eindruck *m*

impressive [im-PRÄSS-iw] *adj*
eindrucksvoll

imprison [im-PRIS-ön] *v*
einkerkern

imprisonment [im-PRIS-ön-
mönt] *n* Einkerkerung *f*

improbable [im-PROB-ö-böl] *adj*
unwahrscheinlich

improper [im-PROP-ö] *adj*
unpassend

improve [im-PRUHW] *v*
verbessern

improved [im-PRUHWD] *adj*
verbessert

improvement [im-PRUHW-mönt]
n Verbesserung *f*

impudent [IM-pju-dönt] *adj*
unverschämt

impulse [IM-palss] *n* Impuls *m*

impulsive [im-PALSS-iw] *adj*
impulsiv

in [in] *adv* hinein; *prep* in

in a hurry [in ö HAR-i] eilig

in advance [in öd-WAHNSS] vorher

in fact [in fäkt] tatsächlich

in front of [in frant ow] *prep* vor

in general [in DƷÄN-ör-öl] im
allgemeinen

in love [in law] verliebt

in order [in OH-dö] in Ordnung

in particular [in pö-TIK-ju-lö]
speziell

in reply [in ri-PLAI] als Antwort

in spite of [in sspait ow] *prep*
trotz

in the meantime [in ðö MIEN-
taim] inzwischen

in time [in taim] rechtzeitig

in writing [in RAIT-ing]
schriftlich

inaccessible [in-æk-SSÄSS-ö-böl]
adj unzugänglich

inaccurate [in-ÄK-jur-it] *adj*
ungenau

inadequate [in-ÄD-i-kuit] *adj*
unzulänglich

incapable [in-KEEJP-ö-böl] *adj*
unfähig

incident [IN-ssi-dönt] *n*
Zwischenfall *m*

incidental [in-ssi-DÄNT-öl] *adj*
zufällig

incline [in-KLAIN] *n* Neigung *f*

include [in-KLUHD] *v*
einschließen

included [in-KLUHD-id] *adj*
eingeschlossen

inclusive [in-KLUHSS-iw] *adj*
einschließlich

income [IN-köm] *n* Einkommen
nt

income-tax [IN-köm-tækss] *n*
Einkommenssteuer *f*

incoming [IN-kam-ing] *adj*
ankommend

incompetent [in-KOM-pi-tönt] *adj*
unfähig

incomplete [in-köm-PLIET] *adj*
unvollständig

inconvenience [in-kön-WIEN-
jönss] *n* Schwierigkeit *f*

inconvenient [in-kön-WIEN-jönt]
adj ungelegen

incorrect [in-kö-RÄKT] *adj*
unrichtig

increase [IN-kriess] *n* Zunahme
f; *v* vergrößern

incredible [in-KRÄD-i-böl] *adj*
unglaublich

incurable [in-KJUHÖR-ö-böll] *adj*
unheilbar
indeed [in-DIED] *adv* wirklich
indefinite [in-DÄF-i-nit] *adj*
unbestimmt
indemnity [in-DÄM-ni-ti] *n*
Sicherstellung *f*
independence [in-di-PÄND-önss]
n Unabhängigkeit *f*
independent [in-di-PÄND-önt] *adj*
unabhängig
index [IN-däkss] *n* Index *m*
India [IN-di-ö] *n* Indien *nt*
Indian [IN-di-ön] *n* Inder *m*
indicate [IN-di-keejt] *v* zeigen
indication [in-di-KEEJ-schön] *n*
Anzeichen *nt*
indicator [in-di-KEEJT-ö] *n*
Winker *m*
indigestion [in-di-DƷASS-tschön]
n Magenverstimmung *f*
indirect [in-di-RÄKT] *adj* indirekt
indistinct [in-diss-TINGKT] *adj*
undeutlich
individual [in-di-WID-ju-öll] *adj*
individuell; *n* Individuum *nt*
indoor [IN-doh] *adj* im Haus
indoors [in-DOHS] *adv* im Haus
industrial [in-DASS-tri-öl] *adj*
industriell
industrious [in-DASS-tri-öss] *adj*
fleißig
industry [IN-döss-tri] *n* Industrie
f
inedible [in-ÄD-i-böl] *adj*
ungenießbar
inefficient [in-i-FISCH-önt] *adj*
wirkungslos
inexact [in-ig-SÆKT] *adj* ungenau
inexpensive [in-ikss-PÄNSS-iw]
adj billig
inexperienced [in-ikss-PIÖR-i-
önsst] *adj* unerfahren
infant [IN-fönt] *n* Säugling *m*

infantry [IN-fönt-ri] *n* Infanterie
f
infect [in-FÄKT] *v* anstecken
infection [in-FÄK-schön] *n*
Infektion *f*
infectious [in-FÄK-schöss] *adj*
ansteckend
inferior [in-FIÖR-i-ö] *adj*
minderwertig
infinitive [in-FIN-i-tiw] *n*
Infinitiv *m*
infirmary [in-FÖHM-ör-i] *n*
Krankenrevier *nt*
inflammable [in-FLÆM-ö-böll] *adj*
entzündbar
inflammation [in-flö-MEEJ-
schön] *n* Entzündung *f*
inflatable [in-FLEEJT-ö-böll] *adj*
aufblasbar
inflate [in-FLEEJT] *v* aufblähen
inflation [in-FLEEJ-schön] *n*
Inflation *f*
influence [IN-flu-önss] *n* Einfluß
m; *v* beeinflussen
influential [in-flu-ÄN-schöll] *adj*
einflußreich
influenza [in-flu-ÄN-sö] *n* Grippe
f
inform [in-FOHM] *v* informieren
informal [in-FOHM-öl] *adj*
unformell
information [in-fö-MEEJ-schön] *n*
Auskunft *f*
infra-red [IN-frö-RÄD] *adj*
infrarot
infrequent [in-FRIEK-uönt] *adj*
selten
ingredient [in-GRIED-i-önt] *n*
Zutaten *fpl*
inhabit [in-HÆB-it] *v* bewohnen
inhabitable [in-HÆB-it-ö-böll] *adj*
bewohnbar
inhabitant [in-HÆB-it-önt] *n*
Einwohner *m*

inhospitable [in-HOSS-pit-ö-böl] *adj* unwirtlich

initial [i-NISCH-öl] *v* abzeichnen; *n* Anfangsbuchstabe *m; adj* erste

inject [in-DʒÄKT] *v* einspritzen

injection [in-DʒÄK-schön] *n* Injektion *f*

injure [IN-dʒö] *v* verletzen

injured [IN-dʒöd] *adj* verletzt

injury [IN-dʒör-i] *n* Verletzung *f*

injustice [in-DʒASS-tiss] *n* Ungerechtigkeit *f*

ink [ingk] *n* Tinte *f*

inlet [IN-lät] *n* Bucht *f*

inn [in] *n* Gasthof *m*

inner [IN-ö] *adj* inwendig

inner tube [IN-ö tjuhb] *n* Schlauch *m*

innkeeper [IN-kiep-ö] *n* Gastwirt *m*

innocent [IN-ö-ssönt] *adj* unschuldig

inoculate [i-NOK-ju-leejt] *v* impfen

inoculation [i-nok-ju-LEEJ-schön] *n* Impfung *f*

inquire [in-KUAIÖ] *v* erkundigen (sich)

inquiry [in-KUAIÖR-i] *n* Nachfrage *f*

inquiry office [in-KUAIÖR-i OF-iss] *n* Auskunftsbüro *nt*

inquisitive [in-KUIS-i-tiw] *adj* neugierig

insane [in-SSEEJN] *adj* wahnsinnig

insanitary [in-SSÆN-i-tör-i] *adj* ungesund

inscription [in-SSKRIP-schön] *n* Inschrift *f*

insect [IN-ssäkt] *n* Insekt *nt*

insect bite [IN-ssäkt bait] *n* Insektenstich *m*

insect repellent [IN-ssäkt ri-PÄL-önt] *n* Insektenschutzmittel *nt*

insecticide [in-SSÄK-ti-ssaid] *n* Insektengift *nt*

insensible [in-SSÄN-ssö-böl] *adj* unempfindlich

insert [in-SSÖHT] *v* einfügen

inside [IN-ssaid] *adj* inner; *adv* drinnen

insides [IN-ssaids] *pl* Eingeweide *nt*

insignificant [in-ssig-NIF-i-könt] *adj* unbedeutend

insincere [in-ssin-SSIÖ] *adj* unaufrichtig

insist [in-SSISST] *v* bestehen

insolent [IN-ssöl-önt] *adj* unverschämt

insomnia [in-SSOM-ni-ö] *n* Schlaflosigkeit *f*

inspect [in-SSPÄKT] *v* inspizieren

inspection [in-SSPÄK-schön] *n* Inspektion *f*

inspector [in-SSPÄK-tö] *n* Aufsichtsbeamte *m*

install [in-SSTOHL] *v* installieren

installation [in-sstö-LEEJ-schön] *n* Einrichtung *f*

instalment [in-SSTOHL-mönt] *n* Abschlagszahlung *f*

instance [in-sstönss] *n* Beispiel *nt*

instant [IN-sstönt] *n* Augenblick *m*

instantly [IN-sstönt-li] *adv* sofort

instead of [in-SSTÄD ow] anstatt

institute [IN-ssti-tjuht] *n* Institut *nt; v* einrichten

institution [in-ssti-TJUH-schön] *n* Institution *f*

instruct [in-SSTRAKT] *v* unterweisen

instruction [in-SSTRAK-schön] *n* Unterweisung *f*

instructor [in-SSTRAK-tö] *n*
Lehrer *m*
instrument [IN-sstru-mönt] *n*
Instrument *nt*
insufficient [in-ssö-FISCH-önt]
adj ungenügend
insulate [IN-ssju-leejt] *v* isolieren
insulation [in-ssju-LEEJ-schön] *n*
Isolation *f*
insulator [in-ssju-LEEJT-ö] *n*
Isolator *m*
insult [in-SSALT] *v* beleidigen; *n*
Beleidigung *f*
insurance [in-SCHUHÖR-önss] *n*
Versicherung *f*
insurance policy [in-SCHUHÖR-
önss POL-i-ssi] *n*
Versicherungspolice *f*
insure [in-SCHUHÖ] *v* versichern
intact [in-TÆKT] *adj* unversehrt
intellect [IN-ti-läkt] *n* Verstand
m
intellectual [in-ti-LÄK-tju-öl] *adj*
intellektuell
intelligence [in-TÄL-i-dʒönss] *n*
Intelligenz *f*
intelligent [in-TÄL-i-dʒönt] *adj*
intelligent
intend [in-TÄND] *v* beabsichtigen
intense [in-TÄNSS] *adj* intensiv
intention [in-TÄN-schön] *n*
Absicht *f*
intentional [in-TÄN-schön-öl] *adj*
absichtlich
interest [IN-trisst] *n* Zins *m*;
Interesse *nt*; *v* interessieren
interested [IN-trisst-id] *adj*
interessiert
interesting [IN-trisst-ing] *adj*
interessant
interfere [in-tö-FIÖ] *v*
einschreiten
interfere with [in-tö-FIÖ uið] *v*
einmischen (sich)

interference [in-tö-FIÖR-önss] *n*
Eingreifen *nt*
interim [IN-tör-im] *n*
Zwischenzeit *f*
interior [in-TIÖR-i-ö] *n* Innere *nt*
interlude [IN-tö-luhd] *n*
Zwischenspiel *nt*
intermission [in-tö-MISCH-ön] *n*
Pause *f*
internal [in-TÖH-nöl] *adj* intern
international [in-tö-NÆSCH-ön-
öl] *adj* international
interpret [in-TÖH-prit] *v*
dolmetschen; auslegen
interpreter [in-TÖH-prit-ö] *n*
Dolmetscher *m*
interrogate [in-TÄR-ö-geejt] *v*
verhören
interrogative [in-tö-ROG-ö-tiw]
adj fragend
interrupt [in-tö-RAPT] *v*
unterbrechen
interruption [in-tö-RAP-schön] *n*
Unterbrechung *f*
intersection [in-tö-SSÄK-schön] *n*
Kreuzung *f*
interval [IN-tö-wöl] *n* Intervall *nt*
interview [IN-tö-wjuh] *n*
Interview *nt*
intestine [in-TÄSS-tin] *n* Darm *m*
intimate [IN-ti-mit] *adj* intim
into [IN-tu] *prep* in
intoxicated [in-TOKSS-i-keejt-id]
adj berauscht
introduce [in-trö-DJUHSS] *v*
einführen; vorstellen
introduction [in-trö-DAK-schön]
n Einführung *f*; Vorstellung *f*
invade [in-WEEJD] *v* eindringen
invalid [in-WÆL-id] *adj* invalide;
n Invalide *m*
invent [in-WÄNT] *v* erfinden
invention [in-WÄN-schön] *n*
Erfindung *f*

inventor [in-WÄN-töl] *n* Erfinder
m

inventory [IN-wän-tri] *n* Inventar
nt

invest [in-WÄSST] *v* investieren

investigate [in-WÄSS-ti-geejt] *v*
untersuchen

investment [in-WÄSST-mönt] *n*
Investition *f*

investor [in-WÄSS-töl] *n*
Kapitalgeber m

invisible [in-WIS-i-böl] *adj*
unsichtbar

invitation [in-wi-TEEJ-schön] *n*
Einladung *f*

invite [in-WAIT] *v* einladen

invoice [IN-weuss] *n* Rechnung *f*

involve [in-WOLW] *v* verwickeln

inwards [IN-uöds] *adv* nach
innen

iodine [AI-ö-dien] *n* Jod nt

Ireland [AIÖ-lönd] *n* Irland nt

Irish [AIÖR-isch] *n* Ire m; *adj*
irisch

iron [AI-ön] *n* Bügeleisen nt;
Eisen nt; *v* bügeln

ironworks [AI-ön-uökss] *n*
Eisenhütte *f*

irregular [i-RÄG-ju-lö] *adj*
unregelmäßig

irritable [IR-it-ö-böl] *adj* reizbar

irritate [IR-i-teejt] *v* irritieren

is [is] *v* (*pr* be)

island [AI-lönd] *n* Insel *f*

isn't [IS-önt] *v* (is not)

isolated [ai-ssö-LEEJT-id] *adj*
abgeschieden

isolation [ai-ssö-LEEJ-schön] *n*
Isolierung *f*

Israel [IS-reejl] *n* Israel nt

Israeli [is-REEJL-i] *n* Israeli m;
adj israelisch

issue [ISS-juh] *v* ausgeben

isthmus [ISS-möss] *n* Landenge *f*

it [it] *pron* es

Italian [i-TÆL-jön] *n* Italiener m;
adj italienisch

italics [i-TÆL-ikss] *pl*
Kursivschrift *f*

Italy [IT-ö-li] *n* Italien nt

itch [itsch] *n* Jucken nt

item [AIT-öm] *n* Posten m

itinerant [i-TIN-ör-önt] *adj*
umherziehend

itinerary [ai-TIN-ör-ör-i] *n*
Reiseplan m

it's [itss] *v* (it is, it has)

I've [aiw] *v* (I have)

ivory [AIW-ör-i] *n* Elfenbein nt

jack [dʒæk] *n* Wagenheber m;
Bube m

jacket [DʒÆK-it] *n* Jacke *f*

jade [dʒeejd] *n* Jade *f*

jail [dʒeejl] *n* Gefängnis nt

jam [dʒæm] *n* Verkehrsstockung
f

January [DʒÆN-ju-ör-i] *n* Januar
m

Japan [dʒö-PÆN] *n* Japan nt

Japanese [dʒæp-ö-NIES] *n*
Japaner m; *adj* japanisch

jar [dʒah] *n* Glas nt

jaundice [DʒOHN-diss] *n*
Gelbsucht *f*

jaw [dʒoh] *n* Kiefer m

jazz [dʒæs] *n* Jazz m

jealous [DʒÄL-öss] *adj*
eifersüchtig

jeans [dʒiens] *pl* Jeans *pl*

jeep [dʒiep] *n* Jeep m

jelly [DʒÄL-i] *n* Gelee nt

jersey [DʒÖH-si] *n* Jersey nt;
Wollpullover m

jet [dʒät] *n* Düsenflugzeug nt

jetty [DʒÄT-i] *n* Pier m

Jew [dʒuh] *n* Jude m

jewel [DZUH-öl] n Juwel nt

jeweller [DZUH-öl-ö] n Juwelier m

jewellery [DZUH-öl-ri] n Schmuck m

Jewish [DZUH-isch] adj jüdisch

job [dzob] n Beschäftigung f

jockey [DZOK-i] n Jockei m

join [dzeun] v verbinden

joint [dzeunt] n Gelenk nt

jointly [DZEUNT-li] adv gemeinsam

joke [dzook] n Witz m

joker [DZOOK-ö] n Joker m

jolly [DZOL-i] adj fröhlich

journal [DZÖH-nöl] n Zeitschrift f

journalism [DZÖH-nöl-ism] n Journalismus m

journalist [DZÖH-nöl-isst] n Journalist m

journey [DZÖH-ni] n Reise f

joy [dzeu] n Freude f

joyful [DZEU-ful] adj freudig

judge [dzadz] n Richter m; v urteilen

judgment [DZADZ-mönt] n Urteil nt

jug [dzag] n Krug m

Jugoslav [juh-goo-SSLAHW] adj jugoslawisch; n Jugoslawe m

Jugoslavia [juh-goo-SSLAHW-jö] n Jugoslawien nt

juice [dzuhss] n Saft m

juicy [DZUHSS-i] adj saftig

July [dzu-LAI] n Juli m

jump [dzamp] v springen; n Sprung m

jumper [DZAMP-ö] n Jumper m

junction [DZANGK-schön] n Autobahnkreuz nt

June [dzuhn] n Juni m

jungle [DZANG-göl] n Dschungel m

junk [dzangk] n Plunder m

jury [DZUHÖR-i] n Preisgericht nt

just [dzasst] adv genau; adj gerecht

justice [DZASS-tiss] n Gerechtigkeit f

juvenile [DZUH-wi-nail] adj jugendlich

keen [kien] adj scharf

* keep [kiep] v halten

* keep off [kiep of] v fernhalten (sich)

* keep on [kiep on] v fortfahren

* keep quiet [kiep KUAI-öt] v still sein

keg [käg] n Fäßchen nt

kennel [KÄN-öl] n Hundehütte f

kept [käpt] v (p, pp keep)

kerosene [KÄR-ö-ssien] n Kerosin nt

kettle [KÄT-öl] n Kessel m

key [kie] n Schlüssel m

keyhole [KIE-hool] n Schlüsselloch nt

khaki [KAHK-i] n Khaki nt

kick [kik] v treten

kick-off [KIK-of] n Anstoß m

kid [kid] v foppen; n Kind nt; Ziegenleder nt

kidney [KID-ni] n Niere f

kill [kil] v töten

kilogram [KIL-ö-græm] n Kilo nt

kilometre [KIL-ö-mie-tö] n Kilometer m

kind [kaind] adj freundlich; n Sorte f

kindergarten [KIN-dö-gah-tön] n Kindergarten m

king [king] n König m

kingdom [KING-döm] n Königreich nt

kiosk [KI-ossk] n Kiosk m

kiss [kiss] n Kuß m; v küssen

kit [kit] n Ausrüstung f

kitchen [KITSCH-in] *n* Küche *f*

kleenex [KLIEN-ökss] *n* Papiertaschentuch *nt*

knapsack [NÆP-ssæk] *n* Rucksack *m*

knave [neejw] *n* Bube *m*

knee [nie] *n* Knie *nt*

* **kneel** [niel] *v* knien

knelt [nält] *v* (*p, pp* **kneel**)

knew [njuh] *v* (*p* **know**)

knife [naif] *n* Messer *nt*

knit [nit] *v* stricken

knitting [NIT-ing] *n* Strickzeug *nt*

knob [nob] *n* Knopf *m*

knock [nok] *n* Klopfen *nt; v* klopfen

knock against [nok ö-GÄNSST] *v* gegenstoßen

knock down [nok daun] *v* niederschlagen

knot [not] *n* Knoten *m*

* **know** [noo] *v* kennen; wissen

knowledge [NOL-idʒ] *n* Kenntnis *f*

known [noon] *v* (*pp* **know**)

knuckle [NAK-öl] *n* Fingergelenk *nt*

label [LEEJB-öl] *n* Etikett *nt; v* beschriften

laboratory [lö-BOR-ö-tri] *n* Laboratorium *nt*

labour [LEEJB-ö] *n* Arbeit *f*

labour permit [LEEJB-ö PÖH-mit] *n* Arbeitsbewilligung *f*

labourer [LEEJB-ör-öl] *n* Arbeiter *m*

labour-saving [LEEJB-ö-sseejwing] *adj* arbeitssparend

lace [leejss] *n* Spitze *f*

laces [LEEJSS-is] *pl* Schnürbänder *ntpl*

lack [læk] *n* Mangel *m; v* mangeln

lacquer [LÆK-ö] *n* Lack *m*

lad [læd] *n* Bursche *m*

ladder [LÆD-ö] *n* Leiter *f*

ladies' room [LEEJD-is ruhm] *n* Damentoilette *f*

lady [LEEJD-i] *n* Dame *f*

lain [leejn] *v* (*pp* **lie**)

lake [leejk] *n* See *m*

lakeside [LEEJK-ssaid] *n* Seeufer *nt*

lamb [læm] *n* Lamm *nt*

lame [leejm] *adj* lahm

lamp [læmp] *n* Lampe *f*

lamp-post [LÆMP-poosst] *n* Laternenpfahl *m*

lampshade [LÆMP-scheejd] *n* Lampenschirm *m*

land [lænd] *n* Land *nt; v* landen

landing [LÆN-ding] *n* Landung *f*

landlady [LÆND-leejd-i] *n* Wirtin *f*

landlord [LÆND-lohd] *n* Hausbesitzer *m*

landmark [LÆND-mahk] *n* Markstein *m*

landscape [LÆND-sskeejp] *n* Landschaft *f*

lane [leejn] *n* Weg *m*

language [LÆNG-guidʒ] *n* Sprache *f*

lantern [LÆN-tön] *n* Laterne *f*

lapel [lö-PÄL] *n* Rockaufschlag *m*

lard [lahd] *n* Schmalz *nt*

larder [LAHD-ö] *n* Speisekammer *f*

large [lahdʒ] *adj* groß

last [lahsst] *v* dauern; *adj* letzt

lasting [LAHSST-ing] *adj* dauerhaft

latchkey [LÆTSCH-kie] *n* Hausschlüssel *m*

late [leejt] *adj* spät

lately [LEEJT-li] *adv* unlängst

later [LEEJT-ö] adj später
latest [LEEJT-isst] adj letzt
Latin America [LÆT-in ö-MÄR-i-kö] n Lateinamerika nt
Latin American [LÆT-in ö-MÄR-i-kön] adj lateinamerikanisch; n Lateinamerikaner m
laugh [lahf] v lachen; n Lachen nt
laughter [LAHF-tö] n Gelächter nt
launch [lohntsch] v in Gang bringen
launderette [lohn-dör-ÄT] n Münzwäscherei f
laundry [LOHN-dri] n Wäscherei f; Wäsche f
lavatory [LÆW-ö-tri] n Toilette f
law [loh] n Gesetz nt
law courts [loh kohtss] pl Gerichtshof m
lawful [LOH-ful] adj gesetzlich
lawn [lohn] n Rasen m
lawyer [LOH-jö] n Rechtsanwalt m
laxative [LÆKSS-ö-tiw] n Abführmittel nt
* lay [leej] v legen
lazy [LEEJS-i] adj faul
lead [läd] n Blei nt; Leine f; v führen
leader [LIED-ö] n Führer m
leading [LIED-ing] adj führend
leaf [lief] n Blatt nt
leak [liek] v lecken; n Leck nt
* lean [lien] v lehnen; adj mager
* leap [liep] v springen
leap-year [LIEP-jöh] n Schaltjahr nt
* learn [löhn] v lernen
learner [LÖHN-ö] n Anfänger m
learnt [löhnt] v (p, pp learn)
lease [liess] n Mietvertrag m
least [liesst] adj kleinste; n Wenigste nt

leather [LÅÐ-ö] n Leder nt
* leave [liew] v verlassen; lassen
* leave out [liew aut] v auslassen
lecture [LÄK-tschö] n Vortrag m
lecturer [LÄK-tschör-ö] n Lektor m
led [läd] v (p, pp lead)
left [läft] adj linke
left luggage office [läft LAG-idʒ OF-iss] n Gepäckaufbewahrung f
left-hand [LÄFT-hænd] adj linke
leg [läg] n Bein nt
legal [LIEG-öl] adj gesetzlich
legation [li-GEEJ-schön] n Gesandtschaft f
leisure [LAʒ-ö] n Muße f
lemon [LÄM-ön] n Zitrone f
* lend [länd] v leihen
length [längΘ] n Länge f
lengthen [LÄNGΘ-ön] v verlängern
lengthways [LÄNGΘ-ueejs] adv der Länge nach
lens [läns] n Linse f
lent [länt] v (p, pp lend)
less [läss] adv weniger
lessen [LÄSS-ön] v vermindern
lesson [LÄSS-ön] n Lektion f
* let [lät] v lassen; vermieten
letter [LÄT-ö] n Brief m
letter of credit [LÄT-ör öw KRÄD-it] n Akkreditiv nt
letterbox [LÄT-ö-bokss] n Briefkasten m
lettuce [LÄT-iss] n Salat m
level [LÄW-öl] adj eben
level crossing [LÄW-öl KROSS-ing] n Bahnübergang m
lever [LIEW-öl] n Hebel m
levis [LIE-wais] n Blue Jeans pl
liability [lai-ö-BIL-i-ti] n Verantwortlichkeit f
liable [LAI-ö-böl] adj

verantwortlich

liberal [LIB-ör-öl] *adj* liberal

liberty [LIB-ö-ti] *n* Freiheit *f*

library [LAIB-rö-ri] *n* Bibliothek *f*

licence [LAI-ssönss] *n* Konzession *f*

license [LAI-ssönss] *v* konzessionieren

lid [lid] *n* Deckel *m*

* **lie** [lai] *v* liegen; *n* Lüge *f*

* **lie down** [lai daun] *v* niederlegen (sich)

life [laif] *n* Leben *nt*

life insurance [laif in-SCHUHÖR-önss] *n* Lebensversicherung *f*

lifetime [LAIF-taim] *n* Leben *nt*

lift [lift] *v* heben; *n* Aufzug *m*

light [lait] *n* Licht *nt*; *adj* leicht; hell; *v* anzünden

light bulb [lait balb] *n* Glühbirne *f*

light meal [lait miel] *n* leichte Mahlzeit *f*

lighter [LAIT-ö] *n* Anzünder *m*

lighthouse [LAIT-hauss] *n* Leuchtturm *m*

lighting [LAIT-ing] *n* Beleuchtung *f*

lightning [LAIT-ning] *n* Blitz *m*

like [laik] *v* gern mögen; *adj* gleich; *prep* wie

likely [LAIK-li] *adv* wahrscheinlich

likewise [LAIK-uais] *adv* ebenfalls

limb [lim] *n* Glied *nt*

lime [laim] *n* Limone *f*

limit [LIM-it] *n* Grenze *f*; *v* beschränken

limited [LIM-it-id] *adj* beschränkt

limp [limp] *v* hinken; *adj* schlaff

line [lain] *n* Zeile *f*; Reihe *f*

linen [LIN-in] *n* Wäsche *f*; Leinen *nt*

liner [LAIN-ö] *n* Linienschiff *nt*

lingerie [LAHNG-ʒör-i] *n* Damenunterwäsche *f*

lining [LAIN-ing] *n* Futterstoff *m*

link [lingk] *n* Verbindungsglied *nt*; *v* verbinden

links [lingkss] *pl* Manschettenknöpfe *mpl*; Golfplatz *m*

lip [lip] *n* Lippe *f*

lipsalve [LIP-ssahw] *n* Lippensalbe *f*

lipstick [LIP-sstik] *n* Lippenstift *m*

liquid [LIK-uid] *n* flüssig

liquorice [LIK-ö-riss] *n* Lakritze *f*

list [lisst] *n* Liste *f*; *v* eintragen

listen [LISS-ön] *v* zuhören

listener [LISS-nö] *n* Zuhörer *m*

lit [lit] *v* (*p*, *pp* light)

literary [LIT-ör-ör-i] *adj* literarisch

literature [LIT-rö-tschö] *n* Literatur *f*

litre [LIE-tö] *n* Liter *m*

litter [LIT-ö] *n* Abfall *m*

little [LIT-öl] *adj* klein

little by little [LIT-öl bai LIT-öl] nach und nach

live [laiw] *adj* lebend; *v* leben

lively [LAIW-li] *adj* lebhaft

liver [LIW-ö] *n* Leber *f*

living [LIW-ing] *n* Leben *nt*

living-room [LIW-ing-ruhm] *n* Wohnzimmer *nt*

load [lood] *n* Last *f*; *v* laden

loaf [loof] *n* Laib *m*

loan [loon] *n* Anleihe *f*

lobby [LOB-i] *n* Vestibül *nt*

lobster [LOB-sstö] *n* Hummer *m*

local [LOOK-öl] *adj* örtlich

local call [LOOK-öl kohl] *n* Ortsgespräch *nt*

local train [LOOK-öl treejn] *n*

Bummelzug m
locality [loo-KÆL-i-ti] n
Örtlichkeit f
locate [loo-KEEJT] v ausfindig
machen
location [loo-KEEJ-schön] n Lage
f
lock [lok] n Schloß nt; v
absperren
lock up [lok ap] v einsperren
locomotive [LOO-kö-moo-tiw] n
Lokomotive f
lodge [lodʒ] v beherbergen
lodger [LODʒ-ö] n Mieter m
lodgings [LODʒ-ings] pl
Unterkunft f
log [log] n Klotz m
logic [LODʒ-ik] n Logik f
lonely [LOON-li] adj einsam
long [long] adj lang
long ago [long ö-GOO] adv vor
langer Zeit
long for [long foh] v sehnen nach
(sich)
longer [LONG-gö] adj länger
longing [LONG-ing] n Sehnsucht f
longitude [LONG-gi-tjuhd] n
Längengrad m
long-playing record [LONG-pleej-
ing RÄK-ohd] n Langspielplatte
f
look [luk] v schauen; n Anblick
m
look after [luk AHF-tö] v
kümmern (sich)
look at [luk æt] v ansehen
look for [luk foh] v suchen
look out [luk aut] v vorsehen
(sich)
look up [luk ap] v heraussuchen
looking-glass [LUK-ing-glahss] n
Spiegel m
loose [luhss] adj lose
loosen [LUHSS-ön] v lockern

lord [lohd] n Lord m
lorry [LOR-i] n Lastwagen m
* **lose** [luhs] v verlieren
loss [loss] n Verlust m
lost [losst] v (p, pp lose)
lost and found [losst önd faund]
Verlust- und Fundanzeigen fpl
lost property office [losst PROP-ö-
ti OF-iss] n Fundbüro nt
lot [lot] n Los m; Menge f
lotion [LOO-schön] n Wasser nt
lottery [LOT-ör-i] n Lotterie f
loud [laud] adj laut
loud-speaker [LAUD-sspiek-ö] n
Lautsprecher m
lounge [laundʒ] n
Gesellschaftsraum m
love [law] n Liebe f; v lieben
lovely [LAW-li] adj schön
love-story [LAW-sstoh-ri] n
Liebesgeschichte f
low [loo] adj niedrig
low season [loo SSIES-ön] n tote
Saison f
low tide [loo taid] n Ebbe f
lower [LOO-ö] adj untere
lower berth [LOO-ö böhΘ] n
untere Koje f
lowland [LOO-lönd] n Tiefland nt
loyal [LEU-öl] adj loyal
lubricate [LUH-bri-keejt] v
schmieren
lubrication [luh-bri-KEEJ-schön]
n Schmierung f
lubrication oil [luh-bri-KEEJ-
schön eul] n Schmieröl nt
lubrication system [luh-bri-
KEEJ-schön ssISS-tim] n
Schmiersystem nt
luck [lak] n Glück nt
lucky [LAK-i] adj glücklich
lucky charm [LAK-i tschahm] n
Amulett nt
luggage [LAG-idʒ] n Gepäck nt

luggage rack [LAG-idʒ ræk] *n*
Gepäcknetz *nt*

luggage van [LAG-idʒ wæn] *n*
Gepäckwagen *m*

lukewarm [LUHK-uohm] *adj*
lauwarm

lumbago [lam-BEEJ-goo] *n*
Hexenschuß *m*

luminous [LUH-min-öss] *adj*
leuchtend

lump [lamp] *n* Stück *nt*

lump sum [lamp ssam] *n*
Pauschalsumme *f*

lumpy [LAMP-i] *adj* klumpig

lunch [lantsch] *n* Mittagessen *nt*

lunch time [lantsch taim] *n*
Mittagszeit *f*

luncheon [LANTSCH-ön] *n*
Mittagessen *nt*

lung [lang] *n* Lunge *f*

luxurious [lag-ʒUHÖR-i-öss] *adj*
luxuriös

luxury [LAK-schör-i] *n* Luxus *m*

lying [LAI-ing] *n* Lügen *nt*

machine [mö-SCHIEN] *n*
Maschine *f*

machinery [mö-SCHIEN-ör-i] *n*
Mechanismus *m*

mackerel [MÆK-röl] *n* Makrele *f*

mackintosh [MÆK-in-tosch] *n*
Regenmantel *m*

mad [mæd] *adj* verrückt

madam [MÆD-öm] *n* gnädige
Frau *f*

made [meejd] *v (p, pp* **make)**

made of [meejd ow] hergestellt
aus

made-to-order [meejd-tu-OH-dö]
adj auf Bestellung gemacht

magazine [mæg-ö-SIEN] *n*
Zeitschrift *f*

magic [MÆDʒ-ik] *n* Zauberei *f*

magistrate [MÆDʒ-iss-treejt] *n*
Friedensrichter *m*

magnetic [mæg-NÄT-ik] *adj*
magnetisch

magneto [mæg-NIE-too] *n*
Magnet *m*

magnificent [mæg-NIF-i-ssönt]
adj prächtig

maid [meejd] *n* Dienstmädchen
nt

maiden name [MEEJD-ön neejm]
n Mädchenname *m*

mail [meejl] *v* aufgeben; *n* Post *f*

mail-box [MEEJL-bokss] *n*
Briefkasten *m*

main [meejn] *adj* wichtigste

main line [meejn lain] *n*
Hauptstrecke *f*

main road [meejn rood] *n*
Hauptstraße *f*

main street [meejn sstriet] *n*
Hauptstraße *f*

mainland [MEEJN-lönd] *n*
Festland *nt*

maintain [män-TEEJN] *v*
aufrechterhalten

maintenance [MEEJN-tin-önss] *n*
Instandhaltung *f*

maize [meejs] *n* Mais *m*

major [MEEJ-dʒö] *adj* größer

majority [mö-DʒOR-it-i] *n*
Mehrheit *f*

* make [meejk] *v* machen

make-up [MEEJK-ap] *n* Schminke
f

malaria [mö-LÄÖR-i-ö] *n* Malaria
f

male [meejl] *adj* männlich

mallet [MÆL-it] *n* Holzhammer *m*

mammal [MÆM-öl] *n* Säugetier
nt

man [mæn] *n (pl* **men)** Mann *m*

manage [MÆN-idʒ] *v* verwalten

management [MÆN-idʒ-mönt] *n*

Verwaltung *f*
manager [MÆN-idȝ-ö] *n* Direktor
  m
mandarin [MÆN-dör-in] *n*
  Mandarine *f*
manicure [MÆN-i-kjuhö] *v*
  maniküren; *n* Maniküre *f*
mankind [mæn-KAIND] *n*
  Menschheit *f*
mannequin [MÆN-i-kin] *n*
  Mannequin *nt*
manner [MÆN-ö] *n* Weise *f*
manners [MÆN-ös] *pl* Manieren
  fpl
manor house [MÆN-ö hauss] *n*
  Herrschaftshaus *nt*
mansion [MÆN-schön] *n*
  herrschaftliches Wohnhaus
manual [MÆN-ju-öl] *adj* mit der
  Hand gemacht
manufacture [mæn-ju-FÆK-
  tschö] *v* fabrizieren
manufactured [mæn-ju-FÆK-
  tschöd] *adj* fabriziert
manufacturer [mæn-ju-FÆK-
  tschör-ö] *n* Fabrikant *m*
manuscript [MÆN-ju-sskript] *n*
  Manuskript *nt*
many [MÄN-i] *adj* viele
map [mæp] *n* Landkarte *f*
marble [MAH-böl] *n* Marmor *m*
march [mahtsch] *n* Marsch *m; v*
  marschieren
March [mahtsch] *n* März *m*
margarine [MAH-dȝör-ien] *n*
  Margarine *f*
margin [MAH-dȝin] *n* Rand *m*
maritime [MÆR-i-taim] *adj*
  maritim
mark [mahk] *v* zeichnen; *n*
  Zeichen *nt*
market [MAH-kit] *n* Markt *m*
market place [MAH-kit pleejss] *n*
  Marktplatz *m*

marmalade [MAH-mö-leejd] *n*
  Marmelade *f*
marriage [MÆR-idȝ] *n* Ehe *f*
married [MÆR-id] *adj* verheiratet
married couple [MÆR-id KAP-öl] *n*
  Ehepaar *nt*
marry [MÆR-i] *v* heiraten
marsh [mahsch] *n* Sumpf *m*
marshy [MAHSCH-i] *adj* sumpfig
marvel [MAH-wöl] *n* Wunder *nt; v*
  wundern (sich)
marvellous [MAH-wil-öss] *adj*
  wunderbar
mascara [mæss-KAH-rö] *n*
  Wimperntusche *f*
masculine [MAHSS-kju-lin] *adj*
  männlich
mass [mæss] *n* Menge *f*
Mass [mæss] *n* Messe *f*
massage [mö-SSAHDȝ] *v*
  massieren; *n* Massage *f*
masseur [mæ-SSÖH] *n* Masseur
  m
massive [MÆSS-iw] *adj* massiv
mass-production [mæss-prö-
  DAK-schön] *n*
  Massenproduktion *f*
master [MAHSS-tö] *n* Meister *m; v*
  beherrschen
masterpiece [MAHSS-tö-piess] *n*
  Meisterstück *nt*
mat [mæt] *n* Matte *f*
match [mætsch] *n* Spiel *nt;*
  Streichholz *nt*
match-box [MÆTSCH-bokss] *n*
  Streichholzschachtel *f*
material [mö-TIÖR-i-öl] *n*
  Material *nt*
mathematics [mæΘ-i-MÆT-ikss]
  n Mathematik *f*
matter [MÆT-ö] *n* Materie *f;*
  Angelegenheit *f; v* von
  Bedeutung sein
mattress [MÆT-riss] *n* Matratze *f*

mature [mö-TJUHÖ] *adj* reif

maturity [mö-TJUHÖR-it-i] *n* Reife *f*

mauve [moow] *adj* hellviolett

* **may** [meej] *v* mögen

May [meej] *n* Mai *m*

May Day [meej deej] *n* der erste Mai

maybe [MEEJ-bie] *adv* vielleicht

mayor [mäö] *n* Bürgermeister *m*

me [mier] *pron* mir; mich

meadow [MÄD-oo] *n* Wiese *f*

meal [miel] *n* Mahlzeit *f*

* **mean** [mien] *v* denken; *n* Durchschnitt *m*; *adj* niederträchtig

meaning [MIEN-ing] *n* Bedeutung *f*

meaningless [MIEN-ing-liss] *adj* sinnlos

means [miens] *pl* Mittel *nt*; Geldmittel *ntpl*

meant [mänt] *v* (*p, pp* mean)

meanwhile [MIEN-uail] *adv* mittlerweile

measles [MIE-söls] *n* Masern *pl*

measure [MÄƷ-ö] *v* messen; *n* Maß *nt*

meat [miet] *n* Fleisch *nt*

mechanic [mi-KÆN-ik] *n* Mechaniker *m*

mechanical [mi-KÆN-ik-öl] *adj* mechanisch

mechanism [MÄK-ö-nism] *n* Mechanismus *m*

medal [MÄD-öl] *n* Medaille *f*

mediaeval [mäd-i-IE-wöl] *adj* mittelalterlich

medical [MÄD-ik-öl] *adj* medizinisch

medical examination [MÄD-ik-öl ig-sæm-i-NEEJ-schön] *n* Untersuchung *f*

medicine [MÄD-ssin] *n* Medizin *f*

Mediterranean [mäd-i-tö-REEJ-ni-ön] *n* Mittelmeer *nt*

medium [MIE-di-öm] *adj* mittlere

* **meet** [miet] *v* treffen

meeting [MIET-ing] *n* Treffen *nt*

meeting-place [MIET-ing-pleejss] *n* Sammelplatz *m*

mellow [MÄL-oo] *adj* mild

melodrama [MÄL-ö-drah-mö] *n* Melodrama *nt*

melody [MÄL-ö-di] *n* Melodie *f*

melon [MÄL-ön] *n* Melone *f*

melt [mält] *v* schmelzen

melted [MÄLT-id] *adj* geschmolzen

member [MÄM-bö] *n* Mitglied *nt*

membership [MÄM-bö-schip] *n* Mitgliedschaft *f*

memo [MÄM-oo] *n* Memorandum *nt*

memorable [MÄM-ör-ö-böl] *adj* denkwürdig

memorial [mi-MOH-ri-öl] *n* Denkmal *nt*

memorize [MÄM-ö-rais] *v* memorieren

memory [MÄM-ö-ri] *n* Gedächtnis *nt*

mend [mänd] *v* ausbessern

men's room [mäns ruhm] *n* Herrentoilette *f*

mental [MÄN-töl] *adj* geistig

mention [MÄN-schön] *n* Erwähnung *f*; *v* verwähnen

menu [MÄN-juh] *n* Speisekarte *f*

merchandise [MÖH-tschön-dais] *n* Ware *f*

merchant [MÖH-tschönt] *n* Kaufmann *m*

merit [MÄR-it] *v* verdienen; *n* Verdienst *nt*

merry [MÄR-i] *adj* fröhlich

mesh [mäsch] *n* Netz *nt*

mess [mäss] *n* Unordnung *f*

mess up [mäss ap] v in
  Unordnung bringen
message [MÄSS-idʒ] n Mitteilung
  f
messenger [MÄSS-in-dʒö] n Bote
  m
met [mät] v (p, pp meet)
metal [MÄT-öl] n Metall nt; adj
  metallisch
meter [MIE-tö] n Zähler m
method [MÄƟ-öd] n Methode f
methodical [mi-ƟOD-ik-öl] adj
  methodisch
methylated spirits [MÄƟ-il-eejt-
  id SSPIR-itss] n (abbr meths)
  vergällter Spiritus m
metre [MIE-tö] n Meter nt
metric [MÄT-rik] adj metrisch
Mexican [MÄKSS-i-kön] adj
  mexikanisch; n Mexikaner m
Mexico [MÄKSS-i-koo] n Mexiko
  nt
mezzanine [MÄS-ö-nien] n
  Zwischenstock m
microphone [MAIK-rö-foon] n
  Mikrophon nt
midday [MID-deej] n Mittag m
middle [MID-öl] adj mittlere
middle-class [MID-öl-KLAHSS] n
  Mittelstand m
midnight [MID-nait] n
  Mitternacht f
midsummer [MID-ssam-ö] n
  Hochsommer m
midway [mid-UEEJ] adv auf
  halbem Wege
might [mait] v (p may); n Macht f
mightn't [MAIT-önt] v (might not)
mighty [MAIT-i] adj mächtig
migraine [MI-greejn] n Migräne f
mild [maild] adj mild
mile [mail] n Meile f
mileage [MAIL-idʒ] n
  Meilenstand m

milepost [MAIL-poosst] n
  Wegweiser m
milestone [MAIL-sstoon] n
  Meilenstein m
military [MIL-i-tör-i] adj
  militärisch
milk [milk] n Milch f
milk-bar [MILK-bah] n Milchbar f
milkman [MILK-mön] n (pl -men)
  Milchmann m
milk-shake [MILK-scheejk] n
  Milchshake m
milky [MILK-i] adj milchig
mill [mil] n Mühle f
miller [MIL-ö] n Müller m
milliner [MIL-in-ö] n Modistin f
million [MIL-jön] n Million f
millionaire [mil-jön-ÄÖ] n
  Millionär m
mince [minss] v zerhacken
mind [maind] v achten auf;
  kümmern um (sich); n
  Verstand m
mine [main] n Bergwerk nt
miner [MAIN-ö] n Bergmann m
mineral [MIN-ör-öl] n Mineral nt
mineral water [MIN-ör-öl UOH-tö] ,
  n Mineralwasser nt
miniature [MIN-jö-tschö] n
  Miniatur f
minimum [MIN-im-öm] n
  Minimum nt
mining [MAIN-ing] n Bergbau m
minister [MIN-iss-tö] n Geistliche
  m; Minister m
ministry [MIN-iss-tri] n
  Ministerium nt
minor [MAIN-ö] adj geringer
minority [mai-NOR-it-i] n
  Minderheit f
mint [mint] n Minze f
minus [MAIN-öss] prep weniger
minute [mai-NJUHT] adj winzig; n
  Minute f

miracle [MIR-ö-köl] n Wunder nt
miraculous [mi-RÆK-ju-löss] adj wunderbar
mirror [MIR-ö] n Spiegel m
miscellaneous [miss-i-LEEJN-i-öss] adj vermischt
mischief [MISS-tschif] n Unfug m
mischievous [MISS-tschiw-öss] adj schelmisch
miserable [MIS-ör-ö-böl] adj elend
misery [MIS-ör-i] n Elend nt
misfortune [miss-FOH-tschön] n Mißgeschick nt
mislaid [miss-LEEJD] v (p, pp mislay)
* **mislay** [miss-LEEJ] v verlegen
mispronounce [miss-prö-NAUNSS] v falsch aussprechen
miss [miss] v verpassen; Fräulein nt
missing [MISS-ing] adj fehlend
missing person [MISS-ing PÖH-ssön] n Vermißte m
mist [misst] n Nebel m
* **mistake** [miss-TEEJK] v verwechseln; n Fehler m
mistaken [miss-TEEJK-ön] adj falsch
mistook [miss-TUK] v (p mistake)
misty [MISST-i] adj neblig
* **misunderstand** [miss-an-dö-SSTÆND] v mißverstehen
misunderstanding [miss-an-dö-SSTÆND-ing] n Mißverständnis nt
mittens [MIT-öns] pl Fausthandschuhe mpl
mix [mikss] v mischen
mixed [miksst] adj gemischt
mixer [MIKSS-ö] n Mixer m
mixture [MIKSS-tschö] n Mischung f
mobile [MOO-bail] adj beweglich

model [MOD-öl] n Modell nt
moderate [MOD-ör-it] adj mäßig
modern [MOD-ön] adj modern
modest [MOD-isst] adj bescheiden
modify [MOD-i-fai] v modifizieren
mohair [MOO-häö] n Mohair m
moist [meusst] adj feucht
moisten [MEUSS-ön] v anfeuchten
moisture [MEUSS-tschö] n Feuchtigkeit f
moisturizing cream [MEUSS-tschör-ais-ing kriem] n Feuchtigkeitskrem f
moment [MOO-mönt] n Augenblick m
momentary [MOO-mön-tör-i] adj augenblicklich
monastery [MON-öss-tri] n Kloster m
Monday [MAN-di] n Montag m
money [MAN-i] n Geld nt
money exchange [MAN-i ikss-TSCHEEJNDʒ] n Wechselstube f
money order [MAN-i OH-dö] n Anweisung f
monk [mangk] n Mönch m
monopoly [mö-NOP-ö-li] n Monopol n
monotonous [mö-NOT-ö-nöss] adj monoton
month [manΘ] n Monat m
monthly [manΘ-li] adj monatlich
monument [MON-ju-mönt] n Denkmal nt
mood [muhd] n Stimmung f
moon [muhn] n Mond m
moonlight [MUHN-lait] n Mondlicht nt
moor [muhö] n Heideland nt
moral [MOR-öl] adj moralisch
morality [mö-RÆL-it-i] n Moral f
morals [MOR-öls] pl Sitten fpl
more [moh] adj mehr
more and more [moh önd moh]

immer mehr
moreover [moh-ROO-wö] *adv*
überdies
morning [MOHN-ing] *n* Morgen *m*
morphia [MOH-fi-ö] *n* Morphium
nt
mortgage [MOH-gidʒ] *n* Hypothek
f
mosaic [mö-SEEJ-ik] *n* Mosaik *nt*
mosque [mossk] *n* Moschee *f*
mosquito [möss-KIE-too] *n*
Moskito *m*
mosquito bite [möss-KIE-too
bait] *n* Moskitostich *m*
mosquito net [möss-KIE-too nät]
n Moskitonetz *nt*
most [moosst] *adj* meist
most of all [moosst öw ohl]
besonders
mostly [MOOSST-li] *adv*
hauptsächlich
motel [moo-TÄL] *n* Motel *nt*
moth [moΘ] *n* Motte *f*
mother [MAð-ö] *n* Mutter *f*
mother country [MAð-ö KAN-tri] *n*
Vaterland *nt*
mother tongue [MAð-ö tang] *n*
Muttersprache *f*
mother-in-law [MAð-ör-in-loh] *n*
Schwiegermutter *f*
mother-of-pearl [MAð-ör-öw-
pöhl] *n* Perlmutt *nt*
motion [MOO-schön] *n* Bewegung
f
motor [MOO-tö] *v* fahren; *n* Motor
m
motorboat [MOO-tö-boot] *n*
Motorboot *nt*
motorcar [MOO-tö-kah] *n*
Kraftwagen *m*
motorcycle [MOO-tö-ssai-köl] *n*
Motorrad *nt*
motoring [MOO-tör-ing] *n*
Autofahren *nt*

motorist [MOO-tör-isst] *n*
Autofahrer *m*
mound [maund] *n* Erhebung *f*
mount [maunt] *v* besteigen
mountain [MAUNT-in] *n* Berg *m*
mountain range [MAUNT-in
reejndʒ] *n* Bergkette *f*
mountaineering [maunt-in-IÖR-
ing] *n* Alpinismus *m*
mountainous [MAUNT-in-öss] *adj*
gebirgig
mouse [mauss] *n* (*pl* **mice**) Maus
f
moustache [möss-TAHSCH] *n*
Schnurrbart *m*
mouth [mauΘ] *n* Mund *m*
mouthwash [MAUΘ-uosch] *n*
Mundwasser *nt*
movable [MUHW-ö-böl] *adj*
beweglich
move [muhw] *n* Umzug *m*; *v*
umziehen
move in [muhw in] *v* einziehen
move out [muhw aut] *v*
ausziehen
movement [MUHW-mönt] *n*
Bewegung *f*
movie [MUHW-i] *n* Film *m*
movie camera [MUHW-i KÄM-ör-
ö] *n* Filmkamera *f*
much [matsch] *adv* viel
mud [mad] *n* Schlamm *m*
muddle [MAD-öl] *n*
Durcheinander *nt*
muddle up [MAD-öl ap] *v*
durcheinanderbringen
muddy [MAD-i] *adj* schlammig
mud-guard [MAD-gahd] *n*
Kotflügel *m*
mug [mag] *n* Becher *m*
mulberry [MAL-bö-ri] *n*
Maulbeere *f*
mullet [MAL-it] *n* Meeräsche *f*
multiplication [mal-ti-pli-KEEJ-

schön] *n* Multiplikation *f*
multiply [MAL-ti-plai] *v*
multiplizieren
mumps [mampss] *n* Mumps *m*
municipal [mjuh-NISS-i-pöl] *adj*
städtisch
municipality [mjuh-niss-i-PÆL-
it-i] *n* Stadtverwaltung *f*
murder [MÖH-dö] *v* morden; *n*
Mord *m*
muscle [MASS-öl] *n* Muskel *m*
museum [mju-SI-öm] *n* Museum
nt
mushroom [MASCH-ruhm] *n* Pilz
m
music [MJUH-sik] *n* Musik *f*
music hall [MJUH-sik hohl] *n*
Varietétheater *nt*
music shop [MJUH-sik schop] *n*
Musikgeschäft *nt*
musical [MJUH-sik-öl] *adj*
musikalisch
musical comedy [MJUH-sik-öl
KOM-i-di] *n* Musical *nt*
musical instrument [MJUH-sik-öl
IN-sstru-mönt] *n*
Musikinstrument *nt*
musician [mju-SISCH-ön] *n*
Musiker *m*
muslin [MAS-lin] *n* Musselin *m*
mussel [MASS-öl] *n* Muschel *f*
* **must** [masst] *v* müssen
mustard [MASS-töd] *n* Senf *m*
mustn't [MASS-önt] *v* (**must not**)
mutton [MAT-ön] *n*
Hammelfleisch *nt*
my [mai] *adj* mein
myself [mai-SSÄLF] *pron* ich
selbst; mich
mysterious [miss-TIÖR-i-öss] *adj*
geheimnisvoll
mystery [MISS-tör-i] *n* Geheimnis
nt
myth [miΘ] *n* Mythos *m*

nail [neejl] *n* Fingernagel *m;*
Nagel *m*
nail-brush [NEEJL-brasch] *n*
Nagelbürste *f*
nail-file [NEEJL-fail] *n* Nagelfeile
f
nail-scissors [NEEJL-ssis-ös] *pl*
Nagelschere *f*
naked [NEEJK-id] *adj* nackt
name [neejm] *v* nennen; *n* Name
m
napkin [NÆP-kin] *n* Serviette *f*
nappy [NÆP-i] *n* Windel *f*
narcotic [nah-KOT-ik] *n*
Rauschgift *nt*
narrow [NÆR-oo] *adj* eng
nasty [NAHSS-ti] *adj* garstig
nation [NEEJ-schön] *n* Nation *f*
national [NÆSCH-nöl] *adj*
national
national anthem [NÆSCH-nöl ÆN-
Θöm] *n* Nationalhymne *f*
national dress [NÆSCH-nöl dräss]
n Tracht *f*
national park [NÆSCH-nöl pahk]
n Naturschutzpark *m*
nationality [næsch-ö-NÆL-it-i] *n*
Staatsangehörigkeit *f*
native [NEEJT-iw] *adj*
einheimisch
native country [NEEJT-iw KAN-tri]
n Heimatland *nt*
native language [NEEJT-iw LÆNG-
guidʒ] *n* Muttersprache *f*
natural [NÆTSCH-röl] *adj*
natürlich
nature [NEEJ-tschö] *n* Wesensart;
Natur *f*
naughty [NOHT-i] *adj* unartig
nausea [NOH-ssjöl] *n* Übelkeit *f*
navigable [NÆW-ig-ö-böl] *adj*
befahrbar

navigate [NÆW-i-geejt] *v* steuern
navigation [næw-i-GEEJ-schön] *n* Navigation *f*
navy [NEEJ-wi] *n* Marine *f*
near [niö] *adj* nahe
nearby [NIÖ-bai] *adj* nahe
nearer [NIÖR-ö] *adj* näher
nearest [NIÖR-isst] *adj* nächste
nearly [NIÖ-li] *adv* beinah
neat [nied] *adj* sorgfältig; unverdünnt
necessary [NÄSS-iss-ör-i] *adj* notwendig
necessity [ni-SSÄSS-it-i] *n* Notwendigkeit *f*
neck [näk] *n* Hals *m*
necklace [NÄK-liss] *n* Halskette *f*
necktie [NÄK-tai] *n* Krawatte *f*
need [nied] *n* Bedürfnis *nt; v* benötigen; müssen
needle [NIED-öl] *n* Nadel *f*
needlework [NIED-öl-uöhk] *n* Handarbeit *f*
needn't [NIED-önt] *v* (**need not**)
negative [NÄG-ö-tiw] *adj* negativ; *n* Negativ *nt*
neglect [ni-GLÄKT] *v* vernachlässigen; *n* Vernachlässigung *f*
negligee [NÄG-lie-zeej] *n* Negligé *nt*
negotiate [ni-GOO-schi-eejt] *v* verhandeln
negotiation [ni-goo-schi-EEJ-schön] *n* Verhandlung *f*
negro [NIE-groo] *n* Neger *m*
neighbour [NEEJ-bö] *n* Nachbar *m*
neighbourhood [NEEJ-bö-hud] *n* Nachbarschaft *f*
neighbouring [NEEJ-bör-ing] *adj* benachbart
neither [NAI-ðö] *pron* keiner von beiden

neither . . . nor [NAI-Θö noh] *conj* weder . . . noch . . .
neon [NIE-on] *n* Neon *nt*
nephew [NÄW-ju] *n* Neffe *m*
nerve [nöhw] *n* Nerv *m*
nervous [NÖHW-öss] *adj* nervös
nest [nässt] *n* Nest *nt*
net [nät] *n* Netz *nt*
Netherlands [NÄð-ö-lönds] *pl* Niederlande *f*
network [NÄT-uöhk] *n* Netz *nt*
neuralgia [njuhö-RÆL-dʒö] *n* Neuralgie *f*
neurosis [njuhö-ROO-ssiss] *n* Neurose *f*
neuter [NJUH-tö] *adj* sächlich
neutral [NJUH-tröl] *adj* neutral
never [NÄW-ö] *adv* niemals
nevertheless [näw-ö-ðö-LÄSS] *adv* nichtsdestoweniger
new [njuh] *adj* neu
New Year [njuh jöh] *n* Neujahr *nt*
New Year's Day [njuh jöhs deej] *n* Neujahrstag *m*
news [njuhs] *n* Nachrichten *fpl;* Neuigkeiten *fpl*
news-agent [NJUHS-eej-dʒönt] *n* Zeitungshändler *m*
newspaper [NJUHS-peej-pö] *n* Zeitung *f*
news-reel [NJUHS-riell] *n* Wochenschau *f*
news-stand [NJUHS-sstænd] *n* Zeitungsstand *m*
next [näksst] *adj* nächstfolgend
next to [näksst tu] *prep* neben
next-door [näksst-DOO] *adv* nebenan
nice [naiss] *adj* hübsch
niece [niess] *n* Nichte *f*
night [nait] *n* Nacht *f*
night train [nait treejn] *n* Nachtzug *m*

night-club [NAIT-klab] *n*
Nachtlokal *nt*

night-cream [NAIT-kriem] *n*
Nachtkrem *f*

nightdress [NAIT-dräss] *n*
Nachthemd *nt*

night-flight [NAIT-flait] *n*
Nachtflug *m*

nightly [NAIT-li] *adj* jede Nacht

night-rate [NAIT-reejt] *n*
Nachttarif *m*

nil [nil] *n* Null *f*

nine [nain] *adj* neun

nineteen [NAIN-tien] *adj*
neunzehn

nineteenth [NAIN-tienƟ] *adj*
neunzehnte

ninety [NAIN-ti] *adj* neunzig

ninth [nainƟ] *adj* neunte

no [noo] nein; *adj* kein

no admittance [noo öd-MIT-önss]
kein Eingang

no entry [noo ÄN-tri] Eintritt
verboten

no longer [noo LONG-gö] nicht
mehr

no more [noo moh] nicht mehr

no one [noo uan] *pron* niemand

no overtaking [noo oo-wö-TEEJK-
ing] Überholen verboten

no parking [noo PAHK-ing]
Parken verboten

no pedestrians [noo pi-DÄSS-tri-
öns] Fußgänger verboten

no smoking [noo SSMOOK-ing]
Rauchen verboten

nobody [NOO-böd-i] *pron*
niemand

nod [nod] *n* Nicken *nt*

noise [neus] *n* Lärm *m*

noisy [NEUS-i] *adj* lärmend

none [nan] *pron* keiner

nonsense [NON-ssönss] *n* Unsinn
m

noon [nuhn] *n* Mittag *m*

normal [NOH-möl] *adj* normal

north [nohƟ] *n* Norden *m*

north-east [nohƟ-IESST] *n*
Nordosten *m*

northerly [NOHð-ö-li] *adj*
nördlich

northern [NOHð-ön] *adj*
Nord . . .

northwards [NOHƟ-uöds] *adv*
nordwärts

north-west [nohƟ-UÄSST] *n*
Nordwesten *m*

Norway [NOH-ueej] *n* Norwegen
nt

Norwegian [noh-UIE-dʒön] *n*
Norweger *m; adj* norwegisch

nose [noos] *n* Nase *f*

nostril [NOSS-tril] *n* Nasenloch *nt*

not [not] *adv* nicht

not at all [not öt ohl] gar nicht

note [noot] *v* anmerken; *n*
Banknote *f;* Notiz *f*

notebook [NOOT-buk] *n*
Notizbuch *nt*

noted [NOOT-id] *adj* berühmt

notepaper [NOOT-peej-pö] *n*
Briefpapier *nt*

nothing [NAƟ-ing] *n* nichts

notice [NOO-tiss] *v* bemerken; *n*
Anzeige *f*

noticeable [NOO-tiss-ö-böl] *adj*
wahrnehmbar

notify [NOO-ti-fai] *v*
benachrichtigen

noun [naun] *n* Hauptwort *nt*

novel [NOW-öl] *n* Roman *m*

novelist [NOW-öl-isst] *n*
Romanschriftsteller *m*

November [noo-WÄM-bö] *n*
November *m*

now [nau] *adv* jetzt

now and then [nau önd ðän] *n*
und wieder

nowadays [NAU-ö-deejs] *adv* heutzutage

nowhere [NOO-uäö] *adv* nirgends

nozzle [NOS-öl] *n* Tülle *f*

nuclear [NJUH-kliö] *adj* nuklear

nuisance [NJUH-ssönss] *n* Unfug *m*

numb [nam] *adj* starr

number [NAM-bö] *n* Anzahl *f*; Nummer *f*

numerous [NJUH-mör-öss] *adj* zahlreich

nun [nan] *n* Nonne *f*

nurse [nöhss] *n* Krankenschwester *f*

nursery [NÖHSS-ri] *n* Kinderkrippe *f*

nut [nat] *n* Schraubenmutter *f*; Nuß *f*

nutmeg [NAT-mäg] *n* Muskatnuß *f*

nutritious [njuh-TRISCH-öss] *adj* nahrhaft

nylon [NAI-lon] *n* Nylon *nt*

oak [ook] *n* Eiche *f*

oar [oh] *n* Ruder *nt*

oats [ootss] *pl* Hafer *m*

obedience [oo-BIE-di-önss] *n* Gehorsam *m*

obedient [oo-BIE-di-önt] *adj* gehorsam

obey [oo-BEEJ] *v* gehorchen

object [öb-DʒÄKT] *v* einwenden; *n* Gegenstand *m*

objection [öb-DʒÄK-schön] *n* Einwand *m*

obligatory [o-BLIG-ö-tör-i] *adj* verpflichtend

obliging [ö-BLAIDʒ-ing] *adj* gefällig

oblong [OB-long] *adj* länglich

observation [ob-söh-WEEJ-schön]

n Beobachtung *f*

observatory [öb-SÖHW-ö-tri] *n* Observatorium *nt*

observe [öb-SÖHW] *v* beachten

obstacle [OB-sstök-öl] *n* Hindernis *nt*

obtain [öb-TEEJN] *v* erhalten

obvious [OB-wi-öss] *adj* offensichtlich

occasion [ö-KEEJ-ʒön] *n* Gelegenheit *f*

occasionally [oo-KEEJ-ʒön-öl-i] *adv* gelegentlich

occupant [OK-ju-pönt] *n* Inhaber *m*

occupation [ok-ju-PEEJ-schön] *n* Beschäftigung *f*

occupied [OK-ju-paid] *adj* besetzt

occupy [OK-ju-pai] *v* besetzen

occur [ö-KÖH] *v* ereignen (sich)

occurrence [ö-KAR-önss] *n* Ereignis *nt*

ocean [oo-schön] *n* Ozean *m*

October [ok-TOO-bö] *n* Oktober *m*

octopus [OK-tö-pöss] *n* Polyp *m*

oculist [OK-ju-lisst] *n* Augenarzt *m*

odd [od] *adj* ungerade; sonderbar

odds [ods] *pl* Chancen *fpl*

odour [oo-dö] *n* Geruch *m*

of [ow] *prep* von

of course [öw kohss] selbstverständlich

off season [of ssIES-ön] außer Saison

offence [oo-FÖNSS] *n* Vergehen *nt*

offend [oo-FÖND] *v* vergehen (sich)

offensive [oo-FÖN-ssiw] *adj* anstößig

offer [OF-ö] *v* anbieten; *n* Angebot *nt*

office [OF-iss] *n* Büro *nt*

office hours [OF-iss auöss] *pl*

Bürostunden *fpl*

office work [OF-iss uöhk] *n*
Büroarbeit *f*

officer [OF-iss-ö] *n* Offizier *m*

official [ö-FISCH-öl] *adj* offiziell

off-licence [OF-lai-ssönss] *n*
Spirituosenladen *m*

often [OH-fön] *adv* oft

oil [eul] *n* Petroleum *nt*

oil fuel [eul FJU-öl] *n* Heizöl *nt*

oil pressure [eul PRÄSCH-ö] *n*
Öldruck *m*

oil-painting [EUL-peejnt-ing] *n*
Ölgemälde *nt*

oil-well [EUL-uäl] *n* Ölquelle *f*

oily [EUL-i] *adj* ölig

ointment [EUNT-mönt] *n* Salbe *f*

old [oold] *adj* alt

older [OOL-dö] *adj* älter

oldest [OOL-disst] *adj* älteste

old-fashioned [OOLD-fæsch-önd]
adj altmodisch

olive [OL-iw] *n* Olive *f*

olive oil [OL-iw eul] *n* Olivenöl *nt*

omit [oo-MIT] *v* auslassen

on account of [on ö-KAUNT ow]
wegen

on approval [on ö-PRUHW-öl] zur
Ansicht

on behalf of [on bi-HAHF ow] im
Namen von

on business [on BIS-niss]
geschäftlich

on credit [on KRÄD-it] auf Kredit

on foot [on fut] zu Fuß

on holiday [on HOL-ö-deej] auf
Urlaub

on the average [on ði ÆW-ör-idʒ]
durchschnittlich

on time [on taim] rechtzeitig

on top of [on top ow] *prep*
obenauf

once [uanss] *adv* einmal

once more [uanss moh] *adv* noch
einmal

oncoming [ON-kam-ing] *adj*
herannahend

one [uan] *adj* ein; *pron* man

oneself [uan-SSÄLF] *pron* selbst

one-way traffic [UAN-ueej TRÆF-
ik] *n* Einbahnstraße *f*

onion [AN-jön] *n* Zwiebel *f*

only [OON-li] *adv* nur; *adj* einzig

onwards [ON-uöds] *adv* vorwärts

opal [OO-pöl] *n* Opal *m*

open [oo-pön] *v* öffnen; *adj* offen

open air [oo-pön äö] *n* im Freien

opener [oo-pön-ö] *n* Dosenöffner
m

opening [oo-pön-ing] *n* Öffnung
f

opera [OP-ör-ö] *n* Oper *f*

opera house [OP-ör-ö hauss] *n*
Opernhaus *nt*

operate [OP-ö-reejt] *v* arbeiten

operation [op-ö-REEJ-schön] *n*
Operation *f*; Funktion *f*

operator [OP-ö-reejt-ö] *n*
Telephonistin *f*

operetta [op-ö-RÄT-ö] *n* Operette
f

opinion [ö-PIN-jön] *n* Meinung *f*

opportunity [op-ö-TJUHN-it-i] *n*
Gelegenheit *f*

oppose [ö-POOS] *v* widersetzen
(sich)

opposite [OP-ö-sit] *adj*
entgegengesetzt; *prep*
gegenüber

optician [op-TISCH-ön] *n* Optiker
m

optional [OP-schön-öl] *adj*
freigestellt

or [oh] *conj* oder

oral [oo-röl] *adj* mündlich

orange [OR-indʒ] *n* Apfelsine *f*;
adj orange

orchard [OH-tschöd] *n*

Obstgarten *m*

orchestra [OH-kiss-trö] *n* Orchester *nt*

orchestra seat [OH-kiss-trö ssiet] *n* Orchestersitz *m*

order [OH-dö] *n* Bestellung *f; v* bestellen; befehlen

ordinary [OHD-nör-i] *adj* gewöhnlich

organic [oh-GÆN-ik] *adj* organisch

organisation [oh-gæn-ai-SEEJ-schön] *n* Organisation *f*

organize [OH-gæn-ais] *v* organisieren

Orient [OO-ri-önt] *n* Orient *m*

Oriental [OO-ri-ÄNT-öl] *adj* orientalisch

orientate [OO-ri-än-teejt] *v* orientienren (sich)

origin [OR-i-dʒin] *n* Ursprung *m*

original [ö-RIDʒ-ön-öl] *adj* originell

orlon [OH-lon] *n* Orlon *nt*

ornament [OH-nö-mönt] *n* Verzierung *f*

ornamental [oh-nö-MÄNT-öl] *adj* ornamental

orthodox [OH-Θö-dokss] *adj* orthodox

other [AÒ-ö] *adj* andere

otherwise [AÒ-ö-uais] *adv* anders; *conj* sonst

** **ought** [oht] *v* sollen

oughtn't [OHT-önt] *v* (**ought not**)

our [auö] *adj* unser

ourselves [auö-SSÄLWS] *pron* wir selbst; uns

out [aut] *adv* hinaus

out of date [aut öw deejt] veraltet

out of order [aut öw OH-dö] funktionsunfähig

out of sight [aut öw ssait] außer Sicht

out of the way [aut öw ðö ueej] entlegen

outboard [AUT-bohd] *adj* Außenbord . . .

outdoors [aut-DOHS] *adv* draußen

outfit [AUT-fit] *n* Ausrüstung *f*

outlook [AUT-luk] *n* Anschauung *f*

output [AUT-put] *n* Ausstoß *m*

outside [aut-SSAID] *adv* draußen

outsize [AUT-ssais] *n* Übergröße *f*

outskirts [AUT-ssköhtss] *pl* Außenbezirke *mpl*

outstanding [aut-SSTÆND-ing] *adj* hervorragend

outwards [AUT-uöds] *adv* nach draußen

oval [OO-wöl] *adj* oval

oven [AW-ön] *n* Backofen *m*

over [OO-wö] *prep* über; *adv* über; *adj* vorbei

over there [OO-wö ðäö] drüben

overalls [OO-wör-ohls] *pl* Arbeitskleidung *f*

overboard [OO-wö-BOHD] *adv* über Bord

overcharge [OO-wö-TSCHAHDʒ] *v* zuviel fordern

overcoat [OO-wö-koot] *n* Mantel *m*

overdue [OO-wö-DJUH] *adj* überfällig

** **overeat** [OO-wör-IET] *v* überessen (sich)

overhaul [OO-wö-HOHL] *v* überholen

overhead [OO-wö-HÄD] *adv* oben

overlook [OO-wö-LUK] *v* übersehen

overnight [OO-wö-NAIT] *adv* über Nacht

overseas [OO-wö-SSIES] *adv* über See

oversight [OO-wö-ssait] *n*

Versehen *nt*
* **oversleep** [OO-WÖ-SSLIEP] *v*
verschlafen
* **overtake** [OO-WÖ-TEEJK] *v*
überholen
overtime [OO-WÖ-taim] *n*
Überstunden *fpl*
overtired [OO-WÖ-taiöd] *adj*
übermüdet
overture [OO-WÖ-tschö] *n*
Ouvertüre *f*
overweight [OO-WÖ-ueejt] *n*
Übergewicht *nt*
overwork [OO-WÖ-UÖHK] *v*
überanstrengen
owe [oo] *v* schulden
owing to [OO-ing tu] *prep* infolge
own [oon] *adj* eigen; *v* besitzen
owner [OON-ö] *n* Besitzer *m*
ox [okss] *n* Ochse *m*
oxygen [OKSS-i-dzön] *n*
Sauerstoff *m*
oyster [EUSS-tö] *n* Auster *f*

pace [peejss] *n* Tempo *nt*
Pacific Ocean [pö-SSIF-ik OO-
schön] *n* Stille Ozean *m*
pack [pæk] *v* packen
pack of cards [pæk öw kahds] *n*
Kartenspiel *nt*
pack up [pæk ap] *v* einpacken
package [PÆK-idʒ] *n* Paket *nt*
packet [PÆK-it] *n* Päckchen *nt*
packing [PÆK-ing] *n* Verpackung
f
packing case [PÆK-ing keejss] *n*
Seekiste *f*
pad [pæd] *n* Polster *nt*
paddle [PÆD-öl] *v* paddeln; *n*
Paddel *nt*
padlock [PÆD-lok] *n*
Vorhängeschloß *nt*
page [peejdʒ] *n* Seite *f*

pageboy [PEEJDʒ-beu] *n*
Hotelpage *m*
paid [peejd] *v* (*p, pp* **pay**)
pail [peejl] *n* Eimer *m*
painful [PEEJN-ful] *adj*
schmerzhaft
painless [PEEJN-liss] *adj*
schmerzlos
pains [peejns] *pl* Mühe *f*
paint [peejnt] *n* Farbe *f*
paintbox [PEEJNT-bokss] *n*
Malkasten *m*
paintbrush [PEEJNT-brasch] *n*
Pinsel *m*
painted [PEEJNT-id] *adj* gemalt
painter [PEEJNT-ö] *n* Maler *m*
painting [PEEJNT-ing] *n* Gemälde
nt
pair [päö] *n* Paar *nt*
Pakistan [pæk-i-SSTÆN] *n*
Pakistan *nt*
Pakistani [pæk-i-SSTÆN-i] *n*
Pakistaner *m*
palace [PÆL-iss] *n* Palast *m*
pale [peejl] *adj* bleich
palm [pahm] *n* Palme *f;*
Handfläche *f*
pan [pæn] *n* Pfanne *f*
panties [PÆN-tis] *pl* Schlüpfer *m*
pants [pæntss] *pl* Hose *f*
pantsuit [PÆNT-ssuht] *n*
Hosenanzug *m*
panty-girdle [PÆN-ti-göhd-öl] *n*
elastische Hose *f*
panty-hose [PÆN-ti-hoos] *n*
Strumpfhose *f*
paper [PEEJ-pö] *n* Zeitung *f;*
Papier *nt*
paper napkin [PEEJ-pö NÆP-kin]
n Papierserviette *f*
paper-back [PEEJ-pö-bæk] *n*
Paperback *nt*
paper-bag [PEEJ-pö-bæg] *n* Tüte
f

papers [PEEJ-pös] *pl* Papiere *ntpl*

parade [pö-REEJD] *n* Parade *f*

paraffin [PÆR-ö-fin] *n* Petroleum *nt*

paragraph [PÆR-ö-grahf] *n* Absatz *m*

parallel [PÆR-öl-äl] *adj* parallel

paralyse [PÆR-ö-lais] *v* lähmen

paralysed [pær-ö-laisd] *adj* gelähmt

parcel [PAH-ssöl] *n* Paket *nt*

pardon [PAH-dön] *n* Verzeihung *f*

parents [PÄOR-öntss] *pl* Eltern *pl*

parents-in-law [PÄOR-öntss-in-loh] *pl* Schwiegereltern *pl*

parish [PÆR-isch] *n* Kirchspiel *nt*

park [pahk] *v* parken; *n* Parkplatz *m*; Park *m*

parking [PAHK-ing] *n* Parken *nt*

parking time [PAHK-ing taim] *n* Parkzeit *f*

parking fee [PAHK-ing fie] *n* Parkgebühr *f*

parking light [PAHK-ing lait] *n* Parkleuchte *f*

parking meter [PAHK-ing MIE-tö] *n* Parkuhr *f*

parking zone [PAHK-ing soon] *n* Parkzone *f*

parliament [PAH-lö-mönt] *n* Parlament *nt*

parsley [PAHSS-li] *n* Petersilie *f*

parsnip [PAHSS-nip] *n* Pastinake *f*

parsonage [PAH-ssön-idʒ] *n* Pfarrhaus *nt*

part [paht] *n* Teil *m*

participate [pah-TISS-i-peejt] *v* teilnehmen

particular [pö-TIK-ju-lö] *adj* besonder

particulars [pö-TIK-ju-lös] *pl* Einzelheiten *fpl*

partly [PAHT-li] *adv* teilweise

partner [PAHT-nö] *n* Partner *m*

party [PAH-ti] *n* Gruppe *f*; Party *f*

pass [pahss] *v* vorbeifahren; *n* Gebirgspaß *m*

pass through [pahss Θruh] *v* durchqueren

pass by [pahss bai] *v* vorbeigehen

passage [PÆSS-idʒ] *n* Durchreise *f*; Reise *f*

passenger [PÆSS-in-dʒö] *n* Passagier *m*

passenger train [PÆSS-in-dʒö treejn] *n* Personenzug *m*

passer-by [pahss-ö-BAI] *n* Passant *m*

passive [PÆSS-iw] *adj* passiv

passport [PAHSS-poht] *n* Paß *m*

passport control [PAHSS-poht kön-TROOL] *n* Paßkontrolle *f*

passport photograph [PAHSS-poht FOO-tö-grahf] *n* Paßphoto *nt*

past [pahsst] *n* Vergangenheit *f*; *adj* vergangen

paste [peejsst] *n* Paste *f*

pastry shop [PEEJSS-tri schop] *n* Konditorei *f*

patch [pætsch] *v* flicken; *n* Flicken *m*

path [pahΘ] *n* Pfad *m*

patience [PEEJ-schönss] *n* Geduld *f*

patient [PEEJ-schönt] *n* Patient *m*; *adj* geduldig

patriot [PEEJ-tri-öt] *n* Patriot *m*

patrol [pö-TROOL] *n* Streife *f*

patron [PEEJ-trön] *n* Kunde *m*

pattern [PÆT-ön] *n* Muster *nt*

pause [pohs] *n* Pause *f*; *v* ausruhen

pavement [PEEJW-mönt] *n* Bürgersteig *m*

pavilion [pö-WIL-jön] n Pavillon m

pawn [pohn] v verpfänden

pawnbroker [POHN-brook-ö] n Pfandleiher m

* **pay** [peej] v bezahlen

* **pay attention to** [peej ö-TÄN-schön tu] v Aufmerksamkeit schenken

pay-desk [PEEJ-dässk] n Kasse f

payee [peej-IE] n Zahlungsempfänger m

payment [PEEJ-mönt] n Bezahlung f

pea [pie] n Erbse f

peace [piess] n Frieden m

peaceful [PIESS-ful] adj friedlich

peach [pietsch] n Pfirsich m

peak [piek] n Gipfel m; Spitze f

peak season [piek SSIE-sön] n Hochsaison f

peanut [PIE-nat] n Erdnuß f

pear [päö] n Birne f

pearl [pöhl] n Perle f

peasant [PÄS-önt] n Bauer m

pebble [PÄB-öl] n Kieselstein m

peculiar [pi-KJUHL-jö] adj eigentümlich

pedal [PÄD-öl] n Pedal nt

pedestrian [pi-DÄSS-tri-ön] n Fußgänger m

pedestrian crossing [pi-DÄSS-tri-ön KROSS-ing] n Fußgängerübergang m

pedicure [PÄD-i-kjuhö] n Fußpfleger m

peel [piel] v schälen; n Schale f

peg [päg] n Kleiderhaken m

pen [pän] n Feder f

penalty [PÄN-öl-ti] n Strafe f

pencil [PÄN-ssil] n Bleistift m

pencil-sharpener [PÄN-ssil-schahp-nö] n Bleistiftspitzer m

pendant [PÄN-dönt] n Anhänger m

penicillin [pän-i-SSIL-in] n Penicillin nt

peninsula [pän-IN-ssju-lö] n Halbinsel f

penknife [PÄN-naif] n Taschenmesser nt

pension [PÄN-schön] n Rente f; Pension f

people [PIE-pöl] n Leute pl; Volk nt

pepper [PÄP-ö] n Pfeffer m

peppermint [PÄP-ö-mint] n Pfefferminze f

per annum [pör ÆN-öm] adv jährlich

per day [pöh deej] pro Tag

per person [pöh PÖH-ssön] pro Person

percent [pö-SSÄNT] n Prozent nt

percentage [pö-SSÄNT-idʒ] n Prozentsatz m

perch [pöhtsch] n Barsch m

percolator [PÖH-kö-leejt-ö] n Kaffeemaschine f

perfect [PÖH-fikt] adj vollkommen

perform [pö-FOHM] v verrichten

performance [pö-FOHM-önss] n Aufführung f

perfume [PÖH-fjuhm] n Parfüm nt

perhaps [pö-HÆPSS] adv vielleicht

period [PIÖR-i-öd] n Zeitabschnitt m

periodical [piör-i-OD-ik-öl] n Zeitschrift f

periodically [piör-i-OD-i-köl-i] adv periodisch

perishable [PÄR-isch-ö-böll] adj leicht verderblich

perm [pöhm] n Dauerwelle f

permanent [POH-mö-nönt] *adj*
dauernd
permanent press [POH-mö-nönt
präss] Dauerbügelfalte *f*
permit [pö-MIT] *v* erlauben; *n*
Genehmigung *f*
peroxide [pö-ROKSS-aid] *n*
Wasserstoffsuperoxyd *nt*
perpendicular [pöh-pön-DIK-ju-
lö] *adj* senkrecht
person [POH-ssön] *n* Person *f*
personal [POH-ssön-öl] *adj*
persönlich
personal call [POH-ssön-öl kohl]
n Telephonanruf mit
Voranmeldung
personality [pöh-ssö-NÆL-it-i] *n*
Persönlichkeit *f*
personnel [pöh-ssö-NÄL] *n*
Personal *nt*
perspiration [pöh-sspö-REEJ-
schön] *n* Schweiß *m*
perspire [pöss-PAIÖ] *v* schwitzen
persuade [pö-SSUEEJD] *v*
überreden
pet [pät] *n* Lieblingstier *nt*
petal [PÄT-öl] *n* Blumenblatt *nt*
petrol [PÄT-röl] *n* Benzin *nt*
petrol pump [PÄT-röl pamp] *n*
Benzinpumpe *f*
petrol station [PÄT-röl SSTEEJ-
schön] *n* Tankstelle *f*
petrol tank [PÄT-röl tængk] *n*
Benzintank *m*
petroleum [pö-TROOL-i-öm] *n*
Petroleum *nt*
petty [PÄT-i] *adj* geringfügig
petty cash [PÄT-i kæsch] *n* kleine
Summen
pewter [PJUH-tö] *n* Zinn *nt*
pharmaceuticals [fah-mö-
SSJUHT-ik-öls] *pl* Arzneimittel
ntpl
pharmacy [FAH-mö-ssi] *n*

Apotheke *f*
pheasant [FÄS-önt] *n* Fasan *m*
philosopher [fi-LOSS-ö-fö] *n*
Philosoph *m*
philosophy [fi-LOSS-ö-fi] *n*
Philosophie *f*
phone [foon] *n* Telephon *nt*; *v*
telephonieren
phonetic [foo-NÄT-ik] *adj*
phonetisch
photo [FOOT-oo] *n* Photographie *f*
photo store [FOOT-oo sstoh] *n*
Photoladen *m*
photograph [FOOT-ö-grahf] *n*
Lichtbild *nt*; *v*
photographieren
photographer [fö-TOG-rö-fö] *n*
Photograph *m*
photography [fö-TOG-rö-fi] *n*
Photographie *f*
photostat [FOOT-ö-sstæt] *n*
Photokopie *f*
phrase [freejs] *n* Redewendung *f*
phrase book [freejs buk] *n*
Sprachführer *m*
physical [FIS-ik-öl] *adj* physich
physician [fi-SISCH-ön] *n* Arzt *m*
physicist [FIS-i-ssisst] *n* Physiker
m
physics [FIS-ikss] *n* Physik *f*
pianist [PIE-ö-nisst] *n* Pianist *m*
piano [pi-ÆN-oo] *n* Klavier *nt*
pick [pik] *n* Wahl *f*; *v* wählen
pick up [pik ap] *v* aufheben
pickerel [PIK-ör-öl] *n* junger
Hecht *m*
pickled [PIK-öld] *adj* gepökelt
pickles [PIK-öls] *pl* Pickles *pl*
pick-up [PIK-ap] *n*
Kleinlieferwagen *m*
picnic [PIK-nik] *n* Picknick *nt*; *vi*
picknicken
picture [PIK-tschö] *n* Bild *nt*
picture postcard [PIK-tschö

POOSST-kahd] *n* Ansichtskarte *f*

pictures [PIK-tschös] *pl* Kino *nt*

picturesque [pik-tschö-RÄSSK] *adj* malerisch

piece [piess] *n* Stück *nt*

pier [piö] *n* Pier *f*

pierce [piöss] *v* durchbohren

pig [pig] *n* Schwein *nt*

pigeon [PIDჳ-in] *n* Taube *f*

pigskin [PIG-sskin] *n* Schweinsleder *nt*

pike [paik] *n* Hecht *m*

pilchard [PIL-tschöd] *n* Sardine *f*

pile [pail] *n* Haufen *m; v* anhäufen

piles [pails] *pl* Hämorrhoiden *fpl*

pilgrim [PIL-grim] *n* Pilger *m*

pilgrimage [PIL-grim-ids] *n* Pilgerfahrt *f*

pill [pil] *n* Pille *f*

pillar [PIL-ö] *n* Säule *f*

pillar-box [PIL-ö-bokss] *n* Briefkasten *m*

pillow [PIL-oo] *n* Kopfkissen *nt*

pillowcase [PIL-oo-keejss] *n* Kissenbezug *m*

pilot [PAIL-öt] *n* Pilot *m*

pimple [PIM-pöl] *n* Pickel *m*

pin [pin] *n* Stecknadel *f; v* befestigen

pinch [pintsch] *v* kneifen

pineapple [PAIN-æp-öl] *n* Ananas *f*

pink [pingk] *n* rosa

pipe [paip] *n* Rohr *nt;* Pfeife *f*

pipe cleaner [paip KLIEN-ö] *n* Pfeifenreiniger *m*

pipe tobacco [paip tö-BÆK-oo] *n* Tabak *m*

pistol [PISS-töl] *n* Pistole *f*

piston [PISS-tön] *n* Kolben *m*

piston-rod [PISS-tön-rod] *n* Kolbenstange *f*

pity [PIT-i] *n* Mitleid *nt;* schade

place [pleejss] *v* stellen; *n* Ort *m*

plaice [pleejss] *n* Scholle *f*

plain [pleejn] *adj* schlicht; *n* Ebene *f*

plan [plæn] *v* planen; *n* Plan *m*

plane [pleejn] *n* Flugzeug *nt*

planet [PLÆN-it] *n* Planet *m*

planetarium [plæn-i-TÄOR-i-öm] *n* Planetarium *nt*

plank [plængk] *n* Brett *nt*

plant [plahnt] *n* Betriebsanlage *f;* Pflanze *f; v* pflanzen

plantation [plæn-TEEJ-schön] *n* Plantage *f*

plaster [PLAHSS-tö] *n* Gips *m*

plastic [PLÆSS-tik] *n* Kunststoff *m*

plate [pleejt] *n* Teller *m*

platform [PLÆT-fohm] *n* Bahnsteig *m*

platform ticket [PLÆT-fohm TIK-it] *n* Bahnsteigkarte *f*

platinum [PLÆT-in-öm] *n* Platin *nt*

play [pleej] *v* spielen; *n* Schauspiel *nt*

player [PLEEJ-ö] *n* Spieler *m*

playground [PLEEJ-graund] *n* Spielplatz *m*

playing-cards [PLEEJ-ing-kahds] *pl* Spielkarten *fpl*

playwright [PLEEJ-rait] *n* Bühnenautor *m*

pleasant [PLÄS-önt] *adj* angenehm

please [plies] *v* gefallen

pleased [pliesd] *adj* erfreut

pleasing [PLIES-ing] *adj* angenehm

pleasure [PLÄჳ-ö] *n* Freude *f*

plenty [PLÄN-ti] *n* Fülle *f*

pliers [PLAI-ös] *pl* Flachzange *f*

plot [plot] *n* Parzelle *f;* Handlung *f*

plough [plau] *n* Pflug *m*

plug [plag] *n* Stecker *m*

plug in [plag in] *v* einstöpseln

plum [plam] *n* Pflaume *f*

plumber [PLAM-ö] *n* Installateur *m*

plural [PLUHÖR-öl] *n* Mehrzahl *f*

plus [plass] *prep* plus

pneumatic [nju-MÆT-ik] *adj* pneumatisch

pneumonia [nju-MOO-ni-ö] *n* Lungenentzündung *f*

pocket [POK-it] *n* Tasche *f*

pocket-book [POK-it-buk] *n* Brieftasche *f*

pocket-comb [POK-it-koom] *n* Taschenkamm *m*

pocket-knife [POK-it-naif] *n* Taschenmesser *nt*

pocket-watch [POK-it-uotsch] *n* Taschenuhr *f*

poem [POO-im] *n* Gedicht *nt*

poet [POO-it] *n* Dichter *m*

poetry [POO-it-ri] *n* Dichtung *f*

point [peunt] *v* hinweisen; *n* Punkt *m*; Spitze *f*

pointed [PEUNT-idl] *adj* spitz

poison [PEUS-ön] *n* Gift *nt*

poisonous [PEUS-ön-öss] *adj* giftig

pole [pool] *n* Pfosten *m*

police [pö-LIESS] *inv* Polizei *f*

policeman [pö-LIESS-mön] *n* (*pl* -men) Polizist *m*

police-station [pö-LIESS-ssteej-schön] *n* Polizeistation *f*

policy [POL-i-ssi] *n* Police *f*; Politik *f*

polish [POL-isch] *n* Schuhkrem *f*; *v* polieren

polite [pö-LAIT] *adj* höflich

political [pö-LIT-i-köl] *adj* politisch

politician [pol-i-TISCH-ön] *n* Politiker *m*

politics [POL-i-tikss] *pl* Politik *f*

pond [pond] *n* Teich *m*

pony [POON-i] *n* Pony *nt*

poor [puhö] *adj* arm

pop in [pop in] *v* hereinplatzen

pop music [pop MJUH-sik] *n* Popmusik *f*

pope [poop] *n* Papst *m*

poplin [POP-lin] *n* Popelin *nt*

popular [POP-ju-lö] *adj* populär

population [pop-ju-LEEJ-schön] *n* Bevölkerung *f*

populous [POP-ju-löss] *adj* dicht besiedelt

porcelain [POHSS-lin] *n* Porzellan *nt*

pork [pohk] *n* Schweinefleisch *nt*

port [poht] *n* Hafen *m*

portable [POHT-ö-böl] *adj* tragbar

porter [POHT-öl] *n* Träger *m*

porthole [POHT-hool] *n* Luke *f*

portion [POH-schön] *n* Portion *f*

portrait [POHT-rit] *n* Porträt *nt*

Portugal [POH-tju-göl] *n* Portugal *nt*

Portuguese [poh-tju-GIES] *n* Portugiese *m*; *adj* portugiesisch

position [pö-SISCH-ön] *n* Stellung *f*; Position *f*

positive [POS-ö-tiw] *adj* positiv; *n* Positiv *nt*

possess [pö-SÄSS] *v* besitzen

possession [pö-SÄSCH-ön] *n* Besitz *m*

possessions [pö-SÄSCH-öns] *pl* Habe *f*

possibility [poss-ö-BIL-it-i] *n* Möglichkeit *f*

possible [POSS-ö-böl] *adj* möglich

post [poosst] *v* aufgeben; *n* Pfosten *m*; Post *f*; Posten *m*

postage [POOSST-idʒ] *n* Porto *nt*

postage stamp [POOSST-idʒ sstæmp] *n* Briefmarke *f*

postal order [POOSST-öl OH-dö] *n* Postanweisung *f*

postal service [POOSST-öl SSÖH-wiss] *n* Postdienst *m*

postcard [POOSST-kahd] *n* Postkarte *f*

poste restante [poosst räss-TANGT] postlagernd

postman [POOSST-mön] *n* (*pl* - men) Postbote *m*

post-office [POOSST-of-iss] *n* Postamt *nt*

postpone [pooss-POON] *v* aufschieben

pot [pot] *n* Topf *m*

potable [POOT-ö-böl] *adj* trinkbar

potato [pö-TEEJ-too] *n* Kartoffel *f*

pottery [POT-ör-i] *n* Töpferwaren *fpl*

pouch [pautsch] *n* Beutel *m*

poultry [POOL-tri] *n* Geflügel *nt*

pound [paund] *n* Pfund *nt*

pour [poh] *v* gießen

powder [PAU-dö] *n* Puder *nt*

powdered milk [PAU-död milk] *n* Milchpulver *nt*

powder-puff [PAU-dö-paf] *n* Puderquaste *f*

powder-room [PAU-dö-ruhm] *n* Damentoilette *f*

power [PAU-ö] *n* Kraft *f*; Macht *f*

power station [PAU-ö SSTEEJ-schön] *n* Kraftwerk *nt*

powerful [PAU-ö-ful] *adj* mächtig

practical [PRÆK-tik-öl] *adj* praktisch

practice [PRÆK-tiss] *n* Praxis *f*

practise [PRÆK-tiss] *v* ausüben

praise [preejs] *v* loben; *n* Lob *nt*

pram [præm] *n* Kinderwagen *m*

prawn [prohn] *n* Steingarnele *f*

pray [preej] *v* beten

prayer [präö] *n* Gebet *nt*

precaution [pri-KOH-schön] *n* Vorsichtsmaßregel *f*

precede [pri-SSIED] *v* vorangehen

preceding [pri-SSIED-ing] *adj* vorhergehend

precious [PRÄSCH-öss] *adj* kostbar

precipice [PRÄSS-i-piss] *n* Abgrund *m*

precise [pri-SSAISS] *adj* genau

prefer [pri-FÖH] *v* bevorzugen

preferable [PRÄF-ör-ö-böl] *adj* vorzuziehend

preference [PRÄF-ör-önss] *n* Vorzug *m*

prefix [PRIE-fikss] *n* Präfix *nt*

pregnant [PRÄG-nönt] *adj* schwanger

preliminary [pri-LIM-in-ör-i] *n* vorläufig

premier [PRÄM-jö] *n* Premierminister *m*

premium [PRIEM-i-öm] *n* Prämie *f*

prepaid [PRIE-peejd] *adj* vorausbezahlt

preparation [präp-ö-REEJ-schön] *n* Vorbereitung *f*

prepare [pri-PÄÖ] *v* vorbereiten

prepared [pri-PÄÖD] *adj* bereit

preposition [präp-ö-SISCH-ön] *n* Präposition *f*

prescribe [pri-SSKRAIB] *v* verschreiben

prescription [pri-SSKRIP-schön] *n* Rezept *nt*

presence [PRÄS-önss] *n* Anwesenheit *f*

present [pri-SÄNT] *v* vorstellen; *adj* gegenwärtig; anwesend; *n* Geschenk *nt*

presently [PRÄS-önt-li] *adv*

sogleich

preservation [präs-ö-WEEJ-schön] n Bewahrung f

preserve [pri-SÖHW] v bewahren

president [PRÄS-i-dönt] n Präsident m

press [präss] n Presse f; v bügeln; drücken

pressed [prässt] adj gebügelt

pressing [PRÄSS-ing] adj dringend; n Bügeln nt

pressure [PRÄSCH-ö] n Druck m

presumably [pri-SJUHM-öb-li] adv vermutlich

pretence [pri-TÄNSS] n Vorwand m

pretend [pri-TÄND] v vorgeben

pretty [PRIT-i] adj hübsch

prevent [pri-WÄNT] v verhindern

preventive [pri-WÄN-tiw] adj vorbeugend

previous [PRIEW-i-öss] adj vorhergehend

pre-war [PRIE-uoh] adj Vorkriegs...

price [praiss] v Preis ansetzen; n Preis m

price list [praiss lisst] n Preisliste f

pride [praid] n Stolz m

priest [priesst] n Priester m

primary [PRAIM-ör-i] adj hauptsächlich

prince [prinss] n Prinz m

princess [prin-SSÄSS] n Prinzessin f

principal [PRIN-ssö-pöl] adj wichtigste; n Direktor m

principle [PRIN-ssö-pöl] n Prinzip nt

print [print] v drucken; n Stich m; Abzug m

priority [prai-OR-it-i] n Vorrang m

prison [PRIS-ön] n Gefängnis nt

prisoner [PRIS-ön-ö] n Häftling m

privacy [PRAIW-ö-ssi] n Privatleben nt

private [PRAIW-it] adj privat

private house [PRAIW-it hauss] n Privathaus nt

private property [PRAIW-it PROP-ö-ti] n Privateigentum nt

prize [prais] n Preis m

probable [PROB-ö-böl] adj wahrscheinlich

problem [PROB-löm] n Problem nt

procedure [prö-SSIE-dʒö] n Verfahren nt

proceed [prö-SSIED] v fortfahren

process [PROO-ssöss] n Vorgang m

produce [prö-DJUHSS] v herstellen; n Ertrag m

producer [prö-DJUHSS-ö] n Produzent m

product [PROD-ökt] n Produkt nt

production [prö-DAK-schön] n Produktion f

profession [prö-FÖSCH-ön] n Beruf m

professional [prö-FÄSCH-ön-öl] adj beruflich

professor [prö-FÄSS-ö] n Professor m

profit [PROF-it] n Gewinn m

profitable [PROF-it-ö-böl] adj einträglich

programme [PROO-græm] n Programm nt

progress [PROO-gräss] n Fortschritt m

progressive [prö-GRÄSS-iw] adj fortschrittlich

prohibit [prö-HIB-it] v verbieten

prohibited [prö-HIB-it-id] adj verboten

prohibition [proo-i-BISCH-ön] *n*
Verbot *nt*

prohibitive [prö-HIB-i-tiw] *adj*
unerschwinglich

project [PRODZ-äkt] *n* Projekt *nt*

promenade [prom-i-NAHD] *n*
Promenade *f*

promise [PROM-iss] *n*
Versprechen *nt; v* versprechen

prompt [prompt] *adj*
unverzüglich

pronoun [PROO-naun] *n* Fürwort
nt

pronounce [prö-NAUNSS] *v*
aussprechen

pronunciation [prö-nan-ssi-EEJ-
schön] *n* Aussprache *f*

proof [pruhf] *n* Beweis *m*

propaganda [prop-ö-GÆN-dö] *n*
Propaganda *f*

propel [prö-PÄL] *v* antreiben

propeller [prö-PÄL-ö] *n* Propeller
m

proper [PROP-ö] *adj* geeignet

property [PROP-ö-ti] *n* Eigentum
nt

proportion [prö-POH-schön] *n*
Verhältnis *nt*

proposal [prö-POOS-öl] *n*
Vorschlag *m*

propose [prö-POOS] *v* vorschlagen

proprietor [prö-PRAI-ö-tö] *n*
Eigentümer *m*

prospectus [pröss-PÄK-töss] *n*
Prospekt *m*

prosperity [pross-PÄR-it-i] *n*
Wohlstand *m*

prosperous [PROSS-pör-öss] *adj*
wohlhabend

protect [prö-TÄKT] *v* schützen

protection [prö-TÄK-schön] *n*
Schutz *m*

protest [prö-TÄSST] *v*
protestieren; *n* Protest *m*

Protestant [PROT-iss-tönt] *adj*
protestantisch

proud [praud] *adj* stolz

prove [pruhw] *v* beweisen

proverb [PROW-öb] *n* Sprichwort
nt

provide [prö-WAID] *v* beschaffen

provided [prö-WAID-id] *conj*
vorausgesetzt daß

province [PROW-inss] *n* Provinz *f*

provincial [prö-WIN-schöl] *adj*
provinziell

provisions [prö-WIZ-öns] *pl*
Vorrat *m*

prune [pruhn] *n* Backpflaume *f*

psychiatrist [ssai-KAI-ö-trisst] *n*
Psychiater *m*

psychoanalyst [ssai-koo-ÆN-ö-
lisst] *n* Psychoanalytiker *m*

psychological [ssai-kö-LODZ-i-
köl] *adj* psychologisch

psychologist [ssai-KOL-ö-dzisst]
n Psychologe *m*

psychology [ssai-KOL-ö-dzi] *n*
Psychologie *f*

pub [pab] *n* Wirtshaus *nt*

public [PAB-lik] *adj* öffentlich; *n*
Publikum *nt*

public announcement [PAB-lik ö
NAUNSS-mönt] *n*
Bekanntmachung *f*

public house [PAB-lik hauss] *n*
Wirtshaus *nt*

public notice [PAB-lik NOO-tiss] *n*
offizielle Bekanntgabe *f*

public relations [PAB-lik ri-LEEJ-
schöns] *pl* Public Relations

publication [pab-li-KEEJ-schön]
n Veröffentlichung *f*

publicity [pab-LISS-it-i] *n*
Reklame *f*

publish [PAB-lisch] *v*
veröffentlichen

publisher [PAB-lisch-ö] *n*

Verleger *m*

pull [pul] *v* ziehen

pull in [pul in] *v* einfahren

pull out [pul aut] *v* abfahren

pull up [pul ap] *v* anhalten

Pullman car [PUL-mön kah] *n* Pullmanwagen *m*

pullover [pul-oo-wö] *n* Pullover *m*

pulse [palss] *n* Puls *m*

pumice stone [PAM-iss sstoon] *n* Bimsstein *m*

pump [pamp] *v* pumpen; *n* Pumpe *f*

pumpernickel [PUM-pö-nik-öl] *n* Pumpernickel *m*

punch [pantsch] *n* Faustschlag *m*

punctual [PANGK-tju-öl] *adj* pünktlich

puncture [PANGK-tschö] *n* Reifenpanne *f*

punctured [PANGK-tschöd] *adj* durchstochen

punish [PAN-isch] *v* strafen

punishment [PAN-isch-mönt] *n* Strafe *f*

pupil [PJUH-pil] *n* Schüler *m*

purchase [PÖH-tschöss] *v* kaufen; *n* Kauf *m*

purchase tax [PÖH-tschöss tækss] *n* Verbrauchssteuer *f*

purchaser [PÖH-tschöss-ö] *n* Käufer *m*

pure [pjuhö] *adj* rein

purple [PÖH-pöl] *n* purpur

purpose [PÖH-pöss] *n* Absicht *f*

purse [pöhss] *n* Portemonnaie *nt*

push [pusch] *v* stoßen

* **put** [put] *v* stellen

* **put off** [put of] *v* verschieben

* **put on** [put on] *v* anziehen

* **put out** [put aut] *v* auslöschen

puzzle [PAS-öl] *n* Rätsel *nt*

pyjamas [pö-DƷAH-mös] *pl*

Pyjama *m*

pylon [PAI-lon] *n* Hochspannungsmast *m*

quail [kueejl] *n* Wachtel *f*

quaint [kueejnt] *adj* seltsam

qualification [kuol-i-fi-KEEJ-schön] *n* Befähigung *f*

qualify [KUOL-i-fai] *v* eignen (sich)

quality [KUOL-it-i] *n* Qualität *f*

quantity [KUON-ti-ti] *n* Quantität *f*

quarantine [KUOR-ön-tien] *n* Quarantäne *f*

quarrel [KUOR-öl] *v* streiten; *n* Zank *m*

quarry [KUOR-i] *n* Steinbruch *m*

quarter [KUOH-tö] *n* Viertel *nt;* Stadtviertel *nt*

quarterly [KUOH-tö-li] *adj* vierteljährlich

quay [kie] *n* Kai *m*

queen [kuien] *n* Königin *f*

queer [kuiö] *adj* sonderbar

query [KUIÖR-i] *v* befragen; *n* Frage *f*

question [KUÄSS-tschön] *n* Frage *f*

question mark [KUÄSS-tschön mahk] *n* Fragezeichen *nt*

queue [kjuh] *v* Schlange stehen; *n* Schlange *f*

quick [kuik] *adj* schnell; *adv* schnell

quiet [KUAI-öt] *adj* still

quilt [kuilt] *n* Steppdecke *f*

quinine [KUIN-ien] *n* Chinin *nt*

quit [kuit] *v* aufgeben

quite [kuait] *adv* durchaus

quiz [kuis] *n* (*pl* quizzes) Quiz *nt*

quota [KUOOT-ö] *n* Quote *f*

quotation [kuoo-TEEJ-schön] *n*

Zitat *nt*
quotation marks [kuoo-TEEJ-schön mahkss] *pl*
Anführungszeichen *ntpl*
quote [kuoot] *v* zitieren

rabbit [RÆB-it] *n* Kaninchen *nt*
race [reejss] *n* Rasse *f;* Rennen *nt*
racecourse [REEJSS-kohss] *n* Rennbahn *f*
racehorse [REEJSS-hohss] *n* Rennpferd *nt*
race-track [REEJSS-træk] *n* Rennbahn *f*
racial [REEJ-schöl] *adj*
rack [ræk] *n* Gepäcknetz *nt*
racquet [RÆK-it] *n* Tennisschläger *m*
radiator [REEJ-di-eejt-ö] *n* Heizkörper *m*
radio [REEJ-di-oo] *n* Radio *nt*
radish [RÆD-isch] *n* Rettich *m*
radius [REEJ-di-öss] *n* (*pl* **radii**) Umkreis *m*
rag [ræg] *n* Lumpen *m*
rail [reejl] *n* Geländer *nt*
railing [REEJL-ing] *n* Gitter *nt*
railroad [REEJL-rood] *n* Eisenbahn *f*
railway [REEJL-ueej] *n* Eisenbahn *f*
rain [reejn] *v* regnen; *n* Regen *m*
rainbow [REEJN-boo] *n* Regenbogen *m*
raincoat [REEJN-koot] *n* Regenmantel *m*
rainfall [REEJN-fohl] *n* Regenschauer *m*
rainproof [REEJN-pruhf] *adj* wasserdicht
rain-water [REEJN-uoh-tö] *n* Regenwasser *nt*

rainy [REEJN-i] *adj* regnerisch
raise [reejs] *v* heben
raisin [REEJS-ön] *n* Rosine *f*
rally [RÆL-i] *n* Versammlung *f*
ramp [ræmp] *n* Rampe *f*
ran [ræn] *v* (*p* **run**)
rancid [RÆN-ssid] *adj* ranzig
rang [ræng] *v* (*p* **ring**)
range [reejnd3] *n* Bereich *m*
range-finder [REEJND3-faind-ö] *n* Entfernungsmesser *m*
rank [rængk] *n* Reihe *f;* Rang *m*
rapid [RÆP-id] *adj* schnell
rapids [RÆP-ids] *pl* Stromschnelle *f*
rare [räö] *adj* selten
rash [ræsch] *n* Ausschlag *m*
rasher [RÆSCH-ö] *n* Schnitte *f*
raspberry [RAHS-bö-ri] *n* Himbeere *f*
rat [ræt] *n* Ratte *f*
rate of exchange [reejt öw ikss-TSCHEEJND3] *n* Kurs *m*
rather [RAH-ðö] *adv* eher
raw [roh] *adj* roh
raw material [roh mö-TIÖR-i-öl] *n* Rohmaterial
ray [reej] *n* Strahl *m*
rayon [REEJ-on] *n* Kunstseide *f*
razor [REEJS-ö] *n* Rasierapparat *m*
razor-blade [REEJS-ö-bleejd] *n* Rasierklinge *f*
reach [rietsch] *v* erreichen
read [räd] *v* (*p, pp* **read**); lesen
readdress [RIE-ö-DRÄSS] *v* umadressieren
reading [RIED-ing] *n* Lesen *nt*
reading-lamp [RIED-ing-læmp] *n* Leselampe *f*
reading-room [RIED-ing-ruhm] *n* Lesesaal *m*
ready [RÄD-i] *adj* bereit
ready-made [RÄD-i-meejd] *adj*

real [riöl] *adj* wirklich

realise [RI-öl-ais] *v* vergegenwärtigen (sich)

really [RIÖL-i] *adv* wirklich

rear [riö] *v* großziehen; *adj* Hinterseite *f*

rear wheel [riö uiel] *n* Hinterrad *nt*

rear-light [riö--LAIT] *n* Schlußlicht *nt*

reason [RIES-ön] *n* Grund *m*

reasonable [RIES-ön-ö-böll] *adj* vernünftig

rebate [RIE-beejt] *n* Rabatt *m*

receipt [ri-SSIET] *n* Quittung *f*

receive [ri-SSIEW] *v* empfangen

receiver [ri-SSIEW-ö] *n* Telefonhörer *m*

recent [RIE-ssönt] *adj* jüngst

reception [ri-SSÄP-schön] *n* Empfang *m*

reception office [ri-SSÄP-schön OF-iss] *n* Rezeption *f*

receptionist [ri-SSÄP-schön-isst] *n* Empfangsdame *f*

recharge [ri-TSCHAHDƷ] *v* aufladen

recipe [RÄSS-i-pi] *n* Rezept *nt*

recital [ri-SSAIT-öl] *n* Solistenkonzert *nt*

reckon [RÄK-ön] *v* halten für

recognise [RÄK-ög-nais] *v* erkennen

recognition [räk-ög-NISCH-ön] *n* Anerkennung *f*

recommence [RIE-kö-MÄNSS] *v* wieder beginnen

recommend [räk-ö-MÄND] *v* empfehlen

recommendation [räk-ö-män-DEEJ-schön] *n* Empfehlung *f*

recommended [räk-ö-MÄND-id] *adj* empfohlen

record [ri-KOHD] *v* aufzeichnen; *n* Akte *f*; Schallplatte *f*

record player [RÄK-ohd PLEEJ-ö] *n* Plattenspieler *m*

record shop [RÄK-ohd schop] *n* Schallplattenladen *m*

recorder [ri-KOHD-ö] *n* Tonbandgerät *nt*

recover [ri-KAW-ö] *v* wiedererlangen

recovery [ri-KAW-ör-i] *n* Erholung *f*

recreation [räk-ri-EEJ-schön] *n* Erholung *f*

recreation centre [räk-ri-EEJ-schön SSÄN-tö] *n* Erholungsheim *nt*

recreation ground [räk-ri-EEJ-schön graund] *n* Spielplatz *m*

recruit [ri-KRUHT] *n* Rekrut *m*

rectangle [RÄK-tæng-göl] *n* Rechteck *nt*

rectangular [räk-TÆNG-gju-lö] *adj* rechteckig

rector [RÄK-tö] *n* Pastor *m*

rectory [RÄK-tör-i] *n* Pfarre *f*

red [räd] *adj* rot

Red Cross [räd kross] *n* Rote Kreuz *nt*

reduce [ri-DJUHSS] *v* herabsetzen

reduction [ri-DAK-schön] *n* Preisnachlaß *m*

reed [ried] *n* Schilfrohr *nt*

reef [rief] *n* Riff *nt*

refer to [ri-FÖH tu] *v* verweisen auf

reference [RÄF-rönss] *n* Referenz *f*

refill [RIE-fil] *n* Ersatzfüllung *f*

reflect [ri-FLÄKT] *v* widerspiegeln

reflection [ri-FLÄK-schön] *n* Spiegelung *f*

reflector [ri-FLÄK-tö] *n* Reflektor *m*

refresh [ri-FRÄSCH] *v* erfrischen

refreshment [ri-FRÄSCH-mönt] *n* Erfrischung *f*

refrigerator [ri-FRIDʒ-ö-reejt-ö] *n* Kühlschrank *m*

refund [ri-FAND] *v* rückvergüten; *n* Rückvergütung *f*

refusal [ri-FJUHS-öl] *n* Verweigerung *f*

refuse [ri-FJUHS] *v* verweigern; *n* Abfall *m*

regard [ri-GAHD] *v* betrachten

regarding [ri-GAHD-ing] *prep* hinsichtlich

regards [ri-GAHDS] *pl* Grüße *mpl*

regatta [ri-GÆT-ö] *n* Regatta *f*

region [RIE-dʒön] *n* Gebiet *nt*

regional [RIE-dʒön-öl] *adj* örtlich

register [RÄDʒ-iss-tö] *v* einschreiben (sich); einschreiben

registered letter [RÄDʒ-iss-töd LÄT-ö] *n* eingeschriebene Brief *m*

registration [rädʒ-iss-TREEJ-schön] *n* Eintragung *f*

registration form [rädʒ-iss-TREEJ-schön fohm] *n* Anmeldebogen *m*

regret [ri-GRÄT] *n* Bedauern *nt*; *v* bedauern

regular [RÄG-ju-lö] *adj* regelmäßig

regulate [RÄG-ju-leejt] *v* regeln

regulation [räg-ju-LEEJ-schön] *n* Vorschrift *f*

reign [reejn] *n* Herrschaft *f*

reimburse [ri-im-BÖHSS] *v* wiedererstatten

reject [RIE-dʒäkt] *n* Ausschuß *m*; *v* zurückweisen

related [ri-LEEJT-id] *adj* verwandt

relations [ri-LEEJ-schöns] *pl* Beziehungen *fpl*

relative [RÄL-ö-tiw] *n* Verwandte *m*; *adj* relativ

relax [ri-LÆKSS] *v* entspannen (sich)

relaxation [ri-lækss-EEJ-schön] *n* Entspannung *f*

reliable [ri-LAI-ö-böl] *adj* zuverlässig

relic [RÄL-ik] *n* Reliquie *f*

relief [ri-LIEF] *n* Erleichterung *f*; Relief *nt*

relieve [ri-LIEW] *v* erleichtern

relieved [ri-LIEWD] *adj* erleichtert

religion [ri-LIDʒ-ön] *n* Religion *f*

religious [ri-LIDʒ-öss] *adj* religiös

rely [ri-LAI] *v* verlassen auf (sich)

remain [ri-MEEJN] *v* bleiben

remainder [ri-MEEJN-dö] *n* Rest *m*

remaining [ri-MEEJN-ing] *adj* übrig

remark [ri-MAHK] *n* Bemerkung *f*; *v* bemerken

remarkable [ri-MAHK-ö-böl] *adj* bemerkenswert

remedy [RÄM-i-di] *n* Heilmittel *nt*

remember [ri-MÄM-bö] *v* erinnern (sich)

remind [ri-MAIND] *v* erinnern

remit [ri-MIT] *v* überweisen

remittance [ri-MIT-önss] *n* Überweisung *f*

remnant [RÄM-nönt] *n* Überrest *m*

remote [ri-MOOT] *adj* entfernt

removal [ri-MUHW-öl] *n* Beseitigung *f*

remove [ri-MUHW] *v* beseitigen

remunerate [ri-MJUH-nö-reejt] *v* entschädigen

remuneration [ri-mjuh-nör-EEJ-schön] *n* Entlohnung *f*

renew [ri-NJUH] *v* verlängern; erneuern

rent [ränt] *v* mieten; *n* Miete *f*
rental [RÄN-töl] *n* Miete *f*
reopen [ri-OO-pön] *v* wieder
  eröffnen
repair [ri-PÄÖ] *v* reparieren
repair shop [ri-PÄÖ schop] *n*
  Reparaturwerkstatt *f*
repairs [ri-PÄÖS] *pl* Reparatur *f*
* **repay** [ri-PEEJ] *v* zurückzahlen
repayment [ri-PEEJ-mönt] *n*
  Rückzahlung *f*
repeat [ri-PIET] *v* wiederholen
repellent [ri-PÄL-önt] *adj*
  abstoßend
repetition [räp-i-TISCH-ön] *n*
  Wiederholung *f*
replace [ri-PLEEJSS] *v* ersetzen
reply [ri-PLAI] *v* antworten; *n*
  Antwort *f*
report [ri-POHT] *v* berichten; *n*
  Bericht *m*
represent [räp-ri-SÄNT] *v*
  vertreten
representation [räp-ri-sän-TEEJ-
  schön] *n* Vertretung *f*
representative [räp-ri-SÄNT-ö-
  tiw] *adj* repräsentativ
reproduce [rie-prö-DJUHSS] *v*
  reproduzieren
reproduction [rie-prö-DAK-
  schön] *n* Reproduktion *f*
reptile [RÄP-tail] *n* Reptil *nt*
republic [ri-PAB-lik] *n* Republik *f*
republican [ri-PAB-lik-ön] *adj*
  republikanisch
request [ri-KUÄSST] *n* Bitte *f*; *v*
  bitten
require [ri-KUAIÖ] *v* erfordern
requirement [ri-KUAIÖ-mönt] *n*
  Erfordernis *nt*
requisite [RÄK-ui-sit] *adj*
  erforderlich
rescue [RÄSS-kjuh] *v* retten; *n*
  Rettung *f*

research [ri-SSÖHTSCH] *n*
  Forschung *f*
resemble [ri-SÄM-böl] *v* gleichen
resent [ri-SÄNT] *v* übelnehmen
reservation [räs-ö-WEEJ-schön] *n*
  Reservierung *f*
reserve [ri-SÖHW] *v* reservieren
reserved [ri-SÖHWD] *adj*
  reserviert
reserved seat [ri-SÖHWD ssiet] *n*
  reservierter Platz *m*
reservoir [RÄS-ö-wuah] *n*
  Reservoir *nt*
reside [ri-SAID] *v* wohnen
residence [RÄS-i-dönss] *n*
  Wohnsitz *m*
residence permit [RÄS-i-dönss
  PÖH-mit] *n*
  Aufenthaltsgenehmigung *f*
resident [RÄS-i-dönt] *n*
  Ortsansässige *m*
resign [ri-SAIN] *v* zurücktreten
resignation [räs-ig-NEEJ-schön]
  n Rücktritt *m*
resort [ri-SOHT] *n* Erholungsort
  m
respect [ri-SSPÄKT] *v* achten
respectable [ri-SSPÄK-tö-böl] *adj*
  ehrbar
respectful [ri-SSPÄKT-ful] *adj*
  ehrerbietig
respective [ri-SSPÄK-tiw] *adj*
  jeweilig
respects [ri-SSPÄKSS] *pl*
  Empfehlungen *fpl*
responsible [ri-SSPON-ssö-böl]
  adj verantwortlich
rest [rässt] *n* Rest *m*; Rast *f*; *v*
  ruhen
restaurant [RÄSS-tö-rongng] *n*
  Restaurant *nt*
restful [RÄSST-ful] *adj* ruhig
rest-house [RÄSST-hauss] *n*
  Erholungsheim *nt*

restless [RÄSST-liss] *adj* unruhig

result [ri-SALT] *v* ergeben (sich); *n* Ergebnis *nt*

retail [RIE-teejl] *v* im kleinen verkaufen

retail trade [RIE-teejl treejd] *n* Kleinhandel *m*

retailer [RIE-teejl-ö] *n* Kleinhändler *m*

retire [ri-TAIÖ] *v* in den Ruhestand treten

retired [ri-TAIÖD] *adj* im Ruhestand

return [ri-TEEN] *v* zurückkehren; *n* Rückkehr *f*

return flight [ri-TÖHN flait] *n* Rückflug *m*

return journey [ri-TÖHN DʒÖH-ni] *n* Rückfahrt *f*

return ticket [ri-TÖHN TIK-it] *n* Rückfahrkarte *f*

revenue [RÄW-in-juh] *n* Einkommen *nt*

reverse [ri-WÖHSS] *v* rückwärts fahren; *n* Rückwärtsgang *m*; Rückschlag *m*

review [ri-WJUH] *v* überprüfen; *n* Zeitschrift *f*

revise [ri-WAIS] *v* überarbeiten

revision [ri-WIʒ-ön] *n* Überarbeitung *f*

revolution [räw-ö-LUH-schön] *n* Revolution *f*

revue [ri-WJUH] *n* Kabarett *nt*

reward [ri-UOHD] *v* belohnen; *n* Belohnung *f*

rheumatism [RUH-mö-tism] *n* Rheumatismus *m*

rhubarb [RUH-bohb] *n* Rhabarber *m*

rhyme [raim] *n* Reim *m*

rhythm [riðm] *n* Rhythmus *m*

rib [rib] *n* Rippe *f*

ribbon [RIB-ön] *n* Band *nt*

rice [raiss] *n* Reis *m*

rich [ritsch] *adj* reich

riches [RITSCH-is] *pl* Reichtümer *mpl*

ridden [RID-ön] *v* (*pp* **ride**)

ride [raid] *n* Fahrt *f*; *v* fahren

rider [RAID-ö] *n* Reiter *m*

ridge [ridʒ] *n* Grat *m*

ridiculous [ri-DIK-ju-löss] *adj* lächerlich

riding [RAID-ing] *n* Reiten *nt*

rifle [RAI-föl] *v* Gewehr *nt*

right [rait] *adj* richtig; recht

right away [rait ö-UEEJ] sogleich

right here [rait hiöl gleich hier

right-hand [RAIT-hænd] *adj* recht

right-of-way [rait-öw-UEEJ] *n* Vorfahrtsrecht *nt*

rights [raitss] *pl* Recht *nt*

rim [rim] *n* Rand *m*; Felge *f*

ring [ring] *n* Klingeln *nt*; Ring *m*; *v* läuten

* **ring up** [ring ap] *v* anrufen

rink [ringk] *n* Eisbahn *f*

rinse [rinss] *n* Haarspülmittel *nt*

ripe [raip] *adj* reif

* **rise** [rais] *v* aufstehen

risen [RIS-ön] *v* (*pp* **rise**)

risk [rissk] *n* Risiko *nt*

risky [RISSK-i] *adj* riskant

river [RIW-ö] *n* Fluß *m*

river-bank [RIW-ö-bængk] *n* Flußufer *nt*

riverside [RIW-ö-ssaid] *n* Flußufer *nt*

roach [rootsch] *n* Plötze *f*

road [rood] *n* Straße *f*

road map [rood mæp] *n* Autokarte *f*

road up [rood ap] Straßenarbeiten

roadhouse [ROOD-hauss] *n* Gaststätte *f*

roadside [ROOD-ssaid] *n*

Straßenseite *f*
rob [rob] *v* rauben
robber [ROB-ö] *n* Räuber *m*
robbery [ROB-ör-i] *n* Raub *m*
rock [rok] *n* Felsen *m*; *v* schaukeln
rock-and-roll [rok-önd-ROOL] *n* Rock-and-Roll *m*
rocket [ROK-it] *n* Rakete *f*
rocky [ROK-i] *adj* felsig
rod [rod] *n* Stange *f*
rode [rood] *v* (*p* ride)
roe [roo] *n* Rogen *m*
roll [rool] *n* Brötchen *nt*; Rolle *f*; *v* rollen
roller-skating [ROOL-ö-sSKEEJT-ing] *n* Rollschuhfahren *nt*
romance [roo-MÆNSS] *n* Romanze *f*
romantic [roo-MÆN-tik] *adj* romantisch
roof [ruhf] *n* Dach *nt*
room [ruhm] *n* Zimmer *nt*
room and board [ruhm önd bohd] *n* Zimmer mit Vollpension
room service [ruhm SSÖH-wiss] *n* Zimmerbedienung *f*
roomy [RUHM-i] *adj* geräumig
root [ruht] *n* Wurzel *f*
rope [roop] *n* Seil *nt*
rosary [ROOS-ör-i] *n* Rosenkranz *m*
rose [roos] *v* (*p* rise); *n* Rose *f*; *adj* rosarot
rouge [ruhʒ] *n* Rouge *nt*
rough [raf] *adj* holperig
roulette [ruh-LÄT] *n* Roulett *nt*
round [raund] *adj* rund
round trip [raund trip] *n* Hin- und Rückfahrt
roundabout [RAUND-ö-baut] *n* Kreisverkehr *m*
rounded [RAUND-id] *adj*

abgerundet
route [ruht] *n* Route *f*
routine [ruh-TIEN] *n* Routine *f*
row [roo] *v* rudern; *n* Reihe *f*; Krach *m*
rowing-boat [ROO-ing-boot] *n* Ruderboot *nt*
royal [REU-öl] *adj* königlich
rub [rab] *v* reiben
rubber [RAB-ö] *n* Gummi *nt*; Radiergummi *m*
rubbish [RAB-isch] *n* Abfall *m*
ruby [RUH-bi] *n* Rubin *m*
rucksack [RUK-ssæk] *n* Rucksack *m*
rudder [RAD-ö] *n* Steuerruder *nt*
rude [ruhd] *adj* grob
rug [rag] *n* Vorleger *m*
ruin [RUH-in] *v* ruinieren
ruins [RUH-ins] *pl* Ruinen *fpl*
rule [ruhl] *v* herrschen
ruler [RUH-lö] *n* Herrscher *m*; Lineal *nt*
rumour [RUH-mö] *n* Gerücht *nt*
* **run** [ran] *v* laufen
* **run into** [ran IN-tu] *v* zufällig begegnen
runaway [RUN-ö-ueej] *n* Ausreißer *m*
running water [RAN-ing UOH-tö] *n* fließendes Wasser *nt*
runway [RAN-ueej] *n* Startbahn *f*
rural [RUHÖR-öl] *adj* ländlich
rush [rasch] *n* Binse *f*; *v* eilen
rush-hour [RASCH-auö] *n* Hauptverkehrszeit *f*
rust [rasst] *n* Rost *m*
rustic [RASS-tik] *adj* ländlich
rusty [RASS-tı] *adj* rostig

saccharin [SSÆK-ö-rin] *n* Saccharin *nt*
sack [ssæk] *n* Sack *m*

sacred [SSEEJK-rid] *adj* heilig

sacrifice [SSÆK-ri-faiss] *n* Opfer *nt*

sad [ssæd] *adj* traurig

saddle [SSÆD-öl] *n* Sattel *m*

safe [sseejf] *n* Safe *m; adj* sicher

safety [SSEEJF-ti] *n* Sicherheit *f*

safety belt [SSEEJF-ti bält] *n* Sicherheitsgurt *m*

safety pin [SSEEJF-ti pin] *n* Sicherheitsnadel *f*

safety razor [SSEEJF-ti REEJS-öl] *n* Rasierapparat *m*

said [ssäd] *v* (*p, pp* say)

sail [sseejl] *v* fahren; *n* Segel *nt*

sailing [SSEEJL-ing] *n* Schiffahrt *f*

sailing boat [SSEEJL-ing boot] *n* Segelboot *nt*

sailor [SSEEJL-öl] *n* Matrose *m*

saint [sseejnt] *n* Heilige *m*

salad oil [SSÆL-öd eul] *n* Salatöl *nt*

salami [ssö-LAH-mi] *n* Salami *f*

salaried [SSÆL-ör-id] *adj* besoldet

salary [SSÆL-ör-i] *n* Gehalt *nt*

sale [sseejl] *n* Verkauf *m*

saleable [SSEEJL-ö-böl] *adj* verkäuflich

sales [sseejls] *pl* Schlußverkauf *m*

salesgirl [SSEEJLS-göhl] *n* Verkäuferin *f*

salesman [SSEEJLS-mön] *n* (*pl* - men) Verkäufer *m*

salmon [SSÆM-ön] *n* Lachs *m*

salon [ssö-LONG] *n* Salon *m*

saloon [ssö-LUHN] *n* Bar *f*

salt [ssohlt] *n* Salz *nt*

saltcellar [SSOHLT-ssäl-ö] *n* Salzfäßchen *nt*

salty [SSOHLT-i] *adj* salzig

salve [ssahw] *n* Salbe *f*

same [sseejm] *adj* selbe

sample [SSAHM-pöl] *n* Muster *nt*

sand [ssænd] *n* Sand *m*

sandal [SSÆN-döl] *n* Sandale *f*

sandwich [SSÆN-uidʒ] *n* Sandwich *nt*

sandy [SSÆND-i] *adj* sandig

sang [ssæng] *v* (*p* sing)

sanitary [SSÆN-i-tör-i] *adj* sanitär

sanitary napkin [SSÆN-i-tör-i NÆP-kin] *n* Damenbinde *f*

sank [ssængk] *v* (*p* sink)

sapphire [SSÆF-aiö] *n* Saphir *m*

sardine [ssah-DIEN] *n* Sardine *f*

satin [SSÆT-in] *n* Seidensatin *m*

satisfaction [ssæt-iss-FÆK-schön] *n* Genugtuung *f*

satisfied [SSÆT-iss-faid] *adj* zufrieden

satisfy [SSÆT-iss-fai] *v* zufriedenstellen

Saturday [SSÆT-ö-di] *n* Sonnabend *m*

saucepan [SSOHSS-pön] *n* Pfanne *f*

saucer [SSOH-ssö] *n* Untertasse *f*

sauna [SSOH-nö] *n* Sauna *f*

sausage [SSOSS-idʒ] *n* Wurst *f*

sausages [SSOSS-idʒ-is] *pl* Würstchen *nt*

savage [SSÆW-idʒ] *adj* wild

save [sseejw] *v* retten; sparen

savings [SSEEJW-ings] *pl* Ersparnisse *fpl*

savings bank [SSEEJW-ings bængk] *n* Sparkasse *f*

saviour [SSEEJW-jö] *n* Retter *m*

savoury [SSEEJW-ör-i] *adj* schmackhaft

saw [ssoh] *n* Säge *f*

* **say** [sseej] *v* sagen

scale [sskeejl] *n* Maßstab *m*

scales [sskeejls] *pl* Waage *f*

scallion [SSKÆL-jön] *n* Schalotte *f*

f

scallop [SSKOL-öp] n
Kammuschel f

scar [sskah] n Narbe f

scarce [sskäöss] adj knapp

scarcely [SSKÄÖSS-li] adv kaum

scarcity [SSKÄÖSS-it-i] n Mangel
m

scare [sskäö] v erschrecken

scarf [sskahf] n Schal m

scarlet [SSKAH-lit] adj
scharlachrot

scatter [SSKÆT-ö] v verstreuen

scene [ssien] n Bühnenbild nt

scenery [SSIEN-ör-i] n Landschaft
f

scenic [SSIE-nik] adj malerisch

scent [ssänt] n Parfüm nt

schedule [SCHÄD-juhl] n Plan m

scheme [sskiem] n Schema nt

scholar [SSKOL-ö] n Gelehrte m

scholarship [SSKOL-ö-schip] n
Stipendium nt

school [sskuhl] n Schule f

schoolboy [SSKUHL-beu] n
Schüler m

schoolgirl [SSKUHL-göhl] n
Schülerin f

schoolmaster [SSKUHL-mahss-tö]
n Schuldirektor m

schoolteacher [SSKUHL-tietsch-ö]
n Lehrer m

science [SSAI-önss] n
Wissenschaft f

scientific [ssai-ön-TIF-ik] adj
wissenschaftlich

scientist [SSAI-ön-tisst] n
Wissenschaftler m

scissors [SSIS-ös] pl Schere f

scold [sskoold] v schimpfen

scooter [SSKUHT-ö] n Motorroller
m

score [sskoh] n Torstand m; v
anschreiben

scorn [sskohn] v verachten; n
Verachtung f

Scot [sskot] n Schotte m

Scotch [sskotsch] adj schottisch

scotch tape [sskotsch teejp] n
Selbstklebeband nt

Scotland [SSKOT-lönd] n
Schottland nt

Scottish [SSKOT-isch] adj
schottisch

scrap [sskræp] n Stückchen nt

scrape [sskreejp] v schaben

scratch [sskrætsch] v kratzen; n
Schramme f

scream [sskriem] v schreien; n
Schrei m

screen [sskrien] n Schutzschirm
m; Filmleinwand f

screw [sskruh] n Schraube f; v
schrauben

screwdriver [SSKRUH-draiw-ö] n
Schraubenzieher m

scrub [sskrab] v scheuern; n
Gestrüpp nt

sculptor [SSKALP-tö] n Bildhauer
m

sculpture [SSKALP-tschö] n
Skulptur f

sea [ssie] n Meer nt

sea-bird [SSIE-böhd] n Seevogel
m

seacoast [SSIE-koosst] n
Meeresküste f

seagull [SSIE-gal] n Möve f

seal [ssiel] n Siegel nt

seam [ssiem] n Naht f

seaman [SSIE-mön] n (pl -men)
Matrose m

seamless [SSIEM-liss] adj nahtlos

seaport [SSIE-poht] n Seehafen m

search [ssöhtsch] n Suche f; v
suchen

seascape [SSIE-sskeejp] n
Meeresblick m

sea-shell [SSIE-schöl] n Muschel f

seashore [SSIE-schoh] n Meeresküste f

seasickness [SSIE-ssik-niss] n Seekrankheit f

seaside [SSIE-ssaid] n Küste f

seaside resort [SSIE-ssaid ri-SOHT] n Seebad nt

season [SSIES-ön] n Jahreszeit f

season ticket [SSIES-ön TIK-it] n Dauerkarte f

seasoning [SSIES-ön-ing] n Gewürz nt

seat [ssiet] n Sitz m; Platz m

seat belt [ssiet bält] n Sicherheitsgurt m

seated [SSIET-id] adj sitzend

sea-urchin [SSIE-öh-tschin] n Seeigel m

sea-water [SSIE-uoh-tö] n Meerwasser nt

second [SSÄK-önd] adj zweite; n Sekunde f

secondary [SSÄK-önd-ör-i] adj untergeordnet

second-class [SSÄK-önd-klahss] adj zweitklassig

second-hand [SSÄK-önd-hænd] adj gebraucht

secret [SSIE-krit] adj geheim; n Geheimnis nt

secretary [SSÄK-rö-tri] n Sekretärin f

section [SSÄK-schön] n Abschnitt m

secure [ssi-KJUHÖ] adj sicher

sedate [ssi-DEEJT] adj gesetzt

sedative [SSÄD-ö-tiw] n Beruhigungsmittel nt

* **see** [ssie] v sehen

* **see to** [ssie tu] v sorgen für

seed [ssied] n Samen m

* **seek** [ssiek] v suchen

seem [ssiem] v scheinen

seen [ssien] v (pp see)

seize [ssies] v ergreifen

seldom [SSÄL-döm] adv selten

select [ssi-LÄKT] adj erlesen

selection [ssi-LÄK-schön] n Auswahl f

self-drive [SSÄLF-draiw] adj ohne Chauffeur

self-employed [ssälf-im-PLEUD] adj selbständig

self-government [ssälf-GAW-ö-mönt] n Selbstverwaltung f

selfish [SSÄL-fisch] adj selbstsüchtig

self-service [ssälf-SSÖH-wiss] n Selbstbedienung f

self-service restaurant [ssälf-SSÖH-wiss RÄSS-tö-rongng] n Selbstbedienungsrestaurant nt

* **sell** [ssäl] v verkaufen

seltzer [SSÄL-tssö] n Selterswasser nt

semicircle [SSÄM-i-ssöh-köl] n Halbkreis m

semicolon [SSÄM-i-KOO-lön] n Strichpunkt m

senate [SSÄN-it] n Senat m

senator [SSÄN-öt-ö] n Senator m

* **send** [ssänd] v senden

* **send back** [ssänd bæk] v zurücksenden

* **send for** [ssänd foh] v kommen lassen

* **send off** [ssänd of] v absenden

sensation [ssän-SSEEJ-schön] n Sensation f; Empfindung f

sensational [ssän-SSEEJ-schön-öl] adj sensationell

sense [ssänss] n Sinn m; Verstand m; v spüren

senseless [SSÄNSS-liss] adj unsinnig

shed

sensible [SSÄN-ssö-böl] *adj*
verständig

sensitive [SSÄN-ssi-tiw] *adj*
empfindlich

sent [ssänt] *v* (*p, pp* **send**)

sentence [SSÄN-tönss] *v*
verurteilen; *n* Urteil *nt*; Satz *m*

sentimental [ssän-ti-MÄN-töl] *adj*
sentimental

separate [SSÄP-ö-reejt] *v*
trennen; *adj* getrennt

September [ssäp-TÄM-bö] *n*
September *m*

septic [SSÄP-tik] *adj* septisch

series [SSIÖR-ies] *n* Serie *f*

serious [SSIÖR-i-öss] *adj* ernst

serum [SSIÖR-öm] *n* Serum *nt*

servant [SSÖH-wönt] *n* Diener *m*

serve [ssöhw] *v* bedienen

service [SSÖH-wiss] *n* Bedienung
f

service charge [SSÖH-wiss
tschahdʒ] *n* Bedienung *f*

service station [SSÖH-wiss
SSTEEJ-schön] *n* Tankstelle *f*

serviette [ssöh-wi-AT] *n* Serviette
f

set [ssät] *n* Gruppe *f*; *v* stellen

set menu [ssät MÄN-juh] *n* festes
Menü

* **set out** [ssät aut] *v* abreisen

setting [SSÄT-ing] *n* Umgebung *f*;
Frisur *f*

setting lotion [SSÄT-ing LOO-
schön] *n* Haarfixativ *nt*

settle [SSÄT-öl] *v* regeln

settle down [SSÄT-öl daun] *v*
niederlassen (sich)

settle up [SSÄT-öl ap] *v* Rechnung
begleichen

settlement [SSÄT-öl-mönt] *n*
Übereinkunft *f*

seven [SSÄW-ön] *adj* sieben

seventeen [SSÄW-ön-tien] *adj*
siebzehn

seventeenth [SSÄW-ön-tienΘ] *adj*
siebzehnte

seventh [SSÄW-önΘ] *adj* siebente

seventy [SSÄW-ön-ti] *adj* siebzig

several [SSÄW-röl] *adj*
verschiedene

severe [ssi-WIÖ] *adj* ernst

* **sew** [ssoo] *v* nähen

* **sew on** [ssoo on] *v* annähen

sewing [SSOO-ing] *n* Näherei *f*

sewing-machine [SSOO-ing-mö-
schien] *n* Nähmaschine *f*

sex [ssäkss] *n* Geschlecht *nt*

shade [scheejd] *n* Farbton *m*;
Schatten *m*

shadow [SCHÆD-oo] *n* Schatten *m*

shady [SCHEEJD-i] *adj* schattig

* **shake** [scheejk] *v* schütteln

shaken [SCHEEJK-ön] *v* (*pp* **shake**)

* **shall** [schæl] *v* sollen

shallow [SCHÆL-oo] *adj* seicht

shame [scheejm] *n* Schande *f*

shampoo [schæm-PUH] *n*
Shampoo *nt*

shan't [schahnt] *v* (**shall not**)

shape [scheejp] *n* Form *f*

share [schäö] *n* Anteil *m*; Aktie *f*;
v teilen

sharp [schahp] *adj* scharf

sharpen [SCHAHP-ön] *v* schärfen

* **shave** [scheejw] *v* rasieren
(sich)

shaver [SCHEEJ-wö] *n*
Rasierapparat *m*

shaving-brush [SCHEEJ-wing-
brasch] *n* Rasierpinsel *m*

shaving-cream [SCHEEJ-wing-
kriem] *n* Rasierkrem *f*

shaving-soap [SCHEEJ-wing-
ssoop] *n* Rasierseife *f*

shawl [schohl] *n* Schal *m*

she [schie] *pron* sie

shed [schäd] *n* Schuppen *m*

sheep [schiep] *inv* Schaf *nt*

sheer [schiö] *adj* dünn

sheet [schiet] *n* Blatt *nt;* Laken *nt*

shelf [schälf] *n* Regal *nt*

shell [schäl] *n* Muschel *f*

shell-fish [SCHÄL-fisch] *n* Schalentier *nt*

shelter [SCHÄL-tö] *n* Schutz *m; v* schützen

shepherd [SCHÄP-öd] *n* Hirt *m*

she's [schies] *v* (**she is, she has**)

* **shine** [schain] *v* strahlen

ship [schip] *n* Schiff *nt; v* versenden

shipping line [SCHIP-ing lain] *n* Schiffahrtslinie *f*

shirt [schöht] *n* Hemd *nt*

shiver [SCHIW-ö] *v* zittern

shivery [SCHIW-ör-i] *adj* fröstelnd

shock [schok] *n* Schock *m; v* schokieren

shock absorber [schok öb-SSOHB-ö] *n* Stoßdämpfer *m*

shocking [SCHOK-ing] *adj* anstößig

shoe [schuh] *n* Schuh *m*

shoe polish [schuh POL-isch] *n* Schuhkrem *f*

shoe-lace [SCHUH-leejss] *n* Schnürsenkel *mpl*

shoemaker [SCHUH-meejk-ö] *n* Schuhmacher *m*

shoe-shine [SCHUH-schain] *n* Schuhputzen *nt*

shoe-shop [SCHUH-schop] *n* Schuhgeschäft *nt*

shone [schon] *v* (*p, pp* **shine**)

shook [schuk] *v* (*p* **shake**)

* **shoot** [schuht] *v* schießen

shop [schop] *v* einkaufen; *n* Geschäft *nt*

shop assistant [schop ö-SSISS-tönt] *n* Verkäufer *m*

shopkeeper [SCHOP-kiep-ö] *n* Ladeninhaber *m*

shopping [SCHOP-ing] *n* Einkauf *m*

shopping bag [SCHOP-ing bæg] *n* Einkaufstasche *f*

shopping centre [SCHOP-ing SSÄN-tö] *n* Einkaufszentrum *nt*

shop-window [SCHOP-UIN-doo] *n* Schaufenster *nt*

shore [schoh] *n* Küste *f*

short [schoht] *adj* kurz

short circuit [schoht SSÖH-kit] *n* Kurzschluß *m*

shortage [SCHOHT-idʒ] *n* Knappheit *f*

shorten [SCHOHT-ön] *v* verkürzen

shorthand [SCHOHT-hænd] *n* Stenographie *f*

shortly [SCHOHT-li] *adv* bald

shorts [schohtss] *pl* Unterhose *f;* kurze Hose

short-sighted [SCHOHT-SSAIT-id] *adj* kurzsichtig

shot [schot] *v* (*p, pp* **shoot**); *n* Schuß *m*

should [schud] *v* (*p* **shall**)

shoulder [SCHOOL-dö] *n* Schulter *f*

shouldn't [SCHUD-önt] *v* (**should not**)

shout [schaut] *n* Schrei *m; v* rufen

* **show** [schoo] *v* ausstellen; beweisen; zeigen; *n* Vorstellung *f*

shower [SCHAU-ö] *n* Schauer *m;* Dusche *f*

shown [schoon] *v* (*pp* **show**)

showroom [SCHOO-ruhm] *n* Ausstellungsraum *m*

shrank [schrængk] *v* (*p* **shrink**)

shriek [schriek'] *n* Gekreisch *nt; v* kreischen

shrimp [schrimp] n Garnele f

shrine [schrain] n Schrein m

* shrink [schringk] v schrumpfen

shrub [schrab] n Strauch m

shrunk [schrangk] v (pp shrink)

shuffle [SCHAF-öl] v mischen

* shut [schat] v schließen;
einschließen; adj geschlossen

shutter [SCHAT-ö] n Fensterladen
m

shy [schai] adj schüchtern

sick [ssik] adj krank

sickness [SSIK-niss] n Krankheit
f

side [ssaid] n Seite f; Partei f

sideburns [SSAID-böhns] pl
Kotelette f

sidelight [SSAID-lait] n
Seitenlicht nt

sidewalk [SSAID-uohk] n
Bürgersteig m

sideways [SSAID-ueejs] adv
seitwärts

sight [ssait] n Aussicht f

sights [ssaitss] pl
Sehenswürdigkeiten fpl

sign [ssain] n Zeichen nt; v
unterschreiben

signal [SSIG-nöl] n Signal nt

signature [SSIG-ni-tschö] n
Unterschrift f

signpost [SSAIN-poosst] n
Wegweiser m

silence [SSAIL-önss] n Stille f

silencer [SSAIL-ön-ssö] n
Auspufftopf m

silent [SSAIL-önt] adj still

silk [ssilk] n Seide f

silken [SSILK-ön] adj seiden

silly [SSIL-i] adj albern

silver [SSIL-wö] n Silber nt

silversmith [SSIL-wö-ssmiΘ] n
Silberschmied m

silverware [SSIL-wö-uäö] n Silber
nt

silvery [SSIL-wör-i] adj silberig

similar [SSIM-il-ö] adj ähnlich

similarity [ssim-i-LÆR-it-i] n
Ähnlichkeit f

simple [SSIM-pöl] adj einfach

simply [SSIM-pli] adv einfach

simultaneous [ssi-möl-TEEJN-
jöss] adj gleichzeitig

since [ssinss] conj seitdem; prep
seit; adv seither

sincere [ssin-SSIÖ] adj aufrichtig

* sing [ssing] v singen

singer [SSING-ö] n Sänger m

single [SSING-göl] adj einzig;
ledig

single bed [SSING-göl bäd] n
Einzelbett nt

single room [SSING-göl ruhm] n
Einzelzimmer nt

single ticket [SSIN-göl TIK-it] n
einfache Fahrkarte

singular [SSING-gju-lö] n Einzahl
f

sink [ssingk] n Ausguß m; v
sinken

siphon [SSAI-fön] n Siphon m

sir [ssöh] mein Herr m

sirloin [SSÖH-leun] n
Lendenstück nt

sister [SSISS-tö] n Schwester f

sister-in-law [SSISS-tör-in-loh] n
Schwägerin f

* sit [ssit] v sitzen

* sit down [ssit daun] v setzen
(sich)

site [ssait] n Gelände nt

sitting-room [SSIT-ing-ruhm] n
Wohnzimmer nt

situated [SSIT-ju-eejt-id] adj
gelegen

situation [ssit-ju-EEJ-schön] n
Lage f

six [ssikss] adj sechs

sixteen [SSIKSS-tien] *adj*
  sechzehn
sixteenth [SSIKSS-tienΘ] *adj*
  sechzehnte
sixth [ssikssΘ] *adj* sechste
sixty [SSIKSS-ti] *n* sechzig
size [ssais] *n* Größe *f;* Nummer *f*
skate [sskeejt] *v* Schlittschuh
  laufen; *n* Schlittschuh *m*
skating [SSKEEJT-ing] *n*
  Schlittschuhlaufen *nt*
skating-rink [SSKEEJT-ing-ringk]
  n Schlittschuhbahn *f*
skeleton [SSKÄL-i-tön] *n* Skelett
  nt
sketch [sskätsch] *n* Skizze *f; v*
  skizzieren
sketchbook [SSKÄTSCH-buk] *n*
  Skizzenbuch *nt*
ski [sskie] *v* Ski laufen; *n* Ski *m*
ski boots [sskie buhtss] *pl*
  Skischuhe *mpl*
skid [sskid] *v* schleudern
skier [SSKIE-öl] *n* Skiläufer *m*
skiing [SSKIE-ing] *n* Skilauf *m*
ski-jump [SSKIE-dʒamp] *n*
  Skisprung *m*
ski-lift [SSKIE-lift] *n* Lift *m*
skill [sskil] *n* Fertigkeit *f*
skilled [sskild] *adj* geschickt
skillful [SSKIL-ful] *adj* geschickt
skin [sskin] *n* Haut *f*
skin cream [sskin kriem] *n*
  Hautkrem *f*
ski-pants [SSKIE-pæntss] *pl*
  Skihose *f*
ski-poles [SSKIE-pools] *pl*
  Skistöcke *mpl*
skirt [ssköht] *n* Rock *m*
skull [sskal] *n* Schädel *m*
sky [sskai] *n* Himmel *m*
sky-scraper [SSKAI-sskreejp-öl] *n*
  Wolkenkratzer *m*
slacks [sslækss] *pl* Hose *f*

slang [sslæng] *n* Slang *nt*
slant [sslahnt] *v* neigen (sich)
slanting [SSLAHNT-ing] *adj* schräg
slave [ssleejw] *n* Sklave *m*
sledge [sslädʒ] *n* Schlitten *m*
sleep [ssliep] *n* Schlaf *m; v*
  schlafen
sleeping-bag [SSLIEP-ing-bæg] *n*
  Schlafsack *m*
sleeping-berth [SSLIEP-ing-böhΘ]
  n Schlafwagenbett *nt*
sleeping-car [SSLIEP-ing-kah] *n*
  Schlafwagen *m*
sleeping-pill [SSLIEP-ing-pil] *n*
  Schlafmittel *nt*
sleepy [SSLIEP-i] *adj* schläfrig
sleeve [ssliew] *n* Ärmel *m*
sleigh [ssleej] *n* Pferdeschlitten
  m
slender [SSLÄN-dö] *adj* schlank
slept [ssläpt] *v* (*p, pp* **sleep**)
slice [sslaiss] *n* Schnitte *f*
sliced [sslaisst] *adj* in Scheiben
  geschnitten
slide [sslaid] *n* Dia *nt;* Gleiten *nt;*
  v gleiten
slight [sslait] *adj* leicht
slim [sslim] *adj* schlank
slip [sslip] *n* Unterrock *m;*
  Fehltritt *m; v* ausrutschen;
  entwischen
slipper [SSLIP-öl] *n* Pantoffel *m*
slippery [SSLIP-ör-i] *adj*
  schlüpfrig
slope [ssloop] *n* Abhang *m; v*
  abfallen
sloping [SSLOOP-ing] *adj* schräg
slot [sslot] *n* Schlitz *m*
slot-machine [SSLOT-mö-schien]
  n Automat *m*
slow [ssloo] *adj* schwerfällig;
  langsam
slow down [ssloo daun] *v*
  verlangsamen

slum [sslam] n Elendsviertel nt

slush [sslasch] n Matsch m

small [ssmohl] adj klein

small change [ssmohl tscheejnd3] n Kleingeld nt

smallpox [SSMOHL-pokss] n Pocken fpl

smart [ssmaht] adj gescheit

* **smell** [ssmäl] v riechen; n Geruch m

smelly [SSMÄL-i] adj übelriechend

smile [ssmail] v lächeln; n Lächeln nt

smith [ssmiΘ] n Schmied m

smog [ssmog] n Smog m

smoke [ssmook] v rauchen; n Rauch m

smoked [ssmookt] adj geräuchert

smokeless [SSMOOK-liss] adj rauchlos

smoker [SSMOOK-ö] n Raucher m

smoke-room [SSMOOK-ruhm] n Rauchzimmer nt

smoking compartment [SSMOOK-ing köm-PAHT-mönt] n Raucherabteil nt

smooth [ssmuhð] adj glatt

smuggle [SSMAG-öl] v schmuggeln

snack [ssnæk] n Imbiß m

snack-bar [SSNÆK-bah] n Snackbar f

snail [ssneejl] n Schnecke f

snapshot [SSNÆP-schot] n Schnappschuß m

sneakers [SSNIEK-ös] pl Turnschuhe mpl

sneeze [ssnies] v niesen

sneezing [SSNIES-ing] n Niesen nt

snorkel [SSNOH-köl] n Schnorchel m

snow [ssnoo] n Schnee m; v schneien

snowstorm [SSNOO-sstohm] n Schneesturm m

snowy [SSNOO-i] adj schneebedeckt

so [ssoo] adv so; conj also

so far [ssoo fah] adv bisher

so that [ssoo ðæt] conj so daß

soak [ssook] v durchnässen

soap [ssoop] n Seife f

soap powder [ssoop PAU-dö] n Seifenpulver nt

so-called [SSOO-kohld] adj sogenannte

soccer [SSOK-ö] n Fußball m

social [SSOO-schöl] adj sozial

socialist [SSOO-schöl-isst] adj sozialistisch

society [ssö-SSAI-ö-ti] n Verein m; Gesellschaft f

sock [ssok] n Socke f

socket [SSOK-it] n Steckdose f

soda-fountain [SSOO-dö FAUN-tin] n Eisdiele f

soda-water [SSOO-dö-UOH-tö] n Sodawasser nt

sofa [SSOO-fö] n Sofa nt

soft [ssoft] adj weich

soft drink [ssoft dringk] n alkoholfreies Getränk nt

soften [SSOF-ön] v mildern

softener [SSOF-ön-ö] n Weichmacher m

soil [sseul] n Erde f

soiled [sseuld] adj beschmutzt

sold [ssoold] v (p,pp sell)

sold out [ssoold aut] adj ausverkauft

soldier [SSOOL-d3ö] n Soldat m

sole [ssool] n Seezunge f; Sohle f; adj einzig

solemn [SSOL-öm] adj feierlich

solicitor [ssö-LISS-it-ö] n Anwalt m

solid [SSOL-id] *adj* fest; *n* Festkörper *m*

soluble [SSOL-ju-böl] *adj* löslich

solution [ssö-LUH-schön] *n* Lösung *f*

solve [ssolw] *v* lösen

some [ssam] *adj* einige

some more [ssam moh] etwas mehr

some time [ssam taim] einmal

somebody [SSAM-böd-i] *pron* jemand

someone [SSAM-uan] *pron* jemand

something [SSAM-Θing] *pron* etwas

sometimes [SSAM-taims] *adv* manchmal

somewhat [SSAM-uot] *adv* ziemlich

somewhere [SSAM-uäö] *adv* irgendwo

son [ssan] *n* Sohn *m*

song [ssong] *n* Lied *nt*

son-in-law [SSAN-in-loh] *n* Schwiegersohn *m*

soon [ssuhn] *adv* bald

sooner [SSUHN-öl] *adv* eher

sore [ssoh] *adj* wund; *n* wunde Stelle

sore throat [ssoh Θroot] *n* Halsschmerzen *mpl*

sorrow [SSOR-oo] *n* Kummer *m*

sorry [SSOR-i] *adj* bekümmert

sort [ssoht] *n* Sorte *f*; *v* sortieren

soul [ssool] *n* Seele *f*

sound [ssaund] *n* Schall *m*; *v* klingen; erschallen

soundproof [SSAUND-pruhf] *adj* schalldicht

soup-plate [SSUHP-pleejt] *n* Suppenteller *m*

soupspoon [SSUHP-sspuhn] *n* Suppenlöffel *m*

sour [ssauö] *adj* sauer

south [ssauΘ] *n* Süden *m*

South Africa [ssauΘ ÆF-ri-kö] *n* Südafrika *nt*

south-east [ssauΘ-IESST] *n* Südosten *m*

southern [SSAð-ön] *adj* südlich

southwards [SSAUΘ-uöds] *adv* südwärts

south-west [ssauΘ-UÄSST] *n* Südwesten *m*

souvenir [SSUH-wö-niö] *n* Andenken *nt*

* sow [ssoo] *v* säen

spa [sspah] *n* Heilbad *nt*

space [sspeejss] *v* in Abständen anordnen; *n* Zwischenraum *m*; Raum *m*

spacious [SSPEEJ-schöss] *adj* geräumig

spade [sspeejd] *n* Spaten *m*

spades [sspeejds] *pl* Pik

Spain [sspeejn] *n* Spanien *nt*

Spanish [SSPÆN-isch] *n* Spanier *m*; *adj* spanisch

spare [sspäö] *v* entbehren; *adj* überschüssig

spare part [sspäö paht] *n* Ersatzteil *nt*

spare room [sspäö ruhm] *n* Gästezimmer *nt*

spare time [sspäö taim] *n* Freizeit *f*

spare tyre [sspäö taiö] *n* Reserveschlauch *m*

spare wheel [sspäö uiell] *n* Reserverad *nt*

spares [sspäös] *pl* Ersatzteile *ntpl*

spark [sspahk] *n* Funken *m*

sparking-plug [SSPAHK-ing-plag] *n* Zündkerze *f*

sparkling [SSPAHK-ling] *adj* funkelnd; perlend

* speak [sspiek] *v* sprechen
special [SSPÄSCH-öl] *adj* speziell
special delivery [SSPÄSCH-öl di-LIW-ör-i] Eilpost
specialise [SSPÄSCH-ö-lais] *v* spezialisieren (sich)
specialist [SSPÄSCH-öl-isst] *n* Spezialist *m*
speciality [sspäsch-i-ÆL-it-i] *n* Spezialität *f*
specimen [SSPÄSS-i-min] *n* Exemplar *nt*
spectacle [SSPÄK-tök-öli] *n* Schauspiel *nt*
spectacles [SSPÄK-tök-öls] *pl* Brille *f*
spectator [sspäk-TEEJT-ö] *n* Zuschauer *m*
speech [sspietsch] *n* Sprache *f*; Rede *f*
* speed [sspied] *v* rasen; *n* Geschwindigkeit *f*
speed limit [sspied LIM-it] *n* Geschwindigkeitsbegrenzung *f*
speeding [SSPIED-ing] *n* überhöhte Geschwindigkeit *f*
speedometer [sspi-DOM-it-ö] *n* Geschwindigkeitsmesser *m*
* spell [sspäl] *v* buchstabieren
spelling [SSPÄL-ing] *n* Rechtschreibung *f*
* spend [sspänd] *v* verbringen; ausgeben
spent [sspänt] *v* (*p, pp* **spend**)
sphere [ssfiö] *n* Kugel *f*; Kreis *m*
spice [sspaiss] *n* Gewürz *nt*
spiced [sspaisst] *adj* gewürzt
spicy [SSPAISS-i] *adj* pikant
* spill [sspil] *v* verschütten
* spin [sspin] *v* wirbeln; spinnen
spinach [SSPIN-idʒ] *n* Spinat *m*
spine [sspain] *n* Rückgrat *nt*
spinster [SSPIN-sstö] *n* alte Jungfer *f*

spire [sspaiö] *n* Turmspitze *f*
spirit [SSPIR-it] *n* Geist *m*; Laune *f*
spirit stove [SSPIR-it sstoow] *n* Spirituskocher *m*
* spit [sspit] *v* spucken
splash [sspläsch] *v* bespritzen
splendid [SSPLÄN-did] *adj* herrlich
splint [ssplint] *n* Schiene *f*
splinter [SSPLIN-tö] *n* Splitter *m*
* split [ssplit] *v* spalten
* spoil [sspeul] *v* verderben
spoke [sspook] *v* (*p* **speak**); *n* Speiche *f*
sponge [sspandʒ] *n* Schwamm *m*
spoon [sspuhn] *n* Löffel *m*
spoonful [SSPUHN-ful] *n* Löffelvoll *m*
sport [sspoht] *n* Sport *m*
sports car [sspohtss kah] *n* Sportwagen *m*
sports jacket [sspohtss DʒÆK-it] *n* Sportjacke *f*
sportsman [SSPOHTSS-mön] *n* (*pl* - **men**) Sportler *m*
sportswear [SSPOHTSS-uäö] *n* Sportkleidung *f*
spot [sspot] *n* Fleck *m*; Platz *m*
spotless [SSPOT-liss] *adj* fleckenlos
sprain [sspreejn] *n* Verstauchung *f*; *v* verstauchen
* spread [sspräd] *v* ausbreiten
spring [sspring] *n* Frühling *m*; Sprungfeder *f*; Quelle *f*
springtime [SSPRING-taim] *n* Frühlingszeit *f*
sprouts [ssprautss] *pl* Rosenkohl *m*
square [sskuäö] *adj* quadratisch; *n* Quadrat *nt*; Platz *m*

squash [sskuosch] *n* Fruchtsaft
m; Kürbis *m*

stable [SSTEEJ-böl] *adj* stabil

stadium [SSTEEJ-di-öm] *n*
Stadion *nt*

staff [sstahf] *n* Personal *nt*

stage [ssteejdʒ] *n* Bühne *f*;
Stadium *nt*

stain [ssteejn] *v* beflecken; *n*
Fleck *m*

stain remover [ssteejn ri-MUHW-
öl] *n* Fleckenreinigungsmittel
nt

stained [ssteejnd] *adj* befleckt

stained glass [ssteejnd glahss] *n*
buntes Glas

stainless [SSTEEJN-liss] *adj*
fleckenlos

stainless steel [SSTEEJN-liss
sstiel] *n* nichtrostender Stahl

staircase [SSTÄO-keejss] *n*
Treppe *f*

stairs [sstäös] *pl* Treppe *f*

stale [ssteejl] *adj* altbacken

stall [sstohl] *n* Sperrsitz *m*

stamp [sstæmp] *v* frankieren; *n*
Briefmarke *f*

stamp machine [sstæmp mö-
SCHIEN] *n* Markenautomat *m*

stand [sstænd] *n* Tribüne *f*; *v*
stehen

standard [SSTÆN-död] *adj*
Standard...

standard of living [SSTÆN-död öw
LIW-ing] Lebensstandard *m*

star [sstah] *n* Stern *m*

starch [sstahtsch] *n* Stärke *f*; *v*
stärken

stare [sstäö] *v* starren

start [sstaht] *n* Anfang *m*; *v*
anfangen

starter [SSTAHT-öl] *n* Anlasser *m*

starting point [SSTAHT-ing peunt]
n Ausgangspunkt *m*

state [ssteejt] *v* darlegen; *n* Staat
m; Zustand *m*

statement [SSTEEJT-mönt] *n*
Erklärung *f*

States, the [öö ssteejtss] *pl*
Vereinigte Staaten *mpl*

statesman [SSTEEJTSS-mön] *n* (*pl*
-men) Staatsmann *m*

station [SSTEEJ-schön] *n* Stelle *f*;
Bahnhof *m*

station master [SSTEEJ-schön
MAHSS-töl] *n* Stationsvorsteher
m

stationary [SSTEEJ-schön-ör-i]
adj stillstehend

stationer [SSTEEJ-schön-öl] *n*
Schreibwarenhandlung *f* ,

stationery [SSTEEJ-schön-ör-i] *n*
Schreibwarenhandlung *f*

statue [SSTÆT-juh] *n* Standbild *nt*

stay [ssteej] *v* aufhalten (sich);
bleiben

steady [SSTÄD-i] *adj* beständig

steak [ssteejk] *n* Steak *nt*

* **steal** [sstiel] *v* stehlen

steam [sstiem] *n* Dampf *m*

steamer [SSTIEM-öl] *n* Dampfer *m*

steel [sstiel] *n* Stahl *m*

steep [sstiep] *adj* steil

steeple [SSTIE-pöl] *n* Kirchturm
m

steering [SSTIÖR-ing] *n*
Steuerung *f*

steering-wheel [SSTIÖR-ing-uiel]
n Steuerrad *nt*

stenographer [sstä-NOG-rö-föl] *n*
Stenograph *m*

step [sstäp] *v* treten; *n* Stufe *f*

sterilize [SSTÄR-i-lais] *v*
sterilisieren

sterilized [SSTÄR-i-laisd] *adj*
sterilisiert

steward [SSTJU-öd] *n* Steward *m*

stewardess [SSTJU-öd-öss] *n*

Stewardess f

* **stick** [sstik] v ankleben; n Stock m

sticky [SSTIK-i] adj klebrig

stiff [sstif] adj steif

still [sstil] adv dennoch; noch; adj still

stimulant [SSTIM-ju-lönt] n Reizmittel nt

* **sting** [ssting] v stechen; n Stich m

stipulate [SSTIP-ju-leejt] v festsetzen

stipulation [sstip-ju-LEEJ-schön] n Klausel f

stir [sstöh] v rühren; bewegen

stitch [sstitsch] n Stich m

stock [sstok] n Aktien fpl; Vorrat m; v vorrätig haben

stock exchange [sstok ikss-TSCHEEJND3] n Börse f

stocking [SSTOK-ing] n Strumpf m

stock-market [SSTOK-mah-kit] n Börse f

stole [sstool] v (p steal)

stomach [SSTAM-ök] n Magen m

stomach ache [SSTAM-ök eejk] n Magenschmerzen mpl

stone [sstoon] n Edelstein m; Stein m

stony [SSTOON-i] adj steinig

stood [sstud] v (p,pp stand)

stop [sstop] v aufhören; n Haltestelle f

stopper [SSTOP-öl] n Stöpsel m

storage [SSTOOR-id3] n Lagerung f

store [sstoh] n Laden m; Vorrat m; v lagern

storey [SSTOH-ri] n Stockwerk nt

storm [sstohm] n Sturm m

stormy [SSTOHM-i] adj stürmisch

story [SSTOH-ri] n Geschichte f

stout [sstaut] adj korpulent

stove [sstoow] n Ofen m

straight [sstreejt] adv geradewegs; adj gerade

straight ahead [sstreejt ö-HÄD] geradeaus

straight away [sstreejt ö-UEEJ] sofort

straight on [sstreejt on] geradeaus

strain [sstreejn] n Anspannung f

strange [sstreejnd3] adj fremd

stranger [SSTREEJN-d3öl] n Fremde m

strap [sstræp] n Riemen m

straw [sstroh] n Stroh nt

strawberry [SSTROH-bö-ri] n Erdbeere f

stream [sstriem] n Bach m

street [sstriet] n Straße f

streetcar [SSTRIET-kah] n Straßenbahn f

strength [ssträngΘ] n Kraft f

stress [ssträss] v betonen; n Betonung f; Spannung f

stretch [ssträtsch] n Strecke f; v dehnen

strict [sstrikt] adj streng

* **strike** [sstraik] v streiken; schlagen; n Streik m

striking [SSTRAIK-ing] adj auffallend

string [sstring] n Schnur f

strip [sstrip] n Streifen m

stripe [sstraip] n Streifen m

striped [sstraipt] adj gestreift

stroke [sstrook] n Schlaganfall m

stroll [sstrool] v bummeln

strong [sstrong] adj stark

structure [SSTRAK-tschö] n Struktur f

struggle [SSTAG-öl] v kämpfen

stub [sstab] n Kontrollabschnitt

m

student [SSTJUH-dönt] *n* Student
  m

study [SSTAD-i] *v* studieren; *n*
  Arbeitszimmer *nt;* Studium *nt*

stuffed [sstaft] *adj* gefüllt

stuffing [SSTAF-ing] *n* Füllung *f*

stuffy [SSTAF-i] *adj* stickig

stung [sstang] *v* (*p,pp* **sting**)

stupid [SSTJUH-pid] *adj* dumm

style [sstail] *n* Stil *m*

subject [SSAB-dʒikt] *n* Subjekt *nt;*
  Staatsangehörige *m; v*
  unterwerfen

subsequent [SSAB-ssi-kuönt] *adj*
  folgend

substance [SSAB-sstönss] *n*
  Substanz *f*

substantial [ssöb-SSTÆN-schöl]
  adj bedeutend

substitute [SSAB-ssti-tjuht] *v*
  ersetzen; *n* Ersatz *m*

sub-title [SSAB-tai-töl] *n*
  Untertitel *m*

subtract [ssöb-TRÆKT] *v*
  subtrahieren

suburb [SSAB-öhb] *n* Vorstadt *f*

suburban [ssö-BÖH-bön] *adj*
  vorstädtisch

subway [SSAB-ueej] *n*
  Untergrundbahn *f*

succeed [ssök-SSIED] *v* gelingen

success [ssök-SSÄSS] *n* Erfolg *m*

successful [ssök-SSÄSS-full] *adj*
  erfolgreich

such [ssatsch] *adv* solch; *adj*
  solch

such as [ssatsch æs] wie zum
  Beispiel

suck [ssak] *v* lutschen

sudden [SSAD-ön] *adj* plötzlich

suede [ssueejd] *n* Wildleder *nt*

suffer [SSAF-ö] *v* leiden; erleiden

suffering [SSAF-ör-ing] *n* Leiden

nt

suffice [ssö-FAISS] *v* genügen

sufficient [ssö-FISCH-önt] *adj*
  genügend

sugar [SCHUG-ö] *n* Zucker *m*

suggest [ssö-DʒÄSST] *v*
  vorschlagen

suggestion [ssö-DʒÄSS-tschön] *n*
  Vorschlag *m*

suicide [SSUH-i-ssaid] *n*
  Selbstmord *m*

suit [ssuht] *v* passen; *n* Anzug *m*,
  Farbe *f*

suitable [SSUHT-ö-böl] *adj*
  geeignet

suitcase [SSUHT-keejss] *n*
  Handkoffer *m*

suite [ssuiet] *n* Zimmerflucht *f*

sum [ssam] *n* Summe *f*

summary [SSAM-ör-i] *n*
  Zusammenfassung *f*

summer [SSAM-ö] *n* Sommer *m*

summertime [SSAM-ö-taim] *n*
  Sommerzeit *f*

summit [SSAM-it] *n* Gipfel *m*

sun [ssan] *n* Sonne *f*

sunbathe [SSAN-beejð] *v* sonnen
  (sich)

sunburn [SSAN-böhn] *n*
  Sonnenbrand *m*

Sunday [SSAN-di] *n* Sonntag *m*

sung [ssang] *v* (*pp* **sing**)

sunglasses [SSAN-glahss-is] *pl*
  Sonnenbrille *f*

sunk [ssangk] *v* (*pp* **sink**)

sunlight [SSAN-lait] *n*
  Sonnenlicht *nt*

sunny [SSAN-i] *adj* sonnig

sunrise [SSAN-rais] *n*
  Sonnenaufgang *m*

sunset [SSAN-ssät] *n*
  Sonnenuntergang *m*

sunshade [SSAN-ssheejd] *n*
  Sonnenschirm *m*

sunshine [SSAN-sshain] *n*
Sonnenschein *m*

sunstroke [SSAN-sstrook] *n*
Sonnenstich *m*

suntan [SSAN-tæn] *n*
Sonnenbräune *f*

suntan oil [SSAN-tæn eul] *n*
Sonnenöl *nt*

superb [ssuh-PÖHB] *adj* prächtig

superior [ssuh-PIÖR-i-ö] *adj*
obere

superlative [ssuh-PÖH-lö-tiw] *adj*
überragend

supermarket [SSUH-pö-mah-kit]
n Supermarkt *m*

supervise [SSUH-pö-wais] *v*
beaufsichtigen

supervisor [SSUH-pö-wais-ö] *n*
Aufseher *m*

supper [SSAP-ö] *n* Abendessen *nt*

supplies [ssö-PLAIS] *pl* Vorrat *m*

supply [ssö-PLAI] *v* liefern; *n*
Lieferung *f*

support [ssö-POHT] *v* stützen; *n*
Unterstützung *f*

support hose [ssö-POHT hoos] *pl*
elastischer Strumpf *m*

suppose [ssö-POOS] *v* annehmen

supposing that [ssö-POOS-ing
ðæt] *conj* angenommen daß

suppository [ssö-POS-i-tör-i] *n*
Zäpfchen *nt*

surcharge [SSÖH-tschahdʒ] *n*
Zuschlag *m*

sure [schuhö] *adj* sicher

surely [SCHUHÖ-li] *adv* sicherlich

surface [SSÖH-fiss] *n* Oberfläche *f*

surfboard [SSÖHF-bohd] *n*
Wellenreiterbrett *nt*

surgeon [SSÖH-dʒön] *n* Chirurg *m*

surgery [SSÖH-dʒör-i] *n*
Operation *f*; Sprechzimmer *nt*

surname [SSÖH-neejm] *n*
Familienname *m*

surplus [SSÖH-plöss] *n*
Überschuß *m*

surprise [ssö-PRAIS] *n*
Überraschung *f*; *v*
überraschen

surprised [ssö-PRAISD] *adj*
überrascht

surprising [ssö-PRAIS-ing] *adj*
überraschend

surround [ssö-RAUND] *v* umgeben

surrounding [ssö-RAUND-ing] *adj*
umliegend

surroundings [ssö-RAUND-ings] *pl*
Umgebung *f*

survival [ssö-WAIW-öl] *n*
Überleben *nt*

survive [ssö-WAIW] *v* überleben

suspender belt [ssöss-PÄND-ö
bält] *n* Hüfthalter *m*

suspenders [ssöss-PÄND-ös] *pl*
Hosenträger *mpl*

suspicion [ssöss-PISCH-ön] *n*
Verdacht *m*

suspicious [ssöss-PISCH-öss] *adj*
verdächtig

swallow [SSUOL-oo] *v* schlucken

swam [ssuæm] *v* (*p* swim)

* **swear** [ssuäö] *v* fluchen

sweat [ssuät] *n* Schweiß *m*

* **sweat** [ssuät] *v* schwitzen

sweater [SSUÄT-ö] *n* Sweater *m*

Swede [ssuied] *n* Schwede *m*

Sweden [SSUIED-ön] *n* Schweden
nt

Swedish [SSUIED-isch] *adj*
schwedisch

* **sweep** [ssuiep] *v* fegen

sweet [ssuiet] *adj* süß; lieb; *n*
Nachtisch *m*

sweetbread [SSUIET-bräd] *n* Bries
nt

sweeten [SSUIET-ön] *v* süßen

sweetheart [SSUIET-haht] *n*
Liebling *m*

sweets [ssuietss] *pl* Süßigkeiten
fpl
sweetshop [SSUIET-schop] *n*
Süßwarengeschäft *nt*
* **swell** [ssuäl] *v* schwellen
swelling [SSUÄL-ing] *n*
Geschwulst *f*
swept [ssuäpt] *v* (*p, pp* sweep)
swift [ssuift] *adj* geschwind
* **swim** [ssuim] *v* schwimmen
swimmer [SSUIM-ö] *n*
Schwimmer *m*
swimming [SSUIM-ing] *n*
Schwimmsport *m*
swimming pool [SSUIM-ing puhl]
n Schwimmbad *nt*
swimming trunks [SSUIM-ing
trangkss] *pl* Badehose *f*
swim-suit [SSUIM-ssuht] *n*
Badeanzug *m*
* **swing** [ssuing] *v* schaukeln
Swiss [ssuiss] *n* Schweizer *m;*
adj schweizerisch
switch [ssuitsch] *n* Schalter *m; v*
wechseln
switch off [ssuitsch of] *v*
ausschalten
switch on [ssuitsch on] *v*
einschalten
switchboard [SSUITSCH-bohd] *n*
Schaltbrett *nt*
Switzerland [SSUIT-ssö-lönd] *n*
Schweiz *f*
sword [ssohd] *n* Schwert *nt*
swore [ssuoh] *v* (*p* swear)
sworn [ssuohn] *v* (*pp* swear)
swum [ssuam] *v* (*pp* swim)
syllable [SSIL-ö-böl] *n* Silbe *f*
sympathetic [ssim-pö-ΘAT-ik]
adj mitfühlend
sympathy [SSIM-pö-Θi] *n*
Mitgefühl *nt*
symphony [SSIM-fö-ni] *n*
Symphonie *f*

symptom [SSIM-töm] *n* Symptom
nt
synagogue [SSIN-ö-gog] *n*
Synagoge *f*
synonym [SSIN-ö-nim] *n*
Synonym *nt*
synthetic [ssin-ΘAt-ik] *adj*
synthetisch
syphon [SSAI-fön] *n* Siphon *m*
syringe [ssi-RIND3] *n* Spritze *f*
syrup [SSIR-öp] *n* Sirup *m*
system [SSISS-tim] *n* System *nt*
systematic [ssiss-ti-MÆT-ik] *adj*
systematisch

tab [tæb] *n* Anhänger *m*
table [TEEJ-böl] *n* Tabelle *f;* Tisch
m
table d'hôte [TAH-böl doot] *n*
feste Speisenfolge
table tennis [TEEJ-böl TÄN-iss] *n*
Tischtennis *nt*
tablecloth [TEEJ-böl-kloΘ] *n*
Tischtuch *nt*
tablespoon [TEEJ-bäl-sspuhn] *n*
Eßlöffel *m*
tablet [TÆB-lit] *n* Tablette *f*
tag [tæg] *n* Etikett *nt*
tail [teejl] *n* Schwanz *m*
tail-light [TEEJL-lait] *n* Rücklicht
nt
tailor [TEEJL-ö] *n* Schneider
tailor-made [TEEJL-ö-meejd] *adj*
nach Maß
* **take** [teejk] *v* nehmen;
einnehmen
* **take away** [teejk ö-UEEJ] *v*
wegnehmen
* **take care of** [teejk käör ow] *v*
kümmern um (sich)
* **take charge of** [teejk tschahd3
ow] *v* übernehmen
* **take in** [teejk in] *v* aufnehmen

* **take off** [teejk of] v starten
* **take out** [teejk autl] v
  ausführen; herausnehmen
* **take place** [teejk pleejss] v
  stattfinden
taken [TEEJK-ön] v (pp take)
take-off [TEEJK-of] n Start m
talcum powder [TÆL-köm PAU-
  dö] n Talkpuder m
tale [teejl] n Erzählung f
talent [TÆL-önt] n Talent nt
talk [tohk] v sprechen; n
  Gespräch nt
tall [tohl] adj groß; hoch
tame [teejm] adj zahm
tampon [TÆM-pön] n Tampon m
tan [tæn] adj braun
tangerine [tæn-dzö-RIEN] n
  Mandarine f
tank [tængk] n Tank m
tanker [TÆNGK-ö] n Tankschiff nt
tap [tæp] n Klopfen nt; Hahn m;
  v pochen
tape [teejp] n Band nt
tape measure [teejp MÆз-ö] n
  Bandmaß nt
tape recorder [teejp ri-KOHD-ö] n
  Tonbandgerät nt
tapestry [TÆP-iss-tri] n Gobelin
  m
tariff [TÆR-if] n Tarif m
tarpaulin [tah-POH-lin] n Plane f
task [tahssk] n Aufgabe f
taste [teejsst] v kosten; n
  Geschmack m
tasteless [TEEJSST-liss] adj
  geschmacklos
tasty [TEEJSS-ti] adj schmackhaft
taught [toht] v (p, pp teach)
tavern [TÆW-ön] n Schenke f
tax [tækss] n Steuer f; v
  besteuern
taxation [tæk-SSEEJ-schön] n
  Besteuerung f

tax-free [TÆKSS-frie] adj
  steuerfrei
taxi [TÆK-ssi] n Taxi nt
taxi-driver [TÆK-ssi-draiw-ö] n
  Taxichauffeur m
taximeter [TÆK-ssi-mie-tö] n
  Taxameter m
taxi-rank [TÆK-ssi-rængk] n
  Taxistand m
taxi-stand [TÆK-ssi-sstænd] n
  Taxistand m
tea [tie] n Tee m
* **teach** [tietsch] v lehren
teacher [TIETSCH-ö] n Lehrer m
teachings [TIETSCH-ings] pl Lehre
  f
teacup [TIE-kap] n Teetasse f
team [tiem] n Mannschaft f
teapot [TIE-pot] n Teekanne f
* **tear** [täö] v zerreißen; n Riß m;
  Träne f
tea-set [TIE-ssät] n (n) Teeservice
  nt
tea-shop [TIE-schop] n Teestube
  f
teaspoon [TIE-sspuhn] n
  Teelöffel m
teaspoonful [TIE-sspuhn-ful] n
  Teelöffelvoll m
technical [TÄK-nik-öl] adj
  technisch
technician [täk-NISCH-ön] n
  Techniker m
technique [täk-NIEK] n Technik f
teenager [TIEN-eejdз-ö] n
  Teenager m
teetotaller [tie-TOOT-lö] n
  Abstinenzler m
telegram [TÄL-i-græm] n
  Telegramm nt
telegraph [TÄL-i-grahf] v
  telegraphieren
telephone [TÄL-i-foon] n
  Telephon nt

telephone book [TÄL-i-foon buk] n Telephonbuch nt

telephone booth [TÄL-i-foon buhðl] n Fernsprechzelle f

telephone call [TÄL-i-foon kohl] n Telephonanruf m

telephone directory [TÄL-i-foon di-RÄK-tör-i] n Telephonbuch nt

telephone operator [TÄL-i-foon OP-ör-eejt-ö] n Telephonistin f

telephonist [ti-LÄF-ö-nisst] n Telephonistin f

telephoto lens [TÄL-i-foot-oo läns] pl Teleobjektiv nt

television [TÄL-i-wiʒ-ön] n Fernsehen nt

television set [TÄL-i-wiʒ-ön sät] n Fernsehapparat m

telex [TÄL-äkss] n Telex nt

* **tell** [täl] v sagen

temper [TÄM-pö] n Wut f

temperature [TÄM-pri-tschö] n Temperatur f

temple [TÄM-pöl] n Tempel m

temporary [TÄM-pör-ör-i] adj zeitweilig

tempt [tämpt] v versuchen

ten [tän] adj zehn

tenant [TÄN-önt] n Mieter m

tend [tänd] v neigen

tender [TÄN-dö] adj zart

tenderloin steak [TÄN-dö-leun ssteejk] n Filet nt

tennis [TÄN-iss] n Tennis nt

tennis court [TÄN-iss koht] n Tennisplatz m

tension [TÄN-schön] n Spannung f

tent [tänt] n Zelt nt

tenth [tänΘ] adj zehnte

tepid [TÄP-id] adj lauwarm

term [töhm] n Ausdruck m; Frist f

terminal [TÖH-min-öl] adj letzt

terminus [TÖH-min-öss] n Endstation f

terms [töhms] pl Bedingungen fpl

terms of payment [töhms öw PEEJ-mönt] pl Zahlungsbedingungen fpl

terrace [TÄR-öss] n Terrasse f

terrible [TÄR-ö-böl] adj schrecklich

terrific [tö-RIF-ik] adj großartig

terrify [TÄR-i-fai] v verschrecken

Terylene [TÄR-i-lien] n Terylene nt

test [tässt] v prüfen; n Test m

text [täksst] n Text m

textbook [TÄKSS-buk] n Lehrbuch nt

textile [TÄKSS-tail] n Textilien pl

texture [TÄKSS-tschö] n Struktur f

than [ðæn] conj als

thank [Θængk] v danken

thankful [ΘÆNGK-ful] adj dankbar

thanks [Θængkss] pl Dank m

that [ðæt] pron das; der; jener; adj jener; conj daß

thatch [Θætsch] n Strohdach nt

thaw [Θoh] n Tauwetter nt

the [ðö] art der

theatre [ΘI-ö-tö] n Theater nt

theft [Θäft] n Diebstahl m

their [ðäö] adj ihr

them [ðäm] pron ihnen; sie

themselves [ðöm-SSÄLws] pron sich; sie selbst

then [ðän] adv damals; dann

theory [ΘI-ö-ri] n Theorie f

therapy [ΘÄR-ö-pi] n Therapie f

there [ðäö] adv dort

there are [ðäör ah] es gibt

there is [ðäör is] es gibt

therefore [ðÄö-foh] *conj* darum

there's [ðääs] *v* (**there is**)

thermometer [Θö-MOM-i-tö] *n*
Thermometer *nt*

thermos [Θöh-moss] *n*
Thermosflasche *f*

these [ðies] *pron* diese

they [ðeej] *pron* sie

thick [Θik] *adj* dick; dicht

thicken [ΘIK-ön] *v* verdicken

thickness [ΘIK-niss] *n* Dicke *f*

thief [Θief] *n* Dieb *m*

thigh [Θai] *n* Oberschenkel *m*

thimble [ΘIM-böl] *n* Fingerhut *m*

thin [Θin] *adj* dünn; mager

thing [Θing] *n* Ding *nt*

* **think** [Θingk] *v* denken

* **think about** [Θingk ö-BAUT] *v*
nachdenken über

* **think of** [Θingk ow] *v* denken
an

* **think over** [Θingk OO-wö] *v*
überlegen

thinker [ΘINGK-ö] *n* Denker *m*

third [Θöhd] *adj* dritte

thirst [Θöhsst] *n* Durst *m*

thirsty [Θöhsst-i] *adj* durstig

thirteen [Θöh-tien] *adj* dreizehn

thirteenth [Θöh-tienΘ] *adj*
dreizehnte

thirtieth [Θöh-ti-iΘ] *adj*
dreissigste

thirty [Θöh-ti] *adj* dreissig

this [ðiss] *adj* dieser; *pron* dieser

thorn [Θohn] *n* Dorn *m*

thorough [ΘAR-ö] *adj* gründlich

thoroughfare [ΘAR-ö-fäö] *n*
Hauptverkehrsstraße *f*

those [ðoos] *pron* jene; *adj* jene

though [ðoo] *conj* obgleich

thought [Θoht] *v* (*p, pp* **think**); *n*
Gedanke *m*

thoughtful [ΘOHT-ful] *adj*
nachdenklich

thousand [ΘAUS-önd] *adj*
tausend

thread [Θräd] *n* Faden *m*;
Drohung *f*; *v* aufreihen

threaten [ΘRÄT-ön] *v* bedrohen

threatening [ΘRÄT-ön-ing] *adj*
bedrohlich

three [Θrie] *adj* drei

three-quarter [Θrie-KUOH-tö] *adj*
dreiviertel

threw [Θruh] *v* (*p* **throw**)

throat [Θroot] *n* Kehle *f*

through [Θruh] *prep* durch

through train [Θruh treejn] *n*
durchgehender Zug *m*

throughout [Θruh-AUT] *adv*
überall

* **throw** [Θroo] *v* werfen

thrown [Θroon] *v* (*pp* **throw**)

thumb [Θam] *n* Daumen *m*

thumbtack [ΘAM-tæk] *n*
Reißnagel *m*

thunder [ΘAN-dö] *n* Donner *m*

thunderstorm [ΘAN-dö-sstohm]
n Gewitter *nt*

thundery [ΘAN-dör-i] *adj*
gewitterschwül

Thursday [ΘÖHS-di] *n*
Donnerstag *m*

thus [ðass] *adv* so

thyme [taim] *n* Thymian *m*

tick [tik] *v* anhaken; *n*
Vermerkhäkchen *nt*

ticket [TIK-it] *n* Karte *f*

ticket collector [TIK-it kö-LÄKT-ö]
n Schaffner *m*

ticket machine [TIK-it mö-
SCHIEN] *m* Fahrkartenautomat
m

ticket office [TIK-it OF-iss] *n*
Fahrkartenschalter *m*

tide [taid] *n* Gezeit *f*

tidy [TAID-i] *adj* ordentlich

tie [tai] *v* binden; *n* Krawatte *f*

tight [tait] *adj* knapp; *adv* fest

tighten [TAIT-ön] *v* straffen

tights [taitss] *pl* Trikot *nt*

tile [tail] *n* Kachel *f*

till [til] *conj* bis; *prep* bis

timber [TIM-bö] *n* Bauholz *nt*

time [taim] *n* Mal *nt;* Zeit *f*

time of arrival [taim öw ö-RAIW-öl] Ankunftszeit *f*

time of departure [taim öw di-PAH-tschö] Abfahrtszeit *f*

timetable [TAIM-teej-böl] *n* Fahrplan *m*

timid [TIM-id] *adj* schüchtern

tin [tin] *n* Büchse *f*

tinfoil [TIN-feul] *n* Stanniol *nt*

tinned food [tind fuhd] *n* Konserven *fpl*

tin-opener [TIN-oo-pön-ö] *n* Dosenöffner *m*

tiny [TAIN-i] *adj* winzig

tip [tip] *n* Spitze *f;* Trinkgeld *nt*

tire [taiö] *v* ermüden

tired [TAIÖD] *adj* müde

tiring [TAIÖR-ing] *adj* ermüdend

tissue paper [TISCH-uh PEEJ-pö] *n* Seidenpapier *nt*

title [TAI-töl] *n* Titel *m*

to [tuh] *prep* nach; bis zu

toast [toosst] *n* Toast *m;* Trinkspruch *m*

tobacco [tö-BÆK-oo] *n* Tabak *m*

tobacco pouch [tö-BÆK-oo pautsch] *n* Tabaksbeutel *m*

tobacconist [tö-BÆK-ö-nisst] *n* Tabakhändler *m*

today [tö-DEEJ] *adv* heute

toe [too] *n* Zehe *f*

toffee [TOF-i] *n* Toffee *nt*

together [tö-GÀð-ö] *adv* zusammen

toilet [TEUL-it] *n* Toilette *f*

toilet water [TEUL-it UOH-tö] *n* Toilettenwasser *nt*

toilet-case [TEUL-it-keejss] *n* Toilettennecessaire *nt*

toilet-paper [TEUL-it-peej-pö] *n* Toilettenpapier *nt*

toiletry [TEUL-it-ri] *n* Toilettenartikel *mpl*

token [TOO-kön] *n* Münze *f*

told [toold] *v* (*p, pp* tell)

toll [tool] *n* Wegegeld *nt*

tomato [tö-MAH-too] *n* Tomate *f*

tomb [tuhm] *n* Grab *nt*

tomorrow [tö-MOR-oo] *adv* morgen

ton [tan] *n* Tonne *f*

tone [toon] *n* Ton *m*

tongs [tongs] *pl* Zange *f*

tongue [tang] *n* Zunge *f*

tonic [TON-ik] *n* Stärkungsmittel *nt*

tonight [tö-NAIT] *adv* heute abend

tonsillitis [ton-ssi-LAIT-iss] *n* Mandelentzündung *f*

tonsils [TON-ssils] *pl* Mandeln *fpl*

too [tuh] *adv* auch; zu

too much [tuh matsch] *adv* zuviel

took [tuk] *v* (*p* take)

tool [tuhl] *n* Werkzeug *nt*

tool-kit [TUHL-kit] *n* Werkzeugtasche *f*

tooth [tuhΘ] *n* (*pl* teeth) Zahn *m*

toothache [TUHΘ-eejk] *n* Zahnweh *nt*

toothbrush [TUHΘ-brasch] *n* Zahnbürste *f*

toothpaste [TUHΘ-peejsst] *n* Zahnpasta *f*

toothpick [TUHΘ-pik] *n* Zahnstocher *m*

tooth-powder [TUHΘ-pau-dö] *n* Zahnpulver *nt*

top [top] *adj* oberst; *n* Gipfel *m*

topcoat [TOP-koot] *n* Überrock *m*

topic [TOP-ik] *n* Thema *nt*

torch [tohtsch] *n* Taschenlampe *f*

tore [toh] v (p tear)

torn [tohn] v (pp tear)

toss [toss] v werfen

tot [tot] n Schlückchen nt

total [TOOT-öl] adj total; n
Gesamtsumme f

totalizator [TOOT-öl-ais-eejt-ö] n
(abbr tote) Totalisator m

touch [tatsch] v berühren;
betreffen; n Tastsinn m

touch up [tatsch ap] v
auffrischen

tough [taf] adj zäh

tour [tuhö] v bereisen; n
Rundreise f

tourism [TUHÖR-ism] n
Fremdenverkehr m

tourist [TUHÖR-isst] n Tourist m

tourist class [TUHÖR-isst klahss]
n Touristenklasse f

tourist office [TUHÖR-isst OF-iss]
n Reisebüro nt

tow [too] v schleppen

towards [tö-UOHDS] prep zu; nach

towel [TAU-öl] n Handtuch nt

towelling [TAU-öl-ing] n
Frottierstoff m

tower [TAU-ö] n Turm m

town [taun] n Stadt f

town centre [taun SSÄN-töl] n
Stadtzentrum nt

town hall [taun hohl] n Rathaus
nt

townspeople [TAUNS-pie-pöl] pl
Städter mpl

toxic [TOKSS-ik] adj toxisch

toy [teu] n Spielzeug nt

toyshop [TEU-schop] n
Spielwarenladen m

track [træk] n Gleis nt; Bahn f

tractor [TRÆK-tö] n Traktor m

trade [treejd] v handeln; n
Handwerk nt; Handel m

trader [TREEJD-ö] n Händler m

tradesman [TREEJDS-mön] n (pl -
men) Geschäftsmann m

trade-union [treejd-JUHN-jön] n
Gewerkschaft f

tradition [trö-DISCH-ön] n
Tradition f

traditional [trö-DISCH-ön-öl] adj
traditionell

traffic [TRÆF-ik] n Verkehr m

traffic jam [TRÆF-ik dʒæm] n
Verkehrsstauung f

traffic light [TRÆF-ik lait] n
Verkehrsampel f

trafficator [TRÆF-i-keejt-ö] n
Winker m

tragedy [TRÆDʒ-i-di] n Tragödie f

tragic [TRÆDʒ-ik] adj tragisch

trail [treejl] n Pfad m

trailer [TREEJL-ö] n Anhänger m

train [treejn] n Zug m; v
ausbilden

train-ferry [TREEJN-fär-i] n
Eisenbahnfähre f

training [TREEJN-ing] n
Ausbildung f

tram [træm] n
Straßenbahnwagen m

tramp [træmp] v wandern

tranquil [TRÆNGK-uil] adj ruhig

tranquilliser [TRÆNGK-uil-ais-ö]
n Beruhigungsmittel nt

transaction [træn-SÆK-schön] n
Transaktion f

transatlantic [TRÆNS-öt-LÆN-tik]
adj transatlantisch

transfer [trænss-FÖH] v
übertragen

transform [trænss-FOHM] v
verwandeln

transformer [trænss-FOHM-ö] n
Transformator m

transistor [træn-SISS-tö] n
Transistor m

translate [trænss-LEEJT] v

übersetzen

translation [trænss-LEEJ-schön]
n Übersetzung *f*

translator [trænss-LEEJT-ö] *n*
Übersetzer *m*

transmission [træns-MISCH-ön] *n*
Sendung *f*

transmit [træns-MIT] *v* senden

transparent [trænss-PÄOR-önt]
adj durchsichtig

transport [trænss-POHT] *v*
transportieren

transportation [trænss-poh-
TEEJ-schön] *n* Transport *m*

trap [træp] *n* Falle *f*

travel [TRÆW-öl] *n* Reise *f; v*
reisen

travel agency [TRÆW-öl EEJ-dʒön-
ssi] *n* Reisebüro *nt*

travel agent [TRÆW-öl EEJ-dʒönt]
n Reisebüro *nt*

travel insurance [TRÆW-öl in-
SCHUHÖR-önss] *n*
Reiseversicherung *f*

traveller [TRÆW-öl-ö] *n* Reisende
m

traveller's cheque [TRÆW-öl-ös
tschäk] *n* Reisescheck *m*

travelling [TRÆW-öl-ing] *n*
Reisen *nt*

travelling expenses [TRÆW-öl-
ing ikss-PÄNSS-is] *pl*
Reisespesen *pl*

tray [treej] *n* Tablett *nt*

treasure [TRÄ3-ö] *n* Schatz *m*

treasury [TRÄ3-ör-i] *n* Schatzamt
nt

treat [triet] *v* behandeln

treatment [TRIET-mönt] *n*
Behandlung *f*

tree [trie] *n* Baum *m*

tremble [TRÄM-böl] *v* zittern

tremendous [tri-MÄN-döss] *adj*
ungeheuer

trespass [TRÄSS-pöss] *v* unbefugt
eindringen

trespasser [TRÄSS-pöss-ö] *n*
Übertreter *m*

trial [TRAI-öl] *n*
Gerichtsverfahren *nt*

triangle [TRAI-æng-göl] *n*
Dreieck *nt*

triangular [trai-ÆNG-gju-lö] *adj*
dreieckig

tribe [traib] *n* Stamm *m*

tributary [TRIB-ju-tör-i] *n*
Nebenfluß *m*

trick [trik] *n* Kniff *m*

trim [trim] *v* stutzen

trip [trip] *n* Reise *f*

triumph [TRAI-ömf] *n* Triumph *m*

triumphant [trai-AM-fönt] *adj*
triumphierend

trolley-bus [TROL-i-bass] *n* Obus
m

troops [truhpss] *pl* Truppen *fpl*

tropical [TROP-ik-öl] *adj* tropisch

tropics [TROP-ikss] *pl* Tropen *pl*

trouble [TRAB-öl] *v* bemühen; *n*
Kummer *m*

troublesome [TRAB-öl-ssöm] *adj*
lästig

trousers [TRAUS-ös] *pl* Hose *f*

trout [traut] *n* Forelle *f*

truck [trak] *n* Lastwagen *m*

true [truh] *adj* wahr

trump [tramp] *n* Trumpf *m*

trunk [trangk] *n* Stamm *m*;
Koffer *m*; Kofferraum *m*

trunk-call [TRANGK-kohl] *n*
Ferngespräch *nt*

trunks [trangkss] *pl* Turnhose *f*

trust [trasst] *v* vertrauen; *n*
Vertrauen *nt*

trustworthy [TRASST-uöh-ði] *adj*
zuverlässig

truth [truhΘ] *n* Wahrheit *f*

truthful [TRUHΘ-ful] *adj* wahrhaft

try [trai] *v* versuchen
try on [trai on] *v* anprobieren
tub [tab] *n* Badewanne *f*
tube [tjuhb] *n* Rohr *nt*
tuberculosis [tju-böh-kju-LOO-ssiss] *n* Tuberkulose *f*
Tuesday [TJUHS-di] *n* Dienstag *m*
tug [tag] *v* schleppen; *n* Schlepper *m*
tumbler [TAM-blö] *n* Becher *m*
tumour [TJUH-mö] *n* Tumor *m*
tuna [TJUH-nö] *n* Thunfisch *m*
tune [tjuhn] *n* Melodie *f*
tune in [tjuhn in] *v* einstellen
tuneful [TJUHN-ful] *adj* melodisch
tunic [TJUH-nik] *n* Tunika *f*
tunnel [TAN-öl] *n* Tunnel *m*
turbine [TÖH-bain] *n* Turbine *f*
turbo-jet [TÖH-boo-DƷÄT] *n* Strahlturbine *f*
turbot [TÖH-böt] *n* Steinbutt *m*
Turk [töhk] *n* Türke *m*
turkey [TÖHK-i] *n* Truthahn *m*
Turkey [TÖHK-i] *n* Türkei *f*
Turkish [TÖHK-isch] *adj* türkisch
Turkish bath [TÖHK-isch bahϴ] *n* Schwitzbad *nt*
turn [töhn] *v* wenden; *n* Biegung *f*
turn back [töhn bæk] *v* umkehren
turn off [töhn of] *v* abdrehen
turn on [töhn on] *v* andrehen
turn round [töhn raund] *v* umdrehen (sich)
turning [TÖHN-ing] *n* Kurve *f*
turning point [TÖHN-ing peunt] *n* Wendepunkt *m*
turnover [TÖHN-oo-wö] *n* Umsatz *m*
turnover tax [TÖHN-oo-wö tækss] *n* Umsatzsteuer *f*
turpentine [TÖH-pön-tain] *n* Terpentin *nt*

tutor [TJUH-tö] *n* Hauslehrer *m*
tuxedo [tak-SSIE-doo] *n* Smoking *m*
tweed [tuied] *n* Tweed *m*
tweezers [TUIES-ös] *pl* Pinzette *f*
twelfth [tuälfϴ] *adj* zwölfte
twelve [tuälw] *adj* zwölf
twentieth [TUÄN-ti-iϴ] *adj* zwanzigste
twenty [TUÄN-ti] *adj* zwanzig
twice [tuaiss] *adv* zweimal
twig [tuig] *n* Zweig *m*
twilight [TUAI-lait] *n* Zwielicht *nt*
twin beds [tuin bäds] *pl* Doppelbett *nt*
twine [tuain] *n* Schnur *f*
twins [tuins] *pl* Zwilling *m*
twist [tuisst] *v* winden
two [tuh] *adj* zwei
two-piece [TUH-piess] *adj* zweiteilig
type [taip] *v* tippen; *n* Typ *m*
typewriter [TAIP-rait-ö] *n* Schreibmaschine *f*
typewritten [TAIP-rit-ön] *adj* maschinengeschrieben
typical [TIP-ik-öl] *adj* typisch
typing paper [TAIP-ing PEEJ-pö] *n* Schreibmaschinenpapier *nt*
typist [TAIP-isst] *n* Stenotypistin *f*
tyre [taiö] *n* Reifen *m*
tyre pressure [taiö PRÄSCH-ö] *n* Reifendruck *m*

ugly [AG-li] *adj* häßlich
ulcer [AL-ssö] *n* Geschwür *nt*
ultra-violet [al-trö-WAI-ö-lit] *adj* ultraviolett
umbrella [am-BRÄL-ö] *n* Regenschirm *m*
umpire [AM-paiö] *n* Schiedsrichter *m*
unable [an-EEJ-böl] *adj* unfähig

unacceptable [an-ök-SSĀP-tö-böl] *adj* unannehmbar

unaccountable [an-ö-KAUN-tö-böl] *adj* unerkärlich

unaccustomed [an-ö-KASS-tömd] *adj* ungewohnt

unauthorized [an-OH-Θör-aisd] *adj* unbefugt

unavoidable [an-ö-WEUD-ö-böl] *adj* unvermeidlich

unaware [an-ö-UÄÖ] *adj* unbewußt

unbearable [an-BÄÖR-ö-böl] *adj* unerträglich

unbreakable [an-BREEJK-ö-böl] *adj* unzerbrechlich

unbroken [an-BROOK-ön] *adj* unversehrt

unbutton [an-BAT-ön] *v* aufknöpfen

uncertain [an-SSÖH-tön] *adj* unsicher

uncle [ANG-köl] *n* Onkel *m*

unclean [an-KLIEN] *adj* unrein

uncomfortable [an-KAM-föt-ö-böl] *adj* ungemütlich

uncommon [an-KOM-ön] *adj* ungewöhnlich

unconditional [an-kön-DISCH-ön-öl] *adj* bedingungslos

unconscious [an-KON-schöss] *adj* bewußtlos

uncooked [an-KUKT] *adj* ungekocht

uncork [an-KOHK] *v* entkorken

uncover [an-KOW-ö] *v* aufdecken

uncultivated [an-KAL-tiw-eejt-id] *adj* unkultiviert

under [AN-dö] *prep* unter

under-age [AN-dör-EEJDȝ] *adj* minderjährig

underestimate [an-dör-ÄSS-ti-meejt] *v* unterschätzen

underground [AN-dö-graund] *adj*

unterirdisch

Underground [AN-dö-graund] *n* U-Bahn *f*

underline [an-dö-LAIN] *v* unterstreichen

underneath [an-dö-NIEΘ] *adv* unten

underpants [AN-dö-pæntss] *pl* Unterhose *f*

undershirt [AN-dö-schöht] *n* Unterhemd *nt*

undersigned [AN-dö-ssaind] *adj* Unterzeichnete *m*

understand [an-dö-SSTÆND] *v* verstehen

understanding [an-dö-SSTÆN-ding] *n* Verständigung *f*

understood [an-dö-SSTUD] *v* (*p, pp* **understand**)

* **undertake** [an-dö-TEEJK] *v* unternehmen

undertaking [an-dö-TEEJK-ing] *n* Unternehmung *f*

undertow [AN-dö-tool] *n* Unterströmung *f*

underwater [AN-dö-uah-tö] *adj*

underwear [AN-dö-uäö] *n* Unterwäsche *fpl*

undesirable [an-di-SAIÖR-ö-böl] *adj* unerwünscht

undid [an-DID] *v* (*p* undo)

undiscovered [an-diss-KAW-öd] *adj* unentdeckt

* **undo** [an-DUH] *v* aufmachen

undone [an-DAN] *v* (*pp* undo)

undress [an-DRÄSS] *v* entkleiden (sich)

undulating [AN-dju-leejt-ing] *adj* wellig

unearned [an-ÖHND] *adj* unverdient

uneasy [an-IES-i] *adj* unruhig

uneducated [an-AD-ju-keejt-id] *adj* ungebildet

unemployed [an-im-PLEUD] *adj*
arbeitslos

unemployment [an-im-PLEU-mönt] *n* Arbeitslosigkeit *f*

unequal [an-IEK-uöl] *adj*
ungleich

uneven [an-IEW-ön] *adj* uneben

unexpected [an-ikss-PÄK-tid] *adj*
unerwartet

unfair [an-FÄO] *adj* ungerecht

unfaithful [an-FEEJϴ-ful] *adj*
untreu

unfasten [an-FAHSS-ön] *v*
aufmachen

unfavourable [an-FEEJW-ör-ö-böl] *adj* ungünstig

unfold [an-FOOLD] *v* entfalten

unfortunate [an-FOH-tschön-it] *adj* unglücklich

unfortunately [an-FOH-tschön-it-li] *adv* leider

unfriendly [an-FRÄND-li] *adj*
unfreundlich

unfurnished [an-FÖH-nischt] *adj*
unmöbliert

ungrateful [an-GREEJT-ful] *adj*
undankbar

unhappy [an-HÆP-i] *adj*
unglücklich

unhealthy [an-HÄLϴ-i] *adj*
ungesund

unhurt [an-HÖHT] *adj* unverletzt

uniform [JUH-ni-fohm] *n*
Uniform *f*

unimportant [an-im-POHT-önt] *adj* unwichtig

uninhabitable [an-in-HÆB-it-ö-böl] *adj* unbewohnbar

uninhabited [an-in-HÆB-it-id] *adj* unbewohnt

unintentional [an-in-TÄN-schön-öl] *adj* unabsichtlich

union [JUHN-jön] *n* Vereinigung *f*

unique [juh-NIEK] *adj* einzigartig

unit [JUH-nit] *n* Einheit *f*

unite [juh-NAIT] *v* vereinigen

United States [juh-NAIT-id ssteejtss] Vereinigte Staaten *mpl*

universal [juh-ni-wÖHSS-öl] *adj*
universal

universe [JUH-ni-wöhss] *n*
Weltall *nt*

university [juh-ni-wÖH-ssi-ti] *n*
Universität *f*

unjust [an-DʒASST] *adj* ungerecht

unkind [an-KAIND] *adj*
unfreundlich

unknown [an-NOON] *adj*
unbekannt

unlawful [an-LOH-ful] *adj*
ungesetzlich

unless [an-LÄSS] *conj* außer
wenn

unlike [an-LAIK] *adj* unähnlich

unlikely [an-LAIK-li] *adj*
unwahrscheinlich

unlimited [an-LIM-it-id] *adj*
unbeschränkt

unload [an-LOOD] *v* abladen

unlock [an-LOK] *v* aufschließen

unlucky [an-LAK-i] *adj*
unglücklich

unmarried [an-MÆR-id] *adj*
unverheiratet

unnatural [an-NÆTSCH-röl] *adj*
unnatürlich

unnecessary [an-NÄSS-iss-ör-i] *adj* unnötig

unoccupied [an-OK-ju-paid] *adj*
unbesetzt

unpack [an-PÆK] *v* auspacken

unpaid [an-PEEJD] *adj* unbezahlt

unpleasant [an-PLÄS-önt] *adj*
unangenehm

unpopular [an-POP-ju-lö] *adj*
unbeliebt

unprepared [an-pri-PÄOD] *adj*

unvorbereitet

unproductive [an-prö-DAK-tiw] *adj* unproduktiv

unprotected [an-prö-TÄK-tid] *adj* ungeschützt

unqualified [an-KUOL-i-faid] *adj* unqualifiziert

unreasonable [an-RIES-ön-ö-böl] *adj* unvernünftig

unreliable [an-ri-LAI-ö-böl] *adj* unzuverlässig

unrest [an-RÄSST] *n* Unruhe *f*

unsafe [an-SSEEJF] *adj* unsicher

unsatisfactory [an-ssæt-iss-FÄK-tör-i] *adj* unbefriedigend

unscrew [an-SSKRUH] *v* abschrauben

unseen [an-SSIEN] *adj* ungesehen

unselfish [an-SSÄL-fisch] *adj* selbstlos

unskilled [an-SSKILD] *adj* ungelernt

unsold [an-SSOOLD] *adj* unverkauft

unsound [an-SSAUND] *adj* ungesund

unsteady [an-SSTÄD-i] *adj* unstet

unsuccessful [an-ssök-SSÄSS-ful] *adj* erfolglos

unsuitable [an-SSUHT-ö-böl] *adj* ungeeignet

untidy [an-TAID-i] *adj* unordentlich

untie [an-TAI] *v* aufknoten

until [an-TIL] *prep* bis

untrue [an-TRUH] *adj* unwahr

untrustworthy [an-TRASST-uöhö-i] *adj* unzuverlässig

unused [an-JUHSD] *adj* ungebraucht

unusual [an-JUHƷ-u-öl] *adj* ungewöhnlich

unwelcome [an-UÄL-köm] *adj* unwillkommen

unwell [an-UÄL] *adj* unwohl

unwilling [an-UIL-ing] *adj* unwillig

unwise [an-UAIS] *adj* unüberlegt

unwrap [an-RÆP] *v* auspacken

up [ap] *adv* hinauf

up and down [ap ön daun] hoch und runter

uphill [AP-hil] *adv* bergan

upkeep [AP-kiep] *n* Unterhalt *m*

upland [AP-lönd] *n* Hochland *nt*

upon [ö-PON] *prep* auf

upper [AP-ö] *adj* obere

upper bed [AP-ö bäd] *n* oberes Bett *nt*

upper berth [AP-ö böhΘ] *n* obere Koje *f*

upright [AP-rait] *adj* aufrecht

upset [ap-SSÄT] *v* stören; *adj* bestürzt

upside [AP-ssaid] *n* Oberseite *f*

upside down [AP-ssaid daun] umgekehrt

upstairs [ap-SSTÄÖS] *adv* oben

upstream [ap-SSTRIEM] *adv* stromaufwärts

upwards [AP-uöds] *adv* aufwärts

urban [ÖH-bön] *adj* städtisch

urgency [ÖH-dƷön-ssi] *n* Dringlichkeit *f*

urgent [ÖH-dƷönt] *adj* dringend

urine [JUHÖR-in] *n* Urin *m*

us [ass] *pron* uns

usable [JUHS-ö-böl] *adj* brauchbar

usage [JUHS-idƷ] *n* Brauch *m*

use [juhs] *v* gebrauchen; *n* Gebrauch *m*

use up [juhs ap] *v* verbrauchen

used [juhsd] *adj* gebraucht

* **used to (be)** [bie juhsst tu] *v* gewöhnt sein

useful [JUHSS-ful] *adj* nützlich

useless [JUHSS-liss] *adj* nutzlos

user [JUHS-ö] *n* Benutzer *m*

usher [ASCH-ö] *n* Platzanweiser
 m

usherette [asch-ör-ÄT] *n*
 Platzanweiserin *f*

usual [JUH-ʒu-öl] *adj* gewöhnlich

utensil [ju-TÄN-ssil] *n* Gerät *nt*

utility [ju-TIL-it-i] *n* Nutzen *m*

utilize [JUH-ti-lais] *v* benutzen

utmost [AT-moosst] *adj* äußerst

vacancy [WEEJ-kön-ssi] *n* Vakanz
 f

vacant [WEEJ-könt] *adj* frei

vacate [wö-KEEJT] *v* räumen

vacation [wö-KEEJ-schön] *n*
 Ferien *pl*

vaccinate [WÆK-ssi-neejt] *v*
 impfen

vaccination [wæk-ssi-NEEJ-
 schön] *n* Impfung *f*

vacuum [WÆK-ju-öm] *n* Vakuum
 nt

vacuum cleaner [WÆK-ju-öm
 KLIEN-ö] *n* Staubsauger *m*

vacuum flask [WÆK-ju-öm
 flahssk] *n* Thermosflasche *f*

valet [WÆL-eej] *n* Diener *m*

valid [WÆL-id] *adj* rechtsgültig

valley [WÆL-i] *n* Tal *nt*

valuable [WÆL-ju-ö-böl] *adj*
 wertvoll

valuables [WÆL-ju-ö-böls] *pl*
 Wertsachen *fpl*

value [WÆL-juh] *v* schätzen; *n*
 Wert *m*

valve [wælw] *n* Ventil *nt*

van [wæn] *n* Lieferauto *nt*

vanilla [wö-NIL-ö] *n* Vanille *f*

vanish [WÆN-isch] *v*
 verschwinden

vapour [WEEJ-pö] *n* Dunst *m*

variable [WÄOR-i-ö-böl] *adj*

veränderlich

variation [wäör-i-EEJ-schön] *n*
 Abänderung *f*

varicose vein [WÆR-i-kooss
 weejn] *n* Krampfader *f*

varied [WÄOR-id] *adj* verschieden

variety [wö-RAI-ö-ti] *n* Auswahl *f*

variety show [wö-RAI-ö-ti schoo]
 n Varietévorstellung *f*

variety theatre [wö-RAI-ö-ti Θi-ö-
 tö] *n* Varietétheater *nt*

various [WÄOR-i-öss] *adj*
 verschiedene

varnish [WAH-nisch] *n* Firnis *m*

vary [WÄOR-i] *v* wechseln

vase [wahs] *n* Vase *f*

vaseline [WÆSS-i-lien] *n* Vaseline
 f

vast [wahsst] *adj* weit

vault [wohlt] *n* Gewölbe *nt;*
 Stahlkammer *f*

veal [wiel] *n* Kalbfleisch *nt*

vegetable [WÄDʒ-it-ö-böl] *n*
 Gemüse *nt*

vegetarian [wädʒ-i-TÄOR-i-ön] *n*
 Vegetarier *m*

vegetation [wädʒ-i-TEEJ-schön] *n*
 Vegetation *f*

vehicle [WIE-i-köl] *n* Fahrzeug *nt*

veil [weejl] *n* Schleier *m*

vein [weejn] *n* Ader *f*

velvet [WÄL-wit] *n* Samt *m*

velveteen [wäl-wi-TIEN] *n*
 Baumwollsamt *m*

venereal disease [wi-NIÖR-i-öl
 di-SIES] *n*
 Geschlechtskrankheit *f*

venison [WÄN-sön] *n* Wildbret *nt*

ventilate [WÄN-ti-leejt] *v* lüften

ventilation [wän-ti-LEEJ-schön] *n*
 Ventilation *f*

ventilator [wän-ti-LEEJT-ö] *n*
 Ventilator *m*

veranda [wö-RÆN-dö] *n* Veranda

f

verb [wöhb] *n* Zeitwort *nt*

verbal [wöh-böl] *adj* mündlich

verdict [wöh-dikt] *n*
Urteilsspruch *m*

verge [wöhdʒ] *n* Rand *m*

verify [wär-i-fai] *v* nachprüfen

verse [wöhss] *n* Vers *m*

version [wöh-schön] *n*
Darstellung *f*

versus [wöh-ssöss] *prep* gegen

vertical [wöh-ti-köl] *adj*
senkrecht

vertigo [wöh-ti-goo] *n*
Schwindelanfall *m*

very [wär-i] *adv* sehr

vessel [wäss-öl] *n* Schiff *nt;*
Gefäß *nt*

vest [wässt] *n* Weste *f*

veterinary surgeon [wät-rin-ör-i
ssöh-dʒön] *n* Tierarzt *m*

via [wai-ö] *prep* über

viaduct [wai-ö-dakt] *n* Viadukt *m*

vibrate [wai-breejt] *v* vibrieren

vibration [wai-breej-schön] *n*
Vibrieren *nt*

vicar [wik-ö] *n* Vikar *m*

vicarage [wik-ör-idʒ] *n*
Pfarrhaus *nt*

vice-president [waiss-präs-i-
dönt] *n* Vizepräsident *m*

vicinity [wi-ssin-it-i] *n*
Nachbarschaft *f*

vicious [wisch-öss] *adj* bösartig

victory [wik-tör-i] *n* Sieg *m*

view [wjuh] *v* besichtigen; *n*
Aussicht *f*

view-finder [wjuh-fain-dö] *n*
Sucher *m*

villa [wil-ö] *n* Villa *f*

village [wil-idʒ] *n* Dorf *nt*

vine [wain] *n* Weinrebe *f*

vinegar [win-i-gö] *n* Essig *m*

vineyard [win-jöd] *n* Weinberg *m*

vintage [win-tidʒ] *n* Jahrgang *m*

violence [wai-ö-lönss] *n*
Gewalttätigkeit *f*

violent [wai-ö-lönt] *adj*
gewalttätig

violet [wai-ö-lit] *n* Veilchen *nt*

violin [wai-ö-lin] *n* Geige *f*

virgin [wöh-dʒin] *n* Jungfrau *f*

virtue [wöh-tjuh] *n* Tugend *f*

visa [wie-sö] *n* Visum *nt*

visibility [wis-i-bil-it-i] *n*
Sichtweite *f*

visible [wis-i-böl] *adj* sichtbar

visit [wis-it] *v* besuchen; *n*
Besuch *m*

visiting card [wis-it-ing kahd] *n*
Visitenkarte *f*

visiting hours [wis-it-ing auös] *pl*
Besuchsstunden *fpl*

visitor [wis-i-tö] *n* Gast *m*

vital [wai-töl] *adj* wesentlich

vitamin [wit-ö-min] *n* Vitamin *nt*

vivid [wiw-id] *adj* lebhaft

vocabulary [wö-kæb-ju-lör-i] *n*
Wortschatz *m*

vocalist [woo-köl-isst] *n* Sänger
m

voice [weuss] *n* Stimme *f*

volcano [wol-keej-noo] *n* Vulkan
m

volt [woolt] *n* Volt *nt*

voltage [wool-tidʒ] *n* Spannung *f*

volume [wol-jum] *n* Band *m*

voluntary [wol-ön-tör-i] *adj*
freiwillig

volunteer [wol-ön-tiö] *n*
Freiwillige *m*

vomit [wom-it] *v* erbrechen

vomiting [wom-it-ing] *n*
Erbrechen *nt*

vote [woot] *n* Stimme *f; v*
stimmen

voucher [wautsch-ö] *n* Gutschein
m

vowel [WAU-öl] *n* Selbstlaut *m*

voyage [WEU-idȝ] *n* Reise *f*

vulgar [WAL-gö] *adj* gemein

wade [ueejd] *v* waten

wafer [UEEJF-öl] *n* Oblate *f*

waffle [UOF-öl] *n* Waffel *f*

wages [UEEJDȝ-is] *pl* Lohn *m*

wagon [UÆG-ön] *n* Waggon *m*

waist [ueejsst] *n* Taille *f*

waistcoat [UEEJSS-koot] *n* Weste *f*

wait [ueejt] *v* warten

wait upon [ueejt ö-PON] *v* bedienen

waiter [UEEJT-ö] *n* Kellner *m*

waiting [UEEJT-ing] *n* Warten *nt*

waiting-list [UEEJT-ing-lisst] *n* Warteliste *f*

waiting-room [UEEJT-ing-ruhm] *n* Wartezimmer *nt*

waitress [UEEJT-riss] *n* Kellnerin *f*

* **wake** [ueejk] *v* wecken

* **wake up** [ueejk ap] *v* aufwachen

walk [uohk] *v* gehen; *n* Spaziergang *m*

walker [UOHK-ö] *n* Spaziergänger *m*

walking [UOHK-ing] *n* zu Fuß

walking-stick [UOHK-ing-sstik] *n* Spazierstock *m*

wall [uohl] *n* Mauer *f*

wallet [UOL-it] *n* Brieftasche *f*

walnut [UOHL-nat] *n* Walnuß *f*

waltz [uohlss] *n* Walzer *m*

wander [UON-dö] *v* umherwandern

want [uont] *v* wünschen; wollen; *n* Bedürfnis *nt*

war [uoh] *n* Krieg *m*

warden [UOH-dön] *n* Aufseher *m*

wardrobe [UOHD-roob] *n* Garderobe *f*

warehouse [UÄO-hauss] *n* Warenhaus *nt*

wares [uäös] *pl* Ware *f*

warm [uohm] *adj* warm; *v* wärmen

warmth [uohmΘ] *n* Wärme *f*

warn [uohn] *v* warnen

warning [UOHN-ing] *n* Warnung *f*

was [uos] *v* (*p be*)

wash [uosch] *v* waschen

wash and wear [uosch önd uäö] bügelfrei

wash up [uosch ap] *v* abwaschen

washable [UOSCH-ö-böl] *adj* waschbar

wash-basin [UOSCH-beej-ssön] *n* Waschbecken *nt*

washing [UOSCH-ing] *n* Wäsche *f*

washing-machine [UOSCH-ing-mö-schien] *n* Waschmaschine *f*

washing-powder [UOSCH-ing-pau-dö] *n* Waschpulver *nt*

wash-room [UOSCH-ruhm] *n* Waschraum *m*

wash-stand [UOSCH-sstænd] *n* Waschtisch *m*

wasn't [UOS-önt] *v* (was not)

wasp [uossp] *n* Wespe *f*

waste [ueejsst] *n* Verschwendung *f; v* vergeuden

wasteful [UEEJSST-ful] *adj* verschwenderisch

wastepaper-basket [ueejsst-PEEJ-pö-bahss-kit] *n* Papierkorb *m*

watch [uotsch] *v* beobachten; *n* Uhr *f*

watch for [uotsch foh] *v* auflauern

watch out [uotsch aut] *v* aufpassen

watchmaker [UOTSCH-meejk-ö] *n* Uhrmacher *m*

watch-strap [UOTSCH-sstræp] *n* Uhrband *nt*

water [UOH-tö] *n* Wasser *nt*

water skis [UOH-tö sskies] *pl* Wasserskier *mpl*

water-canteen [UOH-tö-kæn-TIEN] *n* Feldflasche *f*

water-colour [UOH-tö-kal-ö] *n* Aquarell *nt*

watercress [UOH-tö-kräss] *n* Brunnenkresse *f*

waterfall [UOH-tö-fohl] *n* Wasserfall *m*

watermelon [UOH-tö-mäl-ön] *n* Wassermelone *f*

waterproof [UOH-tö-pruhf] *adj* wasserdicht

waterway [UOH-tö-ueej] *n* Wasserstraße *f*

watt [uot] *n* Watt *nt*

wave [ueejw] *n* Welle *f*; *v* winken

wavelength [UEEJW-läng𝚯] *n* Wellenlänge *f*

wavy [UEEJW-i] *adj* wellig

wax [uækss] *n* Wachs *nt*

waxworks [UÆKSS-uöhkss] *pl* Wachsfigurenkabinett *nt*

way [ueej] *n* Weg *m*; Art und Weise

way in [ueej in] *n* Eingang *m*

way out [ueej aut] *n* Ausgang *m*

wayside [UEEJ-ssaid] *n* Wegrand *m*

we [uie] *pron* wir

weak [uiek] *adj* dünn; schwach

weakness [UIEK-niss] *n* Schwäche *f*

wealth [uäl𝚯] *n* Reichtum *m*

wealthy [UÄL𝚯-i] *adj* reich

weapon [UÄP-ön] *n* Waffe *f*

* **wear** [uäö] *v* tragen

* **wear out** [uäör aut] *v* abtragen

weary [UIÖR-i] *adj* müde

weather [UÄð-ö] *n* Wetter *nt*

weather report [UÄð-ö ri-POHT] *n* Wetterbericht *m*

* **weave** [uiew] *v* weben

weaver [UIEW-ö] *n* Weber *m*

wedding [UÄD-ing] *n* Hochzeit *f*

wedding ring [UÄD-ing ring] *n* Ehering *m*

wedge [uädʒ] *n* Keil *m*

Wednesday [UÄNS-di] *n* Mittwoch *m*

weed [uied] *n* Unkraut *nt*

week [uiek] *n* Woche *f*

weekday [UIEK-deej] *n* Wochentag *m*

weekend [UIEK-änd] *n* Wochenende *nt*

weekly [UIEK-li] *adj* wöchentlich

* **weep** [uiep] *v* weinen

weigh [ueej] *v* wiegen

weighing machine [UEEJ-ing mö-SCHIEN] *n* Waage *f*

weight [ueejt] *n* Gewicht *nt*

welcome [UÄL-köm] *v* bewillkommnen; *n* Willkommen *nt*; *adj* willkommen

welfare [UÄL-fäö] *n* Fürsorge *f*

well [uäl] *adv* gut; *n* Brunnen *m*; *adj* gut

well-done [UÄL-dan] *adj* durchgebraten

well-known [UÄL-noon] *adj* wohlbekannt

well-made [UÄL-meejd] *adj* gutgebaut

went [uänt] *v* (*p* go)

wept [uäpt] *v* (*p, pp* weep)

we're [uiöl] *v* (we are)

were [uöh] *v* (*p* be)

weren't [uöhnt] *v* (were not)

west [uässt] *n* Westen *m*

West Indies [uässt IN-dies] *pl*

Westindien *nt*
western [UÁSS-tön] *adj* westlich
westwards [UÁSST-uöds] *adv*
westwärts
wet [uät] *adj* naß
wharf [uohf] *n* Kai *m*
what [uot] *pron* was
what [uot] *pron* was
what else [uot älss] was noch
what for [uot foh] wozu
whatever [uot-AW-ö] was auch
immer
wheat [uiet] *n* Weizen *m*
wheel [uiel] *n* Rad *nt*
when [uän] *adv* wann; *conj* wenn
whenever [uän-AW-ö] *conj* wann
immer
where [uäö] *adv* wo; *conj* wo
wherefrom [uäö-FROM] *adv*
woher
wherever [uäör-AW-ö] *conj* wo
immer
whether [UÀÞ-ö] *conj* ob
whether . . . or [UÀÞ-ö oh] *conj*
ob . . . oder
which [uitsch] *pron* welcher; der
whichever [uitsch-AW-ö] *adj*
welcher auch immer
while [uail] *conj* während; *n*
Weile *f*
whip [uip] *v* schlagen; *n* Peitsche
f
whiskers [UISS-kös] *pl*
Backenbart *m*
whisper [UISS-pö] *n* Geflüster *nt;*
v flüstern
whistle [UISS-öl] *v* pfeifen; *n*
Pfeife *f*
white [uait] *adj* weiß
whitebait [UAIT-beejt] *n* Breitling
m
whiteness [UAIT-niss] *n* Weiße *f*
whiting [UAIT-ing] *n* Weißfisch *m*
Whitsuntide [UIT-ssun-taid] *n*

Pfingsten *nt*
who [huh] *pron* wer; welcher
whoever [hu-AW-ö] *pron* wer
auch immer
whole [hool] *adj* ganz; *n* Ganze
nt
wholemeal bread [HOOL-miel
bräd] *n* Vollkornbrot *nt*
wholesale [HOOL-sseejl] *n*
Großhandel *m*
wholesome [HOOL-ssöm] *adj*
bekömmlich
wholly [HOOL-li] *adv* gänzlich
whom [huhm] *pron* wem
why [uai] *adv* warum
wicked [UIK-id] *adj* böse
wide [uaid] *adj* breit
widen [UAI-dön] *v* erweitern
widespread [UAID-sspräd] *adj*
weitverbreitet
widow [UID-oo] *n* Witwe *f*
widower [UID-oo-ö] *n* Witwer *m*
width [uidΘ] *n* Breite *f*
wife [uaif] *n* Gattin *f*
wig [uig] *n* Perücke *f*
wild [uaild] *adj* wild
will [uil] *n* Testament *nt;* Wille
m; v wollen
willing [UIL-ing] *adj* willig
***win** [uin] *v* gewinnen
wind [uind] *n* Wind *m; v* winden;
winden (sich)
winding [UAIND-ing] *adj* windend
(sich)
windmill [UIND-mil] *n*
Windmühle *f*
window [UIN-doo] *n* Fenster *nt*
windscreen [UIND-sskrien] *n*
Windschutzscheibe *f*
windshield [UIND-schield] *n*
Windschutzscheibe *f*
windy [UIND-i] *adj* windig
wine [uain] *n* Wein *m*
wine bottle [uain BOT-öl] *n*

Weinflasche *f*
wine-cellar [UAIN-ssäl-ö] *n*
  Weinkeller *m*
wineglass [UAIN-glahss] *n*
  Weinglas *nt*
wine-list [UAIN-lisst] *n* Weinkarte
  f
wine-merchant [UAIN-möh-
  tschönt] *n* Weinhändler *m*
wine-waiter [UAIN-ueejt-ö] *n*
  Kellermeister *m*
wing [uing] *n* Flügel *m*
winkle [UING-köl] *n*
  Uferschnecke *f*
winner [UIN-öl] *n* Sieger *m*
winning [UIN-ing] *adj* gewinnend
winnings [UIN-ings] *pl* Gewinn *m*
winter [UIN-töl] *n* Winter *m*
winter sports [UIN-tö sspohtss] *pl*
  Wintersport *m*
wintry [UIN-tri] *adj* winterlich
wipe [uaip] *v* wischen
wire [uaiö] *n* Draht *m*
wireless [UAIÖ-liss] *n* Radio *nt*
wisdom [UIS-döm] *n* Weisheit *f*
wise [uais] *adj* weise
wish [uisch] *v* wünschen; *n*
  Wunsch *m*
with [uiô] *prep* mit
with reference to [uiô RÄF-rönss
  tu] *prep* hinsichtlich
withdraw [uiô-DROH] *v*
  zurückziehen
withdrawn [uiô-DROHN] *v* (*pp*
  withdraw)
withdrew [uiô-DRUH] *v* (*p*
  withdraw)
within [ui-ôIN] *prep* innerhalb
without [ui-ôAUT] *prep* ohne
without doubt [ui-ôAUT daut]
  ohne Zweifel
without fail [ui-ôAUT feejl] ganz
  gewiß
without obligation [ui-ôAUT ob-

li-GEEJ-schön] unverbindlich
witness [UIT-niss] *n* Zeuge *m*
witty [UIT-i] *adj* geistreich
woke [uook] *v* (*p* wake)
woken [UOOK-ön] *v* (*pp* wake)
wolf [uulf] *n* Wolf *m*
woman [UUM-ön] *n* (*pl* women)
  Frau *f*
won [uan] *v* (*p, pp* win)
wonder [UAN-dö] *v* fragen (sich);
  n Verwunderung *f*
wonderful [UAN-dö-ful] *adj*
  wunderbar
won't [uoont] *v* (will not)
wood [uud] *n* Holz *nt*; Wald *m*
wooden [UUD-ön] *adj* hölzern
woodland [UUD-lönd] *n* Waldung
  f
wool [uul] *n* Wolle *f*
woollen [UUL-ön] *adj* wollen
word [uöhd] *n* Wort *nt*
wore [uoh] *v* (*p* wear)
work [uöhk] *v* funktionieren;
  arbeiten; *n* Arbeit *f*
work of art [uöhk öw aht] *n*
  Kunstwerk *nt*
work permit [uöhk PÖH-mit] *n*
  Arbeitsbewilligung *f*
worker [UÖH-kö] *n* Arbeiter *m*
working day [UÖH-king deej] *n*
  Werktag *m*
workman [UÖHK-mön] *n* (*pl* -
  men) Arbeiter *m*
workshop [UÖHK-schop] *n*
  Werkstatt *f*
world [uöhld] *n* Welt *f*
world famous [uöhld FEEJM-öss]
  adj weltberühmt
world war [uöhld uah] *n*
  Weltkrieg *m*
world-wide [UÖHLD-uaid] *adj*
  weltweit
worm [uöhm] *n* Wurm *m*
worn [uohn] *v* (*pp* wear)

worn-out [UOHN-aut] *adj*
abgenutzt

worried [UAR-id] *adj* beunruhigt

worry [UAR-i] *v* beunruhigen
(sich); *n* Sorge *f*

worse [uöhss] *adv* schlechter; *adj*
schlechter

worship [UÖH-schip] *v* verehren;
n Gottesdienst *m*

worst [uöhsst] *adv* schlechtest;
adj schlechtest

worsted [UUSS-tid] *n*
Kammgarnstoff *m*

worth [uöhΘ] *n* Wert *m*

* **worth (be)** [bie uöhΘ] *v* wert
sein

worthless [UÖHΘ-liss] *adj* wertlos

* **worthwhile (be)** [bie uöhΘ-UAIL]
v lohnen (sich)

would [uud] *v* (*p* **will**)

wound [uuhnd] *n* Wunde *f*; *v*
verwunden

wove [uoow] *v* (*p* **weave**)

woven [UOOW-ön] *v* (*pp* **weave**)

wrap [ræp] *v* einwickeln

wrap up [ræp ap] *v* einhüllen
(sich)

wrapping paper [RÆP-ing PEEJ-
pö] *n* Packpapier *nt*

wreck [räk] *n* Wrack *nt*; *v*
vernichten

wrench [räntsch] *n*
Schraubenschlüssel *m*

wrist [risst] *n* Handgelenk *nt*

wrist-watch [RISST-uotsch] *n*
Armbanduhr *f*

* **write** [rait] *v* schreiben

writer [RAIT-ö] *n* Schreiber *m*

writing [RAIT-ing] *n* Schrift *f*

writing pad [RAIT-ing pæd] *n*
Schreibblock *m*

writing paper [RAIT-ing PEEJ-pö]
n Schreibpapier *nt*

written [RIT-ön] *v* (*pp* **write**)

wrong [rong] *adj* unrecht; falsch;
v unrecht tun; *n* Unrecht *nt*

wrote [root] *v* (*p* **write**)

Xmas [KRISS-möss] *n*
Weihnachten *nt*

X-ray [ÄKSS-reej] *n* Röntgenbild
nt

yacht [jot] *n* Jacht *f*

yacht club [jot klab] *n* Segelklub
m

yachting [JOT-ing] *n* Segelsport
m

yard [jahd] *n* Hof *m*

yarn [jahn] *n* Garn *nt*

yawn [john] *v* gähnen

year [jöh] *n* Jahr *nt*

yearly [JÖH-li] *adj* jährlich

yellow [JÄL-oo] *adj* gelb

yes [jäss] ja

yesterday [JÄSS-tö-di] *adv*
gestern

yet [jät] *adv* noch

yet [jät] *conj* dennoch

you [juh] *pron* Sie; dir; euch; ihr;
du; Ihnen

young [jang] *adj* jung

youngster [JANG-sstö] *n* Kind *nt*

your [joh] *adj* Ihr; euer; dein;
euere

you're [juhö] *v* (**you are**)

yourself [joh-ssÄLF] *pron* Sie
selbst; du selbst; dich

yourselves [joh-ssÄLWS] *pron* ihr
selbst; euch; Sie selbst

youth [juhΘ] *n* Jugend *f*

youth hostel [juhΘ HOSS-töl] *n*
Jugendherberge *f*

you've [juhw] *v* (**you have**)

Yugoslav [juh-goo-ssLAHW] *n*
Jugoslawe *m*

Yugoslavia [juh-goo-SSLAHW-jö]
  n Jugoslawien *nt*

zero [SIÖR-oo] *n* Null *f*
zinc [singk] *n* Zink *nt*
zip [sip] *n* Reißverschluß *m*
zip code [sip kood] Postleitzahl *f*
zipper [SIP-ö] *n* Reißverschluß *m*

zone [soon] *n* Zone *f*
zoo [suh] *n* Zoo *m*
zoological gardens [su-LODʒ-ik-
  öl GAH-döns] *pl* Zoologischer
  Garten
zoology [su-OL-ödʒ-i] *n* Zoologie *f*
zoom lens [suhm läns] *pl*
  Gummilinse *f*

Führer durch die Speisekarte

à la carte à la carte, nach der Speisekarte

à la mode Torte, Obstkuchen oder Kuchen, mit Vanilleeis garniert

Abernethy biscuit Diätbiskuit mit Kümmelgeschmack

allspice Jamaikapfeffer mit verschiedenem Geschmack : Zimt, Muskatnuß oder Nelken

Alma tea cakes in der Pfanne gebackene Kekse

almond Mandel
  ~ paste Mandelteig
  salted ~s Salzmandeln

anchovies Sardellen

angel food cake ein Kuchen aus Eiweiß und Zucker, in einer Auflaufform gebacken

angelica 1) Angelika 2) kandierte Angelikawurzel, die als Garnitur bei Gebäck verwendet wird

angels on horseback «Engel zu Pferde» ; Austern mit Speck am Spieß

appetizers Vorspeisen, Hors-d'œuvres
  assorted ~ verschiedene Vorspeisen, Appetitanreger

apple Apfel
  backed ~s gebackene Äpfel (im Ofen)

  ~ brown Betty pudding Nachspeise aus Apfelschichten, Paniermehl, Gewürzen und Zucker, mit Paniermehl bedeckt und in einer Puddingform gebacken

  ~ charlotte Apfelauflauf, im Ofen gebacken

  ~ dumpling Apfel im Schlafrock, im Ofen gebacken

  Dutch ~ pie Apfeltorte, mit Rohzucker und Butter bedeckt

  ~ fritter Apfelkrapfen

  ~ pan dowdy Apfelscheiben, mit einer Mischung aus Rohzucker und Butter bestreut, mit Melasse und Sirup begossen und im Ofen gebacken

  ~ pie Apfeltorte (oft mit Teig bedeckt)

  ~ sauce Apfelkompott

  ~ snow Apfelkompott mit geschlagenem Eigelb ; mit gezuckerten Meringes bedeckt, kalt serviert

  ~ tart Apfeltorte

apricots Aprikosen

arbroath smokies geräucherter Schellfisch (Schottland)

artichoke Artischocke
  globe ~ Artischocke

Jerusalem ~ Erdartischocke
asparagus Spargel
  ~ **tips** Spargelspitzen
aspic in Gelee, Sülze, Aspik
aubergine Aubergine
avocado (pear) Avocatobirne
bacon Speck
  boiled ~ gekochter Speck
  Canadian ~ geräucherter
  Speck, in dicke Scheiben geschnitten
  ~ **and eggs** Spiegeleier mit
  Speck
  ~ **fat** Schweinefett, -schmalz
  lean ~ magerer Speck
  ~**, lettuce and tomato sandwich**
  Sandwich mit Speck, Tomaten
  und Salat
bagel rundes Brötchen in der
  Form einer Krone
baked im Ofen gebacken
  ~ **Alaska** norwegisches Omelett, Überraschungsomelett
  ~ **apples** im Ofen gebackene
  Äpfel
bakewell tart Kuchen aus gemahlenen Mandeln, Eiern, Mehl,
  zerdrückten Biskuits und Him-
  beerkonfitüre
baking soda doppelkohlensaures
  Natron
banana Banane
  ~ **split** halbierte Banane, verschiedene Eiscreme-Sorten und
  Nüsse
Banbury cakes kleine Kuchen-
  törtchen aus Sahne, Eiern, Zitronenschale, Gewürzen und
  Johannisbeeren
bannocks Brot ohne Hefe, flach
  und rund, in der Pfanne gebak-
  ken (Schottland)
barbecue 1) über offenem Feuer
  grillen 2) Rindfleischgehacktes,

mit pikanter Tomatensauce in
einem Brötchen serviert
~**d spare ribs** aufgeschnittene
Schweinebrust, mariniert, auf
offenem Feuer gegrillt und mit
pikanter Tomatensauce angerichtet
barley sugar Gerstenzucker
barmbrack Rosinenkuchen mit
  getrockneten Früchten (Irland)
basil Basilikum
(sea) bass Wolfsbarsch
basted übergossen
Bath buns kleine im Ofen gebak-
  kene Brötchen aus Eiern, Hefe,
  Zucker und Rosinen
Bath Olivers runde, knusprige
  Kekse
batter geschlagener dünner Eier-
  teig
bay leaf Lorbeerblatt
beans Bohnen
  baked ~ im Ofen gebackene
  weiße Bohnen
  broad ~ Sau-, Puffbohnen
  butter ~ weiße runde Bohnen
  french ~ grüne Bohnen
  green ~ grüne Bohnen
  kidney ~ rote Bohnen
  navy ~ weiße Bohnen
  runner ~ grüne Bohnen
  wax ~ Butterbohnen, Wachs-
  bohnen
beef Rindfleisch
  ~**burger** gehacktes Beefsteak,
  gegrillt und in einem Brötchen
  serviert
  ~ **olives** Rindsrouladen
beetroot rote Rüben
bill Rechnung
  ~ **of fare** Tageskarte, Menü
biscuits 1) Biskuits, Kekse (Großbritannien) 2) eine Art flacher,
  runder Brötchen (USA)

ginger ~ Ingwerbiskuits
savoury ~ gewürzte Kekse
sweet ~ süße Kekse
Bismarck Berliner Pfannkuchen, Krapfen
black currants schwarze Johannisbeeren
black (oder **blood**) **pudding** Blutwurst
blackberries Brombeeren
black-eyed peas Erbsensorte, die in Amerika angebaut wird
bloater leicht gesalzener und geräucherter Hering, meistens gebraten oder gegrillt
blueberries Blau-, Heidelbeeren
boiled gekocht
~ **beef** Siedefleisch, gewöhnlich mit Karotten und Teigklößchen serviert
Bologna (**sausage**) eine Art Mortadellawurst
bone Knochen
~**d** ausgebeint
bortsch(t) Suppe aus roten Rüben und saurem Rahm, oft kalt serviert
Boston baked beans ein Gericht aus weißen Bohnen, Speckwürfeln und Rohzucker
Boston cream pie Schokoladentorte mit übereinandergelegten Cremeschichten
brains Hirn
braised gedämpft, geschmort
bramble pudding Brombeerkompott, dem man oft Apfelscheiben zufügt
brandy snaps Ingwerkekse
braunsweiger eine Art Leberpastete
brawn Preßkopf, Schweinekopfsülze
Brazil nuts Paranuß

bread Brot
brown ~ Schwarz-, Schrotbrot
~ **and butter pudding** Nachspeise aus gebutterten Brotscheiben mit abwechselnden Schichten aus Trockenfrüchten und Eiercreme, meistens im Ofen gebacken
french ~ französisches Weißbrot, Pariser Brot
pumpernickel ~ Pumpernickel, Roggen-Vollkornbrot
rye ~ Roggenbrot
starch-reduced ~ kalorienarmes Brot
~ **sauce** Sauce aus Milch, Paniermehl, etwas Zwiebeln, als Beilage zum Brathuhn oder Truthahn
white ~ Weißbrot
wholemeal, whole wheat ~ Weizen-Vollkornbrot
~**ed** paniert
breakfast Frühstück
bream Brasse
breast Brust
~ **of chicken** Hühnerbrüstchen
~ **of lamb** Lammbrust
brisket Rinderbruststück, mehrere Tage eingelegt
broad beans Sau-, Puffbohnen
brochan Haferbrei (Schottland)
broth Bouillon, Brühe
Scotch ~ Gemüsesuppe aus Hammelkopf mit Graupen
brown pudding Pudding aus getrockneten Früchten, gemahlenen Mandeln, Zimt, Schweinefett, Mehl, Paniermehl und Rohzucker, gekocht
brownie kleiner Kuchen, meistens aus Schokolade und Nüssen
brunch spätes, reichhaltiges Frühstück

Brunswick stew gewürztes Ragout, ursprünglich aus Eichhörnchenfleisch, jetzt meistens aus Hühnerfleisch mit Limabohnen, Mais und Gumboschoten (Virginia)

brussels sprouts Rosenkohl

bubble and squeak Kartoffel- und Kohlpüree (manchmal mit Zwiebeln)

bun 1) kleines Zuckerbrötchen, meistens mit Rosinen oder anderen getrockneten Früchten, manchmal auch mit Kokosnuß und Himbeermarmelade (Großbritannien) 2) kleiner Hefekuchen (USA)

(Kentucky) burgoo Suppe aus Rind-, Schweine-, Kalb-, Lammfleisch, Huhn und Gemüse (Kentucky)

butter Butter

~ **cookie** Butterkeks

fresh ~ frische Butter

~ **milk** Buttermilch

salted ~ gesalzene Butter

~ **scotch** eine Art Karamel aus Rohzucker und Maissirup

cabbage Kohl

cabinet pudding Nachspeise aus Biskuits, kandierten Früchten, Milch, Eiern und Zucker; wird heiß serviert

caerphilly ein Frischkäse aus Wales, sahnig und fein im Geschmack

cake Kuchen, Torte

~ s Kekse, feines Gebäck

calf Kalb

~ **brains** Kalbshirn

~ **feet** Kalbsfüße

Canadian bacon geräucherter Speck, in dicke Scheiben geschnitten

canapé Canapé, Appetitschnittchen

~ **Diane** in Speck eingewickelte Geflügelleber, gegrillt und auf Toast serviert

canary pudding Pudding aus Eiern, Mehl, Butter, Zucker, Natron, Milch und Zitronenschale

candied fruit kandierte Früchte

candy Bonbon, Karamelle, Konfekt

~ **kisses** kleine Schokoladenbonbons

capers Kapern

cantaloupe Kantalupe, Beutel-, Warzenmelone

capercaillzie Auerhahn

caramel Karamel

~ **custard** Karamelcreme

caraway Kümmel

cardamom Kardamom, als Gewürz verwendete Samenkörner einer asiatischen Pflanze

carp Karpfen

carrageen moss Perltang in Gelee (Irland)

carrot Karotte, Möhre

cashews Acajou-, Marknüsse

casserole Kasserolle, gußeiserner Topf

castle puddings kleine Puddings aus Sahne, Butter, Mehl und Backpulver, in Puddingformen serviert

catfish Katzenfisch, Wels

catsup Ketchup

cauliflower Blumenkohl

~ **cheese** gratinierter Blumenkohl, mit Käse überbacken

cayenne pepper Cayennepfeffer

celeriac Knollensellerie

celery Sellerie

braised ~ gedämpfter Sellerie

cereal 1) Getreide 2) Getreide-flocken, zum Frühstück meistens heiß zubereitet als Porridge (Haferflockenbrei); oder kalt als *corn flakes* (oder andere knusprige Getreideflocken) mit Milch und Zucker und manchmal Früchten

char Saibling, Rotforelle

chateaubriand Chateaubriand, doppeltes Lendensteak (Rind)

check Rechnung

Cheddar cheese ein milder, fetter Hartkäse, der auch zum Kochen verwendet wird

cheese Käse

  ~ **biscuits** Käsebiskuits, Käsegebäck

  ~ **board** Käseplatte

  ~ **cake** Käsekuchen mit Vollrahmkäse, Eiern und Zucker

  ~ **straws** Käsestangen, -stäbchen

  ~ **burger** Fleischküchlein und geschmolzener Käse, im Brötchen serviert

Chelsea buns kleine Zuckerbrötchen aus Teig, Hefe, kandierten Früchten und Zucker, bedeckt mit einer Honigglasur

cherry Kirsche

  ~ **tart** Kirschtorte

chervil Kerbel

Chesapeake Bay crab soup Krabbensuppe

Cheshire cheese einer der bekanntesten englischen Käse, von dem zwei Sorten existieren: der weiße und der rote; beide sind ziemlich weich und haben einen leicht süßen Geschmack

chestnut Kastanie

  ~ **stuffing** Kastanienfüllung

chick peas Kichererbsen

chicken Huhn, Hähnchen

  breast of ~ weißes Hühnerfleisch, Hühnerbrüstchen

  ~ **creole** Hähnchen mit einer Sauce aus Tomaten, grünen Paprikaschoten und Gewürzen

  ~ **gumbo** Hähnchen, das zuerst gekocht, dann mit Gumboschoten, Limabohnen, Zwiebeln, Tomaten, Gewürzen geschmort und auf Reis serviert wird

  ~ **leg** Hühnerkeule

  roast ~ Brathähnchen

  Southern fried ~ Hähnchen, in Milch eingetaucht, dann in einen Teig aus Eiern und Milch, in heißem Öl gebraten

chicory Chicorée

chiffon cake Kuchen aus sehr leichtem Teig

chili con carne gehacktes Rindfleisch mit getrockneten roten Bohnen, Piment und Kümmel, im eisernen Topf gekocht (USA)

chips 1) Pommes frites (Großbritannien) 2) Kartoffelschnitzel, Chips (USA)

chitterlings, chittlings, chittlins Schweinekutteln, -kaldaunen

chives Schnittlauch

chocolate Schokolade

  ~ **kisses** kleine, im Ofen gebackene Schokoladenkugeln aus Puderzucker, Schokolade oder Kakao, Eiweiß und Vanilleextrakt

  ~ **pudding** 1) Nachspeise aus Biskuitbröseln, heißer Milch, Butter, Zucker, Kakao, Eiern und Mehl (Großbritannien) 2) Schokoladenschaum (USA)

  ~ **s** Pralinen, Konfekt

(according to) choice nach Wahl
chop Kotelett
    mutton ~ Hammelkotelett
    pork ~ Schweinekotelett
    ~ **suey** ein chinesisches Gericht aus geschnetzeltem Rindfleisch, Reis und Gemüsen
chopped gehackt, geschnetzelt
chowder dicke Fischsuppe mit Muscheln und anderen Schaltieren
Christmas pudding Pudding aus kandierten Früchten, Zitronat, manchmal mit etwas Branntwein
chutney sehr scharfes indisches Gewürz, in dem man Früchte und Gemüse kocht
cinnamon Zimt
cioppino eine dicke Fischsuppe mit Krabben, Langusten, Fisch, Muscheln, Gemüse, Kräutern und Gewürzen (San Francisco)
clam Sandmuschel
    ~ **chowder** dicke Muschelsuppe
cloves Gewürznelken
club sandwich doppeltes Sandwich mit kaltem Hähnchen, gegrilltem Speck, Salat, Tomaten und Mayonnaise
cobbler eine Art Fruchtpastete, heiß serviert
    peach ~ Pfirsichkompott
cock-a-leekie soup (broth) Hühnersuppe mit Lauch (Schottland)
cockles Herzmuscheln
coconut Kokosnuß
cod Kabeljau, Dorsch
    boiled ~ gekochter Kabeljau
    fried ~ gebratener Kabeljau
    ~ **'s roe** Kabeljaurogen
  coffee cake Kaffeekuchen, oft mit

Früchten
Colchester oysters die besten englischen Austern
cold kalt
    ~ **cuts** Aufschnitt
    ~ **meat** kaltes Fleisch
coleslaw Krautsalat
compote Kompott, Brei, Püree
condiments Gewürze
consommé Bouillon, klare Brühe
cooked gekocht
cookies Biskuits, Kekse
coq-au-vin Hühnerragout, in Wein geschmort
coquilles St. Jacques gefüllte und überbackene Jakobsmuscheln
corn 1) Korn 2) Mais (USA)
    ~ **bread** Maisbrot
    ~ **on the cob** Maiskörner am Kolben
    ~ **flakes** geröstete Maisflocken, zum Frühstück serviert
    ~ **flour** Maismehl
    ~ **fritters** Beignets, Krapfen aus Maiskornteig
corned beef Corned beef, gepökelte Rinderbrust
Cornish pasty mit Kartoffeln, Zwiebeln, Rindfleisch und Nieren gefüllte Fleischpastete
Cornish splits gezuckerte Brötchen, mit Konfitüre und Dickmilch gefüllt
cottage cheese frischer, weißer Käse, Quark
cottage pie Hackfleisch, mit Zwiebeln und Kartoffelpüree bedeckt, im Ofen gebacken
Cottenham cheese Doppelrahmkäse, ziemlich fest, blaugeädert, ähnelt dem Stilton
country captain im Ofen gebackenes Hähnchen mit Tomaten, Mandeln, Rosinen, Johannis-

beeren und Gewürzen (Georgia)

course Gericht, Gang

cover charge Preis für das Gedeck, Gedeck extra

cowpea eine Erbsensorte, die in Amerika angebaut wird

Cox's orange pippin Renette (Apfelsorte)

crab Krabbe

~ **apple** Holzapfel

crackers knusprige ungesüßte Kekse

crackling knusprige Kruste von geröstetem Schweinefleisch

cranberry Krannbeere, Preiselbeere

~ **sauce** Krannbeersauce

crawfish, crayfish Krebs, Languste

cream 1) Sahne, Rahm 2) Creme

~ **cheese** Rahmkäse

double ~ Doppelrahmkäse

ice-~ Eis(creme)

~ **puff** Windbeutel

salad ~ Sahnesauce für Salate

sour ~ saure Sahne, Sauerrahm

whipped ~ Schlagsahne

creole auf kreolische Art; meistens stark mit Tomaten, grünen Paprikaschoten und Zwiebeln gewürzt, mit Reis serviert

cress Kresse

crisps Chips, Kartoffelschnitzel

croquette Klößchen, Krokette

crubeens Schweinsfüße (Irland)

crumpet ein Hefebrötchen, mit Butter bestrichen und warm gegessen

cucumber Gurke

Cumberland ham einer der besten Räucherschinken Englands

Cumberland rum butter mit Rohzucker, Muskat und Rum ver-

mischte Butter

cupcake kleiner, runder, mit Glasur überzogener Kuchen

cured geräuchert, gebeizt, eingepökelt (Fleisch)

currant Johannisbeere; Korinthe

~ **bread** Korinthenbrot

curried mit Curry

curry Mischung scharfer indischer Gewürze

custard Pudding aus Milch und Eiern, Eiercreme

~ **baked egg** Eiercreme, im Ofen gebacken

cutlet Kotelett, Schnitzel

dab Kliesche, Scharbe, rauhe Scholle

dace Häsling, Hasel (Karpfenfisch)

damson Damaszenerpflaume

Danish pastry Blätterteiggebäck, zum Frühstück serviert

dates Datteln

deer Hirsch

Delmonico steak Beefsteak aus dem Rückenstück

Derby cheese weißer Käse mit pikantem Geschmack

dessert Nachspeise, Dessert

devilled «teuflisch»; sehr stark gewürzt

~ **kidneys** halbierte Nieren mit Senf, Pfeffer, Chutney gewürzt, gebuttert und gegrillt

devils on horseback «Teufel zu Pferde»; gegrillte, mit Speck umwickelte Austern, auf Toast serviert

Devonshire cream dicke Sahne

diced in Würfel geschnitten

digestive biscuits Verdauungsbiskuits aus Mehl, Eiern, Zucker und doppelkohlensaurem Natron

dill Dill
dinner Hauptmahlzeit, Mittagessen, Abendessen
dish Gericht, Gang
donut Krapfen, Berliner Pfannkuchen in Ringform
double cream Rahm, Sahne
double Gloucester dem Cheddar ähnlicher Käse mit starkem Geschmack
dough Teig
~**nut** Krapfen, Berliner Pfannkuchen in Ringform
Dover sole Dover-Seezunge, gilt als die beste in England
dressing Zubereitung; Füllung; Salatsauce
French ~ Mayonnaise mit Ketchup
Green Goddess ~ Mayonnaise mit Kräutern, saurer Sahne, Sardellen, Essig, Schnittlauch, Petersilie und Estragon (San Francisco)
Italian ~ Sauce aus Öl und Kräutern
thousand island ~ Mayonnaise aus Piment, Nüssen, Sellerie, Oliven, Zwiebeln, Petersilie und Eiern
dripping abtropfendes Bratenfett
drop scones Milchbrötchen, in Kuchenform gegrillt
Dublin Bay prawns Steingarnelen, Langustinen
duck Ente
duckling Entchen
Long Island ~ Entchen von Long Island; die besten in den USA
dumpling Mehlkloß, Knödel, in Suppen verwendet oder mit Früchten gefüllt
Dundee cake Torte aus Mandeln, Kirschen, Dörrobst und Zitronenschale
Dunlop cheese ein dem Cheddar ähnlicher Käse (Schottland)
Dutch apple pie Apfeltorte mit einer Mischung aus Rohzucker und Butter
Easter biscuits mit Korinthen gefüllte Biskuits, manchmal gewürzt
eclair Liebesknochen, Blitzkuchen
chocolate ~ Blitzkuchen mit Schokoladenfüllung
eel Aal
jellied ~ Aal in Aspik
egg(s) Ei(er)
bacon and ~ Eier mit Speck
baked ~ im Ofen gebackene Eier
boiled ~ gekochte Eier
devilled ~ nach Teufelsart, sehr stark gewürzte Eier
fried ~ Spiegeleier
ham and ~ Eier mit Schinken
hard-boiled ~ hartgekochte Eier
~ **mimosa** gefüllte Eier
poached ~ pochierte Eier, verlorene Eier
scrambled ~ Rühreier
soft-boiled ~ weichgekochte Eier
stuffed ~ gefüllte Eier
egg custard Eiercreme, im Ofen gebacken
eggplant Aubergine, Eierfrucht
endive Endivie
English muffin leichtes rundes Brötchen, gegrillt und gebuttert
entrecote Zwischenrippenstück vom Rind
entrée 1) Zwischengericht (Groß-

britannien) 2) Hauptgericht (USA)

escalope Schnitzel

essence Extrakt, Essenz

Eve's pudding Nachspeise aus Apfelscheiben, im Ofen gebacken, mit einer Mischung aus Butter, Zucker, Eiern und Mehl bedeckt

Exeter stew geschnetzeltes Rindfleisch, Karotten, Zwiebeln und Kräuter

extract Extrakt

faggot's Leberfrikadelle

fat Fett

fennel Fenchel

figs Feigen

fillet Filet, Lendenstück
  beef ~ Rinderfilet
  ~ **mignon** Schweinelende
  pork ~ Schweinelende, -filet
  salmon ~ Lachsfilet
  ~ **of sole** Seezungenfilet

Finnian haddock geräucherter Schellfisch (Schottland)

fish Fisch
  ~ **and chips** Fisch und Pommes frites
  ~ **chowder** dicke Fischsuppe
  ~**cake** flaches Fischküchlein

flan Obst-, Käsekuchen

flapjacks dicke Pfannkuchen

flounder Flunder

flour Mehl

fondue Käsefondue

foods Lebensmittel, Nahrungsmittel

fool gekochter Obstbrei mit Zukker, Eiercreme oder Schlagsahne serviert

forcemeat gehacktes Füllfleisch

fowl Geflügel

frankfurter Frankfurter (Würstchen)

french beans grüne Bohnen

french bread französisches Weißbrot, Pariser Brot

French dressing Mayonnaise mit Ketchup

french fries Pommes frites

fresh frisch

fricassee Frikassee

fried gebraten, in der Pfanne gebacken

fritter Beignet, Krapfen

froglegs Froschschenkel

frosting Zucker(über)guß, -glasur

fruit Obst, Frucht
  ~ **cake** Obstkuchen
  ~ **salad** Fruchtsalat

fry 1) Fischfritüre 2) Gekrösefritüre (Herz, Leber, Lunge und Bries, vom Hammel oder Schwein)

fudge eine Art Fondant aus Butter, Zucker und Milch; mit Apfelsinen-, Schokolade- oder Kaffeegeschmack

galantine Sülze

game Wildbret

gammon unteres Stück einer Speckseite

garfish Seenadel, Hornhecht

garlic Knoblauch

garnish Garnierung, Beilage

gelatin Gelatine

Genoa cake Torte aus Rosinen, Zitronenschale, Kirschen und Mandeln

gherkins Essiggurken, Cornichons

giblets Geflügelklein

ginger Ingwer
  ~ **biscuits** Ingwerbiskuits, Ingwerkekse
  ~**bread** Lebkuchen, Pfefferkuchen

girdle (griddle) scones kleine, fla-

che Zuckerkuchen, auf einem Röstblech gebacken
glazed glasiert
Gloucester cheese weißer, milder Streichkäse
goose Gans
  roast ~ gebratene Gans
gooseberries Stachelbeeren
grapes Weintrauben
grapefruit Pampelmuse
grated gerieben, zerrieben
(au) gratin, gratinéed gratiniert, überbacken
gravy Fleischsaft, Bratensaft, Sauce
grayling Äsche (Fisch)
green beans grüne Bohnen
green peppers grüne Paprikaschoten
green salad grüner Salat, Kopfsalat
greengage Reineclaude
greens grünes Gemüse
griddle cakes Art von dicken Pfannkuchen
grill Grill
  ~**ed** gegrillt
grilse junger Lachs
grits Grütze
grouse schottisches Moorhuhn
  roast ~ gebratenes Moorhuhn
gudgeon Gründling
gumbo mit Gumboschoten eingedickte kreolische Suppe, der man Zwiebeln, Tomaten und verschiedene Gewürze zufügt
haddock Schellfisch
haggis gedämpfter Hammelmagen mit Hafermehl-, Zwiebel- und Hackfleischfüllung (Schottland)
hake Meerhecht
half Hälfte
halibut Heilbutt

ham Schinken
  baked ~ im Ofen gebackener Schinken
  boiled ~ gekochter Schinken
  ~ **and eggs** Spiegeleier mit Schinken
  smoked ~ geräucherter Schinken
  Virginia ~ Schinken, dessen Schwarte eingeritzt ist und der mit Ananas, Kirschen und Gewürznelken gespickt und mit dem eigenen Saft glasiert wird
  York ~ einer der besten englischen Schinken, in dünnen Scheiben serviert
hamburger 1) Rinderhackfleisch 2) gegrilltes und in einem Brötchen serviertes Fleischküchlein
hangtown fry Rühreier mit Speck und Austern (San Francisco)
hare Hase
  jugged ~ Hasenpfeffer
haricot beans Gartenbohnen
Harvard beets rote Rüben mit Essigsauce, Gewürznelken und Wein
hash 1) gehacktes oder geschnetzeltes Fleisch, Haschee 2) Gericht aus geschnetzeltem Fleisch mit Kartoffeln und Gemüsen
hazelnuts Haselnüsse
heart Herz
herbs Kräuter
herring Hering
  marinated ~, **soused** ~ eingelegter, marinierter Hering
home-made hausgemacht
hominy grits Maisgrütze
honey Honig
  ~**dew melon** sehr süße Melone mit gelbgrünem Fruchtfleisch

hors-d'œuvre appetitanregende Vorspeise, Hors-d'œuvre

horseradish Meerrettich
~ **sauce** Meerrettichsauce, meist kalt zu Lachs serviert

hot heiß
~**-cross bun** Rosinenbrötchen mit Zuckerguß in Form eines Kreuzes; wird während der Fastenzeit gegessen
~ **dog** heißes Würstchen in einem aufgeschnittenen Brötchen
~ **pot,** ~**ch potch** Eintopfgericht, Gemüsesuppe mit Schaffleisch

huckleberries Heidel-, Blaubeeren

hushpuppy Krapfen aus Maismehl und Zwiebeln (USA)

ice-cream Speiseeis, Eis
butter pecan ~ Pekannußeis
chocolate ~ Schokoladeneis
raspberry ~ Himbeereis
strawberry ~ Erdbeereis
vanilla ~ Vanilleeis
~ **cornet,** ~ **cone** Eistüte

iced eisgekühlt

icing Zuckerguß

in season (je) nach Jahreszeit

Irish moss Perltang

Irish stew Eintopfgericht mit Schaffleisch, Kartoffeln, Zwiebeln und Bier

Italian dressing Salatsauce aus Öl, Essig und Gewürzen

jam Marmelade
~ **roll** Marmeladenroulade

jambalaya Reis-Eintopfgericht mit Garnelen, Schinken, verschiedenen Gemüsen und Gewürzen (New Orleans)

jellied in Gelee
~ **eel** Aal in Gelee

hominy grits Maisgrütze

Jell-o 1) eine Fruchtgelee-Marke 2) eine Geleenachspeise

jelly Gelee, Sülze
~ **doughnut** Berliner Pfannkuchen

Jerusalem artichoke Erdartischocke

John Dory Heringskönig, Petersfisch

joint (of meat) Bratenstück

jugged hare Hasenpfeffer

juice Saft

juicy saftig

juniper berry Wacholderbeere

junket weißer Rahmkäse mit Sahne

kabob Lammspieß mit Tomaten, Zwiebeln und grünen Paprikaschoten

kale Kohl-, Gemüsesuppe

kebab Lammspieß mit Tomaten, Zwiebeln und grünen Paprikaschoten

kedgeree 1) gewürztes Gericht aus Reis, Zwiebeln, Linsen 2) kleingeschnittener Fisch mit Reis, Eiern und Butter, meist als heißes Frühstücksgericht

ketchup Ketchup, pikante dicke Tunke zum Würzen

key lime pie Sahnetorte mit Zitronelle

kidney Nieren
~ **beans** rote Bohnen

kippers geräucherte Heringe

ladies (lady)fingers Löffelbiskuits

lamb Lamm(fleisch)
~ **chop** Lammkotelett
~ **cutlet** Lammkotelett, Lammschnitzel
leg of ~ Lammkeule
loin of ~ Lammkarree
~ **roast** Lammbraten
~ **shoulder** Lammschulter

lamprey Neunauge
Lancashire cheese ein weißer, milder Käse, der mit zunehmender Reife kräftiger schmeckt
Lancashire hot pot Eintopf aus in Scheiben geschnittenen Kartoffeln, bedeckt mit Kotelettstückchen und Nieren, Zwiebeln und Gewürzen ; im Ofen überbacken
lard Schweinefett, -schmalz
larded gespickt
laurel Lorbeer
lean mager
leeks Lauch, Porree
leg Keule, Schlegel
Leicester cheese ziemlich scharfer, orangenfarbiger Käse
lemon Zitrone
~ **buns** Zuckerbrötchen mit Zitronengeschmack
~ **curd** eine Zitronencreme
~ **meringue pie** Schaumtorte mit Zitrone
~ **mousse** Zitronenschaum
~ **pudding** Zitronencreme, Zitronenpudding
~ **sole** Rotzunge
lentils Linsen
lettuce Lattich, Kopfsalat
light weich, leicht
lima beans Limabohnen
lime Zitronelle
key ~ **pie** Sahnetorte mit Zitronelle
liver Leber
~ **and bacon** Leber mit Speck
~ **sausage** Leberwurst
loaf Laib, Brotlaib
lobster Hummer, Languste
loganberries Himbeerenart
loin Filet, Lende
pork ~ Schweinelende, -filet
long john Kaffeegebäck

lox geräucherter Lachs
lunch Mittagessen
~ **eon** Mittagessen mit Geschäftspartnern
macaroni Makkaroni, Teigwaren
~ **and cheese** Makkaroni mit geriebenem Käse
macaroon Makrone
coconut ~ Kokosnuß-Makrone
mackerel Makrele
baked ~ im Ofen gebackene Makrele
grilled ~ gegrillte Makrele
stuffed ~ gefüllte Makrele
maize Mais
mandarin Mandarine
maple syrup Ahornsirup
marinade Marinade
marinated mariniert, eingelegt
marjoram Majoran
marmalade Apfelsinenmarmelade
marrow 1) Mark 2) Markkürbis, Zucchini
~ **bone** Markknochen
stuffed ~ gefüllte Zucchini
marshmallow Art türkischer Honig oder Lederzucker, zu heißer Schokolade, bestimmten Salaten und Nachspeisen hinzugefügt
marzipan Marzipan
mayonnaise Mayonnaise
meal Mahlzeit
meat Fleisch
~ **balls** Fleischklößchen
~ **loaf** Hackbraten, im Ofen gebacken und in Scheiben serviert
~ **pâté** Fleischpastete
~ **pie** in Teig gebackenes Rindfleisch
medium (done) mittel, halb durchgebraten
melon Melone

honeydew ~ sehr süße Melone mit gelbgrünem Fruchtfleisch
musk~ Moschusmelone
water~ Wassermelone
melted geschmolzen
Melton Mowbray pie eine englische Pastete mit einer Füllung aus Schweinefleisch, Zunge, Kalbfleisch und harten Eiern; kalt gegessen
menu Speisekarte
meringue Meringe, Baiser
milk Milch
  ~ **pudding** Reis- und Milchpudding
mince Gehacktes, Hackfleisch
  ~**d meat** Hackfleisch
  ~**meat** Mischung aus eingemachten gewürfelten Früchten, mit oder ohne Fleisch
  ~**meat pie** mit *mincemeat* gefüllte Pastete
mint Minze
  ~ **sauce** Minzsauce, aus feingehackter, in Essig eingeweichter Minze, besonders zu Hammelfleisch
minute steak kurz auf beiden Seiten gegrilltes Steak
mixed gemischt
  ~ **grill** Bratspieß mit Würstchen, Leber, Nieren, Koteletts und Speck, gegrillt
mock turtle soup «Schildkrötensuppe» aus Rindfleisch
molasses Melasse
morrel Morchel
mould Form (für Speisen)
mousse Schaum
muffin 1) kleines, lockeres Teegebäck, geröstet, aufgeschnitten und gebuttert (Großbritannien) 2) kleiner, runder, meistens in einer Papierform ge-

backener Kuchen (USA)
blueberry ~ Heidelbeerkuchen (USA)
mulberries Maulbeeren
mullet Meerbarbe
mulligatawny soup sehr stark gewürzte indische Fleisch- oder Geflügelsuppe mit Karotten, Zwiebeln, Chutney und Curry
mushrooms Pilze
muskmelon Moschusmelone
mussels Muscheln
mustard Senf
mutton Hammel(fleisch)
  ~ **chop** Hammelkotelett
  ~ **cutlet** Hammelkotelett, Hammelschnitzel
  leg of ~ Hammelkeule
  saddle of ~ Hammelrücken
  shoulder of ~ Hammelschulter
  ~ **stew** Hammelragout, -eintopf
napoleon Cremeschnitte
nectarin Nektarine, Nektarinenpfirsich
noodles Nudeln, Teigwaren
nutmeg Muskat(nuß)
nuts Nüsse
  almond ~ Mandeln
  Brazil ~ Paranüsse
  cashew ~ Acajou-, Marknüsse
  chest~ Kastanien
  cob~ große Haselnüsse
  hazel~ Haselnüsse
  pea~ Erdnüsse
oat cakes Hafermehlkekse
oatmeal (porridge) Haferschleim
offal Kaldaunen, Kutteln, auch Innereien
oil Öl
  corn ~ Maisöl
  olive ~ Olivenöl
  peanut ~ Erdnußöl
okra Gumboschoten

olive Olive
~ **oil** Olivenöl
black ~s schwarze Oliven
green ~s grüne Oliven
stuffed ~s gefüllte Oliven
omelet Omelett, Eierkuchen
cheese ~ Käseomelett
ham ~ Schinkenomelett
herb ~ Omelett mit feinen Kräutern
kidney ~ Omelett mit Nieren
plain ~ naturell, einfach
savoury ~ gewürztes Omelett
tomato ~ Tomatenomelett
onion Zwiebel
oppossum Oppossum, virginische Beutelratte
orange Apfelsine
oven-browned gratiniert, im Ofen überbacken
oven-cooked im Ofen gekocht
ox tongue Ochsenzunge
oxtail Ochsenschwanz
~ **soup** Ochsenschwanzsuppe
oyster plant Schwarzwurzel
oysters Austern
pancake Pfannkuchen
paprika Paprika
parkin eine Art Pfefferkuchen aus Hafermehl, Ingwer und Melasse
Parmesan (cheese) Parmesankäse
parsley Petersilie
~ **butter** Petersilienbutter (aus Butter, Petersilie und Zitronensaft)
parsnip Pastinakwurzel
partridge Rebhuhn
roast ~ gebratenes Rebhuhn
pasta Teigwaren, Nudeln
paste Paste, Püree
pastry feines Gebäck
pasty Fleischpastete
patty 1) Törtchen 2) kleine Paste-

te, flach und rund
peach Pfirsich
~ **cobbler** eine Art Pfirsichkompott, mit einer dicken Kruste bedeckt, im Ofen gebacken und warm serviert
~ **melba** Pfirsich Melba
peanut Erdnuß
~ **brittle** mürbes Zuckerwerk aus gerösteten Erdnüssen
~ **butter** Erdnußbutter
~ **butter cookie** Erdnußkeks
~ **oil** Erdnußöl
pear Birne
pearl barley Perlgraupen, für Suppen verwendet
peas Erbsen
~**e pudding** Erbsenpüree mit Gewürzen, Zwiebeln und Eiern
pecan Pekannuß
butter ~ **ice-cream** Pekannußeis (USA)
~ **pie** Pekannußtorte (USA)
pepper Pfeffer
chilli ~ Chilipfeffer
green ~ grüne Paprikaschoten
red ~ rote Paprikaschoten
stuffed ~ grüne, meistens mit Reis und Fleisch gefüllte Paprikaschoten
peppermint Pfefferminz
~ **creams** Pfefferminzbonbons
perch Barsch
persimmon Persimone, Dattelpflaume
pheasant Fasan
roast ~ gebratener Fasan
pickerel junger Hecht
pickled in einer Essiglösung eingelegt
~ **gherkins** Gewürzgurken, Essiggurken, Cornichons
~ **walnuts** in Essig eingelegte Walnüsse

pickles 1) Gemüse oder Früchte, in Essig- oder Salzwasser eingelegt 2) kleine Essiggurken, Cornichons

pie Kuchenart, englische Pastete (meistens mit Teig bedeckt, entweder mit Früchten oder Eiercreme garniert)

pig in a blanket mit Käse gefüllte Wurst, in Speck eingewickelt und in der Pfanne oder im Ofen gebraten

pig's knuckles Schweinshachse

pigeon Taube

pike Hecht

pilchard heringsartiger Fisch; kalifornische Sardine

pimientos süße Paprikaschoten

pizza Pizza

plaice Scholle

plate Teller, Platte, Gang

plover Regenpfeifer

plum Pflaume

poached pochiert
   ~ **eggs** pochierte Eier, verlorene Eier

pomegranate Granatapfel

poor knights «arme Ritter»; in geschlagenes Ei getauchte Brotscheiben, in der Pfanne gebacken und mit Konfitüre und Zucker angerichtet

popcorn Puffmais, geröstete, aufgeplatzte Maiskörner

pork Schweinefleisch
   ~ **chop** Schweinekotelett
   ~ **cutlet** Schweineschnitzel
   roast ~ Schweinebraten
   ~ **sausage** Schweinswurst

porridge Hafer(flocken)brei, besonders zum Frühstück

porterhouse steak Chateaubriand, (doppeltes Filetsteak, aus der Mitte des Filets geschnitten)

possum Oppossum, virginische Beutelratte

pot roast geschmortes Rindfleisch mit Zwiebeln, Karotten und Kartoffeln

potato Kartoffel
   baked ~ **es** im Ofen gebacken
   baked ~ **in its jacket** in der Schale gebacken
   boiled ~ **es** Salzkartoffeln
   chipped ~ **es** Pommes frites
   ~ **chips** Kartoffelchips
   creamed ~ **es** Rahmkartoffeln
   ~ **croquettes** Kroketten
   Idaho baked ~ eine Art Bintje, im Ofen gebacken
   mashed ~ **es** Kartoffelbrei
   new ~ **es** neue Kartoffeln
   ~ **pancake** Kartoffelküchlein
   roast ~ **es** Bratkartoffeln
   sautéed ~ **es** sautierte, in wenig Fett schnell gebratene Kartoffeln
   stuffed ~ **es** gefüllte Kartoffeln

potted shrimp Krabben-, Krevettenterrine

poultry Geflügel

prawn Steingarnele, Krabbe
   ~ **cocktail** Krabbencocktail
   Dublin Bay ~ große Steingarnele

price Preis
   fixed ~ fester Preis

prunes Backpflaumen
   stewed ~ Backpflaumenkompott

ptarmigan Schneehuhn

pudding Pudding; oft eine weiche oder feste Speise aus Mehl, entweder mit Fleisch, Fisch, Gemüse oder Früchten, gebacken oder gedämpft

puff pastry Blätterteiggebäck

pumpkin Kürbis

~ pie flache Kürbistorte
purée Püree, Brei
quail Wachtel
quarter Viertel
queen of puddings Nachspeise aus Eiern, Zucker, Milch, Brotkrümeln und Zitrone, mit Konfitüre bedeckt und im Ofen gebacken
quince Quitte
rabbit Kaninchen
  ~ broth Kaninchenbrühe
  ~ casserole Kanincheneintopf, -ragout
  ~ pie Kaninchenragout, mit einer Teigschicht bedeckt
  ~ stew Kanincheneintopf
radish Rettich
  ~es Radieschen
raisins Rosinen
rare blutig, halbroh
rasher Speckscheibe
raspberry Himbeere
  ~ buns Himbeerbrötchen
ravioli Ravioli
raw roh
red currants rote Johannisbeeren
red mullet Rotbarbe
relish 1) Salatsauce, Mayonnaise 2) Würze aus feingehackten Essiggurken
rhubarb Rhabarber
rib (of beef) Rippe (vom Rind)
rice Reis
  ~ creole Reis mit grünen Paprikaschoten, Piment und Safran
  ~ pudding Reispudding
rissoles Fleisch- oder Fischpastetchen
roach Rotauge, Plötze
roast Braten, gebraten
  ~ beef Rinderbraten
  ~ chicken Brathähnchen

~ lamb Lammbraten
rock cakes Plätzchen aus Mehl, Fett, Zucker und Rosinen
Rock Cornish hen Masthühnchen
roe Rogen, Fischlaich, gewöhnlich vom Kabeljau
roll Brötchen, Semmel
  ~mop herring Rollmops, in Weißwein mariniertes und um eine Essiggurke gerolltes Heringsfilet
roly-poly pudding mit Konfitüre bestrichener, zusammengerollter Teig, gedämpft
round steak Nuß (Stück vom Rinderfilet)
rudd Rotfeder (Fisch)
rum butter mit Rohzucker, Butter, Rum und Muskatnuß verarbeiteter Teig, wird so oder mit Butter bestrichen gegessen (Cumberland)
rump steak Rumpsteak (Rind)
runner beans grüne Bohnen
rusks Zwieback
rutabaga Schwedische Rübe, gelbe Kohlrübe
saddle Rückenstück bei Schlachtvieh
  ~ of lamb Lammrücken
saffron Safran
sage Salbei
  ~ and onion stuffing Füllung aus Zwiebeln und Salbei, gewöhnlich zu Schwein oder Gans serviert
sago Sago, Stärkemehl
salad Salat
  asparagus ~ Spargelsalat
  beetroot ~ Rüben-, Randensalat
  celery ~ Selleriesalat
  ~ cream, ~ dressing Salatsauce aus Sahne

fish ~ Fischsalat
fruit ~ Obstsalat
green ~ grüner Salat
lettuce ~ Kopfsalat
potato ~ Kartoffelsalat
tomato ~ Tomatensalat
salami Salami(wurst)
Sally Lunn leichter Teekuchen, heiß mit Butter gegessen
salmon Lachs
grilled ~ gegrillter Lachs
smoked ~ geräucherter Lachs
~ **steak** Lachsfilet
~ **trout** Lachsforelle
salsify Schwarzwurzel
salt Salz
~**ed** gesalzen
~**y** salzig
saltwater fish Salzwasserfisch, Meerfisch
sandwich Sandwich, zwei Brotscheiben mit Einlage dazwischen
open-faced ~ belegtes Brot
~ **spread** Paste aus Mayonnaise und feingehackten Essiggurken zum Bestreichen von Broten
sardines Sardinen
sauce Sauce
apple ~ Apfelkompott, -brei
bread ~ Sauce aus Paniermehl, Zwiebeln, Margarine, Milch und Gewürzen
brown ~ rotbraune Sauce aus gebundenem Fleischsaft
horseradish ~ Meerrettichsauce
mint ~ Minzsauce
parsley ~ Petersiliensauce
white ~ Béchamelsauce, weiße Sauce
Worcestershire ~ Würzsauce aus Essig und Sojabohnen

sauerbraten in Essig eingelegtes Rindfleisch, mit Pfefferkuchen geschmort (Pennsylvanien)
sauerkraut Sauerkraut
sausage Wurst
~ **and mash** Wurst und Kartoffelbrei
sausage roll Wurst in einer Teigrolle
sautéed sautiert, in wenig Fett schnell gebraten
savoury 1) Würzbissen 2) Zwischengericht
scallops gefüllte, im Ofen überbackene Jakobsmuscheln
scampi Scampi, eine Art große Garnelen
scone kleiner zarter Teekuchen
Scotch broth Brühe aus Rind- oder Hammelfleisch, dem man in Würfel geschnittenes Gemüse zufügt (Karotten, Kohl, Lauch, Rüben und Zwiebeln)
Scotch egg gekochtes Ei in Hackfleisch
Scotch girdle scones flache Milchbrötchen, auf einer Eisenplatte gebacken
Scotch woodcock Art Appetitschnittchen mit feingehackten Eiern, Gewürzen und zerdrückten Sardellen
scrambled eggs Rühreier
sea kale See-, Strandkohl
seafood Meeresfrüchte (kleine Fische, Schaltiere usw.)
~ **gumbo** Art Bouillabaisse mit Langusten, Krabben, Gumboschoten, Tomaten, Gewürzen und Zwiebeln, auf Reis serviert
(in) season (je) nach Jahreszeit
seasoning Würze, Gewürz
seedcake Gewürz-, Kümmelkuchen

semolina Grieß
  ~ **pudding** Nachspeise aus in
Milch gekochtem Grieß
service Bedienung
  ~ **charge** Bedienungszuschlag
  ~ **included** Bedienung inbegriffen
  ~ **not included** Bedienung nicht
inbegriffen
set menu Gedeck, festgelegte
Speisenfolge
shad ein amerikanischer Süßwasserhering
shallots Schalotten
shellfish Schaltiere
shepherd's pie Gericht aus Hackfleisch, in Würfel geschnittenen
Zwiebeln, Karotten, mit einer
dicken Schicht Kartoffelpüree
bedeckt und im Ofen überbakken
sherbet Scherbett, Sorbet, Fruchteis
shoofly pie Torte aus Melasse und
Honig, mit einer Kruste aus
Rohzucker, Gewürzen, Mehl
und Butter
shortbread Mürbekuchen aus
Mehl, Zucker und Butter; im
Ofen gebacken
shortcake kleines rundes Brötchen, Mürbegebäck
  strawberry ~ Art Erdbeertörtchen, mit Eis und/oder Schlagsahne garniert (USA)
shoulder Schulter
shredded wheat Frühstücksnahrung aus Weizenschrot
Shrewsbury cakes Kekse aus Butter, Zucker, Mehl, Eiern und
Zitronenschale
shrimp Garnelen, Krevetten,
Krabben
  ~ **cocktail** Krevettencocktail

~ **creole** in Tomatensauce
geschmorte Krabben mit grünen Paprikaschoten, Zwiebeln
und Gewürzen, mit Reis serviert (USA)
silverside (of beef) Nuß (vom
Rind)
Simnel cake Kuchen aus verschiedenen Trockenfrüchten, Kirschen, Zitronenschale, Gewürzen und Mandelteig, mit einer
dicken Marzipanschicht bedeckt
Singin' Hinny auf einem Röstblech gebackenes Zuckerbrötchen, halbiert und gebuttert
(Schottland)
sirloin steak Lendensteak, Lendenschnitte
skate Rochen
skewer Bratspieß
slice Scheibe
sloppy Joe gehacktes Rindfleisch
mit pikanter Tomatensauce,
im Brötchen serviert
smelt Stint, Spierling (ein Lachsfisch)
smoked geräuchert
snack leichte Mahlzeit, Imbiß
snickerdoodles Zimtbiskuits
snipe Schnepfe
soda Eisnachspeise mit Nuß oder
Sirup, in einem hohen Glas serviert
soda bread aus Mehl, Salz, Buttermilch und doppelkohlensaurem Natron zubereitetes Brot
(Irland)
sole Seezunge
  ~ **au gratin** überbackene Seezunge
sorrel Sauerampfer
soup Suppe
  asparagus ~ Spargelsuppe

barley ~ Gerstensuppe
chicken ~ Hühnersuppe
clear ~ klare Brühe, Bouillon
cream of celery ~ Selleriecremesuppe
cream of tomato ~ Tomatencremesuppe
game ~ Wildbretsuppe
lentil ~ Linsensuppe
lobster ~ Hummersuppe
mock turtle ~ Mockturtlesuppe, falsche Schildkrötensuppe aus Kalbskopf
mulligatawny ~ sehr stark gewürzte indische Fleisch- oder Geflügelsuppe mit Karotten, Zwiebeln, Chutney und Curry
oxtail ~ Ochsenschwanzsuppe
pea ~ Erbsensuppe
potato ~ Kartoffelsuppe
spinach ~ Spinatsuppe
vegetable ~ Gemüsesuppe
sour sauer
~ **cream** Sauerrahm, saure Sahne
~ **dough** Sauerteig, gegorener Hefeteig
~ **dough biscuits** kleine Biskuits aus Sauerteig
~ **dough bread** Brot aus Sauerteig
~ **milk** Sauermilch
soused herring in Essig und Gewürzen eingelegter Hering
spaghetti Spaghetti, Teigwaren
spare ribs Rippenspeer, aufgeschnittene Schweinebrust, Schweinerippchen
spice Gewürz
spinach Spinat
(on a) spit (am) Spieß
sponge cake leichter Sandkuchen aus Eiern, Puderzucker, Weizenmehl und Natron

spotted Dick Rosinenpudding, gebacken oder gedämpft, mit Fruchtsauce serviert
sprats Sprotten, auch kleine Heringe
squash Kürbis, Zucchini
squirrel Eichhörnchen
~ **stew** Eichhörncheneintopf
starter Vorspeise
steak Steak
Delmonico ~ Beefsteak aus dem Rückenstück
~ **and kidney pie** Auflauf aus Rindfleisch und Nieren
minute ~ kurz auf beiden Seiten gegrilltes Steak
porterhouse ~ Chateaubriand (doppeltes Filetsteak, aus der Mitte des Filets geschnitten)
round ~ Nuß (Stück vom Rinderfilet)
sirloin ~ Lendensteak, Lendenschnitte
T-bone ~ T-Bone Steak (größeres Steak mit T-förmigem Knochen, aus dem Filet geschnitten)
tenderloin ~ Filetsteak, Lendenschnitte
steamed gedämpft
stew Ragout, Eintopf
Stilton cheese einer der besten englischen Käse, blaugeädert, mit ausgesprochen scharfem Geschmack, sollte nur reif gekostet werden; es gibt auch einen weißen Stilton
stock Bouillon, Kraftbrühe, Satz
strawberry Erdbeere
~ **shortcake** Art Erdbeertörtchen, mit Eiscreme und/oder Schlagsahne garniert (USA)
streusel Streusel
string beans grüne Bohnen

stuffed gefüllt
stuffing Füllung
submarine sandwich ein mit Pariser Brot zubereitetes Sandwich
suck(l)ing pig Spanferkel
suet Nierenfett, Talg, oft beim Backen verwendet
  ~ pudding Talgpudding (Nachspeise)
sugar Zucker
  brown ~ Rohzucker
  castor ~ Puderzucker
  lump ~ Zuckerwürfel
  powdered ~ Puderzucker
sultanas Sultaninen
summer pudding Nachspeise aus Obst und Brot
summer sausage Dauerwurst
sundae Eisbecher mit Früchten, Nüssen, Schlagsahne und/oder Sirup
supper Abendessen
swedes Schwedische Rüben, gelbe Kohlrüben
sweet 1) süß 2) Nachspeise
  ~ corn Zuckermais
  ~ potatoes süße Kartoffeln
  ~breads Kalbsmilch, Bries, Milken
  ~s Bonbons
swiss cheese Schweizerkäse, Emmentaler Käse
swiss roll Biskuitroulade
swiss steak mit Zwiebeln und Tomaten geschmorte Rindfleischscheiben
swordfish Schwertfisch
syrup Sirup
table d'hôte feste Speisenfolge
taffy Sahnekaramelle, -bonbon
  ~ apple in Sahnekaramel getauchter Apfel
tamale Maismehlteig mit Füllung aus Rinderhackfleisch und Ge-

würzen, oft mit einer pikanten Sauce serviert (USA)
tangerine Mandarine
tapioca Tapioka (Stärke aus den Wurzeln der tropischen Maniokpflanze)
  ~ pudding Tapiokapudding
tarragon Estragon
tart Torte, Obstkuchen
T-bone steak T-Bone Steak (größeres Steak mit T-förmigem Knochen, aus dem Filet geschnitten)
tea cake feines Gebäck oder Brötchen, zum Tee serviert
teal Krickente
tench Schleie
tender zart, weich
tenderloin Filetsteak, Lendenschnitte
thick dick
thin dünn
thousand-island dressing Salatsauce aus Mayonnaise mit Piment, Nüssen, Sellerie, Zwiebeln, Petersilie und Eiern
thyme Thymian
tinned aus der Büchse, konserviert
tip Trinkgeld
toad in the hole Rindfleisch oder Wurst, mit Teig umhüllt und im Ofen gebacken
toast Toast, geröstete Brotscheibe
  ~ed geröstet, gegrillt
  ~ed cheese geröstete Brotscheibe mit geschmolzenem Käse
tomato Tomate
  ~ sauce Tomatensauce
  ~ soup Tomatensuppe
tongue Zunge
tournedos Tournedos, Lendenschnitte
treacle Melasse, Zuckersirup

trifle Nachspeise aus in Sherry oder Branntwein getauchtem Biskuitgebäck, mit Mandeln, Konfitüre, Schlagsahne oder Eiercreme

tripe Kutteln, Kaldaunen
~ **and onions** Kaldaunen mit Zwiebeln

trout Forelle
brown ~ Bachforelle
rainbow ~ Regenbogenforelle

truffles Trüffeln

tuna, tunny Thunfisch

turbot Steinbutt

turkey Truthahn
roast ~ gebratener Truthahn

Turkish delight Geleefrucht, feines Konfekt

turnip Steckrübe, weiße Rübe

turnover halbrundes, gefülltes Törtchen, Tasche
apple ~ Apfeltasche

turtle soup Schildkrötensuppe

underdone blau, sehr blutig

vanilla Vanille
~ **essence,** ~ **extract** Vanilleextrakt
~ **ice-cream** Vanilleeis

veal Kalbfleisch
~ **birds** Kalbsroulade, Kalbsvögel
~ **chop** Kalbskotelett
~ **cutlet** Kalbsschnitzel
~ **fillet** Kalbsfilet
~ **fricassee** Kalbsfrikassee
~ **and ham pie** Kalbfleisch- und Schinkenpastete, wird kalt gegessen
leg of ~ Kalbskeule
roast ~ Kalbsbraten

vegetable Gemüse

venison Wildbret, Reh

Vichyssoise Lauch- und Kartoffelsuppe, wird kalt gegessen

Victoria sandwich Torte aus zwei Teigschichten, abwechselnd mit Konfitüre- und Cremeschichten belegt

vinegar Essig, Weinessig

Virginia ham gekochter Schinken, mit Gewürznelken, Ananasscheiben und Kirschen gespickt und mit dem Saft dieser Früchte glasiert

vol au vent Blätterteigpastetchen

wafer Waffel, Eiswaffel

waffle Art heiße Waffel mit Butter und Melasse, Honig oder Sirup

waiter Kellner

waitress Kellnerin

walnut Walnuß

water ice Fruchteis, Sorbet

watercress Brunnenkresse

watermelon Wassermelone

well-done durchgebraten

Welsh rabbit (oder **rarebit**) geröstete Brotschnitte mit einer Mischung aus geschmolzenem Käse, Milch, Butter und Gewürzen

Wensleydale cheese blaugeäderter, sahniger Käse ; es gibt auch eine etwas mildere Art

whelks Wellhornschnecken

whipped cream Schlagsahne

white weiß
~ **meat** weißes Fleisch
~ **bait** Weißfischchen (Heringsart)

wholemeal Schrotmehl
~ **bread** Schrotbrot
~ **flour** Schrotmehl

wiener schnitzel Wiener Schnitzel

wine list Weinkarte

winkles Meeresschnecken

woodcock Waldschnepfe

Worcestershire sauce Würzsauce aus Essig und Sojabohnen

yam süße Kartoffel, Yamswurzel
yoghurt Joghurt
York ham einer der besten englischen Schinken, in dünnen Scheiben serviert
Yorkshire pudding Pfannkuchen-

teig, im Ofen gebacken, in Vierecke geschnitten und heiß als Beigabe zu Roastbeef serviert
zucchini Zucchini, Kürbischen
zwieback Zwieback

GETRÄNKE

ale 1) helles Bier, kohlensäurearm und schwach gehopft 2) Bier
aperitif Aperitif
appleade alkoholfreies Apfelgetränk
Athol Brose Getränk aus kochendheißem Wasser, das über Hafer gegossen wird und dem man Honig und Whisky zufügt (Schottland)
Babycham Schaumweinmarke
Bacardi 1) ein Rum 2) Mischung aus Zucker, Granatapfelsirup, Zitronellensirup und Rum
barley water Gerstentrank
barley wine stark alkoholhaltiges Gerstenbier
beer Bier
  bitter ~ Bitterbier
  bottled ~ Flaschenbier
  draft ~, draught ~ Faßbier
  lager ~ Lagerbier
  light ~ leichtes, gehopftes Bier
  mild ~ mildes Bier
  mild and bitter ~ Mischung aus stark und aus schwach gehopftem Bier
  pale ~ helles, wenig gehopftes Bier
  special ~ Spezialbier
  stout ~ starkes dunkles Bier

bitter Bitterbier
  ~s 1) Bitteraperitif 2) Angosturabitter
black cow root beer mit Vanilleeis
black and tan Mischung aus Guinness und stark gehopftem Bier
black velvet Mischgetränk aus Guinness und Champagner
bloody Mary Mischgetränk aus Wodka und Tomatensaft
Bourbon (whiskey) aus Mais hergestellter Whisky, nach dem Kreis Bourbon in Kentucky benannt (einige Marken : Jack Daniel's, Ol' Grand Dad, I. W. Harper's)
brandy Branntwein
  ~ Alexander Mischung aus Branntwein, Kakaolikör und Sahne
champagne Champagner, Sekt
  pink ~ rosa Champagner, Sekt
cherry brandy Kirschbranntwein, Kirsch
chocolate Schokolade
  hot ~ heiße Schokolade
cider Apfelwein
  ~ cup Mischgetränk aus Apfelwein, Gewürzen, Zucker und Eis

claret Rotwein aus Bordeaux

cocktail alkoholisches Mischgetränk, vor den Mahlzeiten serviert (z.B. *Manhattan, Martini*)

cocoa Kakao

coffee Kaffee

   black ~ schwarzer Kaffee

   Boston ~ Kaffee mit sehr viel Sahne

   caffeine-free ~ koffeinfreier Kaffee

   ~ **with cream** Kaffee mit Sahne

   iced ~ kalter Kaffee mit Eiswürfeln

   white ~ Kaffee mit viel Milch

cognac Kognak, Weinbrand

cordial 1) süßer, aromatischer Likör 2) bezieht sich auch auf jeden mit Wasser verdünnten Sirup

cups verschiedene Sommergetränke aus mit Wasser verdünntem Wein oder Branntwein

Daiquiri 1) ein Rum 2) Mischgetränk aus Zucker, Zitronellensaft und Rum

double doppelte Portion Whisky

Drambuie Likör aus Whisky und Honig

eggnog Eierlikör

English wines «englische Weine»; werden aus verschiedenen Früchten oder Gemüsen gemacht: Heidelbeeren, Holunderbeeren, Himbeeren, Angelikawurzeln

gin Gin, Kornbranntwein mit Wacholdergeschmack

   ~ **fizz** Mischung aus Gin und Zitronensaft

   ~ **and it** Mischung aus Gin und italienischem Wermut

   ~ **and tonic** Gin mit Tonic

ginger ale alkoholfreies Getränk mit Ingwergeschmack

ginger beer Ingwerbier, Sprudelwasser mit Ingwergeschmack

glass Glas

grasshopper Mischung aus Pfefferminz und Kakaolikör

Guinness Bier aus Dublin; stark, dunkel, fast schwarz, und süßlich

half ungefähr 2 ½ Deziliter (bezieht sich auf Bier)

   ~ **and half** Kaffeesahne

highball Getränk aus Spirituosen mit Soda und Eiswürfeln, manchmal mit einem Fruchtsaft, vor den Mahlzeiten serviert (z.B. *bloody Mary, screwdriver, Tom Collins*)

iced eisgekühlt

Irish coffee Kaffee mit Zucker, Schlagsahne und einem Schuß Whisky

Irish mist irischer Likör aus Whisky und Honig

Irish whiskey irischer Whisky; im Gegensatz zum schottischen Whisky *(Scotch)* wird der irische nicht «geblendet». Er enthält außer Gerste auch Roggen, Hafer und Weizen und wird nicht zweimal, sondern dreimal destilliert; dadurch im Geschmack weicher als der schottische Whisky (Beispiele: *Bushmills, John Power*)

juice Saft

   grapefruit ~ Pampelmusensaft

   lemon ~ Zitronensaft

   orange ~ Apfelsinensaft

   pineapple ~ Ananassaft

   tomato ~ Tomatensaft

lemon squash frisch gepreßter Zitronensaft

lemonade Limonade

light ale leichtes Bier

lime juice Zitronellensaft

liqueur Likör

liquor Branntwein, Spirituosen

long drink alkoholisches Getränk, mit Wasser oder Sprudelwasser verdünnt, Eiswürfel beigefügt

Madeira Madeira

malted milkshake Milchmixgetränk mit Malzzusatz

Manhattan Mischgetränk aus Whisky, trockenem Wermut, Maraschinokirschen und Angostura

Martini 1) Wermutmarke 2) Mischung aus trockenem Martini und Gin

mild Bier, das weniger Alkohol enthält als Bitterbier

~ **and bitter** Mischung aus gleichen Teilen milden und bitteren Biers

milk Milch

cold ~ kalte Milch

hot ~ heiße Milch

~**shake** Milchmixgetränk mit Malzzusatz

mineral water Mineralwasser

mulled ale warmes, gewürztes Bier

mulled wine Glühwein

neat Getränk ohne Eis und Wasser ; unverdünnt, pur

nightcap Schlummertrunk

nip ein Tropfen, ein Schlückchen

noggin ungefähr 1 ½ Deziliter

old fashioned Mischgetränk aus Whisky, Zucker, Angosturabitter und Maraschinokirschen

on the rocks mit Eiswürfeln

Ovaltine Ovomaltine

pale ale leichtes Bier

Pimm's Markenname für alkoholische Getränke

~ **No. 1** aus Gin

~ **No. 2** aus Whisky

~ **No. 3** aus Branntwein

~ **No. 4** aus Rum

pink champagne rosa Champagner, Sekt

pink lady Cocktail aus Eiweiß, Apfelschnaps, Zitronensaft, Granatapfelsirup und Gin

pint ungefähr 5 Deziliter

port (wine) Portwein

porter starkes dunkles Bier (Irland)

potheen schwarz gebrannter Alkohol

punch Punsch

quart englisches Flüssigkeitsmaß, 1,13 Liter (0,94 Liter in den USA)

root beer aus den Wurzeln verschiedener Kräuter bereitetes Getränk

rum Rum

rye (whiskey) Roggenwhisky

Scotch (whisky) schottischer Whisky ; hauptsächlich aus Gerstenmalz hergestellt und meist mit Getreidewhisky «geblendet» (einige Marken : *J & B, Black & White, Johnnie Walker*)

screwdriver Mischgetränk aus Wodka und Apfelsinensaft

shandy Bier mit Limonade oder Ingwerbier, zu gleichen Teilen gemischt

sherry Sherry

short drink unvermischtes, unverdünntes alkoholisches Getränk

shot Schuß Whisky oder Branntwein

sloe gin fizz Schlehenlikör

soft drink alkoholfreies Getränk

sparkling schäumend, sprudelnd

spirits Spirituosen

stinger Mischung aus Branntwein und Pfefferminzlikör

stout dunkles, stark gehopftes Bier (*Guinness* ist die bekannteste Marke)

straight unverdünnt, pur

tea Tee

  China ~ Chinatee

  Indian ~ indischer Tee

  ~ **with lemon** Tee mit Zitrone

  ~ **with milk** Tee mit Milch

toddy eine Art Grog

Tom Collins Mischgetränk aus Zucker, Zitronensaft, Zitronenschale, Selterswasser, Maraschinokirschen und Gin

tonic (water) Tonic(wasser), Sprudel, meist mit Chiningeschmack

vermouth Wermut

vodka Wodka

water Wasser

  mineral ~ Mineralwasser

  soda ~ Sodawasser, Sprudel

  tonic ~ Tonic(wasser)

whiskey, whisky Whisky; Edelbranntwein, aus Getreide destilliert (Weizen, Hafer, Gerste, Roggen, Mais usw.)

  ~ **sour** Mischgetränk aus Whisky, Zitronensaft, Zucker und Maraschinokirschen

wine Wein

  dry ~ trockener Wein

  pink ~ Roséwein

  red ~ Rotwein

  sparkling ~ Schaumwein, Sekt

  sweet ~ Süßwein, Dessertwein

  white ~ Weißwein

  (Unter den Weinen Nordamerikas sind die kalifornischen die bekanntesten; einige Namen: *Cabernet Sauvignon* (Bordeauxtyp), *Pinot noir* (Burgundertyp), *Barbera* (italienisch) für Rotwein, *Sauvignon blanc* (Sauternestyp), *Pinot Chardonnay* (Burgundertyp), *Johannisberger Riesling* (Rheinweintyp) für Weißwein, sowie *Grenache Rosé;* es gibt auch einheimischen Sherry, Portwein und Sekt

ENGLISCHE ABKÜRZUNGEN

AA	Automobile Association	Automobilklub (Großbritannien)
AAA	American Automobile Association	Automobilklub der Vereinigten Staaten
ABC	American Broadcasting Company	amerikanische Rundfunkgesellschaft
A.D.	Anno Domini	nach Christi Geburt
Am	America(n)	Amerika, amerikanisch
a.m.	before noon	vormittags
AT & T	American Telephone and Telegraph Company	Amerikanische Telephon- und Telegraphengesellschaft
ave.	avenue	Allee
BA	bachelor of arts	Universitätsgrad für Geisteswissenschaften
BBC	British Broadcasting Corporation	Britische Rundfunkgesellschaft
B.C.	before Christ	vor Christi Geburt
blvd	boulevard	Boulevard
BR	British Railways	Britische Eisenbahnen
Brit.	Britain, British	Großbritannien, britisch
¢	cent	Teileinheit des Dollars
Can.	Canada, Canadian	Kanada, kanadisch
CBS	Columbia Broadcasting System	amerikanische Rundfunkgesellschaft
CID	Criminal Investigation Department	Kriminalpolizei (Großbritannien)
CNR	Canadian National Railways	Kanadische Bundesbahnen
c/o	in care of	bei...
co.	company	(Handels)gesellschaft
corp.	corporation	Handelsgesellschaft
CPR	Canadian Pacific Railways	Kanadische Eisenbahnen
DDS	doctor of dental science	Doktor der Zahnheilkunde
dept.	department	Abteilung
Dr.	Dr.	Doktor
EEC	European Economic Community	EWG, Europäische Wirtschaftsgemeinschaft
e.g.	for instance	z.B., zum Beispiel
Eng.	England, English	England, englisch
excl.	excluding	ausschließlich
GB	Great Britain	Großbritannien

H.E.	His/Her Excellency, His Eminence	Seine/Ihre Exzellenz, Seine Eminenz
H.H.	His Holiness	Seine Heiligkeit
H.M.	His/Her Majesty	Seine/Ihre Majestät
HMS	His/Her Majesty's ship	wörtlich: Schiff Seiner/Ihrer Majestät
hp	horsepower	Pferdestärke, P.S.
i.e.	that is to say	d.h., das heißt
inc.	incorporated	eingetragen (von Vereinen, Firmen usw.)
incl.	including	einschließlich
£	pound sterling	Pfund Sterling
L.A.	Los Angeles	Los Angeles
ltd.	limited	Aktiengesellschaft
M.D.	medical doctor	Doktor der Medizin
M.P.	Member of Parliament	Mitglied des britischen Parlamentes
mph	miles per hour	Meilen pro Stunde
Mr.	Mister	Herr
Mrs.	Missis	Frau
nat.	national	staatlich
NATO	North Atlantic Treaty Organization	Nordatlantikpakt
N.B.	please note (nota bene)	notabene
NBC	National Broadcasting Company	amerikanische Rundfunkgesellschaft
No.	number	Nummer
N.Y.C.	New York City	New York City
O.B.E.	Order of the British Empire	Orden des Britischen Weltreiches
o/d	on demand	auf Bestellung
p.	page, penny/pence	Seite, Penny/Pence
p.a.	per year	pro Jahr
p.c.	postcard, per cent	Postkarte, Prozent
Ph.D.	doctor of philosophy	Doktor der Philosophie
p.m.	after noon	nachmittags
PO	post office	Postamt
POB	post office box	Postfach
POO	post office order	Postanweisung
pop.	population	Einwohner
prev.	previous	vorhergehend, vergangen

pto	please turn over	b.w., bitte wenden
RAC	Royal Automobile Club	Königlicher Automobil-klub
RCMP	Royal Canadian Mounted Police	berittene Polizei von Kanada
rd	road	Landstraße, Weg
ref.	reference	vergleiche, siehe
Rev.	reverend	Pfarrer
RFD	rural free delivery	Lieferung frei Haus
RR	railroad	Eisenbahn
RSVP	please reply	Antwort erbeten
RT	round trip	Hin- und Rückfahrt
$	dollar	Dollar
Soc.	society	Gesellschaft
SRO	standing room only	nur Stehplätze
St	Saint, street	Sankt, Straße
STD	standard trunk dialling	Selbstwählferndienst
UN	United Nations	Vereinte Nationen
UPS	United Parcel Service	Paketbeförderungsdienst
US	United States	Vereinigte Staaten
USS	United States Ship	wörtlich: Schiff der Vereinigten Staaten
VIP	very important person	wichtige Persönlichkeit
WT	wireless telegraphy	drahtlose Telegraphie
WU	Western Union	amerikanische Telegraphengesellschaft
Xmas	Christmas	Weihnachten
YMCA	Young Men's Christian Association	CVJM, Christlicher Verein Junger Männer
YWCA	Young Women's Christian Association	CVJM, Christlicher Verein Junger Mädchen
ZIP	ZIP code	Postleitzahl

ZEIT UND GELD

Uhrzeit. Die Briten und Amerikaner verwenden nur das 12-Stunden-System (auch für Fahrpläne).

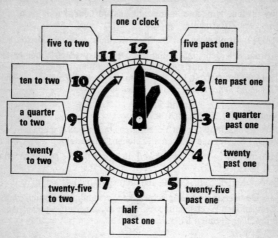

Wenn eine Zweideutigkeit möglich ist, bedient man sich der Ausdrücke *a.m.* und *p.m.* (vor- und nachmittags).

I'll come at two a.m.   Ich werde um zwei Uhr morgens kommen.
I'll come at two p.m.   Ich werde um zwei Uhr nachmittags kommen.
I'll come at eight p.m.   Ich werde um acht Uhr abends kommen.

Die Uhrzeit in Großbritannien ist die gleiche wie in Deutschland, außer im Winter, in dem man sich nach der *GMT*-Zeit (*Greenwich Mean Time*) richtet, die gegenüber der mitteleuropäischen um eine Stunde zurück ist.

In den Vereinigten Staaten (auf dem Festland) gibt es vier verschiedene Zeiten: *PST (Pacific Standard Time), MST (Mountain Standard Time), CST (Central Standard Time), EST (Eastern Standard Time)*. In Kanada kennt man die gleichen Systeme, doch gelten folgende Ausnahmen: Yukon ist eine Stunde hinter der *PST*-Zeit, der östliche Teil der Provinz Quebec, Neu-Schottland und die Prinz-Eduard-Inseln sind der *EST*-Zeit um eine Stunde voraus, und Neufundland ist ihr um anderthalb Stunden voraus.

Wenn es in New York Mittag ist, ist es in San Francisco neun Uhr morgens. Im Sommer werden alle Zeiten um eine Stunde vorgestellt (*Daylight Saving Time*) : *PDST, CDST* usw.

Jahreszahlen. Um eine Jahreszahl auszudrücken, teilt man diese in jeweils zwei Ziffern auf :

   1973 (19/73) *nineteen seventy-three* (wörtlich : neunzehn-dreiundsiebzig)

Währung. Seit der Einführung des Dezimalsystems in der britischen Währung sind die Touristen, die Großbritannien besuchen, von einem großen Problem befreit. Das Pfund (*pound sterling*; Zeichen : £) ist heute in 100 (neue) *pence* (Abk. : p.) eingeteilt.

   Münzen : ½, 1, 2, 5, 10 und 50 p.
   Banknoten : 1, 5, 10 und 20 £.

Die Währungseinheit in der Vereinigten Staaten und Kanada ist der *dollar* (Zeichen : $), der aus 100 cents (Zeichen : ¢) besteht.

   Münzen : 1 ¢ (*penny*), 5 ¢ (*nickel*), 10 ¢ (*dime*), 25 ¢ (*quarter*), 50 ¢ und 1 $.

   Banknoten : 1, 5, 10, 20, 50, 100, 200, 500, 1000 $.

Da die Devisenkurse häufig schwanken, erkundigen Sie sich am besten bei der nächsten Wechselstube (*currency exchange office*) oder Bank nach dem jeweils geltenden Kurs.

ÖFFNUNGSZEITEN

Banken. In Großbritannien sind die Banken von 9.30 bis 15.30 Uhr offen. Abgesehen von einigen Ausnahmen sind sie samstags geschlossen. In den Vereinigten Staaten und in Kanada können die Öffnungszeiten von einem Staat oder einer Provinz zur anderen variieren, manchmal auch von Stadt zu Stadt. Man findet Banken, die bis 21.00 Uhr oder gar die ganze Nacht hindurch offen sind, und für Autofahrer gibt es besondere *drive-in banks*. Am besten erkundigt man sich im Hotel.

Postämter. In Großbritannien sind die Postschalter im allgemeinen von 9.00 bis 17.30 Uhr, an Samstagen bis 13.00 geöffnet. Für Inlandpost gibt es zwei Beförderungsarten: erste Klasse (einen Tag bis zur Ankunft beim Empfänger) und zweite Klasse (zwei bis drei Tage).

In den Vereinigten Staaten hängen Post-, Telegraphen- und Telephonwesen von verschiedenen Gesellschaften ab. Um z.B. ein Telegramm aufzugeben, geht man also nicht zum Postamt, sondern wendet sich an ein Büro der Western Union oder der RCA. Kleinere Postämter haben oft nicht einmal eine Fernsprechzelle. Dies gilt jedoch nicht für Kanada. Der Zahlungsverkehr wickelt sich in beiden Ländern fast nur über die Banken ab.

In der Regel sind die Post-, Telephon- und Telegraphenämter von 8.00 oder 9.00 Uhr bis 18.00 Uhr, an Samstagen bis mittags geöffnet. Erkundigen Sie sich jedoch lieber an Ort und Stelle, denn in einigen Gegenden gelten andere Öffnungszeiten.

Geschäfte. In Großbritannien sind sie meistens von 9.00 bis 17.30 Uhr geöffnet. Einen Nachmittag in der Woche sind sie geschlossen *(early-closing day)*.

In den Vereinigten Staaten und Kanada sind die Öffnungszeiten von Ort zu Ort verschieden. Gewisse Geschäfte sind auch abends oder sonntags geöffnet.

Büros. In den angelsächsischen Ländern sind Büros in der Regel von 8.30 oder 9.00 bis 17.00 Uhr geöffnet und samstags geschlossen.

FEIERTAGE

Dies sind die wichtigsten gesetzlichen Feiertage, an denen in Großbritannien (GB), den Vereinigten Staaten (USA) und Kanada (CDN)
Schulen, Banken, Geschäfte und Büros geschlossen sind. Dazu kommen
noch eine Anzahl Feiertage, die nur für bestimmte Gegenden, Staaten
oder Provinzen gelten.

1. Jan.	**New Year's Day**	Neujahr	USA CDN
1. Juli	**Dominion Day**	Nationalfeiertag	CDN
4. Juli	**Independence Day**	Nationalfeiertag	USA
11. Nov.	**Remembrance Day**	Tag der Erinnerung	CDN
25. Dez.	**Christmas Day**	Weihnachten	GB USA CDN
26. Dez.	**Boxing Day**	St. Stephanstag	GB

Bewegliche	**Good Friday**	Karfreitag	CDN
Feiertage:	**Easter Monday**	Ostermontag	CDN
	Whit Monday	Pfingstmontag	GB
	Washington's	Geburtstag	USA
	Birthday	Washingtons	
	(3. Montag im Februar; ausgenommen		
	Oklahoma)		
	Spring Holiday	Frühlingsfeiertag	GB
	(letzter Montag im Mai)		
	Memorial Day	Tag der Erinnerung	USA
	(letzter Montag in Mai; kein Feiertag in		
	Alaska, Südkarolina, Mississippi; einen		
	Tag später gefeiert in Louisiana,		
	Wisconsin und Süddakota)		
	Late Summer	Spätsommer-	GB
	Holiday	feiertag	
	(letzter Montag im August)		
	Labour Day	Tag der Arbeit	USA CDN
	(erster Montag im September)		
	Thanksgiving Day	Dank- und Bettag	USA CDN
	(4. Donnerstag im November; in Kanada		
	am 2. Dienstag im Oktober gefeiert)		

ZÜGE

Großbritannien. Das Netz der Britischen Eisenbahnen (British Rail) erfaßt das ganze Land. Es gibt Abteile erster und zweiter Klasse. Auf jedem Bahnhof oder in Reisebüros sind zahlreiche Fahrkarten zu ermäßigten Preisen erhältlich (z.B. *round trip tickets, runabout rover tickets*).

Kanada. In diesem Land ist der Zug das Hauptverkehrsmittel. Der größte Teil des Eisenbahnnetzes gehört zwei Gesellschaften, der privaten Canadian Pacific Railway Company und der staatlichen Canadian National Railway System.

Vereinigte Staaten. Beinahe die Hälfte des Eisenbahnnetzes untersteht der Amtrak (National Railroad Passenger Corporation), der vierzehn private Eisenbahngesellschaften vertraglich angeschlossen sind. Die Schnellzüge der Amtrak verkehren zwischen den wichtigsten Städten der Vereinigten Staaten. Dazu gehört auch der *Metroliner,* der in drei Stunden von New York nach Washington fährt.

Außerdem gibt es großartige Turbinenzüge, die Geschwindigkeiten bis zu 300 km/h erreichen.

Es sollte jedoch erwähnt werden, daß man in den Vereinigten Staaten dem Zug meist das Flugzeug oder den Autobus vorzieht.

Express (GB, USA, CDN) oder **intercity** (GB)	Schnellzug, der zwischen den Großstädten verkehrt; hält nur an wenigen Bahnhöfen.
Local (GB, USA, CDN)	Personenzug; Schienenbus.
Motorail (GB); **Piggy-back car train** (USA, CDN)	Autoreisezug.
Pullman (USA, CDN)	Luxuswagen, der auch in einen Schlafwagen umgewandelt werden kann.
Sleeping-car (GB)	Schlafwagen.
Dining-car (GB); **diner** (USA, CDN)	Speisewagen.
Buffet car (GB)	Wagen, in dem Erfrischungen und leichte Mahlzeiten gereicht werden.
Guard's van (GB); **Baggage car** (USA, CDN	Gepäckwagen. In Großbritannien wird Reisegepäck bis zu 70 kg (1. Klasse) und 45 kg (2. Klasse) unentgeltlich befördert. In den Vereinigten Staaten geben Familienfahrkarten das Anrecht auf kostenlose Beförderung von 150 kg Reisegepäck.

VERKEHRSZEICHEN

In Großbritannien, aber vor allem in den USA und in Kanada findet man eine große Anzahl von beschrifteten Verkehrszeichen. Hier die wichtigsten:

Bends for 1 mile (Am.: curves)	Kurven auf 1 Meile
Cattle crossing	Vieh
Danger	Gefahr
Diversion (Am.: detour)	Umleitung
Ford	Furt
Give way (yield)	Vorfahrt beachten
Halt	Halt
Height restriction	Höhenbegrenzung
Keep left	Links einordnen
Level crossing (railroad crossing)	Bahnübergang
Low bridge	Niedrige Brücke
Major road ahead	Hauptstraße, Vorfahrt beachten
No entry	Durchfahrt verboten
No left (right) turn	Links (rechts) abbiegen verboten
No overtaking (Am.: passing)	Überholverbot
No parking	Parken verboten
No through road (Am.: dead-end street)	Sackgasse
No U turn	Wenden verboten
No waiting	Halten verboten
One way	Einbahnstraße
Parking	Parkplatz
Reduce speed	Geschwindigkeit verlangsamen
Road works ahead	Straßenarbeiten
Roundabout (Am.: rotary)	Kreisverkehr
School crossing	Übergang für Schulkinder
Slow	Langsam fahren
Soft verge (Am.: soft shoulders)	Seitenstreifen nicht befahrbar
Steep hill (engage low gear)	Starkes Gefälle (niedrigen Gang einschalten)
Stop	Stop, Halt
Temporary road surface	Provisorische Straßendecke
Weight limit	Gewichtsbeschränkung

Die USA hoffen ab 1976 das internationale System einführen zu können.

TELEPHONIEREN

In Großbritannien findet man zahlreiche öffentliche Telephonzellen, in denen es Anweisungen zur Bedienung des Telephons gibt. Bei Schwierigkeiten ruft man einfach die Zentrale unter der Nr. 100 an. In den meisten Fällen ist der Telephonverkehr automatisiert, und die Leitungen sind für Ferngespräche benutzbar. Die Vorwahlnummer (*dialling* oder *STD code*) findet man im Telephonbuch *(directory)*, oder man fragt das Amt. Die Dauer des Gespräches richtet sich nach der Menge der eingeworfenen Münzen; ein Signal in schnellem Rhythmus zeigt an, daß man erneut Geld einwerfen muß. Telephoniert man vom Hotel aus, verlangt man die Verbindung wie folgt:

> *Can you get me PLaza six/five/four/six/seven?*
> «Können Sie mir PLaza 6-5467 geben?»

Achtung! Werfen Sie kein Geld in den Apparat, bevor Sie die Nummer gewählt haben und die Verbindung zustandegekommen ist.

In den Vereinigten Staaten sowie in den meisten Teilen Kanadas ist der Telephonverkehr automatisiert. Die einzigen Informationen, die man benötigt, sind die Rufnummer und die Vorwahlnummer *(area code)*. In den meisten Fällen besteht die Nummer aus sieben Ziffern, die man nacheinander wählt. In einigen Städten sind die beiden ersten Ziffern durch Buchstaben ersetzt. Telephoniert man vom Hotel aus, verlangt man die Nummer so:

> *Please get me number two/o/two/two/three/four/one/two/seven/five?*
> «Geben Sie mir bitte 202 2341275.»
> *Can you get me PLaza six/five/four/six/seven?*
> «Können Sie mir PLaza 6-5467 geben?»

Um von einem Münzautomaten aus ein Ortsgespräch zu führen, werfen Sie 10 Cents ein. Für ein Ferngespräch ist es am einfachsten, 10 Cents einzuwerfen und die Null zu wählen — die Vermittlung wird Ihnen helfen und Ihnen die Gebühren angeben.

Am Telephon spricht man die Null wie den Buchstaben O aus.

Buchstabiertabelle

A	Alfred	H	Harry	O	Oliver	V	Victor
B	Benjamin	I	Isaac	P	Peter	W	William
C	Charlie	J	Jack	Q	Queen	X	Xray
D	David	K	King	R	Robert	Y	Yellow
E	Edward	L	London	S	Samuel	Z	Zebra
F	Frederick	M	Mary	T	Tommy		
G	George	N	Nellie	U	Uncle		

Merkblatt

Paß Nr. ....

....

Bankkonto Nr. ....

Postscheckkonto Nr. ....

....

Reiseversicherung: **Gesellschaft** ....

    Police Nr. ....

Motorfahrzeugversicherung: ....

    Gesellschaft ....

    Police Nr. ....

Auto: Kennzeichen ....

    Fahrgestell Nr. ....

Kreditkarte: Nrn. ....

Blutgruppe ....

....

....

....

....

Notizen

Personal Data

Passport Nos. ....

....

Checking Account No. ....

Credit Card Nos. ....

....

Car Insurance : Company ....

    Policy No. ....

Travel Insurance : Company ....

    Policy No. ....

Blood Type ....

Licence Plates Car ....

Chassis No. Car ....

....

....

....

....

....

....

Notes